ST. IGNATIUS HIGH SCHOOL FACULTY

VOL. I.

HISTORY
OF
THE SOCIETY OF JESUS
IN
NORTH AMERICA
COLONIAL AND FEDERAL

BY

THOMAS HUGHES
OF THE SAME SOCIETY

DOCUMENTS

VOLUME I

1605–1838

PART I

LONGMANS, GREEN, AND CO.
39 PATERNOSTER ROW, LONDON
NEW YORK, BOMBAY, AND CALCUTTA
1907

All rights reserved

HISTORY OF THE
SOCIETY OF JESUS IN NORTH AMERICA
COLONIAL AND FEDERAL

NIHIL OBSTAT

JOSEPH GRIMMELSMAN, S.J.,
Præpositus Provinciæ Missourianæ S.J.

ST. LOUIS UNIVERSITY,
ST. LOUIS, MO., U.S.A.,
November 28, 1905.

IMPRIMATUR

Si ita placebit R^{mo} Patri Magistro Sacri Palatii Apostolici
JOSEPH PATRIARCHA CO^{pnus} VICESG.

ROMÆ,
Die 12 Jan., 1906.

IMPRIMATUR

FR. ALBERTUS LEPIDI, O.P.
S. P. Ap. Magister.

ROMÆ,
Die 20 Jan., 1906.

HISTORY
OF
THE SOCIETY OF JESUS
IN
NORTH AMERICA
COLONIAL AND FEDERAL

BY

THOMAS HUGHES

OF THE SAME SOCIETY

TEXT

VOLUME I

FROM THE FIRST COLONIZATION TILL 1645

LOUBAT PRIZE
(COLUMBIA UNIVERSITY IN THE CITY OF NEW YORK)

REISSUE

LONGMANS, GREEN, AND CO.
39 PATERNOSTER ROW, LONDON
NEW YORK, BOMBAY, AND CALCUTTA
1908

First printed . . *March*, 1907
Reissued . . . *September*, 1908

PREFACE

THE first portion of the American history, which is herewith laid before the public, belonged properly to the English historian of the Society of Jesus. The whole of this history, like that projected for England, is only one part of a comprehensive historical series, comprising in different languages an authentic account of the Society over the world.

During the first century and a half of Jesuit life and work in the British Colonies of North America, the persons who worked there, as well as the organization of the whole Mission itself, were referred to that unit of Jesuit government which was called the English Province. A number of reasons, however, induced the historian of that Province to seek relief from a piece of historical work, which appeared as dissonant in general tone and temper from English history, as its subject was distant from English soil. Hence, for that first century and a half, it was transferred to the pages of this narrative, which was intended originally to comprise only the Jesuit history of the nineteenth century in the United States and Canada. So transferred, that portion had to be prefixed. And it now supplies an appropriate and even necessary train of antecedents to the later history of the Order in English-speaking North America.

We have taken for our title the official and proper name of this Religious Order, which in the Latin nations of Europe is styled, with a very exact shade of military meaning, "The Company of Jesus," but in the official ecclesiastical Latin, for want of a more precise term, had to be rendered *Societas Jesu*. From the official Latin the English name was taken, and we use it here: "The Society of Jesus." We might have preferred the shorter and popular epithet of "Jesuits," were it not that a well-known volume of Francis Parkman's had appropriated the simpler and easier name for a history of "The Jesuits in North America in the Seventeenth Century."

This was rather a wide undertaking for that brilliant writer; and his performance did not carry it into execution. He treated of the French, and left out the Spanish and English Jesuits in North America. We, for our part, could not pretend to adopt so comprehensive a term. We feel that our title, like our subject, must needs be circumscribed, to distinguish it and exclude from it Spanish and French North America. This we have attempted to do with the aid of two adjectives, "Colonial and Federal," which imply a double stage of history, as before and after the American Revolution, and also include Canada from the time of its being ceded to England. The definition of our subject, by means of these two adjectives, connotes a line of history which was not common to New Spain or to New France.

The requirements of modern studies call for the fullest use of documents, as well as the presentation of all facilities for verifying evidence in its entire context. On this account we have found ourselves under the necessity of accompanying our Text with Documents and Illustrations, such as demanded special attention, and yet could not find accommodation in footnotes or in an appendix of moderate proportions. In another volume, accordingly, we shall reproduce such papers as are indicated in the Table of Contents annexed at the end of this present volume. It will be noticed there that we have not confined ourselves to those historical monuments which are cited in the body of our Text. We have, in fact, taken occasion to put in order a large mass of old documents bearing on Jesuit property and its uses. And we have presented the series in the companion volume as a Documentary Excursus offered on its own merits. The preliminary observations, however, are not to be looked for there, but here.

For Text, Documents, and Excursus all together, for the material employed, its origin, value, and depositories, not a little has to be premised in general or affixed in particular. That which has to be said in general we set forth in the Notices of the Sources and in the Literary Introduction now following. What may occur to be said in particular shall find place on occasion, as called for by the citation of a document or by its reproduction.

For reasons which will appear, there is but little material to be found in published works that could serve to weave the main thread of our history. Yet it may also appear that, in the Introduction and elsewhere, not a little is said about the same matters and publications which we pronounce to be so scanty for our purpose. The fact is that this history of Anglo-American Colonies, being published before that of the English Jesuit Province, is incomplete on the side of the parent stock, and is like a branch detached from its trunk. In the temporary want of an original home account, to which the colonial part of our narrative should have been dutifully appended, we had of necessity to supply, as best we might, with the materials which we needed from that side. This will account for the matter which we have prefixed to complete the relation, and for the form in which we have put it, by way of introducing the Jesuit history of Anglo-American Colonies.

Among the elements that have been of use there is nothing of consequence which we have not endeavoured to draw directly from its source. Some publications merit or aspire to be ranked as sources themselves; such as Brodhead's *Documents relating to the Colonial History of the State of New York*, and divers publications of Historical Societies like that of Maryland. An exceptional book on our general subject, like Dr. J. G. Shea's *History of the Catholic Church within the limits of the United States, from the first attempted Colonization to the present time*, is to be ranked with historical literature, and rated as such.

Of all these matters we undertake to speak in the preliminary chapters which follow.

THE AUTHOR.

Rome,
Collegio P. L. Americano,
January 24, 1906.

CONTENTS

Preface vii

INTRODUCTORY

CHAPTER I

REGISTER AND NOTICES OF THE SOURCES

SECTION I.
- § 1. Register of Sources inedited 1
- § 2. Register of Sources edited 3

SECTION II.
- § 3. Notices of the Sources inedited: Europe (1) to (28) 7
- § 4. Notices of the Sources inedited: America (29) to (50) 24
- § 5. The Maryland Legislature and the Jesuit archives 29

SECTION III.
- § 6. Principles of editing 32
- § 7. List of Generals, Provincials, etc. 32
- § 8. Full titles of books quoted 34
- § 9. Abbreviations used 44

CHAPTER II

HISTORY OF THE ARCHIVES AND THE LITERATURE 46

SECTION I. THE JESUIT ARCHIVES.
- § 1. Preparation of Jesuit archives for a history 47
- § 2. Annual Letters, and their system 49
- § 3. Schedules for Letters and history 53
- § 4. Instruments and deeds up to 1700 55
- § 5. Writing and writers 57
- § 6. Attempts at a history 60
- § 7. Administrative documents in the archives 64
- § 8. Plundering, intercepting, and burning records 66
- § 9. The policy of silence, and its reasons 69
- § 10. Effects on published history; and net results 76

CONTENTS

SECTION II. THE LITERATURE.

§ 11. Criteria drawn from current literature 79
§ 12. Prejudice against our subject 82
§ 13. Political basis of the prejudice 86
§ 14. The first Lord Baltimore and the legal prejudices 92
§ 15. Developments of the literature 99
§ 16. Eighteenth-century literature 104
§ 17. Test Acts and oaths 107
§ 18. Nineteenth-century literature 117
§ 19. Rectifications of history; and results 124
§ 20. The true nature of our subject 129

HISTORY

MARYLAND TILL 1645

CHAPTER III

ANTECEDENTS OF THE MARYLAND MISSION, 1580–1632 . . . 141

§ 1. The first English mission of the Jesuits: 1580 143
§ 2. The motive of religion in colonial enterprises: 1582–1612 145
§ 3. The plan of Catholic migration in 1605 153
§ 4. Andrew White: Vocation: 1605–1606 155
§ 5. The English Province. Formation of a novice 161
§ 6. Father White as a Professor: 1609–1629 168
§ 7. George Calvert and Newfoundland: 1624–1629 176
§ 8. The Propaganda and the English Colonies: 1625–1631 181
§ 9. Propaganda Relations continued: 1625–1631 187
§ 10. Lord Baltimore and the clergy: the Puritans: 1627–1631 193
§ 11. The Bishop, the laity, and Baltimore: 1628–1631 202
§ 12. The crisis of the controversy: 1631 209
§ 13. The friar and the Bishop: 1631 213
§ 14. The Bishop and the monk on the laity: 1631 219
§ 15. End of the laymen's controversy: 1631 224
§ 16. The first Lord Baltimore's last acts: 1631, 1632 232
§ 17. The charter for Maryland: 1632: (1) Dedication of places of worship;
    (2) Ecclesiastical patronage; (3) Elimination of Mortmain Statutes . 236
Facsimile of White's autograph letter to Gerard, Oct., 1606 . *To face* 157
Facsimile of General's autograph draft to White, March, 1629 *To face* 174

CHAPTER IV

FOUNDATION OF THE MARYLAND MISSION, 1633–1640 . . . 244

§ 18. Negotiations for Jesuit missionaries 246
§ 19. Father White as secretary to Lord Baltimore 249

CONTENTS

	PAGE
§ 20. The general Conditions of Plantation: 1633	252
§ 21. Conditions propounded to the missionaries: 1633	255
§ 22. Baltimore's views on religious toleration: 1633	257
§ 23. Baltimore's politico-religious instructions: November, 1633	259
§ 24. The proportion of contributions	263
§ 25. Faculties for Maryland: 1633	266
§ 26. Men for Maryland: 1633–1635	269
§ 27. The voyage to America: 1633, 1634	274
§ 28. The West Indies: 1634	277
§ 29. The western populations	280
§ 30. Puritans, Huguenots, and Anglicans	285
§ 31. Propaganda reports of the Islands: (1) Jesuits; (2) Dominicans; (3) Augustinians and Carmelites; (4) Capuchins; (5) Catholic Merchant Companies; (6) The English Islands; (7) The Jesuit Provinces, West and South	295
§ 32. Propaganda documents about the mainland: British Colonies and French	317
§ 33. The shores of the Potomac	322
§ 34. The Indian tribes	325
§ 35. The soil and climate; fish, flesh, and fowl	329
§ 36. The first missionary establishment: 1634–1638	332
§ 37. Indented servants	340
§ 38. The second and third missionary establishments: 1638–1640	342
§ 39. The college in prospect: 1640	345
Facsimile of the *Relatio Itineris in Marilandiam*, first page . *To face*	276
Map of the Jesuit Missions in the Lesser Antilles . . . . . *To face*	296

CHAPTER V

LORD BALTIMORE AND THE CLERGY, 1635–1640 348

§ 40. John Lewger	350
§ 41. Baltimore's feudal oath for Maryland: 1635, 1636	354
§ 42. Lewger's introduction into the Church: 1635, 1636	359
§ 43. The freemen's code suppressed by Baltimore: 1635–1637	362
§ 44. Copley, Knowles, and missionary aspirants	365
§ 45. Baltimore, Virginia, and a cleavage of parties: 1635–1638	373
§ 46. Baltimore's code suppressed by the freemen: 1638	380
§ 47. Lewger's refitted code: 1638	386
§ 48. The remonstrances: 1638, 1639: (1) The parties; (2) Trade; (3) Landed property; (4) Life and limb	390
§ 49. The attack on the clergy: 1638, 1639: (1) Cornwaleys's protest; (2) Copley's criticism; (3) Copley's requests	404
§ 50. The policy in London: 1638, 1639	416
§ 51. Pressure on the missionaries: 1638, 1639	424
§ 52. The projected Church establishment: 1638, 1639: (1) General standing; (2) Details	427
§ 53. Mistaken and forgotten data: (1) The *Bulla Cœnæ* and excommunications; (2) Coke on Church privileges; (3) The privileges in common and canon law	433

CHAPTER VI

PROGRESS AND CLOSE OF THE FIRST PERIOD, 1639–1645 . . 447

§ 54. The legislation of February–March, 1639 449
§ 55. Jesuit correspondence on the subject: 1639, 1640 457
§ 56. Applications for the Maryland Mission: 1640 460
§ 57. General applications for foreign missions: 1640–1659 466
§ 58. New Maryland missionaries 471
§ 59. Seizure of Church property by Baltimore: 1640 477
§ 60. Jesuit comments on the seizure: 1641: (1) The Maryland Superior Poulton to the Provincial: (2) The procurator Copley's assignment to a layman; (3) Baltimore's counter-observations; (4) Knott the Provincial to Baltimore 480
§ 61. A new clergy for Maryland: 1641 492
§ 62. Baltimore's Conditions of Plantation: 1641: (1) Mortmain and the oath; (2) Baltimore's draft of a Provincial's Certificate; (3) Lewger's Diary on the *Bulla Cœnæ* 499
§ 63. The Provincial Knott on the situation: 1641, 1642: (1) Baltimore's Points; (2) Knott's Observations; (3) Knott's Memorial for Rome . 505
§ 64. Expedition of the new clergy suspended: 1642 518
§ 65. Remonstrance of George Gage: July, 1642 521
§ 66. Invectives and violence: September–December, 1642: (1) The Baltimore draft of a Jesuit assignment; (2) New provisions for ingress and egress; (3) Baltimore's provisions for the incoming clergy 524
§ 67. The chapels 539
§ 68. The Indian missions: 1642–1644 547
§ 69. The General on Maryland: 1643–1644 555
§ 70. Dispersion: 1645 562

APPENDICES

A. OLD ST. MARY'S CITY.
§ 71. Map of Old St. Mary's City (with Explanations) . . . . *To face* 567

B. INDIAN LAND TITLES.
§ 72. Silvius on Maryland 570
§ 73. Kent and others on the general question 573

C. STATUTES OF MORTMAIN.
History of Mortmain before Henry VIII. 578
§ 74. General idea of Mortmain 579
§ 75. Statutes of Mortmain in Catholic times 592
§ 76. The Catholic statutes and the legal status in Maryland 600

INDEX 617

Map of Jesuit Mission and Province in the North-Eastern Colonies and States: 17th–19th centuries . . . . *At end of book*

LIST OF DOCUMENTS, Vol. I. 649

INTRODUCTORY

SOURCES—ARCHIVES—LITERATURE

Sixteenth to Nineteenth Centuries

INTRODUCTION

CHAPTER I

REGISTER AND NOTICES OF THE SOURCES

WE submit a List or Register of the documentary sources or archives which have been consulted for use in this History. In the section which immediately follows, we attach descriptive Notices of the depositories or of the documents. The manner of quotation in our text hereafter shall agree with the order and form adopted in this Register, so as to facilitate reference.

We begin (§ 1) with Europe, and go on to America; then (§ 2) we annex to this List a catalogue of some publications from archives. The numbers prefixed to each head in this Register point to a corresponding head in section the second, or the descriptive Notices (§§ 3, 4).

SECTION THE FIRST.

§ 1. REGISTER OF SOURCES INEDITED.

Europe.

(1) Antwerp: *Archives S.J.*
(2) Brussels: *Archives du Royaume.*
(3)   ,,   *Belgian Province Archives S.J.*
(4)   ,,   *Bollandist Archives.*
    Bruges: *see* under Ghent.
(5) Cambridge, England: *University Library.*
(6) Dublin: *Irish Province Archives S.J.*
(7) *General Archives S.J.*
(8) Ghent: *Archives de l'État* and *de l'Hôtel de Ville.*
(9) Lyons: *Province Archives S.J.*
(10) London: *British Museum MSS.*

(11) London: *English Province Archives S.J.*
(12)   „   *Fulham Palace Archives.*
(13)   „   *Lambeth Palace MSS.*
(14)   „   *Public Record Office.*
(15)   „   *Sion College Library.*
(16)   „   *Westminster Diocesan Archives.*
(17)   „   *[Westminster] Catholic Chapter.*
(18) Paris: *Archives des Colonies.*
(19)   „   *Archives de l'École de Ste. Geneviève.*
(20)   „   *Archives Nationales.*
           „   *Province Archives S.J.* See under Paris: *L'École de Ste. Geneviève.*
(21) Rome: *Barberini Library.*[1]
(22)   „   *Corsini Library.*
(23)   „   *English College Archives.*
(24)   „   *Propaganda Archives.*
(25)   „   *Vatican Archives.*
(26)   „   *Vatican Library.*
(27) *Stonyhurst College MSS.*
(28) Turnhout, Belgium: *Archives S.J.*

We omit any particular notice of certain archives or libraries where we made some special researches, but without result; as in Dublin, with the Irish Franciscans; in Florence, Munich, and Oxford.

America.

(29) *Annapolis Records.*
(30) *Baltimore Diocesan Archives.*
(31) *Georgetown College MSS.* and *Transcripts.*
(32) *Maryland–New York Province Archives S.J.* To these may be referred special collections consulted at—
(33)   Baltimore.
(34)   Bohemia, Md., Eastern Shore.
(35)   Conewago, Pa.
(36)   Fordham, N.Y.
(37)   Frederick, Md.
(38)   Goshenhoppen, Pa.
(39)   St. Inigoes, Md.
(40)   Leonardtown, Md.
(41)   New York.
(42)   Philadelphia.
(43)   St. Thomas's Manor, Md.
(44)   Whitemarsh, Md.
(45)   Woodstock College, Md.

---

[1] This is now to be found in the Vatican Library.

(46) *Missouri Province Archives S.J.* To these may be referred other special collections at—
(47)   St. Charles, Mo.
(48)   Florissant, Mo.
(49)   St. Louis University, St. Louis.
(50) *Canadian Mission Archives S.J.*

The history of the New Orleans Mission S.J., as well as the Diocesan Archives of New York and Philadelphia, will call for a special paragraph in the Notices below (Section II. § 4).

§ 2. REGISTER OF SOURCES EDITED.

Connected with these unpublished collections may be reckoned such published literature as can properly be ranked with archives.

American Archives. Consisting of a Collection of authentick Records, State Papers, Debates, and Letters, and other Notices of Publick Affairs, the whole forming a Documentary History of the Origin and Progress of the North American Colonies; of the Causes and Accomplishment of the American Revolution; and of the Constitution of Government for the United States, to the Final Ratification thereof. In six series, etc. Prepared and published under authority of an Act of Congress [1833]. In fol. Washington. (The Fourth Series is dated Washington, December, 1837; and was published by M. St. Clair Clarke and Peter Force. In the very great variety of papers given, there appears no statement of the sources whence they are derived, nor of their respective values.)

[*American*] *Annals of Congress.* The Debates and Proceedings in the Congress of the United States; with an appendix containing important State Papers and public documents, and all the laws of a public nature; with a copious index. In 8vo. Washington. Vol. 38 is dated 1855.

[*American*] *Congressional Reports.* Senate and Executive documents, etc.

American State Papers. Documents, Legislative and Executive, of the Congress of the United States, etc., March 3, 1789—March 3, 1815. Edited, under the authority of Congress, by W. Lowrie, Secretary of the Senate, and M. St. Clair Clarke, Clerk of the House of Representatives. In fol. Vols. v. and vi., which are, Class ii. Indian Affairs, vols. 1 and 2. Washington, 1832 and 1834.

[*American*] *State Papers and Publick Documents of the United States*, from the accession of George Washington to the Presidency, exhibiting a complete view of our foreign relations since that time, etc. In 8vo. Vol. xi. 3rd edit. is dated Boston, 1819.

[*British*] *Calendars of State Papers: Colonial Series.* Vols. i.–xv. Edited by W.Noel Sainsbury and by the Hon.J.W.Fortescue. 1860–1901. Published by the authority of the Lords Commissioners of His Majesty's Treasury, under the direction of the Master of the Rolls. Large 8vo. London. (The fifteen volumes published up to the present date cover America and the West Indies; East Indies, China, and Japan; East Indies alone; East Indies and Persia. Ten of them belong to our department of America and the West Indies. To form these ten into a distinct series for purposes of quotation, it is necessary to give them a numeration of their own; as is done in the following list, according to which they will be quoted in this work :—)

America and West Indies, 1574–1660 : to be quoted as A. & W.I. i.
 ,, ,, ,, 1661–1668 : ,, ,, A. & W.I. ii.
 ,, ,, ,, 1669–1674 : ,, ,, A. & W.I. iii.
 ,, ,, ,, 1675–1676 :
    and Addenda, 1574–1674 : ,, A. & W.I. iv.
 ,, ,, ,, 1677–1680 : ,, ,, A. & W.I. v.
 ,, ,, ,, 1681–1685 : ,, ,, A. & W.I. vi.
 ,, ,, ,, 1685–1688 : ,, ,, A. & W.I. vii.
 ,, ,, ,, 1689–1692 : ,, ,, A. & W.I. viii.
 ,, ,, ,, 1693–1696 : ,, ,, A. & W.I. ix.
 ,, ,, ,, 1696–1697 : ,, ,, A. & W.I. x.

[*British*] *House of Commons: Reports, Committees.* Committee on Mortmain, 1844, 1851, 1852.

[*British*] *Parliamentary History—Parliamentary Debates* (*Cobbett's*).

[*British*] *Statutes of the Realm.* (The chief editions used are Ruffhead's, and that in massive folios, printed by command of His Majesty King George the Third, in 1819, etc., and covering the period up to Queen Anne. Different editions of the Statutes at Large vary in the paragraphing, numbering of sections, and manner of dating the parliamentary sessions. But the matter did not seem of sufficient consequence to require that the edition should be specified, provided that the exact statute was reached in an authentic text.)

Constitutiones Societatis Jesu latinæ et hispanicæ cum earum declarationibus. Fol. Matriti, 1892.—*Institutum Societatis Jesu.* 3 tt. Florentiæ, 1892–1893.

Constitutions, The Federal and State; Colonial Charters, and other Organic Laws of the United States. Two vols. in fol. Washington, 1878.

Foley, Henry, S.J.: Records of the English Province of the Society of Jesus. Historic Facts illustrative of the Labours and Sufferings of its Members in the sixteenth and seventeenth centuries. In 8vo; twelve series in five volumes; with a supplementary sixth volume on the English College in Rome, and general addenda; and with two further volumes, No. vii. in two parts, containing general statistics, tabulated Collectanea or biographical notices, catalogue of aliases, further addenda; and supplements on the Irish as well as Scotch Missions. London, 1877–1883. (The numbering of the volumes, as thus registered, is to be found only on the title-pages, according to which they will be quoted.)

Gibson, Edmund, D.D.: Codex Juris Ecclesiastici Anglicani; or, The Statutes, Constitutions, Canons, Rubricks and Articles, of the Church of England, etc.; with a Commentary, Historical and Juridical, etc. By Edmund Gibson, DD., Archdeacon of Surrey, Rector of Lambeth, and Chaplain to his Grace the Lord Archbishop of Canterbury. Two volumes, in fol. London, 1713.

Hughes, Thomas, S.J.: Missionary Countries, Old and New. *The American Catholic Quarterly Review*, xxiv. 1–25 (January, 1899).

—— —— The London Vicariate Apostolic and the West Indies, 1685–1819. *The Dublin Review*, cxxxiv. 66–93 (January, 1904).

Hughes, Thomas, S.J.: The Sacrament of Confirmation in the Old Colonies. *American Ecclesiastical Review*, xxviii. 23–41 (January, 1903).

—— —— Educational Convoys to Europe in the olden time. *American Ecclesiastical Review*, xxix. 24–39 (July, 1903).

—— —— A Maryland Marriage Question, A.D. 1713.[1] *American Ecclesiastical Review*, xxvi. 521–538 (May, 1902).

—— —— An Alleged Popish Plot in Pennsylvania: 1756–57. From intercepted correspondence. *Records of the American Catholic Historical Society*, [Philadelphia], x. 208–221 (June, 1899).

—— —— Properties of the Jesuits in Pennsylvania: 1730–1830. *Records of the American Catholic Historical Society*, xi. 177–195, 281–294 (June–September, 1900).

Maryland, Archives of. Published by authority of the State, under the direction of the Maryland Historical Society; editor, W. H. Browne. 1883, etc. In quarto. Baltimore. (The twenty or more volumes, so far announced or published, contain various collections from different dates of Proceedings and Acts of the General Assembly; Proceedings of the Council; Judicial and Testamentary Business of the Provincial Court; Correspondence of Governor Horatio Sharpe; Journal of the Maryland Convention; of the Maryland Council of Safety, etc.)

[*Maryland:*] *Baldwin, J.*: *Maryland Calendar of Wills.* Compiled and edited by Jane Baldwin. Vol. i., 1635–1685. In 8vo. pp. ix.–219; index, i.–lxii. Baltimore, 1901.

Maryland Historical Society: Fund Publications. Various in subjects, authors, and dates. In 8vo. Baltimore, Maryland. We append the numbers and names of the following:—

7. *Relatio Itineris in Marylandiam. Declaratio Coloniæ Domini Baronis de Baltimoro. Excerpta ex Diversis Litteris Missionariorum ab Anno 1635 ad Annum 1638.* Translated by J. Holmes Converse, and edited by Rev. E. A. Dalrymple, S.T.D., pp. 1–100; notes, pp. 101–128. 1874. (Latin text to near the end of the Annual Letter for 1638; then English translation alone as far as the Annual Letter for 1677 inclusively. The series of these letters is not continuous.)

7. Supplement: *Excerpta ex Diversis Litteris Missionariorum ab Anno 1638 ad Annum 1677.* Edited by Rev. E. A. Dalrymple, S.T.D., pp. 1–36; notes, pp. 37–44. 1877. (This Supplement contains the missing Latin text of Publication No. 7.)

As to these publications, No. 7 and its Supplement, and the reproduction of the documents in our accompanying volume, see Notices below: Sources inedited, No. (7), p. 13.

18. [*Johnson:*] *The Foundation of Maryland and the Origin of the Act concerning Religion of April 21, 1649.* By Bradley T. Johnson, pp. 1–161; appendix and index, pp 163–210. 1883.

As to the documents given by General Johnson in No. 18, or referred to by Mr. Streeter in another publication, see below: Sources inedited, No. (7), p. 13.

28. *The Calvert Papers.* (*Number One.*) An account of their recovery and presentation to the Society, December 10, 1888, pp. 1–55. Calendar of the Calvert Papers, prepared by John W. M. Lee,

---

[1] This date should be 1714.

pp. 57–126. The Calvert Papers, First Selection, pp. 127–331. Note, pp. 333–334. 1889.
34. *The Calvert Papers.* (*Number Two.*) Selections from Correspondence, pp. xiv.–263. 1894.
35. *The Calvert Papers.* (*Number Three.*) "A Briefe Relation of the Voyage vnto Maryland," and other Papers, pp. 1–47; appendixes, pp. 49–58. 1899.

[*Maryland:*] *Kilty, John: The Land-holder's Assistant and Land-Office Guide.* Being an exposition of original titles, etc. By John Kilty, Register of the Land-Office for the Western-Shore of the State of Maryland. In 8vo, pp. 1–497; appendix, i.–xliv.; index, i.–vi. Baltimore, 1808.

Massachusetts Historical Society, Collections. Various volumes and series; tome 5. 1798, etc.

[*New York, Brodhead:*] *Documents relative to the Colonial History of the State of New-York.* Procured in Holland, England, and France, by John Romeyn Brodhead, Esq., agent, under an Act of the Legislature, etc. Eleven volumes, large quarto. 1856–1861. Albany, N.Y. Vols. i., ii. contain documents from Holland; iii.–viii., those from London; ix., x., from France; xi., a general and exhaustive index. (Co-editor and superintendent of the publication was E. B. O'Callaghan, M.D., LL.D., who reproduced all the foreign documents in an English dress without the original text. Introductory to each of the three sections may be seen an account of the respective archives whence the compiler derived his documents; as also some historical apparatus relative to the classes of correspondents, such as the Secretaries of State, Board of Trade and Plantations, Colonial Governors, etc. The whole work is characterized by painstaking accuracy.)

[*New York: O'Callaghan:*] *The Documentary History of the State of New York.* Arranged under the direction of the Hon. Christopher Morgan, Secretary of State, by E. B. O'Callaghan, M.D. Four volumes 8vo. 1849–1851. Albany, N.Y. (The matter is arranged in a desultory way, but its merit seems to be of the same order as that ascribed to Brodhead above, whose work was edited a few years later by the same Dr. O'Callaghan.)

Perry, W. S., D.D.: Historical Collections relating to the American Colonial Church [Protestant Episcopal]. Edited by William Stevens Perry, D.D. In large quarto. (The material consists chiefly of manuscripts or transcripts from originals, collected by the Rev. Francis Lister Hawks, D.D., LL.D., from the archives at Lambeth, Fulham, and from those of the Society for the Propagation of the Gospel in Foreign Parts. Bishop Perry apologizes for the imperfect condition of many papers from which he has had to edit the documents:—)

  i. Virginia, pp. xviii.—536; notes, pp. 537–560; index, pp. 561–585.
 ii. Pennsylvania, pp. xxii.–496; notes, pp. 497–586; index, pp. 587–607.
iii. Massachusetts, pp. xxvi.–640; notes, pp. 641–698; index, pp. 699–720.
 iv. Maryland, pp. xii.–348; notes, pp. 349–356; index, pp. 357–370.
  v. Delaware, pp. viii.–140; notes, pp. 141–146; index, pp. 147–151.

Records of the American Catholic Historical Society. In 8vo. 1884, etc. Philadelphia.

[*Records:*] *Historical Records and Studies: United States Catholic Historical Society.* In 8vo. 1899, etc. New York.

[*Researches:*] *The American Catholic Historical Researches.* In 8vo. 1885, etc. Edited since 1887 by M. I. J. Griffin, Philadelphia.

Sommervogel, Carlos, S.J.: Bibliothèque de la Compagnie de Jésus. Première partie—Bibliographie, par les Pères Augustin et Aloys de Backer; seconde partie—Histoire, par le P. Auguste Carayon; nouvelle édition. Bibliographie, Supplément, Anonymes-Pseudonymes, tt. i.–ix. In folio. Bruxelles, Paris, 1890–1900.

Vivier, Alexander, S.J.: Nomina Patrum ac Fratrum qui Societatem Jesu ingressi in ea supremum diem obierunt: 7 augusti 1814—7 augusti 1894. Large quarto, pp. xxiv.–584; index, etc., pp. 585–766. Parisiis, 1897. The entries, in chronological order, number 8311. (A small 8vo edition, pp. xii.–259, reproduces only the summary of names and dates, as tabulated in the index of the full work.)

SECTION THE SECOND.

Following the same numerical order as in the Register (§ 1), we proceed to—

§ 3. NOTICES OF THE SOURCES INEDITED.

Europe.

(1) ANTWERP: ARCHIVES S.J. Three volumes in 8vo, made up and bound in the early part of the nineteenth century by Father Cornelius Geerts, of Antwerp (A.D. 1746–1819). In the third volume, pp. 142–331, there are many extracts or copies made by him of the American correspondence at large, from 1804 to 1809. The subject-matter is the departure and progress of missionaries despatched to America; invoices of goods sent over by Belgian benefactors; reports, etc. There is also, as yet in manuscript, a history of the Jesuit establishment at Antwerp, which shows the activity of missionary emigration to America, between 1835 and 1840. This matter concerns the missionaries who went from the Low Countries in the first half of the nineteenth century, and either reinforced the Jesuit and secular missions in Archbishop Carroll's time, or later, as members of the Missouri Province of the Society, first founded and then carried on with signal success the great Missions of the Rocky Mountains.

To Father Charles Droeshout, S.J., the author of this history, we owe every acknowledgment for his kindness, and also for the gift of another history, which illustrates still more the course of missionary enterprise in America between 1817 and 1840. It is that of the College of Turnhout, and of the apostleship exercised in favour of the new world by a distinguished benefactor, M. Jean Pierre De Nef. The author gave us his own original manuscript, a handsome copy in four great folios being in the possession of Turnhout College.

(2) BRUSSELS: ARCHIVES DU ROYAUME. There is a very large store

of Jesuit documents here; and, as the educational colleges of the English Province were in the Low Countries, no small amount of their original papers are seen to have been swept into this depository at the time of the Suppression. The condition of these Government archives is most unsatisfactory. Several collections of transcripts were made by Fathers Cardwell and Morris, for the service of the English Province in recent times. What we managed to collect in the interest of American history was picked up by a method of the most haphazard divination. We discovered some facts regarding young Americans at St. Omer's in 1764; besides an item relating to the young Calverts, sons of the first Lord Baltimore, in 1629. The papers were original.

(3) BRUSSELS: BELGIAN PROVINCE ARCHIVES S.J. These are very extensive on the same subject as that mentioned under the head of Antwerp. They consist of originals, and also largely of contemporary copies, covering the period 1806–1839. They include copies of letters sent by the Archbishops of Baltimore. The documents offer a very striking testimony to the generosity which Belgian Catholics exercised towards America. The correspondents and agents who transmit the fruits of this generosity are chiefly M. Peemans of Louvain and M. De Nef of Turnhout. The papers are in bundles, in sewed quires, and in bound volumes. The language is either Flemish or French.

For manuscript biographies of Father Peter Malou and Father Théodore De Theux, derived from originals in the possession of their respective noble families, we are indebted to the kindness of the author, Rev. J. F. Kieckens, S.J.; as also for a quantity of material, similarly authentic, and not incorporated in his biographies. These latter are in a condition to be translated and published.

(4) BRUSSELS: BOLLANDIST ARCHIVES. Matter, which was supplied to us from the Museum Ignatianum of the Bollandists, Brussels, was largely blended with that of the Belgian Province, as described above; and we need add nothing special to the foregoing number (3).

(5) CAMBRIDGE, ENGLAND: UNIVERSITY LIBRARY. Here is to be seen a small manuscript quarto, of about 100 pages, the notes or drafts beginning at both ends. It is the private Note and Letter Book of Father John Warner, who was Provincial of the English Province during the latter period of the Titus Oates agitation. He furnishes several items of information on American affairs, 1680–1684. Further particulars about the book are given in Foley's *Collectanea*, under the name, "Warner, John."

(6) DUBLIN: IRISH PROVINCE ARCHIVES S.J. There are papers gathered here, chiefly by the Rev. Edmund Hogan, S.J., upon subjects which illustrate the early nineteenth century, and, at a subsequent date, bear upon Father Peter Kenney's ministry in behalf of the American mission. The American correspondence is original; and the writers are Father Ferdinand Farmer, Archbishop Carroll, Father Benedict Fenwick,

besides others. Moreover, at the critical period of the Society's restoration, the general course of events in Ireland, as well as in England, afforded grounds for a useful comparison with parallel experiences on the American side of the ocean. These papers were kindly put at our service by Father Hogan.

(7) GENERAL ARCHIVES S.J. Of these we shall speak at some length in Chapter II. of this Introduction, when we sketch the history of the Jesuit archives. There are documents which concern us in the three divisions of (a) Letters from the Generals of the Order; (b) Letters and Documents of others; (c) Catalogues or Registers of Persons.

(a) *Anglia: Epistolæ Generalium.* Three volumes, stout, small folio, made up of unequal quires, bound in half pig-skin, like all the rest of these documents; and not paginated.[1] The binding seems to be recent; probably of the early part of the nineteenth century. The letters are the original authentic drafts, in the hand of the General himself, or in that of a secretary; and from them the copies were taken and despatched. Hence they are nearly chronological in their arrangement; though sometimes the fact of a letter appearing out of its place shows that the record was entered afterwards from a loose draft. The injury which is being done by time and corrosive ink to these invaluable papers is partly discounted now by the complete photographic reproduction which we have caused to be made of the three volumes. Upon American affairs, as treated chiefly through the English Provincial, there are letters, or rather paragraphs in letters, throughout the entire series after the first mention of English America, till 1744—some 111 years. And again, after this latter date, where the main series ends, there are some more paragraphs directed or relating to Americans and American missionaries, in an appendix of answers to very private letters addressed *Soli*, that is, for the General's eye alone. They reach as far as April 1, 1769.

A facsimile specimen is presented below of a normal draft as made by the General Muzio Vitelleschi. It shows in the process of composition his very first letter on Anglo-American affairs. (See *infra*, *History*, § 6 : "Father White: a Professor;" reproduction of General's letter, 1629, March 3, to Father Andrew White, at Liège.)

(b) *Anglia: Historia.* Seven large folio volumes, besides two quartos, which latter contain respectively Father Christopher Grene's notes, records, etc., and Father Bartoli's materials for his work on England. In the seven folio tomes there are to be seen the *Relatio Itineris*, Annual Letters, and other documents of value. Those which concern us are all autograph or original copies, coming down from their respective dates. The binding of these volumes, like that of the Generals' Letters, is recent. To direct the binder, some one wrote in pencil upon the fly-leaf, apparently in an Italian hand, *Anglia—Historia*, adding the

---

[1] The first tome contains ff. 528; the second, ff. 577 the third, ff. 399; in all, ff. 1504.

dates of the period covered by the volume. This the binder reproduced on the back as *Anglia Histor.*, or *Anglia Hist.*, adding the dates. To avoid confusion with the Stonyhurst documents entitled *Anglia*, we have kept rigidly to this form of citation.

Father Thomas Glover, who discharged various functions in Rome from 1825 to 1849, compiled two volumes of Excerpts from Annual Letters, etc., and he quotes from *Angl. Hist.* But the dates, which he affixes as part of the title to the tomes, do not agree with those of to-day. From this it would appear that they have been reconstructed since then.

The material proper to America underwent a process of division at some time, possibly with the dispersion of the Society in the Roman Revolution of 1849, and the return of Father Glover to England.[2] A short series of papers which are about America may now be found in the Stonyhurst MSS., called *Anglia A*, with a great quantity of other papers, which were evidently of the General's fund, and related to England. Dr. George Oliver, who died some thirteen years after Father Glover's return, is credited with having put these documents into their present form of binding. A portion of the American documents, the *Relatio Itineris*, the *Declaratio Coloniæ*, etc., remained where they had been originally, and are in the volumes of the General Archives before us: *Anglia—Historia*.

A facsimile specimen from this collection is given below, where a page of Father White's Narrative, *Relatio Itineris*, may be seen in the official hand of the General's Roman copyist, with some marks by Father Southwell's hand abridging and excluding matter for his own redaction (cf. *infra*, Introduction, Chap. I. § 6). (See *infra*, History, § 27: "The Voyage to America;" reproduction of *Relatio Itineris*, first page.)

(c) *Angliæ Catalogi.* Fifteen volumes, large quarto, thick and thin, some containing the Catalogues or registers of persons for a single triennial set of reports, others comprising large collections of annual or short Catalogues. These, supplemented by a large volume of Catalogues now bound up in the English Province Archives, under the title *Catalogi Varii Provinciæ Angliæ S.J.*, are adequate to fill up with registers the entire period of a hundred and forty years between the foundation of Maryland and the Suppression of the Society (1633–1773).

As to what comes under the name of "triennial" reports, covering the normal period from one Provincial Congregation to another, all that may be aptly described in the words of a General, Father Retz, to an English Rector of Liège, Father Henry Bolt, who was acting as Vice-Provincial on the Continent. He says he will "repeat" what he has stated in several letters recently: There are desired a Catalogue of the members deceased since the last Provincial Congregation, also of those dismissed,

---

[2] However, a division for a temporary purpose may have taken place earlier, to meet some demands of M. Crétineau-Joly. (See below, No. (19), Paris, Ste. Geneviève.)

as well as of books published; copies likewise of foundations [title-deeds], of contracts, at least such as are more important, of professions, and vows of spiritual and temporal coadjutors; finally, Annual Letters, with the supplement of the History, and with the data for the Menology of the Society. Strictly speaking, he says, there should also be an information regarding subjects with a view to their filling posts as superiors; but he foregoes demanding a repetition within three years of an information, if the subject is being proposed for a post of authority a second time within such a period of three years.[3]

To the annual and triennial reviews of the Province was added the particular report about each house, immediately after the formal visitation made by the Provincial in the course of his circuit each year; as well as the collateral information contained in the reports at stated seasons from the four councillors attached to the Provincial; and from those, usually four in number, assigned to each local superior.

(d) [America:] *Epistolæ Generalium*. The Generals' Letters concerning America in the nineteenth century, when there was no longer the old connection between that country and England, are mingled as far as 1830 with correspondence directed to other parts of the world. Being of a modern cast and numerous, they will be treated specially when we come to use them.

It is to be understood, as a matter of course, that letters sent by the Generals or sent to them are regularly in Latin. While the material is so limited as it is for the first main division of our history, that is to say, up to the Suppression of the Society (1773), or till near the date of the American Revolution, all that we find, as dating originally from Rome, can be reproduced in our companion volume of *Documents*, I. After that, the quantity becomes too considerable to re-edit, apart from our use of it in the text. For that older period, therefore, the codices or volumes, as we have described them above, may be tabulated as follows:—

(a) Anglia: *Epist. Gen.* 1605–1641.
    ,,   ,,   1642–1698.
    ,,   ,,   1698–1744. *Soli*, 1681–1769.

The first of these volumes contains the correspondence for Great Britain in general till 1623, in which year the English portion, having been first a Mission, and then a Vice-Province, was raised to the grade of a full Province.

(b) Anglia: *Histor.* 1550–1589, ff. 583, pp. 585–599, to be cited as I.
    ,,   ,,   1590–1615, ff. 466, pp. 467–732   ,,   ,, II.
    ,,   ,,   1616–1627, *Litteræ annuæ* 1623–1649, ff. 495, to be cited as III.
    ,,   ,,   1628–1644, pp. 927, to be cited as IV.
    ,,   ,,   1645–1678, pp. 857   ,,   ,, V.

[3] General Archives S.J., *Anglia, Epist. Gen.*, 1741, April 8.

Anglia: Histor. 1679–1761, pp. 797 to be cited as VI.
,,   ,,   Monum. Hist. Suppl., pp. 509, to be cited as VII.
Hist. Angl. Suppl. I. [Grene's papers]   ,,   ,,   VIII.
Hist. Angliæ, Suppl. II. [Bartoli's materials]   ,,   ,,   IX.

In Glover's Excerpta (Stonyhurst MSS., B.I. 16, vol. 1, 2), such quotations as the following are used for Annual Letters: (vol. i. p. 1) *Ex tomo, cui titulus, Angl. Hist.*, 1635, 1649, *in Archivio Domus Professæ Soc. Jesu Romæ*; (ibid., p. 107) *Excerpta e tomo cui titulus, Angl. Histor.*, 1645–1677; (ibid., p. 331) *Ex tomo cui titulus, Angl. Hist.*, 1631–1717, etc.

(c) Angl. Catal., 1623–1639, Catal. Brev. et Trienn.
Angliæ Catal., 1639, 1649.
,,   ,,   1622, 1649.
,,   ,,   1651, 1658.
Ang., 1678, C. 1, 2.
Ang. Catal., 1, 2, 1681.
Angliæ Catal., 1665, 1675 [all 1 and 2].
Angl. Catal., 1685 [1 and 2].
Angl. Cat., 1690 [1 and 2].
Angl. Cata., 1693 [1 and 2].
Angliæ Catal., 1696 [1 and 2, to which is added, as a matter of course, Catal. 3 *Rerum*].
Angl. Catal., 1632–1680 [all *Catalogi breves*].
Anglia Cat. Brev., 1682–1758.
Anglia Cat. Trien., 1700–1727.
Anglia Cat. Trien., 1730–1767.

The "first" and "second" Catalogues are full triennial reports regarding the members. The "third" or "brief" one is drawn up annually to record the situation and offices of members, but triennially in what regards temporalities or property.

The manner of quoting from the General Archives S.J. is indicated below, § 9: *Abbreviations*.

In the accompanying volume containing a redaction of documents, and to be cited as *Documents*, I., we propose to give the following elements from the archives:—

First, the entire series of excerpts out of the Generals' Letters, from the time when the first mention of an American expedition occurs in the correspondence to the last item which we find on American topics prior to the Suppression, that is to say, from March 3, 1629, to May 23, 1744.

Secondly, the amended and augmented series of Annual Letters, as far as we have found them, with the addition of property accounts, sent in triennially.

Thirdly, an authentic redaction of those papers, now found at Stonyhurst, which pertain to the controversy between Lord Baltimore and the Jesuits in Maryland, 1640–1649.

The first of these heads will furnish matter perfectly new,—that of the Generals' correspondence.

The second will revise and complete the editions of Jesuit Annual Letters, etc., for which we are indebted to the Maryland Historical Society; originally, as translated in 1847, by Nathan C. Brooks, LL.D.; subsequently, as re-edited, English and Latin together, by the Rev. E. A. Dalrymple, S.T.D., in 1874–1877. These included as their chief documents the *Relatio Itineris* and the *Declaratio Coloniæ*. The copy from which the gentlemen edited was not equal to the original, from which we make our redaction. The first translation appeared in Peter Force's Collection of Historical Tracts, vol. iv. No. 12; the second was issued as the Maryland Historical Society's Fund Publication, No. 7, 1874, and No. 7 Supplement, 1877.[4] We shall take occasion in a subsequent paragraph to mention the Act of the State Legislature of Maryland, and the correspondence pursuant thereto, which led to these literary labours.

The third will present the proper text of documents cited by General Bradley T. Johnson, in Fund Publication, No. 18, on "The Foundation of Maryland and the Origin of the Act concerning Religion of April 21, 1649" (Baltimore, 1883, pp. 210). Mr. B. U. Campbell, in 1846,[5] and Mr. S. F. Streeter, in 1852, by the courtesy of Mr. Campbell,[6] made use of some portion of these documents, relating to the controversy between Lord Baltimore and the early Jesuit missionaries.

(8) GHENT: ARCHIVES DE L'ÉTAT; ARCHIVES DE L'HÔTEL DE VILLE. In the State archives deposited at Ghent may be seen the registers of the large and small Jesuit colleges at Bruges, as they stood when the Emperor of Germany put in execution the Brief of Clement XIV., dissolving the Society of Jesus. The commissary, whose eye is exclusively on the property, pensions, etc., closes his account on the 5th day of November, 1773; and, in his statement regarding scholars, with their debits and credits, not a few West Indian and Maryland names appear. Another account, given by P. Augustin Noël, Priest and Regent of the College at Bruges, 1775, carries on for two years more the record of receipts, etc. The volumes are numbered 82, 83, 88, in which the records or inventories cover respectively 211 pp., 385 pp., and about 200 pp. in folio.

The Municipal Archives, at the Hôtel de Ville, contained nothing special.

(9) LYONS: PROVINCE ARCHIVES S.J. We found here a trace of what seems to be correspondence between the newly consecrated Bishop Carroll (September, 1790) and Father Pierre Picot de Clorivière, who was a candidate for the American missions. Other letters from Clorivière addressed to young Father John Bolton at Bruges (1766–1768) are preserved in the Maryland–New York Province Archives.

---

[4] See prefaces of Dalrymple to Fund Publication, No. 7, and No. 7 Supplement.
[5] B. U. Campbell, *Historical Sketch of the Early Christian Missions among the Indians of Maryland*.—St. Inigoes Record Book; a copy, pp. 57–74.
[6] S. F. Streeter, *Maryland Two Hundred Years Ago*, p. 32, note.

(10) LONDON: BRITISH MUSEUM MANUSCRIPTS. This great collection of MSS., in every line of political and religious thought and activity, has served us in three ways: first, in the same researches as we made in the Public Record Office, to discern the political movements of the American Colonies; secondly, in certain questions of a general religious character or with reference to Jesuits in particular, whether in the old English Colonies or in the newly acquired Canada, during the period up to the nineteenth century; thirdly, in finding out the characters and tracing the fortunes of the Calverts, George and Cæcilius, the earliest Lords Baltimore. However, many of the political documents which interested us seemed to be only duplicates of the materials in the fuller depository, the Public Record Office.

(11) LONDON: ENGLISH PROVINCE ARCHIVES S.J. These, which are still kept separate from the Stonyhurst MSS., are a large collection of bound and unbound documents, papers, note-books, besides a valuable set of English procurators' ledgers and waste-books, dating from 1730. We gathered much information about Fathers in America, and about the young Americans of both sexes, who flocked to the colleges and convents in Belgium and France. This occurred especially between 1747 and 1769. The money accounts, too, of Maryland and Pennsylvania with the parent Province appear from 1731 till 1818. Here may be seen a fair portion of Carroll's correspondence with Father Charles Plowden; the remainder, now found in the Maryland Province Archives, evidently formed part of this series.[7] There is a set of extracts made in Rome by Father John Thorpe, from letters of the Provincials, etc., and affording us points of information on America from 1713 to 1759. There is also much correspondence belonging to the nineteenth century—Grassi's, Kohlmann's, Bishop Milner's, etc.; all of which is important, because of a strange and irregular connection, made in the years 1822-1830 by persons outside of the Order, between the affairs of the Jesuits in England and those of the Jesuits in America.

(12) LONDON: FULHAM PALACE ARCHIVES. The muniment-room, in which we were permitted to work by the late Anglican Bishop of London, Dr. Mandell Creighton, was in no orderly condition. It is impossible to cite with any degree of precision masses and bundles of papers, among which certain piles were inscribed as relating to parts of North America. Several interesting papers came to hand, of a kind which were likely to be of more interest to us than to Dr. Hawks or to Dr. Perry, who had

---

[7] Cf. below, under No. (19), Paris, Ste. Geneviève: on Grassi and Dubuisson. In the English Province Archives, Portfolio 6, now a bound volume, entitled *Maryland*, consisting of ff. 137, with other documents inserted, contains letters or papers of John Carroll (thirty-three in number, from January 23, 1772, to October 15, 1815); Leonard Neale, Charles Sewall, Grassi, Kohlmann, Grivel, Christian Mayer (Mannheim, April 24, 1778), John Ashton, W. Strickland, Ambrose Maréchal, Austin Hill (Cincinnati, April 12, 1825). The correspondents are Ellerker (Liège), Charles Plowden, Nicholas Sewall, Strickland, Stone, Peter Jenkins, Korsak, Tristram, and Lord Arundell of Wardour.

used these archives. We were much indebted to his lordship for his courtesy.

(13) LONDON: LAMBETH PALACE MANUSCRIPTS, in the library of the Archbishop of Canterbury. Three folio volumes on the American colonies contain a large quantity of religious matter from the side of Protestant authorities and organizations. The question of the Indians receives no mean illustration from the tenor of a controversy, which was rather actively pursued in 1762-1763 by the Anglican ministers in New England and New York on the one side, under the guidance of Archbishop Secker of Canterbury, as against Congregationalist preachers on the other. Then an untimely fate befell the new-born Boston Society for Propagating Christian Knowledge among the Indians of North America. Other volumes throw light upon the perpetual difficulty of settling a bishop in America; on the efforts of Dr. Thomas Bray, Commissary of the Bishop of London, to establish parish libraries, and to feed a Virginia College by means of free schools in Maryland. The three folio volumes on the American colonies are numbered, 1123; and seem to have been well thumbed. Vol. I., documents 1-87, has some early papers of A.D. 1641, 1642, then 1693-1725; but is chiefly filled with documents of 1750-1754. Vol. II., documents 88-215, covers A.D. 1755-1760. Vol. III., documents 216-336, comprises A.D. 1760—December 20, 1763. Other volumes that may be named are Nos. 711, 941, 942, and 953.

(14) LONDON: PUBLIC RECORD OFFICE. In the Literary Search Room of the new building, it appears from the superintendent's special list that there are between two and three thousand volumes on hand, relating to American colonial affairs, those of British Canada included. The general divisions are: *Colonial Papers*, or the correspondence sent from the colonies; the *Colonial Entry Books*, or official bound minute-books, etc., transmitted to the home Government; *Colonial Office Transmissions; Colonial Correspondence;* the *Board of Trade's* correspondence from the colonies, or specifically from the Leeward Islands of the West Indies; *Proprieties,* etc. The merest contingencies of business and accident governed the growth and assortment of these documents. The process of calendaring the papers on America and the West Indies had, in the years 1897, 1898, reached as far as 1680 in the records; and in 1901-1902 further progress had been made to the year 1692. While undergoing such process of calendaring, all volumes, which were not originally bound books, were broken up and reconstructed into new books, on a strictly chronological plan; and, while in this state of reconstruction, the old volumes were represented only by residual fragments. After the point of time to which the calendaring had reached, there was nothing for a student to do but to proceed by guess-work, helped by the general name of a tome, and perhaps by a table of contents within. By this method of research we examined strictly and accurately some two hundred

volumes relating to Maryland, New York, New England, Massachusetts, the Leeward Islands, Canada, etc.

Since the records are open to the public only as far as the year 1802, and the Jesuit question of the old Canadian landed property was not yet finished at that date, we received permission from the Secretary of the Colonies, Mr. Chamberlain, to continue that question even as far as 1820, if necessary. We desisted, however, at 1809, leaving Governor Craig and Lord Castlereagh to settle the matter of those estates as best they might with the Indians and the Educational Commissioners of Canada.

The ten volumes of Calendars so far published on America and the West Indies, and tabulated above in the second article of our Register,[8] are of a high order of accuracy, though they do not satisfy the minds of critics on the score of technical finish. Not content with merely describing papers, they frequently reproduce important parts or entire documents; and, when they profess to do this literally, there is, as far as we have observed, but little reason for suspecting any error. Such literal reproduction is naturally rare, and very seldom in the line of our researches. Nor was it even to be expected that general statements or abstracts of papers would satisfy an inquirer who was following a very particular scent. So vast is the territory to be explored in such a world of historical documents, that the paths to be struck out by searchers form a network of lines, no one following the same as his neighbour, and all beyond the scope of an archivist who is sketching for general purposes.

Along with the Calendars, to supplement investigation among these London papers, there are the volumes of Brodhead's *Documents relative to the Colonial History of the State of New York*, registered above;[9] the published archives of other States, especially Maryland,[10] etc. Mr. Brodhead has given an account of how he used the London documents of the State Paper Office, now called the Public Record Office.[11] But since then everything has been changed—the locality, the system, and the results thence accruing for the convenience of the public.

For the *Transcripts from Rome* in the Public Record Office, see below, No. (21), Rome, Barberini Library.

(15) LONDON: SION COLLEGE LIBRARY. In this library of the Anglican clergy we were favoured with the manuscripts relating to Dr. Thomas Bray, appointed Commissary for Maryland by the Bishop of London in April, 1696.

(16) LONDON: WESTMINSTER DIOCESAN ARCHIVES. With the permission of His Eminence Cardinal Vaughan, we examined these extensive

---

[8] Register, *supra*, § 2, p. 4.—Another volume is issued, October, 1905.
[9] *Ibid.*, p. 6.
[10] *Ibid.*, pp. 5, 6.
[11] Brodhead, *Documents relative to the Colonial History of New York*, i. pp. xxii.-xxiv., xxvii.-xxx.; iii. pp. xix.-xx.

records for some distinct objects, and we were rewarded with several papers of consequence, especially on the Indian land question in Maryland. These archives are well cared for by the Rev. Fathers of the Oratory.

(17) LONDON: [WESTMINSTER] CATHOLIC CHAPTER. This remnant of antiquity, which, as we understood, has no connection with the organization of the Westminster archdiocese, still keeps several ancient papers; and, among them, a document on the expedition of secular clergymen to Maryland in 1642. The secretary, the Rev. R. Stanfield, afforded us every facility for securing a careful transcript.

(18) PARIS: ARCHIVES DES COLONIES. In the French colonial archives relating to New France, we endeavoured to investigate a question about the Jesuits, French and English, at the time of Dongan's governorship in New York. Here notes and signs, very irregularly inscribed on the documents themselves in the archives, show that some scribes of crude and primitive notions had copied documents for Mr. Parkman and M. Marmette.

(19) PARIS: ARCHIVES DE L'ÉCOLE DE SAINTE GENEVIÈVE, S.J. These we might call at once the archives of the Province of France. But, as they were deposited in the College of the Rue des Postes or Rue Lhomond, and since Père C. de Rochemonteix quotes them as archives of that college,[12] we keep the same form. There was a very large collection of Jesuit papers here, well preserved and bound, relating chiefly to the affairs of New France and the French Antilles, but also to those of British Canada and the English colonies. Omitting the valuable old French relations and ancient documents, we observed here a set of papers in French or in Italian, which treated of British America and the United States, and had a very special value for us. The French papers we refer to the authorship of Father Stephen Dubuisson, a Maryland Jesuit, who from 1827 onwards till his death in 1864 did considerable service in Rome and elsewhere in Europe. The Italian notes we should ascribe to Father John Anthony Grassi, were they written in his hand. After being Rector of Georgetown and Superior of the Maryland Mission, he spent the rest of his life, from 1817 to 1849, in Italy and Rome, where he was Assistant to the General. The French papers are various and of different dates. The Italian notes are called by the writer *Cenni sulla Chiesa Cattolica nella Colonia di Maryland negli Stati Uniti per quello che riguarda la Compagnia di Gesù*. And there are other *Cenni*, or Notes, on particular parts of the same subject. Where we ourselves have verified the statements in these sketches and outlines, we have found them to be perfectly correct. And the knowledge which the writers show of documents both in Europe and America, besides their personal acquaintance with transatlantic affairs, makes still more clear

[12] P. Camille de Rochemonteix, S.J., *Les Jésuites et la Nouvelle-France au XVIIᵉ Siècle*.

the authorship and authenticity of the papers. The occasion for all this drafting seems to have been a demand from M. Crétineau-Joly, the writer of a well-known *Histoire de la Compagnie de Jésus*.[13] For, at the close of a lengthy French document on Maryland and Missouri, a note is appended in the same language: "We send with these sheets a MS. of P. Dubuisson, *Notice on the Jesuits in the United States*. It contains the following heads;" and, after enumerating the heads, the writer continues with the following pertinent observation: "M. Crétineau will find, I think, many things and thoughts useful for history. He is requested meanwhile to take care, that both the MS. of P. Dubuisson, and these sheets on Maryland, are sent back to Rome; since what is here is not an extract from a history of the Province or from Annual Letters; but a collection of notes [which we have found] scattered in hundreds of private letters." [14]

The Italian writer, in his *Cenni*, or Notes, gives a very full biographical sketch of Mgr. Carroll; and, in the course of it, he affords us a clue to the process by which some archives came to be divided, part from part, at this date. He quotes from Father John Carroll's correspondence with Father Charles Plowden. As the latter had lived in England, this series of correspondence is represented to-day in the London Provincial archives.[15] But only a fragment of it is there. The portion which is quoted by the Italian writer on the fiftieth of his 52 pages of *Cenni* is to be seen no longer in England, but in the archives of the Maryland–New York Province of the Society, and is taken from the third letter out of one hundred and eighty-six of Carroll's in that collection; of which, however, only a portion is correspondence with Charles Plowden. Thus the letters received by Plowden in England are in the American Province archives, while the letters received by Carroll in America from that same correspondent are not there. It would appear that an English bundle of letters had found its way across the ocean. The Italian-American writer probably received the loan of them, for the service which he was rendering to Crétineau-Joly; and they drifted to America, which gained so much without losing anything. The French writer lent his own valuable Notes and the Dubuisson MS. to M.

[13] An English rendering and abridgment of Crétineau-Joly's six 8vo. volumes may be seen in the two 8vo. volumes of B. N. (Barbara Neave, Countess de Courson), *Foundation and History of the Society of Jesus*.

[14] "M. Crétineau trouvera—à ce qu'il me paraît—bien des choses et des pensées utiles à l'histoire ; il est prié pourtant d'avoir soin, que tant le MS. du P. Dubuisson, que ces feuilles sur le Maryland soient renvoyées à Rome : puisque ce n'est pas un extrait d'une histoire de province ou de Lettres Annuelles, mais une collection de notices dispersées dans des centaines de lettres particulières." End of the document, "2. États-Unis ; 2°, (a) Maryland (jusqu' en 1845) : " consisting of seven double folios.

[15] London : English Prov. Archives, Portfolio 6, beginning with Carroll, Rome, to Fr. Ellerker, Liège, January 23, 1772, and ending with the last of Carroll's that is extant in our hands, sc. Carroll to Plowden, October 13, 1815. There are 125 folios of original American correspondence, though not all from Carroll's pen, nor all to Plowden.

Crétineau-Joly, with the strict injunction to send them back to Rome; but they drifted into the Province archives of France, which gained so much and lost nothing. The English Province had lent its Carroll-Plowden correspondence to the Italian writer; and never received the papers back, losing so much. But, at this or some other date within this period, it received from the General at least as many as two hundred and seventy-seven documents, which are now in the Stonyhurst Archives, excepting one part presented to the Irish Province.[16] Thus the English depository gained more than it lost. The only source which lost all round and gained nothing was that to which the best and largest part of everything was due—the General Archives, from which all felt at liberty to get what they could, and to keep what they got.[17]

(20) PARIS: ARCHIVES NATIONALES. There were various pieces here illustrating the history of what became Upper Louisiana. But the most piquant morsel, which was served out to us by the superintendent at his own choice, was a violent Jansenistic production against the French Jesuits in America, all put into the mouth of M. de la Salle in the course of an interview, while that traveller was in France.[18]

(21) ROME: BARBERINI LIBRARY. This was of interest to us in conjunction with the Roman *Transcripts* by Stevenson, deposited in the Public Record Office, London; whereof two volumes, xvi. and xvii., are entitled *Barberini*, and the second of the two contains Panzani's correspondence, 1635-1636. The material, however much reason there was to investigate it, afforded us little occasion to use it, and that was only in relation to the course followed by the second Lord Baltimore, whom Panzani represents as elaborating some oaths—the same, we presume, which were proffered in Maryland not long afterwards. John Lewger also is described at the time when he entered the Catholic Church.

The Stevenson *Transcripts* here are wanting in references. The reason for this may have been that, as we ourselves experienced, the documents were brought out under the appearance of special favour and secrecy. But our esteemed colleague, the Rev. J. H. Pollen, S.J., instituted a complete verification, which we supplemented in the restricted field proper to ourselves. Now that the entire Barberini Library has been acquired by the Vatican (A.D. 1902), consultation will be easier.

(22) ROME: CORSINI LIBRARY. Some documents here relate to the Propaganda and missions; in particular, there are several copies of Urbano Cerri's *Relation*, made in 1678, to Innocent XI., on the state of missions in the whole world. A review of North America is attempted

[16] Stonyhurst old Catalogue, p. (28): "March 1868. J. Hayes."—Cf. above (7), p. 10.
[17] In 1905 the French Archives of the Society are in a state of dispersion, owing to the application of the Associations Law passed against the Religious Orders.
[18] Paris: Archives Nationales, K 1232, 1, pp. 111, carefully written, possibly in the interest of the traders who were baulked by the missionaries. Pages 1–56 recount the manners, etc., of the savages; pp. 57–98, *L'Histoire de M. de la Salle*; pp. 99–111, *Mémoire de la conduite des Jésuites en Canada*.

in it. This account was done into English by the Anglican Bishop Hoadly, in 1716, and published under Sir Richard Steele's name.

(23) ROME: ENGLISH COLLEGE ARCHIVES. Through the courtesy of Mgr. Giles, Rector, our colleague Father Pollen was able to exhaust much of the matter in the archives of the English College. A portion of the materials belonging to a very late date treated of an American question (1821–1828) relating to the American Jesuits. Copies of these he handed over to us, after due verification. Matter of the same kind appears concurrently in the Propaganda, at Baltimore, and in Georgetown College. It may be seen in our companion volume of *Documents I.*

(24) ROME: PROPAGANDA ARCHIVES. A general sketch of the material to be found in the Propaganda has been given by Dr. A. Pieper, in two articles of the *Römische Quartalschrift*, i. Jahrgang 1887: "Propaganda Archiv," pp. 80–99, pp. 259–265. Also reference may be made to I. Kollmann, in the Review, *Časopis musea Královstvi českého*, 1892, s. 423 ff.: "O archivu Sv. Kongregace de propaganda fide." A large collection of papers relating to America were copied for Dr. J. G. Shea, under the patronage, and no doubt through the munificence, of the late Archbishop Corrigan, as appears from a communication among the papers. These are now among the Georgetown College *Transcripts*. But the copies seem not to have been accurately revised, or indeed revised at all, when taken from the originals. This Shea series we used freely. But we rely upon the work of our colleague, Rev. Louis Schmitt, S.J., whose ample schedules on the series of American volumes and others which happened to concern us, besides his revision of our old copies from Georgetown, and his procuring the accurate transcripts of further material for us, put us finally at our ease in doing justice to the Propaganda Archives. We are also indebted to the Rev. Canon D. Pietro Semadini for valuable services.

Before subjoining a table of the volumes which we have chiefly used, we may say a word to explain the character of their titles. The system adopted in conducting the business of the Sacred Congregation of the Propaganda led, in the course of time, to a distribution of documents, which ran on in parallel series. There were the letters or documents which came in from the missions; and these, being put together in volumes, formed a series of what we shall call simply, as their title imports, *Lettere*. Pieper calls these "Letters not reported" (*Lettere non riferite*). In the earlier times, however, not a few of these letters were reported and acted upon, as the endorsements show. Next, there was a selection made out of this general mass of correspondence, for reporting at the committee meetings of writers, who received directions what to answer. These papers, being set apart, have made up the series of volumes called "Papers reported in the Committees" (*Scritture riferite nei Congressi*). There was a still further refinement, in the selection of papers for presentation at the full board of Cardinals, or what is properly called a " General Congregation." These writings had all to be original or else authenticated by some competent and responsible authority. Hence their full denomination is " Original Papers reported in the General Congregation" (*Scritture Originali riferite in S. Congregazione Generale*). The mere names of other series will suggest a sufficient explanation of their nature: "Acts of Special Committees," which are called *Congregazioni Particolari*; "Letters of the Sacred Congregation;" "Acts" of the same; "Audiences of His Holiness."

Apart from the express authentication of documents required for certain processes, we must take the authentic or original character of other papers just as we find them or can best estimate them. A very great number are original and autograph letters; others are duplicates sent for security's sake by the writers; others again are office copies; and a large quantity are impersonal in their form, like petitions and relations. For these latter we may or may not find covering letters from the Nuncios or other persons who despatched them.

The following table will show what codices or volumes have principally been of use to us. We had proposed to give at least as much as the full title of each codex used. But, as that would require too much space, we must limit the indications to the forms sufficient for subsequent quotation :—

LETTERE—

    America 3 Canada. 256.
       ,,   4 usque 22 and 23. 257. 4 Cayenna.
       ,,   1° 2°. Arequipa, Bresile e S. Salvatore. 258.
    I. America, 259.
    II.   ,,   260.

SCRITTURE RIFERITE NEI CONGRESSI—

    America Centrale dal Canada all' Istmo di Panama. Dal 1673 a tutto il 1775. [Cited by us: America Centrale. I.]
       ,,   Centrale . . . 1776–1790. [America Centrale. II.]
       ,,   ,,   . . . 1791–1817. [America Centrale. III.]
       ,,   Antille. Dal 1634 a tutto il 1760. I.
       ,,   ,,   ,, 1761 al 1789. II.
       ,,   ,,   ,, 1790 a tutto il 1819. III.
       ,,   Settentrionale. Canada. Nuova Brettagna. Labrador. Terra Nuova. Dal 1668 al 1791. I.
       ,,   Settentrionale . . . Dal 1792 al 1830. II.

LETTERE—

    I. Anglia. 347. [1622–1647.]
    II. ,, et Scotia. 297. [1622, 1632, 1649–1656.]
    Settentrione 33 Scotia. 308. [1658–1668.]

LETTERE RIFERITE—
    D'Inghilterra, Spagna, Portogallo, Fiandra, Francia, Indie, Ibernia, Alsazia, Amburgo, Etiopia, etc., 101 [A.D. 1626], 129 [1627], 102 [1628], 131 [1629], 132 [1630], 100 [1631], 150 [1632], 133 [1633], 134 [1634], 105 [1635], etc., 141 [1642], etc.

SCRITTURE RIFERITE NEI CONGRESSI—

Anglia I. 1627–1707.		Anglia VI. 1801–1817.	
,, II. 1708–1727.		Irlanda. Dal 1625 al 1668.	I.
,, III. 1728–1740.		,, 1669–1671.	II.
,, IV. 1741–1760.		,, 1672–1675.	III.
,, V. 1761–1800.		,, 1676–1683.	IV.

SCRITTURE NON RIFERITE—

Ibernia.	1684–1699.	V.	Ibernia.	1761–1772.	XI.
,,	1700–1707.	VI.	,,	1773–1776.	XII.
,,	1708–1718.	VII.	,,	1777–1778.	XIII.
,,	1719–1727.	VIII.	,,	1779–1780.	XIV.
,,	1728–1740.	IX.	,,	1781–1784.	XV.
,,	1741–1760.	X.	,,	1785–1787.	XVI.

SCRITTURE RIFERITE—

Irlanda.	1788–1801.	XVII.	Irlanda.	1811–1815.	XIX.
,,	1802–1810.	XVIII.	,,	1816–1817.	XX.

Other series follow of the Particular Congregations, held upon the affairs of Ireland, of England, as also North America, etc.; as well as the Acts (*Atti*), of the General Congregations, during the seventeenth and eighteenth centuries. All these are collateral sources of documents.

(25) ROME: VATICAN ARCHIVES. These are the private documents, or, as the Italian word expresses it, the "secret" archives, of the Holy See. In such a vast treasury, covering the world at large and chiefly the great centres of activity and power, not much was to be expected relating to a far-off mission in an English part of the American continent, whence papers came to an English Provincial, and through him to the General of the Society, and only in a very incidental way might ever come under the notice of the Propaganda; while the merest accident alone could bring them to the Vatican. Yet, such as it is, a short-lived Nunciature, which goes under the name of England, has afforded us some very important documents on the subject of the earliest controversy in Maryland, that between Lord Baltimore and the Jesuit missionaries. They were the papers of the Nuncio Extraordinary at Cologne, Mgr. Rosetti, who was raised to the purple in 1643. These documents furnish a very substantial supplement to the original papers at Stonyhurst on the same subject. The volumes which have been of use to us are chiefly the following:—

INTROD. I. § 3.   NOTICES OF SOURCES INEDITED (26)-(28)   23

  Nunziatura d'Inghilterra, 4. Rosetti, 1639-1681.
     „   „   5. Panzani, 1634-1636.
     „   „   6. Con, 1636-1637.
     „   „   7. „ 1638-1639.
  Nunziatura di Colonia, 20, 21, 22.   Rosetti, 1641-1643.

 The Nunziatura di Fiandra, 56, 57 (Carlo Agretti secretary, Mgr. Abbate Airoldi Internuncio), 1668, 1669, ought seemingly to have contained the report of Agretti, December 14, 1669, in which that secretary gives an account of his interview with Lord Baltimore upon the ecclesiastical affairs of Maryland.[19] But we have found no copy of the text, save that in vol. xxxiii. pp. 233-354 of the Westminster Diocesan Archives. Of Airoldi's report, dated November 29, 1670, after his own journey to England, we found a copy in the Corsini Library; but there is nothing in it on America.

 (26) ROME: VATICAN LIBRARY. This great library, which is entirely distinct from the Vatican Archives, supplied us with a few supplementary documents on the earliest years of the first Lord Baltimore's enterprise in America, and on the second Lord Baltimore's controversy with the Jesuits. We also drew from volumes, relating to the missions and the Propaganda, various points of illustration for the text of our work.

 The Prefect of the Vatican Library, the Rev. Franz Ehrle, S.J., has rendered us the most important services in directing our historical researches and in revising our text.

 (27) STONYHURST COLLEGE MANUSCRIPTS. There are here ample collections of the old English Province documents, besides acquisitions made in modern times, as was stated above (No. (7) General Archives S.J.). A central series of such ancient papers is that which is called *Anglia A*, in nine morocco-bound folio volumes. Chiefly in volumes iii. and iv. occur the Maryland papers to which we have frequently referred; and we took pains to have them photographed. There is also American correspondence dating from the nineteenth century. There are old wills which had reference to the Jesuit property in Maryland and Pennsylvania, showing its origin in several instances by heritage or bequest, and its line of descent through members of the Order. Other papers were interesting and instructive in every line of research; but, as they were incidental only for American purposes, they call for no distinct mention here. Nor is it necessary for us to describe these valuable archives at large.

 For a specimen in facsimile, taken from the Stonyhurst documents, see *infra, History*, § 4, 1605: "Andrew White, Vocation;" reproduction of White's letter, 1606, October 27, to Father Gerard.

 (28) TURNHOUT COLLEGE ARCHIVES. Missionaries who toiled in the

---

[19] W. M. Brady, *The Episcopal Succession in England, Scotland, and Ireland*, iii. 116.

Western States and Rocky Mountain Missions came from this little town; or at least they were formed here by M. De Nef, who laboured at this educational work from 1817 till after 1840. In 1845 his institute became what is now the Jesuit College of Turnhout. Writing the history of this College, the Rev. Charles Droeshout, S.J., described fully its antecedent American connection. And, as mentioned before (No. (1), Antwerp), he placed entirely at our disposal his own original manuscript.

We have not paused to record here any unsuccessful quests made in Europe, as, for instance, an attempt to throw more light upon the Franciscan expeditions to Maryland, 1670–1720; or to recover correspondence which the German Fathers in Pennsylvania, 1730–1773, may have kept up with members of their former Provinces on the Upper and Lower Rhine; or other such subjects of investigation. Hence we pass over Florence, Munich, Oxford, the Franciscan archives in Dublin, etc.

§ 4. Notices of the Sources Inedited.

America.

Coming now to America, we record in like manner some general results of our search there.

(29) ANNAPOLIS RECORDS. These were of consequence to us only in the matter of landed property which the Society possessed. We verified several points; and for others we owe our acknowledgments to the Rev. J. T. Hedrick, S.J. We take this occasion to express our appreciation of the general services rendered us by the Rev. E. I. Devitt, S.J., of Georgetown University, D.C.

(30) BALTIMORE DIOCESAN ARCHIVES. To these the kindness of his Eminence the Cardinal-Archbishop gave us access; and we endeavoured to find the originals of some of the transcripts made in Dr. Shea's own hand, as well as to supplement certain papers of our own. But these ample and orderly archives are of more service to an historian of the Catholic Church in the nineteenth century than to one who treats of old Jesuit missions, which are not represented.

(31) GEORGETOWN COLLEGE, D.C. The archives here, as now arranged with the efficient aid of the Rev. Francis Barnum, S.J., are divided into *Manuscripts* and *Transcripts*. The *Manuscripts* comprise some original papers of the eighteenth century throughout; some of Charles Carroll's (1752-1756); Father Beeston's *Ledger of Bohemia*, 1791, continued by the Sulpician Fathers; Brother Joseph Mobberly's *Diaries*; Archbishop Maréchal's correspondence, etc. The *Transcripts*, which we may note here are first those of B. U. Campbell, and secondly those of J. G. Shea. Both have drawn on other Jesuit

archives in the Province. The Shea Collection may be roughly divided into the two classes of what he obtained, as we mentioned before, from the Roman archives of the Propaganda, and what he procured elsewhere, transcribing either with his own hand or with the help of others. As to the Roman Transcripts, we cannot speak with unqualified approbation of them; for they seem to have been communicated after copying, without any further revision—which always means inaccuracy. But we have taken pains to have our material which was derived from the Shea transcripts collated with the originals in the Propaganda, as stated above, No. (24). The other class of transcripts Dr. Shea has taken without adding an indication of their source. Intimate acquaintance, however, with his work has shown us that he personally was a trustworthy investigator and writer. At the same time, his field was much wider than ours; it required a more varied class of documents, and afforded less room or time for the minuter investigation of particular facts, difficulties, and episodes generally. Hence the same documents have concerned him and ourselves in a different way and to a varying degree—an observation which applies to work and workers even on the same general line in all large depositories of documents.

We arranged all papers here as nearly as possible in a chronological order; and we quote them accordingly.

As to Dr. Shea's omission of his sources, there is a strange remark made by him in a paragraph of the Preface to his *History*. It is at the solicitation of a venerated friend, he says, that he gives authorities in his notes, "although scholars generally have been compelled to abandon the plan by the dishonesty of those who copy the references and pretend to have consulted books and documents they never saw, and frequently could not read."[1] Nothing may be truer than this, as some recent publications professing to treat of the Jesuits in England have strikingly illustrated. But nothing could be more at variance with the principles and practice of critical editing in our days. We have travelled far from the time when Lord Palmerston practically refused Mr. Brodhead, the literary agent of New York, all access to the public records of Great Britain.[2] We have reached the new era, when the Popes admit every one into the private archives of the Holy See.

(32) MARYLAND–NEW YORK PROVINCE ARCHIVES S.J. These rank next to the General Archives of the Society, in contributing materials for ancient colonial history. A part comes down from the seventeenth century, a very considerable portion from the eighteenth, and the rest is abundant for the nineteenth century. This bare statement shows how young in history America is,—and in historical collections. The matter may be broadly distinguished as "financial," in the American sense of that term, or pertaining to money matters, landed property, etc.; and

[1] John Gilmary Shea, *The Catholic Church in Colonial Days*, preface v.
[2] Brodhead, *Documents, etc.*, I. xxiii., xxiv.

historical, comprising all other matters. These funds of documents, which were separate till recently, are now put together; but, having been distinct before, they are kept so still; while other funds have been added. Fortunately, before many fires and accidents had destroyed the remains of antiquity at the residences of St. Thomas's, St. Inigoes, and elsewhere, the zeal of one or two Provincials like Father James Ryder had suggested the removal of local records to a safer centre. What was permitted to remain in the more important localities must be considered as hopelessly lost; though some relics may still be seen. Such monuments as old Baptismal Registers are to be found in mission stations, which have been resigned by the Jesuits to bishops for the settlement of secular parish priests.

Among the seventeenth-century papers are contemporary copies of documents from Lord Baltimore and John Lewger; if, indeed, one or other of these be not original and autograph. There is a series of autograph applications on the part of young English Jesuits, asking to be sent on the Maryland Mission. Both these sets date from the years 1639-1642. There are original parchments of land grants at Bretton's Neck to William Bretton, 1640 and 1658. There is an old, oblong, narrow day-book, bound in pig-skin, very much worn throughout in every way, which we call " L. 1," and which consists of " Old Records." The principal memorandum-writers in the book seem to be Father Peter Attwood, who flourished in Maryland, 1711-1734, and Father George Hunter, who laboured there 1747-1779. There are all kinds of important memoranda here, as valuable as they are varied. It is written in from both ends; and, at about the middle starting from one side, it capriciously numbers p. "100" to p. "109;" while, from the other end, it numbers nearly a score of pages straight on from unity. Here, as well as in other record-books, ledgers, day-books, and the like, both those of the missionaries and those of persons like the Carrolls and Fenwicks, one may discern not a little of the Catholic colonial life in Maryland during the eighteenth century. Many of the books are much dilapidated. Over and above all these, there is a quantity of papers proper to the general business of the mission, which grow in number as the date advances. There are original and autograph letters of Charles Carroll and Ignatius Digges, in the name of divers Catholic gentlemen on the one side, and of John Ridout, by order of Governor Sharpe on the other, treating of the legislative assault made between 1750 and 1760 on the property of Catholics and their rights as citizens. The history of the Maryland Corporation of ex-Jesuits, chartered to secure the old Jesuit property, is satisfactorily covered; and papers to complete this episode lie in the Government archives.

Everything that was not in the nature of a bound book we arranged in chronological order, as far as we felt free to do so, without disturbing any series of portfolios or bundles that might already be catalogued.

INTROD. I. § 4. NOTICES OF SOURCES INEDITED (33)-(49) 27

Hence the general business of the mission, which is historical, need only be referred to by the date. The portfolios, bundles, or envelopes are indicated by a number (covering, as a rule, historical matter) or by a letter (covering "financial" matter of deeds or accounts).

In two large series of folio transcripts, respectively of 98 pages and of 34, a very complete copy of American documents at Stonyhurst and in London was sent over by Henry Foley, at the request of Maryland Provincials, in 1874 and 1883. They are in Portfolio 4; and they were used by Dr. Shea. These Anglo-American documents have been an object of attention with the State authorities of Maryland and with the Jesuits there, since 1837. We shall sketch the progress of inquiry in a paragraph further on.[3]

Having intimated what was the fate of documents scattered in the Jesuit residences, we need only class all the local archives there as being comprised in the general treasury of the Province. But since we found papers still lying in local depositories, and we cannot affirm that they have been or will be removed to the central archives, we rank those places here in order without further comment :—

(33) BOHEMIA, Md., Eastern Shore.
(34) BALTIMORE.
(35) CONEWAGO, Pa.
(36) FORDHAM, N.Y.
(37) FREDERICK, Md.
(38) GOSHENHOPPEN, Pa.
(39) ST. INIGOES, Md.
(40) LEONARDTOWN, Md.
(41) NEW YORK.
(42) PHILADELPHIA.
(43) ST. THOMAS'S MANOR, Md.
(44) WHITEMARSH, Md.
(45) WOODSTOCK COLLEGE, Md.

(46) MISSOURI PROVINCE ARCHIVES S.J. Under this head may be ranked at once several local centres, for the period of history which we take in hand at present. They are—
(47) ST. CHARLES, Mo.
(48) FLORISSANT, Mo.
(49) ST. LOUIS UNIVERSITY, St. Louis.

The papers in the Missouri Province Archives date from 1820, a little before the foundation in 1823 of the Western Mission. Though they become rich in matter from the time when the entire western country was comprehended in the field of Jesuit labour, and the Missouri Mission itself was separated from Maryland, still up to the date where we stop at present—that is, about 1830—the papers are very limited, and they

[3] *Infra*, § 5.

have to be supplemented by those in the Maryland Mission Archives. The direction of the western movements during these years was vested in the eastern superior. The best part of the papers in the east are those which became available only on the death of Father John McElroy in 1894, seventy years and more after the events which they cover and reveal. This venerable Father had been a procurator in Maryland; and he kept papers safely up to our day. His documents on western matters begin with 1813; and the more important instruments relating to the foundation of the Missouri Mission are to be found in his papers, Portfolio 21, of the Maryland–New York Province Archives.

As to the New York Diocesan Archives, we were informed by the late lamented Archbishop Corrigan, that there were no documents prior to the time of Archbishop Hughes, except a scrap of Father Kohlmann's. Hence we infer that a collection of papers, which we have found in the Jesuit Archives tabulated above, may rank among the fullest Catholic records of the northern metropolis for the second decade of the nineteenth century. The same is to be observed, but for several decades, of the following centre.

At Philadelphia, we were kindly informed by his Grace Archbishop Ryan, that there were no diocesan records before the time of Archbishop Kenrick. And we find a Shea transcript of a letter, written by the Right Rev. Francis Patrick Kenrick to B. U. Campbell, Esq., under date of January 29, 1845, wherein his lordship, after discussing the Sir John James's Fund and some other points, says briefly and sadly, "I have no archives to explore."[4]

As to the documentary literature at Harvard, or in the hands of the Massachusetts Historical Society, or in the Carter-Brown Library at Providence, it was not of a kind to engage our researches; because, as might be expected, where Jesuits appeared they were those of French Canada, not of the English settlements. It was not within our scope to enter a field so well occupied. Nevertheless, while we enjoyed the advantage of working in foreign parts, and found new elements of history in English sources, we thought it was due to our own colleagues not to omit any items which, after all, might be used only in French history.

New Orleans or the Louisiana Jesuit Mission of the nineteenth century, considered either as an organization or as a depository of documents, belongs to a development just later than the period at present before us; and it will form a conspicuous element at the opening of the subsequent missionary era. The New Orleans foundation

[4] Georgetown College *Transcripts*, 1748: on the Sir John James's Fund.

was signalized by establishments in the direction of Kentucky, New York, and Canada. In this last-named country we found an accumulation of documents, which invites us to say a word. We have, indeed, nothing very special to mention with regard to Quebec; but there remains Montreal—

(50) CANADIAN MISSION ARCHIVES S.J. These are deposited at St. Mary's College, Montreal. They have been admirably cared for and arranged; and the custodian at the time we consulted them, the Rev. Arthur Jones, S.J., is well known for his competency in French Canadian history. If, in the hundred odd portfolios of documents arranged chronologically, we have not found such English elements as would serve ourselves, it is because the archives are amply filled with what they profess to contain, materials on the old French Missions of New France and Louisiana; as also on later English issues, which do not enter yet into the limits of our actual subject.

§ 5. We have referred to some action taken by the Legislature of the State of Maryland with regard to old Jesuit archives. We proceed to sketch the correspondence, and the subsequent action taken by different persons and officials thereupon—

At a session of the General Assembly of Maryland, begun and held at the city of Annapolis on the last Monday of December, being the twenty-sixth day of the said month, in the year 1836, and ended on the twenty-second of March, 1837, his Excellency Thomas M. Veazey Esquire being Governor, Bill No. 56 was passed by the House of Delegates on March 20th, 1837, to the following effect; that, whereas it has been ascertained by means of certain extracts, which have been taken from documents relating to the first settlement and early history of the Province of Maryland, which now remain among the Archives of the Jesuits at Rome, that "an interesting and authentic narrative or history of Maryland, composed in Latin by Father Andrew White, the first Missioner of Maryland, and fellow-voyager with Leonard Calvert, in manuscript, is easily accessible," the State Librarian is "authorized and required to solicit the Rev[d.] William McSherry of Charles County the now Provincial of the Jesuits to use his endeavours to procure for the State of Maryland an accurate transcript of the said narrative or history, and of any other document relating to the early history of Maryland, that may chance to be lodged in the said archives or in other Jesuits' house in Europe, and to contract for procuring such transcript at any expence not exceeding five hundred Dollars;" and the Treasurer is hereby authorized and required to advance such sums to the same Librarian, as may be required. And such transcript or transcripts are to be deposited in the State Library.

This Bill, passed by the House of Delegates, was concurred in by the Senate next day, March 21, 1837. A certified copy, with seal affixed by the Court of Appeals, 24th day of March, A.D. 1837, was forwarded to the Jesuit superior on the same day, with the following letter:—

"State Library, Maryland,
"Annapolis, March 24th, 1837.

"To the Revd. William McSherry, Charles Co., Md.

"Reverend and Dear Sir,

"Herewith I transmit you an office Copy of a Preamble and Resolutions passed by the Legislature at its recent Session. Happy in being selected as the organ of our liberal and enlightened Legislature on this interesting occasion, I hasten to carry into effect, on my part, their very laudable and praiseworthy intention. May I indulge the hope, My Dear Sir, that you will give me your valuable aid, in procuring the documents indicated in the Resolutions; and which are deemed so necessary and important to the elucidation of the early history of Maryland. I shall be happy to hear from you, and am,

"Reverend and Dear Sir,
"With great Respect,
"Your ob^{t.} serv^{t.}
"D. Ridgely—Librarian."[1]

Father McSherry had already his own copy of the Latin *Relation*, obtained by himself in Rome a few years before. But, as the Act of the Legislature looked further afield for other documents, he communicated promptly with the former superior and Visitor of Maryland, Father Peter Kenney, then stationed at Upper Gardiner Street, Dublin, who wrote immediately to Stonyhurst, England, Father James Brownbill being Rector there. After a full statement of the case, Father Kenney went on to say: "As the Mission of Maryland was constantly supplied and governed by the English Provincial up to the Suppression in 1773, much valuable information may be contained in the correspondence of the Missioners with their Superiours and brethren in England and Flanders during that long period. Many doubts now affecting the property of their missions might possibly be cleared up, as well as such information obtained as would be appreciated by the compilers of the history, which the Legislature seems desirous to proc[ure]. At your convenience you will let me know if there exist any hope that you or Fr. Norris [the Provincial] possess in your respective archives sources, whence the desired information may be drawn."[2]

[1] Md.-N. Y. Province Archives; Portfolio 3; 1837, March 20–24: Ridgely correspondence.
[2] Stonyhurst College MSS., *Varia A*, ii. 21, document 68: Peter Kenney [to the Rector of Stonyhurst], Dublin, 1837, November 9. Endorsed, "F. Kenny, rec^d Nov. 10. Ans. Nov. 22." 4 pp. 4to.

Father McSherry died in 1839; and under his successor the question was revived by Father Francis Vespré, who, writing from Georgetown College, October 21, 1840, to Father Kenney, says that, in consequence of the Legislature's request, "Fr. McSherry wrote in 1837 or 1838 to Fr. James Brownbill, if I am not mistaken, then President of Stonyhurst College, to beg the communication of any notices they might have on such a subject. As far as I know, no direct answer was received. However, Fr. Ryder says, he understood that something was written to some one or other in these parts importing that all what [that] could be found had been sent to Your Rev$^{ce.}$ with request to forward it to Fr. McSherry. At any rate, nothing having appeared, I beg leave to request you would be so kind as to let me know something about it."[3]

As we mentioned before,[4] when speaking of the General Archives, a translation of the Latin *Relation* and other McSherry papers was made in 1847 by Nathan C. Brooks, LL.D., and subsequently published in Peter Force's Collection of Historical Tracts, vol. iv. No. 12; and another translation and edition was made in 1874 and 1877, by Dalrymple, in No. 7 and No. 7 Supplement of the Fund Publications of the Maryland Historical Society. But since we observe, as we mentioned in the same place, that B. U. Campbell in 1846, and B. F. Streeter in 1852, had under their eyes documents which we find at Stonyhurst, we may infer that Father Kenney was able to communicate something through the kindness of the Rector of Stonyhurst.

The date of Dalrymple's edition of the Latin documents in 1874 coincided with the date of Henry Foley's first contribution of copies from England to the Provincial of Maryland.[5] Then in his third volume of *Records of the English Province*, issued in 1878, Foley published a number of such papers, translated rather indifferently.[6] In 1883, he sent over a second consignment, as we have already stated; and this date agrees with Bradley T. Johnson's Fund Publication No. 18, on the *Foundation of Maryland*, etc.; wherein appears for the first time a series of controversial documents concerning the second Lord Baltimore and the Jesuits.[7] But many of these were only English translations, more or less accurate. A list of the Maryland Historical Society's publications relative to this matter has been given above.[8]

[3] Irish Province Archives: Francis Vespré to Peter Kenney, Georgetown, 1840, October 21.
[4] Above, § 3 (7), p. 13.
[5] Above, § 4 (32), p. 27. Father Joseph Keller was then Provincial
[6] H. Foley, *Records*, iii. 320–400.
[7] Above, § 3 (7), p. 13. General Johnson makes his acknowledgments to the English and American Jesuit authorities for the communication of these papers Fund Publication, No. 18, Appendix A, p. 163.
[8] Above, § 2, p. 5.

SECTION THE THIRD.

§ 6. As to our manner of treating what we have taken from archives, we have set apart the accompanying volume of *Documents* for the reproduction of original pieces or extracts. The use made of this original matter in our own text is that which is suited to the general reader. Therefore, whether we use them literally or in synopsis, we introduce them in the vernacular.

The documents which belong to our period of history are not very ancient either in their calligraphy or in their literary style. Hence they have imposed no special hardship on us in the effort to reproduce them. We have consulted modern usage and the convenience of the modern printer in the matter of capitals and small type, of paragraphs and punctuation, preserving, however, the original spelling. Abbreviations are written out in full, if they are obvious. Any interpolations on our part are always enclosed in square brackets.

Since most of our work is derived from papers in other languages than English, we cannot do justice to them all by reproducing them and multiplying tomes. We trust, however, that the account given either in the notes to our text, or in the companion volume, will be found sufficient to justify the use which we make of them, or to direct the reader in doing justice to them himself.

As to our method of using published literature, we do not undertake to explain any particular method of ours, because we make so little use of that literature in weaving the web of our narrative. The reasons for this will appear in the second chapter of these introductory remarks, where we sketch the history of the literature.[1]

§ 7. As reference is constantly made to the superior who occupies the post of General of the Society or of Provincial in the English Province, while no further reason may occur for specially naming the person, we append at once so much of the information needed as will serve to identify such official personages for use in this first volume—

GENERALS OF THE SOCIETY OF JESUS.

I. St. Ignatius Loyola, 1541–1556.
II. James Laynez, 1558–1565.
III. St. Francis Borgia, 1565–1572.

[1] See below, Introduction, Chap. II. section ii.

IV. Everard Mercurian, April 23, 1573—August 1, 1580, under Gregory XIII.
V. Claudius Aquaviva, February 19, 1581—January 31, 1615; Gregory XIII., Sixtus V., Urban VII., Gregory XIV., Innocent IX., Clement VIII., Leo XI., Paul V.
VI. Mutius Vitelleschi, November 15, 1615—February 9, 1645; Paul V., Gregory XV., Urban VIII., Innocent X.
VII. Vincent Carrafa,[2] January 7, 1646—June 8, 1649; Innocent X.
VIII. Francis Piccolomini, December 21, 1649—June 17, 1651; Innocent X.
IX. Alexander Gottifredi, January 21, 1652—March 12, 1652; Innocent X.
X. Goswin Nickel, March 17, 1652—July 31, 1664; Innocent X., Alexander VII.
XI. John Paul Oliva, July 31, 1664—November 26, 1681; Alexander VII., Clement IX., Clement X., Innocent XI.
XII. Charles de Noyelle, July 5, 1682—December 12, 1686; Innocent XI.
Etc.

Provincials of the English Province S.J.

Father Robert Parsons, 1580–1610; Father Thomas Owen, 1610–1618; Prefects of the Mission, residing in Rome.

Fathers Jaspar Haywood, William Weston, Henry Garnett, Richard Holtby, Robert Jones, Richard Blount; Vice-Prefects residing in England.

Father Richard Blount, Vice-Provincial, 1619–1623.

1. Richard Blount, appointed Provincial, January 21, 1623.
2. Henry More, about September, 1635.
3. Edward Knott (Matthew Wilson), about August, 1639.
4. Henry Silesdon (H. Bedingfeld), about October, 1646.
5. Francis Forster, about March, 1650.
6. Edward Knott, March 22, 1653.
7. Richard Barton (R. Bradshaigh), April 25, 1656.
8. Edward Courtney (E. Leedes), July 15, 1660.
9. John Clarke, January 14, 1664.
10. Joseph Simeon (Emmanuel Lobb), November 14, 1667.
11. George Gray, May 22, 1671.
12. Richard Strange, September 16, 1674.
13. Thomas Harcourt (T. Whitbread), about February, 1678.
14. John Warner, October 26, 1679.
15. John Keynes, July 1, 1683.
Etc.

---

[2] We take this spelling from Father Carrafa's Register of Letters, *Anglia, Epist. Gen.* The same is used in the Acts of the Eighth General Congregation.

For further lists, as well as particulars and statistics of membership, houses, ways and means, compare H. Foley, *Records*, vii., *Collectanea, Historical Introduction*.

§ 8. To avoid prolixity in the footnotes, we add here to the Register of published sources, given above in section i. § 2, a list of other books to which reference is made.

Full Titles of Books quoted.

ACOSTA, JOSEPHUS, S.J. "De Natura Novi Orbis," libri duo : et "De Promulgatione Evangelii apud Barbaros, sive De Procuranda Indorum Salute," libri sex. 8vo, pp. 581. Coloniæ Agrippinæ, 1596.

ALLEN, WILLIAM. "An Apologie and True Declaration of the Institution and Endeavours of the two English Colleges, the one in Rome, the other now resident in Rhemes : against certaine sinister informations given up against the same." 8vo, ff. 123. Mounts in Henault, 1581.

ALSOP, GEORGE. "A Character of the Province of Mary-Land." 16mo, pp. xviii., 118. London, 1666.

American Archives. See above, § 2, Sources edited.

"Ancient Laws and Institutes of England." Published by the Record Commission, 1840 ; edited by B. Thorpe. Fol.

ANDERSON, J. S. M. "The History of the Church of England in the Colonies and Foreign Dependencies of the British Empire." 8vo, 3 vols. London, Brighton, 1845–1848.

ANGELL & AMES. "A Treatise on the Law of Private Corporations Aggregate." 8vo. 3rd edition. Boston, 1846.

"Annales de la Société des soi-disans Jésuites; ou, Recueil historique-chronologique de tous les Actes . . . contre la doctrine . . . des soi-disans Jésuites." 4to, t. iii. Paris, 1767.

ANSTEY, T. C. "A Guide to the Laws of England affecting Roman Catholics." 8vo, pp. ix., 195. London, Dublin, 1842.

"The Apostate Protestant. A Letter to a Friend, occasioned by the late reprinting of a Jesuites Book, about Succession to the Crown of England, pretended to have been written by R. Doleman." Small 4to, pp. 59. London, 1682.

ARGENTO, JOANNES, [S.J.] "De Rebus Societatis Jesu in regno Poloniæ, ad Serenissimum Sigismundum Tertium." 12mo. Edit. 3ª. Cracoviæ, 1620.

"Articles of Christian Religion. Approved and passed by both Houses of Parliament, after advice had with the Assembly of Divines, by authority of Parliament sitting at Westminster." Small 4to, pp. 50. London, 1648.

ASTRAIN, P. ANTONIO, S.J. "Historia de la Compañía de Jesús en la Asistencia de España ; tomo I., San Ignacio de Loyola, 1540–1555." 8vo, pp. xlv., 714. Madrid, 1902.

BACON, FRANCIS. "Works." 8vo, 10 vols. London, 1803.

BACQUET, JEAN. "Des Droicts du Domaine," t. ii. partie 4 ; "Du Droict d'Amortissement." Œuvres in 5 tt. fol. Paris, 1664.

BALDWIN, JANE. "The Maryland Calendar of Wills," vol. i., 1635–1685. 8vo, pp. ix., 219, lxii. Baltimore, 1901.

"The Lord Baltemore's Case, concerning the Province of Maryland, adjoyning to Virginia in America. With full and clear Answers to all material Objections, touching his Rights, Jurisdiction and Proceedings there. And certaine Reasons of State, why the Parliament should not impeach the same. Unto which is also annexed a true Copy of a Commission from the late King's eldest Son to Mr. William

Davenant, to dispossess the Lord Baltemore of the said Province, because of his adherence to this Common-Wealth." Small 4to, pp. 20. London, 1653.

[The Lord Baltamore's Case.] "Virginia and Maryland ; or, The Lord Baltamore's printed Case, uncased and answered. Shewing the illegality of his Patent and usurpation of Royal Jurisdiction and Dominion there," etc. Small 4to, pp. 51. London, 1655.

BANCROFT, GEORGE. "History of the United States." 10 vols.; divers editions. 1834, *seqq.*

BERINGTON, REV. JOSEPH. "Reflections addressed to the Rev. John-Hawkins, to which is added an exposition of Roman Catholic Principles, in reference to God and the Country." 8vo, pp. xiv., 121. London, 1785.—The same. "The History of the Decline and Fall of the Roman Catholic Religion in England, during a Period of 240 years from the Reign of Elizabeth to the present time; including the Memoirs of Gregorio Panzani, Envoy from Rome to the English Court, in 1634-5-6, with many interesting particulars relative to the Court of Charles the First, and the Causes of the Civil War. Translated from the Italian Original." 8vo, pp. xliii., 473. London, 1813.

[BLACKSTONE:] STEPHEN'S "New Commentaries on the Laws of England, partly founded on Blackstone." 4 vols. 7th edition. London, 1874.—EWELL, M.D. "Essentials of the Law: A Review of Blackstone's Commentaries." Small 8vo, pp. xii., 611. Boston, 1889.

BODINI, JOANNIS, ANDEGAVENSIS. "De Republica," libri sex. Fol. Parisiis, 1586.

BOEHMERI, JUSTI HENNINGII, "Jus Ecclesiasticum Protestantium, usum modernum Juris Canonici juxta seriem Decretalium ostendens," etc. 4to, 5 tt. Halæ, 1714-1736.—The same. "Jus Parochiale ad fundamenta genuina revocatum." Edit. 2da. Halæ, 1716.

BONACINÆ, MARTINI, "Opera omnia in tres tomos distributa." Fol. Venetiis, 1693.

BOUCHER, JONATHAN. "A View of the Causes and Consequences of the American Revolution ; in thirteen Discourses, preached in North America between the years 1763 and 1775 ; with an historical preface." 8vo, pp. xcvi., 596. London, 1797.

BOWYER, GEORGE. "Commentaries on Universal Public Law." 8vo, pp. xii., 387. London, 1854.

BOZMAN, JOHN LEEDS. "The History of Maryland, from its first settlement in 1633 to the restoration in 1660, with a copious introduction, and notes, and illustrations." 8vo, 2 vols. Baltimore, 1837.

BRADY, W. MAZIERE. "The Episcopal Succession in England, Scotland, and Ireland, A.D. 1400-1875." 3 vols. Rome, 1876, 1877.

BRODHEAD, J. R. "Documents relative to . . . New York." See above, § 2, Sources edited, under "New York."

BROWNE, WILLIAM HAND. "Maryland, the History of a Palatinate." Boston, 1884. In the "American Commonwealth" series, edited by Horace E. Scudder.—The same, editor of "The Archives of Maryland." See above, § 2, Sources edited.

BROWNSON, ORESTES A. "Review." Vol. I. New York series, 1856.

DE BUCK, VICTOR, S.J. "Examen Historicum et Canonicum Libri R. D. Mariani Verhoeven, Prof. Publ. Ord. SS. Can. in Univ. Lovanien., de Regularium et Sæcularium Clericorum juribus et officiis." 8vo, pp. vi., 620. Gandavi, Bruxellis, 1847.

"Bullarium Diplomatum et Privilegiorum SS. Romanorum Pontificum." Editio Taurinensis. Fol. 24 tt. Augustæ Taurinorum, 1857-1872.

"Bullarium Patronatus Portugalliæ Regum in Ecclesiis Africæ, Asiæ, atque Oceaniæ." Fol. 3 tt. Olisipone, 1868-1873.

[Bulario—Hernáez.] "Coleccion de Bulas, Breves y otros Documentos relativos a la Iglesia de America y Filipinas dispuesta, anotada e ilustrada por el P. Francisco Javier Hernáez de la Compañia de Jesús." Fol. 2 tt. Bruselas, 1879.

[Bullarium—Propaganda.] "Juris Pontificii de Propaganda Fide Pars Prima, complectens Bullas, Brevia, Acta, a Congregationis institutione ad præsens . . . disposita, cura et studio Raphaelis de Martinis." Fol. 7 tt. in 8 part. Romæ, 1888-1897.

BURK, JOHN. "The History of Virginia, from its first settlement to the present day." 8vo, 4 vols. Petersburg, Va., 1804.

BURNAP, GEORGE W. "Leonard Calvert." Vol. xix. of "Library of American Biography," edited by Jared Sparks. Boston, 1846.

BUTLER, CHARLES. "Historical Memoirs of the English, Irish, and Scottish Catholics, since the Reformation," etc. 8vo, 4 vols. 3rd edition. London, 1822.

"Calvert Papers, I., II., III." See above, § 2, Sources edited, under "Maryland Historical Society, Fund Publications."

"Calendars of State Papers: Colonial Series." See above, § 2, under "British Calendars."

CAMPBELL, BERNARD U. "Biographical Sketch of Father Andrew White and his Companions, the first Missionaries of Maryland; with an historical account of the first ten years of that Mission." In the Metropolitan Catholic Almanac and Laity's Directory. Baltimore, 1841.—The same. "Historical Sketch of the Early Christian Missions among the Indians of Maryland." Read before the Maryland Historical Society, January 8, 1846.—The same. "Review of the Hon. John P. Kennedy's Discourse on the Life and Character of George Calvert, the First Lord Baltimore." 8vo, pp. 32. Baltimore, 1846.

CANES, J. VINCENT, O.S.F. "Fiat Lux. A General Conduct to a right understanding and charity in the great Combustions and Broils about Religion here in England. Betwixt Papist and Protestant, Presbyterian and Independent. To the end that Moderation and Quietness may at length hapily ensue after so various Tumults in the Kingdom." 12mo, ff. 4, pp. 396. 1662.

CARAYON, P. AUGUSTE, S.J. "Documents Inédits concernant la Compagnie de Jésus. Document M: Le Père Pierre Chaumonot." Pp. 199-225: "Catalogue par ordre chronologique des membres de la Compagnie de Jésus, envoyés dans les missions du Canada et de la Louisiane (1611–1800)." 8vo. Poitiers, 1869.

CARNE, JOHN. "Lives of Eminent Missionaries." 12mo, 3 vols. London, 1832.

CARREZ, LOUIS, S.J. "Atlas geographicus Societatis Jesu, in quo delineantur quinque ejus modernæ assistentiæ, provinciæ tres et viginti, singularumque in toto orbe missiones, necnon et veteres ejusdem Societatis provinciæ quadraginta tres cum earum domiciliis, quantum fieri licuit." Parisiis, 1900.

CERRI, URBANO. See below, under HOADLY.

CHALMERS, GEORGE. "Political Annals of the Present United Colonies, from their Settlement to the Peace of 1763; compiled chiefly from Records, and authorized often by the insertion of State Papers." 4to, pp. 695, besides preface. London, 1780.

CHILD, GILBERT W. "Church and State under the Tudors." 8vo, pp. xix., 281; appendix, pp. 283-429. London, 1890.

COBBETT'S "Parliamentary Debates." 8vo, vol. ix.

COKE, LORD. "The Lord Coke His Speech and Charge [at Norwich, Aug. 4, 1606]. With a discoverie of the Abuses and Corruptions of Officers." 4to, not paginated [64 pp.]. London, 1607.—The same. "Coke's Littleton: 2 Institutes." London, 1628-1669.—"Coke's Littleton," edited by Francis Hargrave and Charles Butler, with notes. 2 vols. London, 1823.

"Compendium (Breve) Privilegiorum et Gratiarum Societatis Jesu. Ex majori Compendio [1585] extractum." 16mo, pp. 72. Romæ, 1586.

"Compendium Privilegiorum et Gratiarum, quæ Religiosis Societatis Jesu et aliis Christi fidelibus, in utriusque Indiæ regionibus commorantibus, a Summis Pontificibus conceduntur." 12mo, pp. 70. Romæ, 1737.

"Constitutiones Societatis Jesu latinæ et hispanicæ cum earum declarationibus." See above, § 2, Sources edited.—"Institutum Societatis Jesu." See *Ibid.*

"Constitutions, the Federal and State." See above, § 2, Sources edited.

CORDARA, J. C., S.J. "Historiæ Societatis Jesu, Pars sexta, complectens res gestas sub Mutio Vitellescho." Fol. 2 tt. Romæ, 1859.

COTTON, SIR ROBERT. "Twenty Four Arguments, whether it be more expedient to suppress Popish Practises against the due Allegeance of his Majesty, By the Strict

Executions touching Jesuits and Seminary Priests; or, to Restrain them to Close Prisons during life, if no reformations follow." 16mo, f. 1, pp. 111-159. London, 1651.

"Court and Times of James I." 8vo, 2 vols. London, 1848.

CRÉTINEAU-JOLY, J. "Histoire religieuse, politique, et littéraire de la Compagnie de Jésus, composée sur les documents inédits et authentiques." 8vo, 5 tt. Paris, 1844.

DAHLMANN, JOS., S.J. "Die Sprachkunde und die Missionen. Ein Beitrag zur Charakteristik der ältern katholischen Missionsthätigkeit (1500-1800)." 8vo, pp. xi., 128. Freiburg im Breisgau, 1891.

DALLAS, R. C. "The New Conspiracy against the Jesuits, detected and briefly exposed: with a short account of their Institute; and observations on the danger of systems of education independent of religion." 8vo, pp. xxii., 374. London, 1815.— The same. "A Letter to Charles Butler, Esq., relative to the New Conspiracy against the Jesuits." 8vo, pp. 75. London, 1817.

DARREL, WILLIAM, S.J. "A Vindication of St. Ignatius (Founder of the Society of Jesus) from Phanaticism; and the Jesuites from the Calumnies laid to their Charge in a late Book, entitul'd, 'The Enthusiasm of the Church of Rome.'" Small 4to, ff. iv., pp. 40. London, 1688.

DAVIS, GEORGE L. L. "The Day-Star of American Freedom; or, the Birth and Early Growth of Toleration in the Province of Maryland; with a sketch of the colonization upon the Chesapeake and its tributaries, preceding the removal of the Government from St. Mary's to Annapolis; and a Glimpse of the Numbers and general State of Society, of the Religion and Legislation, of the Life and Manners of the men, who worshipped in the wilderness, at the first rude altar of liberty." 8vo, pp. 290. New York, Baltimore, 1855.

"Declaratio Catholicorum Laicorum Angliæ, circa Authoritatem, etc., Episcopi Chalcedonensis. Exemplar Epistolæ Catholicorum Laicorum Rmo. Chalcedonensi Episcopo missæ, cujus in præcedenti Declaratione fit mentio. (Acta et attestationes.)" Small 4to, pp. 23. Bruxellæ, 1631.

"Dialogue (A) betwixt a secular Priest and a lay Gentleman. Being an Abstract of the most important matters that are in controuersie betwixt the Priests and the Spanish or Jesuitical faction." 16mo, pp. 134. Rhemes, 1601.

[DODD, CHARLES.] "The Church History of England, from the year 1500 to the year 1688," etc. Fol. 3 vols. in 8 parts. Brussels, 1737-1742.—The same, edited by M. A. Tierney. 8vo, 5 vols. London, 1839-1843.

DORSEY, K. G. "Life of Father Thomas Copley." In *Woodstock Letters*, xiii., xiv.

DOUGLASS, WILLIAM. "A Summary, Historical and Political, of the first Planting, progressive Improvements, and present State of the British Settlements in North America; with some transient Accounts of the Bordering French and Spanish Settlements." 8vo, 3 parts in 2 vols. Boston, 1747-1750.

DOYLE, J. A. "The English in America, Virginia, Maryland, and the Carolinas." 8vo. London, 1882.

ERASTUS, THOMAS. "Explicatio Gravissimæ Quæstionis, utrum Excommunicatio, quatenus Religionem intelligentes et amplexantes a Sacramentorum usu propter admissum facinus arcet, mandato nitatur Divino, an excogitata sit ab hominibus." Small 4to, pp. xiv., 63. "Thesium Confirmatio in sex libros . . . .," etc. Pp. 65-390, cum indice. Pesclavii, 1589.

EWELL, MARSHALL D. "Essentials of the Law." See above, BLACKSTONE.

FERRARIS, L. "Prompta Bibliotheca Canonica, Juridica," etc. 4to, 10 tt. Venice, 1782.

FIELD, THOMAS W. "An Essay towards Indian Bibliography: being a catalogue of books," etc. 8vo, pp. iv., 430. New York, 1873.

FINLASON, W. F. "An Essay on the History and Effects of the Laws of Mortmain, and the Laws against Testamentary Dispositions for Pious Purposes: comprising an account of the Debates in Parliament, and the inquiries of Select Committees of the House of Commons, and the most interesting cases which have occurred in courts of law: with an appendix containing the reports of the Select Committees, and digests of the evidence," etc. 8vo, pp. viii., 268. London, 1853.

"Florus Anglo-Bavaricus." 4to, pp. 205. Leodii, 1685. (Author, Father John Keynes, S.J.)

FOLEY, HENRY, S.J. "Records of the English Province of the Society of Jesus." See above, § 2, Sources edited.

FROUDE, JAMES ANTHONY. "History of England from the Fall of Wolsey to the Defeat of the Spanish Armada." 8vo, 12 vols. London, 1897.

GAMS, PIUS BONIFACIUS, O.S.B. "Series Episcoporum Ecclesiæ Catholicæ," etc. Fol. Ratisbonæ, 1873.

GARDINER, SAMUEL R. "History of England from the Accession of James I. to the Outbreak of the Civil War, 1603–1642." 8vo, 10 vols. London, 1883–84.

GIBSON, EDMUND. "Codex Juris Ecclesiastici Anglicani." See above, § 2, Sources edited.

GILLOW, JOSEPH. "A Literary and Biographical History, or Bibliographical Dictionary of the English Catholics, from the breach with Rome, in 1534, to the present time." 8vo, 5 vols. London, New York, 1885, *seqq*.

GOODMAN, GODFREY, Bishop of Gloucester. "The Court of King James the First." Edited by John S. Brewer. 8vo, 2 vols. London, 1839.

GROTIUS, HUGO. "Introduction to Dutch Jurisprudence." Rendered into English by Charles Herbert. 8vo, pp. xx., 548.

"Growth of Knavery (An Account of), under the Pretended Fears of Arbitrary Government, and Popery. With a Parallel betwixt the Reformers of 1677 and those of 1641, in their Methods and Designs. In a Letter to a Friend." Small 4to, pp. 72. Extract from "Growth of Popery," pp. 65–72. London, 1678.

HAKLUYT, RICHARD. "The Principall Navigations, etc., of the English Nation," etc. Fol. 3 vols. London, 1599.

HALLAM, HENRY. "The Constitutional History of England, from the Accession of Henry VII. to the Death of George II." 8vo, 3 vols. 3rd edition. London, 1832. —The same. "View of the State of Europe during the Middle Ages." 8vo, 3 vols. 6th edition. London, 1834.

HAMMOND, JOHN. "Hammond versus Heamans; or, An Answer to an audacious Pamphlet, published by an impudent and ridiculous Fellow, named Heamans, etc., In which is published His Highnesses absolute (though neglected) Command to Richard Bennet, Esq., late Governour of Virginia and all others, not to disturb the Lord Baltamores Plantation in Maryland." Small 4to, pp. 17. London, [1655].—The same. "Leah and Rachel, or, The Two Fruitfull Sisters, Virginia and Maryland: Their Present Condition, Impartially stated and Related. With a removall of such Imputations as are scandalously cast on those Countries, whereby many deceived Souls chose rather to Beg, Steal, rot in Prison, and come to shamefull deaths, then to better their being by going thither wherein is plenty of all things necessary for Humane subsistance." Small 4to, pp. 32. London, 1656 [1655].

HAMY, ALFRED, S.J. "Documents pour servir a l'histoire des domiciles de la Compagnie de Jésus dans le monde entier de 1540 à 1773;" collationnés par le P. Alfred Hamy, S.J. Fol. pp. iv., 97. [No date.]

HARTWELL, ABRAHAM. "A Report of the Kingdom of Congo, a Region of Africa, etc. Drawen out of the writings and discourses of Odoardo Lopez, a Portingall, by Philippo Pigafetta. Translated out of Italian." With Epistle Dedicatory to John, Archbishop of Canterbury; from Lambehith, January 1, 1597. Small 4to, ff. 11, pp. 220. London, 1597.

HAWKINS, WILLIAM. "A Treatise of the Pleas of the Crown." 8vo, 4 vols. London, 1795.

HAWKS, FRANCIS L. "Contributions to the Ecclesiastical History of the United States of America." 8vo, 2 vols. New York, 1836, 1839.

HEAMAN, ROGER. "An additional brief narrative of a late bloody design against the Protestants in Ann Arundel County, and Severn, in Maryland in the Country of Virginia, as also of the extraordinary deliverance of these poor oppressed people." Small 4to, pp. 14. London, 1655.

HERGENROETHER, JOSEPH CARDINAL. "Kirchengeschichte." 8vo, t. ii. Freiburg, 1879.

"Historical Manuscripts Commission: Second Appendix to Fifth Report;" "Appendix to Sixth Report;" and "Fifth Appendix to Tenth Report."

[HOADLY, BISHOP BENJAMIN—STEELE, SIR RICHARD.] "An Account of the State of the Roman Catholic Religion throughout the world, written for the Use of Pope Innocent XI. by Monsieur Cerri, Secretary of the Congregation de Propaganda Fide." 8vo, pp. 184, preceded by introduction, preface, etc. London, 1715.—The same. French translation. 16mo, pp. 307, after introduction, etc. Amsterdam, 1716.

"House of Commons: Reports, Committees: Mortmain:" 1844, 1851-2.

HUGHES, THOMAS, S.J. "Loyola and the Educational System of the Jesuits." 8vo, pp. x., 298. New York, 1892.

HUME AND SMOLLETT. "History of England." 8vo, 18 vols. London, 1854.

HUONDER, ANTON, S.J. "Deutsche Jesuitenmissionäre des 17 und 18 Jahrhunderts. Ein Beitrag sur Missionsgeschichte und sur deutschen Biographie." Ergänzungshefte zu den Stimmen aus Maria-Laach, 74. 8vo, pp. iv., 230, with indexes. Freiburg im Breisgau.

HURTER, HUGO, S.J. "Nomenclator Litterarius recentioris theologiæ Catholicæ. . . ." 8vo, 5 tt. Editio altera. Œniponte, 1892-1903.

"Jesuits (The) Reasons Unreasonable; or, Doubts proposed to the Jesuits upon their paper presented to divers persons of honor, for non-exception from the common favour voted to Catholicks." 4to, ff. iv. pp. 101-131. London, 1662.

JOHNSON, BRADLEY T. "The Foundation of Maryland," etc. See above, § 2, Sources edited, under "Maryland Historical Society, Fund Publications, No. 18."

KELLISON, MATTHEW. "A Treatise of the Hierarchie and divers orders of the Church against the anarchie of Calvin." Small 8vo, ff. 22, pp. 420. Doway, 1629.

KENNEDY, J. P. "Reply of J. P. Kennedy to the Review of his Discourse on the Life and Character of Calvert, published in the *U.S. Catholic Magazine*, April, 1846." Baltimore, May 15, 1846.

KENT, JAMES. "Commentaries on American Law." 8vo, 4 vols. 13th edition. Boston, 1884.

KILTY, JOHN. "The Landholder's Assistant, and Land-Office Guide; being an exposition of original titles, as derived from the proprietary government, and more recently from the State of Maryland," etc. 8vo, pp. 498, xliv., vi. Baltimore, 1808.

KILTY, WILLIAM. "A Report of all such English Statutes as . . . have been found applicable to . . . local and other circumstances [of Maryland]," etc. 4to, pp. viii., 10-289. Annapolis, 1811.

KIP, WILLIAM INGRAHAM. "The Early Jesuit Missions in North America; compiled and translated from the letters of the French Jesuits, with notes." 8vo, in two parts, pp. xv., 321. London, 1847.—The same. "Historical Scenes from the Old Jesuit Missions." 8vo, pp. xiv., 375.

[KNOTT, EDWARD, S.J.] "Charity Mistaken, with the want whereof Catholicks are unjustly charged; for affirming, as they do with grief, that Protestantcy unrepented destroies Salvation." 16mo, pp. 130. 1630.

LANGFORD, JOHN. "A just & cleere Refutation of a false & scandalous Pamphlet, entituled, Babylons Fall in Maryland, &c. And, A true Discovery of certaine strange & inhumane proceedings of some ungratefull people in Maryland, towards those who formerly preserved them in time of their greatest distresse. To which is added a Law in Maryland concerning Religion, and a Declaration concerning the same." Small 4to, pp. 35. London, 1655.

LECKY, WILLIAM E. H. "A History of England in the Eighteenth Century." Vol. iii. 2nd edition. London, 1879.

"Letter (A) from a Gentleman of the Romish Religion, to his Brother a Person of Quality of the same Religion; persuading him to go to Church, & take those Oaths the Law directs, Proving the Lawfulness thereof by Arguments not disagreeable to the Doctrines of the Roman Church." Small 4to, pp. 47. London, 1674.

[LEWGER, JOHN.] "Erastus Senior, scholastically proving this Conclusion that (admitting their Lambeth Records to be true) those called Bishops here in England are no Bishops, either in Order or Jurisdiction, or so much as Legal," etc. 24mo, pp. 104, with preliminary pp., etc. 1662.

LINGARD, JOHN. ["The History of England, from the first invasion by the Romans to the accession of William and Mary in 1668." 8vo, 10 vols. 6th edition. London, Manchester, 1855–1868.

M. G. "An Account of the Jesuites Life & Doctrine." 16mo, pp. 150. 1661.

MAITLAND, F. W. "Roman Canon Law in the Church of England." 8vo, pp. viii., 184. Cambridge, 1898.

MAITLAND-POLLOCK. "The History of English Law, before the time of Edward I. By Sir Frederick Pollock, Bart., M.A., LL.D., Corpus Professor of Jurisprudence in the University of Oxford . . . and Frederick William Maitland, LL.D., Downing Professor of the Laws of England in the University of Cambridge." 8vo, 2 vols. 2nd edition. Cambridge, 1898.

MAMACHI, THOMAS M. "Del Diritto libero della Chiesa di acquistare e di possedere beni temporali sì mobili, che stabili, libri tres." 8vo, 5 tt. Romæ, 1769–70.

(DE) MARTINIS, RAPHAEL. "Jus Pontificium de Propaganda Fide." See Bullarium—Propaganda, *supra*.

"Maryland, Archives of.—Historical Society, Fund Publications." See above, § 2, Sources edited.

"Massachusetts Historical Society, Collections." See above, § 2, Sources edited.

MAYHEW, JONATHAN. "Popish Idolatry: a Discourse delivered in the Chapel of Harvard College, Cambridge, New England, May 8, 1765. Lecture founded by the Honourable Paul Dudley, Esq." 8vo, pp. 52. Boston, 1765.

McLAUGHLIN, FAIRFAX. "College Days at Georgetown." 16mo, pp. 229. Philadelphia, 1899.

McMAHON, JOHN V. L. "An Historical View of the Government of Maryland, from its colonization to the present day." 8vo, pp. xvi., 539.

MEJER, OTTO. "Die Propaganda, ihre Provinzen und ihr Recht." 8vo, 2 vols. Göttingen, 1852–53.

MILNER, JOHN. "Ecclesiastical Democracy Detected," etc. 8vo, pp. xvi., 318. London, 1793.

MONTANUS, FRANCISCUS. "Apologia pro Societate Jesu in Gallia, contra Antonii Arnaldi Advocati Parisiensis Philippicam." 16mo, pp. 359. Ingoldstadii, 1596.

MORRIS, JOHN G. "The Lords Baltimore." 8vo, pp. 61. Fund Publication, No. 8. Baltimore, 1874.

MORUS, HENRICUS. "Historia Missionis Anglicanæ Societatis Jesu, ab anno salutis 1580. . . . Vice-Provinciæ . . . Provinciæ, ad 1635." Fol. pp. 516 and ff. 8 index. Audomari, 1660.

MURY, PAUL, S.J. "Les Jésuites à Cayenne: Histoire d'une mission de vingt-deux ans dans les pénitenciers de la Guyane." 8vo, pp. xvi., 283. Strasbourg, 1895.

N. B. [NEAVE, BARBARA, COUNTESS DE COURSON]. "Foundation and History of the Society of Jesus." 8vo, 2 vols. London, 1879.

NARES, EDWARD. "Life of Lord Burghley." 4to, 3 vols. London, 1828–1831.

NEILL, EDWARD D. "The Founders of Maryland, as portrayed in manuscripts, provincial records, and early documents." 8vo, pp. 193. Albany, 1876.—The same. "Terra Mariæ, or Threads of Maryland Colonial History." 8vo, pp. 260. Philadelphia, 1867.

O'CALLAGHAN, E. B. "The Documentary History of the State of New York." See above, § 2, Sources edited, under "New York, O'Callaghan."

OLDMIXON, J. "The British Empire in America, containing the History of the Discovery, Settlement, Progress, and Present State of all the British Colonies on the Continent and Islands of America." 8vo, 2 vols. London, 1708.

OLIVER, GEORGE. "Collections illustrating the history of the Catholic religion in the counties of Cornwall, Devon, Dorset, Somerset, Wilts, and Gloucester." 8vo, pp. 576. London, 1857.

"Ordinances and Orders (All the several), made by the Lords & Commons assembled in Parliament, concerning Sequestring the Estates of Delinquents, Papists, Spyes, & Intelligencers, Together with Instructions for such Persons as are imployed in sequestring of such Delinquents Estates. Very useful for those whom it doth or may concern." Small 4to, pp. 86. London, 1650.

PALGRAVE, FRANCIS. "The Rise and Progress of the English Commonwealth. Anglo-Saxon Period," etc. 4to, 2 vols. Text; Proofs and Illustrations. 1832.

PARKMAN, FRANCIS. "The Jesuits in North America in the Seventeenth Century." 8vo. Boston, 1867.

PARSONS, ROBERT, S.J. "A Treatise tending to Mitigation towardes Catholicke-Subjectes in England. Wherein is declared, That it is not impossible for Subjects of different Religion (especially Catholickes & Protestantes) to live togeather in dutifull obedience and subjection, under the government of his Majesty of Great Britany. Against the seditious wrytings of Thomas Morton, Minister, and some others to the contrary," etc. 8vo, pp. 556, followed by index. 1607.

[PASQUIER, STEPHEN.] "The Jesuites Catechisme, or Examination of their doctrine. Published in French this present year 1602, and nowe translated into English." Ff. 10, pp. 238. 1602.

PAYNE, JOHN ORLEBAR. "Records of the English Catholics of 1715." 8vo, pp. xvi., 182. London, 1889.

PERKINS, JOHN. "Booke . . . treating of the Lawes of this Realme," etc. 16mo, ff. 3, 168. Londini, 1555.

PERRY, WILLIAM STEVENS. "Historical Collections relating to the American Colonial Church." See above, § 2, Sources edited.

PETRE, EDWARD—HUSENBETH, F. C. "Notices of the English Colleges and Convents established on the Continent after the Dissolution of Religious Houses in England." Small 4to, pp. vi., 105. Norwich, 1849.

PIEPER, A. "Propaganda Archiv." See above, § 3, Sources inedited, (24), "Rome, Propaganda Archives."

POLK, JOSIAH F. "The claim of the Church of Rome to the exercise of religious toleration, during the proprietary government of Maryland, examined." 8vo, pp. 32. [1846.]

"[Propaganda] Collectanea S. Congregationis de Propaganda Fide, seu Decreta, Instructiones, Rescripta pro apostolicis missionibus, ex tabulario ejusdem Sacrae Congregationis deprompta." Fol. pp. x., 924. Romae, 1893.

PUGH, ROBERT. "Blacklo's Cabal Discovered in severall of their Letters, clearly expressing designs inhumane against regulars, unjust against the laity, schismatical against the Pope, cruel against orthodox clergy men, and owning the nullity of the Chapter, and their opposition of episcopall authority." Small 4to, pp. viii., 127. 1680.

"Records of the American Catholic Historical Society." 8vo. Philadelphia, 1884, seqq.

"Records (Historical) and Studies. Published by the United States Catholic Historical Society." 8vo. New York, 1899, seqq.

"Relations des Jésuites, contenant ce qui s'est passé de plus remarquable dans les missions des Pères de la Compagnie de Jésus dans la Nouvelle-France." 8vo, 3 tt. Québec, 1858.

"Relations, The Jesuit." Edited by Reuben Gold Thwaites. 8vo, 73 vols. Cleveland, 1896-1901.

[Relations or pamphlets touching Maryland:] "Objections answered touching Maryland." 16mo, pp. 9-16, "Finis." [London, 1633?]—Reproduced by Bradley T. Johnson. "Foundation of Maryland." Pp. 24-30. Taken from the Stonyhurst MSS., *Anglia*, A iv. No. 108E.

"Relatio itineris in Marilandiam," [1634]. See above, § 2, Sources edited, under "Maryland Historical Society, Fund Publication, No. 7."

"A Briefe Relation of the Voyage unto Maryland." See *Ibid.*, No. 35, "Calvert Papers, iii.," pp. 26-45.

"Relation (A) of the successfull beginnings of the Lord Baltemores Plantation in Mary-Land. Being an extract of certaine letters written from thence by some of the Adventurers to their friends in England. . . . To which is added, The Conditions of

Plantation propounded by his Lordship for the second voyage intended this present yeere, 1634." Small 4to, pp. 10. 1634.

"Relation (A) of Maryland; Together with a map of the countrey, the Conditions of Plantation, his Majesty's Charter to the Lord Baltemore, translated into English." Small 4to, pp. 1-56, 1-25. 1635.—Reproduced in Sabin's Reprints, with comments by F. L. Hawks. 4to, No. 2. New York, 1865.

[Other Relations analogous.] "Present State of Virginia, by Hugh Jones." Sabin's Reprints in 8vo, No. 5. 1724.

"The Indians of New England, by Henry Whitfield." Sabin's Reprints in 4to, No. 3. 1651.

"Certain inducements to well-minded people, who are strained in their estates or otherwise (. . . to go to the West Indies . . .) for the propagating of the Gospel and increase of trade." *Ibid.* No. 4 (1643). With "Objections answered."

"Whitfield's (further progress among Indians)." "New England's first fruits," etc. *Ibid.* Nos. 5, 6, 7 (1643-1658). With letters of John Eliot; theses for the Commencers in their Public Acts, Cambridge, 1643, etc.

[Researches.] "The American Catholic Historical Researches." See above, § 2, Sources edited.

ROBERTSON, WILLIAM. "A view of the progress of society in Europe, from the subversion of the Roman Empire to the beginning of the sixteenth century." 8vo. London, 1825.

ROCHEMONTEIX, P. CAMILLE DE, S.J. "Les Jésuites et la Nouvelle-France au xviie siècle, d'après beaucoup de documents inédits." 8vo, 3 tt. Paris, 1895-96.

SACCHINI, FRANCISCUS, S.J. "Historiæ Societatis Jesu pars quinta, sive Claudius; t. i. Res extra Europam gestas et alia quædam supplevit Petrus Possinus ex eadem Societate." Fol. Romæ, 1661.

SCHARF, J. THOMAS. "History of Maryland from the earliest period to the present day." 8vo, 3 vols. Baltimore, 1879.

SCOBELL, HENRY. "A collection of several acts of Parliament, published in the years 1648, 1649, 1650, and 1651: very useful, especially for Justices of the Peace," etc. Fol. ff. 5, pp. 224, ff. 3. London, 1651.

SHEA, J. GILMARY. "A History of the Catholic Church within the limits of the United States, from the first attempted colonization to the present time [1866]." 8vo, 4 vols. New York, 1886-1892.—The same. See under WINSOR, JUSTIN, below.

SILVIUS, FRANCISCUS. "Resolutiones Variæ in alphabetico ordine digestæ." 4to, 2 tt. Duaci, 1641, 1644.

SMITH, C. ERNEST. "Religion under the Barons of Baltimore, being a sketch of ecclesiastical affairs, from the founding of the Maryland Colony in 1634 to the formal establishment of the Church of England in 1692, with special reference to the claim that Maryland was founded by Roman Catholics as the seed plot of religious liberty." 8vo, pp. xiii., 384. Baltimore, 1899.

SMITH, WILLIAM. "The History of the Province of New York, from the first discovery to the year 1732; to which is annexed a description of the country, with a short account of the inhabitants, their trade, religious and political state," etc. 4to, pp. xii., 255. London, 1757.—Same work with a continuation, up to 1747. In 8vo, pp. 512. Albany, 1814.

SOMMERVOGEL, CARLOS, S.J. "Bibliothèque de la Compagnie de Jésus," etc. See above, § 2, Sources edited.

SOUTHWELL, NATHANIEL, S.J. "Bibliotheca Scriptorum Soc. Jesu: opus inchoatum a R. P. Petro Ribadeneira, S.J., 1602; continuatum a R. P. Philippo Alegambe, S.J., usque ad 1642; recognitum et productum ad annum jubilæi, 1675." Fol. pp. xxxvi., 982. Romæ, 1676.

SPELMAN, HENRY. "Of the Law Terms." 24mo, ff. 2, pp. 88. London, 1684.

"Statutes of the Realm." See above, § 2, Sources edited: "British Statutes."

"Stephen's Blackstone." See above, BLACKSTONE.

STEVENSON, JOSEPH. "Preface to the Chronicon Monasterii de Abingdon." No. 2 of Rolls Series, "Chronicles and Memorials of Great Britain and Ireland, during the Middle Ages." 8vo, preface, pp. iii.-lxxxv. London, 1858.

INTROD. I. § 8.   TITLES OF BOOKS QUOTED   43

STOCKBRIDGE, HENRY. "The Archives of Maryland, as illustrating the spirit of the times of the early colonists." 8vo, pp. 87. Baltimore, 1886.—Maryland Historical Society, Fund Publication, No. 22.

STRAFFORD'S (THE EARL 'OF) "Letters and Dispatches." Fol. 2 vols. London, 1739.

STREETER, SEBASTIAN F. "Papers relating to the Early History of Maryland." 8vo, pp. 315. Baltimore, 1876. Maryland Historical Society, Fund Publication, No. 9.—The same. "Two Hundred Years Ago." 8vo, pp. 76. Baltimore, 1852.

STRONG, LEONARD. "Babylon's Fall in Maryland: A fair warning to Lord Baltamore. Or, A Relation of an Assault made by divers Papists & Popish Officers of the Lord Baltamore's against the Protestants of Maryland; to whom God gave a great victory against a greater force of Souldiers & armed men, who came to destroy them." Small 4to, pp. 11, 2. 1655.

STUBBS, WILLIAM. "The Constitutional History of England, in its Origin and Development." 8vo, 2 vols. Oxford, 1874.—The same. "Select Charters and other Illustrations of English Constitutional History:" a third vol. attached to the above.

SUAREZ, FRANCISCUS, S.J. "Defensio Fidei Catholicæ adversus Anglicanæ sectæ errores, cum responsione ad apologiam pro juramento fidelitatis, et epistolam ad principes Christianos serenissimi Jacobi Angliæ regis." Operum, tom. 24. In fol. Parisiis, 1859. Liber sextus, "De juramento fidelitatis regis Angliæ," pp. 660-735.

"Summary Account (A) of all the Statute Laws of this Kingdom, now in force, made against the Jesuites, seminary Priests and Popish recusants; drawn up for the Benefit of all Protestants. Done by a Protestant, to inform such of his Fellow-subjects, that are ignorant of these Laws, and would be willing to do their Duties, where, and when the Laws enjoyn them." Small 4to, f. 1, pp. 14. London: Printed in the year 1666, and reprinted with Additions, in 1673. Accompanied by notes and additions in manuscript. 16 ff. same size. British Museum MSS., Add. 17,022.

[Again:] "An Abstract of all the Statute-Laws of this Kingdom, now in force, made against Jesuites, Seminary Priests, and Popish Recusants." 4to, pp. 21. London, 1675.

"Synopsis Actorum in causa Societatis Jesu, 1540-1773." 8vo, 2 vols. Florentiæ, Lovanii, 1887-1895.

TAUNTON, ETHELRED L. "The English Black Monks of St. Benedict: A sketch of their history from the coming of St. Augustine to the present day." 8vo, 2 vols. London, 1897.—The same. "History of the Jesuits in England, 1580-1773." 8vo. London, 1901.

[TAYLOR, NATHANIEL.] "The History of Popish-Sham-Plots from the reign of Elizabeth to this present time. Particularly of the Present Popish Plot. Being an account of the several methods the Papists have used to stifle it," etc. 12mo, pp. 179. London, 1682.

TERTRE DU, J. B., Ord. Præd. "Historie Générale des Ant-Isles, habitées par les François, enrichie de cartes et de figures." 4to, 4 tt. Paris, 1667-1671.

THADDEUS, FR., O. F. M. "The Franciscans in England, 1600-1850; being an authentic account of the second English Province of Friars Minor." 8vo, pp. viii., 352. London and Leamington, 1898.

THOMAS, JAMES WALTER. "Chronicles of Colonial Maryland." 8vo, pp. 323. Baltimore, 1900.

THURLOE'S "State Papers." Fol. vol. v. London, 1742.

TIERNEY, MARK A. "Dodd's Church History of England," etc. See above, DODD.

VANE, THOMAS. "A Lost Sheep returned home; or, The Motives of the Conversion to the Catholike Faith of Thomas Vane, Doctor of Divinity, and lately chaplaine to his Majesty the King of England," etc. 12mo. Paris, 1648.

VATTEL—ROYER-COLLARD. "Le Droit des Gens . . . Par Vattel . . . Traduit en français par M. P. Royer-Collard." 8vo, 3 tt. Paris, 1835-1838.

VICTORIA, F. DE, O.P. "Relectiones Undecim. [4th] De Indis, prior; [5th] De Indis, posterior, sive De Jure Belli." 12mo, 2 tt. in 1. Salmanticæ, 1565.

"Virginia and Maryland." See above, "Baltamore's Case."

"Virginia's Cure; or, An Advisive Narrative concerning Virginia. Discovering the true Ground of that Churches Unhappiness, and the only true Remedy. As it was presented to the Right Reverend Father in God Guilbert Lord Bishop of London, September 2, 1661. Now published to further the Welfare of that and the like Plantations: by R. G." Small 4to, pp. 5, 22. London, 1662.

[WATSON, WILLIAM.] "A Brief Historical Account of the Behaviour of the Jesuites & their Faction, for the first twenty five years of Q. Elizabeth's Reign." 4to, pp. 1–41. "Important Considerations which ought to move all true and sound Catholicks, who are not wholly Jesuited, to acknowledge without all Equivocations, Ambiguities and Shiftings, that the Proceedings of Her Majesty, and of the State with them, since the beginning of her Highnesses Reign, have been both Mild and Merciful. Published by Sundry of us, the Secular Priests, in dislike of many Treatises, Letters and Reports, which have been written and made in places to the contrary. Together with our opinions of a better Course hereafter, for the promoting of the Catholick Faith in England." 4to, pp. 43–72. Printed in the year 1601, and reprinted in the year 1688.

WELDON, BENNET, O.S.B. "Pax; Chronological Notes on the English Congregation of the Order of St. Benedict." 4to, pp. 253, and appendix, pp. 14. Worcester 1881.

WHEATON, HENRY. "History of the Law of Nations in Europe and America; from the earliest times to the treaty of Washington, 1842." 8vo, pp. xiv., 797. New York, 1845.

WILHELM, LEWIS W. "Sir George Calvert, Baron of Baltimore." 8vo, pp. 172. Baltimore, 1884. Maryland Historical Society, Fund Publication, No. 20.

WINSOR, JUSTIN. "Narrative and Critical History of America." 8vo, 8 vols. Boston and New York, 1889. Among the contributors of the monographs are—

 Brantly, William J., on "Maryland."
 Brock, Robert A., on "Virginia."
 Davis, Andrew McFarland, on "Canada and Louisiana."
 Deane, Charles, on the "Voyages of the Cabots," and on "New England."
 De Costa, Benjamin F., on "Norumbega."
 Ellis, George E., on the "Religious Element in New England."
 Hale, Edward E., on "Hawkins and Drake."
 Henry, William Wirt, on "Sir Walter Ralegh, Roanoke and Guiana."
 Keen, Gregory B., on "New Sweden."
 Rivers, William J., on "The Carolinas."
 Shea, John Gilmary, on "Jesuits, Recollects, and Indians."—The same, on "Ancient Florida."
 Stevens, John Austin, on the "English in New York."

WOOD, ANTHONY à. "Athenæ Oxonienses." Edition 1721.

"Woodstock Letters." 8vo, vol. i., *seqq.* Woodstock College, Maryland, 1872, *seqq.*

§ 9. We employ the following method of abbreviation:—

GENERAL ARCHIVES S.J.—
 Anglia, Epist. Gen. 1633, June 4
  = Letter sent by the General under that date, as contained in the Register for England.
 Anglia, Catal. 1 (or 2), 1633
  = Triennial Catalogue of members, first (or second), for England, under said date.
 Anglia, Catal. 3 (or *brevis*), 1633
  = The Annual Catalogue, 1633.
 Anglia, Epist. 1, v. (with date)
  = Letter sent to the General, to be found in the department for England, vol. 1, fasciculus v.
 Anglia, Litt. Ann., 1633
  = English Annual Letter, 1633.
 Md.-N.Y. Prov.
  = Maryland-New York Province, S.J.

Mo. Prov.
    = Missouri Province, S.J.

MARYLAND, ARCHIVES OF—
  Proceedings of the Assembly (or Council)
    = According to page in the volume corresponding to the date.
  Provincial Court, Judicial and Testamentary Business
    = Ditto.

LONDON—
  P. R. O. = Public Record Office, according to the series and volume noted.
  Ante med.; med.; post med.; ad calcem
    = Designating the locality of a quotation on the folio or page cited.
  Cf.   = *confer*, compare.
  F. 25ᵛ. = folio 25 *verso*, otherwise designated, f. 25*b*.
  Ibid.   = *ibidem*, in the work or tome already cited.
  Loc. cit. = *loco citato*, in the passage just cited.
  Passim = Here and there, recurring often.
  s.d.   = *sine data*, without date.
  s.v.   = *sub voce*, under the name or word.
  seq. or sq. = And in the rest of the passage, or in what follows.
Documents, I. = The accompanying first volume of Documents.
History, I. = This first volume of Historical text.

CHAPTER II

HISTORY OF THE ARCHIVES AND THE LITERATURE

From the foregoing notice of the sources, it will have appeared that the materials used in this history are chiefly such as have belonged to the Society itself, and therefore such as originally lay in Jesuit archives. To a certain extent, the materials have come from sources outside. It may seem to the minds of persons conversant with historical documents, that the portions here derived from Jesuit archives are of such particular value as on their own account to be worthy of a special publication. If so, our present undertaking is justified, even though it effected no other purpose than that of giving publicity to private papers of no ordinary value.

Among the interesting features of these old manuscripts, there is one aspect under which they can serve us well, before our History professes to use them at all. It is that, if we wish to know how to use them, we have only to begin by consulting them. For there is scarcely a preliminary observation which we should desire to make, but is already made for us in those archives; besides other significant remarks, which we should never have thought of ourselves. The information so obtained will, we imagine, be the more agreeable on another account. It will suggest the answers to several questions which have been prompted by historical interest, and have been repeated not unfrequently during the last century by persons worthy of consideration in the United States.

We shall be answering such questions if, after the technical account of the archives as given above, we set up for our guidance some principles of historical narrative; and, for this purpose, consult not any modern nor quote any ancient author, but simply stay within the circumscription of these Jesuit papers, and see what they will tell us.

The points which we select are naturally such as the following:

Whence do the records come, and what is their degree of authenticity? Are any documents wanting? If so, why? Amid directions given on the manner of employing materials, we find the principle inculcated that there must be, not only fidelity on the part of original records in themselves, but fidelity to original records in the use made of them. How this must be attained in the manner and style of writing is a subject of frequent observation. Over and above all this, we hear persons reminded of what they should carefully avoid.

So much being done for unpublished archives in the first section of this chapter, we intend, in the next section, to do as much, or something proportionate, for published literature. We shall advert to the condition in which we find such published materials, whether in England or in America, as far as they relate to our subject. We ought to indicate the reasons which we have had for using published works so little; and the requirements which none the less we must meet, if we would satisfy in a moderate degree the expectations of a critical public.

SECTION THE FIRST.

§ 1. Preparation of Jesuit archives for a history. § 2. Annual Letters, and their system. § 3. Schedules for Letters and history. § 4. Instruments and deeds up to 1700. § 5. Writing and writers. § 6. Attempts at a history. § 7. Administrative documents in the archives. § 8. Plundering, intercepting, and burning records. § 9. The policy of silence, and its reasons. § 10. Effects on published history, and net results.

§ 1. Just about the time when American history commenced, the General of the Order wrote from Rome to the recent Provincial of England, Father Richard Blount, desiring him and some others whom he named to gather materials for a history. *Dignity and utility of the subject.* He urged as an incentive "the dignity of the subject-matter, as well as the singular utility which may justly be looked for in such a work."[1] It was not the first time the General touched this key. And, as regards Father Blount's competency at the time to furnish materials, he had but lately held the office of Provincial or Superior of the English Mission during eighteen years. To Father Andrew White, founder of the Maryland establishment, the General wrote in the same sense: "The history of that Mission, which you have begun, will be," he said, "most acceptable to me; and I doubt not but it will be of use in arousing the zeal of many towards undertaking such expeditions."[2]

[1] General Archives S.J., *Anglia, Epist. Gen.*, 1637, January 24.
[2] *Ibid.*, 1639, October 1.

The correspondence shows that he was not a little gratified at the assiduity with which Father Henry Bedingfeld, *alias* Silesdon, wrote to him constantly in 1627. However, the state of affairs in England was critical, and not to be taken in at a glance. Silesdon himself was master of novices at Watten, in Belgium. The character of his functions, and the remoteness of his situation from the field of action, did not qualify him to report either as an actor or as a keen-sighted eye-witness. Hence the General, while courteously making his acknowledgments for many lengthy epistles received, went on cautiously to say that "all did not offer the same degree of certainty." He added some useful advice: "To the end that, in labouring to write out such long letters, you or others whose help you employ may not go to undue lengths, I would have you know that I do not desire you to send hither all the reports which are rehearsed wholesale every week by the scribblers of news. When we want such letters, we can easily get them here [in Rome] from others. But I would have you make a selection out of all the news available, and then communicate to us what you have ascertained to be more authentic, what is of greater consequence, and particularly all that concerns the condition of Catholic interests, and matters connected therewith. To this, when you can, you might add the expression of your own judgment."[3] Among the permanent records of the English Province, we find a standing memorial of this period, conceived in the following terms: "From the letter of Father General Mutius [Vitelleschi], January 26, 1636. . . . The older Fathers should be reminded to write out all that they themselves know, or what they have heard from persons worthy of credit, so that in due time a history of the mission can be composed."[4]

Authentic matter.

Though the Generals departed this life, the traditions of their office did not change. Thirty years later, the fifth successor of Father Mutius Vitelleschi, whom we have just been citing, wrote to the Provincial of the time, Father Simeon, and admonished him of a serious omission: that brave men were passing away, and no diligence was shown in putting upon record, with accuracy, the events of their lives. "Please," he wrote, "provide a remedy for this evil; and let not oblivion bury the good deeds which your workmen accomplish day after day, unto the glory of God and the honour of the Society. These memoirs will be most effective incentives, spurring on all of

---

[3] General Archives, S.J., *Anglia, Epist. Gen.*, 1627, June 5: ". . . *sed ut certiora ex iis majorisque momenti, et quæ præcipue ad statum rei Catholicæ aliaque illi connexa pertinent, excerpta, addito etiam ubi poterit suo judicio nobiscum communicet.*"

[4] Stonyhurst MSS., A, v. 1, f. 32ᵛ.

ours to follow in such footsteps; and for posterity they will be monuments to commemorate the virtues that adorned our predecessors." On the same day, the General wrote to the Rector in London, Father Maurice Newport, directing attention to the same matter.[5]

When times of special trial and anxiety had come and gone, as after the subsidence of the Titus Oates agitation, a new General wrote to the Rector of St. Omer's, who had lately been Provincial in England; and he said that the latter might now, at odd moments, put together a complete history of the plot, and of the martyrdom suffered by the Jesuit Fathers. He observed judiciously that the time was now ripe for such a record. He added: "This labour, undertaken by you, will, as I said, be a tribute to the glory of our martyrs, and will be particularly useful yet for the history of the Society."[6] Then the General followed the course of the monograph, which was undertaken after repeated solicitations; and the Vicar-General, who succeeded him, acknowledged the receipt of it, a year and a half later. This urgency to have an ample and well-considered narrative drawn up was the more noteworthy, as we find that, in the very midst of the turmoil, ample reports concurrent with the events had been sent in by men of authority—such as Father William Morgan, who, escaping across the Channel, seems to have written from Ghent, and Father Gervase Mumford, who was procurator at Antwerp.[7]

The ripe moment for writing out materials.

§ 2. Meanwhile there were always in progress those letters which are called "Annual," and are intended to embody the most exact contemporary record of stations and ministries. We may listen to the Generals speaking of them incidentally, and then we shall describe their contents.

Word is sent from Rome to the English Provincial, that the Annual Letter for 1631 is wanting. This is in the year 1651. He is desired to bring a copy with him on his approaching visit.[1] A new General, Father Goswin Nickel, reverts from time to time during many years to the subject of Annual Letters. At the commencement of his administration in

The urgency for Annual Letters.

---

[5] *Anglia, Epist. Gen.*, 1668, September 15: the General Oliva from Rome.

[6] *Ibid.*, 1685, July 7: the General De Noyelle, Rome, to J. Warner, Rector, St. Omer's.

[7] *Ibid.*, 1679, March 18: the General Oliva to W. Morgan, Ghent.—1679, March 25, *et seq.*: same to G. Montfortius, Antwerp.

[1] *Ibid.*, 1651, September 16: Vicar-General, Rome, to Provincial, Foster, Ghent.

VOL. I.

1652, he begins to discuss that question. Twice in the course of 1654 he desires the Provincial Father Knott to rouse the men who should be sending in the Annual Letters; and to have these on hand promptly; and he is waiting for the "Annuals" of 1651 and the two following years.[2] This admonition points to a double stage in the composition of such letters; the first being that of the local reports for a year, which are despatched from the different posts to the Provincial or his secretary; and the second being that of the comprehensive redaction, which is made in the Provincial's name and forwarded to the General. The next year, writing to the same Provincial, Father Nickel is concerned at not hearing that any one has been appointed to draw up a select recital ("*selectiora*") out of the materials now massed in the Annuals.[3] In the following year again, he urges promptness in despatching the reports. And in 1657 he goes over the whole subject once more. From a remark of his made to the Provincial's secretary, or *socius*, it may appear that the archives of the Province itself were suffering as much as the General's from a dearth of Annuals; for he writes in 1655 to Father George Gray, the secretary: "When your procurator arrives, we shall examine all the papers which he brings, and of which you have now sent us a list ahead. We are sorry that the Annuals are wanting; and we desire that they be made up as soon as possible."[4] This may mean that he will give orders for copies to be taken in his own general archives and sent back to England, whence the originals had come.

A general redaction of Annuals.

Now we have occasion to hear the General speak of the Propaganda. This reference is interesting, because the existence of the Roman board, called the Sacred Congregation *de Propaganda Fide*, was a determining factor in the foundation of several other societies, which were intended to counteract the Catholic propagation of the faith, and were projected under titles comprising the word "propagation" as a characteristic element.

The Propaganda and the Annual Letters.

Thus, to speak of the very date from which we are about to quote, a society of this kind received its patent of incorporation on February 7, 1662, under the name of "The Society or Company for Propagation of the Gospel in New England and the parts adjacent in America."[5] These societies sprang up in England, Scotland, and New England.

[2] *Anglia, Epist. Gen.*, 1654, May 23, August 29.
[3] *Ibid.*, 1655, March 27.
[4] *Ibid.*, 1655, October 16.
[5] Public Record Office, *Patent Roll*, 14 Car. II., part 11, No. 17.

The notion, indeed, entertained by them of the Roman Propaganda was generally somewhat confused with that of Religious Orders, as appears at times by the mention of Generals and Provincials in the documents.[6]

The Congregation of the Propaganda received copies of the Annual Letters from the General of the Society, who informed the Provincial, Father Edward Courtney (May 13, 1662), that he had the matter of the Annuals drawn out under separate heads, so as to make the relation of what had been done come properly sorted and parcelled out before the eyes of the Congregation *de Propaganda Fide*.[7] A week later he explains this by comparison with the reports sent in from Austria: "The Annual Letters sent by the Austrian Province to the Congregation of the Propaganda met with high commendation, for this special reason among others, that the number of converts to the faith was not given only in sums-total, but in detail, so many in such a city, so many in such a mission, so many in another district. I should like the same to be done by you too. For, though it may not perhaps be expedient to name the persons of the Province, still the provinces [the counties] themselves, the districts, etc., can be stated, and so the account be made more authentic. I expect you will do so; and then we shall deliver such a copy rather than the one on hand, which is good; but the other will be better."[8] It is not clear from this language whether the suppression of names in the accounts from England concerned only the Jesuits in the English Province, or other persons also in the provinces, that is the counties, of England. The same prudential reasons would apply to both classes of persons in times of persecution. In any case, we have a reason here indicated for the absence of proper names in the Letters.

The dangers of betrayal.

In 1665 the General tells the Provincial, Father John Clarke, that he had received and delivered the Annuals destined for the Congregation of the Propaganda, and he expects that they will "give great pleasure on account of the extraordinary spiritual fruit produced by so many conversions." But he is waiting for a copy to lay up in his own archives.[9] And to the next Provincial, three years later, while acknowledging the receipt of a double copy,

[6] Cf. British Museum MSS., *Harl.* 1220, fol. 61: *A Tract wherein means are proposed to prevent the growth of Popery in England*, etc.
[7] *Anglia, Epist. Gen.*, 1662, May 13.
[8] *Ibid.*, 1662, May 20: "... Nam licet personas nominare Provinciæ forte non expediat, possunt tamen exprimi provinciæ, districtus, etc.; ita res fidem facilius impetrabit ...."—*Documents*, I., No. 6, S².
[9] *Ibid.*, 1665, May 16: the General Oliva.

he subjoins: "I congratulate [all of] you most heartily on such holy labours; and I advise you also to keep up the custom of writing out what is accomplished." [10]

Those motives of prudence, which had prompted the writers to be indistinct in their reports, came to acquire a preponderating influence, and threatened the very policy of duplicating the copies sent to Rome. To Father Simeon, the Provincial last mentioned, the General wrote, a year afterwards: "I received your letter, dated at the end of May, and the Annual Letter of the Province, and also that which you directed to the Sacred Congregation of the Propaganda. I do not wish that, on account of the communication made thereof to the aforesaid Congregation, the Society should come to be exposed to greater perils. The Sacred Congregation itself is not to be understood as desiring anything of the kind. But, suppose the letter be drawn up at the time when you are in Belgium, making the visitation of the houses there, that might be a way of keeping clear of the danger. However, if the letter cannot be guaranteed against risk, then drop it." [11]

Here we have several reasons alleged, either against the multiplication of copies, or at least against too minute a distinctness in the accounts. One is the danger of copies drifting abroad; another is the risk incurred by persons, if proper names are put down in black and white. As it was really never intended that the names of persons concerned should be unknown, they were left to be supplied or inferred from other papers, or from some copy of the same letter, duly annotated. To these reasons we may add a third, which operates even where no danger threatens on the score of betrayal. Considering the various uses or abuses to which these letters are liable in passing from hand to hand, it may not be advisable to connect too closely with the names of individuals the work which is being described as that of the Society. Contingent circumstances, affecting both the present and the future, seem to make it preferable that what is public and official be officially impersonal. As to the further measure of putting the letters in print, and the fate which attended the publication of them under the name of "Relations," that does not concern our subject. But we may refer to the published Relations of New France, and the story thereof, as told elsewhere.[12]

The indistinctness of Annual Letters.

[10] *Anglia, Epist. Gen.*, 1668, April 28: General to Simeon.
[11] *Ibid.*, 1669, July 6.
[12] C. de Rochemonteix, *Les Jésuites et la Nouvelle-France*, I. pp. xlii.–l.

Omitting subsequent references to the duty which the Propaganda exacted of all Provincials, that a report should be returned every year of the work accomplished in the missions,[13] we may remark another and kindred form of document which was sometimes demanded. In an ecclesiastical crisis of 1679, the General desired Father John Warner, Vice-Provincial, to have a statement of the whole case drawn up and sent to him: "It will be of use to me," he said, "with the Sacred Congregation of the Propaganda." [14]

<small>Controversial Briefs.</small>

The policy of this had been well explained, half a century before, by Father Mutius Vitelleschi, with respect to an ecclesiastical controversy, in which George Calvert, first Lord Baltimore, was seen combating very actively on the same side as the Jesuit Fathers of England. A memorial had been sent to the Pope, about the accuracy of which the General entertained some doubts; and he expressed his regrets to Father Silesdon—the same who was so diligent in keeping him well informed—that no full answer to the various heads of the memorial had been despatched along with the copy of it; for those heads, he observed, "comprise statements of events that are said to have occurred in England; and no refutation is possible, except at the hands of persons to whom the facts are perfectly well known." Then he went on to lay down the general rule: "As the omission in this case is just what frequently occurs in cases that are similar, I would wish you to remind those who send hither papers of a kind that call for a precise refutation,[15] to annex thereunto supplementary papers, containing the points that are altogether necessary for understanding such documents and refuting them." [16]

§ 3. Two schedules which may be of very different dates, but belong in general to the period before us, retail in the first instance the heads of information proper to Annual Letters; and, secondly, the points to be obtained from the older Fathers, in the interests of a general History. The syllabus for the Annuals is short, and will apply to America in most points:—

<small>Schedule for Annual Letters.</small>

"Note for the Annual Letters.

"1. How many have been reconciled to the Church? how many baptized?

---

[13] *Anglia, Epist. Gen.*, 1676, April 18: General to Strange, Provincial.
[14] *Ibid.*, 1679, September 25.
[15] "... *quæ refutanda apte essent* ..."
[16] *Ibid.*, 1632, April 10 (one of fourteen autograph drafts to English Fathers, same day; 7 pp. fol., on the most diverse subjects).—Cf. *infra, History*, § 15, pp.229-231.

"2. How many general confessions heard?

"3. Anything remarkable in confirmation of the Catholic faith?

"4. How many personal feuds adjusted by means of the missionaries?

"5. Anything singular on behalf [*pro bono*] of the Society?

"6. How many have entered seminaries or monasteries, through the influence of the Fathers?

"7. What assistance has been rendered to Catholic captives and the poor?

"8. If ours have exhibited any remarkable example of virtue either in death or in life?

"9. What alms have been given to the Society?"[1]

For the purposes of a history we find a document entitled: "Some heads on which information is to be sought, especially from the older members, for the purpose of writing the history of the Province." The date of it seems to coincide with that of the foundation of Maryland; and the substance of the ten points is confined to the antecedents of the parent Province. A few, however, will concern us for the things they say; and all of them for the principles which they involve.

<small>Schedule for a history.</small>

"1. On the beginnings of the Mission; of the Vice-Province; the Province; what part they themselves have taken therein; what they have heard from others worthy of credence;—points that deserve notice and have not yet been adequately consigned to posterity.

"2. On the first Fathers of the Mission in particular."

Here follow items with regard to individuals and martyrs. The information called for is that about facts, either as witnessed by the informants, or as received from competent witnesses. So, in the active ministry among souls, let them report the fruits of their labours; their perils, imprisonment, the circumstances of their capture, the number of times they were taken, the particulars of their deliverance or of their escape. Notable converts or penitents of the Fathers; particularly those who ended their life as martyrs. The books they have written in defence of the faith. The virtues and lives of certain Fathers and of the chief benefactors. The public disputations held with heretics; or private ones, if of greater moment. The difficulties between parties in the Church and the Society, the conferences, vexations, agreements, "which it may be expedient to

---

[1] Stonyhurst MSS., A, v. 1, f. 39, a quarto volume, containing instructions, memorials left by Provincials, list of faculties, etc., covering over eighty years, from the coming of Parsons and Campion, till 1663; all copies.

§ 4. INSTRUMENTS AND DEEDS TILL 1700

commit to writing for the greater glory of God, and for the defence of themselves as well as of the Society." The foundation of colleges. Persons who abandoned the Society or were dismissed from it.

"10. Anything else worthy of historical record. It is requested that, as far as possible, the years be noted in which events took place, the names too of localities, of persons, etc." [2]

§ 4. Besides all this material, which might yet be published, there were the authentic deeds to be preserved. The General, Father Piccolomini, wrote to Father Foster, Provincial: "Some one has wisely observed that it concerns the highest interests of the Province, if on the first occasion and with the utmost care, when times are so turbulent there and nothing is safe from the persecution and the assaults of the persecutors, you would cautiously have withdrawn from England, and stored up safely in Belgium, all authentic writings and letters, or archives of the colleges of England; materials too for history, books in fine, and other articles of greater value." [1] A few months later, the General added the following point: "It would be worth while having authentic documents, and such like papers, copied out by Notaries-Apostolic (of whom it is said there are some among our own members); or else by other trustworthy persons; so that one copy could be transferred, for safety's sake, to Belgium." [2] This care was called for as well by the interests of business as by another motive, that of keeping on record the religious obligation of gratitude and charity towards benefactors.

The preservation of deeds, etc.

Twenty-two years later, the General writes that funds, foundations, and accounts must all be exactly recorded and kept on the Continent; and, as to movable property and the like, local superiors must send information every year to the Provincial, so that, in any sudden emergency or in case of death, there may be no uncertainty as to what this property consists in, and where and how everything stands. He continues: "Of this the remoter superiors should take the more exact notice, as all their property is subject to greater risks, by reason of the circumstance that it has not come in anybody else's way to learn what these distant superiors have possibly received in the successive years of their management." [3]

Annual business statements.

---

[2] Stonyhurst MSS., A, i. 29, No. 1, a folio volume: "*Catholic Affairs*, 1600-1800."
[1] *Anglia, Epist. Gen.*, 1650, August 27.
[2] *Ibid.*, 1650, October 29.
[3] *Ibid.*, 1672, March 12: the General Oliva to J. Gray, Provincial.

There was always a race being run between the Governmental dilapidators and the religious property-owners; the former rushing in from all sides with legal warrants to wreck and confiscate, the latter taking more or less the precautions requisite to screen and save; the former rushing back again, fortified even with some itemized account furnished them by a brow-beaten trustee, the latter, in that case, having nothing else to do but to stand back and look on, while all the property assigned to religion and charity went by the board.

<small>Government and religious proprietors.</small>

When, in the course of the Titus Oates agitation, the provincial archives had been broken into and the Provincial himself, Father Harcourt, ended his days on the gallows at Tyburn, the temporary substitute, Father Warner, who was himself appointed Provincial soon afterwards, seems to have applied himself on the spot to the work of reconstructing the archives; but whether in England or on the Continent is not said. After hearty congratulations on the late splendid spectacle of the martyrdoms and the effects thereof, the General notes with approval Father Warner's purpose of "taking on himself, with the aid of his secretary, the labour which he observed would devolve upon the future Provincial, that of putting the Province records in order."[4]

With the final and permanent success of the Orange Revolution, all hopes of Catholics arriving at any degree of emancipation were buried for generations to come. Hence we may pause at the year 1700, at which date we meet with an account of the archives drawn up for the General by Father Sheldon. We see by preceding correspondence of the Generals that St. Omer's on the Continent had been a depository of papers. There too was a *typographium*, or printing-office.[5] Wherever Father Sheldon may happen to be, he answers a circular addressed to the Provinces on January 2 by the General, Father Thyrsus Gonzalez. The nature of the circular may be inferred from the endorsement on the reply: "The letter of Father Henry Sheldon on annual reports and documents that may serve for the history of the Society. The Annual Letters of England, Anno 1700. And an Index of Papers, etc."[6] Towards the close of the paper, the writer begins the index of documents with our Maryland archives in these terms—

<small>The archives in 1700.</small>

---

[4] *Anglia, Epist. Gen.*, 1679, October 7.
[5] *Ibid.*, 1694, August 7-14: the General Gonzalez to the Provincial; to J. Clare, Watten; to J. Persall, Rector, Liège.
[6] General Archives S.J., *Anglia, Historia*, vi. pp. 509-517. It is in the form of a letter, but without signature.

"An Index of the chief writings, which might seem to be of any use for the Father Historian, regarding the English Province.

"1. We have some that pertain to the Mission of ours in Mary-Land. That is a colony in America, belonging to the Kingdom of England. The Society has worked there almost alone, not indeed for the salvation of the native Indians, but of the English themselves, who are found there in great numbers." [7] He says nothing more about America, but proceeds to the documents concerning England. Not adverting any further at present to his paper, or to the judicious reflections which he makes on Father More's history, we shall return at once to some more instructions given by the Generals on the subject of writing and writers.

§ 5. Such was the material. Writing is one of the functions for which the Society was instituted; and there has never been a lack of good will, on the part of chief authorities, to see that ministry actively prosecuted, though the expression of such good will on their part may not often be necessary, if members are not wanting in zeal and energy themselves. The high standard of excellence, set up as a necessary condition for stamping a work with the approval of the Order, was quite noteworthy at this time in relation to English affairs. On the score of both learning and taste, a distinguished place was accorded to national English culture; and the General insisted on the necessity of not permitting anything to issue, if it should fall below such a high level. "Otherwise," said the Father General Oliva to Father Richard Ashby of St. Omer's, who desired to publish a collection of college pieces in prose and verse, "it will rather impair than improve the renown of your erudition and education among the English, who at this time are so accomplished." [1] Wherefore he requires the opinions of the local revisers in the Province to be forwarded to Rome; and the last word, as to publishing the book, shall be given from there. In the same year the publication was projected of an *opus academicum* or literary work, which should contain the poems and orations of Father Grant. In December the General declined to give his authorization. In the following January he allowed it.[2] On a similar principle, when under the last Stuarts that Jesuit

Literary and scientific excellence.

---

[7] General Archives S.J., *Anglia, Historia*, p. 515.
[1] *Anglia, Epist. Gen.*, 1677, February 20: "*Ea tamen esse oportebit admodum selecta et prorsus excellentia; nam alioqui eruditionis institutionisque vestræ famam apud Anglos hac tempestate adeo eruditos imminuent potius quam augebunt.*"
[2] *Ibid.*, 1677, December 11; 1678, January 8: General to R. Strange, Provincial.

institution was opened on the Strand, London, called the College of the Savoy, and became an eye-sore to the non-Catholic zealots both of Maryland and of England, the General recommended that the most particular attention should be paid to the selection of the professors. These should answer and surpass the expectations formed by the adversaries of the Society, "especially as now you are laying the foundation of that prestige which will contribute most effectually to the conversion of souls." [3]

These matters concerned rather literary excellence. And here we may observe that, when we speak of literature in the seventeenth century, and of what concerns European interests and reputation, it is the Latin and Greek literature, with a corresponding style, that is in question; for such were the studies of the learned and such the means of communication among them. Owing to the anglicizing of Latin pronunciation, the English were suffering now from their insularity among the nations of Europe; and it was only at the end of the nineteenth century that their tenacity began slowly to yield, in favour of recovering their franchise of intelligible Latin speech among the cultured classes of Europe. But what we note once for all is that the great fund of literature then, and still more the fund of archives which belonged to a centre like Rome, was in form classical and Latin. As in other countries, so in Rome itself, papers in the vernacular, or in a language known to the parties, might be passed to and fro; but for international communication the vehicle was Latin. And all our ancient papers from the Generals or to them are in that tongue.

Chiefly a Latin literature.

If mere literary excellence met with so much regard from busy men, it will readily be understood that the substantial material of history, philosophy, and theology, was the object of much more jealous attention. One of the Generals found fault with the hasty publication of Father Floyd's book against Mark Anthony de Dominis, before it had been sent for revision to Rome. Father Joseph Cresswell, then at Watten, excused the circumstance by sending to his Paternity a copy of the Cardinal's authorization for the publication; and argued that prejudice would ensue to business, if answers to mischievous books were not promptly written and promptly published. This reflection we find repeated constantly, and very naturally, throughout the whole of the seventeenth

Solidity as against speed.

---

[3] *Anglia, Epist. Gen.*, 1687, July 28 [?] : the General De Noyelle to J. Keynes, Provincial : ". . . *præsertim cum fundamentum nunc ponatur illi nomini, quod ad conversionem animorum* [sic] *maximum pondus est habiturum.*"

§ 5. *WRITING AND WRITERS* 59

century. The reply of the General we may consider to be officially characteristic. After admitting the force of the argument, he continued: "Notwithstanding all that, we must bear in mind that the refutation is quick enough if it is good enough," *sat cito, si sat bene;* "and therefore every effort must be made that solidity be not sacrificed to speed."[4]

The writer, Father John Floyd, was no ordinary man. Though thus criticized, he is the very person whom the same General, at a later period, selects to answer in the name of the Society a book, which, in its first edition, had been met by no less a personage than Paul Laymann, the celebrated moralist.[5] And, in a letter to the Provincial, he had said that, while strength and age permitted it, Father Floyd should lay all other cares aside, and devote himself to writing out, for the benefit of posterity, what he had accumulated and originated in his capacious mind.[6] So, too, the General Oliva in a later generation wrote of Father William Morgan, just liberated from his attendance on an Apostolic Nuncio: "I should wish," he says to the Provincial Simeon, "that you would avail yourselves of the services of a man so eminently learned, for fear his intellectual attainments go without producing their proper fruit; for we shall be culpably responsible if we dig down and bury out of sight the talents which have been entrusted to the fidelity and industry of our administration."[7]

Realizing resources.

In spite of all this, there was nothing that gave so much trouble as this question of books. To a distinguished author, Father Michael Alford or Griffith, on the subject of his book about Constantine, the General wrote: "There is scarcely anything in this age which throws us into greater difficulties than the publication of books; and so you must not be surprised if we feel bound to use more and more circumspection and care as time goes on, especially in the case of those books which touch the burning controversies of the day."[8] Hence he requires the work in question to be sent for revision to Rome.

The troubles over Jesuit books.

[4] *Anglia, Epist. Gen.*, 1620, December 5: the General Vitelleschi to J. Cresswell, Superior, Watten: "... *sed illis non obstantibus cogitandum etiam sat cito illos refutari si sat bene: ideoque studium omne adhibendum ut celeritas responsionis soliditati non officiat.*"

[5] *Ibid.*, 1638, July 17: General to J. Floyd, St. Omer's: on answering the *Astrum Inextinctum*, a work by the Rev. R. Haye, O.S.B. Father Vitelleschi refers Floyd for information and materials to a Rector at Cologne, Goswin Nickel, the same who succeeded in the Generalate, fourth in order after Father Vitelleschi's death.

[6] *Ibid.*, 1635, August 18: General to Blount "or his successor, Fr. Henry More, Provincial."

[7] *Ibid.*, 1670, March 1: "... *nam et aliorum talenta defodere culpa non vacat* ..."

[8] *Ibid.*, 1625, August 25: the General Vitelleschi.

The vicissitudes of fortune, through which an important work of this Father passed, are particularly instructive as to the cramped conditions of Jesuit publications at that time. A new General, Father Goswin Nickel, conferred with Father Alford about his *Annals* of the Church in England. Just then the author died, in 1652; and his work, now posthumous, was revised and approved by the English censors and the Provincial. The General desired to have the judgment of those revisers forwarded to Rome. A couple of years passed, and he asked the next Provincial what had become of Alford's *Annals;* but, he went on to say, if the book treated of St. Ursula against Father H. Crombach, S.J., it would be better to omit that as likely to give offence. The two next years register similar reminders from the General, respecting Alford's *Ecclesiastical Annals* and the tardiness which marked the proceedings in England. Five or six years had now glided by. Eleven years passed; and then the General wrote to the Provincial of the time: "The *Annals* of Father Alford should contain no root of bitterness. No spark should be carelessly left in smouldering embers, for fear of a future conflagration, which would teach us, all too late, that it would be better if the book had never seen the light. If it cannot be published without danger, let it be suppressed. This," he added, "is a melancholy conclusion to come to; but it is a necessary one for that prudence which forecasts the future—unless you and your councillors can suggest some other expedient to me." [9] In the same year the *Annals* appeared, in four volumes folio, and took a high place among learned works of their kind.

It is quite clear that, if such sensitiveness towards whatever came from Jesuit pens was developed among Catholic doctors and controversialists on subjects like Constantine and St. Ursula, the tone of the times would be high-pitched indeed when the subject happened to be the Society itself. Then every word was fuel for a flame, in the Church and out of it, a fire that never went out and is still ablaze,—whether the Society was living or dead, was waking or sleeping, was the infant of a day or the veteran of nearly four hundred years.

§ 6. It must have been in pursuance of the General's urgency to have a select recital—*selectiora*—drawn up out of the materials now massed in the Annual Letters,[1] that the first attempt which we

[9] *Anglia, Epist. Gen.*, 1652, May 25, to 1663, March 17: General to Alford, Foster, Knott, Courtney.
[1] *Supra*, § 2, p. 50.

find was made at a History. Father Henry More, when spending the last years of his life in the Low Countries, was the writer. He adopted the very term, *Selectiora*, for his title. And the date of his manuscript, as completed, we put down for the period between 1656 and 1661. For he records the death of Father Andrew White, who died in 1656; and he himself died at the latter date, five years after. The whole period just follows the time when, in 1655, the General, Father Nickel, was urging that the work should be done.

First redaction of Annual Letters.

The paper is only twenty-four folio pages long. And the writer begins it in a very inauspicious fashion. He entitles it, "The more select points regarding the Province of England, such as are extant for the years 25 to 45 [of the seventeenth century.]"[2] Then he commences in these terms: "When it came to gathering the more select material out of the records of the English Province, one circumstance faced us for which we must beg indulgence at the outset. It is that the letters belonging to many years either have perished entirely or were sent to Rome and are kept there; and no copies are found here. So it should be no matter of surprise if many things are passed over here in silence. In fact, I find nothing at all from the year 15 [1615] to the year 23 [1623]. The year 23 passed more auspiciously, inasmuch as our Mission, though shaken by many storms at home and abroad, had nevertheless grown up to a respectable number of members and of houses; and, having been first erected into a Vice-Province, was in this latter year declared a Province." Thus far all that Father More has written, including the title, is crossed out by another hand, or encircled with a line for exclusion. The next sentence is not so marked for omission. It runs thus: "By those who worked at the harvest in England, 2630 persons were numbered who had been brought over from heresy to the Catholic faith, since the persecution had moderated somewhat in view of the Spanish match." The next sentence follows with an item about Belgian houses, and is excluded. And so the document undergoes a new redaction at the hands of another person.[3]

Meanwhile, looking over his twenty-four pages, we observe that, after only five of them, the writer notes the years 26 and 27 as void of records, and says not another word about them; 29 and 30 are

---

[2] "*Provinciæ Angliæ selectiora quæ extant ab anno* 25° *ad* 45um."

[3] General Archives S.J., *Anglia, Historia*, iv. pp. 125–140 and 857–864: a MS. draft in the handwriting of H. More.

vacant; the letters of 32 and 33 are lost. These latter are the years in which Lord Baltimore's Maryland project was set on foot, his invitations to the colony and description of it formulated, and the expedition itself despatched. Yet Father More attempts not a word on the subject. The next year, 1634, to which Father White's "*Relation of the Voyage*" belongs,[4] has four lines and a half to its credit, and those are on Wilson's death; 35 is wanting; 37 also; 41 has perished; 42 is honoured with two lines; 43 is wanting; and 45, the last, gives one original item regarding the Maryland missionaries. There is no signature anywhere; but the handwriting is Father More's, who, though an actor, an eye-witness, a superior, during these times, still, in default of authentic monuments, gives us only twenty-four pages on twenty years.

It is clear that, if the record is poor for history, the credit won for what he does write is of the highest. Father Sheldon, in the document cited before,[5] speaks of Father More and his published History, which no doubt followed soon after this manuscript sketch, and he says: "Father More was certainly one of the first Fathers of this Province, having discharged almost all the offices in it with singular credit, and been more or less an eye-witness of all those events which he has committed to the press. . . . He brings down his History to the year 1635; and the foundation of all the colleges in Lower Germany [Belgium] is narrated with sufficient accuracy, as well as many other events which took place in England itself. To this we on our part can add very little, seeing that we no longer possess many of the writings which he used. Now, should anybody find this History of Father More's scant enough in materials, let him consider the causes of this penury, as given by the same author in book v., No. 43." Father Sheldon goes on to state that the deficiency in Father More's work has largely been made good by Fathers Bartoli, Sacchini, Alegambe, Tanner. He mentions the contributions of Father Nathaniel Southwell; of Father Warner, Provincial of England, who, when attending the twelfth General Congregation of the Order in Rome, assisted Father Tanner in his book on the Titus Oates Plot; also of Father Courtney, and others, who supplied particulars on different points. Then Sheldon continues, expressing to the General a hope that, through these publications, they may "supply in great part the want of other authentic instruments, a large portion of which has perished,

More's published History.

---

[4] "*Relatio Itineris in Marilandiam.*"—Cf. *supra*, § 2, p. 5, No. 7.
[5] *Supra*, § 4, p. 56.

not so much through the carelessness of ours, as through the inevitable losses of the times."[6]

The volume which Father More published is entitled by him a History of the English Mission and Province of the Society, from 1580 to 1635, and he calls himself modestly a "collector" of the materials. The work was published at St. Omer's, in the year 1660,[7] one year before he died. Both the manuscript, which we described above, and the copy for this published work, went to Rome; but they met with different treatment. The General returned promptly the copy for publishing the History. Father Nathaniel Southwell took the manuscript of twenty pages, and beginning at the very title he altered it from Father More's "Selections," between the years 25 and 45, to the "English Province, 1623 to 48." He then drew lines round different sentences of the text, to exclude or include, as the case might be. He did the same with all the papers which he found in the Roman archives, with Father White's *Relation* and the Annual Letters, leaving out the titles, with entire paragraphs, pages, and sections; numbering the pieces which were to be preserved and put together in one consecutive story; and thus by attaching together, with just a word of transition, some one or two hundred extracts, he obtained a new redaction, consisting of sixty-three folio sheets, that is to say, one hundred and twenty-six pages, instead of Father More's twenty folio pages.

Southwell's manner of redaction.

Had Father More received this before publishing his work, the last ten years of his History would have been much richer, and have comprised the foundation of Maryland. Then, proceeding to the ten years which he did not treat in his printed work, he could have touched on a fair portion of the historical elements in the first twelve years of the Maryland colony. In one instance, Father More himself is the original authority for what happened to the Maryland missionaries, White and Copley, on their capture in the colony and their trial in London, 1645. And here More's bad hand—though he wrote distinctly enough for one who knows the word, "Coppleius," as the family name of Father "Fisher"—led Father Southwell's copyist into the error of writing "Cappecius, the family name of Fisher," a conceit which was destined to exercise the ingenuity of so many

[6] General Archives S.J., *Anglia, Historia*, vi. pp. 514, 515.
[7] *Historia Missionis Anglicanæ Societatis Jesu, ab Anno Salutis, MDLXXX. ad DCXIX. et Vice-Provinciæ primum, tum Provinciæ, ad ejusdem sæculi annum XXXV. Collectore Henrico Moro, ejusdem Societatis Sacerdote. Audomari: typis Thomæ Geubels MDCLX.*; in fol., frontispiece, pp. 518, indexes, etc., pp. 18.

worthy investigators of American records. This piece about Copley and White on trial in London, taken by Southwell from the last leaf of More's twenty-four pages, is the 118th excerpt, as numbered by him in the archives before him.[8]

Father More's manuscript for publication as a History ran through a simpler course. On May 20, 1656, the General wrote to the new Provincial, Father Richard Barton, successor of Father Knott, that it would give him pleasure to see the History of the Province when completed by Father Henry More. To the author himself, six months later, he said that he liked the plan of More's being recalled to Belgium for the purpose of finishing the History of the Province: "Apply yourself diligently to the work." Then, three years afterwards (October 6, 1659) he sent back from Rome the opinions of the revisers in general, supplementing them later (December 6, 1659) with the judgment of one in particular. In both letters he submitted the final judgment upon the merits of the criticism and of the work to the Provincial and his advisers, saying: "You can see how far you need defer to this opinion. As far as I am concerned, once those points are amended, which you shall consider to need amending, the History may be published, provided that all precautions be taken against anything appearing in it which will give ground for invidious criticism or offence, to the annoyance of the Society and its friends."[9]

The General's final criticism on More.

At some time or other, a note from the chief administration required some one to find out all that the general archives contained on the subject of English America. The slip, which is inserted amid the documents of this early date, reads to the following purport: "England. Father General desires Father Compagnoni to look in the archives for information regarding the origin and condition of the Mission of Maryland in America, belonging to the English Province."[10]

§ 7. The materials which we have considered, in the form of Annual Letters, or in the redaction of a History, were of their own

---

[8] General Archives S.J., *Anglia, Historia*, iii. ff. 173–236. It is the copyist's transcript, who reproduces the numbering of the excerpts, as he is following them in the documents. He prefixes the title, *Provincia Anglicana*, to which, in Father Southwell's hand, is appended the limitation: "1623 *usque ad* 48." The White and Copley incident, which in More's MS. is to be found, *Anglia, Historia*, iv. pp. 863–864, A.D. 1645, is in the Southwell redaction, *Ibid.*, iii. f. 227ᵛ, 228, A.D. 1645.

[9] *Anglia, Epist. Gen.*, 1656, May 20; 1659, December 6: the General Nickel to R. Barton, Provincial; 1656, October 28: to H. More.—Stonyhurst MSS., A, iv. 13 (iii.), pp. 1115–1116.

[10] Inserted in *Anglia, Epist. Gen.*, 28 Junii–Julio, 1636: "... *Missionis Marinlandiæ* [sic] *in America, pertinentis ad Provinciam Anglicanam.*"

nature available for publication. There were other private reserves, precious in the highest degree for understanding the course of history. One was the correspondence of the members with the Generals. Another was that of the Generals with the members. These were documents appertaining to internal administration. We have just given some specimens in connection with the materials themselves.

There is little extant of what the Jesuits in England or Flanders wrote to Rome. As far as the course of American affairs entered into the communications of the English Provincials with headquarters, we find only a few data for our history preserved through that channel. There are the official Catalogues of persons with accounts of temporalities (*rerum*); and the formal or Annual Letters, which we have already described. Documents on America to the Generals.

Of what the missionaries in America wrote to the Provincials or direct to the Generals, in the way of administrative or of private correspondence, there is barely a specimen left. And, if there were, we may be allowed to remark here that really we should not expect to find what has recently been so much coveted by certain commemorative associations of America. The business of men so employed as the missionaries were, dealing with far-off superiors who were engaged as Provincials and Generals were, would not admit of details and particulars, regarding localities and personalities and places of burial, such as none were in a position to identify, or at least to appreciate. The duty of the Society towards its departed members was abundantly discharged in every instance. Their lives and deaths were taken over as so much capital, and funded in the record of family merits, for posterity to live on and to increase. But this was as independent of the material conditions or monuments which we should prize now, as the simplicity of religious funerals is foreign to the solemnity of stately functions.

Of greater consequence than either of these departments, which have been so utterly effaced by the injuries of time and, worse than time, by the injuries of men, is that collection of despatches which were written in reply, and were the counterpart of the other correspondence. These we have. They are the letters which the Generals wrote to their men. Here we have the expression of opinion, the formal directions and explicit guidance, given officially by the head of the Society. Now others might err, as judged by the gauge of the institute; and their conduct might leave much to desire, when confronted with the standard set up for them. Criticism, reproof, or repudiation might be their part in the bureau of administration, as it may be in the tribunal of history. But the General, representing in an eminent degree that conservative and responsible authority of which he is the adequate depositary and can alone commit any share to subordinates, must be held to represent the action of the Society itself, in the direction which he impresses on affairs, or in the judgment which he passes upon them. On this account we have omitted nothing that emanated from the chief superior of the Society. Even though it did not concern America in the first instance, but only had bearings to fit an American case, we have preferred to pick up such a clue for exploring historical events, rather than merely deduce rules from general premises.

The letters of the Generals are extant in the original authentic Registers. These are either autograph, corrected by the writer, and passed on to the copyists for despatch, or, having been written under orders by a secretary, they remain as they were approved, and were handed over for transcription. In the years from 1629 to 1769, *Elements on America.* during which we find the more ancient records available for American affairs, we have used the utmost diligence in gathering from three very closely written and large folio tomes of such Registers every sentence and word that bears on America. The data of history which they afford us are incorporated in our narrative, and the original text of the documents may be seen in the companion volume.

As the chief value of the letters is owing to the official character of the writer, we have thought it of less importance to repeat a personal name than to indicate his position as General. The same reason has led us to speak in a general way of the Provincial, since the personal names of a series changing every few years in England would impart no special definiteness to their superintendence over America.[1]

§ 8. Having accounted for the origin of some stores, we proceed to explain the absence of others from the archives. The writer who *Chronic violence, 1685.* draws up the Annual Letter for 1685 concludes in these terms: "Much more could be said about our English Mission, but the violence of the last persecution [that of the Titus Oates Plot] did away with almost all our documents; whole libraries

[1] See above, § 7, p. 33, for the personal names of Generals and English Provincials.

§ 8.   PLUNDERING AND BURNING RECORDS   67

of ours were pillaged; all our desks with their papers and notes were robbed; so that it is not strange if much is wanting here, which we hope is written in the book of life." [1]

A more sweeping disaster attended the Orange Revolution of three years later; and one who had been a missionary in Maryland seems to have been culpably responsible. Father Tidder or Ingleby was at this time in charge of affairs at the new College of the Savoy. Of him and his conduct in this connection, the General says to the Provincial's secretary, Father Francis Sanders: "Among so many deplorable occurrences exciting the deepest commiseration, there is in the first place that misfortune, which you write about, the destruction of all that had been set on foot there, and at such great expense, for the advancement of the Catholic faith; and then there is the seizure of our papers through the carelessness and negligence of Father Edward Ingleby, and the sequestration of them by the secular magistrate." [2]   The British Museum manuscript department and the Cambridge University Library have some documents now, which may have been part of the booty gathered in on this occasion.[3]

1688.

A few years later, things had settled down permanently into the most hopeless condition. The Annual Letter for 1705, written on the continental side of the English Channel, begins thus: "The Province of England is in a condition of such difficulty that, whenever a more violent persecution breaks out, or when wars rage, the services rendered by our men and the sufferings undergone are indeed of a more arduous and brilliant kind than at other times; but, as to reporting them even when the Provincial is himself in England, that is either not attempted at all, or it is done in so cryptic and elliptical a style, that there is no making out what it means. The use of even ciphers is unsafe over there. Then, if the Provincial receives accounts, it is seldom that he can find any means of forwarding them to the Continent. At all events, just lately the Provincial's secretary wrote that he had reminded the local superiors in good time to send the material which regarded the Annual Letters; and they had in fact sent him accounts. But, for fear of being caught off their guard to some one's prejudice,

The embargo on correspondence.

---

[1] General Archives S.J., *Anglia, Historia*, vi. p. 204: Annual Letter, 1685.

[2] *Anglia, Epist. Gen.*, 1690, May 27: ". . . *deque scripturis nostris ex incuria et negligentia P. Edwardi Inglebæi arreptis, atque ad Magistratum sæcularem delatis.*" The General implies some grave reasons for complaint.

[3] Cf. Foley, *Collectanea*, under "Warner, John." This Father's draft MS. on the Titus Oates Plot is: British Museum, *Harl.* 880. A fair copy of the same, autograph, and his *Note and Letter Book* are in the Cambridge University Library.

they had drawn up the papers in such an enigmatical and concise fashion, that no exact transcript could be made of the matter. And, supposing all the points were extended in the manner desired, it is still impossible to face the peril of despatching them hither, because, if intercepted, they would create a situation of imminent danger for many persons." Then the writer, who is no doubt the Vice-Provincial acting on the continental side of the Channel, proceeds to report about the houses in Flanders, premising that all this matter is monotonous and void of incident, since there are scarcely any Fathers engaged in external ministries outside of the domestic precincts.[4]

A business trouble of a few years after this shows us how men in office could dispose of important papers. Father Edmund Plowden was English procurator in Paris, before 1718. On leaving Paris, he became procurator of the Province; and, after residing at different times in England or in Belgium, he was called upon to give an account of a certain money difficulty which he had tried to settle with a French Province a good many years before. The question had reference to the expenses of a Father Galloway, who had served the French mission of Martinique. Now, this is the manner in which he addresses himself to the requisition. It is in 1733, and he is writing to Father Retz, fifteenth General of the Society, who had been Assistant to the previous General, Father Tamburini, and had been Plowden's correspondent on this very issue of the Anglo-French dispute. "It is extremely unfortunate," he says, "that, when I came back to England, I burnt all the letters of your Paternity. At the present moment, nothing more would be necessary than to write out your answers and send the copies back to Rome. I can scarcely venture to hope that the manifold letters which I wrote to your Paternity upon that subject are still kept on file with you."[5] He goes on to say that he kept a short syllabus of all his own letters, and he will give an abstract of them in order. Thus the Assistant's letters had passed off in smoke. So, too, had the General's; for he proceeds: "Meanwhile, I sent frequent letters to the Father [General] Tamburini, imploring his assistance. He answered several times; and kindly. The letters themselves, as I

A procurator burning papers. 1718-1733.

---

[4] General Archives S.J., *Anglia, Historia*, vi. p. 603: Annual Letter for 1705.

[5] His apprehension was unfounded. The papers were safe in the General Archives. Approving of the account he gave, Father Retz, the General, said in reply: "*Cum et penes nos extet informatio illius actorumque in ea, Reverentiæ Vestræ pro solatio respondeo*. . . ." *Anglia, Epist. Gen.*, 1733, August 29: Leodium, P. Edmundo Plowden, Rectori.

said at the beginning, have been burnt; but I can recover the substance of them well enough from my own minutes."[6]

Among the most sweeping and far-reaching causes of destruction was the Suppression of the Society in 1773 by Clement XIV. When it was revived a generation afterwards by Pius VII., the French Revolution and other episodes being then recognized as having been intimately connected with the phase of its suspended vitality, there could be restored to the Society its status, its work, and its privileges in the Catholic Church; but not the property that had been appropriated or squandered by every agency in Europe. Of books, papers, and archives only a fraction remained to be returned by His Holiness. And, since that time, we know that important collections among them have been exposed to constant danger even during the nineteenth century; and have led such a migratory life to escape pillage, that one very important depository has had to be emptied secretly, and its contents hurried away, no less than nine times. Such was one tribute to enlightenment and toleration on the part of the latest century.

The havoc at the Suppression, 1773.

§ 9. It might be thought that records have been put in print at one time or another, and so have been preserved. But we must point to another cause which operated against any notable advantage accruing to us from that quarter. We refer to the policy of silence, imposed oftentimes upon the writers of the Society, that their contributions might not add fuel to the flame of domestic controversy. It is a policy which has often been suppliantly appealed to by open adversaries or masked foes, on the plea that some one or other must desist or there will be no end to the fury of dispute; and none can do it more naturally or gracefully than the Jesuit Fathers, who alone are under control. Rome itself has frequently counteracted the rebellious attitude of a Gallican Sorbonne and other such domestic enemies, by desiring not another word to be said. Of course, in all such contingencies, it has been only a closely bound organization like that of the Society which is found responsible enough not to say another word.

A writer, at the date of the Restoration of Charles II., explained that there were three sorts of adversaries ranged against the Order. "The first and worst of all," he wrote, "are some Catholicks, who have such a tooth against the Jesuits

Classes of adversaries.

---

[6] General Archives S.J., *Anglia, Historia*, vi. pp. 753-756: E. Plowden to General, 1733, July 25.

that they cannot afford them one good word." He does not undertake to write for these. A second sort, he observes, are those whose watchword is "Root and Branch;" the King being for them a Papist, "the Pope a monster, and the Jesuites his horns." There is nothing to be expected of these either. The third sort are "adversaries of the Society of Jesus, not out of malice, but prevented by a prejudicate opinion;" and he adduces a good many reasons for the prejudice, which he does not despair of removing.[1]

This policy of suppressing literature in the interest of peace introduces us to a new chapter of directions, which are to be followed in the employment of materials. We shall quote some of the formulas adopted by the Generals in these proscriptive measures.

There was that controversy which, as we observed before, saw George Calvert, first Lord Baltimore, actively enlisted in the fight.

Directions against writing.
A whole mass of literature had been thrown on the market. The General wrote to Father Blount, Provincial: "I judge that no books should be written in self-defence against the libels and treatises, by means of which your opponents there endeavour to cast odium upon ours along with other regulars. That would be but a feeble defence against assaults of such a kind. And then it only invites more mischief to the regulars than is the evil which they are trying to ward off. And I need scarcely mention that it gives great displeasure to the Apostolic See and to many dignitaries of the Church, who have deliberated upon issuing an order, that no more discussions and altercations of the kind shall be issued in print. Wherefore I earnestly recommend you to restrain all your men from composing or publishing such-like vindications and refutations."[2]

A month passed, and the General repeated this admonition against writing. Four months later he applied what salve he could to feelings wounded by adversaries and left without any protection.[3] Certain effects of Father Knott's very temperate publications, about 1631, confirmed the General in his view; and so did the remark of Father John Percy, a famous controversialist, who said in a letter that the libellers were hurting themselves more than the Jesuits. His Paternity persisted in the opinion that to publish answers would only be like throwing oil upon the flames. At the end of 1632 he commended the Provincial for his firmness in applying the

[1] M[artin] G[rene], *An Account of the Jesuites Life and Doctrine*, pp. 59, seqq.
[2] *Anglia, Epist. Gen.*, General, Mutius Vitelleschi, 1631, February 15.
[3] *Ibid.*, 1631, March 22; July 19.

restrictions, as desired by higher authorities, and in particular for refusing to allow of any answer being published to refute *Petrus Aurelius*, a work issued by the chief of the new Jansenistic sect in France. Of this work we shall have occasion to hear again.[4]

There were deeper reasons for such a policy of abstention; but they were not always discernible at the time by men who, being on the spot, were blinded by the dust of the affray. Indeed, this is one of the prudential reasons in sound organization for having men placed higher, to see further, and to check the movements below. Beyond the actual issue, there was always another practical question—how far or to what extremities your opponents would go. And, if they would go any lengths whither you could not follow them, it were as well not to start out with them.

<small>Eschewing controversy in certain conditions.</small>

An excellent instance was furnished by the experiences of the same Father Knott. He published a book in 1636 on doctrinal matters for the benefit of Mr. Chillingworth and Protestants generally, with whom his relations seem to have been quite smooth and to have continued so. At once a campaign opened against him. There was no party question touched in his book; but all the party rancour discharged upon him six years before was poured out anew. It was represented that the Protestants ought to feel insulted by "this man and his brood;" that the Protestant "State should look to this man and his abbettors;" and the Protestant king should banish Knott from the kingdom.[5] The papal envoy in England, George Con, wrote to Rome, that the men who were playing this game "had no love for one another, but they readily clubbed together for such enterprises." And, forwarding the book itself, the envoy observed to the Cardinal: "The author is held to be one of the most learned and prudent men in England, by the admission of his very accusers."[6] The significant feature of this assault, which Father More, Provincial at the time, interpreted as a blow at the Society,[7] was the method of bringing down a hostile Government on one's brethren in arms; which any one can do who

<small>Father Knott's experiences.</small>

---

[4] *Anglia, Epist. Gen.*, 1632, October 23: to Blount.—For *Petrus Aurelius*, cf. *infra, History*, § 13, pp. 216, 217, note 8.

[5] Stonyhurst MSS., *Anglia A*, viii. No. 109, f. 126: Jo. Ha?, November 9 [1636].

[6] Vatican Archives, *Nunziatura d'Inghilterra*, 6, f. 102.—London, Public Record Office, *Transcripts from Rome*, vol. 97: Con from Hampton, 1636, December 11.—Among the critics he mentions the name of Price. Con names there the two great parties to the *Concordia*, or Concordat, and alludes felicitously to the Jesuits' happy mission of bringing foes together: " *Quali* [li due corpi più grandi della *Concordia*] *seguitano à lacerarsi bravemente, nè si accordano in alcun punto fuorchè nell' oppugnare li Giesuiti.*"

[7] Vatican Archives, *Ibid.*, f. 129^v: Con from Hampton, 1637, January 7.

will choose to do it; which the irresponsible do the more largely as the hostile Governments become more numerous; and which Dr. Pugh characterized as a game of "throwing a stone to dash another man's brains out, and hiding your hands that you may seem to have done nothing."[8] But there was no escaping for Father Edward Knott. When three years afterwards he was made Provincial, all the fury broke out again to work the same external agencies and have the king demand that the new Provincial be deposed. And now we arrive at the General's observations on this stage of the proceedings. We select only a sentence or two: "I hear that the old causes of quarrel are now being raked up again, and from the side of those where it should least have been expected; and the sons of our mother the Church are fighting against us by the hands of outsiders; they are agitating his deposition from office: and this is the reward they allot him for his defence of the purity of faith."[9]

Such were the experiences of one Jesuit as an individual object of resentment, showing what thicker sediment was ever ready to rise if the medium around was only stirred up a little more. The prohibitions had been repeated against all further writing, especially on occasion of the protest signed and issued by the Catholic peers, among whom George Calvert was one to affix his signature. If the Fathers wanted to write for the press, it was ordered that their manuscripts should be submitted for revision at Rome. Meanwhile adversaries were not silent, the Jesuits were restive, and the Lords Baltimore and Somerset took pains to express indignation at the statements given out in print.[10] At the end of 1632 the embargo upon the Jesuit writers was stated by the General to be a precept binding all of them. His view of the peers' protest was not cheering; he feared it would only make the pamphleteers wilder.[11] To the Rector of St. Francis Xavier's and his men in Wales he wrote: "That the example of others may not seduce you and your Fathers there from the path of due observance, I would have you consider that dereliction of duty on the part of others should not be allowed to have more weight with us than the authority of the Holy See."[12] He informed the Provincial, however, that he

The precept of silence imposed.

---

[8] R. Pugh (1680), *Blacklo's Cabal*, p. 75, note: on Holden's letter against Dr. Leyborne [1647].

[9] *Anglia, Epist. Gen.*, 1640, January 14: General to P. J. Suffren, London.

[10] General Archives S.J., *Anglia, Historia*, iv. pp. 289, 290: George Baltimore to Lord Petre, August 8, 1631; 2 pp. fol.; a contemporary copy: *Documents*, I. No. 3.— Cf. *infra, History*, § 12, pp. 209–211.

[11] *Anglia, Epist. Gen.*, 1631, April 26, to 1632, December 18: General to Blount, Provincial.

[12] *Ibid.*, 1633, January 15: General to Charles Brown, Rector.

§ 9. THE POLICY OF SILENCE

desired to receive answers himself to any mischievous papers, which might be transmitted for circulation in Rome.[13]

The whole situation under this skirmishing fire was like that forced upon the General in the face of a certain marquis, who was steadily fighting the Society for an unpardonable sin, inasmuch as his own son had chosen to become a Jesuit. The General remarked tersely to Father Silesdon in London: "It is hard to shut the mouth of the ill-disposed. Whatever you do, whatever you don't do, they find fault with it all the same; not because it is wrong, but because they are not right." However, as the Right Honourable Marquis was not in such a category as that, the General would propose another adjustment.[14] Discounting only this compliment, the marquis and the pamphleteers were quite in the same category; and, if the Jesuit did not want to go the same lengths with them, he had only to let them go alone. *Hard to please.*

There is a curious set of instructions which show how far it was thought necessary to humour a perennial irritation or ulceration, and to buy off vexation by suppressing in England books current and quite classical in other parts of Europe. Indeed, in other lands there was nothing to match the undisciplined state of ecclesiastical affairs during the Stuart period in England. For, if things as bad or worse were published in other countries, still there was some authority on the ground to stigmatize measures as irresponsible, or statements as unauthentic; to note some balance and to keep some check as betwixt the good and the bad; to direct minds in the present, and instruct history for the future. It is the good fortune of history in America that, while we may find little to help us in products from the other side of the ocean, we also find little to embarrass us in any native growth of old publications and so-called Church history, which we should have to scrape away as a preliminary to reaching the surface, and still more the inside, of authentic facts. *Translations into English forbidden.*

In 1630 the General wrote to the Provincial, Father Blount: "I understand that one of ours is thinking of translating the History of our Society from Latin into English. We consider that to be inexpedient. Hence you will not grant any one the permission to undertake it."[15] This was Orlandini's and Sacchini's great History,

---

[13] *Anglia, Epist. Gen.*, 1632, July 31.
[14] *Ibid.*, 1640, December 22: "*Arduum est malevolis os obstruere; quidquid egeris, aut omiseris, reprehendunt, non quia pravum sit, sed quia ipsi malevoli. In eorum numero cum non sit Ill^{mus} Dominus Marchio [de Vieilleville],*" etc.
[15] *Ibid.*, 1630, March 30.

of which three tomes had been published during the last sixteen years. In 1666 Father Bartoli's History of the Society in England was ready in Italian, and the General spoke in the highest terms of the work; but he was of the same mind as several revisers in doubting whether it was a safe thing to publish it at present. In the following year, English Fathers both in Rome and in England examined and passed on their observations to head-quarters.[16] And then it was published in Italian. In 1670 the general policy to be adopted was stated thus to Father Simeon, Provincial: "When books already published are translated into another language, even though our own members be the authors, still we should be consulted about the new edition; for we should prefer that some books had never been published at all, and therefore we do not desire them to come out in different languages. Often, too, the very best works are translated in a style not altogether worthy of the originals, lessening the credit due to them. As to calumnious books against the Society, if they treat of some particular issues which can easily be pilloried for falsehood, refutations may be published at once. But, if they attack our affairs in general, I should not wish the vindication to be published before approving of it myself." [17]

Bartoli's History of the Society in England.

Anti-Jesuit libels.

The Order had been bearing the brunt of the fight against Gallicanism. Now the whole army of Jansenism was on its hands for a hundred years to come; and the war was not to end for the Society save in its temporary defeat by a Suppression, nor for the victorious sect save by its immediate extinction in revolution and infidelity. In 1657 the General wrote to Father Thomas Carwell, Rector of the London residence: "As to that libel against the Society called the *Provincial Letters,* if you can send us a copy we shall be glad to see it. For the rest, we trust the Society will not suffer more damage at the hands of this new slanderer than it has incurred heretofore at the hands of so many others, whose libels can furnish a copious library." [18] Then follows correspondence on the refutations published in France, and the republication of the *Provincial Letters* in England.[19]

Jansenism.

From what has been said, it may rightly be inferred, that a constitutional reason was operating to limit the supply of Jesuit papers

[16] *Anglia, Epist. Gen.*, 1666, December 11: General, John Paul Oliva, to J. Clarke, Provincial.
[17] *Ibid.*, 1670, September 6.
[18] *Ibid.*, General, Goswin Nickel, 1657, December 1.
[19] *Ibid.*, 1657, December 22: to the same Carwell; 1659, February 22: to George Gray, secretary or *socius* of the Provincial.

directed to persons outside of the Order. This is a circumstance to be borne in mind when, in archives, like those of the Vatican or Propaganda, a reader sees so much about the Society, and yet sees so little from it. In the Vatican one may examine minutely fifty volumes or *codices* of those miscellaneous documents called the "Letters of Individuals,"[20] as distinguished from the collections of nuncios, princes, bishops, etc., and he will be struck by the rarity of communications during a hundred and thirty years from members of the Order, while he hears not a little about them, and often in a critical or incriminating sense. The tendency of what is written about them may be obvious; the charges perhaps less so; but the papers of the Jesuits are scarcely to be found, and, least of all, in the line of incriminating others. So, too, in the Propaganda for twenty years after its foundation, beyond which period this first volume of ours does not profess to reach, we reckon that only a twentieth part of the business touches the Society directly; and there is barely a slight contribution proceeding from the Jesuits, though they were labouring in most of the missionary countries over the globe. About an entire third of the business is Capuchin, and consists in sending men on missions, providing for them, governing them to all intents and purposes just as a chapter of regulars might superintend its own community. Indeed, the Cardinal who became Prefect in 1632, ten years after the foundation of the Propaganda, was himself a Capuchin, Antonio Barberini, Cardinal di Sant' Onufrio, brother to the reigning Pope, Urban VIII. Another third part or more of the business concerns other Orders, exclusive of the Society. About a fourth relates to the secular clergy. And a little fraction remains for the Jesuits, or for those pontifical colleges among which the Society had charge of not a few. At the same time, the same archives contain many complaints about these Jesuits, in most lands where they are found, concerning many things that they are doing, or are supposed to be doing or intending. But, though their cause is usually in the dock however casually or by implication, they are scarcely there themselves.

The reason for all this was constitutional with them. They were a military body, always organic, in order, and under discipline; habitually transacting business with their own superiors; and, as to the privilege of dealing directly with higher authorities in the Church, habitually leaving such affairs to the higher authorities in the Society. Where this family characteristic fails in particular instances, it will

[20] *Lettere di Particolari.*

also, as a rule, be apparent that other traits of the Society's spirit are wanting.

§ 10. The effects of the systematic silence and abstention from writing were no doubt threefold. First, there was that which Rome and the General intended, that so much extra fuel was, in point of fact, not thrown to feed the flames of domestic discord. Secondly, great violence was certainly done to the feelings of the Jesuits on the ground, who had only to salve their wounds as best they might, and nurse the compensating virtues. Thirdly, equal violence was done in a negative way to published literature, which thus has handed down a history lacking on one side and therefore false on the other.

Three effects of this silence.

As to their injured feelings, the Vice-Provincial Warner wrote to the Cardinal of Norfolk about a vicious book, which was coming out against the Society in 1680. He said: "I have hitherto hindred all publick mention of this, and will continue so as long as I can. But it is a hard matter to act always the anvil, and receive rude blows from those persons, without returning any, when they lye open to such mortall wounds. What I here say is knowne to many: and I feare very much some may be provoked to discover for self-defence, what I wish may remaine secret for the good of religion." And he goes on to quote the words of the Apostle: "If we bite and eat one another up, we shall be mutually consumed." Nor does it seem to have been much of an alleviation that further plans to bring the Protestant Government down upon them were understood to fail—"that businesse," the same writer observed, "by which they offend Rome, and get nothing in England."[1]

As to the effects on historical literature, that result was inevitable which we find the sequel actually to have been. The actors disappeared; posterity came; it found the printed letter which remained, and did not find the letter which had not been printed. Printed, a libel stood out; and to him who found it the document was history because he found it; and it might even be mistaken for Christian doctrine. Thus the reader of our day will find the Gallicanism of that time implicitly endorsed in modern books, and Sorbonne decrees reverentially taken as Catholic faith, for want of any remote suspicion on the part of the twentieth-century compiler that he is rehearsing crude Gallicanism. In the

The effect on published literature.

---

[1] Cambridge University Library, Warner's *Note and Letter Book*: drafts of letters, September 27 and May 1, 1680, to Cardinal Howard of Norfolk.

§ 10.   *EFFECTS ON PUBLISHED HISTORY*   77

literature itself one may verify the condition as described in a contemporary Information, and exhibited to the Sacred Congregation of the Inquisition in 1663: "Nothing," it says, "does so unsettle the minds of Catholics as the manifold example for imitation offered by our neighbour, France. Whatever the Parliaments there have enacted, or the Sorbonne decreed, or other universities adopted, which in any way opposes the legislative and coercive power of the Pope, or his infallibility in defining matters of faith, or the immunity and liberty of the Church; whatever measures have been taken to counteract [the Jesuit] Bellarmine or his books against Barclay, or to do away with the Defence of the Faith by [the Jesuit] Suarez, which book was publicly burnt by the hangman in Paris; whatever happened in [the Jesuit] Sanctarelli's case; whatever has been advanced against the authority of the Pope, or to the prejudice of the Apostolic See;—all this they rake together, and pile up in their books, and present under one comprehensive view." Then, going about the houses of the English Catholic laity, they worry the latter with the argument that what is good enough for Frenchmen ought in all conscience to be good enough for Englishmen, who are suffering so much under penal laws. "And with this fraud and sophistry they have entrapped great numbers."[2]

Now, we shall find all this recurring under phases of its own in Maryland. For it was during a crusade of this kind in England, and under the influence of men prominent therein, that John Lewger, destined to be first secretary of the transatlantic colony, was introduced into the Catholic Church, and that he resigned his benefice only to be inducted into these principles. The consequences were of no slight moment to the consciences of Catholics and to the history of a plantation, which survives under some legislative aspects in the present State of Maryland. Lord Baltimore himself, from the time at least when he engaged the services of Lewger, began to manifest views and sympathies in ecclesiastical affairs quite at variance with those of George Calvert, his father, and apparently differing from those which he himself had favoured at the first foundation of the Catholic colony. *Lewger and Baltimore.*

In summing up the net results of influences acting on our archives, we must take into account certain mechanical and material difficulties arising from the penmanship, the ink, the paper, and

---

[2] General Archives S.J., *Anglia, Historia*, v. pp. 659-661; *Sac. Cong^{ne} Sti. Officii. De Periculoso statu Rei Catholicæ in Anglia. Informatio facti*, etc. Anno 1663; pp. 647-670.

at times eventual loss in the transmission of documents. Some letters took a year to travel from England to Rome; and then arrived "obsolete," as the General would call them. There was the damp; there was the bad paper, bad ink, bad writing. Father Vitelleschi besought Father Henry More to form his letters *perfectius et distinctius*, more accurately and more distinctly; he said the paper used was too transparent, allowing the characters on both sides of it to show through. In a case of our own, we mentioned before that Father More's written word, perfectly clear to one who knows, "Coppleius," became in the transcripts an optional variation, "Coppecius" or "Cappecius;" and Father Southwell, in editing this material, wrote out again between Father More's lines some of the words for the relief of the copyist; as, for instance, the name of Father White himself, "*Vitum*." The General did well to suggest that, where possible, this Provincial might very properly employ another person's hand.[3] To More's immediate successor, Father Knott, the same General said of two letters just received, that it was at the cost of labour he had read them, "all blurred, whether through the fault of the paper or of the ink."[4] It is noteworthy how, if their paper is not of the same kind as that which was used in Rome, it seems to be invariably inferior, with a graduation in its declension, according as it is presumably Belgian or English. To Father Francis Forcer an intimation is given that "it was with the greatest difficulty I could decipher your two letters of the 2nd of August; they were so spotted over with rusty stains from the damp."[5] Nor is the same theme wanting to the same key a long generation later, with quite other men in office. The General, Father Oliva, writes to Father Sir John Warner, *alias* Clare, who became Provincial afterwards like his namesake John Warner: "I have received both your letters, and I laboured not a little to catch the fleeting characters, which were distinguishable only as pale marks upon a white ground."[6]

We are living now in the third century since those times. Hence it is no wonder if bundles of corroded papers have become undecipherable. The documents gape vacantly there where separate letters, words, and lines have left their places, and, subsiding like an abraded rust of inky paper, have been coffined by a reverential hand in envelopes; while the ghastly moulding,

[3] *Anglia, Epist. Gen.*, 1638, April 17: General to More.
[4] *Ibid.*, 1639, December 24.
[5] *Ibid.*, 1640, October 27.
[6] *Ibid.*, 1677, July 17.

which remains around the vacant panel of a page, threatens to crumble at the barest touch, and follow whither its only reason for existence has gone before.

Were it not for the preservation of the archives originally belonging to the General, and still existing in the degree and in the scattered places or parts mentioned above, we might have found it useless for American history to try and peer into the obscurity of the seventeenth century. So we may finish this first section of our Introduction by recalling what it was that we undertook to show—the origin of the records and their degree of authenticity; how far they are wanting, and why so; and what directions governed the use of them, or dictated a prudential abstention from use.

SECTION THE SECOND.

§ 11. Criteria drawn from current literature. § 12. Prejudice against our subject. § 13. Political basis of the prejudice. § 14. The first Lord Baltimore and the legal prejudices. § 15. Developments of the literature. § 16. Eighteenth-century literature. § 17. Test Acts and oaths. § 18. Nineteenth-century literature. § 19. Rectifications of history, and results. § 20. The true nature of our subject.

§ 11. Thus far we have been using such materials of criticism as came to hand in the archives themselves. It is proper not to omit such other criteria for our guidance, as are suggested by the published and standard literature lying about us. There is enough of the literature and of the criteria to be suggestive and directive on our topic.

This review will also help in some degree to meet a difficulty, inherent as well in our subject as in every other which dates from before the American Revolution. In the frame of the general reader's mind there is observable an absence, *The critical sense of time* not indeed of interest, but of just appreciation. The *and place.* interest may be so lively and genuine as to originate flourishing societies and found a body of literature relating to colonial times. But it is only too plain, even from respectable productions of recent date, that the interest outruns the power of appreciation; and by this we mean the realization of circumstances, of environment, and habits of thought, which prevailed in the plantations at a distance from our day of only two or three full human lives. Thus so dominant with us are the modern ideas of freedom and government, where neither conscience enters to control politics nor politics to control conscience, that we have drifted a world away from the right historical bearings to understand oppression for conscience' sake and persecution for religion's sake. Not far from our doors there may be a full recrudescence of those experiences; and there are contemporaries of our own who have only too much reason to acquire, even under the forms of a republican government, a live and bitter realization of social conditions, which the American is apt to consider as rather prehistoric. In fact, a realization of them is not among his intellectual or sentimental acquisitions. Yet, if the vital intuition to appreciate the past is wanting, the history too is wanting; consisting as this does, not in a number of hard positive facts like a trail of pebbles in the bed of a river run dry, but in the current of principles, of causes and effects, continuous in the flow of events. It may be added that, if the principles and operative causes of history are missed, neither is the faculty acquired of recognizing them as they reappear, identical in substance, though disguised under the altered conditions of new times.

Among the first original documents which offer themselves for use in our narrative, one gives occasion for an historian to illustrate in a mild form a manner of treatment which, if not punctiliously accurate, has none the less a technical air of critical acumen about it. Mr. Doyle writes on the English in America; and he says of the Maryland expedition, that to one of the Jesuits, "Father Andrew White, we owe a picturesque, though not always trustworthy account of the voyage and of the early days of the settlement."[1] This is all that the gentleman has to say about the critical value of Father White's *Relation*—that it is "not always trustworthy." Having thus condemned it, he proceeds to use it. There is no citation of facts, nor indication of intrinsic or extrinsic evidence to show Father White's untrustworthiness. There is no author cited, nor any contemporary monument. Since the gentleman wrote, an additional document has indeed come to light: *A Briefe Relation of the Voyage vnto Maryland*, which, however, though qualified to be a tell-tale, tells no tale of untrustworthiness.[2] It is not probable that the historian presumed to impeach Father White's facts from his own personal experience; for, if he ever did cross the ocean and set foot in America, he came into the world a few centuries too late for Father Andrew White. The only ground which we can discover for this jaunty manner of writing on the part of one person

J. A. Doyle on Father White.

[1] J. A. Doyle, *The English in America*, p. 377.
[2] *The Calvert Papers*, No. 3, pp. 26–45.—Cf. *supra*, Chap. I. § 2, p. 6, No. 35.

at the expense of another is the tone, not the facts, of Father White. It is that which the Rev. E. D. Neill refers to when he says respectfully of a document similarly composed: "The journal of the early Jesuit mission in Maryland abounds in religious sentiment."[3] It is that living personality of the Catholic priest which is apparent in the narration, and which could expand freely because, in the Latin letter, he was writing to his own superior, and never expected to be caught and fixed in the revelation of a printed page for the non-Catholic world. This circumstance, which adds vitality, vivacity, and a distinct value to what might otherwise have been a mere colourless report, seems not to have pleased the historian whom we have cited. It means nothing less than that he himself must be caught in the revelation of a printed page, as borrowing from a Catholic priest and a Jesuit. Such a condescension on the part of one who, being ignorant, must borrow, is made amends for by depreciating the other, who knows indeed, but of course must be false. This kind of literary treatment is uncritical and illiberal.

However, that was a slight case, as the performance itself was slight. And we do not mean to imply that, if an author of this description had exchanged his own manner for any of the other forms of uncritical writing, he would have been doing better. He might have done very much worse.

Omitting divers other specimens, there is that insidious form of pretending to justify statements in one's text by a show of references in one's notes; which go to betray the implicit confidence of the reader, until, being verified, they are found to discredit the writer. Of such a practice Mr. Hallam says that, when it proceeds from prejudice, it "is a glaring violation of historical integrity, and tends to render the use of references, that great improvement of modern history, a sort of fraud upon the reader."[4] Of the practice itself no one affords better instances than Mr. Hallam himself; so that a distinguished lawyer, giving testimony before a Committee of the House of Commons on a Catholic question, found no more pertinent samples, to illustrate the abusive manner of quoting Catholic writers, than those furnished by Mr. Hallam and Dr. Robertson in their employment of monastic originals.[5]

The deceptive use of references.

---

[3] E. D. Neill, *Terra Mariæ*, p. 71. The Rev. Mr. Neill was not a Catholic clergyman.
[4] H. Hallam, *View of the State of Europe during the Middle Ages*, ii. 224.
[5] W. Burge, before the *Mortmain Committee*, July, 1844, p. 172 (690), Qu. 1394. The falsification is that of making out that the clergy were so ignorant as not to be able to "read," whereas the document quoted speaks of quite another thing, that of

With respect to all things Roman, Catholic and Jesuit, there have been three stages of evolution in the manner of writing history.

<small>A threefold attitude towards Jesuit history.</small> The first period was that which for its duration, covering as it did all our colonial times and extending before and after, may be called the classical period, one which was persistently conservative in maintaining an attitude of intolerance. Though it drags out a protracted existence still, it is not supposed to be in fashion. A second was the transitional period, which began in the nineteenth century, and, with the majority, led onwards and forwards to an atmosphere of liberality, or at least of indifference; while, with some, it found a wrong issue, and reverted backwards to a more melancholy frame of mind, as if the truth were too brutal if the facts were too fair. A third stage is that of the modern renaissance, which, in the publishing world of America far more than in that of England, endeavours to strike a proper tone, or at least not to strike discordant notes, when the theme is Catholicism, sacerdotalism, or even Jesuitism. Of this we have many instances. Suffice it to mention as a specimen that collection of monographs by different writers in Justin Winsor's *Narrative and Critical History of America*; or again the publications of historical societies, not a few treating expressly of Jesuit questions.

§ 12. It is our privilege in this work, so far as we look outside and beyond the limits of the Catholic body, to be addressing a public <small>Views still prevalent.</small> which represents the third and liberal stage of historical thought and civility. At the same time, it is our misadventure, and one inseparable from the entire subject of this History, that most of the published literature, which in any way dates from within the limits of our period, belongs unmistakably to the other two stages of thought, and is either of the intolerant classical type, or does barely attain to the modified toleration of the transitional form. Hence, that we may not seem to be wantonly sombre, and to be throwing gratuitously an atmosphere of gloom over some parts of our subject, we must even now explain what phases of thought and policy this double period of literature covered. And so we hope to meet with indulgence if subsequently we take things as we find them.

Besides, we observe, at the opening of the twentieth century, that

---

"chanting well." Yet a writer like this can afford to tell the reader that, as between the "monkish chroniclers" and himself, the reader should believe him and not the chroniclers: "*experto credite*," he says. Hallam, *Middle Ages*, ii. 224.—Cf. *infra*, p. 615.

some of the most odious products of the more ancient creed of history are rehearsed by persons very remote in their tenor of thought from such illiberality. The reason is obvious. They have copied what they supposed to be correct, because they have heard it always; and it is said to be in a thousand books; and it does stand out clearly in the cyclopædias and abridgments, whereof Bacon said even in his time, that the advocate, unable to master so many original books, gives them up and takes to second-hand compends. If the inquirer did rise from the digest and go back for once to the original, he would find the very formulas of constitutional history, which he has met so often that he knows them off by heart, to be word for word the production of some one man's brain. But behind the figments bred there, some hundred and fifty years ago, when has any one thought fit to go and pry? After all, it was only some matter of Christianity or Popery.

No one could justly take it to be invidious, but many would find it tedious, if we brought forward here some examples from recent publications, and showed how far well-meaning men can go in a false presentation of other people's doctrine and practice. It is not really their own presentation which they are exhibiting, nor that of the other people on whom it is fathered; but it is that of some third party, one oftentimes as remote from us now as the twilight of fable, whom they should first have run down with the hounds of criticism, before beginning to follow up such a blind lead. These recent authors are persons whom we should mention only with respect. And, were we in want of such an argument, we might derive from their works a plausible induction, that scant indeed must be the authentic literature on Church history, canon law, mortmain, præmunire, marriage, testaments, and the like, if such accounts can be repeated as history, without a sign of misgiving or critical doubt. Over and against all this, there are now modern works scientifically composed, which treat these hackneyed subjects in an original way, making them as good as new, because the old lines are demonstrably false. But, in spite of all such masterly efforts at mental illumination, made by the universities and made by the Bar, we must only presume that the enlightenment has not yet penetrated so far as to reach every one among us, and impart something of what that ancient sage desiderated in the Greeks—a little of the antiquity of knowledge and of the knowledge of antiquity.[1]

Persons with whom tradition prevails.

[1] Compare the works on English Law, on Canon Law, on Constitutional History,

84   INTROD. II.   THE ARCHIVES AND LITERATURE

This, perhaps, is vague, and the subject we have touched on is wide. Not to leave vastness and vagueness together hanging on our borders, let us define our meaning with a sample, and pass on. We should not be surprised to see sprung upon us at any moment language like that used by so responsible an American jurist as Wheaton, when he happens to light upon such antiquities as the Christian Church and Catholicism. This author, writing on the history of the Law of Nations in Europe and America, conceives it to be a happy circumstance that the Romish priesthood found it worth their while somehow to respect the laws of justice; that the Pope's authority in Christendom was good, but only as a substitute for nothing; and that the Catholic clergy, by inventing casuistry, came within hail of the science of ethics.[2] These things are said by the author in quite a temperate tone, and are perhaps the more flagrant on that account. We are reduced to the necessity of supposing that not a word of such pages has been derived from original study; for that supposition is milder than the only other alternative left. Add a Sir James Mackintosh on Suarez, as quoted there by Wheaton;[3] add a Lord Macaulay on Macintosh and Hallam, pronounced to be men of eminently judicial mind; add the whole series of standard and canonical books;—and it is no wonder if the old tradition is still accepted by the busy generations. In short, original research is too slow and costly.

Wheaton's view on the Church.

Our very language has taken into its framework the concrete results of such history. Its idiom is redundant with phrases, and its vocabulary is deficient in terms, according as the religious movement contemporary with its formation shaped and trimmed this

by F. W. Maitland (Cambridge), Sir Frederick Pollock, W. Stubbs (Oxford), etc. The English Government publications might be referred to, whether the Introductions to the editions of medieval British writers, or those prefixed to divers volumes of *State Paper Calendars*. As a sample, take the Preface, pp. iii.-lxxxv., to the second volume of the *Chronicon Monasterii de Abingdon*, No. 2 of the *Rolls Series*, edited by the Rev. Joseph Stevenson.

[2] H. Wheaton, *History of the Law of Nations in Europe and America*, etc.: "It may be considered as a favourable circumstance for the revival of civilization in Europe, that the interests of the priesthood, in whom all the moral power of the age was concentrated, induced them to cherish a certain respect for the rules of justice. The spiritual monarchy of the Roman pontiffs was founded upon the want of some moral authority to temper the rude disorders of society during the middle age. . . . The compilation of the canon law, under the patronage of Pope Gregory IX., contributed to diffuse a knowledge of the rules of justice among the Catholic clergy; whilst the art of casuistry, invented by them to aid in performing the duties of auricular confession, opened a wide field for speculation, and brought them to the confines of the true science of ethics."—Introduction, pp. 33, 34. Had he meant in these passages the technical art of administering justice and a formal science of ethics, still he was lawyer enough to express what he meant; and even so the passages would have been improved by an infusion of historical knowledge.

[3] *Ibid.*, p. 51.

modern English. Take the grafting on it of terms which are anti-Jesuit, all freighted with opprobrious meanings. They will occur to any one, or they may be seen at large in the solemn lexicons of the tongue, as a valuable part of the national patrimony.[4] Take the decline of idioms, which had so well expressed in English, no less than in other Christian tongues, the points of Christian doctrine encased in home-made phrases, as they had been embodied in domestic life and religious faith during a thousand years before. They disappeared; or they stood as archaic forms in Shakespeare, calling for an editor's footnote to explain them; or they are recovered to-day by students to enrich again a language which should never have been impoverished. The Catholic child thenceforth was foredoomed to be instructed in a large part of the faith of its fathers by means of a Latinized dialect invented for Catholic expediency.

The English language on Jesuits.

Of philosophy there was none, from the time when that of Christendom was rejected, and when Latin speech, the means of communication among the learned, was debased into an English cant. The powers of abstraction became commensurate with materialism; and metaphysics as a science became proverbially contemptible. In our day, the philologist or philosopher may well ask in wonderment, which is the more lamentable feature in a language so exuberant, whether the self-inflicted state of privation which has reduced it to the condition of a mendicant, begging phrases and words for abstract thought and Christian doctrine; or the social and political narrowness, which has enclosed and petrified in it the timidity and the hate, the terror and the cruelty, inspired by the presence of the old clergy and the logic of the new Jesuits—"a logic," says Hallam, quietly, "in whose labyrinth the most practical reasoner was perplexed."[5] Logic, like other sciences, came to be overlaid with a multitude of contemptuous epithets or synonyms, which threw discredit on the art of reasoning itself. And, whenever a Jesuit fell into the hands of those who sought to seize his person but to evade his logic, their primary idea of equal terms seems to have been that he should lie on the rack so that they might stand on their feet. It was an adaptation of the old argument,

[4] Similar invidious meanings may be seen attached to other names, but an apology also may be seen carefully appended by modern lexicographers. Cf. "Dutch auction," "Dutch courage," "Dutch defence,"—"probably due," say the lexicographers, "to the animosity consequent on the long and severe contest for the supremacy of the seas between England and Holland in the seventeenth century." Cf. *Imperial Dictionary* ; *Century Dictionary*.

[5] Hallam, *Constitutional History of England*, ii. 84, edit. 1832.

a verbis ad verbera—from words to blows, when you have nothing further to say. On one occasion a witty Jesuit answered the preliminary skirmish of an importunate disputant, by begging him to get stretched out first on a rack alongside, and then they could try conclusions more on a par.[6]

§ 13. It was natural that the question should be asked—Why all this intolerance? or, using another term which is employed by modern historians, Why all this persecution? It was asked in Maryland and in North America generally, both before and after the American Revolution. It is not, indeed, a question which Catholics put. They take the answer to be about as plain as the fact, which is transparent from every point of view. But the query is proposed by others, who do not mince the matter even when they are no friends of Catholicism, and who are not always over-nice in their statement of the crude fact. "Persecution," says one, "is the deadly original sin of the Reformed Churches; that which cools every honest man's zeal for their cause, in proportion as his reading becomes more extensive."[1] It is pronounced to be "somewhat an humiliating admission;" still the humiliating admission is made, "that the Protestant faith was imposed upon our ancestors by a foreign army." This was when German Lutheran troops were sent for from Calais to force the new religion down the throats of English people, although, as one of the governing ring said, "The use of the new religion is not yet printed in the stomachs of eleven out of twelve parts of the realm, whatever countenance men may make outwardly to please them, in whom they see the power resteth."[2] We are correctly told that "the rack seldom stood idle in the Tower for all the latter part of Elizabeth's reign."[3] Between one hundred and ninety-one and two hundred and four Catholic martyrs suffered under Elizabeth, besides many others who died of hardship in the Tower, in the Clink, in the Fleet, or in Newgate.[4] The long series of statutes was inaugurated, having the clear purpose of impoverishing all Catholics, and keeping them by force of legislation in the state of penury to which legislation reduced them.[5] For the whole monastic and

The question mooted about persecution.

---

[6] Father Thomas Strange. Cf. H. Foley, *Records*, iv. 4, note.—Cf. *infra*, *History*, § 4, note 11.
[1] Hallam, *Constitutional History of England*, i. 130, 131.
[2] *Ibid.*, pp. 127, 128: note on Paget writing to Somerset, from Strype.
[3] *Ibid.*, p. 201.
[4] *Ibid.*, p. 222.
[5] Cf. *Ibid.*, p. 210, text and note. But for specimens of the facts which Hallam so

ecclesiastical organization of the country having been dismantled and despoiled, there remained only the real estate and personalty of individual Catholics to prey upon and devour; and in this chase, for two centuries to come, all joined heartily and merrily—monarchs, commons, and informers; the only class that fell out of the hunt being the poor, as well as impotent soldiers, who had originally been mentioned as part beneficiaries of Catholic plunder. This had been the new and cheap way, along with stripes and slavery, of shelving the pauperism and vagabondism which had recently come into existence, and was spreading through the nation.[6] But soon the poor disappeared from among the beneficiaries. The informer became the favoured character, with perquisites that were enormous and so privileged that, though the Crown might remit its own debts, it could not remit the informer's fee.[7] This amounted to as much as £50 sterling for a single discovery of a priest being harboured or of Mass being said, etc.[8] And a new department of literature sprang eagerly into existence, having the same purpose as the following:— "A viewe of the revenewe [which] may be brought to His Majesties coffers by recusants convicted in the tyme of the late Queen by a favourable and mylde course," A.D. 1607.[9] *Exploiting a new source of revenue.* In the papers (A.D. 1608–1612) of Sir Julius Cæsar, Chancellor of the Exchequer, one may obtain some clear insight into the plan of operations against Catholic gentlemen and ladies, against "all weomen recusants," yeomen and the rest, who are being preyed upon in the counties; how, for instance, a man named John Thornbury, Bishop of Bristol, is campaigning as President of the Council in Yorkshire; and how the same class of men signalize themselves in Derbyshire, Staffordshire, Monmouthshire, Herefordshire, Durham, Northumberland, and Lincolnshire. The pursuivants and all others manifest an extreme solicitude to "increase his Majesty's revenue," and do other good things.[10] Some of the correspondents are large-minded enough to comprise even honour and justice among the motives for robbery; thus: "for our best profit with honour and justice." [11]

anxiously minimizes, see Lingard, *History of England*, vi. 258, 259, and appendix, note YY; vii. pp. 182, 183, and appendix, note LLL; edit. 1855.—Cf. *infra*, *History*, § 7, note 5.

[6] 29 Eliz., c. 6, § 7, 1586–1587; 35 Eliz., c. 1, § 8; where the assignment of other people's property is said to be for "good and charitable uses."
[7] 2 Blackstone, *Commentaries*, 437: on Title by Judgment in Actions Popular.
[8] 3 Jac. I., c. 5, § 1, 1605.
[9] British Museum MSS., *Lansdowne*, 153, ff. 101, 102.
[10] *Ibid.*, *Lansdowne*, 153, ff. 319 of original papers.
[11] *Ibid.*, Class Catalogue, No. 5, *Church History*, vol. i. p. 295, *seqq*.

Men's consciences were pried into by the public court of justice for direct answers to speculative questions, as to what they would do if such and such a contingency occurred; and, upon not returning the answers required, the accused were visited with the extreme penalties of the law, as convicted traitors,—for theoretical " possibilities," says a writer with just sarcasm, "which may or may never be, things on which not even God passes judgment."[12] On such an indictment, ten Catholic priests were murdered at one time.[13] Catholic ladies did not escape the most brutal kind of torture, one being even pressed to death under the government of that virgin queen who gave Virginia its name.[14] And, while Catholic heiresses lay under the same incapacities for life as heirs, married women, as being the stronghold of the faith in Christian families, became, under the gallant Parliament of James I., the particular object of assault by Parliamentary laws.[15]

Cross-examining conscience on possibilities.

In virtue of divers statutes, the name of "Popish recusant convict" became applicable by a short process of law to any person whose conscience was superior to violence; and, from that moment forward, legal processes could be discarded in abusing almost every natural and civic right of a person so labelled. Like a test case decided, like the *res judicata* or *la chose jugée* which had passed as a precedent into law, the man or woman who was dubbed a "Popish recusant convict," became, not indeed a person judged, but a person prejudged, one on whose head judgment need not be passed, and who, to a number of intents and purposes, was already proscribed and condemned. A blow, too, was struck at the rights of posterity not yet born; and, prior to the Act of Catholic Emancipation in 1829, no acquisition or purchase of real estate or interest therein, under any title whatsoever, was valid on behalf of a Papist, whatever proviso might be made in favour of his heirs or posterity.[16] But, in favour of such children as might have an eye to sharp practice against their own parents and the rest of a Catholic family, premiums for apostasy were dangled before their eyes. And this scheme either worked so well, or else afforded such a peculiar satisfaction to those who drove the cold steel right through the heart of a Christian family, that it was carefully reproduced in Maryland; "dissolving

The character of "Popish recusant convict."

---

[12] Sacchini, *Historia Societatis Jesu*, V. ii. §§ 127–129, 1582.
[13] Hallam, as above, i. 223.—Lingard, vi. 167–169.
[14] Margaret Clitheroe (Middleton) and others. Lingard, *Ibid.*, 169, note, and appendix, note AAA.
[15] 7 Jac. I., c. 6, 1609–1610; and on widows, 3 Jac. I., c. 5, § 8, 1605–1606.
[16] 11 Gul. III., c. 4, § 4, etc.

the filial obligations," as the Protestant Rector, Dr. Hawks, observes, and offering " to a wayward child a premium for youthful hypocrisy."[17] There were not a few eventual premiums for such a promising scion, who became, by virtue of his hypocrisy or apostasy, the Protestant next-of-kin, and so, by virtue of the law, entered into the franchise of being able to oust the whole family out of all inheritances, out of all devises of lands or tenements, " within the kingdom of England, the Dominion of Wales, or the town of Berwick-upon-Tweed."[18]

This was another franchise too precious to forego in Maryland, and so was re-enacted there; and we shall have occasion to rehearse the sentiments of high glee which Governor Seymour in great privacy gave expression to when writing to the Board of Trade, and particularly his gratification at having engineered such legislation through when the delegates who voted for it thought they were voting for something else. The delegates were Americans. The Governor himself was what he described himself to be at this very date. " Take notice," he said to Fathers Brooke and Hunter, "that I am an English Protestant gentleman, and can never equivocate." Other legal pieces of that epoch—1704 and later—were in like manner staple enactments conveyed from England to Maryland; as that of awarding £100 to any informer who should convict a priest of having said Mass; perpetual imprisonment for any priest guilty of such an enormity; the same for any Catholic who presumed to teach; a fine of £100 on any one who should send a child abroad to be educated in the Catholic faith.[19] *Reproductions in Maryland.*

While held in durance by so many statutes enacted against the Papist as such; while, among the members of Dissenting denominations, he was found ultimately to be the only one enveloped in the disabling laws which made a show of being passed against all Dissenters; shut out by name from the benefit of so many royal amnesties, which remitted all manner of "treasons, felonies, offences," etc., but which declared the Catholic to be "foreprised out of this generall Pardon;" expunged with legal circumspection from the various bills proposed by the Commons "for the ease of the subject" against royal or judicial aggression, but not for the ease of "Popish Recusants or for or concerning Popish Recusancy;" ground down as only natives can *Terms of acquittal for recusants.*

[17] J. T. Scharf, *History of Maryland*, i. 370.
[18] T. C. Anstey, *A Guide to the Laws of England affecting Roman Catholics*, p. 61.
[19] Cf. J. Scharf, *History of Maryland*, i. 368-370.

be by a paternal government, but taxed doubly as only aliens were without representation—a point to be jealously reproduced in the new world;—still, be it added in justice, the Catholic, in spite of all this hardship, and in spite of being worse off than the murderer in royal amnesties, did actually find himself better off when it came to executing the law with its penalties. For, at any moment and at any stage, when the noose was already about his neck, and that the neck of a priest or a Jesuit, and the knife was ready to cut him open while still alive, and the fire was burning there to show him his entrails broiling till they should kindly cut out his heart, he remained quite free all this while to walk off a rehabilitated man. Unlike any condemned murderer, he was at liberty to walk off acquitted; not merely pardoned, but innocent. The terms on which his injuries were thus redressed coincided very closely with those on which absolution for real sin is imparted in the Sacramental system of the Church. He should repent and "acknowledge his Faulte," and "refuse his said wilfull obstinacie," and "fullye reconcyle hymself to the true Religion established by Order of Lawe within this Realme, declaring that his Reconciliation to the Bysshopp of the Diocesse, and shewing the same openly by comyng to the Devyne Servyce by Order of this Realme appoynted, and receavyng the Holy Comunion;" and he should "continue in such his conformity and due obedience towards her Majestie." That is to say, the terms were contrition, confession, and satisfaction; the Queen being his confessor and the bishop her substitute; if it were not rather that the Queen's majesty was the divinity offended, and the bishop her vicar among men.[20]

More singular still was it that the spoils of the Papist's property, though already sequestered and enjoyed by other people; the heritage already impropriated out of the rightful hands of Catholic heirs and heiresses into those of Protestant substitutes or next-of-kin; the advowsons or rights of patronage and presentation to ecclesiastical livings already well covered by the appropriating grip of the universities;—all these things came floating back to the owner as from a wreck, and practically intact, if he would only

Indemnification.

[20] 23 Eliz., c. 16; 27 Eliz., c. 30, and other general pardons.—21 Jac. I., c. 4; cf. other Acts for ease of the subject, in same year.—3 Car. I., c. 8; cf. other subsidy Acts on to William and Mary.—13 Eliz., c. 3, against Catholic fugitives beyond sea.—As to the extraordinary whitewashing of Jesuits, priests, etc., their pupils beyond sea, their receivers, their benefactors, who are all pell-mell made traitors and felons respectively, but who shall become absolutely spotless on the instant, if they will take the oath of supremacy, cf. 27 Eliz., c. 2: "*An Acte againste Jesuites, Semynarie Priestes, and such other like disobedient Persons.*"

§ 13.   POLITICAL BASIS OF THE PREJUDICE

conform. Conformity was the beginning, middle, and end of justice and legislation drawn round the Catholic conscience. It was the dividing line between treason and patriotism. It was a cordon tightly drawn, bristling with oaths, Sacraments, surety bonds, declarations as to how he treated purgatory and how he would treat transubstantiation. It was as easy for the timorous crowd to pass in and make itself comfortable on the safe side, as it was painful for the brave heart and upright conscience to stay outside, exposed to the packs of prowling treasons, felonies, disabilities, disfranchisements, imprisonments, confiscations, for what he did and what he did not do, for what he intended and what he did not intend, for what he and his children were likely to do and what they were never likely to do. Thus one elaborate statute, explaining another, legislates that the real intention of a Catholic absentee, who has gone over the seas, is "not materyall," as being only his "secrete thoughte;" but that his subsequent action in staying beyond the seas shall be taken as a sufficient proof that he had such an intention to stay away when he went away; and therefore his estates shall be forfeited accordingly, for an intention which he may never have had.[21] "*Durum est torquere leges,*" says Bacon, "*ad hoc ut torqueant homines:*" "'Tis a cruel thing to be torturing laws to make them torture men."

The test of rehabilitation.

Secret intentions and forfeitures.

If a Catholic had an ambition to enjoy a public office or post, the advice given by William Cecil, Lord Burleigh, relative to oaths and Sacraments, came in to bar all advance, and effectually operated during three centuries against him and his posterity. It was to the effect that "from the highest counsellor to the lowest constable, none shall have any charge or office but such as will really pray and communicate in their congregation, according to the doctrine generally received into this realm." This advice, given to the Queen in 1583, is considered by the historian Hallam to have been "not only sagacious," but, he adds, "just and tolerant."[22] The advice was effectual, and gave the tone to the generations. And so, when two centuries later the Quebec Act of Toleration for Canada was under discussion, and Lord Chatham took that stand which won for him the admiration and imitation of the Continental Congress in Philadelphia, his words re-echoed the very phrases of Burleigh, as he conjured the House of Lords not to break down "the safeguards

The oath and the Sacrament for constable and peer. 1583.

1774.

---

[21] 14 Eliz., c. 6, explaining 13 Eliz., c. 3, "*Agaynst Fugytyves over the Sea.*"
[22] Hallam, *Constitutional History*, i. 207, 205, approving the advice in general.

and barriers against the return of Popery and of Popish influence, so wisely provided against by all the oaths of office and of trust, from the constable up to the members of both Houses, and even to the Sovereign, in his coronation oath."[23] Burleigh and his kind made much of an oath for Catholics, because they had consciences.[24] He said of them in the same memorial: "That they make conscience of an oath, the trouble, losses, and disgraces that they suffer for refusing the same do sufficiently testify."[25] As to Burleigh's own conscience, this founder of the Cecil family, who was a good type of the statesmen for generations to come, was so singularly delicate of sentiment and moderate in his desires, that he left behind him "only three hundred distinct landed estates," though he might "have left much more"![26] Where he got them all, the biographer does not venture to state; but perhaps the Papists might be able to say.

Suppose, however, a Catholic did not aspire to any post, and merely wanted to be left alone, neither then could he escape; since it was not doing nothing or going alone that the State wanted. For example, just eight years before Maryland was founded, the Attorney-General Heath argued before the Commons that they should not demand for Hampden and his fellow-knights the privilege of a *habeas corpus* writ, which gave the right to a trial. Having employed several arguments ineffectually, he adverted "with more success to the number of Papists and other State prisoners, detained for years in custody for mere political jealousy. 'Some there were,' he says, 'in the Tower who were put in it when very young; should they bring a *habeas corpus*, would the court deliver them?'"[27]

Habeas Corpus.

§ 14. On the political basis everything else rests. If it is not strong enough to bear everything else, it will be made so by

---

[23] *American Archives*, Fourth Series, i. col. 212, col. 912, etc.; the House of Lords, June 14, 1774; Continental Congress, Philadelphia, October 14, 1774, etc.

[24] Compare the commentary of Shakespeare, who was writing at this very time—

> "For I know thou art religious,
> And hast a thing within thee called Conscience,
> With twenty popish tricks and ceremonies,
> Which I have seen thee careful to observe—
> Therefore I urge thy oath."
>
> *Titus Andronicus*, act v. sc. 1.

[25] Hallam, *Constitutional History of England*, p. 206.

[26] Cf. Macaulay, essay on *Burleigh and his Times*, from Nares, *ad init.*—Nares says: "As nearly as possible three hundred. We must not, however, suppose from this that his gains were exorbitant, or his fortunes greater than his services had merited," etc. *Life of Lord Burghley*, iii. 496.

[27] Hallam, *Ibid.*, i. 527 (1625).

§ 14. CALVERT AND THE LEGAL PREJUDICES

supplementary legislation. And the legal men and the literary men alike will take their stand there.

But, notwithstanding all that, the question will still return— Why was the persecution itself necessary, which made new politics necessary and new law, to come in and justify the persecution? It will not rectify a vicious circle like this to say that everybody persecuted in those times, and hence there is no need of saying anything more about it. *The fallacy that every one persecuted then.* This is one of the loose generalizations so favoured by those who popularize history; and, if their language is grandiose enough, it seems to satisfy not only the vulgar but the literary mind. Thus George Bancroft devotes a half-page to some assertions of his own and to some others taken from Fra Paolo Sarpi or from Grotius, which call only for a little verification to pare them all away as apocryphal or irrelevant—without even leaving him the Spanish Inquisition, or Charles V., or the Netherlands, to keep the legends decently alive.[1] It is a discovery of panegyrists or apologists in our time, that everybody was persecuting in those times; for the principal actors in England do not seem to have known it themselves. On the contrary, it is remarked by a modern that "such excessive severities, under the pretext of treason, but sustained by very little evidence of any other offence than the exercise of the Catholic ministry, excited indignation throughout a great part of Europe;" and that Lord Burleigh wrote two pamphlets in justification, one of which makes Hallam blush for the "contempt" and "detestation" due to it; but in neither did the pamphleteer justify the practices, by appealing to the customs or principles of those times.[2] The Catholic Emperor Ferdinand intimated to Elizabeth that his own toleration of Protestants might be influenced for the worse, if she continued in her system of intolerance.[3] *Protests of Catholic Courts.* She replied by affirming in explicit terms the same principle of intolerance,[4] which, in the famous protestation made at Spires, had fixed the name of "Protestants" on the protesters against toleration.[5] When there was question in France of admitting the Huguenot Henry IV. to the throne, a tract was published by English Catholics for the benefit of the French, to enlighten them on the risk they ran of losing their religion altogether, and experiencing what English

---

[1] G. Bancroft, *History of the United States*, etc., i. 455, edit. 1859.
[2] Hallam, *Constitutional History of England*, i. 202–205.
[3] *Ibid.*, p. 161.
[4] *Ibid.*, p. 162.
[5] *Ibid.*, p. 131, note.

Catholics were suffering, if they permitted a heretic to mount the throne.[6] When the Spanish match of 1622 was being adjusted by James I. for his son Charles, a stipulation was made by the Spanish Court, requiring that every effort should be made in England to stop the execution of Catholic priests for their religion, and to begin the practice of toleration.[7] In the subsequent negotiation of the French match, which put upon the throne of England, as the King's consort, Henrietta Maria, a daughter of Henry IV., and gave through her a name to Maryland, a condition was inserted by the French Court that the Spanish stipulation should hold good in behalf of toleration;[8] or, as the terms seem to have been: "The Frenche kinge insistethe to haue the same freedome for His Majesties subiectes that are Romaine Catholiques, that the Frenche Protestants haue in France;" and again, in other words: "As much toleration as he graunteth his Hugonots in France."[9]

One of the letters, from which we take these phrases, and some other letters of the same date, announce from the English priests to their agent in Rome, that George Calvert has just entered the Catholic Church, and that he has been made an Irish peer. One writer states that Calvert is going to Newfoundland.[10] These letters are dated February, 1625. Thus, through the midst of political persecution, we arrive at the remote occasion of the Maryland Catholic colony, in the person of this new convert, who must now endeavour to make his way, or at least to keep on his feet, in spite of the weight of prejudice bearing down upon him; the whole setting and the whole practice of English politics and law being against toleration, and therefore against him; while the whole practice of Catholic countries outside of England was declared to be in favour of toleration and quiet forbearance.[11]

The occasion for a new American Colony. 1625.

[6] Hallam, *Constitutional History of England*, i. 202, note.
[7] Lingard, *History of England*, vii. 120.
[8] *Ibid.*, p. 138.
[9] Stonyhurst MSS., *Anglia A*, viii. f. 206: Roper to More, February 24, 1625; *Ibid.*, f. 182: Muskett to More, March 4, [1625].
[10] *Ibid.*, f. 206: Roper to More; *Ibid.*, f. 186: Nelson to More in Rome, February 21, [1625].
[11] Cf. Dodd, *Church History*, ii. 448, (o): "Part of King James I.'s Answer to the Commons, concerning Popish recusants, 1621." "¶ . . . The first, and the greatest point is that of religion; concerning which, at this time, we can give you no other answer than in general: which is, that you may rest secure, that we will never be weary to do all we can for the propagation of our religion, and the repressing of Popery. But the manner and form you must remit to our care and providence; who can best consider of times and seasons, not by undertaking a public war of religion through all the world at once; which, how hard and dangerous a task it may prove, you may judge . . . But, as we already said, our care of religion must be such, as on the one part we must not, by the hot persecution of our recusants at home, irritate foreign princes of contrary religion, and teach them the way to plague the Protestants in their dominions, with whom we daily intercede, and at this time

§ 14.   CALVERT AND THE LEGAL PREJUDICES   95

But if, in answer to the question—Why all this persecution? it will not do to shut one's eyes and take a blind leap, asserting roundly that everybody persecuted in those times, neither will it be convenient to make for the other extreme and claim that there was no persecution at all, at least in England. This seems to be the discovery lately made by a Baltimore writer of 1899, who, explaining the reasons why George Calvert came to Virginia and sought a home in Maryland, takes some pains to affirm that there was no reason of intolerance in England impelling him or other Catholics to seek a refuge in America.[12] At the first blush, this might appear to be a relapse into a more ancient style of writing historical anecdotes than is suited to history at the beginning of the twentieth century. Still, there is an authentic touch about the style, as if really derived from the spirit, if not from the history, of Calvert's age. For no characteristic stood out more clearly in the prolonged persecution, even under Elizabeth and Burleigh, and much more so under the Stuarts, than that of their smarting under the imputation of being persecutors. This is the sentiment which, in part, if not wholly, caused the penal statutes to be cast into the shape of visiting a number of religious acts as if they were high treason and felony, in order not to be seen visiting religion itself with the penalties. Indeed, the policy is older still. It dates back as far as the time of Julian the Apostate, of whom St. Gregory Nazianzen says, in his speech against that tyrant: "There is one thing the apostate wants, to do violence and not to be thought to do it"—to persecute and not to acknowledge it.[13] The contention, therefore, of the Baltimore writer, that there was no sufficient reason of intolerance to influence Calvert's action, is a very just reflex, though probably he did not know it, of the intolerant spirit of Calvert's age.

Fallacy that nobody persecuted then in England.

Evading the imputation of persecution.

principally, for ease to them of our profession that live under them; yet, upon the other part, we never mean to spare from due and severe punishment any Papist, that will grow insolent for living under our so mild a government." The King then proceeds to declare his policy against all Catholic education of Catholic children, at home or abroad; and continues: "And, as in this point, namely, the good education of Popish youth at home, we have already given some good proofs, both in this kingdom and in Ireland, so will we be well pleased to pass any good laws, that shall be made either now or at any time hereafter, to this purpose."—Cf. L. W. Wilhelm, *Sir George Calvert, Baron of Baltimore*, p. 93, who refers to a passage about James's reluctance to "kindle a war of religion through the world, and by hot persecutions of Catholics provoke foreign princes to persecution of Protestants."—In Gardiner's *History of England*, and Lingard's *History of England*, the tenor of this Answer, as given above, seems to have escaped notice.

[12] C. E. Smith, *Religion under the Barons of Baltimore*, ch. i.-iv. The book is dedicated to the ladies and gentlemen of his congregation, "already familiar with many of the statements made in its pages."

[13] 1 *Contra Julianum*, § 58.

But we are not at present engaged with the unfolding of the first Lord Baltimore's history. We wish to regard only the formation and development, in his time and later, of that English literature which **Justification of the persecution.** had the political state of intolerance for its basis, and had its solid substructures built in by lawyers like Sir Edward Coke. He was a contemporary of Calvert's. His name is most sacred in English law as that of the acutest of lawyers, whatever he may be in general history as a man and a zealot. In his capacity of a zealot, whether as serving Elizabeth or as exploiting for James I. a Gunpowder Plot, the conduct of this Attorney-General arraigning Father Robert Southwell, or of this Lord Chief Justice railing against Catholics, furnishes some typical scenes of what Hallam describes as "those glaring transgressions of natural as well as positive law, that rendered our courts of justice in cases of treason little better than the caverns of murderers," the prosecutor being "virulent," while the "judge was hardly distinguishable from the prosecutor except by his ermine;" and both found a precious foil in a "passive pusillanimous jury."[14]

Coke's prosecution of Father Southwell, in 1594, contains a justification of the penal code which was now being applied to the martyr. **Coke, 1594.** In few words, his contention runs thus: Her Majesty had made it treason to attribute any authority to the Pope; who then sent over Bulls and other trifles, and the law met them and made them treason; and he sent over Agnus Deis and prayingbeads and other such nonsense, and the law met them with retribution; and he sent over the firebrands of books, and the law made them a felony; and, worst of all, he sent over these swarms of Jesuits and seminary priests. As Attorney-General, Coke demanded judgment on the prisoner at the bar; who accordingly was condemned to be hanged, cut down alive, to be made to see his entrails burned before his face, and then to be killed.[15]

A few years later, Lord Justice Coke delivered a charge at the assizes held in Norwich on August 4, 1606. It was just after the Gunpowder Plot. From the ninth to the thirty-fifth page, which is nearly one-half the address, his theme is an unremitting tirade against **A fictitious Bull. 1606.** Popery. He is descanting upon the contents of a papal Bull published against Elizabeth and against her possible successor, James I., by Pope Clement IX. Coke's Bull of Clement IX., now supposed to be defunct, against Elizabeth also defunct,

[14] Hallam, *Constitutional History of England*, i. 313.
[15] *Anglia, Historia*, ii. f. 78.—Cf. an English account in H. Foley, *Records of the English Province S.J.*, i. 364–375.—Cf. Hallam, *ubi supra*, i. 222, note, on the barbarity.

was that of a Pope who may possibly have been born about this time, but who certainly did not ascend the papal throne for sixty-six years to come. Since at a later date this Lord Chief Justice repudiated the published address, as unauthorized, crude, and, he said, incorrect in rendering his every phrase, though he did not repudiate it for any infidelity in rendering the general sense of his discourse, we refer to it because, while attaching credit to a fiction, it furnished lawyers with an express formula of intolerance, which then was quoted as an authority. It sentenced Catholics thus: "It is not then a toleration only which they seeke, nor could they have bene contented therewith (although so much shall never be granted unto them). They may, therefore, easily despaire of the rest, though they (the Pope and the Divell) doe never so much conspire to bring their Hell-borne practises to passe." [16]

This fiction, with which the Lord Chief Justice of England was plying his trade, seems to have been different from another which was going the round of Ireland, not apparently among the people, but in the hands of the judges and ministers. They were using it as a weapon for what Dr. James White, Vicar-Apostolic of Waterford, called *intolerabilis persecutio*, "an intolerable persecution;" and they would give no account of the original, nor return any answer as to whether it was in Latin, or how it appeared. It purported to be "Imbulled at Rome, the 7th of December, [1605]." It exhorted the faithful to rise in arms, and it said: "Furthermore, in that we tender our greate zeale unto the Catholick fayth, we doe by our authority from God fully and wholy absolve and remitt unto you and every of you all your synnes from your byrth untill the tenth of June next ensuing." Dr. White wrote to His Holiness, supplicating him to send some information about the strange matter. But possibly he had not seen such a copy as the Lord-Deputy of Ireland, Sir Arthur Chichester, sent over to Cecil, the Earl of Salisbury, adding his own opinion, that the Bull, he wrote, is "of hytselfe so grosse and absurde I can hardly believe" it ever came from Rome. This copy was signed "Sixtus Papa." Now, Sixtus Papa, who signed this Bull on the 7th day of December, 1605, had then been in his grave just fifteen years.[17]

Another forged Bull. 1605.

---

[16] *The Lord Coke his Speech and Charge*, etc., London, 1607, small 4to, some 64 pp. not paginated.—Cf. Coke, Preface to 7 Rep.—British Museum MSS., Add. 17,022, *Notes concerning Recusants; or, A Summary Account of all the Statute Laws*, etc., *against the Jesuites*, etc.; f. 3: "Cooke's Charge at Norwich, A.D. 1606. It is not then a toleration only which they seeke, nor could they have been contented therewith (although so much shall never be granted them)."—Cf. *infra*, Introduction, Chap. II. § 16, p. 107, note 10.

[17] Public Record Office, State Papers, *Ireland, James I.*, vol. 208, document 34.—

98 INTROD. II. THE ARCHIVES AND LITERATURE

This growth of forgeries cannot be considered as having attained its fullest and rankest development at the time of which we are speaking. But we have had enough of it to show one important element of fertilization for the tender annuals and hardy perennials of anti-Popish literature. All this spurious material we may despatch with the words which were written by an old summarist about a certain manuscript, and are now printed by the British Museum in relation to the same,—a manuscript entitled, "The voluntary Confession of John Browne a Romish Priest of the age of seventy-two years, a prisoner in the Gate House; twice examined by a Committee of Six from the Honorable House of Commons, A.D. 1641." The summarist's view is to the following effect: "In this Confession it is intended to discover secret intrigues, with relation to the Jesuites; to the Queen's court; to Archbishop Laud; to the Popes aspiring to the temporal monarchy of these kingdoms; and the restraining the English Papists from selling their lands, and sending their money beyond the Seas. But though the Jesuits and Popish Clergy were bad enough (whether this was Browne's Confession or was made by the Committee of Six), 'tis plain that it is a most impudent Libel." [18]

A forged confession. 1641.

Observe, however, the condition in which a convert like George Calvert found himself to be. For, according to the prejudice he had incurred, he should be found devising his remedy, whenever that came to consist in his settling outside of England as a Catholic colonist. The kind of colonial charter, which had suited him as a Protestant adventurer speculating in Newfoundland, should have to be otherwise conceived and composed if he would found a colony anywhere as a Catholic.

George Calvert's situation as a Catholic. 1625-32.

The situation was technically this. Even supposing that a Catholic was not declared a "Popish recusant convict," and lost not his life nor the ordinary franchises of citizenship, still, morally speaking, he was in a state of destitution. The secret relic in his most private cabinet, the crucifix in a lady's trinket, were as much at the mercy of the legal pursuers who could break into one's premises and assault his person at any hour, as all the great endowments of Catholicism were already in the grip of the spoilers. The cathedral which stood pointing to the skies, whither Catholic hands had directed its pinnacles, was not for him; nor the university college,

---

Cf. Historical MSS. Commission, fifth appendix to tenth report, pp. 340-379; *Archives of the Jesuits in Ireland*, pp. 342, 345, No. 3.

[18] British Museum MSS., *Harl.* 1219; Class Catalogue, No. 5, *Church History*, vol. i. p. 313.

§ 15. DEVELOPMENTS OF THE LITERATURE   99

nor the elementary school, built for rich and poor by Catholic charity. Nor could he keep a schoolmaster at home, nor have his child learn A B C at school, except at the price of its soul. One must be a Protestant or be illiterate; he must conform or be destitute. As the laws against him professed to be in behalf of God's true religion and of the commonwealth also, his religion was declared to be a conspiracy against the State as well as against religion; and the penal laws were to receive the most liberal interpretation against him, in grinding him down relentlessly, because *summa est lex quæ pro religione facit,* "that law has precedence which makes for religion." [19] How George Calvert, first Lord Baltimore, protected himself by a charter against a repetition in Maryland of such sanguinary and predatory intrigues, we shall have occasion to see in a subsequent paragraph of our History.

§ 15. The succession in the legal ministry was not unworthy of Coke as a sire of English law. Let us, however, mention in particular the man who condemned to death the Catholic Irish Archbishop Plunket for complicity in a Popish Plot. This, as usual, had been first conceived and then happily discovered by the same persons, who merited well of the nation by finding out and slaughtering the innocent. The arraignment of Oliver Plunket was among the last scenes of the Titus Oates Plot and of the judicial murders consequent thereupon. The Lord Chief Justice Pemberton, who condemned the venerable Archbishop, went out of his way to condemn his religion also, and to declare that it was ten times worse than paganism. Upon this a modern Protestant writer makes the following observation: "That a Chief Justice from the Bench should thus have denounced a religion which, until one hundred and fifty years before, had been acknowledged by all Christendom, and was then acknowledged by three-fourths of it— to which we owe our comparative immunity from the cruelties, the superstitions, and the impurities of paganism—to which More had been a martyr, and which Pascal, Fénelon, and Bossuet then professed and adorned—that he should have dared to proclaim such a religion ten times worse than the worst heathenism, is a proof of the intolerance of the speaker, and, we must add, of the audience, which nothing but a contemporary record would lead us to credit." [1]

Lord Chief Justice Pemberton.

[19] Cf. Anstey, pp. 40–42, 109, where a brief summary is given of decisions by oracles of the law in the course of time. These may be said to culminate for recusant convicts in the application to them of the writ against excommunicated persons, of that against lepers, and of the writ *præmunire.*
[1] *Edinburgh Review,* xciii. 120, 121, on "Lord Campbell's *Chief Justices,*" ii. 38.

A school of such men and such traditions, with a growth of public profligacy and social impiety which sank religion and manners under the Georges to as low a depth as perhaps they have ever reached, made the time ripe, in the middle of the eighteenth century, for a Blackstone to incorporate this new kind of history into a pleasing and successful text-book. He borrowed the inspiration of preceding misrepresentations and fictions.[2] While expounding the jurisprudence of a nation now maturely Protestant after two centuries of reform, he threw behind his subject as a background, and he hung upon its borders and edges, all the travesties of Catholic times and history, of which the shortest account to give is that his presentation may be seen everywhere in lawyers' books, in their texts, compends, encyclopædias. American law-books of the latest date, omitting so much that is now antiquated, insert the rest unverified, whether as from Blackstone or not; for it is now matter of common formulas. And so it comes to pass that much of what he wrote on mortmain, præmunire, canon law, testamentary administration, ecclesiastical jurisprudence, and other such mixed questions, is found recurring everywhere in his own terms,—well put and elegant, if only it were true.

Justice Blackstone.

When, a hundred years after his time, Serjeant Stephen undertook to modernize Blackstone's *Commentaries* as being "a work now falling into decay," he wished indeed to save the pieces as much as he could; but, he tells us, seldom was he "able to pursue the text for several pages in succession, without the introduction (more or less extensively) of matter from my own pen;" because Blackstone's "exposition of particular subjects appeared to me to be often deficient in depth, in fulness, or in precision, and in some instances to be even chargeable with positive inaccuracy."[3] Yet, with all this expurgation and correction, we may say in general that, whatever Blackstone had expounded against the Catholic Church, against Christian history or religion, or the spirit of piety in general, remains there in Stephen's edition, a libel on the history of the Church and of Christendom;—not, we presume, because it was too precious to be sacrificed, but because a lawyer is too busy with his law to do more for Christian history than to take with thanks

Serjeant Stephen.

---

[2] Cf. a specimen in W. F. Finlason, *Essay on the History and Effects of the Laws of Mortmain*, etc., pp. 71–73: note on Blackstone copying from Lord Chief Baron Gilbert.—Cf. *Ibid.*, pp. 65, 68: similar matter from the Chancellor Lord Hardwicke, promoter of the Mortmain Law, 9 Geo. II.

[3] Stephen's *New Commentaries on the Laws of England, partly founded on Blackstone.* Preface to first edition, *ad init.*

whatever is served out to him.[4] Such pieces of by-matter, very necessary for the understanding of other things, he accepts as postulates understood; just as he accepts those historical or explanatory preambles to penal and other dubious statutes, which make up the history for the laws to repose upon; and the statutes and the other matters, thus enabled to stand upon something else, may be trusted to do the rest.

It is the fallacy which Bacon characterized as "picking out some plausible traits, to put a fair face on the matter and make it go down."[5] In' commentaries, no less than in preambles, history has been used as a coating for something else to make it go down, as Bacon intimates. And it has known uses viler still, such as Shakespeare has seen in noble clay; it has gone to stop up many a gap in reason, logic, and law. Whence has resulted what Lactantius so vividly described: "*Nec veritas cum vi nec justitia cum crudelitate.*"—Violence and cruelty; neither justice nor truth![6]

The American Colonies took after the mother country. Just as in England, from Land's End to Berwick-on-Tweed, so in America, from Cape Cod to the Ashley River, the dulness of life was varied and enlivened with the resonance of "Popish Plots." These came echoing from England, and re-echoing from Barbados and Jamaica, and most of all from the "back" of the plantations, where the Indians and the French were supposed to be. And thence dim and far came whispering Popish Plots and Jesuit intrigues from every cliff and scar of the Alleghanies. Governors addressed houses, houses addressed Governors, both addressed the Crown. Politics and history were growing bigger and bigger with that spirit of patriotism, otherwise called revolution, which had already gloated over the deposition of an English King, and which was soon to throw off the whole British domination. But bigger still, to judge by its duration, was the eternal plot of the unpatriotic Papists, and that Jesuit peril which, like a weakness that Socrates speaks of, or like a frailty that the inebriate knows, was altogether too dear a foible to forego. It was so fascinating a peril and so necessary an evil, the emphasis being understood to lie on the fascinating necessity

Popish Plots in America.

---

[4] Cf. the extraordinary specimen of Christian history, under the head of "*Præmunire*;" 4 Stephen's *Commentaries*, 168–185. It is history turned inside out, like that other account, by Blackstone, of Mortmain, as a "Title by Forfeiture." 2 Blackstone's *Comm.*, 268–274.—For this latter, cf. *infra*, Appendix C, §§ 74–76.

[5] "*Sæpe enim præambulum arripit nonnulla ex maxime plausibilibus et speciosis ad exemplum.*" *De Augm. Scient.*, lib. viii.; *Aphor. de font. juris*, 70.—"*Non tam ad explicationem legis, quam instar suasionis ad perferendam legem in Comitiis, et rursus ad satisfaciendum populo.*" *Ibid.*, 69.

[6] Lactantius, *De Div. Instit.*, V. xx.

of the thing and not on the reality of it, that, amid all phases of public fortune, it was still indispensable for the happiness of life to season politics with some genuine Popish Plot. So, as late as the middle of the nineteenth century, while the Know-nothings in America were engaged in their well-known campaign, Disraeli remarked with alarm in England, that the Whigs were going to govern still "by a perpetual Popish Plot;"[7] which thus had so many lives, or had a life so often renewed that, from the time of its first alleged importation by the Jesuits Parsons and Campion into the hapless British domain, down to the time of Disraeli and Lord Russell, it had attained the respectable age of well-nigh three centuries. Dr. Johnson in his day is reported to have said that they who cried out "Popery" then would have cried out "Fire" in the time of the Deluge.

In New York, as Chancellor Kent observes, "so extremely strong and so astonishingly fierce and unrelenting was public prejudice on this subject" of the Catholic Church, "that we find it declared by law, in the beginning of the last [the eighteenth] century,[8] that every Jesuit and Popish priest who should continue in the colony after a given day, should be condemned to perpetual imprisonment; and, if he broke prison and escaped and was retaken, he should be put to death. That law, said Mr. Smith, the historian of the colony, writing as late as the year 1756,[9] was worthy of perpetual duration."[10] In the same place the same authority takes note that "as late as 1753 the Legislature of Virginia passed an Act extremely severe upon Popish recusants, placing them under the most oppressive disabilities."[11]

New York and Virginia. 18th century.

However, the genuine priests and Jesuits seem to have been in default when requisition was made to hang them. Not even under Lord Bellomont, who had that law passed, and who had inherited from his father, Colonel Coote, a name blood-red for dragonades against the Irish Papists—nor under the conspirator and traitor, Lord Cornbury, who at the head of his cavalry had deserted his colours and broken his oath of fidelity to King James II.—do we find any record that either had

Governors Bellomont and Cornbury.

---

[7] In the matter of the so-called Papal Aggression, on the appointment of a Catholic hierarchy in England. Compare a recent speech of the Count de Mun upon the law against the religious Congregations in France: "*Voici que l'anticléricalisme est redevenu le grand moyen de gouvernement*" (close of his speech in Chamber of Deputies, January 21, 1901).

[8] *Colony Laws*, i. 38, Livingston's and Smith's edition.

[9] Smith's *History of New York*, 111.

[10] 2 Kent's *Commentaries*, 73 : "Of Aliens and Natives."

[11] *Ibid., loc. cit.*, note.

the pleasure of hanging a priest in New York or Boston. Bellomont did his best to get accommodated. He took the principal sachems of the Iroquois apart, and solicited them to gratify his tooth with a morsel of the French Jesuits from their country; and he would pay them one hundred pieces of eight for every priest brought down. He said: "Wee have a law in this Province for the seizing and securing all Popish Priests and Jesuits, and I would very glad[ly] put that Law in Execution against those disturbers of mankind, and I hope you will take special care exactly to comply;" and, if so, then he tells them that they will serve the King well and deserve Bellomont's particular friendship. The next day, in similar private conference, the sachems assure his lordship that they will do nothing of the kind. And the savages read his lordship several severe lessons that same morning.[12] *The sachems and the Jesuits.*

In default of the genuine priest or Jesuit, they were content to put up with the next remove; they took an Anglican, John Ury, and hanged him for a Popish Plot. And, however pathetic as regards the poor victim, the literature here becomes positively interesting under other aspects. After the trial, Judge Horsmanden relieved his mind and his nerves of the strain imposed upon them by his immaculate discharge of justice, and he took a trip up the Hudson, "on board Admiral Winne;" and, near the mouth of the Highlands, he indited a long letter to Christopher Colden. "By way of amusement," as he calls it, he tells of having run to death thirty negroes and the fourth white, in the person of John Ury, with whom they will stop for the time being and draw breath. With perfect self-complacency he says that "Popery was at the bottom" of the New York plot of this date, 1741; "and," he continues, "the old proverb has herein also been verified, that there is scarce a plot but a priest is at the bottom of it, or as the like pert priest Eury said upon his defence at his trial (though sarcastically) 'according to the vogue of the world, where there is a plot, the first and last links are especially fastened to the priest's girdle;' but he must excuse us in this case, if the last link be fastened to his neck; for he is convicted as one of the conspirators, and is condemned to be hanged on next Saturday sevennight."[13] *The Anglican victim, Ury.*

[12] Public Record Office, *America and West Indies*, 580, ff. 114, 115: Albany, August 26 to September 4, 1700.—Cf. Brodhead, *Documents relative to the Colonial History of State of New York*, iv. 736, 737.—Cf. *infra*, History, § 66, p. 536.
[13] Georgetown College *Transcripts*: 1741, August 7, a proof copy.—Cf. *American Catholic Historical Researches*, xiii. pp. 2-4.—Cf. Geo. Bancroft, Boston, May 8, 1844, to B. U. Campbell, Esq., Ellicott Mills, Md., autogr.: Georgetown College *Manuscripts*, inserted in Campbell's 4to blank book. Bancroft transmits "a full and exact copy of the very extraordinary letter of Judge Horsmanden."

In all this amusement of the colonial judge, there was one feature awry. It was that the priest should have been sarcastic where his hangman was serious, while his hangman should make merry over taking a life, about which its owner was quite serious.

§ 16. We have drifted into the eighteenth-century literature. We may depict what remains of it just so far as to show its tone of morality on our present subject, and its religious idiosyncrasies. There was an author, William Douglass, a doctor of medicine, whose fly-sheets, subsequently gathered into books, treated historically and politically of the British settlements, and were much in vogue during the latter part of the eighteenth century. On religious topics they conveyed no small share of the practical economics which the writer had brought over from the Great Britain of his time. Whenever he lights upon the inoffensive Catholics, he cannot keep his wild untutored spirit within any decent bounds. He writes: "The Roman Catholics, commonly called Papists, in all well-regulated Governments, from most evident civil political reasons, ought to be excluded: the constitution of their religion renders them a nuisance in society; they have an indulgence for lying, cheating, robbing, murdering, and not only may, but are in Christian duty bound, to extirpate all mankind who are not of their way of thinking; they call them hereticks." He continues his tirade against the Pope and the Catholic Church in a style of which the manner is out-Heroded only by the matter.[1] It would not be worth while quoting more, were it not that in the next century we find the Maryland historian, John Leeds Bozman, following in the same vein.

Dr. W. Douglass. 1750.

This wild writer, then, delivers himself thus: "It is not easily to be accounted for, that the British Government are not more sedulous, in purging off by lenitives, not by drasticks, the pernicious leaven of Popery (their doctrine of no faith to be kept with hereticks or dissenters from them, destroys all society), which prevails in Montserrat, Maryland, and Ireland."[2] What he refers to here, that gentle methods of persecution are preferable to drastic, was exactly the policy which distinguished eighteenth-century intolerance from the hangings and quarterings and imprisonments of the two centuries before. Elsewhere

The persecution by lenitives.

---

[1] W. Douglass, *A Summary, Historical and Political, etc., of the British Settlements in North America*, i. 225, note. The printing and punctuation are crude, like the matter and style.
[2] *Ibid.*, ii. 381, note.

§ 16. EIGHTEENTH-CENTURY LITERATURE

he says: "Toleration of all Christian professions of religion is the true ecclesiastical constitution of our American Colonies: the Roman Catholic only is excepted; the nature of our Constitution, the horrid principles of that religion, and at present the Popish claims to our Royal succession, can by no means admit of it; and the Papists of Maryland, Pensylvania, and Montserrat seem to be too much indulged."[3] As a specimen of the political honesty which Americans should practise, he recommends that the charters of Maryland and Pennsylvania be broken by the British Parliament just so far as to shut out Catholics: "As the grants of Maryland and Pensylvania do actually tolerate the publick exercise of the Roman Catholic religion, and as that religion is pernicious to human society in general, and tends to subvert our happy Constitution; why may it not be suppressed as to publick worship, by an Act of the British Parliament? without giving any umbrage to the other good grants and charters at home and in the plantations."[4] He slights the notion that intolerance was ever practised in America. Boston and the Congregationalists did never persecute, as is proved by the one instance which he adduces. It is that of "town assessors being imprisoned for failing in their public duty as assessors."[5]

Such was the mental pabulum purveyed for the American colonists, and, to judge by its popularity, enjoyed by them, prior to the War of Independence. An Episcopalian minister of the time said in a sermon, which he delivered repeatedly in different colonies: "Unwilling or unable either to think or to read deeply, our age has the merit of having found a most palatable substitute in what is called light reading; and there are no subjects to which the principle is not now applied."[6]

If we pass over from the Scottish medical adventurer and his "light reading" to the material worthy of a university in a Congregationalist discourse, and listen to a Dudley Lecture delivered in Harvard College chapel by Dr. Jonathan Mayhew, we may find the style somewhat better and the matter somewhat worse. His subject, chosen in accordance with the terms of the lectureship foundation, is just what it ought to be. It is "Popish Idolatry." He begins by skirmishing on his title-page

Dr. Jonathan Mayhew.

---

[3] W. Douglass, *A Summary, Historical and Political, etc., of the British Settlements in North America*, i. 224, 225.
[4] *Ibid.*, ii. 146, note.
[5] *Ibid.*, ii. p. 157.
[6] Jonathan Boucher, *A View of the Causes, etc., of the American Revolution: Discourses, preached in North America, 1763-1775*, p. 58: "On Schisms and Sects."

with four frightful texts, of which the last and the shortest may be taken as a sample: "'Without are dogs—and idolaters.'—Apostle John." In a fifty-two page octavo pamphlet he proceeds to treat, as one who knows, of Transubstantiation, of Saints and Angels, of Pictures and Images; and, did we regard only the grossness of the production, we might leave it on the same level as the ignorance of a Douglass. But there is a twist and obliquity put upon things which really suggests something else than ignorance. At the end he makes a few reflections, which show that he does not agree with the eighteenth-century policy of "lenitives, not drasticks," that is, the slow-file system of a wearing persecution as considered preferable to the halter and the knife. He says: "Popery is now making great strides in England, as great perhaps as it did in the reign either of Charles or James the Second; I pray God, things may not at length be brought to so bad a pass! Thousands of weak and wicked Protestants are annually perverted to an impious, horrid system of tyranny over the bodies and souls of men, which less deserves the name of religion than that of an outrage on the senses and most valuable rights of men, and a satire upon God. If we may believe those who pretend to know, and probably do, Popish priests, Jesuits, and other emissaries, are very open and bold in our mother country of late years; and even Popish bishops reside there, and go about to exercise every part of their function without offence. It seems," he continues, "there is far less good old Protestant zeal than were to be wished and expected. Many who call themselves Protestants look upon Popery as an harmless, indifferent thing, notwithstanding its inherent restless, intolerant malignity and most destructive tendency. Heaven only knows what the end of these things will be; the prospect is alarming!"[7]

The end seems to have come already, as we must admit with all who know Boston and Massachusetts to-day. There may be a touch of poetic justice about its coming. For in times nearer to the beginning, as Dr. Mayhew intimates, the founder himself of this lectureship, the Honourable Paul Dudley, late Chief Justice of the Province, did grace his own pious and liberal foundation with "a learned dissertation" relative to the Church of Rome's infallibility; and his text had been: "'On slaves and souls of men.'—Rev. xviii. 13."[8] On this beginning had waxed strong and full the spirit which we have

[7] Jonathan Mayhew, D.D., Pastor of the West Church in Boston: *Popish Idolatry*, May 8, 1765.
[8] *Ibid.*, p. 49.

seen exemplified in the annual lecture of a Dr. Mayhew. And the end accordingly may seem in our generation to be poetically just.

But, to appreciate fully the historical fitness of things, it should be added that the Popish idolatry in question, whereon they floated, was of their own invention and inflation. So we are told by the constitutional historian of our day, that "this name of idolatry" had been "adopted in retaliation for that of heresy."[9] And we may catch the Puritan lawyer of Dudley's age telling us very much the same when commenting in secret notes on the Popish penal statutes. He says: "Wee charge the prelatical [*i.e.* the Anglican] clergy with Popery to make them odious, though wee know they are guilty of no such thing. Just as heretofore they called images Mametts, and the Adoration of Images Mametry, *i.e.* Mahomets and Mahometry: odious names when all the world knowes the Turks are forbidden Images by their religion:"[10] Here this writer's secret note stops, probably because his memory will need no reminder to draw the plain conclusion from such premises. He has given two angles of his triangle, with the line of fiction drawn between. We know at once all the rest: "Hence we charge Popery with idolatry to make it odious, though we know it is guilty of no such thing."

The manufacture of idolatry.

§ 17. In the year 1736 an effort was made in the House of Commons to repeal the Test Act of the 25th year of Charles II., passed, as the text ran, "for preventing dangers which may happen from Popish recusants." This was the precise chord on which Maryland anti-Catholic legislation was playing during the same eighteenth century.

The mover of the repeal, Mr. Plumer, argued that it was persecution to force an oath from a man, making him "subscribe to an

[9] Hallam, *Constitutional History of England*, i. 131.
[10] *Notes concerning Recusants*, a small 4to, consisting of 16 ff. of a lawyer's MS. notes upon 14 pp. of a printed pamphlet enclosed, probably the same man's production, entitled, "*A Summary Account of all the Statute Laws of this Kingdom, now in force, made against the Jesuites, seminary Priests, and Popish Recusants; drawn up for the Benefit of all Protestants. Done by a Protestant, to inform such of his Fellow-subjects, that are ignorant of these Laws, and would be willing to do their Duties, where, and when the Laws enjoyn them.*" London: Printed in the year 1666, and reprinted with additions in 1673. Cf. *supra*, Introduction, Chap. I. § 8, "*Summary*."—The pious solicitude to do one's duty, shown in all such literature, is strictly connected with pecuniary emoluments which accrue from the hunting down of Papists. Unless the Papist was hunted down to conviction, the bonus did not become due to the spy, informer, or domestic traitor. However, in justice be it added, oftentimes even a higher motive supervenes to urge the plucking of the blooming flower or of the fruit mature. It is an altruistic regard for successors in one's office, and even for posterity at large. Few legal spoilers have failed to cant in that key.

opinion which he thought inconsistent with the Christian religion;" or to force him "to join in any ceremonies of public worship which he thought sinful or perhaps idolatrous;" and then, in case he did not do both these things, by taking the oaths of supremacy and allegiance and receiving the Sacrament of the Lord's Supper according to the usage of the Church of England, to declare him incapable of holding any office in the State or of receiving any inheritance in his family. "I am surprised," he said, "that the Sacrament of the Lord's Supper should ever have been turned to such prophane use, as that of qualifying a man for being an adjutant to a regiment, or the bailiff of a little borough." Sir Robert Walpole replied that there was no persecution here; it was only a misfortune for the victim; because, he said, it was necessary that a governing party should lay the other party "under some hardships;" and "when those hardships are no greater than what are absolutely necessary for the end intended, they are just and reasonable, and such as those who are subjected to them ought not to complain of." Mr. Holden replied that in Scotland, Holland, and several other Protestant countries, Dissenting bodies of Protestants at least were not held incapable of public office; that the measure was consequently unnecessary; and "therefore this hardship must in the strictest sense be called persecution, even according to the meaning put upon it by the honourable gentlemen who have spoken on the other side of the question."[1] Had it served their purposes for debate, they might have adduced the example of Catholic countries. We have found the Puritan lawyer, who was referred to above, objecting to himself privately: "The Protestants in France bear office in the State;" and he can devise no other answer to meet the difficulty, except that the Protestants in France have only one King, whereas the Catholics in England must have two, one of them being the Pope,[2]—which this lawyer says makes all the difference; but which the Protestant writer Dallas says is all "a begging of the question."[3]

The House of Commons debate, 1736.

The fruitless pursuit of toleration in the House of Commons did but add to the historical literature of profanity and profanations.

[1] Cobbett's *Parliamentary Debates*, vol. ix.: 9 George II., 1736, col. 1046-1059.
[2] *Notes on Recusants*, as above.
[3] R. C. Dallas, *A Letter to C. Butler, Esq., Relative to the New Conspiracy against the Jesuits*, etc., p. 12. "This," he says, "I read very lately in a note of a book expressly written against the Society of the Jesuits, and in reply to the volume which I did myself the honour of publishing in their behalf. It is surely begging the question, or rather the question has been for some time settled both on facts and principles." And he refers to the Catholics in Russia, in the United States, in Canada.

§ 17. TEST ACTS AND OATHS

Mr. Plumer adverted with feeling to the "terrible indecencies," the "great abominations," the "scandal" given to the truly devout by the merely legal or formal communicants, and the consequent subversion of the morals of the vulgar. But a special value attaches to the whole debate, inasmuch as we find that Walpole's style of reasoning on behalf of penal legislation against the Catholics was adopted by Dr. William Paley, the standard moral and political philosopher of England for the end of the eighteenth and for the coming nineteenth century. This classical author, writing in the interest of ethics, morality, and politics, indoctrinated the learned youth of the universities with principles in the sense of the following argument. *Walpole's argument and Dr. Paley's.*

He says: There is no reason for punishing Catholics on account of their religion. But there is reason for punishing them on account of their Jacobitism; that is, their sympathies with the deposed and exiled Stuart kings. Now, they happen to be so faithful and loyal as to commit no visible or overt acts of Jacobitism; and there is no danger visible in their conduct, for which they could be punished. Therefore the Government is justified in taking their religion as an overt sign of that Jacobitism, which is not visible enough, and of that danger which is invisible; and it "is well warranted in fencing out the whole sect from situations of trust and power." *Abstract of Paley's argument.*

Such is Dr. Paley's argument, which is sufficiently remarkable in itself. It becomes more so for the observations, glosses, provisos, which he attaches to it, covering it all up in a bundle of verbiage. He says: "It should be observed, that it is not against the religion that Government shuts its doors;" but against "those political principles," which may be quite "independent of any article of religious faith." "Nor," he goes on to say, "would the legislator make religious tenets the test of men's inclinations towards the State, if he could discover any other that was equally certain and notorious." That is to say, if the legislator could discover any certain and notorious sign of disloyalty, he would take that as a test; he would take the overt acts, the offences, which are alone the object of municipal law; not the intendments or intentions, which are private matter of conscience. However, in default of acts, the legislator takes religion, which is independent of such acts, and is "independent" even of political "principles," and is not a sign at all; but still is something "certain and notorious." Paley hastens to repeat: "It is not to Popery that the laws object, but to Popery *His glosses.*

as the mark of Jacobitism; an equivocal indeed and fallacious mark, but the best and perhaps the only one that can be devised." All this means that the penal laws against Catholicism must be; and the only concern of legislator and philosopher alike is to find the best hook on which to hang them. To show how refined is the sense of justice all round, Paley adds with delicate sympathy: "As the connection between Popery and Jacobitism, which is the sole cause of suspicion and the sole justification of those severe and jealous laws, which have been enacted against the professors of that religion, was accidental in its origin, so probably it will be temporary in its duration; and these restrictions ought not to continue one day longer than some visible danger renders them necessary to the preservation of public tranquillity."[4]

This argument of Dr. Paley's was reproduced, at least in a note, by the Maryland preacher, the Rev. Mr. Jonathan Boucher, when treating of the Toleration of Papists. But he did not vouchsafe a word of comment on the distinguished want of sense which runs through the text of the very distinguished Dr. Paley.[5] The argument undertakes to justify that *illaqueatio malitiosa prætextu legis*, that "malignant entrapping under the colour of legality," which, with the violence dictating the law and the virulence animating it, constitutes for Lord Bacon the triple fount of social injustice.[6] That very kind of penal legislation which the noble Chancellor stigmatizes in the words of a Prophet: "He shall

The glosses of others.

---

[4] W. Paley, D.D., *The Principles of Moral and Political Philosophy*, book vi. ch. 10: "Of Religious Establishments and of Toleration," pp. 452-454. The passage is long, even in its barely essential statement. But the comment passed upon it in our text renders its reproduction necessary. The essential part of Paley's argument runs textually thus: ". . . If the generality of any religious sect entertain dispositions hostile to the constitution, and if Government have no other way of knowing its enemies than by the religion which they profess, the professors of that religion may justly be excluded from offices of trust and authority. But even *here* it should be observed, that it is not against the religion that Government shuts its doors, but against those political principles which, however independent they may be of any article of religious faith, the members of that community are found in fact to hold. Nor would the legislator make religious tenets the test of men's inclinations towards the State, if he could discover any other that was equally certain and notorious. Thus, if the members of the Roman Church, for the most part, adhere to the interest or maintain the right of a foreign pretender to the crown of these kingdoms; and if there be no way of distinguishing those who do from those who do not retain such dangerous prejudices, Government is well warranted in fencing out the whole sect from situations of trust and power. But, even in this example, it is not to Popery that the laws object, but to Popery as the mark of Jacobitism," etc., as above. It should be observed that Jacobitism began in the year 1688, with James the Second's deposition at the end of the Stuart dynasty; the penal laws had begun in the middle of the Tudor dynasty.

[5] J. Boucher, *ubi supra*, *Discourse on the Toleration of Papists, preached in Queen Anne's Parish, Prince George's Co., Maryland, in* 1774, p. 271, note.

[6] Bacon, Aphorism 1, "*De fontibus juris.*"

rain snares upon them," [7] Paley loftily dignifies with the noble title of "severe and jealous laws"! The substance of his argument is that which Hallam correctly describes as an "odious and hypocritical subterfuge;" and it consists in the equivocation, that a man is not persecuted for his religion, merely because some one else gives that religion another name, and then persecutes him for that; [8] what St. Augustine speaks of as *simulata æquitas—duplex iniquitas*, putting on the guise of equity and cloaking a double iniquity.[9] Under another aspect, it is what Macaulay styles "the most vulgar legerdemain of sophistry," to make it a ground of accusation against a whole class of men that they are unpatriotic.

Not to mention other fallacies and conceits of Paley's, as, for instance, that of men who happen to hold the reins of government presuming to "test other men's inclinations" with a view to letting them in or putting them out of the State,[10] and ousting them from their private estates, the rights of citizens and the rights of nature, we are quite taken aback by the historical assumption to which he harnesses the argument. It is what is called in learned phrase a *hysteron-proteron*, that is, the hindmost foremost. He places Jacobitism ahead of the penal laws, as "the sole cause of suspicion and the sole justification" of them. Now, Jacobitism, or the interest and party of the deposed Stuart King, James II., came into being with the deposition of the same King in 1688. The penal laws had begun with Henry VIII.'s schism from Rome, one hundred and fifty years before; they had been operating, waxing stronger and multiplying, during a century and a half. And they had been so efficacious that, instead of the one-twelfth who under Edward VI., as Paget told Somerset, had favoured the new doctrines, not one-twelfth now remained to favour the old.

The penal laws and Jacobitism.

It was computed that there was one Catholic in every fifty of the population, when the intruding dynasty of William III. had taken

---

[7] Bacon, *Aphor.* 53: "*Dicit Propheta: Pluet super eos laqueos. Non sunt autem pejores laquei quam laquei legum, præsertim pœnalium, si numero immensæ, et temporis decursu inutiles, non lucernam pedibus præbeant, sed retia potius objiciant.*"
[8] Hallam, *Constitutional History*, i. 223.
[9] Cf. St. Thomas Aquinas, *Summa Theologica*, 2da 2^{dæ} qu. 89, a. 5 ad 3^{m}.
[10] Compare the modern democratic statement of the same principle, as made by the Premier, M. Waldeck-Rousseau, when declaring the programme of war against the Catholic religious Orders or Congregations; Toulouse, October 29, 1900: "*Il ne suffit pas qu'il [le gouvernement] soit animé au sommet de l'esprit démocratique, il faut que le même esprit préside au fonctionnement de chacun de ses rouages, et ils sont trop complexes et trop nombreux pour que la plupart d'entre eux n'obéissent pas surtout à l'impulsion propre de ceux qui les dirigent.*" This policy was enlarged on in his speeches and those of others, and was carried into effect by the dissolution and expulsion of the Catholic religious Congregations and Orders.

the place of James II.; that is, some hundred thousand Catholics, men, women, and children, in a population of about five millions. This latter multitude, constituting the great world, represented the final outcome of that vast movement executed successfully, by means of one hundred and fifty years of coercion on five generations. A contemporary apologist of theirs, writing to his Catholic brother, dissuading him from losing by forfeiture £2000 sterling a year out of his £3000 merely for conscience' sake, and persuading him to follow suit and conform to law and Church like himself, puts the case very plainly, and, among many other arguments, offers a salve to conscience thus: "Suppose all here said nothing to the purpose, but what 'tis likely many would be changed in time, and become Protestants; What is that to you or I, Brother, or indeed to any rational lay Catholick in England? for he, whose case it should be, need not much repine that his conscience should lead him into a more advantageous religion as to this world; and, for the other, he would no doubt be as confident of a good place there, if he acted purely on the score of faith, as ever whilst he remained Papist." And the same writer says of himself that when he saves two-thirds of his estate by becoming a "heretick," he does "what in itself is lawful," because of "the laws commanding it."[11] Now, this gentleman's outcry against being squeezed into poverty, or out of the country, or in a "scavenger's daughter," or on a gibbet, occurs at the latter end of five generations, that had been so bound, tightened, and straitened, as to be unable to breathe any longer. His outcry is published fourteen years before Jacobitism begins. Yet, says Dr. Paley, who is no vulgar writer, but a standard philosopher, and who is not digressing into any other field, but is expressly on his own ground of political philosophy, this Jacobitism at the end of the seventeenth century started the penal laws in the middle of the sixteenth. So was his argument fabricated that the history had to be fabricated too, in the face of facts, dates, and common sense.[12]

The history of oaths extorted kept pace with the history of Sacraments inflicted; for both were contained in Test Acts. We have heard described in the House of Commons the enforced profanation

[11] *Letter from a Gentleman of the Romish Religion, etc.* (1674), pp. 17, 18. The writer's assumption of having been a Papist may be only a literary device.

[12] Compare the following from *Blackwood*: "The greatest mischief which a man with a ready command of rhetoric can do is to wrap up selfish or ignoble aims in the cloak of a generous and imposing vocabulary. The abominations of the French Revolution were in large measure due to the combination of high-flowing language, about universal brotherhood and the regeneration of humanity, with an insatiable predatory instinct." *Blackwood's Edinburgh Magazine*, March, 1900, end of article on "Mr. Ruskin."

§ 17. TEST ACTS AND OATHS

of the Lord's Supper by Protestants. The essential text of oaths after 1643, enjoined the formal blasphemy of the Lord's Supper by Catholics. The instinct was perfect, no less with regard to the central mystery of Catholic ministrations, the Holy Eucharist, than with regard to the sign of the central mystery of Christian redemption, the Cross or the crucifix. *The Sacrament as well as oaths.*

The administration of oaths was not indeed for Catholics alone. It was for all, but it was effectual in catching the Papists, while Dissenting sects were allowed to slip through. The perpetual profanation of oaths, being carried on into the most comprehensive form of public and unabashed perjury, gave occasion to a remarkable scene. It was that which was acted in Parliament, immediately after the assumption of power by William III. The class of men who had been outlawing Catholics as disloyal, and had been applying oaths to do so, had now deliberately broken their own oaths of loyalty to their King, and had brought in an intruder. They proceeded to dispense themselves from their allegiance to a sovereign already forsworn, and from their oaths to God already violated. And, in the very same Act, they went on to "appoint other oaths."[13] These, as usual, were for others to keep, and for them to keep others out with. Subsequently, the same men who had perjured themselves, as against the Stuart King, went on to treat with James and perjure themselves anew as against the Orange usurper. Here historians cannot find language strong enough to express their abhorrence of such "extraordinary and abandoned treachery," of the "ambition and rapacity in the motives," of the "treachery and intrigue in the means," employed by so "great a man" even as Churchill, Lord Marlborough.[14] But, when the same man, just a little while before, betrayed his legitimate sovereign James II., to bring in the usurper William, at the cost of every virtue and with the exhibition of unblushing vice, the language employed by one historian runs as follows: "This conduct was a signal sacrifice to public virtue of every duty in private life; and required ever after the most upright, disinterested, and public-spirited behaviour to render it justifiable," that is, to render justifiable a policy of perjury and iniquity, which Mr. Hume is in the act of calling an exercise of "public virtue."[15] *Breaking, abrogating, and appointing oaths.*

Now, this passage of Mr. Hume, where he designates acts of

---

[13] 1 Gul. & Mar., c. 8: "*An Act for the Abrogating of the Oathes of Supremacy and Allegiance and Appointing Other Oathes.*"
[14] Hallam, *Constitutional History of England*, iii. 167, text, p. 169, note.
[15] Hume, *History of England*, vi. 447. See context for further abuse of language.

VOL. I. I

treachery and perjury by the euphemism of "sacrifices to public virtue," does still appear to another historian, Mr. Hallam, to be quite

The justification of perjury. "severe."[16] Both of them, however, consider that subsequent fidelity to the later oaths would have made the former perjuries "justifiable,"—not merely excusable or pardonable, inasmuch as sins once committed are ever sins, though afterwards remitted. No; they consider the perjuries justifiable; that what was once a sin becomes an act of virtue retrospectively, if something else happens to be done afterwards. This is a kind of retroactive indulgence, such as never was heard of in any other code of morality.

And of the end justifying the means. It is, however, a development of the doctrine elsewhere laid down, that the end justifies the means; as, when arguing against his co-religionists, and trying to defend the spoliation of the monasteries by Henry VIII., Mr. Hallam rebukes them plainly for not observing that the end might never have been reached if more laudable means had been used, and legality was only then possible when violence had gone before, to clear the way for Protestantism.[17]

In the Colonies, the course of revolution with the fall of the Stuarts followed the lead of the old country. The new oaths imposed under the Orange dynasty immediately went into operation,

The Colonies and the principle of revolution. starting, like the forged Bull in Ireland, an intolerable persecution, which at times made life in Maryland almost impracticable for priests and laity alike. The question of justifying that disloyalty and perjury which had brought about the Revolution of 1688 gave no occasion for even a second thought in the Colonies at that date. And when, in our own times, the modern historian reverts, in the midst of a very philosophical and high-flown disquisition, to the essential merits of the Orange Revolution, he takes the whole of it as perfectly correct—beginning, middle, and end; and that, merely because people did it. Bancroft says, that by deposing their King, they annihilated his right; that by disfranchising a dynasty for its Catholicity, they had a right to disfranchise it; that by breaking a contract, they had a perfect right to break it; and, by establishing new conditions, they had a right to

---

[16] Hallam, *Constitutional History of England*, iii. 169, note.
[17] "Nor could the Protestant religion have easily been established by legal methods under Edward and Elizabeth without this previous destruction of the monasteries. . . . In many, the violent courses of confiscation and attainder which accompanied this great revolution excite so just an indignation, that they either forget to ask whether the end might not have been reached by more laudable means, or condemn that end itself either as sacrilege or at least as an atrocious violation of the rights of property," etc. Hallam, *Ibid.*, i. 100.

go back upon a contract and reform it *ex post facto*.[18] In all this the historian affords not the slightest inkling of a latent consciousness that possibly there is some obligation imposed by allegiance, truth, fidelity, or solemn oaths. The fact of breaking all these obligations is a general dispensation from them. It is the philosophy of the accomplished fact. The end attained justifies the means. That end he states to have been "a successful insurrection against legitimacy and authority over mind."[19]

What resulted thence was what might have been expected. Oaths met the same fate in the Colonies as in the old country. Even Douglass cannot help observing the general blight that had settled on truthfulness, fidelity, and reverence for the name and witness of God. He says that the way solemn oaths are taken "renders them nearly upon a par with common profane swearing; the many oaths in the several branches of the revenue, particularly in the customs, are of bad effect; hence the proverb, 'A custom-house oath,' that is, an oath that may be dispensed with. Oaths give a profligate man of no religion (that is, who does not think himself bound by an oath) a vast advantage over an honest, conscientious, religious man. The same may be said of the Sacramental tests of conformity, and occasional conformity practised by the Church of England."[20] *The fate of oaths in the Colonies.*

When the United States of America had evolved out of the British Colonies, and the spirit of liberality began to breathe where it had so long been suffocated, there was still observed an imminent danger in divers directions that the oaths as tests would be kept in full force against Catholic priests, against their holding any landed property, and against granting the citizen's full franchise to Catholic laymen.[21] *The threatened continuance of test oaths in U.S.*

But the palm remained and was to remain for a long while with

[18] "By resolving that James II. had abdicated, the representatives of the English people assumed to sit in judgment on its kings. By declaring the throne vacant, they annihilated the principle of legitimacy. By disfranchising a dynasty for professing the Roman faith, they not only exerted the power of interpreting the original contract, but of introducing into it new conditions." G. Bancroft, *History of the United States*, iii. 7, 15th edit.

[19] *Ibid., loc. cit.*

[20] Douglass, *Summary*, i. 203, note.

[21] Dr. John Carroll alluded with concern to this danger, while the corresponding political movements were in progress. Cf. *Documents*, I. No. 144: Carroll to C. Plowden, 1783, September 26.—But the following illustration from Kent will suffice. He quotes several cases in point, and says: "The Constitution of New York, as it was originally passed, required all persons born out of the United States, and naturalized by the Legislature, to take an oath abjuring all foreign allegiance and subjection in all matters *ecclesiastical* as well as civil. This was intended, and so it operated, to exclude from the benefits of naturalization Roman Catholics, who acknowledged the spiritual supremacy of the Pope," etc. 2 Kent, *Comm.*, 73.

Great Britain. An Englishman wrote at this time (1795): "In no country under heaven is to be found that multiplicity of oaths which are at every turn administered in Great Britain." This English writer continued, adding sarcasm to censure: "It should seem as if the Legislature had discovered something so infamously base in the character of an Englishman that nothing but the most extraordinary ties could bind him to his duty. Is he to be admitted to any office, civil or military; is he to receive any pay by patent or grant from the King; is he to enter on any command or place of trust? etc., etc., the Sacrament must be taken. But this will not suffice: he must then take the oath of allegiance, then that of supremacy, then that of abjuration. But he is not yet to be trusted; he must declare that he does not believe in transubstantiation. God in heaven!" However, he goes on to observe, "some of them serve to keep the Papists in a state of bondage, and the views of legislators are thus fulfilled." [22]

Continuance of oaths in Great Britain. 1795.

The permanent conspiracy of Papist men, women, and children, 100,000 all told, against the great State, with its Legislature, Executive, army and navy, seems to have exercised the patience and long-suffering of the British empire till the year 1871, or 34th–35th years of Victoria. Jacobitism was long since dead, and could no longer have furnished a William Paley with a subterfuge to mystify an argument or a university. The American Republic was already emancipated during well-nigh a century from the servitude of swearing against Popery. And, when at last in England the time for repeal could be put off no longer, never in the history of Christianity had a nation been found that was surcharged with such an accumulation of oaths as then was exhibited in the bill of repeal. This is named "*An Act to repeal divers enactments relating to Oaths and Declarations which are not in force, and for other purposes connected therewith.*" It proceeds to enumerate thirty-six English Acts, now wholly repealed, and forty partly repealed; six Scotch Acts wholly, and three partly repealed; eight Irish Acts wholly, and ten partly repealed; and, in one further schedule, ninety-six annual indemnity Acts totally repealed.[23] This made the sum-total of one

Abolition of test oaths in 1871.

---

[22] Rev. Joseph Berington, *Reflections addressed to the Rev. J. Hawkins*, etc., pp. ix., x.—*Ibid.*, pp. x.-xii., Berington adverts to a small pamphlet against the Church of Rome by Dr. Porteus, Bishop of Chester: "The contents of this tract, the worthy Prelate informs us, he extracted from Archbishop Secker's *Five Sermons against Popery*. . . . *Five Sermons against Popery!* . . . When has a Primate of France left behind him *Sermons against Protestants?*"

[23] 34 & 35 Vict., c. 48, cited as "*The Promissory Oaths Act*, 1871." The last schedule enumerates briefly the annual indemnity Acts "from 11 Geo. III., c. 18, to 30 & 31 Vict., c. 88."

hundred and ninety-nine Acts of Parliament; of which only six dated back to Catholic times, and they concerned exclusively justices, clerks of chancery, sheriffs, and corporations. Hence, from the time when Henry VIII. began this culture on leaving the Catholic Church, one hundred and ninety-three Acts of Parliament had blossomed with Sacraments and oaths, which it was necessary for decency's sake to prune away or to root out. If Popery had been responsible for this, it would be proper for some one to make an apology. But, as it was anti-Popery, there is nothing further to say.

§ 18. Next to the literature of the eighteenth, that of the nineteenth century came to be scanned while we were looking about wistfully, to see if perchance some pages in print might yet fall to our share and help us in the course of this History. A remarkable change did come over the spirit of writing, not quite at the beginning of the century, but as the age wore on and tardy day began to divide the mental sky with lingering night. *The new age and the change.* Men who saw what was coming ran out of the ranks to be ahead of their fellows, and salute the rising sun of liberality, as if they introduced it into the world. Many great things indeed would seem to have existed only from the time when some people found them, and took out a brevet of distinction for the merit of creation. With these the past is nothing beyond the point where they are something.

The old style of history, however, was still in possession as late as 1837. For a witness we have the *History of Maryland* by John Leeds Bozman, published in that year. In the Introduction, extending over three hundred and fourteen pages, *J. L. Bozman, in 1837.* the writer undertakes to treat of the general religious antecedents in England and elsewhere, and then he discusses in section the ninth the " causes of the severe statutes against Roman Catholics in England under Elizabeth."[1] He affirms that principles of assassination were common among Catholics, and that they were endorsed by plenary indulgence from the Pope; and he strews other such amenities about. His notes are as remarkable as his text. To justify his accounts of Catholicity, of the Gunpowder Plot, and the like, he discerns authorities unimpeachable in men like Bayle and Hume.[2]

[1] J. L. Bozman, *History of Maryland*, i. 222, *seqq*.
[2] In Note Q, pp. 294, 295, he quotes at length from Bayle, *Historical and Critical Dictionary*, article "Elizabeth." He considers that author a competent critic on Catholics, because he was a "Free-thinker;" and "for this reason," says Bozman, " his [Bayle's] character was assailed by the bigots and fanatics, both of the Catholics and the Calvinists; but, for the same reason also, his opinions, like those of Mr. Hume, are to be respected as of the most impartial authority in all historical

For to have the mind not merely unattached to Catholicity, but quite foreign and inimical to it, appears to be taken as a mellow and necessary condition for knowing all about other people's affairs. And, the compliment not being turned round the other way, a Catholic is not presumed to know anything either about his own mind and affairs, or any body else's.[3] However, in Bozman's time, the vapours of Hume's historical conceptions had not yet faded from view; nor had general archives been as yet opened to public use; nor would the treatment of them, upon such subjects as Bozman rushes into with such assurance, seem to be altogether within the competency of that gentleman. His is a residual specimen of what Sir Francis Palgrave calls "traditionary opinions," or old stories many times told, and taken blankly on trust.

A gentleman of culture has recently described what this school looked like, so late as the nineteenth century. The "ascendency," says Mr. Child, " of Protestantism in England, from the reign of Elizabeth to a time within the memory of living men, was so complete and so universal, that all the questions concerning it had come to be looked upon by the mass of Englishmen as finally settled, and had ceased to be a subject of study or interest even with the majority of educated persons, who were mostly bred up with the notion that all the right was, and had always been, on the Protestant, and all the wrong on the Roman side of all questions between the two parties."[4] Then this gentleman finds that there were two great temporary causes which led to a reversal of all this; first, the institution of historical societies with the facilities granted in all directions for the consultation of records; "and, secondly, the extension to England of the great Catholic reaction, which began on the Continent towards the close of the last [the eighteenth] century, and dates with us from the rise of what is known as the Tractarian Movement in 1833."[5]

The process of change.

No insignificant cause of this ungracious awakening had been the historical labours of Dr. John Lingard, Professor in the Catholic seminary at Ushaw, whose chief production, the well-known *History of England,* began to appear in 1819. The work was a revelation, and the mingled sentiments excited by

Dr. John Lingard.

controversies between these two sects of religion." Possibly all this is merely a form of excuse for taking history from a dictionary.

[3] Thus an *Encyclopædia Britannica,* ninth edition, commits the writing of an article on the Jesuits, not to any one antecedently competent on any visible ground, but to a Protestant and anti-Jesuit, Dr. R. F. Littledale.

[4] G. W. Child, *Church and State under the Tudors,* p. 213.

[5] *Ibid., loc. cit.*

it in the public mind led to several noteworthy results. One was the irritation which became visible in the immediate generation of writers afterwards. The Philistines themselves kept their temper better at the spectacle of the Hebrews "coming forth out of the holes wherein they were hid." Another result was that of the inevitable, which was recognized as such, and which had to be accepted; for the revelation had been made, as some felt it should never have been. Hence a fair face was put upon the matter by a new and self-asserting propagandism of liberality. Some of these forced liberals, like Hallam, are the very men who are smarting most under the irritation, particularly as caused by Lingard.

But, according to Mr. Child and Mr. Froude, all this sympathy with the down-trodden Papists was only the swinging back of a pendulum which had swung long and far in the other direction. Now, towards the end of the century, it had gone too long and too far in the new direction. They enter their protests, and they write their books. Mr. Froude says that High Churchmen on one side, Liberal statesmen and political philosophers on the other, were assailing the English Reformers with "equally violent abuse." Lord Macaulay had come in and "attacked Cranmer as one of the basest of mankind. It had become the fashion to speak with extreme severity of the persecution of the Catholics by Elizabeth. Even writers on the whole favourable to the Reformation described the English branch of it as a good thing badly done." Mr. Froude has quite a different opinion, and he writes his extensive *History of England* to rehabilitate Elizabeth at least, and others too, if so he may.[6]

J. A. Froude.

Mr. Child makes his observations on Church and State rest on historical records more or less, but not with the professional character of an historian; and we should be glad if he had claimed as much immunity from the traditional temper which has waited on historical literature as he modestly submits to on the score of new historical information, when he begs to be excused from exhibiting any. So late in the cultivation of manners as 1890, we find in this book of a dignified Master of Arts some specimens of writing and language, which might be considered a survival of Zwinglian free speech. What he chooses to set as an earmark on the literature of the Puritans, that he takes care to exemplify in his own pages, to wit, a "bitter and cantankerous style," as he says, and

G. W. Child.

[6] J. A. Froude, *History of England from the Fall of Wolsey to the Defeat of the Spanish Armada*, preface. London: June, 1870.

a "perverse and impracticable character."[7] He couples Jesuits with "Thugs;" tells stories of an unnamed Catholic preacher, a convert from Protestantism, counselling assassination at a date unnamed; and he tells of the Pope giving "precepts" to assassinate.[8] Such assertions he introduces with the bluff assurance: "The evidence of all this," says he, "is unimpeachable, and comes from their own side. There is no room for reasonable question or doubt about it." This asseveration is in the line of protesting too much, as his references and also his want of references proceed at once to betray.[9]

Language and manners apart, we fear that something which comes to hand from Maryland exhibits the best reversionary title, among all modern samples of the older times renewed. For, in the worst efforts of irresponsible literature, old or new, there is one head that seems to be notably wanting in the wholesale indictment of the Jesuits. They may be painted as murderers, assassins, traitors, merchants, Indian chiefs, or Bedouins in disguise. They may be, as an ancient reports it, "now a cobler, now a preacher, now a tinker, now a courtier, now a peason [peasant], now a states-man, and what not."[10] They may be as the author of the *Apostate Protestant* indignantly describes them, in the words of Father Watson: "Of all sects and religions (saith Father Watson) the Jesuit and the Puritan come nearest, and are fittest to be coupled like dogs and cats together. And so he [Father Watson] goes on comparing them, for their schismatical humour," etc., until the author of the *Apostate Protestant* winds up the twenty-four heads of indictment by saying of Jesuit and Puritan together, in Watson's words, "You will find them, that, as they came into the world much about a time, so they have been sworn brethren from the womb."[11] Thus the Jesuits may be said to be all that the coarse literature of those times put to their account, while it strictly observed the rubric to "rove in general propositions, crying out against all without being able to instance in any."[12] Or, as a modern writer, always observing strictly the same cautious rubric, charges them in round names, periods, and terms: "Subtle alike and intrepid, pliant in their direction, unshaken in their aim, the sworn, implacable, unscrupulous enemies of Protestant governments, the Jesuits were a

The Jesuit in tradition.

---

[7] G. W. Child, *Church and State under the Tudors*, p. 234.
[8] *Ibid.*, pp. 215, 216.
[9] *Ibid., loc. cit.*
[10] M. G., *An Account of the Jesuites Life and Doctrine*, 1661: "To the Reader."
[11] *The Apostate Protestant: a Letter to a Friend*, p. 49; from Watson's *Quodlibets*, p. 27.
[12] M. G., *ubi supra, loc. cit.*

§ 18.   *NINETEENTH-CENTURY LITERATURE*   121

legitimate object of restraint." And the scrupulous gentleman harps at length on the same sympathetic theme, which seems almost to become true by repetition.[13] Our pages would not tolerate the summing up made by a modern lawyer, where the legal language quoted comprises worse expressions than "the tails of Samson's foxes," "lepers," "tongues set on fire by hell," till the very climax of iniquity is reached in these words: "saying Mass, administering the Sacrament, hearing Confessions."[14] But, with all this, it is noteworthy how few efforts were made to bespatter the personal integrity of life in the Company of Jesus. Possibly their power, like Lucifer's, left them no time to be weak. And the world, like a hound on a nobler scent, left that offal to other mongrels.

In the last year of the nineteenth century, a writer in Baltimore started on the other scent. He was imprudent enough to discard the time-honoured rubric of "roving only in general propositions," when assaulting the Jesuits. He was particular, and he formulated the charge of libertinism against a Jesuit, and he named the Jesuit—Father Thomas Copley, or Fisher, well known among the first missionaries of Maryland. This he did under those colours, which are so usual now-a-days, of flying in his preface the flag of documents and archives. "Increased historical research," he says, "the publication of the Maryland Archives; above all, the recovery and publication of the *Calvert Papers*," etc.[15] And this gentleman, the Rev. C. E. Smith, informs the ladies and gentlemen of his flock, to be whose Rector he very properly considers "no slight privilege," that they "are already familiar with many of the statements made" in these printed pages. He says to them, that the crime in question "is credited" to Copley. This which is credited he takes for granted. He assumes it as a fact, for he says that Copley, "notwithstanding this *mésalliance*, acquired a potent voice in Maryland affairs." He sets down a reference to "Neill, *Terra Mariæ*, p. 70."[16]

An additional trait in the Jesuit.

C. E. Smith, 1899.

Now, the Rev. E. D. Neill said something very different. He did not "credit" Father Copley with anything of the kind for which the Rev. Ernest Smith quotes him. But he threw out a tentative suggestion, offensive enough when the ground of it was confessedly ignorance, whether our Maryland Father may

E. D. Neill.

---

[13] Hallam, *Constitutional History of England*, i. p. 225.
[14] Anstey, as above, *Guide to the Laws of England affecting Roman Catholics*, p. 109; from *Campian's Case*, 1 Howell's *State Trials*, 1053.
[15] C. E. Smith, *Religion under the Barons of Baltimore*, p. vii.
[16] *Ibid.*, pp. 203, 204.

not have been "the Father Copley who, when domestic chaplain of Lord Montague, fell in love with the nursery-maid, and, forgetting his vows, was married, and, of course, as long as his wife lived, could only serve in secular affairs."[17] This last suggestion alludes to the fact of Father Copley being the temporal administrator or procurator of the Maryland Mission. Now, all this surmising was not worthy of modern research and criticism. But Neill lived half a century ago in darker times, before the archives were opened; and he made no pretension even to that small dealing in big things, which consists in putting very full labels on empty canisters. Like a magazine gossip, he doubted about an identity between two persons on the very slight affinity of a family name being common to both, who were living more or less in the same age of the world; which process of logic, if exercised even among so small and select a class as that of American writers like Mr. Smith on Jesuit affairs, might still land us in some ambiguities and embarrassments. Yet so did it come to pass that a senior John Copley, priest, some fifteen or twenty years ahead, became one in the mind's eye with a boy of sixteen, Thomas Copley, or Fisher, who was studying philosophy then at Louvain.[18] The former was never a Jesuit, the latter was. The mistake thus fledged, Mr. Neill was incautious enough to leave flapping its wings in his pages, a feeble doubt just essaying to poise itself in the air. The fluttering timid creature caught the eye of the Rev. Mr. Smith, who brought it down at once as a peremptory fact. But a lady of Maryland had written long before this: "Neill quite strangely confounds this apostate with Father Thomas Copley of Maryland." She quotes what was reported from London, January 29, 1611, that the decayed priest, "one Copley," and the "ancient Catholic maid," who had charge of Lord Montague's children, "had left their profession and fallen to marriage." Then, as an object of favour, this Copley was presented by Abbot, Archbishop of Canterbury, to a Protestant living, as Rector of Blethersden, in Kent; and later on he was Rector at Pluckley. But he was "always in trouble with the lord of the manor, Sir Edward Dering, who as late as 1614 speaks of his 'currishness' and 'face.'"[19] We may now leave this specimen of recent historical research in the hands of the competent Catholic lady and of the Camden Publication Society.

The two Copleys.

[17] E. D. Neill, *Terra Mariæ*, p. 70.—Cf. *The Court and Times of James the First*, i. 134: John Chamberlain, London, January 29, 1611, to Sir Dudley Carleton.
[18] Foley, *Records*, vii., *Collectanea*, p. 165, *sub voce* "Copley, Thomas;" "Fisher, Philip."
[19] Mrs. K. C. Dorsey, of Washington, *Life of Fr. Thomas Copley*, published in the *Woodstock Letters*, vol. xiv. p. 223.

But we have dwelt upon the case because it occurred while we were writing, and because it was so honestly peculiar as to be definite—an indiscretion which will probably be avoided next time.

Some writers, like Bancroft and Parkman, belonging to a liberal date and school, brought eminent talents to the service of literature; and they did not omit Catholic interests, exploits, and history. The results were insinuating, and yet disappointing. *G. Bancroft and Parkman.* There were brilliant descriptions; there was touching pathos; there was the cultivation of new fields, which proved a very oasis of literature in the artistic barrenness of the times. That is to say, it was in large part a literary school, writing for effect, and able to write Catholicity up instead of down, because, while the nature of the subject invited it, the spirit of the day permitted it. They allowed themselves oftentimes to come under the full influence of Catholic subjects. Like genuine artists, they took the very pick of the noble, the pathetic, and the sublime, which they knew how to cull amid a luxuriance of Jesuit Relations or other Catholic records. But we cannot say that their workmanship enhanced the subject. While they expressed well the parts and disposed well the whole, they seemed to make it a principle to sacrifice at the end both the whole and the parts to something else, which they had found in neither. Over a beautiful narrative, over a soul-stirring picture of heroic and supernatural virtue, which went straight to the heart because it came from the human heart of the subject, they would incontinently draw a gross line, as a painter might make a gross daub, declaring suddenly and capriciously, as if to dispel the effects, that it was all superstition, or enthusiasm, or fanaticism. And, having dashed their picture thus, they would pass on to find other brilliant pages in a subject-matter which they meant still to spoil, painting the virtue for art's sake and calling it vice for the sake of prejudice. This manner of proceeding was not more offensive to Catholic sentiment which probably they never regarded, or more agreeable to the latent prejudice which certainly they were fondling, than it was an error on the score of art. *Prejudice and art.* Their contribution sprang neither from the subject nor from its belongings nor from its suggestions. It was only an ill-matched offset, as being quite gratuitous. And it was a lapse too in literary integrity. For to take what did not belong to them, the Catholic sentiment or heroism, and then spoil it into something which did belong to them, by an unwarranted slur upon it, was a kind of intellectual plagiarism, which disguised and claimed other people's property, not on account of improvement but of damage done. It is just what we see all over England to-day, in the beautiful Catholic monuments of other ages, from cathedrals to market-crosses, from niches in the door-ways to the tombs of kings in the sacred crypts. They are subjects of national pride; but they are all broken or defaced. They were too beautiful not to leave there, and yet too Catholic to leave in their beauty. On this score we find scarcely more to profit by in an Irving or a Longfellow, besides the authors whom we have mentioned, than in a Macaulay or a Byron.

§ 19. And now, if we come to the reckoning up of such literature in general, we may easily infer how little is likely to be found for the purposes of Catholic history. But to formulate the inference, we prefer not to speak in our own character; just as, in supplying the antecedents above, we have preferred to use, not our own language, but that of men acknowledged to be representative in matters of law, politics, and history. One, whom we have quoted often, because his *Constitutional History* has been so long a standard university work, will inform us what may not be expected in such a literature since the time of the Reformation. Mr. Hallam happens to find himself suffering from want of documents on Elizabeth's reign, owing to the forced silence imposed on muzzled writers. He gives vent to his temper in the following terms, not meaning the passage for our benefit, but for his own solace: "This forced silence of history," he says, "is much more to be suspected after the use of printing and the Reformation, than in the ages when monks compiled annals in their convents, reckless of the censure of courts, because independent of their permission. Grosser ignorance of public transactions is undoubtedly found in the chronicles of the Middle Ages; but far less of that deliberate mendacity, or of that insidious suppression, by which fear and flattery and hatred and the thirst of gain have, since the invention of printing, corrupted so much of historical literature throughout Europe."[1] As to the chances of Catholic literature, he says of the same age: "It was penal to utter, or so much as to possess, even the most learned works on the Catholic side; or, if some connivance was usual in favour of educated men, the utmost strictness was used in suppressing that light infantry of literature, the smart and vigorous pamphlets with which the two parties [the Catholic and Calvinistic], arrayed against the [Anglican] Church, assaulted her opposite

Shortcomings of the literature.

---

[1] Hallam, *Constitutional History of England*, i. 337, 338.

flanks." [2] And, not being allowed to be present, these absent writers were, of course, always in the wrong.

As to Hallam himself, and men of his school, who posed as liberals when it was no longer fashionable to be intolerant, we may borrow a critical estimate from another constitutional historian and lawyer, one raised far above the level of that school, both in scientific attainments and professional prestige. Sir Francis Palgrave was giving evidence before a Committee of the House of Commons upon the subject of mortmain. Speaking of a class of men whom he called "popular but shallow and prejudiced writers," and of the confusion introduced by them into a subject like mortmain, which was supposed to touch the power of "the Romanists," he said that the main cause for all this trouble may be found in "the habit of taking traditionary opinions upon trust." [3] He remarked: "I should only wish that my evidence should be considered as the means of leading others to consider the question impartially, and especially to examine the propriety of submitting any longer to the thraldom of the traditionary opinions (if I may use the expression) which have arisen during the last [eighteenth] century. We are now wholly governed by the traditions of Blackstone, Delolme, and Robertson, and other writers of that description. I may also add, of Adam Smith, whose opinions are taken entirely as law, without the slightest investigation as to their truth and relevancy." These men, he affirmed, had only "fettered public opinion," and "prevented that freedom of thinking which results from the investigation of facts." [4] Reverting to the subject of "what Guizot calls historical traditions," he continued: "Our notions of Church authority, and of the influence of the Church in general, are gained almost in our earliest youth, from the first educational works which fall into our hands. The influence of these educational works continues to affect the minds of the majority during life." And, after some severe animadversions on the historian Robertson, whom he names "as the type of agencies," he characterizes the policy of those agencies in these words: Robertson, "in his well-known work, from which most people obtain their ideas with regard to the Middle Ages, represents, on the whole, Church influence as an antagonist principle to the progress of society; whereas, without entering into any doctrinal

---

[2] Hallam, *Constitutional History of England*, p. 323.
[3] House of Commons, *Reports, Committees*, vol. x., 1844: "Mortmain," qu. 151, pp. 29 (547), 30 (548).
[4] *Ibid.*, qu. 143, p. 22 (540).

126   INTROD. II.   THE ARCHIVES AND LITERATURE

question, and simply considering the Church as [a] fact, it was the great means of both civil and intellectual improvement." [5]   After Sir Francis Palgrave, Mr. Burge, a distinguished colonial lawyer and author, had occasion to reinforce the evidence and opinion of Sir Francis, by citing as a typical case a page of Mr. Hallam's, where this latter was merely a blind copyist of Robertson, and Robertson was misrepresenting the original.[6]

Burge.

Thus the old landmarks of so-called history are being swept away, by the advancing tide of criticism, from the imaginary posts where they have been kept so long by a reverence for tradition, by a professional unconcern for things unprofessional, or simply by the illusions of an undying superstition. They were landmarks of a kind which may be witnessed of a morning on the ocean, those rocks and cliffs and mountains, marshalled and serried and piled on high, only to be dissolved, the fabric of a vision, by the advancing noon. Nevertheless, quite recently, while treating some questions about the Jesuits and the second Lord Baltimore, one or two Maryland authors have adverted with respect to several of these ancient dogmas, and have made them the basis of a long argumentation. And yet, before these articles of a creed were last repeated, they had already been expunged from the creed, though not from the cyclopædias.

The traditions reappearing in Maryland.

For instance, there is that doctrine of the great and noble efforts made by the English people in Catholic times to withstand the Pope and the canon law, and to save their monument of reason, the English common law. It was just in this spirit, so the account goes, that Cæcilius Lord Baltimore nobly withstood the Jesuits and their endeavours to introduce the same canon law into Maryland on the plea of a Divine right. It may appear, in some chapter of ours following here, that there was no Divine right in question, and that there was no such measure in question as the introduction of canon law. But, as to the theory behind such a statement, it has already been shown by professors of Cambridge and Oxford, that the English people never took any such stand as that with which they are credited; that the laity and clergy were not opposed to one another on any such issue; and that the figment is one of Blackstone's propagation, though not perhaps of his production. Professors Pollock

---

[5] House of Commons, *Reports, Committees*, vol. x., 1844: "Mortmain," qu. 1225, pp. 150 (668), 151 (669).

[6] *Ibid.*, qu. 1394, p. 172 (690). See above, § 11, note 5.—A fair digest of the evidence furnished to the Mortmain Committees, both of 1844 and of 1851–2, is given, but without observing exactly the order of the reports, by Finlason, *History, etc., of Laws of Mortmain*, Appendix, pp. 169-245.

and Maitland inform us that "Blackstone's picture of a nation divided into two parties, 'the bishops and clergy' on one side contending for their foreign jurisprudence, 'the nobility and the laity' on the other, adhering 'with equal pertinacity to the old common law,' is not true.[7] It is by 'Popish clergymen' that our English common law is converted from a rude mass of customs into an articulate system; and when the 'Popish clergymen,' yielding at length to the Pope's commands, no longer sit as the principal justices of the king's court, the creative period of our medieval law is over."[8] *Pollock and Maitland.*

In like manner, some other old materials have been imported into Maryland history, to explain how Lord Baltimore fell out with the Jesuits. Medieval bishops are dragged in, and scant courtesy is paid them on the score of common honesty. It is said of their action under the canon law: "Taking exclusive cognizance of all causes testamentary, the clergy, under this law, paid legacies to the Church or to pious uses before they paid creditors, heirs, or legatees; and, assuming sole control of administration of the estates of decedents, the Ordinary never rendered any account whatever of such estate, and it was absorbed to the uses of the clergy."[9] The worthy author of this passage never verified what he wrote here; for there are eight errors in six lines. And, as this is not an unusual proportion in unverified history, we may be allowed to note them as a mere sample. First, the Bishop could not be said to "assume" an office, which was constitutionally his by every law. Secondly, the clergy did not take an exclusive cognizance of all causes testamentary. Thirdly, they did not pay legacies to the Church or to pious uses, before paying creditors; as all canon law and moral theology say precisely the contrary. Fourthly, a clerical executor was accountable according to his grade and state. But, fifthly, the Bishop, who was officially the executor of pious legacies, was the ordinary judge, who is not expected to report but to decide; and, when statutes came to impose a personal representation of testators and intestates, then did they require the Bishop to appoint some one, as an administrator, who could appear as a responsible party. Sixthly, when the Church is a *Catholic bishops in Maryland literature.*

---

[7] 1 Blackstone, *Comm.*, 19.—Cf. 1 Stephen, *Comm.*, 13.

[8] Pollock and Maitland, *History of English Law*, i. 133: on Roman and Canon Law.

[9] B. T. Johnson, *The Foundation of Maryland and the Act concerning Religion of April 21, 1649*, p. 59. The main part of General Johnson's theory has been reproduced textually by Mr. J. W. Thomas, member of the Maryland Historical Society, in *Chronicles of Colonial Maryland*, pp. 87–90, note. The former wrote in 1883; the latter in 1900.

legatee and her legacy is paid, it is incorrect to say that she is paid before legatees. Seventhly, creditors being paid first, if then there was not enough for all legacies, canonists held that the Church had no right to preference, but should take her share *pro rata*, as one of the legatees at large, sacred and profane together. Eighthly, if by "decedents" are meant intestates, then, according to civil and canon law, the kinsfolk of such intestates succeeded as heirs, unto the tenth degree of kindred inclusively; hence such estate was not "absorbed to the uses of the clergy;" and much less were the estates of testators.[10]

J. V. L. McMahon.

Finally, as a last instance, we may cite the words of a Maryland lawyer upon the measure introducing mortmain, which Lord Baltimore applied to missionary property in the early government of Maryland. To throw light upon some obscurer topic, McMahon brings forward, as an illustration perfectly luminous and axiomatic, "the Statutes of Mortmain, the simple object of which," he says, "was to prevent the alienation of lands to the all-absorbing clergy, whose ingenuity, prompted by their avarice and thirst for dominion, for ages kept the statute law lagging behind them."[11] This characteristic and slashing declaration of traditional opinions calls only for the characteristic answer of modern history. What McMahon asserts to have been "the simple object" of those laws, seems to have been nothing of the kind, as the text of the original Magna Charta, quoted from itself and not from the cyclopædias or abridgments, abundantly shows.[12] Hence, in keeping with the text of Magna Charta and with the correlative facts, the Oxford and Cambridge professors explain how the "simple object" of the Laws of Mortmain was to be found in the acts of the laity, not of the clergy.[13] Or, to put the statement in plainer terms with the

[10] For a good specimen of the history, as pertaining to intestacy, cf. Pollock-Maitland, as above, ii. 356-363.—For the statements of canon law, cf. Bonacina, who was the author referred to by John Lewger, in the Maryland dispute: *Theologia Moralis*, ii., "De Restitutione in Genere;" Disp. I. qu. viii. punctum 2, "De ordine quo facienda est restitutio," etc., nn. 12, 13, 35; "De Contractibus," Disp. III. qu. xvii., "De testamentis et legatis," p. 3, n. 23, "Quinam succedant ab intestato;" *Ibid.*, p. 8, § 2, "Quodnam dicatur legatum pium," etc., n. 4, quinto, sexto; *Ibid.*, § 6, n. 5, "Quo ordine solvenda sint debita;" *Ibid.*, § 10, "Quisnam sit competens judex circa solutionem legatorum," nn. 1, 2; *Ibid.*, qu. xviii., "De executoribus," etc., p. 3, n. 6, "An religiosus executor teneatur reddere rationem executionis, et cui;" *Ibid.*, p. 4, n. 3, "An executor teneatur rationem reddere administrationis."—For Blackstone's libel on the clergy, with reference to intestacy, see his 2 *Comm.*, 494.—With the usual fidelity, Blackstone's successors, while they take liberties with his text in other matters, reproduce such history intact. Cf. 2 Stephen, *Comm.*, 182-184; Ewell's *Essentials of the Law*, i. 298 (Boston, 1889).—Cf. *infra*, Appendix C, § 74, p. 591.
[11] J. V. L. McMahon, *An Historical View of the Government of Maryland, from its Colonization to the Present Day*, p. 110.—Cf. *infra*, Appendix C, § 76 (9) (*a*), pp. 611-613.
[12] 2 Henry III., A.D. 1217; 9 Henry III., 1224-1225; 25 Edward I., 1297.
[13] Pollock and Maitland, as above, i. 333, note.

constitutional historian Dr. Stubbs, the laws of mortmain originated in the frauds of laymen, who were imposing upon the Church and were imposing upon their higher landlords, and, giving nothing to the former while taking all from the latter, they passed their lands fraudulently under the name of the Church and took all they could from their duties to the State.[14] This was not robbing Peter to pay Paul; but it was robbing Peter, Paul, and Cæsar all together. Such was the origin of mortmain legislation. Some further illustrations on this matter will be noticed hereafter, when called for by the controversy between Lord Baltimore and the early Jesuit missionaries.[15]

§ 20. As to our theme, the Jesuits, it is to be observed that there are two essential points of view in the question, because there are two essential qualifications of the subject. One is that of the Catholic priest, the other is that of the regular or religious. Both of these are contained in the legal and canonical definition of "regular clerics," or "clerks regular."

Now, as to the place and importance of the first element, that is, the priesthood, it has always been understood, that nothing was really effected against the Catholic Church, however much might be inflicted upon her, so long as the priesthood was left on its feet. *(The priesthood.)* This, which impresses a certain historian's mind, gives rise to a piece of typical reasoning in his pages. He says: 'Tis true that "the Romish scheme of worship" attaches more importance than the Protestant to "ceremonial rites" in public and united prayer (and therefore should seem to be more social than the Protestant); *(Hallam's commentary.)* yet it is also true that, with the suppression of its ceremonial rites and public worship, the Romish scheme does still survive, where the Protestant would expire; which happens if a priest is allowed to remain in touch with the Romish faithful. Here we should expect the reasoner to conclude, that therefore there must really be something in the priesthood and something in the Church, over and above its ceremonies and social worship. No, he baldly states that the Roman worship is "far less social" than the Protestant; and there his argument ends, contradicting its own premises.[1]

[14] W. Stubbs, *The Constitutional History of England*, iii.; *Select Charters, etc.*, p. 457, A.D. 1279: *Statute of Mortmain.*—Cf. *infra*, Appendix C, § 75 (1), pp. 593–595.
[15] Cf. *infra*, *History*, § 53, "Mistaken and Forgotten Data," Nos. (2), (3); and Appendix C, §§ 74–76, "History of Mortmain," etc.
[1] Hallam, *Constitutional History*, i. 163, 164: "The Romish scheme of worship, though it attaches more importance to ceremonial rites, has one remarkable difference from the Protestant, that it is far less social; and consequently the prevention of

VOL. I. K

From the same premises we should draw a different conclusion. It is that the priest is the embodiment of an institution, and that, where Catholicity and the priest are not, there is not this institution. We should infer that the priesthood, ministering what nothing else can supply, supplies for what other things cannot minister, and for some things which they can; that it makes up for the social character of other forms of worship, as well as for that of its own when constrained to do without it; while the sociability of other forms does only try to make up for the priest that is wanting, and leaves nothing behind when itself is not there.

Nor was it by the springs of "fascinating wiles," which, says the same imaginative writer, were touched " by the skilful hands of Romish priests, chiefly Jesuits," that " Protestant clergymen in several instances, but especially women of rank, became proselytes to a religion so seductive to the timid reason and sensible imagination of that sex; " and were brought over from the plain page of Scripture by means of " superstitious illusions," self-congratulation at the charm of their own folly, splendid vestments, incense, harmony and sculpture—not to mention something about " romantic tenderness," and some other romantic satisfaction enjoyed in " privation and suffering."[2] Such is the *ripieno*, or, in plain English, the padding of a page on the Catholic priesthood in a *Constitutional History of England*. It would seem that the scientific requirements for writing such history were not very exacting.

To those who prefer a plain page of Scripture, there will readily occur more than one description of the priesthood, to which is attributed the dispensing of the mysteries of God, the instructing in the law, the organizing of Christ's mystical body upon earth. And the place of the Church is not vacated till that of its priesthood, head and members, is left vacant, or else till their liberty is supplanted.

A State Church. Then will a State bureau be next in order; a national department of decorous exchange, giving patronage and receiving homilies; a sacerdotal college of imperial augurs, whether Russian, Greek, Gallican, or Anglican, presided over by the lay man or woman who happens to preside over the State. By this local and collegiate substitution for a universal priesthood which should be coextensive in its functions with natural society, the religious

---

its open exercise has far less tendency to weaken men's religious associations, so long as their individual intercourse with a priest, its essential requisite, can be preserved." The premises of the more or less " social " are involved in this one sentence.

[2] *Ibid.*, ii. 83, 84. Hallam is speaking here of the numerous conversions, which, he says, were " the news of every day," in the time of Charles I.

organization shrinks into one of those "bodies politic which have no point of unity of their constitution beyond the limits of the country in which they are situated." They "are in the nature of *collegia*, that is to say, bodies politic or societies wholly within the civil community, and therefore of a municipal nature."[3] And, according to Hooker's opinion, adopted by Mr. Gladstone in his work on State and Church,[4] the same persons make up both Commonwealth and Church in England,[5] the same heads being counted twice over to form two different local societies, coextensive with the length and breadth of the island.

When, therefore, Mr. Davis, expounding his theory of the "Day-Star of American Freedom," endeavoured so sympathetically to throw light upon the religious situation in Maryland, and explain the points at issue between the Jesuits and Lord Baltimore, he took a very lofty stand indeed when he stated the following universal proposition: "The Church of no Christian country," he wrote, "is prepared, either upon the Protestant or upon any other basis, to acknowledge the supremacy of the State, or surrender the jurisdiction it exercises over questions of faith and ethics—questions which touch the very heart of humanity, and connect us with the invisible world; but work, at the same time, such deep changes in states and empires." And, to show that the English Church, however much enslaved, has never acknowledged the supremacy of the civil magistrate, he quoted Magna Charta.[6] But he did not seem to notice that the Magna Charta, which begins by guaranteeing the liberties of the Church and then passes on to other liberties, just as London and other borough charters commence with the Church's franchises whereon to ground the rest,[7] was nothing less than a Catholic instrument of Catholic times, penned like so much English law by Catholic priests, and under their leadership extracted by the barons from a tyrant. When, after a score of solemn confirmations of the Great Charter, the priesthood was separated from its head, and the Church with its Christianity became fractional and local, then that fundamental article of Magna Charta was never renewed in favour of a mere national "college." There was no reason why it should be; since

marginalia: G. L. L. Davis; Magna Charta.

---

[3] G. Bowyer, *Commentaries on Universal Public Law*, p. 127.
[4] Gladstone, *The State in its Relations with the Church*, pp. 7, 8, 11, 12.
[5] G. Bowyer, *loc. cit.*
[6] G. L. L. Davis, of the Bar of Baltimore, *The Day-Star of American Freedom; or, The Birth and Early Growth of Toleration in the Province of Maryland*, etc., p. 16.
[7] Cf. 14 Edw. III., stat. i. c. 1.

there was no reason for liberty except in the lay head, to do as he or she liked; and a charter was not needed for that. It was only in the little assembly of freemen transplanted to Maryland that the provision of a free Church was repeated and Magna Charta saved, in the years 1639 and 1640.[8] This was the spirit which a modern historian, without any sign of disapprobation, calls cosmopolitan, " extra-national," or " supernational." [9] A Catholic would add something more—he would say "supernatural."

Besides being priests, the Jesuits are regulars. This, which is the second element in their definition, means that they follow a rule of life approved by the Catholic Church; and they are bound down by voluntary vows, some of which are common to other religious Orders, and some are special to themselves. A particular instance of these latter is their solemn act of self-dedication to the Church in any part of the world, as the Pope shall desire. Before them, the Orders of St. Francis and St. Dominic had penetrated into both hemispheres; and those of St. Augustine and Carmel, not to mention others with names perhaps less familiar, were to be found advancing the outposts of Christianity and civilization together. All such institutes represented in their proper place a reaction and reformation which was called for specifically by the age, and was furnished by themselves in the right time and manner. So too the Order or Company of Jesus was the embodiment of a famous reaction and reformation, that of a movement directed outwards against the Protestant reform, and reacting inwardly on many lines. Indeed, its captain, he of Pampeluna, received a papal commission somewhat wider than that of the two and thirty captains who were bidden to fight against none, great or small, save the King of Israel only. The militant commission conveyed to his Company equipped them with powers to evangelize infidels in every clime of the known world. It appointed them to various departments of education in school, college, and university. It distributed them liberally among the sacred ministries and works of charity, without guaranteeing at the same time either thanks or reward on this side of the grave. The reinforcements thus sent in to aid the militant Church drew the brunt of the attack upon themselves, as every land has witnessed.

When they allude to Jesuits and other regulars, we find that Protestant writers will become apologists for the Catholic Church,

---

[8] *Archives of Maryland : Proceedings, etc., of the General Assembly, etc.*, 1637-1664, pp. 40, 85, 96.—Cf. *infra*, History, § 54.
[9] F. W. Maitland, *Roman Canon Law in the Church of England*, p. 8.

§ 20. *SUBJECT OF THIS HISTORY* 133

and for " both the laity and the secular priesthood," as against these intrusive reformers; albeit these intrusive reformers came, as a rule out of the secular priesthood. It is said that they lent the Popes " a powerful aid towards subjecting both the laity and the secular priesthood;" and none were like " that new militia which the Holy See had lately organized," in carrying on with " restless activity " this and many other unholy avocations.[10] They excelled as " good and faithful janissaries of the Church." [11] *Defence of the secular priesthood.*

A glance at the fate and prospective final destiny of these " janissaries " serves a useful purpose in economic science. At every turn withstood and expelled by main force, the history and fate of the Jesuits show us that, as all social economy resolves itself ultimately into a prime motive power of finding bread and shelter, so all the economics of religious and intellectual disputation resolve themselves into an ultimate motive power of brute force to get the best of an argument. If these men have been, as is affirmed, " superior in learning and ability," and in their "emulous zeal, their systematic concert, their implicit obedience," then they have paid the price of what is never forgiven and what never ceases to provoke. We are told elsewhere that " in times of barbarous violence, nothing can thoroughly compensate for the inferiority of physical strength and prowess." [12] Now, though the writer of these words is speaking of the Middle Ages, we find that in our own times, which consider themselves the very pink of liberty and progress, the same supremacy of brute force is, we do not say the last, but oftentimes the very first, argument employed against the Jesuits. The difference is only between a medieval robber-baron, who probably died repentant, and a constitutional machine which *The ultimate and prime argument.*

---

[10] Hallam, *Constitutional History*, i. 224, 225.
[11] As this apparent antagonism between the secular priesthood and the Society of Jesus is made to appear, not only in the non-Catholic kind of literature just referred to, but in many documents from which subsequent pages of our History are taken, we may pass a comment on it here,—a comment not very different in substance from that which will occur below in another chapter, on a like semblance of antagonism between one regular Order and another: First, during the period which is covered by this volume, the Society of Jesus in England was made up chiefly of secular priests, who had chosen the life of the Jesuit Order. Secondly, any individuals or party in the general body of the secular priesthood who were disposed, for some particular purpose or out of some antecedent difficulty, to busy themselves with Jesuit interests and affairs, were also prone to put themselves forward as " the secular clergy," leaving quietly in the background the other priests who had nothing to do with them in furthering such purposes and plans. Thirdly, these latter clergymen, engaged peaceably in their duties, and constituting most properly a " secular clergy," need scarcely be looked for in the documentary literature cited, of which so much is contentious, and deals with the difficulties started by agitators.—Cf. *infra, History*, § 31 (2), pp. 303, 304.
[12] Hallam, *View of the State of Europe during the Middle Ages*, ii. 207, 208.

grinds and never repents. Where adversaries are in the majority, as in the Protestant empire of Germany and the Protestant republic of Switzerland, the Society of Jesus is banned; and any chance individual Jesuit who may come by is an outlaw, or is under the special supervision of the police, to be quenched like a firebrand.[13] If adversaries are in a minority, as in France and Italy, they may climb to power, as any determined little swarm can clamber over a big people; and then the Jesuits at least, and many other Orders too (including nuns), are flanked again by brute force, are relieved of their property and sent adrift. Nor, if one looks along the whole line, from the Gallican wing inside the Catholic Church to that other wing fading away undistinguishably in the farther distance, will he fail to find that pretexts for violence are never wanting, as if drawn from the heart of Catholicity itself, and that abettors are never lacking when sought for, even in the sanctuary. Thus we have heard the author of the *Apostate Protestant* quote a Watson on the Jesuits, or we may find a Bishop Burnet listening complacently to a Friar Walsh as "the honestest Papist the Bishop ever knew," because, says Burnet, "he was in all points of controversy almost wholly a Protestant."[14] And the liberal-minded Jonathan Boucher, preacher in Maryland, helps himself to a selection of Catholic writers whom he considers representative and commendable for something like a genuine Protestant ring.[15] Indeed, we scarcely find fault with this. Things within the homestead, as seen from the outside, may all appear to be equally bright or equally dark; and the criterion of distinction and preference for outsiders is apt to be something which either comes home to a sentiment, or at least proffers the compromise of a meeting half-way.

So, turning back to the point from which we started in this literary Introduction, we need spend no words on declaring our inability to appreciate the sneer of Mr. Doyle at Father White's narrative. We feel somewhat at a loss in face of such an assumption, as that, if a Jesuit wrote a memoir

---

[13] By the Kulturkampf legislation, till March, 1904, four classes of persons could be excluded by the police from the present German empire: professional vagabonds, paupers, criminals liable to extradition, and Jesuits. We quote the *résumé* as quoted from a German jurisconsult: "*Der Aufenthalt im Deutschen Reiche kann folgenden Personen polizeilich verboten werden:* 1. *gewohnheitsmässigen Bettlern und Landstreichern;* 2. *gänzlich Subsistenzlosen;* 3. *auszuliefernden Verbrechern;* 4. *Mitgliedern des Jesuitenordens.* (Professor Laband, *Reichsstaatsrechte,* Bd. i. Seite 159.) This last head included divers classes of cultured nuns.

[14] J. Milner, *Ecclesiastical Democracy detected,* p. 242, note; from Burnet, *History of his own Times,* i. 194–196.

[15] *Discourses,* p. 279, note; viz. Peter Walsh, Berington, [C.] Butler, O'Leary.

§ 20. SUBJECT OF THIS HISTORY

or writes a history, another gentleman is at once justified in rejecting it—rejecting it as false, while using it as true. A Jesuit might opine that, if it suits the gentleman to adopt such a postulate, it will suit himself to reject it. And the seeming implication that a Catholic, to be acceptable, must be colourless and discreetly dun, having no hue in his cheek or light in his eye, if thought worthy of being insinuated by a university man, is worthy of being brushed aside by a sensible man. Much as the Jesuit will profess his respect for the learned, the judicious, and the critical of this world, he does not imagine that any deliberate judgment of theirs requires him, if he wishes to speak, to put off what he is and to affect some manner whereof he is not. Lightly as a mundane judgment may pretend to value him, doling out oftentimes but a scant share of the respect so cheaply current in the world, nevertheless, when it comes to truth and sincerity, he does not think lightly of himself, nor profess there that spirit of effacement, nor take any vow of that poverty and destitution, which we have seen more than sufficiently instanced in the paragraphs above, from seventy authors of ten successive generations.

Hence, for reasons now passably clear, we must in general part company with history that is published, in order to publish history that is authentic. And, looking back wistfully at those golden vases of literature which we would gladly rescue from their contents, we must even rest satisfied with a plainer service, and present such entertainment as documents afford us. Without special difficulty, and certainly without disguise, we expect to make manifest from the documents the varied sides and bearings of our subject, which, while not too small to fill continents, is not too large to show its features in a colonial Maryland or Pennsylvania. *Barrenness of published literature.*

A theology is presupposed here, but it calls for no special statement. It is that which, they say, was discovered by some German pastors at Frankfort Fair, when they lighted upon a copy of the Jesuit *Constitutions*, and devoured the book with avidity. But, having duly digested it, they said they did not find anything very wrong there, except only the Roman religion. That is irremediable, and it is original with the Jesuit. It must be confessed from the beginning, for he will never outgrow the conditions of his origin.[16] *The theology presupposed.*

[16] Compare the reflections of Dr. O. Mejer, in his work, *Die Propaganda, ihre Provinzen und ihr Recht* (1852-53). This worthy Lutheran Professor of Canon

Nor, as to the philosophy of the subject, is there any need of discussing that here. Only it is considerably different from the principles of conduct which, as Mr. Lecky tells us, governed the life and policy of a well-known English moral philosopher, the same whom we heard a while ago descanting on Papist penal laws and Jacobitism. Dr. Paley claimed that he was "too poor to keep a conscience;"[17] so, clinging to the Thirty-Nine Articles, he kept his living instead. And then he wrote on morality. He became the very oracle of pure ethics. Very different, indeed, is the moral philosophy which governs a call to the Catholic priesthood or to the Orders. Here a man may already have enjoyed not only a living, but rank, wealth, or professional success, and that under the Thirty-Nine Articles themselves, or under the Presbytery; and yet he has been willing to make himself poor, in order to keep a conscience, and to keep it well. And, having given this pledge to fortune, to the world, and to God, or, in the case of the Jesuit, having also faced the history of a past with struggles, suppressions, expropriations, and slanders, in the teeth of every form of revolution except that of the law of conscience, he has not paid such a price, taken his post by such a standard of sacrifice, and appropriated that history as his own, only to turn round then and pay some other price, forfeiting all he has won by lapsing into the likeness of all he has spurned.

The philosophy.

There is a fixed policy throughout the subject of our history. And here we come to matters of great interest, which we shall derive, not so much from the formal *Constitutions* of the Order and the general rules obliging the members, as from the original papers of the chief authorities in the Society directing local action.

The policy expounded.

Finally, there is the carrying out of that policy by the local

Law, after devoting one volume of his work to the policy and history of the Propaganda, where his documents, including Urbano Cerri's pamphlet, present the Jesuits in a rather sorry light, conspicuous for no Christian virtue in their dealings with the Pope, the Propaganda, other regular Orders or the Roman Catholic Church generally, nevertheless commences his second volume with a Preface, or *Vorrede*, in which he lays marked stress upon a truth "never to be forgotten," that "the spirit, which the Catholic Church as such has maintained ever since she rejected the Reformation in the sixteenth century, is none other than the spirit of the Jesuit Order, whose strength lies precisely therein, that it is the embodiment of this spirit. Not for a moment," he continues, "must it be forgotten in these days that the two things are identical—*Roman Catholic* and *Jesuit*—"

"*Vor Allem davon nehmen wir Act, dass es* [*das Vorwort der Evangelischen Kirchenzeitung*] *anerkennt, wie der Geist, welchen die katholische Kirche als solche behalten hat, nachdem sie die Reformation des sechszehnten Jahrhunderts von sich gewiesen, kein anderer ist, als der Geist des Jesuiten-Ordens, dessen Macht eben darauf, dass er diesen Geist selber darstellt, beruhet. Die Identität von römisch-katholisch und jesuitisch soll man heute keinen Augenblick vergessen.*" Ibid., ii. p. v.

[17] W. Lecky, *History of England in the Eighteenth Century*, iii. 498.

sections of the Order, and by individuals in the exercise of their ministries. This execution, or putting of principle into practice, may have been right or wrong; it may have been properly or improperly conceived; it may have been conformable to the Society's plans or unconformable. Disorders at different times in the normal routine of corporate life and action have resulted from irregular administration on the part of local sections or of individuals. *Local administration.*

While tracing the general course of events and the peculiar variations introduced rightly or wrongly by individual initiative, we may observe that the Maryland settlement of America exhibited the first specimen of a political and social condition which is now largely normal in the world. It is the social condition of a non-Catholic environment, with the political condition of practical toleration. This novelty of circumstance was attended from the first with a series of alterations, not all for the best, in the life of a religious Order; and they were such as the Society had never known in Catholic surroundings. One very full episode was certainly of a kind which it had never passed through elsewhere. Whether it is to experience the like again, on an equal or a larger scale, is part of the perspective of the future. *Maryland a novel experiment.*

The fact is that the experiences of the Order, which in spite of its elasticity found itself so uncongenially placed, whether in the England or America of the time, were the same which have since become the record of every clime in our day. One great republic, then but undeveloped English Colonies, one large empire, then an insular Protestant monarchy, supply the data for judging now of a dozen European monarchies, empires, or republics, in the matter of general religious politics, and of the particular destiny that may wait on religious institutes. The formative period preparatory to an American Republic, which some maintain has Christianity for its basis, but which others declare is based on nothing of the kind, is no unfavourable field for observation on the life and destiny of one religious institute, which is not insignificant within those ample borders.

However that be, if this religious Order is fated to decay, its decline and fall do not seem likely to occur through agencies from without. Were such a final destiny probable, past defeats and temporary annihilation should have brought that about already. But they did not, since it is clear that men would not continue in these busy days to be fighting with the *Prospective destiny of the Order.*

138   INTROD. II.   THE ARCHIVES AND LITERATURE

defeated or strangling the departed. No; the possibility of decline must be limited to the alterations of internal life or the process of decay from within.

And thus from every side of right and wrong, of prosperity or decadence, we address ourselves, under the form of historical narrative, to a subject which has invited the study of many minds. That is to say, the principles of growth, preservation, efficiency, and longevity, as exhibited in this religious Order.

We shall endeavour to be objective and let facts speak for themselves. But the reason and method of things, which inquiring minds may expect from a member of the Order, cannot be omitted when called for. In that case they shall be introduced expressly to meet such demand as the passing occasion may seem to make upon the author.[18]

[18] At the moment of consigning these pages to the press, we are confronted with a noteworthy illustration of several statements formulated above : (p. 77) that what is good enough for Frenchmen ought in all conscience to be good enough for Englishmen, if it be to the prejudice of Catholicism ; (p. 134) that pretexts for doing violence to the Church are never wanting, as if drawn from the heart of Catholicity itself; (p. 117) that the opinions or guidance of an anti-Christian or atheist on Catholic matters are of more consequence than those of Catholics themselves, whether laymen or ecclesiastics.

On receiving a great deputation of Catholic parents from Leeds, Bradford, Sheffield, Birstal (March, 1906), who, as ratepayers, parents, and citizens, submitted the claims of their consciences to be regarded in the new Education Bill, Mr. Birrell, Liberal President of the Board of Education, after listening to full explanations, declined the responsibility of attempting to "give pleasure to everybody. He at once deprecated any notion of being able to perform such a task. He had to deal with the question as ecclesiastical differences had made it, and he had no control over those ecclesiastical differences. He could not do more than attempt to lay before Parliament, after full approval of his colleagues, some scheme which should at all events do justice all round, if that were possible. The fact was sometimes overlooked that those difficulties had arisen in other countries besides this ; and he did not know that they [Catholics] could derive any profound satisfaction from the way in which other countries had solved those difficulties. (A Member of the Deputation : They are not solved.) Mr. Birrell said that, at any rate, they would not like the State to solve them, as they had been attempted to be solved elsewhere. Those difficulties had arisen in other countries, which had been far longer Catholic than this country; and, therefore, they must not treat those difficulties as if they rose here for the first time, and as if they were not very far-reaching in their consequences." (*The Yorkshire Post* :—London Tablet, April 7, 1906, p. 551.)

This answer omitted all mention of the way in which the Protestant Empire of Germany had solved the question to the perfect satisfaction of Catholics, and in a manner not unknown to Englishmen (*The Times*, March 29, 1906 : "Catholicus"). But, leaving a liberal Protestant Empire aside, the Liberal Minister of England referred exclusively to such an anti-Christian Ministry as had brought up the question in Catholic France, and had cut it through with the "far-reaching consequences" of expelling the Catholic religious Orders, of confiscating their property, and of mobilizing in all directions the gendarmes and dragoons.

HISTORY

MARYLAND TILL 1645

CHAPTER III

ANTECEDENTS OF THE MARYLAND MISSION, 1580-1633

§ 1. The first English mission of the Jesuits. § 2. The motive of religion in colonial enterprises. § 3. The plan of Catholic migration in 1605. § 4. 1605. Andrew White: Vocation. § 5. The English Province. Formation of a novice. § 6. Father White as a Professor: 1609-1629. § 7. George Calvert and Newfoundland: 1624-1629. § 8. The Propaganda and the English Colonies: 1625-1631. § 9. Propaganda Relations continued: 1625-1631. § 10. Lord Baltimore and the clergy: the Puritans: 1627-1631. § 11. The Bishop, the laity, and Baltimore: 1628-1631. § 12. The crisis of the controversy: 1631. § 13. The friar and the Bishop: 1631. § 14. The Bishop and the monk on the laity: 1631. § 15. End of the laymen's controversy: 1631. § 16. The first Lord Baltimore's last acts: 1631, 1632. § 17. The charter for Maryland: 1632: (1) Dedication of places of worship; (2) Ecclesiastical patronage; (3) Elimination of Mortmain Statutes.

Manuscript Sources: (Brussels), Archives du Royaume, *Archives Jésuitiques.*—General Archives S.J.: *Anglia, Epistolæ Generalium; Anglia, Historia,* ii., iii., iv., vii.; *Anglia, Catalogi.*—(London), British Museum MSS., *Sloane,* 3662.—English Province Archives S.J., *Roman Letters,* ii.—Public Record Office, *Colonial Papers; Rolls and Patents; Transcripts from Rome,* xvii.—(Rome), Barberini Library, *Lettere.*—Corsini Library, cod. 283.—Propaganda Archives: *I America,* 259 ; *America Centrale,* I.; *Lettere,* 100, 101, 102, 129, 131, 132, 150, 297, 347 ; *Scritture riferite nei Congressi, Anglia,* I.—Vatican Archives, *Nunziatura d'Inghilterra,* 5.—Vatican Library, *Ottoboni,* 2536.—Stonyhurst College MSS.: *Anglia A.,* iii., iv., viii., ix.; A. I. 40.—Georgetown College *Transcripts.—* Maryland-New York Archives S.J., old Catalogues.

Published Sources: G. Bancroft, *History of the Colonization of the United States,* i.—*Calendars of State Papers, Colonial Series, America and West Indies,* i., iv.; London, Public Record Office.—*Constitutiones Soc. Jesu;* and *Institutum Soc. Jesu.*—(Maryland), *Archives of Maryland: Pro eedings of the Council,* 1636-1667.—H. Morus, *Historia Missionis Vice-Provinciæ, Provinciæ Anglicanæ Soc. Jesu.*—T. Scharf, *History of Maryland,* i.—J. G. Shea, *History of the Catholic Church within the Limits* *of the United States,* i.—J. Winsor, *History of America,* iii. : C. Deane, *Voyages of the Cabots;* E. E. Hale, *Hawkins and Drake;* W. W. Henry, *Sir Walter Ralegh;* R. A. Brock, *Virginia,* 1606–1689; B. F. de Costa, *Norumbega and its English Explorers.*

THE rise of the Society of Jesus in England dated from the year 1580. Its introduction into the new sphere of colonial activity took place in 1633, fifty-three years later. Between these two dates, the spirit of colonial enterprise, which had scarcely asserted itself before the earlier one, pressed forward and took possession of the Atlantic sea-board in America, from Newfoundland to Carolina, and to the isles of the Antilles farther south. Amid the various motives which were set forth as actuating these undertakings, that of propagating the Christian religion was given a prominent place. And, in theory, the dictates of religion and morality were so far respected, that the ostensible right of a Divine religion to be preached everywhere did not ostensibly deny the rights of aboriginal natives to keep a footing of their own somewhere. Whether for moral motives or prudential reasons, the natives did not suffer damage all at once.

With a religious society or Order of the Catholic Church, the necessities of colonists in point of religious practice and worship operated as a prime incentive to go out and lend assistance. And, with a missionary society, the claim of barbarous nations on the zeal and charity of priests commended a prompt acceptance of the invitation not to lag behind, when temporal and secular interests were running on so fast and far before. The Society of Jesus had already entered into every other uncultivated field of the world; and we find non-Catholic historians acknowledging without reluctance that it had served well as an advanced founder and accomplished manager of Catholic missions.[1] For the conduct of missionary life in particular, the Society had as much of a method as for the preservation of its own life in general, or for the right application of its principles in the most diversified conditions of places, times, and persons. Its missionary spirit and means were precisely an essential part of itself and its organization; and hence were always to be found wherever it existed.

In this chapter we propose to sketch the antecedents of the American foundation, in which the Jesuits took part; to touch on the

[1] " *Ein neuerer deutscher Geschichtschreiber* [Dr. P. Wittmann] *hat—nicht ohne einigen Schein—den Nachweis unternehmen können, dass an allen Puncten der katholischen Mission das rechte Leben erst mit den Jesuiten gekommen sei.*"—O. Mejer, *Die Propaganda,* i. 57.

characteristic principles of formation which qualified them as missionaries; to note the public events in England which cast their reflection on the Catholic enterprises of Newfoundland and Maryland; and especially as they did so through the instrumentality and personality of George Calvert, first Lord Baltimore. Some salient features in his course of action were determined by certain religious disputes in which he became involved. Probably before this controversy, but certainly during it, he was in close contact with members of the Society. Hence our topic is, at present, foreign colonies and Jesuit recruits; religion in the cold of a Newfoundland winter, and religion in the heat of a London controversy.

§ 1. It was late in the history of the English Reformation when the Jesuits first set foot in England. The fortieth year was just beginning to run its course since Henry VIII. had enacted the law for " abolishing diversity in Opynions," and had *1580.* imposed upon the nation six Catholic dogmas of his own particular choice. Imprisonment and fines, and ultimately the pains due to felony, were to be inflicted " for not confessing and communicating at the time comonly accustomed in the Churche of Englonde."[1] And thus the new department of Sacraments and oaths was instituted by the Tudor sovereign, and was added to the administration of the royal exchequer or of the royal executioner.

Forty years likewise had passed since the Society of Jesus had been founded by St. Ignatius of Loyola, and, offering itself to succour the militant Church, had received the approbation of the Holy See.

And it was just forty years since Edmund Campion had first seen the light of day in London, that now he came in 1580, as companion of Robert Parsons, to invade the old country *Parsons and* with the old faith, which had won himself back to its *Campion.* fold, and Parsons also; and in the same city where he had drawn his first breath, there in the course of a short year he was to heave his last sigh, hanged and butchered at Tyburn.[2]

Both of these brilliant men had known what it was to taste the sweets of time-serving and preferment. But, abandoning that decent policy of opportunism, they entered the Catholic Church, and then they entered the Society of Jesus. Parsons, ordained priest in Rome, offered his services for the Indian missions. Campion, ordained at Prague, became a Professor of Rhetoric and Philosophy. Both, like so many English, Irish, and Scotch Jesuits of the time, were prepared

[1] 31 Hen. VIII., c. 14.   [2] December 1, 1581.

to spend their lives in foreign parts, among either civilized or barbarous nations. But the Holy See judged that the exigencies of the moment called for the assistance of the Society in England. Pope Gregory XIII. despatched Parsons thither. Campion was summoned to bear the missioner company. And the two penetrated safely into the kingdom on June 12, 1580. From this time forward English Jesuits were always to be found working among the English population, as several intrepid Irish Jesuits were already braving death on the perilous Irish mission.

While the two Jesuit pioneers were running their short course of apostolic ministry in the island, the President of the English College at Rheims, Dr. William Allen, afterwards Cardinal, wrote *An Apologie and true Declaration of the Institution and endeuours of the two English Colleges, the one in Rome, the other novv resident in Rhemes; against certaine sinister informations giuen vp against the same.*[3] In this book Dr. Allen explains the policy of having called the Jesuits into the English field of work; and we cannot state his reasons better than in his own words. He says—

Dr. W. Allen's Apologie.

"These mens order in deede and rule of life is nevv, but their faith and doctrine is the same that our forefathers and al the Church had, and hath. They are hated of Heretikes, vvhich S. Hierom coumpteth a singular glorie."[4] Referring to the small contingent now in England, the Doctor proceeds: "Alas, poore men, thees same fevv that you there haue, might as vvel haue been sent to the Indes, or to any part of Turkey or Heathenesse, if it had been their lotte and their Superiors commaundement, as vvel as to you. For thither they go vvith no more danger then to England."[5] He then describes how they were demanded for the English mission, and how a general spirit of emulation rose, fostered by the example of the splendid work already accomplished through the colleges in Rheims, Doway, and Rome.

Ambition to serve in England.

"We therefore seeing, both before and novv these late daies, some euen of our Countrie sent to the Indes: motion vvas made to their Superiors, that those of our Nation might rather be employed vpon their ovvne Countrie: vvherevnto after good deliberation they did most charitably condescend, much moued by the example and profitable endeuours of the Priests of both the Colleges."[6]

"And to tell you al, vvhen it was once secretly bruted among

[3] W. Allen, *An Apologie*, etc., printed at Mounts, in Henault, 1581.
[4] *Ibid.*, f. 82. [5] *Ibid.*, f. 82ᵛ. [6] *Ibid.*, f. 83.

the Fathers (vvhom men call Iesuites) that hereafter some of the Order vvere like to be deputed, in times and seasons, for England, it is incredible to tell (but before Christ it is true) hovv it vvas sued and sought for, of diuers principal learned men, strangers, no lesse then of our ovvne, vpon their knees, vvith teares and affection exceeding extraordinarie: that they might haue the lotte, either to dispute vvith the Protestants in their Vniversities, or to die for the profession and preaching of their faith, in so noble a Countrie, vvhich they pitied to see deceiued vvith so improbable and barbarous heresie.

"Yea diuers learned men strangers, neither Iesuites nor Priests, seing at the same time the Scholers of the English Colleges giue their promis and profession so promptly and zelously, ... vvere much inflamed to hazard their person in the same spiritual aduenture. ... And being told, that the dealing in England (in such cases specially) for strangers vvas much harder then in the Heathen Countries, vvhere there vvere no such exquisite lavves against religion, as in the Countries reuolted: they replied, that they had no feare of dangers, nor deaths, nor miseries vvhatsoever, but that they vvould sell their ovvne persons to any seruitude, and for vvhat vvorke so euer. . . .

"But hauing so many of our ovvne Nation inflamed vvith the like holy desires, it vvas not thought needful nor meete easily to admitte the said strangers for this time: but rather to employ our ovvne, of the same Colleges specially, and of the Societie of Jesus.

Englishmen preferred to foreigners.

"Into vvhich order, because it is most agreeable to the Churches and our Countries seruice in this time, diuers of our Nation of al sortes haue yielded them selues, and novv the rather, for that they trust to be rather employed vpon their ovvne Countrie, then vpon the Indes or other Nations in like distresse. Trusting that so these companies, with the help of our zelous Countriemen in many places both at home and abrode, shalbe able to supply al vvants that may fall in England from time to time, by the deaths, executions, or enprisonments, of such as novv be, or hereafter shalbe, by vvhat extremitie so euer, restrained from the vvorke of our Lord." [7]

§ 2. In the twenty-third year of Elizabeth, 1580-1, a session of Parliament was closed with a usual act of grace and pardon as the Queen's acknowledgment of a Subsidy Act. The pardon covered

[7] W. Allen, *An Apologie*, etc., ff. 83-85.

every kind of crime with its penalties, from treason and hanging down to petty larceny and the stocks. But there were exceptions made in the pardon, and among them appeared the new sin and crime of not conforming to the Queen's religion.[1] And a special date was mentioned, since which time no offence committed on the score of Common Prayer and the Sacraments was to be condoned, in favour of any persons "lawfully indicted or convicted." This date was "the twentieth of June last past."[2] The 20th of June, 1580, was just within eight days after the actual landing of Father Parsons at Dover, and the invasion of England by him and Campion.

1580-1581. The crime of non-conformity.

The weight of persecution bearing down so heavily on the Catholic nobility and gentry, as well as the searching discrimination practised against them under every form, made some of the victims willing to leave the country; and, as they were numerous still, the Queen and her Council appeared willing to let them go. Later on it was not so, especially under James I. They and the constant fines exacted of them were coveted and wanted as a perennial fund of "debts" to the King, and of taxes to the country. But in the time of Elizabeth the spur of persecution, when applied to some bold spirits like Sir Thomas Gerrard, Sir George Peckham, and others, would seem to have been among the first incentives that started the colonizing enterprises of Great Britain. This we infer from a clear passage of Father Parsons, in a document of 1605, soon to be quoted.[3] And from a State Paper we gather that Sir Humphrey Gylberte himself, who, as far back as 1574, stood at the head of all these undertakings, was hand and glove with the "Papists" in looking for relief to a new world.

The incentive for Catholics to look abroad.

In 1574 the first steps had been taken by Gylberte, Peckham, and others towards discovering and claiming settlements in the northern parts of America. Such claims were to be in the lands of savage and heathen people, whom it was proposed to reclaim from idolatry to Christianity; and the enterprise was not to prejudice the rights of any Christian prince or friendly country. The interests of trade, national honour and glory, with other similar motives, were put forward. In due time letters patent were issued to Sir Humphrey Gylberte, of Compton, county Devon, and to his heirs and assigns (June 11, 1578).

Colonial enterprises of Gylberte, Peckham, etc. 1574-1578.

[1] Cf. *supra*, Introduction, Chap. II. § 13, pp. 89, 90.
[2] 23 Eliz., 1580-1, c. 16, § 11.
[3] *Infra*, § 3, p. 154, "Thirdly."

We quote one passage from these patents, as showing the reference made to Papists in the clauses of Gylberte's charter. It is to be observed that, at this time, the Catholics who refused to conform, and were suffering pains and penalties in consequence, had during the last seven years been subjected to a very special inquisition, lest, not conforming, they should also escape by flight. This new and special restraint was devised by the "*Acte agaynst Fugytyves over the Sea;*" in virtue of which Act persons who did not "return and repent," and "acknowledge their faulte," and "submit themselves to the Queenes Majesties Obedyence, and fullye reconcyle themselves to the true Religion established by Order of Lawe within this Realme," and make public satisfaction by "shewing their Reconciliation openly" and "comyng to the Devyne Servyce by Order of this Realme appoynted, and receavyng the Holy Comunion,"—all such recalcitrants and delinquents became disfranchised, their lands and goods being forfeited, and their families being left at the mercy of Chancery.[4] Now the hard case of these recusants and the interests of Sir Humphrey Gylberte himself were directly met by a provision conceived in his charter, derogating from this statute in particular; or, as the clause reads: "The statute or Actes of Parliament made against fugytyves or against such as shall departe, remayne or contynue out of our Realme of England without licence, or anye other Acte, statute, lawe, or matter whatsoever to the contrary in any wise notwithstandinge."[5] *Gylberte's patent providing a refuge for recusants.*

Four years later, after the failure of a first attempt, this same Sir Humphrey Gylberte, of Compton, county Devon, made articles of agreement with "Sir Thomas Gerrard of Bynne, county Lancaster, and Sir George Peckham of Denham, county Bucks." He communicated to them the privileges of his former charter, adding special stipulations, under the date of June 6, 1582. While this contract was maturing, an informer submitted to the Secretary of State, Sir Francis Walsingham, a "secret advertisement" to the following effect: "There is a mutterynge among the papists that Sir Humfraye Gylberde goithe to seeke a newefounde lande; Syr George Peckham and Syr Thomas Gerarde goithe with hym. I have harde it said among the papistes that they hope it wyll prove the best journeye for England that was maide these fortie yeares."[6] *The Gylberte, Gerrard, Peckham venture. 1582.*

---

[4] 13 Eliz., 1571, c. 3.—Cf. *supra*, Introduction, Chap. II. § 13, p. 90.
[5] Public Record Office, *Patent Roll*, 21 Eliz., part 4, membr. 8, 1578, June 11.
[6] *Ibid., Dom. Eliz.*, vol. 153, No. 14, 3 pp. 4to, p. 3, 1582, April 19.

Gerrard and Peckham presented in their own name some articles of petition to the Secretary, Sir Francis Walsingham. They pray that certain classes of persons may be allowed to go with them. Among six items, the first mentions the "families" of persons, whose names shall be put down "in a booke indented made for that purpose;" and that such "families," no less than themselves, may come and go. The second item asks that "the recusantes of abilitie that will travell as beforehande maie have libertie, uppon discharge of the penallties dewe to her Majestie in that behallffe, to prepare themselves for the saide voiage. Item, that other recusantes" also, who are not able to pay the fines and penalties due for the practice of their religion, shall still be allowed to go, "untill souche tyme as God shall make them able to paie the same." And the last point is: "Item, that the xth [10th] person which they shall carrie with them shalbe souche as have not any certainetie whereuppon to lyve or maintaine themselves in Englande."[7] This last clause means liberty for a tenth part of the whole company to consist of servants or able-bodied retainers.

Recusant gentry and dependants for the Colonies.

The intentions of Sir Humphrey Gylberte were liberal towards gentlemen adventurers, towards future tenants and lessees, and not least in behalf of the Church, of schools and charities. After mentioning "thirteen Councillors to be chosen by the people," he requires that every minister, of whatsoever degree, shall give yearly out of his portions the full twentieth part of his whole living, and every landlord, "beinge a temporall man," shall give for ever the fortieth part of his land, to be indifferently appointed toward the maintenance of maimed soldiers, and of learning, lectures, scholars, and other good and godly uses, in such sort as shall be from time to time thought most meet, "by the consente" of the chief magistrates and law-makers of those countries; not employing the same to any other end than as is hereby meant. Then every country parish shall contain just three English miles square; and the church is to be in the middle thereof. Every minister is to have his tithes, and three hundred acres of good land besides, which shall be as near to the church as conveniently may be, with allowance of common of pasture in the waste, and other privileges. Thus "the said rates before specified" are "to be established forever without alteration for the mynysters; the lorde of the parishe beinge alwaies charged to alott oute of his owne land, in sorte as is aforesaid, the glebe land before specified, at

Gylberte's liberality towards religion, education, and charity.

---

[7] Public Record Office, *Dom. Eliz.*, cxlvi., No. 40; without date or signature.

the fyrste devidinge of the parishes; which, beinge so appoynted, shall alwayes remayne in fee symple to the church, subiecte to noe mans alteration; neither yett shall the clergy have power to lease any of the same, other then for the present incumbent his lief [life] at the farthest; nor soe neither to be good in lawe, but with reseruation of soe mutch rent, as it shalbe adjudged worth by the iudgemente of twelve of the beste sorte of his parishioners. And no mynyster to have at one tyme above one benefice, nor any at all excepte he be resident thereon at the leaste sixe whole monethes in the yeare." Every bishop shall have ten thousand acres in one seigniory, two thousand of which are to be "tythe free;" and an archbishop shall have two seigniories of ten thousand acres each, with three thousand for his demeanes tythe-free.

At the commencement of the charter there is the power conveyed to make laws, of which it is said: "And also so as they be not agaynste the true Christian faythe or religion now professed in the Church of England."[8] *Gylberte's profession of religion.*

In the following year, 1583, Gylberte with a little fleet was in Newfoundland; and, in the presence of adventurers and sailors from many nations who were already there before him, he took formal possession of the country in the Queen's name. He then enacted three laws, of which the first provided "for religion, which in publique exercise should be according to the Church of England."[9]

Gylberte sailed from Newfoundland to Norumbega, an undefined country on the coast of Maine.[10] He re-embarked for England, but went down with all hands on the high seas. Now there followed a succession of maritime enterprises, which resulted finally in establishing a colonial empire for Great Britain. The same motives in general which had led Spain and Portugal on their course of appropriation and conquest stirred the breasts of Englishmen, who were separated from those *The founding of a British colonial empire.*

---

[8] Public Record Office, *Close Roll*, 24 Eliz., part 7, m. 8: "Writing indented" of Sir Humphrey Gylberte, 1582, July 9.

[9] R. Hakluyt, *Principal Navigations*, etc., iii. 151.—Cf. J. S. M. Anderson, *History of the Church of England in the Colonies and Foreign Dependencies of the British Empire*, i. 71.—Cf. also J. A. Doyle, *The English in America*, p. 66. Except for the romantic story of Gylberte's adventures, derived by these writers from Hakluyt, the general features of this first great colonizing expedition may be scanned in the *Calendars of State Papers*, Public Record Office; *Colonial Series, America and West Indies*, vols. i. and iv., *ad init.*, according to the catalogue as given in the Register and Notice of Sources, *supra*, Introduction, Chap. I. § 2, p. 4. As may be noted in our text, there is a difference between the language of Gylberte's charter and that of Gylberte's law, in defining the religion to be exercised.—Cf. *infra*, § 17, (1).

[10] B. F. De Costa, *Norumbega and its English Explorers*, in J. Winsor, *History of America*, iii. 171.

nations in faith, were rendered emulous of them by ambition, and hostile by national policy. Especially jealous of Spain, whose star was so soon to decline, Englishmen began a series of maritime adventures, largely piratical on the Spanish main, but brilliantly successful elsewhere in founding a new nation. Courtiers like Sir Walter Ralegh, captains and pirates like Hawkins and Drake, buccaneers who could vie with Cromwell himself in preaching and praying while cutting men's throats,[11] did more than overbalance the declining energies of that comprehensive Spanish empire, which had taken in the new world from Chili to New Mexico and Florida. And, on the other side, they kept pace with the intrepidity of those French colonists to the north, who now sailed over the ocean to establish a New France amid the snows and the Indians of Canada.[12]

So rapid was the development of colonial activity, when the first English settlements had been made, that, in the course of eighty years from the time of Gylberte's adventures, fifty-nine charters were granted by the British Crown for what had cost the British Crown nothing.[13] The settlements so authorized were seen to range from the northern latitude of the Gulf of St. Lawrence to the equatorial line at the mouth of the Amazon river, comprising territories as diverse in climate, soil, and size, as New England and Barbados. Nor was the unfailing source of African slavery passed over in the gracious grants of indolent sovereigns or in the pious solicitude of a Lord Protector Cromwell. Guinea in Africa figures grimly aside of Guiana, the Sugar Islands and the northern colonies in America.

Fifty-nine charters in eighty years.

To this period, then, belongs the settlement of Virginia, under the patent of 1606; the establishment of divers colonies in New England, beginning in 1620, and including within ten years Plymouth, Salem, Massachusetts Bay, New Hampshire, and Maine; then the foundation of Maryland in 1633–1634, followed within a couple of years by Connecticut and Rhode Island in 1636. More to the south, French Huguenots negotiated for Carolina in 1630. And to the same period a number of West Indian islands attach themselves; among which, just to mention some names appearing in our pages, there were St. Christopher, Barbados, Martinique, Guadeloupe, Antigua, Montserrat, besides a score of others. They were granted to the Earl of Carlisle on July 2, 1627.[14]

The order of settlement.

---

[11] E. E. Hale, *Hawkins and Drake*, in J. Winsor, *History of America*, iii. ch. ii.
[12] J. G. Shea, *History of the Catholic Church in U.S.*, i. 217.
[13] *Calendars of State Papers, A. & W. I.*, i. Preface, p. viii., note.
[14] The fluid condition of nomenclature in which these islands floated may be

No one of these islands seems to have been appropriated as yet by any other Power.

Some of the original charters merit a moment's attention on account of the religious motives set forth in behalf of colonial expansion.

Letters patent were issued by James I. to Sir Thomas Gates, Richard Hakluyt, Prebendary of Westminster, and others, granting them licence to lead out a colony and found a plantation in Virginia and other parts of America. The King commended their project, which might by the providence of Almighty God hereafter tend to the glory of His Divine Majesty, in propagating the Christian religion among people as yet living in darkness, etc.[15] The patent was dated April 10, 1606. *Religious clauses in the patents. Virginia, 1606.*

It was just at this date that the Gunpowder Plot of the previous November was being exploited against the Catholics. The Earl of Salisbury was a prime manipulator of the whole prosecution. Now to this same Robert Cecil, Earl of Salisbury, with many others,[16] an enlargement of the foregoing Virginia franchise was granted, at their request, on May 23, 1609; and we find that the simple motive of religion in the former charter was treated to a strong infusion of anti-Popery. And thus it is served out in the following pious reflections, at the close of a long roll of eight membranes—

"And lastly, because the principall effect which Wee cann desier or expect of this Action is the conversion and reduction of the people in those partes unto the true Worshipp of God and Christian Religion, in which respect Wee would be lothe that anie person should be permitted to passe that Wee suspected to affect the superstitions of the Churche of Rome, Wee doe hereby declare that it is oure Will and pleasure, that none be permitted to passe in anie voiage from time to time to *Anti-Popery clauses. Virginia, 1609.*

---

seen in the *Patent Roll,* 14 Car. II., part 20, in letters patent to Francis Lord Willoughby, November 18, 1662, where a list is given of the Caribbee islands in this form: "St. Christopher's *alias* St. Aristovall, Granado *alias* Granada, St. Vincent, St. Lucy *alias* St. Lucre, Barbidas *alias* Barbadoes *alias* Barbados, Mittalania *alias* Martenico, Dominico, Margalanta *alias* Marigallanta *alias* Marigante, Desseada, Todo Fantes *alias* Todo Santes, Guardalupe, Antigoa *alias* St. Antigoa, Montserat, Redendo, Barbido *alias* Barbada, Mevis, St. Bartholomew's *alias* St. Bartholomeo, St. Martin's *alias* St. Martin, Angilla *alias* Angvilla, Sembrera *alias* Sembroa *alias* Essembrera, Enegada *alias* Enegeda, and Estatia, and all other islands," etc. This list of islands is identical with that alluded to in our text, as conveyed in the original grant to the Earl of Carlisle, July 2, 1627.—Compare *Calendar, A. & W. I.,* ii. No. 387; i. p. 85.—For a sketch of the Lesser Antilles, see *infra,* § 31, from the Propaganda Archives.

[15] Public Record Office, *Patent Roll,* 4 Jac. I., part 19.

[16] There is a list of earls, lords, knights, city companies, etc., occupying three membranes of the roll.

be made into the saide countrie, but such as firste shall have taken the oath of suprematie; for which purpose Wee doe by theise present give full power and authoritie to the Tresorer for the time beinge, and anie three of the Counsell to tender and exhibite the said Oath to all such persons as shall at anie time be sent and imploied in the said voiadge. Although expresse mention, etc. In witness whereof, etc. J. r. [Jacobus Rex] apud—xxiii. die maij. Per ipsum Regem." [17]

In the following year, 1610, a grant was made of the southern and eastern parts of Newfoundland to adventurers of London and Bristol; and the identical formula was used on the score of religion, as in the Virginia patent just quoted. But, with regard to savages, a parenthesis contained the expression of a doubt whether any such heathen were to be found in most parts of the said island.[18]

Newfoundland, 1610.

A confirmation of the Virginia charter, dated March 12, 1612, contained an improvement upon the foregoing documents; and the list of adventurers became much more imposing. Instead of merely lay lords, knights, and merchants, such as had been speculating heretofore, there now appeared also lords spiritual and ladies: " George lord Archbishopp of Canterbury," then " William lord Bishopp of Duresme [Durham], Henry lord Bishopp of Worcester, John lord Bishopp of Oxonford," with earls, countesses, etc. Aliens and all kinds of strangers might be admitted to the full franchise of the colony. But, instead of only the oath of supremacy, King James's oath of allegiance could also be administered. This was an additional religious test, impossible for the Catholic conscience. Hence, while all nationalities and religions were permitted to take root in Virginia, the English native, if a Catholic, was excluded by the barrier of a double oath. The text runs to this effect, that the Treasurer, his deputy, or any two others of the Council, " shall have full power and authoritie to minister and give the oath and oathes of supremacie and allegiaunce, or either of them, to all and euery person and persons, which shall att anie time and times hereafter goe or passe to the said Colonie in Virginia." [19]

Virginia, 1612.

Additional anti-Popery oath.

These may suffice as specimens of the religious policy and motives put forward in the early and typical charters.[20] A distinct

[17] P. R. O., *Patent Roll*, 7 Jac. I., part 8, 1609, May 23.
[18] *Ibid.*, 8 Jac. I., part 8, 1610, May 2.
[19] P. R. O., *Patent Roll*, 9 Jac. I., part 14, 1612, March 12.
[20] Compare G. E. Ellis, *The Religious Element in the Settlement of New England*, in J. Winsor, *History of America*, iii. ch. vii.

variation will be seen in the letters patent of June 20, 1632, drawn up from a Catholic point of view for the colony of Maryland. Meanwhile a Catholic colony for Norumbega had been projected in 1604–5, just a little before the date of the first Virginian charter given in the series above. *The Maryland charter, 1632, a variation from the type.*

§ 3. Father Robert Parsons, stationed as Rector of the English College in Rome, was consulted by a Mr. Winslade on the subject of a Catholic migration to the new world. The formation of the plan submitted must have been about 1604, and the occasion, no doubt, was the utter disappointment of all hopes entertained by the distressed Catholic body when Elizabeth died. These hopes had been dashed to the ground by the conduct of her successor, James I.

As to Mr. Winslade, there was a Catholic gentleman, "Wyslade," alluded to by the Attorney-General, Sir Edward Coke, in his prosecution of Father Garnett, some twelve months after the date of Parsons' letter. In the course of his sweeping declamations against the Pope, the Spaniards, and Garnett, the Attorney-General spoke of a great navy that was to be despatched by the King of Spain. Then he went on to say: With the Spaniards "was a consultation holden, whereof was the Cardinall of Austria, the Duke of Medina, and others, amongst whome was one Wyslade, an Englishman, but with a Spanish and traitorous heart," etc.[1]

Winslade's plan regarded rich Catholics and poor. One thousand of the poorer sort, husbandmen, labourers, and craftsmen, should muster in some foreign port, Catholic princes being appealed to for assistance, and contributions being solicited from the pulpits of the Continent. The substantial and rich Catholics should sell their lands and turn over the proceeds. And, in the first and last place, the object should be that of converting barbarous people to the faith of Christ. These elements of the project we infer from the paper which Father Parsons in reply dated the 18th of March, 1605, and entitled, " My iudgement about transferring Englishe Catholiques to the Northen partes of America for inhabitinge those partes and converting those Barbarous people to Christianitie." [2] The sum and substance of this paper was well expressed by Father Christopher *Winslade's plan of migration.* *Parsons' criticism. March 18, 1605.*

---

[1] Cf. H. Foley, *Records*, iv. 169, in the document cited at length from the British Museum MSS., Add. 21, 203, Plut. ciii. F, "Papers relating to the English Jesuits."

[2] Stonyhurst MSS., *Anglia A*, iii. document 52, ff. 109, 110; contemporary copy, endorsed by a contemporary hand: "A copye of f. Persons answere to Mr. Winslade touching Norimbega."

Grene, who read more in the document than appears on the face of it. Entering it among Parsons' letters, he wrote: It " shows the plan proposed by him [Winslade] to be morally impossible, to wit, that a whole body of English Catholics [3] should migrate to some parts of the West Indies not yet occupied by Europeans, where they should have the free exercise of the Catholic Religion, and should propagate the faith among barbarians." [4]

Father Parsons first pays a merited compliment to the author of the plan, for " the good and godly endes proposed by hime and diuerse good particularities of meanes and helpes, whereby to arriue to these endes, discreetly and piously put downe." Nevertheless, he adds that, " for the executione and puttinge in vse the enterpriz it self," he finds many great difficulties, which seem to him " scarsly to be superable; as amonge others these that folowe."

First, the King and Royal Council would never allow of it, apprehending the same as not only dishonourable to them, but dangerous also. Hence no permission would be granted to go forth, to sell lands, to make over money, and the like. Secondly, to induce the Catholics to go would be a difficult matter; for the rich would disdain to hear of leaving their wealth, commodities, and country; and the poorer dependent sort would be of small consequence, without the rich on whom to rely.

Parsons' reasons.

Thirdly, if the proposal were first made known to foreign and friendly princes, without taking counsel at home, Catholics would be much offended " to haue, as it were, theire exportatione to barbarous people treated with Princes in thire name, without theire knowledge and consente; the hereticks also would laughe and exprobrate the same vnto them, as they did when Sr George Peckhame and Sr Thomas Gerrarde, about xx yeares gone, should haue made viage to Norembrage by the Queene and counselles consente, with some euacuatione of Papistes, as then they called them; which attempte became presently most odiouse to the Catholicke partie."

Fourthly, prejudice would be done to the cause of Catholicity in England, by the diminishing of the Catholic body, and by exasperating the public authorities, who would proceed to tighten the restraints upon priests, and interfere more effectually with Catholic scholars passing over to the foreign seminaries. Fifthly, Father Parsons finds difficulties in the foreign elements which enter the

---

[3] " *Catholici pleriq. Angli.*"
[4] Stonyhurst MSS.; Christopher Grene, S.J., *Collectanea*, part i. f. 337*b*.—Grene died at Rome, November 11, 1697, æt. 68.

plan, such as the mustering of a thousand husbandmen, labourers, and craftsmen, in some foreign port; sixthly, in the jealousy of the King of Spain; seventhly, in the consequent incapacity of other Catholic princes to give help, if Spain did not approve. Then, to have the cause of English Catholics preached as an object of charity from the pulpits of the Continent would be open to many objections from other sides. Lastly, the paper closes in these terms—

"Finally, what thire successe would be amongest those wilde people, wilde beasts, vnexperienced ayre, vnprouided lande, God onely knoweth. Yet, as I sayd, the intentione of conuertinge those people liketh me soe well and in soe high a degree, as for that onely I would desire my self to goe in the iorney; shuttinge my eyes to all other difficulties, if it were possible to obtayne it; but yet, for that wee doe not dele here for our selves onely, but for others also, wee moste looke to all other necessary circumstances; whereof the first and of moste importance are, in my opinione, that the matter be broken in England and Spain; wherein for many reasons I may not be the breaker; but, if these ii [two] were once optayned, I would then be willinge to doe in Rome what lieth in me; and this is all that I canne say in this matter. Christ Jesus keepe you in health; this 18th of March, 1605." [5]

§ 4. Eight months after Father Parsons had written the foregoing document, a new direction was given to the course of events by the Gunpowder Plot, and by the machinery which the Government put in motion against the entire Catholic body, old and young and of both sexes. At this date, not a few of the threads that go to weave our American history may be picked up for future use. Father Andrew White, a young secular priest, twenty-six years of age, being expelled from England, entered the Society. George Calvert, subsequently first Lord Baltimore, was already somewhat conspicuous in the public service, under the high patronage of Sir Robert Cecil, who, like his father, Lord Burleigh, was a deadly political enemy of the Catholics and the Jesuits. Married to Anne Mynne, of a Hertfordshire family, Sir George was blessed about this date by the birth of a son and heir, "who was cristened by the name of Cecill, but was afterwards confirmed by the name of Cæcilius." [1] The

Andrew White, secular priest, 1605.

George and Cecil Calvert.

---

[5] For full text, see *Documents*, I. No. 1.
[1] British Museum MSS., *Sloane*, 3662, ff. 24-26: on the two first Lords Baltimore,—a paper drawn up in 1670, probably by Cæcilius himself, or under his direction.

Christian name so adopted from such a patron's surname might be thought to presage no friendly relations with Jesuits or with Catholics, on the part of this future founder of the Maryland colony. While Cæcilius passed on through his early education, and before the date when his name occurs again, he formed at Oxford a new connection **John Lewger, minister.** with a Protestant minister, John Lewger, whose official career in Maryland, after his conversion to the Catholic Church, gave occasion for quite a lively episode in American affairs. However, Lewger and Cæcilius will not cross our path now for a good span of years. The first and most important personage at present is Andrew White, whose earlier career as a Jesuit opens a page full of instruction on the methods and customs of the Society. Next to him moves in the busy round of public administration or of private management the prominent figure of Sir George Calvert, on whose conversion to the Catholic faith followed the title of Baron of Baltimore as a public honour, and the title to an American province as a private estate.

Andrew White was born in London about the middle of Queen Elizabeth's reign, in 1579. At the age of sixteen or thereabouts he **White's antecedents.** entered St. Alban's College, Valladolid, one of the English seminaries founded by Father Parsons to supply priests for England. At a later period he was in the college at Seville,[2] another of the English seminaries founded by the indefatigable Parsons. Then in the year 1605, being twenty-six years of age, he was engaged in the ministry on the English mission, when he was caught up in the storm occasioned by the Plot, and, with forty-five other priests, had to leave the kingdom. Having applied for admission into the Society, he was accepted, and was apparently designed to be one of the "foundation-stones" of the new novitiate at Louvain, which was opened in the following year, 1607.

Two autograph letters of his belong to this period; they bear the same date of October 27, 1606.[3] They are addressed respectively to Father Parsons and to Father Gerard, both of whom are in Rome; and the latter is requested, with much persuasive language, to further **White's letters. 1606.** the object which, in more official guise, is being submitted to the former. He writes on behalf of his friend, Father Richard Greene, who has petitioned for admission into the Society; but whereas others, who petitioned later, have been accepted,

---

[2] White to Gerard, October 27, 1606: as *infra*, note 4.
[3] Stonyhurst MSS., *Anglia A*, iii. documents 69, 70, ff. 138, 139: White to Parsons and to Gerard ("Garret"), Rome.

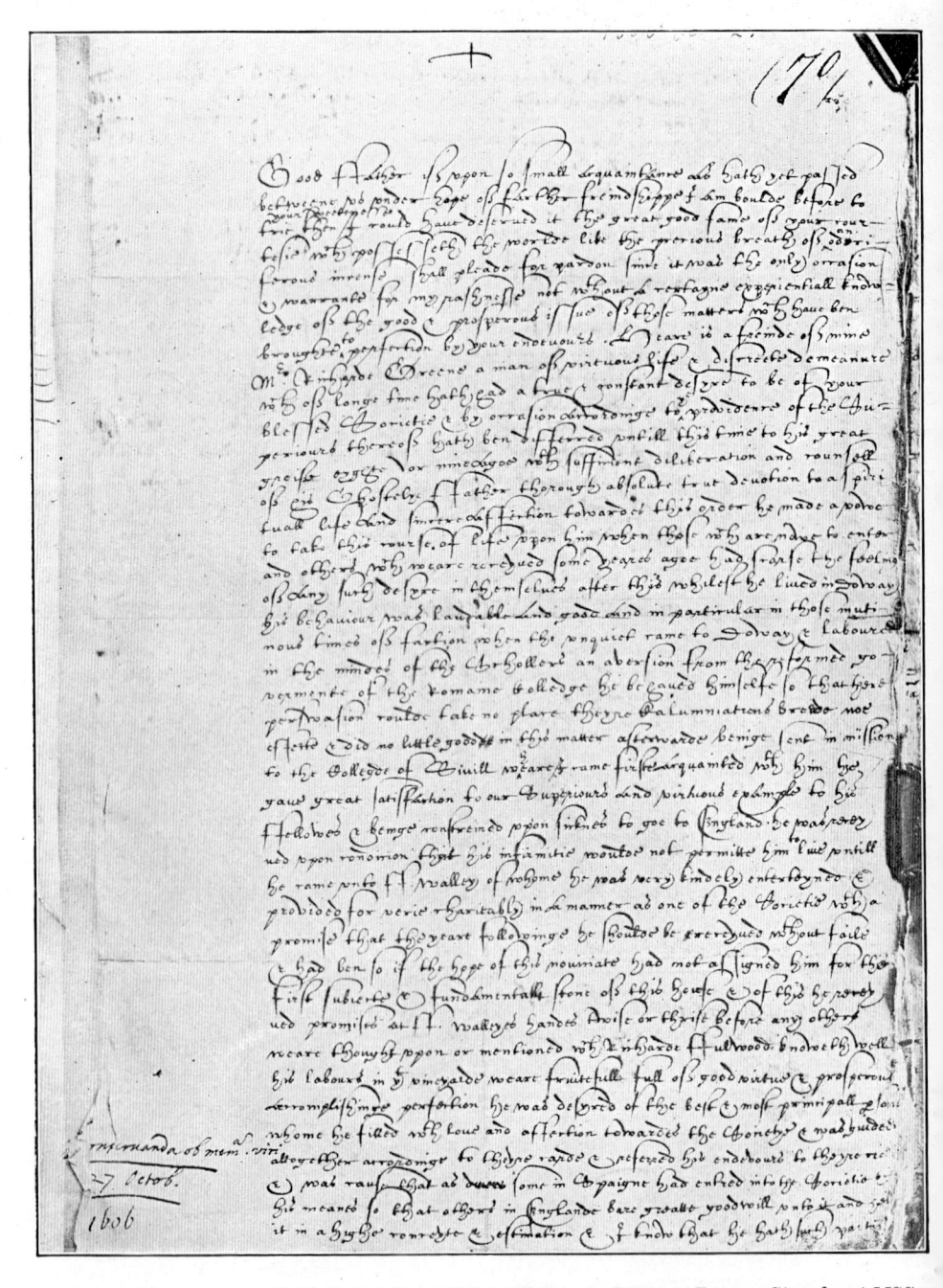

Father A. WHITE, (Louvain?), 27 October, 1606, to Father J. GERARD, Rome. Stonyhurst MSS., Anglia, A, iii. 70, f. 139. With Father CHR. GRENE's (?) note in the margin. (⅔ scale of the original.)

[To face p. 157.

and Father White is evidently one of the favoured ones soon to be admitted, Father Greene is still left out of the list. The value of these two letters consists rather in the glimpse which they afford us of the young man's character. If we knew no more about him than what they betray, we should still be justified in drawing some conclusions from the manifest pains taken in their composition, the consideration and reverence shown in the care with which they are so beautifully written out, the youthful exuberance of fancy rather beyond the limits of an epistolary style, and the expansion of sentiment, warm, courteous, and religious—certainly a worthy combination of qualities in a young man. We must not omit to adorn our text with one of these letters. Though the longer one to Father Gerard furnishes more lines of a personal portrait than the shorter official one to Father Parsons, we merely affix here a specimen in facsimile of White's first page to the former,[4] and we subjoin the other at once. He says—

☩

"REUEREND FATHER,

"Had not matters fallen out crosse since the receypt of your last comfortable letter, wherein you yielded such comforte and sweetenesse vnto the suite of my dearest freinde as was beyond expectation, I thinke I shoulde haue lett more time passe, before that eyther I rendered thankes for this fauour obteyned or woulde haue ben boulde to haue stopped the line of your more serious imploiments with an other letter of like efforte. But now pardon me Father, if I follow the vaine of goulde, where I see the colour glitter in the sandes, if I hope for sommer when I see store of blossomes one early tree, if I expecte the center when I feele my desyres to be in strongeste motion drawinge to the ende of theyre pretenses with a speed[y] foote of execution: and lastely if, by these pledges of charitie I lastly receyued,[5] I am boulde to entreate you for a perfecte accomplishmente of a virtuous contente. Mr. Greene hath spoken with Father Baldwin after the consolation he had from you; but findinge himselfe to be putt of vntill an other time hath geuen himselfe to excessiue greife, altogether vncapable of comforte, vnlesse your charitie assiste his desolation.

To Parsons. Oct. 27, 1606.

---

[4] See reproduction opposite.—See entire letter, *Documents*, I. No. 2: White to Gerard, October 27, 1606.—Cf. also Foley, *Records*, iii. 268, 269. *Ibid.*, 270, is a portion of the letter to Parsons given here in our text.—An indication of [Father Christopher Grene's] industry in saving the documents now extant may be seen in the marginal note of the reproduction : " To be preserved for the memory of the man."
[5] Possibly including the acceptance of himself as a candidate.

He hath gone longest with his desyres, eyght or nine yeares, since with consell of ghostely Father he made a vowe of this Order, and hath liued euer since with greate virtue and good example. Three yeares since he was in sicknes receued vnder the condicion that he died, though he him selfe doubteth whether it weare absolutely or no.[6] He hath ben occasion that other haue embraced and entred into the same religion [*i.e.* religious Order]. In Englande his labours where happie and effectuall in gaininge soules and breedinge in them religious spirittes and encreasinge the number of the Societies freindes. F. Walley[7] loued him well and promised him to receyue him, the Christemas was tweluemonth after he came to Englande. Then, the hope of this noviciate[8] beinge conceiued, he was assigned by F. Walley and Father Antonie,[9] and so, as is to be thought, by the grauest Fathers in Englande, to be the very firste for this place. He had the day assigned him for his departure, but, thinges heare not beinge in a readinesse, he was stayed and soone after imprisoned, which without doubt doth not a little aduaunce his good deseruinges. I beseech you, good Father, sende some solid and effectuall confortes to the alleuation of his greifes, to the encrease my ioy, to adde obligations of duety towardes you, that he may eyther be receyued now, or else may haue a promise to be the next that entreth. Otherwise this springe he intendeth to goe to Roome to urge his suite him selfe. So desyringe your blessinge I ende, this St. Simon and Judes Eaue.

"Y[rs] obedient Childe,
"ANDREW WHITE."

Address: "To the Reuerend Father
and his assured good Freind
F. Robert Persons
geue these
att Roome."

Endorsed by Parsons: "f. Andrew White 27 8[ber] 1606, answered;" [by Christopher Grene?]: "27 Octob. 1606."[10]

---

[6] That is, he was received into the Society on the supposition that he lay on his death-bed; but not to any effect or purpose on the contrary supposition, that is, "absolutely."

[7] Henry Garnett, superior of the English Jesuits, who was put to death six months before the date of this letter.

[8] St. John's, Louvain.

[9] Father Anthony Rivers apparently, who was the secretary or "*socius*" of the superior, Father Walley or Garnett. See Foley, *Collectanea, sub voce* "Rivers;" also his *Records*, i. 4, *seqq.*, 676. The disappearance of his name, which Foley could not account for, will be explained below; for we find in a Propaganda document that he went to Newfoundland, no doubt as a secular priest.—See below, § 7, note 12.

[10] Father Parsons has underlined several passages in the letter.

We meet with some old memoranda about the departure of young Father White from England and his entrance into the Society. One, in the shape of a note scribbled at the moment on the back of a letter to Parsons, or inscribed there later from a contemporary memorandum, gives seven categories of priests who had to leave England after the Gunpowder Plot. It begins: "Banished out of the Tower," and it mentions some six persons, among whom Father Thomas Garnett appears.[11] It proceeds: "Out of the Gatehouse," and two are named; "Out of the Kinges Bench," and four are mentioned, among whom is the Father Floyd, writer of the Society, referred to on a former page;[12] "Out of the Marshalsea," one name appears; "Out of the Clink," five prisoners; "Out of Neugate," ten more, among whom we see the name of "Mr. Greene," undoubtedly the gentleman for whom Andrew White pleaded; "Out of Bridwel," two more. Thus there are so far thirty names. Then follows the last category: "Others that came but not banished," and it contains fifteen names, among which appears: "14. Andrew White." In all, the memorandum contains forty-five entries on the roll.[13]

Expatriation.

Another document records Father White's formal admission into the Order, some four months after the date of his letters to Parsons and Gerard. It is a note from the Master of Novices at St. John's, Louvain, Father Thomas Talbott, to Father Henry Silesdon, who has written from Rome for particulars about the new novitiate. The answer is given a little after February, 1609. The Novice-Master tells of twenty-one candidates received in two years since the opening of this novitiate, which was the first establishment of the kind for English Jesuits. His statement, though not official in this familiar letter to his friend, is still characteristic of the Society in the manner of regarding and of recording the probation of candidates. We quote some phrases from the closely written folio page. He says—

Admission into the Order, Feb. 1, 1607.

"Reuerend good father,

"I receiued yours of the last of February, and, desirous to doe you any seruice, I haue sett down here the names of thos which haue been receiued hear according as you demanded.

---

[11] "Mr. Rookwood, other 2, viz. father Thomas Garnett, fr. Strang remayneth ther still. Mr. Alabaster and other two Laymen." As to Father Thomas Strange, mentioned here, cf. *supra*, Introduction, Chap. II. § 12, p. 86.

[12] *Supra*, Introduction, Chap. II. § 5, p. 59.

[13] Stonyhurst MSS., *Anglia A*, iii. f. 148.—Cf. Foley, *Records*, ii. 482, in biography of Father Thomas Garnett; note on the forty-six priests named by Challoner, *Memoirs*, ii. 14.

"Anno Dni. 1607, the first of February, F. Thomas Garnett, Priest, now Martyr of blessed memory, of the countrey of Middlesex & age of 22 years, was heer admitted to his probation (hauing been admitted into the Society the year 1604, the 29 of 7^{ber} by F. Henry Garnett of holy memory). He made his vowes the 2. of July, the same year of 1607.

The Novice-Master on the candidates, 1609.

"The same year and daye F. Andrew White, Londoner, of the age of 28 years; F. Thomas Lathwait, of the countrey of Lancaster and age of 29 years; F. Henry Lanman, countrey of Suffolk [and age] of 34 years; F. James Blundell, of the countrey of Lancaster, of age 29; Thomas Beuerige, of the country of Darby, age of 24; and John Laward, commonly called Fettiplace, of Buckinghamshire, age of 33, were admitted into the Society; the last for a temporall Coadiutour."

These were the foundation-stones of the first English novitiate; wherein Father Andrew White appears as the second novice, following in order a distinguished martyr. The writer goes on to tell of the later accessions; among whom is recorded for the same month and year Michael Alford, Londoner, aged 22, of whom we have heard before.[14] "The 19 of Nouember in the same yeare, Henry More of Essex, 21 years old, entered into the Society." Several temporal coadjutors or lay-brothers are in the list: "The 18 of June the same year [1607], Edward Rigbye, of the country of Lancaster, of age 26, was admitted for a temporall Coadiutour. And the same daye and year Francis Griffith of Middlesex, about 24 years old, was admitted for a temporall Coadiutour; and the next year in the end of Julye he was dismissed."

In the year 1608, after the priests, Michael Freeman and Charles Yelverton, respectively of 29 and 33 years of age, "Hughe Sheldon of Staffordshire, of age 42 (hauing been admitted at Tournay the 24 of August the year 1603, and sent into England for his health), entred now the second time into the Society for a temporall Coadiutour." "The 16 of 10$^{ber.}$ Michael Roper of Yorkshire, & age about 8 or 9 and twenty, was admitted for a temporall Coadiutour; but, being found to haue a great impediment in his eyes, and that he was like to lose them within a short time, he was within a little after dismissed."

Finally, after twenty-one such entries, numbered down the margin either by the writer or his correspondent, Father Talbott has occasion now, two years having elapsed since the beginning of the

[14] *Supra*, Introduction, Chap. II. § 5, pp. 59, 60.

novitiate, to count the first fruits which he had just gathered, in the previous month of February. His last paragraph runs thus—

"F. Francis Thomson *alias* Yates made his vowes on the 9 of 9^(ber) A. 1608. F. Lanman, commonly [called] F. Butler, F. White, F. Blundell, the 2. of febr. 1609. F. Laithwait, *alias* F. Scott, in England the same daye. B. [Brother] Thomas Beuerige the next daye after. F. Robert Bastard and B. Michael Allford, *alias* Griffith, the 1. of March the same yeare." [15]

§ 5. In this account we are favoured with a glimpse of that Jesuit Mission or incipient Province, into which Father White was admitted; how it was gradually built up from the modest proportions of twenty-seven years before, when it consisted of the two solitary Jesuits coming into England; and what were the elements of its composition, after so many years had been spent by others in trying to root it out. Not taking into consideration those applicants who might be received through foreign novitiates, the accessions, within the walls of the first English novitiate during its first two years, amounted, as we have seen, to ten priests as novices; three young men, among whom Alford and More became very distinguished Fathers in the course of time; and eight temporal coadjutors, or lay-brothers, of whom two, not being admitted to take their vows, were sent back to the world. Temporal coadjutors before this date seem to have been extremely rare; probably because there were not as yet any normal residences, nor any scholasticates or houses of studies, nor even a novitiate, in which they could be placed, and their handicraft or art be put to use. After this time, that form of life became rather an object of desire with many a gentleman who would prefer it for its opportunities of domestic quiet and devotion to the bustle of a distracting ministry. Still, it was considered that the grade of lay-brother was not in place on the English side of the Channel, owing to the disturbed and irregular kind of life which had to be led there.[1]

Elements making the English Province of Jesuits.

[15] Stonyhurst MSS., *Anglia A*, iii. f. 188: Thomas Talbott, Louvain, to H. Silesdon, Rome [March or April], 1609. Endorsed: "The names of some receaved from the beginninge to 1609. *De Thoma Garnetto M. ex registro Nouitiatus.*"

[1] A memorial given to the superiors of the English Vice-Province, after the first Congregation held in 1622, contains the following paragraph: "*Necessarium videtur, ut Coadjutores perraro admittantur in Anglia; et non nisi diligentissime instructi de Instituto. Exercitia spiritus quotannis faciant, et reliqua de more Societatis.*" Stonyhurst MSS., *A. V*, i. f. 34.—A situation somewhat similar may be seen in Maryland, one century later. The Provincial, Father John Turberville, wrote to the American superior, Father George Thorold, on November 10, 1728: "As for Br. Clemson, who desires to be re-admitted, I'm entirely against it; but am for his being imploy'd, if you find him fit, in some of your houses; and, if after some triall

The entire membership of the Mission was already so large that in the following year, 1610, fifty-three were in England alone, all being priests except one who was a prisoner.[2] In 1633, just a short generation of twenty-three years later, when the fully developed Province was mature enough to send out a mission to America, there were not less than three hundred and thirty-eight members referred to this Province as their own;[3] while, counting exiled German Jesuits who took refuge there, no fewer than three hundred and sixty-four members were counted, as forming the entire body of the English Province at the end of 1633.

The total membership, 1610, 1633.

About this time the proportion of younger men, who were accepted as scholastics or students, became more considerable; still, in the annual supply of novices, priests were one-fourth or one-fifth of the number.[4] The roll of death thus far had been adorned with the sacrifice and martyrdom of sixteen members at Tyburn, or in St. Paul's Churchyard, or on the rack.[5]

Scholastics.

Martyrs.

The considerable accession of members from the clergy at large to the ranks of the regular clergy did not please every one of those who, witnessing this movement on the part of their fellow-priests to adopt the life of regulars, found not such a step to be to their own liking. To judge by not a few pages that were printed in those times, we should infer that some individuals felt aggrieved at this condition of things as between their fellow-men and the religious Orders. They even expressed resentment that such a communication in spirit and life should be allowed to exist, when they did not partake. Hence may be seen curious pages that were published in consequence.[6]

Accessions from the secular clergy.

you think fit, you may take him as oblate [in French, *donné*]; which degree I take to be the most proper for your Factory." Md.-N. Y. Province Archives, L. 1, p. 14.

[2] Cf. Foley, *Collectanea*, Historical Introduction, p. lxix.

[3] General Archives S.J., *Angliæ Catalogi*, vol. 1623–1639; *Catalogus Tertius Rerum Prouinciæ Angliæ Societatis Jesv, Anno* 1633. These 338 are distributed "*in novem domicilia et residentias septem*," nine houses and seven residences. We quote from a triennial report, which extends, however, to a quinquennium of five years past; and the first general summary of the *personnel* closes with: "*Admissi in Societatem hoc quinquennio* 69, *dimissi duo, vita functi* 26," leaving a net increase during five years of 41 members. Thirteen German exiles are not counted in the 338. The report is signed by the Provincial, Father Richard Blount. He does not mention as a distinct element the small colony of three sent to Maryland this year, 1633, and put down by himself as a detachment apart in the annual or short Catalogue of the same year; the reason being that this triennial report was meant for an earlier date, but wars and other circumstances delayed its delivery two years, till the procurator of the Province actually went to Rome. The delay affected seriously the Maryland Mission. But we mention it at present to account for a different sum-total, 364, given by Foley, *Collectanea*, Historical Introduction, p. lxxv., as the membership for 1633.

[4] Cf. Foley, *Ibid.*, p. lxxv.

[5] *Ibid.*, pp. lxiii., lxiv.

[6] Dodd's *Church History of England*, etc., iii. 81, edit. 1742. Speaking of Father

If that question be proposed which has so often been put—What is the nature of the formation given? we can add at once another query—Whether there is sufficient reason for keeping priests as novices during two years? And we may devote here a few paragraphs to answering both inquiries together.

There was but slight difference between younger and older persons in facing such a practical question as that of assuming this form of life or vocation. No theoretical approbation of the life, nor any practical acceptance of it, would avail without exercise. And so much exercise was requisite, to say the least, as is necessary for any serious profession, which is never mastered save by the labour of apprenticeship. Different might be the attractions inducing one or other candidate to offer himself for the life of the Order. With some a motive might be the missionary organization of the Society, with others the divers functions which appealed to men of various talents. But, with all this, the personal formation to be assumed and embodied in the religious character of a Jesuit was not differentiated in the least by such remote attractions or original suggestions; nor could it be discounted by any amount of fervid approval or excellent intentions. A large measure of practical experimentation was necessary. *The need of probation or apprenticeship.*

The general end in view embraced all. Co-extensive with the end was the missionary organization, which likewise enveloped all. To these many means were subordinated. At the very threshold the statement was made to the candidate: *The end in view.*

"The end of this Society is to labour with the Divine grace for one's own salvation and perfection; and also, with the same Divine

---

Edmund Arrowsmith, Dodd says: If he really did become a member of the Society a few days before suffering martyrdom, "as he is not the only one of the clergy that made that step, I will not dispute the fact. 'Tis a serviceable expedient, to encrease the catalogue of men of merit in that Order," and so forth; reflecting on the Society which admitted secular clergymen; on the clergymen who applied for admission, especially when they were enjoying a competency; and on the religious vow of poverty which they preferred to their competency and comfort. He does not explain whose was the device of this " serviceable expedient, to encrease the catalogue of men of merit" in the Society, when men of merit chose to live the life of the Order, or when, by choosing it, people allowed themselves to be made men of merit. We observe that he prints at length a Brief of Alexander VII., who regulated the entrance of students from Pontifical Colleges into religious Orders, and, by reason of their existing obligations to such Pontifical foundations, imposed various conditions on the said students or foundationers (*pontificiorum collegiorum alumni*), both before and after they entered the religious life. This Brief Dodd gives verbatim in Latin (*Ibid.*, iii. 376); but he prefixes to it in English the apocryphal title : " A Brief of Pope Alexander VII., whereby the Clergy are prohibited to enter into any Religious Order." We note further that a recent *Bibliographical Dictionary and Biographical History of the English Catholics*, by Mr. Joseph Gillow, who describes himself as an unassisted layman, has adopted and reissued the materials, the statements, and the spirit of this kind of literature without further question or any misgiving.

assistance, to work intensely for the salvation and perfection of others."[7] After this, one of the governing conditions was stated, and it was precisely that of the missionary organization: "It is according to the nature of our profession and our manner of procedure that we always be ready to go to this or that part of the world, whithersoever the Sovereign Pontiff or our immediate Superior shall order us."[8] The lasting obligation of vows, promising to God the perfect observance of poverty, chastity, and obedience, supplied a solid basis for all this, a stable ground on which to stand, or what is technically called a "state of life."

The stability requisite for a state of life.

This implied an adjustment of one's self to a life under rule, which rule is the organic necessity and development of a life under vow. It meant also devotion to the apostolic ministry of preaching and administering the Sacraments, with the entire equipment of those means for influencing one's neighbour, which ranged from the solid work of education to the lighter exercise of social qualities in casual intercourse. The two elements of priestly ministry and religious rule are expressed technically in the name, under which the Church recognizes the Order, to wit, Regular Clerics or Clergy of the Society of Jesus. In this accurate denomination, the most general class to which the Order belongs is the clergy; the subordinate genus is that of clergy who are regulars, or who live under rule; and the specific body, which is thus classed, is the Company or Society of Jesus. So constituted, it has a moral personality and exclusive rights, like other coordinate institutes. The personality and rights of such moral entities in the Church are quite absolute; so that we may note how, at the date when the Society was going to acquire rights in Maryland, those old Orders in England, which had been stripped of their property by the suppression of the monasteries a hundred years before, could still in canon and moral law be absolute masters of that property; and, if they were not accessible to receive amends offered them, they were to be replaced only by the poor.[9]

Rule of the regular.

Ministry of the priest.

Regular clerics or clergy.

Specification.

Corporate entity and rights.

---

[7] "*Primum ac generale examen iis omnibus qui in Societatem Jesu admitti petent proponendum.*" Cap. i. § 2.

[8] *Ibid.*, iv. § 35, etc.

[9] Public Record Office: *Transcripts from Rome*, xvii., *Barberini*, ii., document 1; faculties for Panzani, October 24, 1634: "17. *Dispensandi cum conversis ad fidem Catholicam super fructibus bonorum ecclesiasticorum male perceptis, facta aliqua eleemosyna in usum Religionis illius, cujus ante schisma erant bona, si ibi adsit illa; sin minus in Catholicos pauperes.*"—Cf. *Documents*, I. No. 61: "The ultimate and juridical basis of Jesuit tenure."

Such was the Order or Company of Jesus, and to enter it God gave the vocation and added qualities corresponding. The formation imparted by the Society had to be in keeping, and its aim was to make the individual capable of the work and functions in prospect. The result was to be that of making him reliable, when thrown on his own resources, whether moral, intellectual, or material, in the sense and spirit of a greater man who said, when speaking of his material circumstances alone: "I have not coveted any man's silver, gold, or apparel, as you yourselves know; for, such things as were needful for me and them that are with me, these hands have furnished." [10] *Scope of personal formation.*

This does not mean that the recent recruit or the new religious was thus to be thrown on his own resources. To be put in a state of forwardness for that, it was first necessary to be put into a form and moulded, whence the subject was to issue so as never to lose that mould and form, and thus to become reliable. For, indeed, there is scarcely anything so unreliable in creation or so wanting in consistency as human character unformed. Every art demands some formation, in matters much slighter than that of character. Grammar goes before composition, to the effect that composition shall never issue out of the mould of grammar. And if any one imagined that the shaping of a Jesuit in a novitiate, so as never thenceforth to outgrow the rules fitted on and embodied in life, was altogether too much of a servitude for a man to tolerate, the same critic might probably think that it was too much of a slavery for a public speaker or writer never more to outgrow the fixed rules of grammar once incorporated in his style; even as a certain stylist is reported to have said, and probably with a strong touch of vanity, that, if he tried, he could not be ungrammatical. Trying or no trying, it was essential for the successful member of the Order to be never otherwise than regular and thoroughbred. And, in the general organization of men homogeneously trained, and ready alike to go out in all weathers even when unsupported and alone, it was intended that a programme should be found in operation which was comprehensive indeed, but withal circumscribed; to the effect that all were to have full play in executing all that was good; but, the moment they fell foul of any principle, they should relapse under check and control.[11] *No abridgment of the formation.*

The field of action comprehensive, yet circumscribed.

[10] Acts xx. 33, 34.
[11] *Constitutiones S.J.*, parte decima, § 8: "*Ita ut omnes ad bonum omnia possint, et, si male agerent, omnino subjecti sint.*"

The apprenticeship of a novice comprised various exercises. First, there was the constant practice of prayer, meditation on Divine truths, examination of conscience, reception of the Sacraments. Then, to occupy well the ground which was to give him his state of life, he should experience the effects of poverty—not only using nothing as his own, nor having anything for his own convenience in the hands of others, but knowing how to abound and how to suffer penury with equal self-possession and self-restraint. Hence, among other practices, to travel for a month without scrip or wallet, and live entirely on alms, was an integral part of a noviceship formation. In the midst of abundance, he was still to love poverty "as a mother," which meant that he would always prefer the effects of poverty to comfort, which is the effect of abundance. As to obedience, everything was cast into that mould, of which two general results were that he should learn how to govern himself and know how to govern others. The sanctity of personal integrity, which is signified by chastity, admitted of no modification in any particular, and for any compromise here there was no place in the Order. Hence, as in all religious institutes, the life was one of austerity. And whatever appearance of a man of the world might be assumed for the sake of dealing naturally with the world, the Jesuit life interiorly was to keep in austere and mortified correspondence with the exigencies of this virtue; or else the life was not genuine.

The three vows: poverty, obedience, chastity.

On all these accounts, and for the multitude of particulars which they comprehend, the time of the novitiate might well be common to all, whether priests or not; nor be unduly long, though it lasted two entire years. If one left untilled in any part the field of his future activity and usefulness as a spiritual man, he forfeited so much for ever; since all things have their time, and this was the time for ploughing and planting. It was not the season or place even for study, which belonged to the colleges. It was the time and place for such a probation as precluded the further advance of those who, even with a real vocation, could not bring themselves to do without real defects, to the prejudice in the future of order and union. A *turba* or "crowd" was not even allowed to set foot in the novitiate—that is to say, a number of men, however gifted or distinguished they might be, who were unfit for the institute.[12]

Exacting conditions of the novitiate.

[12] *Constit. S.J.*, parte x. § 7 : " *Ut perpetuo totius hujus corporis status conservetur, confert plurimum, quod in prima, secunda, et quinta parte dictum est, de turba et hominibus ad nostrum Institutum ineptis ne ad probationem quidem admittendis.*"

Then for such as were approved and admitted to their first vows, these two years were counted as the beginning of ten years' practice in the ministries of the Society and in the use of their attainments, after which they were advanced to a final grade in the Order. But, if they had not pursued their higher studies of philosophy and theology before entering the Society, the seven years required for such courses were added to the ten spent in the exercise of divers functions, and only then could the final profession be granted. It was the original intention of the founder, as shown in the choice of his nine first companions, to accept none but men already qualified by their virtue and learning; "but," he wrote, "as those who are good and learned are comparatively few, and of these few the greater number would now rather rest from their labours," he adopted a larger plan from the beginning. It was that of admitting younger men, to make of them the virtuous and learned members whom he desired to have.[13] Thus he proceeded to legislate about scholasticates and colleges, which were attached to universities, or to which public schools were attached.

<small>Formation continued during ten or seventeen years.</small>

As to the relevancy of the observations which we have made here, the questions frequently mooted on such topics may show their point. Besides, with regard to America, the spectacle of such members as laboured there, men who were evidently qualified for many posts, yet who sacrificed themselves on a far-off mission, will help to indicate the application of these principles in the lives of clergymen at that time.

However, against a uniform and consistent adoption of such maxims in everyday management, there was always militating a set of difficulties, which arose from the pressure of much handiwork and many calls, with fewness of hands to respond, —a consideration which ever weighed upon the minds of immediate superiors, and tended to relax the conditions for accepting new men. But, if immediate superiors bent to the force of opportunism, a counter-pressure was felt from the side of the remoter and higher administration; which, as being wider in its views, and less subject to the change of incumbents, looked not merely nor so much to present expediency, but regarded steadfastly the general good and the future. With one illustration out of many, to show such restraining action on the part of the higher and wider government, we close this account of the novitiate.

<small>The handicapping of opportunism.</small>

Writing to the Provincial, Father Edward Courtney, on October

[13] *Constit. S.J.*, parte iv., procem., decl. A.

14, 1662, the General Father Oliva said: "I hear that few are being admitted into the Society in your parts. Lately I gave you authorization to receive [as many as] ten. But, I beg of you, let them be most select; so that they suit the greatness of the Province, and that they walk worthily in the footsteps of the eminent Fathers who have flourished there in times gone before. Be more free in letting men go betimes, if any seem to be of a difficult character, or to be useless for keeping up the Mission in spirit and learning. It is better to have one good one than ten inept, about whom we are always in a state of trepidation. I should wish very much that your Reverence would take this matter to heart. It is better for us to be in fewer posts, than to have some risked here and there out of our sight, who are only a danger to us."[14]

<small>Quality to be guaranteed.</small>

§ 6. We return now to the sequence of events. After taking his first vows of religion in 1609, Andrew White was sent back as a missionary to England. In 1610 we do not see his name inserted among those of the Fathers labouring in England;[1] still two years later he was in London. At some time or other he was sent to the seminary which Parsons had founded in Lisbon. While passing through Spain, he addressed the King and Prince Royal, thanking them for the benefits conferred upon St. Omer's College in Flanders. On June 15, 1619, twelve years after his admission to the novitiate, he took the four final vows of profession. The rest of his time was largely spent in the duties of a professor, teaching Sacred Scripture, Dogmatic Theology, Greek, Hebrew; and he was in charge of the higher courses as Prefect of Studies at Louvain and Liège. At intervals he was engaged on the English mission in Suffolk, Middlesex, Devonshire, and Hampshire.

<small>White, 1610-1629.</small>

---

[14] *Anglia, Epist. Gen.*, 1662, October 14: "*Audio paucos admitti apud uos in Societatem. Nuper dedi R⁰ V⁰ facultatem ut decem admittat. Sed quæso selectissimos; ut respondeant magnitudini Provinciæ, ac impleant magna insignium qui olim istic floruere Patrum uestigia. Sit liberalior in dimittendis tempestiue, si qui difficiles futuri videantur, aut inutiles missioni cum spiritu ac doctrina sustinendæ. Præstat unum bonum habere, quam decem ineptos, et de quibus semper simus in trepidatione. Valde uelim id R⁰ V⁰ cordi esse. Præstat nos esse in locis paucioribus quam periculosos aliquos hinc inde extra oculos collocari.*" Among the salutary effects of such testing would be that of cutting through the tendrils of a parasitism, which can attach to religious organisms; if they have a name in the world for something which is attractive, and offer to self-love a hold for getting by the way what the world might never have granted in any way.—Compare a practical judgment on this subject, expressed by the Rector of the College at Vienna, Father Victoria, S.J., in a letter to Father Peter Canisius, October 24, 1561. O. Braunsberger, S.J., *B. Petri Canisii, S.J., Epistulæ et Acta*, iii. 268.

[1] Foley, *Collectanea*, Historical Introduction, p. lxix.

And it is at the residence of St. Thomas, in the district of Hants, that we find he was stationed when deputed for the American mission.[2]

Father White was a prominent divine. In a manuscript volume, containing some seventeen opinions rendered by divers theologians on a few cases of conscience, we find his name and opinion among those of Leonard Lessius, S.J., Ægidius, S.J., Dr. Francis Silvius Father Crathorne, S.J., De Coninck, S.J., and Peter Wading, S.J. He signs as "Andrew White of the Society of Jesus, Professor of Sacred Theology at Louvain. 1623, 3rd day of August."[3]

In speculative or dogmatic theology, the trend of his system and manner of thought seems to have been of an excessively conservative kind. He adhered so rigidly to the interpretation of St. Thomas Aquinas that, had his method been more common among Jesuits of that age, the Society might never have given birth to the works of a Suarez or a Bellarmine. His Thomist party at Liège made stringent demands in the direction of exclusiveness. The General, while respecting the good intentions, did not quite appreciate the policy of the party. Father White found himself in a difficult position, the more so as he had the management or supervision of the studies. On several occasions, we observe, his professorial career was cut short by a trip to England in a missionary capacity. Thus, at some date about 1622, he was in the catalogue of London missioners; in 1623 he was professor at Louvain; in 1625 he was on the Suffolk mission;[4] and then, in the same year, becoming Prefect of Studies at Liège, he remained at that post till the middle of 1629, when he was certainly relieved of his office for his rigorous and exacting theological views.[5]

His Thomism.

We may quote some passages of the General's letters to Father Andrew White at different periods. In 1617 he wrote about the proposals, no doubt made by Father White himself, to call over from England Fathers Price, Batford, and others, for the purpose of rousing a spirit of ardour in the studies at Louvain. The General says he

[2] General Archives S.J., *Anglia, Catalogi.*—Foley, *Collectanea*, s.v. "White, Andrew;" and Second Appendix, p. 1458.

[3] Stonyhurst MSS., *A*, i. 40, document 17; two minutely and elegantly written folio pages, signed: "*Ita Censeo saluo meliori iudicio. Andreas Vitus, Societ^{is}. Jesu, Sacræ Theologiæ Professor Louanij.* 1623, *die* 3 *Aug^i*." There is no intimation of its being a transcript, yet the handwriting is entirely different from that of the letters to Parsons and Gerard, seventeen years before. He wrote then in the old Elizabethan hand; this paper is in the new style. The question is about destitute nuns, who have sunk their dowries or funds: Whether they can borrow in their necessities, and so contract new debts.

[4] Foley, *Collectanea*, s.v. "White, Andrew."

[5] General Archives, *Catalogi.*—Also *Anglia, Epist. Gen.*, as given *infra*.

will reflect upon the matter, and he drops some remarks about maintaining the order of studies, and not making too many alterations.[6] Passing over some intermediate business, we find his Paternity, two years later, conferring with Father Henry Silesdon at Louvain, about Father White's desire to cross over into England, and also about his doctrine and manner of teaching.[7] On the same day he discusses the subject with Father John Price, another professor at the same scholastic house of studies, and he speaks distinctly of "propositions" advanced by Father White. Finally, under the same date, he addresses the latter directly upon this topic, as well as on the proposal that the Father resume his missionary work in England. Six months afterwards this subject of correspondence closes all round, for the reason that White is now in England, where the General writes to him and alludes to the valiant exploit of "having penetrated through perils into the midst of perils"—*per pericula in pericula pervenit*. Indeed, on the very same day he indites an epistle to Father John Percy "in prison"—*in carcere*.[8]

Less than four years afterwards White's services were in demand again; but people found themselves at cross-purposes with regard to him. Father Joseph Creswell, whose name is not unknown in British statutes,[9] had just died at Ghent; and the General, writing to Father Edward Knott at Liège, who was the Provincial's vicar on the Continent, signified his consent that Andrew White should take the post vacated, which was that of instructing the young priests of the Society in their last year of formation.[10] But to the Provincial, Father Blount, he says on the same day, that he had sent Father White to teach Scripture at Louvain, who now has been designated by the Vice-Provincial to become instructor of the young Fathers. Let Father Blount provide for one or other place, as he shall think fit to determine.[11] White's co-operation as professor seems to have been more indispensable; hence we find him confirmed in that position, which he occupies for several years to come, no longer at Louvain, but at the new foundation of Liège. In 1625 his record is that of having filled heretofore the offices of Professor of Theology, minister, that is, assistant in the management of some college, superior of the Mission of Devon, and

Proposed for divers posts. 1623.

---

[6] *Anglia, Epist. Gen.*, 1617, February 18: General to White at Louvain.
[7] *Ibid.*, 1619, February 16: General to Silesdon, Rector, Louvain.
[8] *Ibid.*, 1619, February 16: General to John Price, White; and 1619, September 7: to White in England.
[9] Cf. 3 Jac. I., c. 2, 1605-6.
[10] As *Instructor tertii anni probationis*.
[11] *Anglia, Epist. Gen.*, 1623, April 8.

councillor; now he is Prefect of Studies and Professor of Sacred Scripture at Liège.

In this latter capacity, as superintendent of the courses in the scholastic house of studies, he opened again the old question about method and principles in theological training. The debates which follow are interrupted twice by the proposal to call White to Rome, as confessor of the English College there. On the first occasion the result of a conference between the General and Father Thomas Fitzherbert, Rector of the College in Rome, is to the effect that Father White will not suit for the post; and the statement would seem to imply that Fitzherbert had applied for White, but that the Provincial Blount had declined to accede.[12] Three years later, on the death of Father Hall, the actual incumbent in Rome, a successor had to be found as confessor in the college, and also as procurator or manager of the temporalities. So the General proposed "Father Stafford as very suitable; and I add," he wrote, "Father Andrew White, and also Father Edward Knott himself. But, if you cannot conveniently send any one of these three, see if you can find some one who, besides other endowments of prudence and charity, is also fluent in speaking Italian."[13] The person actually sent by the Provincial was one who is well known in Jesuit bibliography, Father Nathaniel Bacon, or Southwell, who became at a later period secretary to several of the Generals, and published his *Bibliotheca Scriptorum Societatis Jesu*. In the notice which Southwell inserted about Andrew White and his Indian writings, we have the testimony, not only of a contemporary, but of one who, besides running closely in the same career with White for a time, was afterwards in a position to receive and file the missionary's relations and other writings.

For Rome. 1624, 1627.

Thus ended the incident of his Roman opportunities. Meanwhile, as a professor and also a councillor of the house at Liège, he has touched again the question of old theological difficulties. The General acknowledges the Father's criticism in these terms: "20 April, 1624. To Liège, to Father Andrew White. . . . In the method of teaching theology, I do not think that any change need be introduced into the ordinances of

The General on White's Thomism. 1624.

---

[12] *Anglia, Epist. Gen.*, 1624, July 20: General to Richard Blount, Provincial: "Jam locutus sum cum P. Thoma Fitzherberto de P. Andrea Vito, eum nempe pro confessario Seminarii Anglicani Romani minus commodum esse. Quare rogat ipse mecum R. V. ut pro eo alium officio confessarii (quod postulat virum valde prudentem et paucorum verborum) conquirat, et ubi aliquem designarit nos de eo admoneat." After the words "*minus commodum*," the original draft has the following words cancelled: "*esse. Est enim pro eo munere—esse. Quare non amplius eum a R. V. petet.*"

[13] *Ibid.*, 1627, April 24: General to Blount, Provincial.

our *Ratio Studiorum* [programme of studies], which is now adopted almost everywhere. I shall be happy to recommend to Father Provincial the step of desiring the Rector of that college, or rather the Prefect of Studies, not to allow the professors there to recede farther from the doctrine of St. Thomas than their rules permit. The sense of these rules is, I think, sufficiently clear to call for no further explanation. What is needed is the watchful care of the prefect, for fear the professors overstep the bounds set for them. I shall take pains to have this seriously brought to their notice. And now would you please salute in my name Fathers George Morley and Thomas Southwell, and let them know that I was sincerely gratified at receiving their letters."[14] This acknowledgment refers to their official letters, as councillors of the Rector. Father White himself is the Prefect of Studies, whose hands are to be strengthened by a reminder from the Provincial to the professors.

From 1623 to 1626 then, his position at Liège, under the Rector, Father Owen Shelley, was that of Prefect of Studies, Professor of Sacred Scripture, councillor of the house, besides assisting in the spiritual care of the community and presiding at the conferences on moral theology. In April, 1626, he was engaged in some laborious writing, to which the General kindly alluded. But, at the end of that year, his whole situation was changed. He became Professor of Dogmatic Theology in place of Father John Crathorne. The General wrote to the Vice-Provincial Knott: "I hope that Father Crathorne and Father Andrew White will give perfect satisfaction in the offices which they now occupy at Liège; and I doubt not but Father Lawrence Worthington will also fill the place of Father White with signal ability in expounding Holy Scripture, if only his interest in that occupation does not flag."[15]

The question of studies and method now came to a crisis, and we may infer from the General's language, in answering White, that the latter considered himself to be on the defence, in the stand which he took up to maintain St. Thomas or some Thomist method of treating theology. Two letters, separate in date by two years, will explain the situation, and bring us to the first announcement of an American expedition.

On December 11, 1627, the General wrote to Father Andrew White at Liège: "Since the book, in which the *Ratio Studiorum* of

[14] *Anglia, Epist. Gen.*, 1624, April 20.
[15] *Ibid.*, 1626, December 12: Worthington took the double post of White as Professor of Scripture, and councillor of the Rector. Crathorne became the spiritual director of the house.

our Society is contained, shows clearly enough what the points are in which our professors may recede from the doctrine of St. Thomas, and prescribes that, in the rest, the said holy Doctor's opinion is to be exactly followed, I do not think that any one can go beyond bounds in following him, provided he keep within the range marked out by the Society. Wherefore, as in this matter you have always conformed your judgment to the rules laid down for ours, so I would have you continue to do so, and spare no pains that others do likewise. Thus the Divine Majesty will bless the efforts which you make in carrying out the desires of your superiors; and the fruit which is looked for will be abundant." The letter goes on to convey an expression of thanks for the information conveyed about the college; and then adds that, if there are further communications to be made, the Father will be pleased to put them down in writing or in cipher, for the General's use: "Do not wait, please, till you can tell me face to face, since I see no opportunity at present of your being able to meet me."[16] This was the time when Father Nathaniel Southwell had been selected for service in Rome. The tone of the letter just given implies that Father White was still Prefect of Studies, although the Catalogue of the year before omits that circumstance; and other Catalogues are wanting for several years afterwards.

The General in favour of liberty, against White. 1627-1629.

The next letter which we quote was the last addressed to White in his professorial career. The General says, under date of March 3, 1629: "I have received three letters written by your Reverence in the month of January; and I was highly gratified to see in each one of them a proof of your solicitude, that nothing should escape my notice which could be of use in serving the Society. Be assured that the pains you have taken shall not be fruitless. I will do my part and turn to good account the information which you have favoured me with, for rectifying what I understand to be amiss. And, in the first place, I shall be happy indeed to insist on what you have recommended several times, that all our professors should follow most scrupulously the doctrine of St. Thomas, according to the provisions laid down in the system of studies.[17] If you think that any one wanders farther away from that standard and more independently than the Society intends, as is clearly explained in

---

[16] *Anglia, Epist. Gen.*, 1627, December 11.
[17] Here the following words were added, but erased: "in the explanation of which you [expressed] some doubt."

the said *Ratio Studiorum,* I would have you inform Father Provincial of the circumstance or, if you like, myself, mentioning distinctly the opinions which you judge to be foreign to St. Thomas's doctrine. It is in this way that any undue liberties may be controlled more easily than by adding new explanations to the laws already enacted." Such are the General's administrative directions for the control of studies.

He then passes on to make mention for the first time of America: "For the rest, as to that holy readiness of soul that has made you offer yourself to Father Provincial for the mission of instructing the American colonies of the English in Catholic doctrine, I do not doubt but he is as much pleased with it as I am.[18] And, since I ardently desire that Divine Providence will yet offer your Province a suitable opening for carrying such designs into execution, I make it an object of my earnest prayers. Herewith I commend myself to your holy Sacrifices and prayers; and I would ask you to salute cordially on my behalf Father Thomas Southwell, Father Thomas Colford, Father John Crathorne and Father Thomas Babthorpe; and let them know that their letters gave me particular pleasure. To Father Thomas would you say moreover from me, that I was delighted to hear of the desire which he also has been inspired with to go on the American mission; and I trust that God will add the means for satisfying such a desire. And, commending myself again to your holy Sacrifices, and those of each of the Fathers named, [I remain . . .] Rome, March 3, 1629."[19]

First mention of America. March 3, 1629.

Who the Father Thomas was that applied for the American mission with Father White, is not clear from the draft; since out of the four names just mentioned by the General three are Thomas. However, one of them, that of Father Thomas Colford or Cooke, nephew of the famous Sir Edward Cooke the lawyer, was inserted above the line afterwards; hence the text must refer to either Thomas Southwell *alias* Bacon, or to Thomas Babthorpe. If the missionary spirit ran in the family, we should be inclined to surmise that it was rather Southwell who was meant; seeing that his brother Nathaniel, lately called to Rome, never ceased during many years to ask for the foreign missions.

In view of the embarrassment caused by three men out of four having the same name, and that name Thomas, we may notice that

---

[18] Here a few words are crossed out, about "undertaking the expedition"—"*cujus expeditionis suscipiendæ ut diuina.*"

[19] *Anglia, Epist. Gen.,* 1629, March 3: *Documents,* I. No. 5, A.—See reproduction opposite. This is one of eight letters for the English Province, dated the same day.

The General, M. VITELLESCHI, Rome, 3 March, 1629, to Father A. WHITE, Liège. General Archives S.J., *Anglia, Epist. Gen.*, i. f. 290ᵛ. Autograph draft. First mention of English America. (⅔ scale of the original.)

[*To face p.* 174.

at a later date, as we see by the *Calvert Papers*, Father White himself appears to have abandoned his own name Andrew for that same appellative, Thomas.[20] Hence we go out of our way to mention a singular circumstance in English antecedents, which had scarcely changed in this respect even till our own day. An Englishman had but one Christian name or baptismal patron. By it the members of the Society were listed in the Catalogue. In 1633 we find the sum-total of membership for the English Province reported at the figure 349. Of these no fewer than sixty-eight follow one another in an unbroken row as John, forty-eight as Thomas, thirty-four as William, and twenty-two as Francis. One hundred and seventy-two persons distributed those four Christian names among them; with no other to distinguish them save the surname. When the family name also agreed, the manner adopted for distinguishing was by the use of "senior" and "junior," as with Molyneuxes, Parkers, and with this very Thomas Babthorpe mentioned here, who was a senior with reference to another of the same name and same knightly family.[21]

Christian names and patron saints.

Father Thomas Babthorpe was evidently of the same theological bent as Father White. Hence, before the epistle just quoted had reached Liège, another was dated from there by Babthorpe, and duly answered by the General eight weeks later. In his usual courteous style, the latter declines to interfere with the liberty of the professors, where they are using their right; and he quotes the example of the Dominican Fathers, who, though bound to follow their great chief, "do still deviate from the teaching of St. Thomas in some points," or at least, when in contradiction with other Thomists, do still maintain on both sides that they are all strictly following the same Doctor.[22]

White's party discarded. 1629.

The conclusion of the whole debate is shown in a letter to the Rector of Liège, Father Robert Stafford, only two months later: "I do not think," says the General, "that there is much ground for fearing anything more from that doctrine of Father Andrew White,

---

[20] *Calvert Papers*, i. 211: Tho. White to Lord Baltimore, February 20, 1638.

[21] General Archives, *Anglia, Catal.* 1622-1649, triennial 1 and 2 for 1633. The other names which tempt our arithmetic are: Richard, 19 persons; Henry, 18; Edward, 17; Robert, 16; George, 10; which comprise 80 more persons. Thus 252 members distribute only 9 names among them. Twelve more names embrace 52; they are, in order, from 7 down to 3, Peter, Christopher, Charles, James, Lawrence, Edmund, Joseph, Michael, Alexander, Andrew (3), Anthony, Nicholas. The remaining 45 individuals stand out in sporadic independence, by ones and twos.—This binominal system for individuals may be seen illustrated at length in divers Subsidy Acts of Parliament, as well as in American colonial records.

[22] *Anglia, Epist. Gen.*, 1629, April 28.

seeing that he has now been removed from the office of teaching and has crossed over to England. If anything further is observed at any time, and if, in maintaining Father White's opinions, any one there is more contentious than is convenient, it will be easy, I expect, to find a remedy. For the present, I am pleased that you have taken note of the troubles resulting from that doctrine, and that you are anxious to avert them." [23] So ended Father White's professorial career.

§ 7. We have already pointed to the development of English colonization along the coast of North America, from Newfoundland to Virginia and beyond. Moreover, in the circles of statesmanship at home, we left the young George Calvert entering on a career under the patronage of Cecil, first Earl of Salisbury. Sir George becomes now a chief character in our narrative; and, if his position as that of a statesman at home is prominent, his ulterior action as that of a Catholic, and one successful in originating an American colony, is of much more consequence for the unfolding of our story.

George Calvert. 1605-1623.

In the year of the Gunpowder Plot, 1605, and soon after his marriage, he was honoured with the degree of Master of Arts at Oxford, in company with his patron, and in presence of the King. Then, from being private secretary to Salisbury, he attained to the post of Secretary of State in 1619. A domestic difficulty, which had beclouded the circumstances of Sir Thomas Lake's dismissal from that high office, formed a marked contrast with the domestic felicity of Calvert in his family, consisting of his wife and ten children.[1] But in August, 1622, he lost this his first wife.

Meanwhile he was deeply engaged in the secret negotiations for bringing about the marriage of Charles, heir-apparent, with a Spanish princess. He arrived at the height of his fortune in 1623, when the Spanish match was abandoned for a French one; and ultimately Charles I. was married to Henrietta Maria. Calvert himself eventually took in second wedlock a lady whom he was to lose on the high seas, with several of her little children, in 1630.[2]

---

[23] *Anglia, Epist. Gen.*, 1629, June 2: *Documents*, I. No. 5, B.

[1] "She is a good woman," said Calvert to the King, "and has brought me ten children; and I can assure your Majesty, she is not a wife with a witness." J. G. Morris, *The Lords Baltimore*, pp. 10, 11.—L. W. Wilhelm, *Sir George Calvert*, p. 41. —The phrase so employed by Calvert would seem to be a play upon words: "with a witness," that is, as we should say, "with a vengeance;" and "with a witness," that is, not like Lady Lake, whose witnesses had paraded in the recent difficulty, leading to her husband's dismissal.—Cf. Lingard, *History of England*, vii., A.D. 1618, 1619, p. 99.

[2] Philip Calvert, who was at a later period Governor of Maryland, is said to have

Like other men of station and means, he was much interested in American ventures or colonizing enterprises. Newfoundland, the original foothold for English adventure, still remained the object of fitful zeal with speculators, who took it up from time to time, only to drop it. Calvert in 1620 bought the south-eastern peninsula of the island from Sir William Vaughan; and on April 7, 1623, he was favoured with a formal charter by King James I. for the territory which was called in his patent the Province of Avalon.[3] Now, since we called attention before to the religious aspect put upon colonization in general, we may quote at once the phrases which are to a similar purport in this charter.

The second paragraph runs thus: "Whereas our right trusty and well-beloved Counsellor Sir George Calvert, Knight, our principall Secretary of State, being excited with a laudable and pious zeale to enlarge the extents of the Christian world, and therewithall of our empire and dominion, hath heretofore to his greate cost purchased a certain region or territory hereafter described, in a country of ours scituate in the west part of the world, commonly called Newfound Land, not yet husbanded or planted, though in some parts thereof inhabited by certaine barbarous people wanting the knowledge of Almighty God; and intending now to transport thither a very greate and ample colony of the English nation, hath humbly besought our kingly Majesty to give, grant, and confirme all the said region. . . . Know yee therefore," etc. In the fourth section there are granted to Calvert "the patronages and advowsons of all churches, which, as Christian religion shall increase within the said region, isles, & limitts, shall happen to be erected," with all kinds of rights and privileges, such as "any Bishop of Durham within the Bishopprick or county palatine of Durham in our kingdome of England hath at any time heretofore had," etc. Finally, as to the meaning of this charter, a paragraph at the end provides "that no interpretations bee admitted thereof, whereby Gods holy and truly Christian religion, or allegiance due unto us, our heirs and successors, may in any thing suffer any prejudice or diminution."[4]

The charter for Avalon, on religion. April 7, 1623.

As to Calvert's own attitude towards religion, we have to record now that, within a year and a half after the date of his Newfoundland

---

been one of the surviving children by the second wife. J. T. Scharf, *History of Maryland*, i. 47, note.

[3] Cf. Scharf, *Ibid.*, i. 31-33. The charter of Avalon follows, *Ibid.*, pp. 34-40.

[4] Scharf, *Ibid., loc. cit.*

178   CALVERT AND NEWFOUNDLAND   [CHAP. III

charter, he became a Catholic, in spite of certain signs of the times, and of clouds that were gathering.

The times were indeed not at all secure. James I. had but lately been fencing off the aggressions of the intolerant House of Commons. The orators nevertheless expressed their fears at the alarming growth of Popery in the land; they declared that connivance at the evil would beget toleration; that toleration would be followed by equality; that equality would soon be improved into ascendancy—points which rather seemed to express a high esteem of the intellectual and moral powers of Catholics. And the Commons prayed that all laws made or to be made against Papists should be put in force; that His Majesty would order all children, whose fathers and mothers were Catholic, to be taken from their parents and brought up Protestants; and that he would on all accounts annul those pecuniary compositions or bargains, which were made in favour of recusants unto the saving of their estates. The pious gentlemen lamented with delicate sensibility the iniquitous character of pecuniary compositions; not because it was legal blackmail, but because it was only blackmail. And one of them, for example, who complained that Thomas Tankard, Esq., of Yorkshire, was let off with a fine of £200 sterling a year for being a Catholic, was able, a few years later, to buy the whole of Mr. Tankard's estate from the Commonwealth, which had confiscated it; and he bought the whole for £600 sterling—which indicated that the annual fine under the blackmail process had been equal to one-third of the estate's entire value.[5] It was in the face of these gathering clouds, which followed a season of brighter prospects, that the Secretary of State entered the Catholic Church.

Calvert's conversion to Catholicity.

To judge by the tenor of divers letters, written by English priests to the Roman agent of the clergy in the first half of 1625, it would seem that the news of his conversion penetrated very slowly among the Catholics themselves. Thus, on January 20, 1625, one writes to Rome: "Secretary Caluert hath surrendered his place and on [one] Sir Albert Morton sometimes Secretary to the Lady Elizabeth is to succeed him."[6] On February 21 another says: "Sir George Caluert is made an Irish

Date of Calvert's conversion [1625].

---

[5] On the Commons, cf. Lingard, *History of England*, vii., A.D. 1621, p. 117.—Also L. W. Wilhelm, *Sir George Calvert*, p. 93.—On the Tankard incident, and Rushworth's complaint, with his subsequent purchase, see Lingard, *Ibid.*, note LLL on ch. iv., A.D. 1631.—Cf. *supra*, Introduction, Chap. II. § 13, note 5.

[6] Cf. J. R. Brodhead, *Documents, Colonial History of New York*, iii. p. vii., who dates Calvert's resignation, February 9, 1624/5.

Baron, that the world shold not conceyue he was put from his secretariship in disgrace." Neither correspondent so far seems to have heard of Calvert's conversion. A third writes a few days afterwards, on February 24: "Sir G. Coluerte, I am tolde, is *rectus* in C. R. [*receptus*, that is, received into the Catholic Religion], and it is sayed he intendes to goe a viage to the new founde land where he hathe a share in that plantation.' Finally, some three or four months later, another sends the information from Paris to the clergy agent at Rome, but as at second-hand from the Vicar-Apostolic in England: "Your old freind Sr Geo. Caluert professed himselfe openly a Catholique before the councell: and, as my L. of C. [Lord of Chalcedon] writes to me, had continued in the councell, if he would haue taken the oath of allegiaunce, which is tendered to Caths [Catholics]." [7]

As to Sir George's religious life after this, the Protestant Bishop Goodman describes it for us, and adds something about the Secretary's integrity in the previous discharge of his public office. Speaking of the Spanish negotiations in view of the royal match, this Bishop of Gloucester writes: "The third man who was thought to gain by the Spaniard was Secretary Calvert; and, as he was the only Secretary employed in the Spanish match, so undoubtedly he did what good offices he could therein for religion's sake, being infinitely addicted to the Roman Catholic faith, having been converted thereunto by Count Gondomar and Count Arundel, whose daughter Secretary Calvert's son [Cæcilius] had married. And, as it was said, the Secretary did usually catechize his own children, so to ground them in his own religion; and in his best room having an altar set up with chalice, candlesticks, and all other ornaments, he brought all strangers thither, never concealing anything, as if his whole joy and comfort had been to make open profession of his religion. Now, this man did protest to a friend of his that he never got by the Spaniard so much as a pair of pockets; which, it should seem, is a usual gift among them, being excellently perfumed, and may be valued at twenty nobles or ten pounds price." [8]

Calvert's faith and devotion.

---

[7] Stonyhurst MSS., *Anglia A*, viii. f. 175: Muskett, January 20, 1625, to Thomas More, Rome; f. 186: Nelson to same, February 21; f. 206^v: Roper to same, February 24; f. 140: Ireland, Paris, to Thomas Rant, "à St. Louis à Rome," June 5, same year.

[8] G. Goodman, *The Court of King James the First*, i. 376, 377. As to being "infinitely addicted to the Roman Catholic faith," there were many specimens of this habit of mind, even among people who were still Anglicans. Goodman himself, if we may believe Panzani—"Gudman, Vescovo di Golcestria"—favoured all kinds of Catholic practices, which, with the demands he made for certain spiritual

180 CALVERT AND NEWFOUNDLAND [CHAP. III

The steps which Calvert, now Lord Baltimore, took after his conversion may be mentioned as they are told in his own letters, and also in an account which we ascribe to his son Cæcilius. Writing to his friend, Sir Thomas Wentworth, Bart., later the famous or notorious Earl of Strafford, Lord Deputy of Ireland, he said, on May 21, 1627: "Sir, I am heartily sorry that I am farther from my hope of seeing you before my leaving of this town, which will be now within these three or four days, being bound for a long journey to a place which I have had a long desire to visit, and have now the opportunity and leave to do it. It is Newfoundland I mean, which it imports me more than in curiosity only to see; for I must either go and settle it in a better order than it is, or else give it over, and lose all the charges I have been at hitherto for other men to build their fortunes upon. And I had rather be esteemed a fool by some for the hazard of one month's journey, than to prove myself one certainly for six years by past, if the business be now lost for the want of a little pains and care. At Michaelmas I hope to be with you again, God willing." [9]

Voyage to Newfoundland or Avalon. [May to July], 1627.

A note of Dr. John Southcote's, a contemporary, gives us the following item: "1627. The first mission into New Foundland was begun by Mr. Anthony Smith and Mr. Thos. Longville, priests of the secular clergy, who put to sea the 1 of June and landed there the 23 of July with my Lord of Baltimore." [10]

The priests in Calvert's company.

Another contemporary document gives us a variation in the reading of the priests' names. It says: "There set out two priests of the secular clergy, the Rev. Mr. Anthony Rivers, and the Rev. Mr.

privileges from the Pope, read like a comedy. However, Goodman became a Catholic later. Instead of saying "Count," that is, Earl Arundel, Bishop Goodman should have spoken of Thomas, Baron Arundel of Wardour. At this time, Thomas Howard, Earl of Arundel, was reckoned by Catholics as a schismatic, that is, a temporizer, one who conformed to the Established Church in outward practices to save his temporal interests. A man of that kind was not likely to do much good to anybody. But the other lord, Thomas Arundel, Baron Wardour, was ranked as a practical Catholic. He was the father-in-law of Cecil, Lord Baltimore. For Panzani on Goodman, see Vatican Archives, *Nunziatura d'Inghilterra*, 5, f. 194, Febr. 6, 1636. For the religion of the two lords, Thomas Howard and Thomas Arundel, cf. Stonyhurst MSS., *Anglia A*, ix. document 1; general list of 155 English peers, about 1630–1640; No. 3: "*Thomas Houardus, Comes Arundeliæ Angliæ Mariscallus et Eques Periscellidis, Schismaticus*. . . . No. 127: *Thomas Arundelius Baro de Vardour, Catholicus*."

[9] *The Earl of Strafford's Letters and Despatches*, i. 39: Geo. Baltimore, Savage, May 21, 1627, to Sir Thomas Wentworth, Bart.

[10] "Extract from the note-book of Dr. John Southcote, second son of Sir John Southcote of Merstham, Surrey (*obiit* May, 1637). In the possession of the Bishop of Southwark." Appended to Notes from the Westminster Diocesan Archives, communicated [by Dr. Knox?] to Dr. J. G. Shea.—Georgetown College *Transcripts*, under date.

Thomas a Longavilla."[11] The first-named of these two secular priests was an ex-Jesuit, and he seems to have had the two names of Rivers and Smith, with others besides.[12]

§ 8. The religious history of Newfoundland under Lord Baltimore's management may be told from sources not yet touched by historians. Fra Simon Stock, an Englishman, belonging to the Order of Discalced or Barefooted Carmelites, entered into a correspondence with Dr. Francis Ingoli, secretary of the newly founded Sacred Congregation at Rome, called De Propaganda Fide. The style of Fra Simon calls for some explanation. However, he writes in Italian, and hence his manner of expressing himself is perhaps excusably crude.

Fra Simon Stock and the Propaganda. 1625.

At the end of the year 1625, which had witnessed Calvert's accession to the Catholic Church, Stock sent a letter from Chelsea, London, saying to the authorities of the Congregation: "The island about which I wrote to your Excellencies has been a subject of so

---

[11] Propaganda Archives; *I America*, 259, f. 2: *Nova Anglia sive Terra recens inventa;* a report sent by the Brussels Nuncio, September 21, 1630. See *infra*, § 10, p. 196.

[12] See above: "Father Antonie," referred to by Andrew White, in his letter to Parsons, October 27, 1606, this chapter, § 4, p. 158, note 9. Other names of Rivers, or Anthony Smith, were Roger Bernard (General Archives S.J., *Hist. Angl. Suppl.*, i. viii. 315*b*), Thomas Blewett (Foley, *Collectanea*, p. 938). But in a certain *Relation* (Barberini Library, lvi. 136, f. 19ᵛ) there occurs a passage which distinguishes Rivers from Smith: "*Uno già Giesuita, hora cacciato da essi, detto Revers, sente le confessioni, per quanto si dice, senz' alcuna autorità. Un tal Antonio Smiter pur già Giesuita, doppo hauer preso il giuramento, si dice pure senta le confessioni* . . ." This is in the *Relation* of Panzani, who wrote after his return from England in 1636. He knew very little at first-hand, and may well add, *si dice pure*, "so people say again." And he understood very little at second-hand, as we shall see later in the affairs of the first and second Lords Baltimore. The very similarity of the two sentences just quoted, one following the other, seems to indicate that he had noted as a double fact what had merely been mentioned under a double name. As to this Anthony Smith, it is not clear whether he may not have been a Jesuit still at the date of his going out with Baltimore in 1627. For the Rev. Mr. Clerk, five years later, counts him among those who had left the Society within the previous three years. He writes to Fitton, agent of the secular clergy in Rome: "Those seauen [seven] Jesuits putt out of their order here in England within the space of 3 yeares, my lord [Bishop of Chalcedon] can best name unto you; three or 4 I remember, videlicet Rob. Rookood, Anthony Smith, John Dukes, Ferdinando Pulton" (Stonyhurst MSS., *Anglia A*, viii. f. 74: Clerk to [Fitton], July 13, 1632). As to the Rev. Mr. Thomas Longueville, of whom so little seems to be known, we meet him here on the Newfoundland mission; and again, in 1632, we find him in England writing a long and bitter lamentation that, owing to the Jesuits, he can find no fixed place; and in particular because, as he says, "Mr. Wigmore, *alias* Momfort, one of those Jesuits receaued here in England, hath throughout al the countrie where I liue so blased and published the Breue which is, as he saieth, against our Bishop and Clergie, that he hath therby endeauored much to alienate our friends from vs" (Stonyhurst MSS., *Ibid.*, f. 164: Longueville to Fitton, April 27, 1632). The Brief in question is that of 1631, which closed the controversy to be mentioned later in connection with Lord Baltimore. From all this it appears that Longueville was never a Jesuit.

much satisfaction to that knight our friend, that in the spring he went there; he stopped there; and I have managed to get him made governor of the island. He writes wonderful things about it, and incredible things about the quantity of fish. The inhabitants are few and of a kindly temperament; and, though all are idolaters, they do no harm to strangers. I trust that, as you have promised, your Excellencies will not fail to send missionaries expressly for this mission.

"Two of our [Carmelite] religious are come; one for that new mission, but he is old and incapable; the other is sent by the superior, and he has no experience or sufficient knowledge; and, if you do not take this mission of ours in England under your protection, I shall be forced to abandon it. I have put down the reasons in another letter herein enclosed." And with this he signs himself their most humble servant, "✝ Simon Stock, Chelsea, 30 October, 1625."[1]

We may say once for all that the tenor of Stock's correspondence is monotonous. He himself chose his post in England, and it was only to serve there that he entered the Order of Carmelites; but he finds that he enjoys no advantages there, neither convents, nor chapters, nor a novitiate, all of which he desires to have, and none of which can he obtain from the General. Hence on several occasions he proposes to leave his Order, as in this letter he threatens to leave England. Meanwhile he takes things into his own hands generally, has a governor appointed in Newfoundland, has secular priests sent over there; and his influence seems to be considerable, though history is rather silent on that subject. Still, he reports and links together some facts which we do not find elsewhere; and for these we cite him.

The Sacred Congregation of the Propaganda took action upon this letter, and proposed to his Holiness that the General of the said Order "should on all accounts be required to despatch those missionaries whom he had already intended to send to that island, in company with the two English nobles, that were to take the missionaries out at their expense. In this way a relation at least will be obtained by their means, regarding the inhabitants of those parts; and perchance, with the help of God, who makes very easy that which seems impossible to the human mind, he [the General] will open a way for his workmen to convert not only the natives, but also the heretics who have established colonies there."[2]

[1] Propaganda Archives, *Lettere d'Inghilterra*, etc., *riferite*, 101 [A.D. 1626], f. 21; his *Cause* or Reasons, etc., f. 22.
[2] *Ibid.*, f. 21ᵛ: "*Die 6 Februarii*, 1626, *Cong.* 51: *Ad Ill. Millinum, pro sequenti coram Sanctissimo, Num.* 5."

At this date the Sacred Congregation of the Propaganda had been organized for several years. In the Constitution of Gregory XV., published June 22, 1622, the board had been appointed, consisting of thirteen Cardinals, two prelates, a religious in the person of the Vicar-General of the Discalced Carmelites, and a secretary. One of the prelates was John Baptist Agucchi, a papal secretary and apostolic notary. The secretary of the new Congregation was Dr. Francis Ingoli, a priest of Ravenna, who remained in this post during more than a quarter of a century, from 1622 till 1649. The object set before this great Congregation was, as the Pope declared in his Constitution, "to superintend all missions for preaching and teaching the Gospel and Catholic doctrine; to appoint and change necessary ministers."[3] Mgr. Agucchi was promoted soon afterwards to the nunciature of Venice; and the distance between the secretary, Ingoli, and the Nuncio at Venice gave rise to a correspondence. Mgr. Ingoli communicated items of information; and, as the material rapidly grew on his hands, he conceived the plan of putting the relations together in order; on which account he invoked the aid of the Venetian Nuncio, with much of the respect usually entertained by a disciple towards his master. The confidence was evidently not misplaced, on the score of literary taste and historical criticism.[4]

The institution of the Propaganda.

Secretary Ingoli and the Nuncio Agucchi.

On December 27, 1625, just before official cognizance was taken of Simon Stock's letter, secretary Ingoli wrote to Mgr. Agucchi, giving him an account of "the affairs of the Congregation in summary;" and he distributed the subject of the epitome under five heads: (1) Sweden; (2) Avalon; (3) Bohemia and Moravia; (4) Alexandria and Cairo; (5) Grisons. His paragraph on Avalon runs thus—

" 2°. There has been discovered by the Discalced Carmelites of England a new and great island, very fertile and full of sensible people. It is called by them Avallonia, and is half-way on the voyage from England to North America. A great lord thereof has already been converted from paganism;[5] and he has asked for two

[3] Cf. *Collectanea S. Congregationis de Propaganda Fide*, No. 3.
[4] Vatican Library, *Ottoboni* 2536, a volume of Agucchi's letters and his own drafts; a large 4to, ff. 24–337.—*Ibid.*, *Vaticano-Latino* 6696, a small folio, ff. 1–147, may be one of Ingoli's redactions. It is a uniform copy of relations or of summaries thereof, supplied by persons who have been asked for them in Rome or in divers parts of Europe. We have not lighted upon a corresponding volume for this date treating of the Indies and America.
[5] " *Una nuova Isola grande, fertilissima e piena d'huomini sensati... S'è conuertito già dalla gentilità un sig[nor]e grande di quella.*"

Barefooted Carmelites, who have already come from Flanders to England." [6]

But Simon Stock had applied himself to the enterprise in the wrong way. He had undertaken it without reference to his superiors, which was a measure the more futile, as he had no subjects to send without their co-operation; and, indeed, he seems to have had no authority to dispose of members at all. The Congregation consulted his superiors in his stead. These latter would appear to have consulted other Carmelites in England, over Stock's head. The said Carmelites returned a reply which is filed in the archives, and is not gratifying unto Simon's pretensions.

The report begins with much historical and geographical variety of landscape, wherein three colonies are spoken of as having been founded in North America since 1603; Virginia and New England blend into one hazy view; the fishing for cod on the shore of Newfoundland might appear to be flourishing in the latitude of Virginia; and the two Catholic cavaliers, on whom Simon's enterprise depends, are among those who have a footing at large somewhere in this extensive territory. The three colonies can boast respectively of fifty houses, of twenty, and of fifteen; and Simon and the cavaliers are probably involved in the fifteen-house undertaking. But there are no Catholics there, except the two said gentlemen; and they do not live there, but here. And the Protestants who are there make no show of being obliging in the face of a Catholic invasion. The writer has spoken to his two companions, Fathers Eliseus and Elias, desiring them to go, if only to gather intelligence about those parts; but both are of one mind that the basis of operations, as laid down by Fra Simon, is not substantiated in fact; and they decline to go, making the pertinent observation that, as Fra Simon has taken up the business to treat of it with the Sacred Congregation, he may as well carry it out by going himself. The writer offers to set out himself, if he shall receive an intimation to that effect, and if he can only find the two cavaliers who are to supply the wherewithal for the journey. But one is in Ireland, the other he knows not where. Neither is in London, because the plague is raging there.[7]

Stock's account of Avalon revised.

[6] Vatican Library, *Ottoboni* 2536, f. 45: Ingoli, Rome, December 17, 1625, to Agucchi.
[7] Propaganda Archives, *America Centrale*, I. ff. 5-6: " *Relazione auuta dalli PP. Carmelitani scalzi, che sono in Inghilterra intorno alla Missione proposta . . . dal P. F. Simone Stock . . . nel Paese della Virginia che chiamano nuoua Inghilterra, ad istanza di due Caualieri Cattolici . . .* "

Fra Simon had followed his former letter with another, in which he enclosed a memorial on the manner of conducting missions properly and effectually. The policy therein laid down consisted in furnishing him with such faculties in England as other regulars enjoyed; in giving him licence to found a novitiate, to have active and passive voice as other religious of his Order had, with the confirmation of certain constitutions for the good management of missions; and all this he demanded for "Holy Church, which was losing its honour by founding chimerical missions, without a basis on which to rest, or means to produce fruit." [8]

In his letter he stated that "in Virginia the English heretics have founded a college to infect America with heresy. *Virginia.*

"I humbly beg of you to remember the mission of Avalon, because, if the faith be not planted there now, all will become infected heretics, to the great detriment of Holy Church. Many Catholic friends of ours will go to live there, if they have religious men provided on purpose to go with them. From the beginning I wrote to your Excellencies, that there is no [Carmelite] Father of ours here for the purpose; and you promised by a letter of March 16 to send missionaries, and you have not sent any except this one, who is infirm and without faculties sufficient to keep up relations with the Ordinary of England; seeing that Avalon is at least 2000 miles distant from here." [9]

On these premises, the action taken in the Propaganda was manifold. As to Fra Simon's account of the King's "edict unto the propagation of Calvinism in Virginia, Vermudes, New England, and Nova Scotia," it was considered necessary to send a mission out on the part of the Sacred Congregation, for the evangelizing " of those provinces, and of the Philippines, China, and East Indies;" for "it was easy to cross over from North America to the Philippines, China, and the East Indies." Wherefore it was ordered that the Generals of the "Dominicans, Observantines, Augustinians, or Jesuits" should be consulted about despatching a mission "from the nearer parts of North America to the aforesaid provinces of the same America," and their answers be reported.[10] *Virginia, Vermudes, New England, Nova Scotia.*

The Congregation learnt from the Carmelite General that the two

[8] Propaganda Archives, *Lettere*, 101, as above, f. 24: London, December 15, 1625.
[9] *Ibid.*, f. 23: London, December 5, 1625.
[10] *Ibid.*, *Acta*, 3, *Congregatio* 39, July 21, 1625, *Coram Sanctissimo*, No. 25, f. 245.

missionaries in London were now in prison; and, with this and other data on hand, a reply was drafted for Father Stock to the effect that, "since the missionaries who were to have been sent to Avalon have been imprisoned, and since of Simon's own Order there are no other subjects who know the language and are competent, it is necessary that he himself get ready to go thither with the companion whom the General will give him from here. The necessary faculties will be sent him." And their Eminences proceed to say that at least they will be able to procure through him a full and trustworthy account, and so be enabled to take further steps; and, if his own Order shall not be able to supply the men needed, others no doubt will. And they thank him for his correspondence.[11]

Stock deputed as missionary to Avalon.

The Nuncio at Brussels, having been referred to on the subject, had no encouragement to give, but said to the Congregation about Simon's project of an English novitiate which was discountenanced by Simon's own Order: "I fear that inconveniences will ensue, if, while his Order disapproves of his plan, you give him the faculties to execute it in these States." Referring to a note which had been sent him by the Congregation, and in which the Carmelites had set forth the inexpediency of following Stock's programme, the Nuncio observed that some one who was versed in the affairs of their institute should be commissioned to examine the case.[12]

Pondering also on the memorial sent by Simon as to the manner of conducting missions, the Congregation approved of ten rules, whereof four relate to dignities in the missions, binding superiors under oath to promote the more worthy subjects, etc., and the others regard spiritual exercises and the observance of conventual rules, etc., as befitted the respective Orders. But the most obvious value of the memorial suggesting these rules is that of its showing how some good people brought themselves under the favourable notice of the Propaganda, and, at the cost of third parties, made their way into the counsels of that Sacred Congregation.[13]

In a series of communications from 1626 to 1631, we find Stock sending a long account of the new world, on the authority of a pilot, whose name he does not mention; with an accompanying map,

---

[11] Propaganda Archives, *Lettere*, 101, f. 23, endorsed: "*Die* 17 *Martii*, 1626, *Cong.* 53;" Cardinal Millini being reporter.

[12] *Ibid.*, f. 78: Nuncio, Brussels, March 14, 1626. The reference to "these States" implies that the institution projected should have to be organized in the Low Countries.

[13] *Ibid.*, *Acta*, 4, *Cong.* 53, March 17, 1626, *Coram Sanctissimo*, No. 7, f. 30.

correcting the former one despatched to their Eminences. He holds out the prospect that the people of the new country "will, in a few years, become themselves good missionaries, and priests, and religious, without needing further supplies from Italy or other parts." [14] The Sacred Congregation repeats its thanks, gives expression to its hopes, and presumes that Stock has received the intimation of its desire that he should go himself to America; and then, on his return from Avalon, the mission will be abundantly provided with subjects, "if not of your own Order, which is rather scant of men, then at least of some other, that is to say, Capuchins or Recollects, if you think these would suit." [15]

Maps.

This was not at all what Stock wanted. He writes that he has received the faculties, and they are not what he expected. He expresses his disgust at their insufficiency. He has planted the faith in many places where there was not a single Catholic Christian before, notably in Canterbury, a principal city. He therefore expected rather that His Holiness would have granted him privileges, "and not have deprived him of necessary faculties." [16]

With another map which he sends, to show how the English heretics have occupied the best part of North America, he tells how "men and women of that country have been here in England, and they are like those of Europe; and one of them was in these last wars of Bohemia; and nothing is wanting but holy faith to make them like the Italians.

"Among the other plantations which the English heretics have made in North America, on the same line and elevation of the Pole, and same latitude as that of Rome, they have built a town upon hills like those of Rome, and a fort, where for three years now there have been two ministers or preachers; and more will be gone soon to infest that people with heresy. In that map, this town is called Plimouth." He directs their attention to the 32nd degree of longitude on the map.[17]

Plymouth, New England.

§ 9. At this point, quite a new turn is given to the friar's relations. He sets his face against the General of his own Order, and against the religious Orders that be. He introduces the business of a violent controversy which has begun to rage in

---

[14] Propaganda Archives, *Lettere*, 101, ff. 15, 16: London, March 7, 1626.
[15] *Ibid.*, f. 16ᵛ, endorsement: "*Die 4 Maii*, 1626, *Cong.* 56."
[16] *Ibid.*, ff. 13, 17, April 2, June 30, 1626; from London.
[17] *Ibid.*, f. 14, April 22, 1626.

England. At the same time, he speaks of Lord Baltimore's movements. This noble lord on his part enters actively into the same ecclesiastical controversy, if not on behalf of the regular Orders, at least not against them. Affairs generally become embroiled.

Simon Stock continues in the same letter, after speaking of Plymouth as above: "Our Father General has written to me, that your Excellencies have recommended him to send me alone to that island."

A disappointed missionary.

Upon this preamble he proceeds to establish a thesis, that he must first be authorized to found the Carmelite mission in England, as other Orders have done, with novitiates and temporal means, with competent superiors, with the right of active and passive voice, with adequate faculties; otherwise, says he, alluding to the General's communication, "it is of no use running after chimeras in sacred things and, through want of discretion, making the conversion of infidels more difficult than it is, and rendering apostolic missions odious, through the want of success [which should rest] on proper foundations and means."[1] And, after some more language in the same mood, he puts himself in the hands of the Sacred Congregation for anything that is desired, "provided they give him licence to observe the laws and customs of Holy Church, and give him the necessary means to produce fruit and to save his soul." The endorsement on this letter says that "Fra Simon Stock gives a curious relation, which should be read *in extenso*."[2] The good man returns later with indefatigable persistence to the same theme: "It is better not to send out any mission, than to do so without form or foundation; wherefore I most humbly beg your Excellencies to take this mission under your protection, and be pleased to recommend to our superiors that they follow in the footsteps of Holy Church, as do the Jesuit Fathers, the Benedictine Fathers, the Fathers of St. Francis, and all that are here, with fruitful results."[3]

Eight months later he says: "During two years now I have been humbly soliciting the aid of your Excellencies for the mission of Avalonia and for that of England; and up to the present nothing has yet been done for one or other mission. Thus those Christians of Avalonia have come here, but with the intention of returning in the spring to Avalonia." This was the expedition with which Lord Baltimore

Lord Baltimore's expedition of May —July, 1627.

---

[1] "*Per il malo successo supra debiti fundamenti et mezzj.*"
[2] Propaganda Archives, *loc. cit.*
[3] *Ibid.*, f. 18, June 30, 1626.

was about to take ship for Newfoundland. The friar goes on to speak of the immense difficulties caused him by the persecution, "and the indiscreet obedience and bad government of the superiors of the Order, which prevents me much more from producing fruit in converting souls to the Lord than the persecution does; for they deny me the licence to use the means necessary for the work, such as Holy Church has always used, depriving me of assistance, and afflicting me with impertinent commands; and it is now fourteen or fifteen years since I began to be oppressed in this manner; and there is no hope for anything better under the obedience of the Order. Wherefore I humbly supplicate the Sacred Congregation to grant me permission to live under the obedience of the Bishop of Chalcedon, Vicar-Apostolic of England; and this will be a special favour to me; and with his permission and counsel I shall easily accomplish something for the good of this my afflicted country." [4]

The disappointment from which the missionary was suffering appeared evidently enough in these communications. The Congregation first replied that, "as to the novitiate of the English which your Reverence has claimed during so many years past, your superiors not judging that measure expedient for the Order, no resolution has been come to of the kind you desire; and the Sacred Congregation is accustomed to do no violence to the superiors of Orders, finding that to run counter to their wishes always embarrasses the management of business. As to the mission of Avalon, no resolution has been made for want of subjects; and since you, who are informed, have not thought fit to accept the charge, the Congregation does not know whom to send, if you do not propose some fit person either of your own or another religious institute." [5] When Stock began to ply his new idea of leaving his own Order, founding a monastery, and putting it "under the obedience of Bishops, as in the primitive Church," the Congregation answered: "As to the desire you manifest of living under the obedience of the Bishop of Chalcedon, since it is not becoming in a good religious to withdraw from the obedience due to his superiors, it is well to persevere in your vocation, and do your best to help souls in those countries, where there is so much need of labourers." [6]

Speaking evidently of Baltimore's first trip to the new world with the Rev. Messrs. Longueville and Smith, Stock says, in October,

[4] Propaganda Archives, *Lettere*, etc., 129, f. 208: London, February 12, 1627.
[5] *Ibid.*, endorsed: "*Die* 12 *Julii*, 1627, *Cong.* 77."
[6] *Ibid.*, 102, f. 10, endorsed: "*Die* 19 *Januarii*, 1628," on Stock's letter of October 10, 1627.

1627: "No religious having been sent for the new mission, about which I have written so much, I did not want to lose the occasion; <small>Longueville and Smith.</small> so I managed that two secular priests should go, one to be with the Catholics who are there, and who number about twenty, the other to come back here with the hope of obtaining more assistance in the spring."[7] And, in the <small>More maps.</small> following June he resumes: "I send to your Excellencies the map which you desire to have, and I send two sorts, one printed in the year 1624, and the other in the year 1628, which is the darker of the two. I did not write that I sent religious to the new mission; because I had none to send. But the two who went last year were secular priests; and this year there are others gone; and with them he of whom I wrote when first I spoke to you of this mission; as well as other spiritual sons of mine; and I have given them the advice that, when they have settled the mission a little, they should send some one to Rome to give an account and to ask assistance of Holy Church; and they will do so; and, when any of them come back hither, and the times are more tranquil, I will write at greater length.

"Here there is a great discord between the secular and the regular priests. As they have been so long without bishops, and in <small>The controversy in England. 1628.</small> such liberty that they did what they liked, and much more than they ought, the name of a bishop and of any degree of subordination is ungrateful." Simon Stock here takes occasion to extend his former idea of leaving the Order to which he belonged, and he intimates the propriety of dissolving the missionary Orders altogether, and substituting diocesan monasteries for them. He says: "In the end, your Excellencies and Holy Church will find no better means for quieting these contentions and establishing missions, than by founding monasteries and making missions of religious under the obedience of bishops, as in the primitive Church; and of commencing missions in the way in which they require to be continued and settled: so great is human misery, that it is easier to plant a new church and the faith where it has never been, than to bridle the liberty once granted."

Upon this text of Simon Stock's, the secretary, Mgr. Ingoli, writes a lengthy annotation for Cardinal Barberini, in which, speaking of <small>Ingoli's thesis.</small> the missions, he declares himself against the exemption of religious from the jurisdiction of bishops; he disagrees with the application of the principle of exemption, as laid down by

[7] Propaganda Archives, *loc. cit.*

the Council of Trent and carried out by the Congregation of the Holy Office, unless the regulars are living in community "conventually," and not if they are engaged as missionaries abroad; and he closes the disquisition with the urgent note: "To his Eminence, Cardinal Barberini. For the next audience of His Holiness. Would your Excellency condescend to read and consider well this writing, because it is of importance?" Finally, the Sacred Congregation itself, taking action on the letter, "ordered thanks to be returned to the aforesaid friar for the maps and for his admonition against regulars."[8] The Cardinal Barberini, who reported the correspondence, would seem to have been the Capuchin named Antonio Cardinale di Sant' Onufrio, and not his nephew, Cardinal Francesco Barberini, Secretary of State and Protector of England.

Soon after his last letter, Stock wrote again about Avalon, and his friend the pilot, and his expectation of seeing some one back from that country in the same year, 1628. For this he was thanked again; his further communications were solicited, and an account in particular asked of "the progress of the Bishop of Chalcedon and other missionaries, and especially of the regulars," etc.[9]

Amid much correspondence of the friar, we notice the distinctly new American item, which he gives one year later, July 2, 1629. He says: "In the want of missionaries for the new mission, two Fathers of the Society of Jesus are gone there; and so from them your Excellencies shall have some relation of what is going on there, and what can be done." And, on August 9 he promises: "Two Fathers of the Society on the return of the ships, which shall be in September, will give a good account to you."[10] *(Jesuits gone to Avalon. 1629.)*

Eight months passed and the friar wrote expressing his gratification that "the difference between his lordship the Bishop of Chalcedon and the regulars was settled in the Holy Office," or Congregation of the Inquisition; it was "now three years since this dispute had commenced," and the long delay in settling it had prejudiced "the reputation of the [Roman] court, among infidels. A great number of the sect of Puritans are gone from here, to live in the northern parts of America—4000 or more; and they will infect with their heresy those infidels who, as I have understood from the people that come thence, want to be *(4000 Puritans to North America.)*

---

[8] Propaganda Archives, *Lettere*, 102, ff. 11–13: Simon Stock, June 27, 1628, endorsed: "*Die* 24 *Novembris*, 1628, *Cong.* 100, *Nu?* 20."
[9] *Ibid.*, 131, f. 187: Simon Stock, July 28, 1628, endorsed: "*Nu?* 31, *Die* 12 *Januarii*, 1629, *Cong.* 103."
[10] *Ibid.*, 131, ff. 186, 188.

Christians; and they are numberless populations, and they are near to Europe. Since peace is concluded between France and England, the persecution has increased here." [11]

This letter was unsatisfactory. The Congregation wrote, asking about Avalon, which had been so conspicuous in his correspondence before. He answered on January 1, 1631: "The letter of your Excellencies, dated June 22, came to hand only in December. As to the affairs of Avalon, two Fathers of the Society went there about Easter, in the year 1629, and returned here before the feast of Christmas following; and they brought with them to England practically all the Catholics who were there, leaving behind them about thirty heretics, and two or three Catholic women, without priest or minister of any kind. They say, the winter before they reached there was extremely cold; and the land is barren." Then, apparently alluding to Lord Baltimore, but mistaking Baltimore's purpose of founding a new colony in the direction of Virginia for a longing to see Newfoundland again, Stock goes on to say: "I have spoken with the principal gentleman of that place; and he is sorry to come back; and he says, he means to return there again; and that the Fathers of the Society have a mission or commission specially for those parts of America." [12] As this letter is dated January 1, 1631, some particular negotiations regarding a Jesuit mission in America must have been set on foot in 1630 or earlier; and not improbably from the time that the two Jesuits went, in 1629, to Avalon. The arrangement does not seem to please Simon Stock, for he continues—

Baltimore, Virginia, and the Jesuits. [1630.]

"As now those parts of the world are more or less at peace, and the English, French, and Scotch have colonies in those parts of America; if his Holiness would be pleased to settle there a colony of Italians with a bishop and religious of the greatest poverty who are accustomed to suffer, and so plant the holy faith in those parts of the world, which are as large as Europe and near and opposite to Europe, nor yet converted anywhere, it would be a work redounding to the honour of Holy Church, and withal most useful in the course of time, and most opportune for converting them."

Simon then closes with some observations on the controversy between the Bishop of Chalcedon and the regulars: the decree has not yet been published; there is no saying what effect it will have;

---

[11] Propaganda Archives, *Lettere*, 132, f. 141: Stock, April 28, 1630.
[12] "*E che li Padri della Compagnia tengano missione o comissione particulare per quelli loci d'America.*"

in the present interval of suspense, the evils of the debate are multiplying. He promises to send a report of how the decree works, as soon as it is known what the decree says.[13]

The summary of this letter records merely: "That to the island of Avalon, in 1629, there went at Easter two Jesuit Fathers, etc." The Sacred Congregation ordered an answer to be sent in this sense: "Acknowledge the receipt, and bid him go on steadily informing the Sacred Congregation of all that he shall happen to learn about Avalon; the Congregation having already ordered thither a mission of English and French Capuchins; and likewise let him send word about the particulars of the contentions between the regular clergy and the Bishop of Chalcedon, to suggest to the Congregation of the Inquisition such means as shall appear effective for stopping the disputes; it is high time."[14] *Capuchins instead of Jesuits for Avalon. 1631.*

Here for the present we may leave Simon Stock's relations, such as they were. Some other reports were being received by the Propaganda, and were being acted upon at Rome. Some steps too had been taken by Lord Baltimore in America and England, of which Stock either knew or said nothing.

§ 10. When Lord Baltimore arrived in Avalon for the second time, bringing with him the priest Hacket, it would appear that the colony became uncomfortable for a resident Protestant clergyman there, one named Erasmus Stourton. He was not the first incumbent in the island, the Rev. Mr. James having tried it, with its "eight or nine months' winter, and upon the land nothing but rocks, lakes, or morasses like bogs, which one might thrust a spike down to the butt-head." Mr. James abandoned the place for the more congenial post of librarian to Sir Robert Cotton, in England.[1] So too the Rev. Mr. Stourton left it in August, 1628, arrived at Plymouth in the old country, and forthwith volunteered an information or denunciation of the Catholic lord. *Deserting and denouncing Avalon. 1628.*

This business of denunciation on the score of religion was not considered a discreditable occupation, any more than the eventual gathering in of the spoils, which might follow as a perquisite. We just mention the circumstance to save the reader's susceptibilities, when he sees the avocation so patronized by people of condescending moods; and when he finds the most respectable names of gentlemen

---

[13] Propaganda Archives, *Lettere* 100, ff. 150, 151: Stock, London, January 1, 1631.
[14] *Ibid., loc. cit.*, endorsed.
[1] E. D. Neill, *Terra Mariæ*, pp. 46, 47: from Mead (1629).

associated for more than a century with the assiduous telling of tales either in the court of a magistrate or in the King's council-chamber. And, as a proper counterpart thereto, the more irresponsible people were, or the more cheaply moved by fitting considerations, so much the more were they egged on to tell all the stories they could about others; while they were free, in presence of a flattering auditory, to say all the nice things they might about themselves. The dun and repulsive character of great masses of documents in the archives of administrative bureaus is a monumental commentary on this ply of the human heart.

Accordingly, this good gentleman, being Lord Anglesea's chaplain, offered himself promptly for examination, and did depose as follows:

The delinquencies imputed. "That my Lord of Baltamore arryved there agayne and brought with him one other seminary preist whose name is Hacket." Proceeding with conscientious frankness to the substance or body of the crimes committed, the examinee did continue: "The sayd Hacket and Smith every Sunday say Masse and doe vse all other ceremonies of the church of Rome, in as ample manner as is vsed in Spayne. And this Examinant hath seene them at Masse, and knoweth that the childe of one William Poole," a Protestant, was baptized a Catholic, "contrary to the will of the sayd Poole, to which childe the sayd Lord was a witness."[2]

To this reverend gentleman and informer the noble lord, so mightly traduced at so great a distance, did not fail to send a bouquet of his compliments. Writing to his most gracious and dread sovereign, in the August of the following year, he returned thanks for protection from calumny and malice, uttered to his prejudice by "persons notoriously lewd and wicked. Such a one," he continued, "is that audacious man, who, being banished the colony for his misdeeds, did the last wynter (as I understand) raise a false and slanderous report of me at Plymouth," etc.[3]

What happened in the course of domestic life at Avalon, we may gather from a document which secretary Ingoli of the Propaganda procured in 1630 from the Nuncio at Brussels, and *"New England or New Found Land."* which then he communicated to his friend Agucchi, for use in the volume of missionary relations. The document forwarded from Brussels is called: "New England or New Found Land," a form of synonymous nomenclature which does

[2] Public Record Office, *Colonial Papers, A. & W.I.*, iv. No. 59, 1 p. fol.; stamped "*Conway Papers;*" October 9, 1628.
[3] *Ibid.*, v. No. 27: Geo. Baltimore, Feryland, August 19, 1629, to the King.—Cf. Scharf, i. pp. 44, 45.

not agree with our modern geography. Still, it was sufficiently accurate just then. Ten years before, a patent of incorporation had been granted to the Duke of Lenox and others, for the foundation of a Plymouth colony, lying between 40 and 48 degrees of north latitude, and to be called "New England."[4] That range of territory would comprise Avalon in Newfoundland, besides Nova Scotia, the modern New England, New York, and Pennsylvania. And it is with an extension like this that we find the term used afterwards by the Maryland missionaries, when they speak of New England as the next plantation north of their own.

The occasion and purport of the Belgian Nuncio's report are explained in his accompanying letter, addressed to Cardinal Ludovisi, Prefect of the Propaganda: "I have arranged to procure the information, which your Eminence was pleased to order by your letter of July 20, regarding the English Puritans who have betaken themselves to North America; and what I have ascertained may be seen in the relation enclosed. The French missionaries will be very useful by going there to stop at once the progress of the said Puritans; nor will it be difficult, when necessary, to send some from here [Belgium], as there are many religious qualified for the purpose. But, for the sake of the language, priests English themselves will be best. Of these at present two only could be sent; and their reports might then be looked for; so that the Sacred Congregation could take such action as it judged more serviceable for the propagation of the faith in those parts. One might solicit the aid of the ambassadors of France and Spain, who are stationed in London, to ensure the said missionaries against any let or hindrance being put in their way. I will see to what your Eminence will proceed to order, and will execute it duly. And I remain . . . Brussels, 21 September, 1630. The Archbishop of Consa."[5]

The report, so introduced, describes the topography of New England or New Found Land. The vast undefined region is sketched in terms proportionately general, and we may say approximately true; for each part of a vague description may naturally suit some part or other of a diversified continent. Then the particulars of the history are given to the effect, that Count Baltimore, George Calvert, first King James's Secretary, and afterwards a Catholic, having sent out adventurers to explore, obtained permission "some four years ago" to conduct a

The Nuncio's report on North America. September, 1630.

[4] Cf. *Calendar of State Papers, Colonial, A. & W.I.*, i. 24: November 3, 1620.
[5] Propaganda Archives, *I America*, 259, f. 1, original.

colony thither, "in company with another gentleman of about the same rank, but a heretic." To secure harmony, the King himself defined the limits between the two. "Calvert took with him not only Protestants, but some Catholics, who were happy to travel thither and escape the rising storm of persecution in England." Then, after stating that the priests who went with Calvert were the secular clergymen, Anthony Rivers and Thomas a Longavilla, and that the land was utterly uninhabited, the report continues—

"As to the practice of religion, that was carried on under Calvert's roof; in one part, Mass was said according to the Catholic rite; in another, the heretics performed their functions.[6] Not long afterwards, Calvert and the two priests, along with divers Catholics, returned to England; and some too of the other colony of the heretics." Here no mention is made of the double or triple reinforcement of priests, after Rivers and Longueville; first Hacket, and afterwards the two Jesuits in Newfoundland. And in what follows the Relation confounds the glowing reports of Baltimore returning from Virginia with the notorious disappointment attending the Avalon enterprise. It says: "When they came back from the new found Land, they were eloquent in its praises; and so others caught the idea of seeing that region, if an occasion offered. About five months ago, some Puritans made up their minds to emigrate. They are supposed to have been prompted to this by religious zeal. For, when they saw the chapel of her Majesty the Queen thrown open, and the Catholic religion practised there freely; and Capuchins to boot, who had come into England with the King's consent; believing that the end of their evangelical doctrine was in sight, they made up their minds in considerable numbers to go and settle a New England. Among them were not a few distinguished for birth and wealth. The number of those who set out is said to have reached about two thousand." The report closes with a reference to the oaths of allegiance and supremacy, exacted of the Puritans before they started. "Most took both oaths; some declined the latter one" of supremacy, that which professed

Celebrating under the same roof with heretics.

---

[6] About this time the Propaganda formulated a decree against missionaries using churches in which heretics held divine service: "*Referente eodem Illustrissimo D. Magalotto litteras fratris Ignatii Capuccini, S. Cong. censuit, non debere missionarios divina celebrare in ecclesiis, in quibus simul hæretici sua profana et sacrilega exercitia habent; ut tamen Catholicis fiat satis, super altaribus portatilibus in privatis domibus positis sacrum peragendum esse.*" *Acta*, 4, *Cong.* 75, Maii 21, 1627, *Coram Sanctissimo*, No. 15, f. 222.—But, seven years later, the question was opened again with regard to Rhætia (Tyrol): *Ibid.*, 10, *Cong.* 190, Mart. 13, 1634, *Coram Sanctissimo*, No. 25.

"the Archbishop of Canterbury to be the true and legitimate primate of England." It was "foreign to the anarchy of the Puritans," that is, to the Presbyterian or Independent system, which admitted no prelacy in the Church.[7]

Upon the Relation and the accompanying letter of the Brussels Nuncio, reported formally to the Congregation of the Propaganda by the Cardinal of Tivoli, an order was issued "to treat with the Procurator-General of the Capuchins, who should arrange, through Father Joseph of Paris, that a mission be sent to the said New England under the usual conditions, to wit, that the said Father Joseph be required to signify the names of the prefect and of the missionaries, and their number in all; and in due time also the progress made. To the Nuncio of Flanders acknowledgment should be made of his letter, and the information be given that his report was brought to the notice of His Holiness, who derived satisfaction from it, as well as to the notice of the Cardinals, who gave orders as in the above decree."[8] No mention was made of the Jesuits.

A full abstract of the Relation was promptly sent by the secretary Ingoli to his friend Agucchi, on December 28, 1630: "Your Excellency will receive herewith the writing from Morocco, and a Relation about New England in North America, with two other papers about two notable miracles, that you may take advantage of them to enrich our letters, which I think will receive a noteworthy contribution in these particulars. I have thought proper to send you also at the same time some resolutions, which have been passed regarding the Indies, in consequence of which I hope to see great progress made."[9]

Ingoli and Agucchi on New England, 1630, 1631.

---

[7] Propaganda Archives, *I America*, 259, f. 2. The "latter oath" is misapprehended.

[8] *Ibid.*, f. 4ᵛ, endorsed.—Also *Ibid.*, Acta, 7, Cong. 132, Nov. 22, 1630, *Coram Sanctissimo*, No. 10, f. 164ᵛ; with the Cardinal reporter's proper name, Bentivoglio, cited in the decree.

[9] Vatican Library, *Ottoboni*, 2536, f. 150: Ingoli to Agucchi, December 28, 1630, ff. 154–157; minutes of the resolutions at the particular congregation of November 18, 1630, General Congregation of November 21, same year, and papal audience relative thereto, all distributed in Ingoli's text and marginal notes. They are on the subject of fifteen articles submitted by the Collector of Portugal; and they concern the training of a native clergy, throwing open missionary fields to all religious Orders, suppressing the slave-trade, and other matters that touch chiefly the Spanish and Portuguese Indies. The throwing open of missionary fields has reference, without a doubt, to the Jesuit reservation in the Far East. And, in a preceding letter to Agucchi, the secretary mentions two other distinct points with reference to the Society; one being that of universities, which the Sacred Congregation desires to have thrown open to all religious Orders, the other being the question of Jesuitesses: "*Nell' Indie s'è sparsa la fama di essa [viz. la Congregazione] e con grand' allegrezza si darà principio à nuove conquiste de' popoli : solo perchè gl' operarij hauranno doue far capo ne' bisogni delle Missioni. Mi spiace solo, che questa Congregazione da padri Giesuiti non sia ben intesa, nè credo potrà mai essere : perchè spesso occorrono materie di disgusto loro, massime [nel] punto dell' uniuersità, che la Sacra Congregazione uuole,*

Mgr. Agucchi did not attach any special value for actual use to the New England Relation. He wrote: "With your letter of the 28th of last month, I received the papers you sent me; and of all that is to the point I will enter the proper notices in their own places. The account of New England, submitted by Mgr. the Nuncio of Flanders, came to hand some time ago; but it does not seem to me that, as far as the Congregation is concerned, there is anything of consequence there. However, I took note of the abstract, for the purpose of attaching it to America, if it fits in. I should be sorry to see heretics making such an advance there. However, the Dutch are making much more." Among other pieces of advice and criticism he says: "Take care also not to be too ready to believe all that the missionaries write; for they willingly amplify their relations." [10]

While George Calvert was in Newfoundland, he corresponded with Father Andrew White at Liège; and, among other things, said to the Father that he would divide with him "every and the very last bitt." [11] At that time, Father White addressed himself to the Provincial, applying for the American mission; and he was complimented by the General upon his spirit of sacrifice. Father Thomas, one of his colleagues, had also applied.[12]

Calvert and the Avalon Jesuits.

Now, it appears that some Jesuits were actually despatched to Newfoundland at that very date, in the spring of 1629; for so has Simon Stock expressly told us; and besides we see traces in the history of some Fathers, though no trace remains in the Catalogues extant. It is said of Father Alexander Baker, a rather famous character of those times, that twice he undertook journeys to the remotest parts of the Indies—assuredly the West Indies, not the East.[13] But, for 1634, we have it recorded in the Catalogue that he was out in Maryland then; and he never appeared

Fathers Baker and L. Rigby.

---

che siano libere à tutte le Religioni, et in materia delle Giesuitesse, che per il mondo si uanno disseminando, con colleggi de' medesimi istituti della Società," etc. Ingoli to Agucchi, November 3, 1629. *Ibid.*, ff. 71ᵛ, 72.—For the resolutions, etc., cf. also Propaganda Archives, *Acta*, 7, *Cong.* 132, Nov. 22, 1630, *Coram Sanctissimo*, No. 33, ff. 172-178.—The name of the Nuncio, diversely spelt, is engraved "Agucchi" on his tomb in Sant' Onufrio, Rome.

[10] Vatican Library, *Ottoboni*, 2536, f. 242: Agucchi, Oderzo, January 11, 1631, to Ingoli, Rome; a draft.

[11] *Calvert Papers*, i. 205; White, Maryland, February 20, 1639, to Cæcilius, second Lord Baltimore; quoting the first lord.

[12] Cf. *supra*, § 6, p. 174: General to White at Liège, March 3, 1629.

[13] Foley, *Collectanea, sub voce* "Baker, Alexander;" on the authority of "*Summary of the Deceased S.J.*," which we have never been able to identify, at least for this particular item.

again in that country. Hence the other journey which he took must have been earlier than 1634.

In like manner, we find it expressly stated that Father Lawrence Rigby had been in English America before the date of the Maryland foundation; and he was never there again. In 1633 it is said of him that "he had been on the mission, in that part of America which is subject to England." But, seeing that in the year 1633 he had been only four years in the Society, was thirty-three years of age, and was then teaching rhetoric at St. Omer, it does not seem possible that he could have been a Jesuit priest when out in America on a mission. However, arriving in England from Rome at the latter end of 1628, if then he started out with the Jesuit, Father Baker, in the spring of 1629, he would have been reputed a Jesuit, and would have substantiated that report by actually entering the Society on his return from Avalon, towards the close of the same year.[14]

Of two priests no distinct account is left us; that is to say, of Rivers, whom we take to be the same as Anthony Smith, and of Hacket. It is true, they could have returned to England with any of the convoys of 1628 and 1629; but Simon Stock made no mention of them, though he did mention the Jesuits. One or both might have gone with Lord Baltimore and his lady on the trip to Virginia; and it is extremely unlikely that George Calvert went sailing on the high seas, in company with his wife and little children, without the attendance of a chaplain; or that he should have left the precious charge behind him in Virginia, destitute of such spiritual aid.

Rivers or Smith and Hacket.

However that may be, we merely call attention to such circumstances, probable or improbable, for the sake of throwing light on a curious old record, which appears in two venerable American manuscripts, and not in the same form. It would seem to have been copied independently into either of them from an older document. It runs thus: "Father White, Andrew: came hither about 1630 before Lord Baltimore; built a chapel at White's Neck, but had no house." In the other form it reads:

An American tradition.

[14] *Triennial Catalogue of Persons*, 1633, p. 50, No. 9. *Seminarium Audomarense*: "*P. Laurentius Rigbæus . . . fuit in missione ad eam Americæ partem quæ paret Angliæ.*" In a similar Catalogue for 1645, p. 15, No. 23, he is in the College of St. Aloysius, or the Lancashire and Staffordshire mission, and the entry runs: "He teaches grammar; has taught humanities; has been on the mission 10 years." In the short Catalogue of persons for 1648, p. 14, he appears thus: "*Dimissi: P. Laurentius Rigbæus . . .*" then in another [Foley's] hand: "*vere* Morley, Henry;" under which name a sufficient account of his antecedents may be seen in Foley's *Collectanea; Records*, iii. 776, note; *Ibid.*, vi. 295, 296, Diary of the English College, Rome.

"First Maryland missionary; came hither to the Irish exiles with Lord Baltimore; built a chapel at White's Neck," etc.[15]

The statements are so plain and circumstantial, that, taking exception only to the identity of the missionary, whom we cannot admit to have been Father Andrew White, we seem justified in accepting an inferential basis of fact. A priest came "hither," that is to Maryland or the region of the Chesapeake, before the second Lord Baltimore's expedition of 1633 was organized. He came "about 1630," that is to say, in 1629, with the first Lord Baltimore; and, if he stayed till 1630, then he attended Lady Baltimore and the children. He found "Irish exiles" here, and assisted them, remaining so long that he had a congregation of some kind, and "a chapel at White's Neck." But, the whole ministry being very precarious in the Virginia which turned the first Lord Baltimore away because he was a Papist, the missionary "had no house" or settlement; he was only chaplain to a visitor. Indeed, if he did stay with Lady Baltimore and depart with her, he must have been lost at sea with the family.[16]

Let us now finish with the Newfoundland enterprise, for, as we have seen, at Rome itself the view of Avalon is dissolving rapidly into that of the Puritans at Plymouth. "Having disbursed neare 20,000 lbs.," said his son Cæcilius some four years later, George Calvert, "finding Avalon by reason of the great colds there in winter to disagree with his constitution, goes from thence to Virginia in the yeare 1629, where he found a much better clymate; and leaving his lady (his then second wife) and some of his children by her there,

---

[15] Maryland-New York Province Archives S.J.: *Liber continens*, etc., a folio blank book, of about 150 sheets, with a number of Catalogues transcribed; inscribed outside in the hand, apparently, of John McElroy, S.J., and probably so labelled about the second decade of the nineteenth century, or a little later, when he had charge of such-like books at Georgetown. There is a companion volume in the Georgetown College Archives; and to this also we refer in the text. It contains the first or briefer notice cited. All the copies of older records, inserted in these volumes with current registers, we take to be of the same date, more or less, as McElroy's inscription.—As to the identification of persons in connection with this question, cf. E. I. Devitt, S.J., *Woodstock Letters*, xi. 18, *seqq*.

[16] We have the Catalogues of persons for 1630, 1631, 1632, 1633. Father White is in the mission of St. Thomas, Hants, and Father Alexander Baker is in that of St. Ignatius, London, till they appear in Maryland.—There are divers hypotheses that might be formed respecting those old entries. Thus the whole might be a confused tradition, referring, in fact, to Father White's experiences among the Irish of the West Indian Islands, in the course of his cruise from England to Maryland, November to March, 1633–1634. But we leave the entries just as they stand. Immediately after that about Father Andrew White, there appears the following: "1632. F. Starkey, F. Coply Thomas, and F. Ferret, came hither and lived at the farm of St. Inigoes"—"1632. *P. Starkey, P. Coply Thomas, & P. Ferret, huc apulerunt et vixerunt in Praedio Sti Ignatii.*" In this both manuscripts agree. The ancient way of abbreviating "apulerunt" is significant.

comes himselfe to England to procure a pattent of some part of that continent; and some while after sends for his lady, who, together with her children that were left with her, were unfortunately cast a way in their returne: in which shipp his Lordship lost a great deal of plate and other goods of a great vallue." Meanwhile, "vpon his arriuall in England [his Lordship] became an humble sutor to his Majestie for that part of Virginea which lyeth between the river of Passamagnus and the present Plantation of Virginea on James Riuer towards the South." [17]

Avalon abandoned for Virginia. 1629, 1630.

At the same time, Lord Baltimore applied to Father Richard Blount, Provincial of the English Jesuits, for a detachment of missionaries to send out with the new colonizing expedition. He seems to have told Simon Stock so, in terms which intimated that he counted with certainty on their cooperation; inasmuch as "the Fathers of the Society had a mission or commission specially for those parts of America." [18]

Jesuits applied for. 1630, 1631.

Father Blount made reference to the General, asking for "authorization to despatch some of ours, in company with English gentlemen or merchants, who were contemplating new settlements in the West Indies, beyond the limits of territory occupied by the Catholic King [of Spain]." The General replied that the proposal was "a subject meriting grave deliberation, for fear of offending those who will perhaps claim that this runs counter to rights conferred on them by the Apostolic See;" and he called therefore for "more particular information on the whole matter." [19] With this we reach the end of 1631.

In the same year there reached England a decree passed by the Sacred Congregation of the Inquisition, and published by Pope Urban VIII. on May 7, 1631. It decided a controversy of the gravest moment, in which Richard Smith, Bishop of Chalcedon, the regular clergy, and the Catholic laity had all been deeply involved. George Calvert, Lord Baltimore, was engaged in it, almost, if not quite, as a

---

[17] British Museum MSS., *Sloane*, 3662, f. 25 (A.D. 1670); and *Calvert Papers*, i. p. 222, in Cæcilius, Lord Baltimore's *Declaration to the Lords* [A.D. 1634]. The two documents, penned at a distance from one another of thirty-six years, supplement one another, as in the text. It is to be observed that the £20,000 disbursements were incurred by the first Lord Baltimore on account of Newfoundland, not by the second lord on behalf of Maryland. Cæcilius computes the sums "disbursed by himself and his freinds" together on the settlement of Maryland to be only "aboue tenn thousand pounds"—*Calvert Papers*, *Ibid.*, p. 228.

[18] Cf. *supra*, § 9, p. 192, note 12: Stock, January 1, 1631.

[19] *Anglia, Epist. Gen.*, 1633, June 4: General to Blount, Provincial, rehearsing the correspondence of a "year or two before"—"*ante unum alterumve annum.*"—Cf. *infra*, § 18, p. 246.

leader. What effects in the direction of new views, regarding the spiritual authority of the clergy and the temporal power of the laity, may have been produced in his mind by the tenor of the dispute, we cannot infer with any degree of precision from his new Maryland charter. But, as to his son Cæcilius, a young man of about twenty-five years of age, who was soon to inherit the charter and the palatinate from his father, certain features in the colonial legislation advanced by him within the next ten years are too closely connected with the matters of the controversy, not to suggest a relationship between this agitation and the subsequent legislation.[20]

A London controversy and Maryland politics.

§ 11. Just about the date when George Calvert entered the Catholic Church, Dr. Richard Smith was appointed, on the 2nd of January, 1625, to succeed the first Bishop of Chalcedon,[1] and take charge of ecclesiastical affairs in England. Consecrated on the 12th of the same month by the Nuncio Spada at Paris, he passed over to the new scene of his labours, where, as Cardinal Albizi related in a memorial to Pope Innocent X.,[2] he created new vicars, archdeacons, notaries, registrars; erected a tribunal before which he required last wills and testaments to be produced, with juridical supervision over pious legacies, marriages, and baptisms, and with the power of visiting the private houses of Catholics. The faithful were not to receive the Sacraments, even in case of necessity, save from such as he designated. No one could hear confessions, unless approved by himself, in accordance with the enactment of the Council of Trent and the Bull of Pope Pius V. He

The Chalcedon controversy.

---

[20] Some forty-six years after these events, a memorial was presented to Pope Innocent XI. (Odescalchi), by Mgr. Urbano Cerri, who was secretary of the Sacred Congregation of the Propaganda at that time (1675–1679), and among the one hundred and forty countries or territories reviewed, Virginia, Avalon, and Maryland appear; but their characters have become confused. With regard to the Puritans of "Virginia, called also New England," where the two noblemen settled, one Catholic and the other heretical, it is stated that, to withstand the progress of the Puritans who emigrated thither in 1630, "the General of the Capuchins was bidden to send out a mission of his Order; and French and English religious went there; as also in 1650," etc. As to Avalon, "Father Simon Stock, a discalced Carmelite, got leave of the Congregation to found there a mission of his Order, and, notwithstanding the difficulties put in his way by his General, missionaries were ordered thither in company with two English gentlemen," etc. Corsini Library, cod. 283 (40 F. 30), ff. 223, 224. This is the memorial which was published in English by Dr. Hoadly, under the name of Sir Richard Steele, in 1715, London. It was then translated into French, and published the following year in Amsterdam.—For the sake of comparison with another specimen of Cerri's style given below, notice may be taken of his slighting remark about the Carmelite General at the same moment when he is betraying entire ignorance of the facts. Cf. § 31 (1), 300, note 20.

[1] William Bishop, by name.

[2] W. M. Brady, *The Episcopal Succession in England, etc.*, iii. 77, *seqq.*

exacted of the laity an annual pension for himself, the clergy, and parish priests, and ordered them to receive his ministers and officials. He was very severe on the regulars, and appointed their enemies to high posts.

Father Henry More remarks in his History: "All grades of Catholics were alarmed when, in addition to the daily persecution from the side of heretics, such a novel limitation, one never heard of since the time of the schism, was thus imposed, so that Christians were deprived of the liberty of using any assistance they pleased in their last moments; and their property was put in greater jeopardy than ever before; more priests having to be admitted there where, without the greatest peril to life and fortune, it was sometimes hard to give admittance to one."[3]

In July, 1627, the lay Catholics of England submitted to his lordship the Bishop of Chalcedon what was in form and substance a searching and minute interrogatory on the subject of his claims, and on the relation of the same to Catholic practice and faith. Their letter of remonstrance, presented to him in the next year, 1628, rehearses in great part what these "articles or questions" contain.[4] *The Catholic laymen's interrogatory. July, 1627.*

Cardinal Albizi goes on to tell how Pope Urban VIII. was displeased at the exceeding indiscretion of the Bishop; and, by a decree of the Inquisition conveyed privately through the French Nuncio and the English Queen's confessor, Dr. Smith received information that he was not the true Ordinary Bishop of England, but he was Bishop of Chalcedon in Asia, with delegated and limited faculties for England; that, in the matter of confessors, he could not invoke the Council of Trent or Pius V.; that his approval was not necessary for priests having jurisdiction from the Pope; that there was no place for contentious jurisdiction in England; and his deputation of vicars was impracticable.

This private admonition, dated December 16, 1626, produced no effect in allaying the storm of controversy which had arisen in public. And in the next year, 1628, a number of lords and gentry signed a letter of remonstrance, whereof we shall proceed to give an extract. Since Lord Baltimore went out on his second trip to Newfoundland in the spring of this year, and stayed away *The remonstrance. 1628.*

---

[3] Morus, *Historia Provinciæ Anglicanæ*, lib. x. § 9, p. 457, edit. 1660.
[4] Propaganda Archives, *Lettere, I Anglia*, 347, ff. 207, 208: "*Articoli o questioni proposte dalli Cattholici laici al Vescovo di Calcedonia nel mese di luglio, 1627, tradotti verbatim dalla copia inglese.*" The articles are followed, *Ibid.*, ff. 208-210, by "*Considerationi del Padre Don David sopra li detti articoli.*"

for a couple of years, we take it that his signature was appended to the document at the beginning of 1628. It may be that he not only signed it, but composed it. His subsequent action in the controversy, and his antecedent qualifications as a Privy Councillor and Secretary, agree perfectly with the policy adopted and the statements made in this letter of remonstrance, which runs thus—

"RIGHT REV. FATHER IN CHRIST,

"We have seen the letter of your Lordship, dated the 16 October, addressed to the lay Catholics of this kingdom. We are glad to pass over that part of it which does not proximately touch us. But there are other matters in it, which do concern us in the highest degree; they concern ourselves, our offspring, and whatever can be dear to us in this world. Wherefore with the greatest humility we will state to your Right Reverend Lordship, what is our sentiment and opinion thereupon.

"Your letter consists of four parts. It is the second of these which chiefly regards us, that wherein you speak of your power as Ordinary, which you describe in these terms: 'As to the authority, in virtue of which I made these exactions, it is as great as the authority of any Ordinary is or can be in his own city or diocese for exacting so much from regulars. Secondly, His Holiness makes me Judge in the first instance. Thirdly, on this same account he has constituted me as truly and absolutely Ordinary in England, as are other Ordinaries in their dioceses. Fourthly, it is manifest from my papal Brief, that His Holiness has made me delegate for all causes,[5] a characteristic of Ordinaries. Fifthly, in the letters of their Eminences the Cardinals of the Propaganda, I am called the Ordinary of England and Scotland.' This passage, and the entire scope of the second part of your Lordship's letter, show plainly that you claim as much authority over the Catholic laity of England and Scotland as the Ordinaries of old exercised, when the Catholic religion was established here, and as much as they now possess in Catholic countries. With your good pleasure, we beg of you to hear for a moment from us, how far such authority assumed over the laity does extend.

"First, Ordinaries have the power of examining and proving last wills and testaments; secondly, of granting letters of administration for disposing of the effects of the deceased; thirdly, of deciding questions and controversies about tithes; fourthly, of passing

[5] "*Ad universalitatem causarum.*"

judgment in the matter of contracts, marriage, divorce, alimony, legitimacy; fifthly, of doing so in the matter of defamation and other such issues, in all of which examinations are wont to be carried on under oath, with censures and judgments to correspond. Controversies of this kind appeal to a mixed power, being partly temporal over our property and fortunes; and, as such, this authority has by our laws and statutes been made the subject, in varying circumstances, of various ordinances, confirmations, and alterations, no less in the reigns of Catholic than of Protestant kings, as seemed expedient in the eyes of ecclesiastical and political powers here. The body of such statutes has now passed so fixedly into use and custom, that any innovation may well be considered fraught with danger, since it militates against the various laws of the kingdom, both ancient and recent. To set up any new tribunal with certain forms for the administration of justice, differing from or foreign to what is already established by law, or, still worse, contrary to the same, is the crime of high treason. Those who recur or submit to such a tribunal are involved in the same guilt. The slightest complicity therein is a capital crime, entailing forfeiture of all property and perpetual imprisonment." *Status of Chalcedon before the law.*

The letter then adverts to the impossibility of keeping such a tribunal secret; and the consequent embittering of the general persecution; and it proceeds: "Your Lordship, then, may easily infer what a perilous thing it would be for the Catholic laity to submit to such a power and conform to its decisions; nay, how prejudicial it is for us to have kept silence so long, seeing that you have actually put forward the claim, and have promulgated it to everybody." Then, after some further remarks on the conflict inevitable between such a tribunal and the courts of the nation, a gentle allusion seems to be made to the Roman authorities, in the following words:—

"If these things had been as evident to persons at a distance as to ourselves,[6] if they had known what we have suffered thus far, and in what a depth of misery we are sunk, we are convinced that a new authority of this kind would never have been imposed upon us; nor can we be induced to believe that it is a question of faith, or of the profession of faith, to submit to this new tribunal; or that we lie under any obligation to acknowledge it, at the cost of our fortunes and to the ruin of our posterity; seeing that neither the Catholic faith itself, nor any necessary profession thereof, does impel us thereto. *The laity's exceptions to the mixed power.*

[6] "*Quæ si exteris æque ac nobis perspecta fuissent.*"

"We ask your Lordship to believe that this is the mind of the laity; and we desire it to be known to all at home and abroad. That we should change our convictions in the matter is not possible in the premises. But as to the rest of your letter, since it does not affect the general condition of the laity, but the case of the regular clergy, we humbly request that no further prejudice be done to us on that account, and that we be not dealt with more hardly than in the time of your predecessor; and that controversies of this kind be conducted with charity, sweetness, candour, secrecy, and without noise; to the end that your pious desires, in conjunction with the wishes of all of us, may the more surely attain their object for the good of all, in the present afflictions of our country.

"Your Right Reverend Lordship's most dutiful servants,

"THE LAY CATHOLICS OF ENGLAND."

Here follow the names of four earls, one marquis, two viscounts, twelve or thirteen barons, the last name being that of Baltimore; and the clause is added: "And others, knights and gentry without number, as well as all pious and prudent persons." [7]

The Baron of Baltimore went off to Newfoundland. He abandoned it in the autumn of the following year, 1629. Then we find that on the 24th of November, 1629, "ten boys, three of them being sons of the Lord Baron of Baltimore," were in the English Channel, crossing over to St. Omer's College, under the charge of Jesuits. The little vessel was overhauled and attacked by Netherlanders. An exciting scene followed. Nobody was killed; but the convoy of harmless passengers was robbed of everything; and then landed in safety on the 28th of the same month at Nieuport, whence they reached St. Omer's on December 6.[8]

Three young Calverts at St. Omer's. 1629.

---

[7] General Archives S.J., *Anglia, Historia*, iv. pp. 41–43, endorsed: "*Anglia*, 1628. *Litteræ Catholicorum Nobilium ad Ep͡m Chalcedonensem.*" It is a MS. copy sent to Rome. As the printed pamphlet of 1631, to be mentioned hereafter (p. 209, note 14), reproduces this letter in its Latin text, beginning: ". . . *Vidimus epistolam* . . ." and ending: ". . . *observantissimi Laici Catholici Angliæ* . . ." the original would seem to have been in that language. The names in our MS. copy are in cipher, and are then deciphered letter by letter on a slip of paper, the writing of which is singularly like that of the General himself, Father Mutius Vitelleschi: "[*Comites*] *Salopiæ. Rutlandiæ. Riuers. Clanricard. Marchio. Vintoniensis. Dicki de sancto. Ioanne. Vicecomites. Sommerset. Sauagio. Barones. Herbert. Abergefenni. Vindesor. Morley. Mordart. Petreus. Tenham. Votton. Vaux. Stourion. Dunchelly. Poro. Baltimor. Equites aliique nobiles sine numero, atque adeo omnes pij simul et prudentes.*" The last clause, as well as a few syllables before, were not put in cipher.

[8] Bruxelles, Archives du Royaume: *Archives Jésuitiques*, Inventaire 80, carton 29; one sheet 4to, MS., a narrative of the attack: "*Decem omnino numero, ex quibus tres fuerunt filii D͡ni Baronis de Baltimore.*" The assailants were "*Flandri.*"

At the very same date, the liberal-minded Council of Virginia, Pott, Mathewe, Smyth, and Claybourne, indited a letter to the King's Privy Council, telling how they had blocked the Papist lord's design of settling among them. They had done it by interposing that oath which, if Baltimore had a conscience to take it then and please them, he might rather have used as a passport, four years before, not to a desolate British colony and its farms, but to the highest honours of the British court, with substantial assets to boot.[9]

Back in England, to which not only the rebuff in Virginia but a written command of the King, under date of November 22, purported henceforth to confine him, he showed himself the undisguised Catholic he ever was. Writing to the Viscount Wentworth, Lord President of the North, on occasion of the birth of "our Prince," he tells how the Spanish court, which had no reason whatever to rejoice over affairs concerning the English court and the Anglo-French Queen Henrietta, did nevertheless rejoice exceedingly; and "solemn Masses and prayers" were said for his [the young Prince's] health and prosperity everywhere. "Thus," he adds pleasantly, "your Lordship sees that we Papists want not charity towards you Protestants, whatsoever the less understanding part of the world think of us."[10]

But, as to the ecclesiastical controversy in which he had embarked before he left, he found it and his own name in a refractory condition. The controversy had been raging. And one issue now was that he must have been a forger; or else his name and those of all the rest had been forged by the Jesuits.

Baltimore and the Jesuits compromised together 1630-1631.

A long series of pamphlets and works was being published on either side of the episcopal question; and those who wrote for the bishop were reinforced by all the anti-Jesuitism of the Gallicans and Jansenists of France, including the whole body of the Sorbonne. At the same time, all the Jesuit forces were recalled from the field of controversy by the orders which the General issued, as we narrated on a former occasion, when speaking of the policy of silence and its reasons.[11] How Baltimore and the Jesuits were compromised together

---

[9] Cf. Scharf, i. pp. 47, 48.—Compare also the remark of Burk on the "fear and antipathy to the principles and persons of the Papists. This narrow and impolitic spirit," he says, "qualified in the mother country by a thousand circumstances which softened its rigour and severity, had the fullest scope in the colonies for displaying its malignity. In small communities all attachments and prejudices are stronger and more lasting." J. Burk, *History of Virginia*, ii. 25, 26, on Lord Baltimore's arrival in Virginia.

[10] *Earl of Strafford's Letters*, etc., i. p. 53: 1630, August 12.

[11] Above, Introduction, Chap. II. § 9, pp. 70, 71.

will appear from the title of one work, which has the singular merit of publishing the author's name: "*A Manifestation regarding the Declaration of the English Jesuits, falsely put forward under the name of the Lay Catholics of England.* Author, William Price. Printed at Cologne, 1631." [12] And in another "Manifestation" as it is again named, in which the recall of all Jesuits from England was demanded of the Pope, ostensibly by the lay Catholics, and in which every evil that had occurred, "these forty yeares more or lesse," with "other great evills" still possible before the end of time, were all fathered on the Jesuits, this precise charge was brought to their door, that a list of performances purporting to be those of the laymen were really exploits of the Jesuits; and at least two salient phrases from the letter of the Catholic lords given above were ostentatiously introduced. One is the following: "For which reasons it might perhaps bee worthily said of vs, that it seemeth lesse safe for vs to have bin hitherto so long silent;" the other is, that, in the premises so rehearsed, "wee cannot recede from our judgement and resolution herein." There seems to have been no question of real signatures to this production, which, among other things, invoked his Protestant Majesty and the Puritan Parliament as arbiters of the destiny of the Society.[13]

Manifestations and Declarations.

The first thing to do for a man of bureaucratic habits, like the ex-Secretary Lord Baltimore, was to bring papers back to their proper offices, and to have them attested by such official signatures as were prudently available. And, this being done, a pamphlet was published in the spring of 1631, containing a "Declaration of the Lay Catholics of England," on the subject of the authority of Chalcedon, etc.; besides a copy of their letter to the bishop in 1628, given above; and an account of the steps now taken with the various

---

[12] "*Manifestatio circa Declarationem Jesuitarum Anglorum falso editam sub nomine Laicorum Catholicorum Angliæ. Auctore Gulielmo Priceo: impressa Coloniæ,* 1631." *Anglia, Historia,* iv. p. 194; in Urban VIII.'s catalogue of books to be suppressed, on one side and the other, 1631.

[13] Stonyhurst MSS., *Anglia A,* ix., documents 27 and 27*a*, first in Latin then in English, ff. 89, 89 *bis.* The paper is made the subject of correspondence between Cardinal Barberini, Secretary of State, and Signor Panzani, who at first professes to believe that it is genuine, then, a week afterwards, admits the real authorship in part, and says that the enterprise of procuring subscriptions is dropped. He describes it as "made to the likeness of the manifesto against the Bishop"—"*simile al Manifesto fatto contro il Vescovo.*" Five such papers, emanating from laymen, are cited in the Manifestation, and are fathered on the Jesuits. Two or three of them we identify as those in which Baltimore had a hand. Vatican Archives, *Nunziatura d'Inghilterra,* 5, f. 153: Panzani, London, December 12, 1635; f. 159ᵛ, December 19, same year.—The "Manifestation" begins in the Latin: "*Cum receptio Jesuitarum in Anglia . . .;*" in English: "Forasmuch as the admittance of the Jesuitts in England . . .;" ending in the Latin: ". . . *facile præscindentur;*" in English: ". . . will easily bee taken away." It is dated June 23, 1635.

ambassadors in London, such as the French Marquis de Fontenai and others, to rebut the calumnies circulating about the Catholic lords and their previous action.[14]

But there are few games which two cannot play, even though one party plays amiss. And so the action of the lords with their attestation was taken off in an opposition document, of which we shall let Lord Baltimore himself tell the story and sequel.

§ 12. The French ambassador, the Marquis de Fontenai, was now found in print, as having lent his attestation to the opposition document, which, contradicting all that the lords had done, stated that it made a contrary declaration in the name of "the better and greater part" of the British laity. The very name of the document, which was in French, gave the gist of the question: *General Disavowal by the lay Catholics of England, contrary to a Declaration which has been falsely published in their name.*[1] Lord Baltimore, like a man who has the reins of the business in his own hands, relates to Lord Petre, in a circumstantial letter, what line of action Viscount Somerset and himself now thought fit to pursue—

Baltimore, Somerset, and Fontenai. July, 1631.

"Your Lordship shall therefore understand, that my Lord Somerset and I, hearing that the Ambassador was gone from London

---

[14] General Archives S.J., *Anglia, Historia*, iv. pp. 197–224; small printed 4to, p. 224: "*Bruxellæ. Apud Viduam Huberti Anthoni*, etc., 1631." Pp. 197–212 (1–16): "*Declaratio Catholicorum Laicorum circa Authoritatem . . . Chalcedonensis . . . ;*" and *Rationes Redditæ*, to the French ambassador extraordinary, Chasteauneuf; (16–20): "*Exemplar Epistolæ Catholicorum Laicorum Rᵐᵒ Chalcedonensi Episcopo missæ, cuius in præcedenti Declaratione fit mentio.* ¶ *Rᵐᵉ in Xto. Pater. Vidimus Epistolam . . '. ;*" (20): "*. . . consequantur. Rᵐᵃ D.V. observantissimi Laici Catholici Angli.*" No names are published. Then (21–23) the report of their action with the French ambassador, Marquis de Fontenai, and other ambassadors and agents in London. Finally, four pages of official testifications, 3–15 Martii, 1631, about this last action of theirs, with the documents in Latin. The Spanish ambassador extraordinary, Coloma, appears as testifying to the *Declaratio.*—Cf. *idem*, in Stonyhurst College Library, Z, 7 (10).—Also in British Museum Library, 860, I, 25.—But the title-page of the latter refers the pamphlet to the Plantin printing-office, Antwerp. "*Antverpiæ, ex officina Plantiniana, Balthasaris Moreti, M.DC.XXXI.*"

[1] A violent paper of this description—a *Désaveu*—is analyzed in a long note by the Jansenistic compilers of *Annales de la Société des soi-disans Jésuites*, iii. 425–427, reference being made for a Latin version to M. d'Argentré, Collect. Jud. ii. part ii. p. 34. The marginal sub-heads show the style of the whole school and of the *Désaveu* itself: "*Les Jésuites fabricateurs de fausses Lettres.—Défenseurs d'une cause infâme* (the Voltairian phrase of the day).—*Fripons, mettant sur les autres les iniquités dont ils sont capables. . . .—Menteurs, indignes de toute foi et de toute croyance.—Hérétiques . . . Cause de tous les maux par leurs friponneries.—Faux et trompeurs dans leurs protestations de respect pour l'autorité épiscopale.*"—The text and succeeding notes in the same place do not quite make short work of Knott, Floyd, and the English Jesuits at large; because, being so long, there is practically no end to them.—Cf. *infra*, § 13, pp. 216, 217, note 8.

VOL. I. P

to his villa at Twittnam, we went thither to waite on him vppon Saterday last was fortnight, being the xxiii[th] of the last moneth [July 23, 1631], where he receaued vs with much courtesy, and humanity. After we had rested a while, and the vsuall ceremonyes of complements past, we tould him, that we were come to acquaint his Excellency with a matter, wherewith not only our selues then present, but many other Catholickes of this kingdome, as well Noblemen, as principall gentlemen and others (diuers of them being then, or very lately in London, and at whose entreaty we came to wait vppon him) were very much scandalized, and offended. That some there were, who to [too] eagerly and passionately pursuing theyr own ends of advancing the Lord Bishop of Chalcedons pretended authority, as Ordinary of England, had caused to be printed a certayn pamphlet or manifest in French, entitled, *General desadueu des Catholiques lais d'Angleterre contre vne declaration qui à este faussement publiée a leur nom.* Which Disavow not only endeauours to discredit a former Declaration set forth against the said pretended iurisdiction of Ordinary, but besides cast many vnworthy aspersions vppon such Catholiques as haue oppugned the said iurisdiction; and that, to authorize this Disavow abroad in the world, we told him they had published it with a subscription, in the nature of an Attestation vnder his Excellencyes hand and seale, purporting that he had seene the same, and acknowledging that it had been presented vnto him, *au nom de la plus grande, et meilleure partye des Catholiques d'Angleterre.* This, we told him, seemed so exceeding strang to many that had seene it, as they could not possibly beleeue, that a person of so much honour and candour, as his Excellency was conceived to be, could be drawn to lend his hand or his credit to such a paper. First, for that the very title of *General Desadueu* (which must necessarily be vnderstood to comprehend all Catholiques) can with no colour be iustified, since so many Catholiques of prime quality had formerly eyther beene with his Excellency or otherwise made known vnto him theyr sense and opinion clearely against the said pretended authority of Ordinary, wherein we appealed to his own remembrance. Next, that the wordes of restriction which follow afterwards in the Attestation, of *la plus grande et meilleure partye*, are as farr from truth, which way soeuer the wordes be taken, whether for number or quality, as will most easely be made manifest; and certayn it ys (as his Excellency himself could not but know) that diuers of those Catholique Lords, who appeared vnto him to oppose the said pretended authority, were of the most eminent ranke of nobility in this kingdome. Besides the paper it self ys very contumelious, imputing odious thinges to the dissenting party, without all manner of proofe, or coulour of reason: which we hoped his Excellency would not beleeue, much lesse patronize with his name."

Not to pursue the detailed narration, which may be seen in its proper place, we merely recapitulate the steps then taken. The ambassador declared he had never seen any such document; that he had testified to having been visited by persons who favoured the bishop's claims; that there was no question of paper or pamphlet. But Baltimore had the paper with him. Then began a new series of polite manœuvres, till the marquis mentioned that he had not his notes with him; once in town, he would look over them; he desired his visitors to have patience just for two or three days. In town, Baltimore waited on the ambassador; he wrote to him. Under one excuse or another, the marquis could not yet state what he did attest or did not. "I wonder at the stopp," said Lord Baltimore with considerate charity; "but, what the reason of it ys, I know not." So, in default of knowing more as yet, he lets Lord Petre know what he has learnt thus far. Apologizing for the long discourse, he concludes: However, "yf I should measure your disposition by myne own, I haue not in that respect for which to aske your Lordship pardon, because particulars are to me always gratefull, and generalls vnsatisfactory. And soe God haue your Lordship in his holy keeping. From my lodging neere to Lincolnes Inne. 8 August 1631.

"Your Lordshipps very affectionatly,
"To serue you,
"GEORGE BALTIMORE." [2]

Since nothing in the way of a written document was to be extracted from the French ambassador, and he had contributed to

---

[2] General Archives S.J., *Anglia, Historia*, iv. pp. 289, 290; an elegant copy in Elizabethan hand, with the superscription of the original transcribed in these terms: "Endorsed To the right Hon[ble.] my very good Lord The Lord Petre."—See *Documents*, I. No. 3.—Panzani was told in due time that the French ambassador had borne "public" witness to the foul play practised by "some particular Catholics," that is, Baltimore and the rest; and accordingly he entered this item of history in a letter of May 14, 1636, containing a character of the recent French ambassador at the English court. He wrote to Cardinal Barberini: "*Testificò [il Fontenai] publicamente sotto la sua mano, che diversi Cattolici principali, così in nome loro, come della maggiore e meglior parte delli altri, li havevano protestato contro la dichiaratione fatta da alcuni Cattolici particolari, e falsamente in nome di tutti publicata contro l'autorità del Vescovo di Calcedonia.*" Vatican Archives, *Nunziatura d'Inghilterra*, 5, f. 283.

the case of the indignant laymen only a futile shaking of his head, Baltimore and others proceeded to more effectual measures against him and his and the other party. This became the more urgent in their eyes, because a papal Brief had now been published, in which the case of the bishop and the regulars was set to rights; and yet never a word appeared of the issue between the bishop and the laity.

Information sent by the laity to the Pope. [August],1631.

The whole question, regarding the exercise of a mixed temporal and spiritual jurisdiction over them, and the expediency of admitting it in the actual circumstances of England, was now pared down to one fine point; and that point was: Who these laymen were that judged it inexpedient; and what their opinion was worth? To use their own language, they had now to complain that a paper had recently been presented to the Pope, " or at least had been addressed by its author to those who were appointed by His Holiness to take cognizance of the case, in which the author assailed with calumny and contumely certain noblemen, precisely the ones deserving best of the Catholic cause; and then went on to count up the lords, who stood for the Right Rev. Chalcedon in the dispute." And among these the said paper, which was styled, "A true and sincere Information about the sentiments of Catholics in England towards the Bishop of Chalcedon," proceeded to rank " as favouring the pretended authority of the said bishop, certain earls and barons, at least six in number, namely, John Earl of Shrewsbury, Henry Earl of Worcester, Thomas Earl Rivers, William Lord Howard, Henry Baron Abergavenny, George Baron of Baltimore." In order to meet such reckless assertions, they took the provisional measure of addressing His Holiness at once, begging him, in terms of the most profound respect, to suspend judgment and delay action, until in the following month of October the Catholic lay gentry should have returned to town, and they could then submit to His Holiness some considerations that were positive and authentic.[3]

While they are waiting to draw up the decisive paper in October, 1631, we may scan some characteristic documents, which are being despatched from England to Rome. We shall thus arrive at the last acts of George, Lord Baltimore, when he sets his name and seal to the protest in the episcopal controversy; is ready to do the same

[3] General Archives S.J., *Anglia, Historia*, iii. ff. 372-375: *Status Controversiæ inter Episcopum Chalcedonensem et Laicos Angliæ Catholicos*; a contemporary MS. copy of a document accompanying the protest subsequently sent, and addressed to His Holiness as an "Information" explaining the protest. It rehearses the facts as given in the text.

to his great new charter for the province of Maryland; leaves a palatinate as a princely heritage to Cæcilius, second Lord Baltimore; and so closes the chapter of antecedents to our Maryland history.

§ 13. Our old friend, Simon Stock, wrote from London to the Sacred Congregation of the Propaganda, on the 4th of February, this year, 1631— *Stock's suggestions.*

"YOUR EMINENCES,

"Thus far the decree of the Holy Office [the Inquisition], in the case of the Bishop of Chalcedon, is not yet published. The contention and discord betwixt one and other party is great, with the writing of books one against the other, to the prejudice of Holy Church and the scandal of the simple-minded. And, as that proposal of appointing two other Bishops, one being of the Society of Jesus, the other of the Order of St. Benedict,[1] does not meet with the approbation of the Sacred Congregation, it will be useful at least if the Congregation forbid both parties to write any more books, one against the other; and to command his lordship the Bishop to send you in writing what it is that he claims, and the reasons why, and the consistency of such demands with a time of persecution; and, on the other side, to order the heads of the regulars to send you, in writing, what authority they are content to give the Bishop, and the reasons and appropriateness of not allowing more; and so the differences betwixt the two can easily be seen, and be adjusted to some extent;[2] otherwise they will go on contending for ever, to the great damage of Holy Church. And, with profound reverence, asking your blessing, I am,

"Your Eminences' most humble servant,
"FRA SIMON.
"London, February, 4, 1631."[3]

Simon Stock seems to have known very little of what was in progress behind the scenes, when he desired that his lordship the bishop should be encouraged to write and enlighten the Sacred Congregation. During the last six years the bishop's letters have been about as numerous as his own, but in an elegant Latin style which contrasts strongly with the friar's eclectic Italian and infelicitous manner of expression. *The Bishop of Chalcedon's correspondence on the Jesuits.*

[1] Cf. Propaganda Archives, *Lettere*, 132, f. 144: S. Stock, London, July 25, 1630 It was a notion of his own.
[2] "*Et determinarla con una mediocrità.*"
[3] Propaganda Archives, *Lettere*, 100, f. 151.

Though numerous, they have been very uniform in their general scope, while diversified in the points of business treated. Thus his lordship has discussed the intimate connection of the Jesuits with the Gunpowder Plot, with heretical opinions, with schismatical doctrines, with the abandonment of the plague-stricken; with inducing the laity to take the condemned oath of allegiance, and inducing young clerics of the English colleges to follow the life of religious perfection; with hearing confessions without faculties, at least when Jesuit members cease to be Jesuits; with writing on both sides of his own question, both for and against him, in the anonymous books which must be theirs; with their enrolling lay people in the sodality of the Blessed Virgin; and finally, not to mention other points in his voluminous correspondence, he charges the Jesuits with using the names of the lay gentry only to score some advantage for themselves.[4] In the letter now to be quoted, he assails Lord Baltimore and other lords for their complicity, or duplicity, in this Jesuitical business. Fra Simon then was not well informed; and the Sacred Congregation of the Propaganda took no special notice of his suggestions about improving its intelligence department, but simply rewarded him well with commendations for his own co-operation. The assessor of the Holy Office or Inquisition reported his letter, and a reply was ordered in this sense—

"This Sacred Congregation can take no measures to settle the controversies, which you state are becoming more and more bitter between the secular and regular clergy, because the matter has been committed to the Holy Office; and it is from there a remedy must be counted on for the scandals which you record. What this Sacred Congregation can do is to continue imparting to that of the Holy Office such information as comes to hand from those parts; that in the exercise of its prudence it may provide," etc.

The Propaganda no longer the competent tribunal.

---

[4] Propaganda Archives; on the Jesuits and the Gunpowder Plot, heresy, error, sedition: Bishop of Chalcedon to the Propaganda, December, 1630, No. 100, ff. 134, 135; on their abandoning the plague-stricken, *pridie Calend. April.*, 1626, No. 101, ff. 7, 8; *excerpta*, February 1, 1626, *Ibid.*, f. 9. The other charges are commonplace and appear *passim* in the bishop's correspondence as well as in that of others, with more points than would repay the trouble of enumeration. That, however, about the Jesuits being Proteus-like, and writing for the Bishop as well as against him, is in relation to a book which he names: *Apologia Jesuitarum pro Episcopo Chalcedonensi.* Propaganda, *Ibid.*, 100, f. 144, A.D. 1631, June 14.—To this book, in the list of works prohibited by Urban VIII., we find a brief description attached, which ends with the words: "*et censetur Episcopus Chalcedonensis esse Auctor.*" Four other anonymous works in the list have the same note appended. General Archives S.J., *Anglia, Historia*, iv. p. 195: *Catalogus librorum*, etc., *prohibitorum ab Urbano VIII.*—The *Apologia Jesuitarum* is a thesis against the Jesuits by way of an argument *ad hominem*. Small 16mo, pp. 46, British Museum Library, 860, K, 24 (3).

The reply makes special allusion to the incongruity of quarrels within and persecution without, flourishing together about the same ecclesiastical body.⁵ Simon is invited to continue his correspondence.

In the following month information was sent to his lordship of Chalcedon that the board of reference at Rome had been altered for the settlement of his dispute. He replied—

"Your Eminences,—I received the letter directed to me under date of April 26; and I was exceedingly sorry to understand that the affair of my controversy with certain regulars was entirely transferred from your tribunal, where I doubt not it would have been settled long before this. I do persuade myself that you are not inhibited from defending your two decrees; in one of which your Eminences bid me take cognizance of the faculties of missionaries, sent or to be sent into England; and in the other you desire the Jesuits to suspend their sodality of the Conception of the Blessed Virgin until God shall grant better days to the English.⁶ It touches your honour nearly that you should maintain your own decrees, and not suffer them to be contemned by regulars, of whom some have had the effrontery to declare that your Congregation has no authority over them; and it is a question also that concerns the necessity and the indigence of this afflicted Church and clergy. For, if regulars are not bound to show me their faculties, they can go on hearing confessions without any jurisdiction, as five of them have done already and one is doing still; and so deceive souls to their damnation. And it is very important likewise to the clergy that the Jesuits be not allowed, under pretext of the said sodality, to draw the laity away to themselves as confessors. [*Chalcedon's plea for the Propaganda.*]

"In Catholic countries the clergy have either patrimonies or benefices for their support; and these are the titles under which they are promoted to Holy Orders; and consequently they do not depend at all upon their penitents for a living. The English clergy are advanced to Holy Orders, only under the title of the Mission, and they have no other maintenance except at the hands of penitents; and therefore to withdraw these, under any pretext [*For the quasi-benefices.*]

---

⁵ Propaganda Archives, *Lettere*, 100, f. 151: Stock to the Cardinals, London, February 4, 1631; endorsed by Ingoli, with reply, etc., " March 27, 1631, *Cong.* 137, No. 26."

⁶ Compare Stonyhurst MSS., *Anglia A*, iv. ff. 78, 79; Sir Thomas Leeds prefect, Sir Ralph Babthorpe secretary, petition the General of the Society to be aggregated under the title of the "Immaculate Conception;" from Louvain, July 7, 1617.

whatever from the clergy, is to take the bread from their mouths. Your Eminences know that the English clergy was the first to be sent by the Apostolic See into this vineyard; that it has spent more blood and sweat upon tilling it than all the regulars together; that it has no home except in England; whereas the English regulars have monasteries outside of England, where they can go to; and therefore it is an injustice that the laity should be withdrawn from the clergy, under pretext of greater faculties or apostolic privileges.

"I beseech your Eminences therefore to maintain your decrees: let our regulars feel that your Congregation has authority over them; reassure our English Catholics on the subject, that the regulars they confess to have really competent faculties for hearing confessions;[7] preserve to the clergy the children they have begotten in Christ, and do not suffer them to be drawn away by pedagogues.[8] Do not allow the title under which they were ordained to come to nothing; and themselves, after so much sweat

Against "pedagogues."

---

[7] That is, furnish the Catholics with a criterion (in the bishop's approbation) by which they may be able to reassure themselves, etc.

[8] This is an allusion to 1 Cor. iv. 15. The phrase thus used implied the theory of religious priests being merely outsiders in the Church, as pedagogues or "hirelings," to use Hallier's application of St. John x.; they were merely superfluities, excrescences, afflicting the Church's organization. The work of Dr. Matthew Kellison's, which in 1629 had started the whole war of pamphlets and books, and was entitled *A Treatise of the Hierarchie and divers orders of the Church against the anarchie of Calvin*, was wholly a plea for the Bishop of Chalcedon, but was half taken up with the anarchy of the Church, if regular priests were supposed to belong to its hierarchy. In answer to the English Jesuits, Fathers Floyd and Knott, Dr. Kellison, who lived in France, was supported at great length by the leading Gallican, Francis Hallier, and by the founder of the sect of Jansenists, the Abbé de St Cyran; the former in his book, *De Hierarchia ecclesiastica*, the latter in volumes published under the assumed name of *Petrus Aurelius*. This work of *Petrus Aurelius* was adopted in the solemn assembly of the French clergy, and the expenses of publishing its three volumes in folio were defrayed by them, on October 2, 1635, in 1642, and in 1646; it was lauded by the Sorbonne, but was suppressed by the King. (*Les Annales . . . des soi-disans Jésuites*, iii. 431, 470, 471, 473, notes; Hurter, *Nomenclator litterarius*, ii. 69, note.) The Jansenistic compilers of the *Annales de la Société des soi-disans Jésuites* devote to the exposition of the doctrine laid down by Hallier and St Cyran or Petrus Aurelius a series of notes, occupying the greatest part of forty-five quarto pages, double column, in small print. Besides the tenets of these gentlemen, in defence of Kellison as against Floyd and Knott, we find in this Jansenistic collection other English documents, interesting in their character, and mounted in their proper setting. The book of Dr. Kellison's, though not at all so explicit nor extreme as the ample literature of his supporters, comprises some of the essential doctrine in their position, and exemplifies some of their characteristic ways of presentation.

Thus to give a few instances both of matter and manner, Dr. Kellison repeats continually in divers forms that regulars cannot exercise the functions of priests, except in virtue of their being priests, and not in their capacity of being regulars (pp. 224, 246, 256, 257, etc.). If there are regular Orders of clergy, that is, religious who are priests by profession, then "these Orders [of clergy] are indeed instituted to that purpose, but yet to helpe onlie and assist the clergie; and to this they [these Priests] were not ordained by the divine law as Bishops and Priests are, but by the Churches institution" (pp. 257, 258). They "are ordained to helpe and assist Bishops and pastours in preaching and hearing confessions, as the pastours shall desire and need, or as their priviledges shall permit them" (p. 225). The life of

and blood shed for the Church, to be reduced to a shameful mendicancy, with dishonour to their priestly character.

"The Jesuits, I know well, will pretend that it is not a question here of their interest, but of the glory of God and of the good of souls; and would that they not only made the pretence, but that we had in fact the experience of finding by the erection of the said sodality they were not working for their own ends, drawing disciples after them, fostering a faction against the clergy. And your Eminences also may judge, whether this bit of a pretext of the honour of God and the good of souls, is of such great importance that, with such damage to the clergy, with such offence taken by them, with such detriment to charity, it should meet with any notice; especially at this disastrous time, and in the midst of such exasperation; and whether it were not more for the honour of God and the good of souls that the sodality be suspended, until it could be kept up without grave damage to the clergy, or offence taken by them."

Now his lordship proceeds to the laity, and to our friend Baltimore, whom he brushes aside. The transition thus made here from the regular clergy maintained with chaplaincies by the laity, whose private houses furnished the refuge or home for the chaplains, is strict and correct. The gist of the controversy was to be found in the unduly close connection between the laity and the regulars. The peers did not seem to know this. They persisted in taking legal views and punctilious exceptions

<small>Misconception of the peers.</small>

---

a curate is one of heroic perfection, as he may be required to lay down his life for his flock; "but the religious, as religious, by his state is not obliged to this heroicall charitie" (p. 327). "Yea and all they [all Priests] who are lawfullie called to converte or govern soules by preaching, teaching and ministring the Sacraments (especiallie if in performing these offices they expose their lives, landes, or liberties) have a more perfect calling then the religious [Priests, preachers and teachers] as religious have, because the religious man by his calling seeketh onlie to save his own soule, not the soules of others" (p. 328). "Onlie the pastour not Bishop, though he have a perfecter calling then the religious as religious, yet he hath not so perfect a state, as the Bishop or religious hath" (p. 329). "When a religious man is made a Bishop or a pastour, he is preferred to an higher calling, and to a vocation of greater perfection" (p. 333). From the practice of St. Francis Xavier, a Jesuit, and from the rules of the Society of Jesus, which inculcate great reverence in dealing with bishops, this writer concludes: "Therefore these titles of Patriarches, Archbishops, Priests and pastours are not titles or orders of religious, as they are religious, but onlie of the secular clergie and hierarchie of the Church" (p. 230). And, not to quote his extraordinary statements, that regular priests cannot be allowed to act as priests in preaching to the far-off Gentiles, "but by priviledge and extraordinarilie," inasmuch as they are priests ordained (pp. 246, 329), we finish with his thesis that lay people themselves, who stay in the world, are called to real perfection, while enjoying all the good things of life; but religious who leave all to follow Christ, who practise the evangelical counsels and vow a life of perfection, do not practise perfection thereby. They only adopt "an instrument of perfection" (p. 322); while with lay Christians, "to leave all in preparation of mynd is perfection, because it either is the love of God, or is joyned with it" (p. 322)—which presumably is never to be assumed of a religious.

to his lordship's implied claims regarding mixed powers, which they jealously and emphatically refused to acknowledge. He could not well disabuse them by explaining such nominal claims away, unless he also explained where the state of the question really lay. Four years had now passed since the laity had proposed to him their doubts and questions;[9] and they were none the wiser, but only more emphatic than ever, with the embassies of France and Spain involved on one side and the other. The gentlemen had never caught the issue, that it was the franchise of their own houses which was in question, as between the portion of the clergy under his lordship's immediate jurisdiction and the other portion of the clergy under the Pope's direct authority; and the objective was that one should be supplanted by the other. Hence would issue a consequence, which could never be put into words for them, that, as the great majority of the regular clergy then in the English service, that is to say, of the hundred and sixty Jesuits, one hundred Benedictines, twenty Franciscans, seven Dominicans, five Carmelites, two Minims,[10] had previously been secular clergymen, who had simply passed over into the ranks of the regulars, such a transferring of one's self henceforth, on the part of any secular clergyman, would be tantamount to incurring a sentence of disfranchisement and exile from his own co-religionists; for, as his lordship had expressed it, religious should "go to their monasteries outside of England," and disencumber the ground. Many of these religious priests were, not merely friends, but members of the noble families; and the Jesuits in particular were always noted as bound up by relationship with the nobility.[11]

---

[9] Propaganda Archives, *I Anglia*, 347, ff. 207, 208 : *Articoli o questioni proposte dalli Cattholici laici al Vescovo di Chalcedonia nel mese di luglio*, 1627, *tradotti verbatim dalla copia inglese*, July, 1627. Cf. *supra*, § 11, p. 203.

[10] According to Panzani's computation.—According to Foley, the number of Jesuit Fathers in England for the same time was 163 in 1634, and 176 in 1636. *Records*, viii. *Collectanea*, Historical Introduction, pp. lxxvi., lxxvii.

[11] Thus, among the very earliest documents of the Propaganda, we find this point taken notice of by Fra Angelo Raffaele da Raconigio, Capuchin preacher. On September 29, 1622, he states that there are here in England "at least 1200 priests, of whom more than half are Jesuits, who govern the greater part of the Catholic nobility," and where they are there is no room for any one else, though every one is welcome on passing. On October 29 of the same year, he repeats this complaint with variations; adding that one circumstance or reason is because "some [of the Jesuits] belong to the most noble families," *per esser alcuni di loro delle più nobili famiglie*. He mentions an aggravating circumstance, which evidently he does not understand : "In the same house there are oftentimes two or three regularly, besides the chance comers," *senza i forestitij*; and he puts in a parenthesis by way of excusing them for their clannishness, and then proceeds with his complaint. The good man did not observe that, in the midst of persecution, the Jesuits had the foresight and means to live in little communities, and keep in tone and vigour the fibre and nerve of their Order; which is nothing, if it have no centres and ganglia to maintain organic life. "Thou art poured out like water: grow thou not!" (Gen.

§ 14. So the Right Reverend Bishop of Chalcedon went on to treat the case of the laity in the same letter: "I also beg your Eminences most earnestly not to believe that either a third part of the Catholic lords of England were represented by those lords, who as Don Carlos Coloma, late Spanish ambassador here, affirms in that attestation of his, printed by the Jesuits and scattered about everywhere, did come to him and affirm that they could not submit to my episcopal authority; or that other Catholics, who agree with them, are the hundredth part of the Catholics of England.[1] For, not to mention that all those Catholic lords who refuse to submit to me are penitents of the regulars, and that during two entire years [after my consecration] no one opposed me, until I had taken action in the matter of the approbation of regulars, the fact is that only seven, or at most eight, English lords approached his Excellency the French ambassador on this subject, and no more could have approached the Spanish ambassador on the same topic. Now, two of these, that is to say, Somersett and Baltimor, are not lords of England, but of Ireland; the third, to wit, Herbert, is not a peer of the English Parliament; and a fourth, who is the chief among them, when he was correctly informed afterwards of the power which I claim over the laity, sent his brother at once to the said French ambassador, to protest that he did not object to my authority. Seeing, then, that there are in England twenty-four Catholic lords, how small is the number of those, whom the said Don Carlos could attest had declared against my authority, when their number is compared with all the Catholic lords of England![2] But if, by actual trial, I wanted to get the votes of the other Catholics who accept most willingly the episcopal authority, and who are highly indignant that this opposition should be made to it in the name of the Catholics of England, my adversaries would surely be ashamed of such a shameful imposture.[3]

The bishop's estimate of Baltimore, etc.

"But I, trusting in the justice of my cause and in the prudence of the Apostolic See, would never have the episcopal authority submitted to the judgment of laymen. Moreover, those laymen who are

xlix. 4). Propaganda Archives, *Lettere, I Anglia*, 347, ff. 21, 246, 255. A testimony of the Jesuits to the charity and devotion of English Catholics, in maintaining priests for their spiritual service and for the Divine worship in private, may be seen in the triennial report for 1655. *Documents*, I. No. 8, S.—It may be noted that, in Fra Angelo's computation, some 112 Jesuits then in England figured as over 600.

[1] "*Ne credant vel Magnates illos Anglos, quos Don Carolus Coloma Orator . . . profitetur ad se accessisse . . . esse tertiam partem Catholicorum Magnatum Angliæ.*"

[2] There may have been as many as eight, he says, who protested; therefore, twenty-four being the total, they could have been one-third.

[3] "*Puderet sane adversarios meos tam pudendæ imposturæ.*"

opposed to me never consented to meet me, though often invited by me to come and get the right information about my authority and intentions;[4] but they would only listen to my adversaries. And certainly they have not been rightly informed, since they pretend that the ground of their opposition is my purpose of setting up a tribunal, contrary to the courts of England; of proving testaments, gathering tithes, settling priests anywhere as I choose; of declaring confessions made without my approbation to be null, and other things of this kind; all of which are most foreign to the truth and to my intention; so that they are really attacking, not me, but a fiction of the regulars, and it is that which they refuse to submit to." In another couple of pages, his lordship relates how the Spanish ambassador has declared against him, for his sympathy with the French and for being intimate with Cardinal Richelieu; how he himself would be glad indeed to escape from his episcopal troubles and retire to France; but he is forced to stand his ground in the teeth of heretics and regulars, if only to save the Apostolic See from infamy, the episcopal dignity from dishonour, and other bishops from danger and scandal, not to speak of the whole English clergy with the greatest part of the laity. He concludes: "I send also herewith to your Eminences a blasphemous censure of the Creed, which the Jesuits have given out, and have had publicly sold among the heretics;[5] so that from this, as well as from their other libels which they pour out of the press, your Eminences may understand how necessary it is to establish here the episcopal authority as a rampart against their unbridled assaults. May God preserve your Eminences.

"Your most humble servant in Christ,
"R. Bishop of CHALCEDON.[6]

"London, 14th June, O.S., 1631."

To this letter the Sacred Congregation gave orders, on August 26, for a reply to be couched in the following sense: "To the Bishop of Chalcedon, in Latin.

"That Cardinal Barberini, Protector of England, has reported his lordship's letter in the Sacred Congregation of the Propaganda; and inasmuch as one part of it discusses the issue between him and the regulars, a case already settled by the Holy Office, as he must have seen by this time in the Brief published by His Holiness under date

---

[4] "*De mea authoritate ac proposito.*"
[5] Cf. *Annales de la Société des soi-disans Jésuites*, iii. 429–437, note.
[6] Propaganda Archives, *Lettere*, 100, ff. 142, 143; an original, of which only the signature is autograph.

of the 9th May, this year, a copy of his letter is [merely] sent to the same Holy Office. Then, as to the matter of the sodality of the Conception[7] of the Blessed Virgin and the decree of the Sacred Congregation issued with respect to it, Cardinal Cajetan has been commissioned to treat thereof with the Father General of the Jesuits, for the purpose of coming to some suitable resolution." [8]

The Brief so published, under the date of May 9, 1631, decided the point which was mentioned by Cardinal Albizi as most important,[9] and which regarded as well the position of the regulars in England as the relation of the laity to them. It said: "We declare that the confessions heretofore heard by priests of the regular clergy were valid, and such in the future shall be valid. For, since they acted by virtue of Apostolic authority, and will continue to do so, ordinary faculty and approbation is not and shall not be necessary to them. And every missionary shall use his faculties and privileges in the same manner and by the same authority as he did before these controversies, and in the times of Gregory XIII. and Paul V. of happy memory." The entire controversy was herewith ordered to be stopped; and recourse should be had to the Holy See for all further enlightenment and decisions.[10]

The Papal Brief. May 9, 1631.

On receipt of the Brief from Rome, four representatives of the regular Orders proceeded to have a copy authenticated by an English Notary-Apostolic, Dr. Southcot, whom on occasion we find, in company with George Fisher and Thomas White or Blacklow, representing the Bishop of Chalcedon.[11] They called upon him, sending word by the head of the house why they

Southcot, Fisher, and Blacklow.

---

[7] As appears above, the Jesuits' own title for their sodality was that of the "Immaculate Conception." *Supra*, § 13, p. 215, note 6.

[8] *Ibid.*, f. 143ᵛ: "*die 26 Augusti*, 1631, *Cong.* 146, No. 33;" summary and reply in Secretary Ingoli's hand.—This disagrees with Chalcedon's statement, p. 215, med.

[9] Cf. Brady, *Episcopal Succession*, etc., iii. 77.

[10] More, *Historia Provinciæ Anglicanæ S.J.*, lib. x., §§ 9, 10; where the text is given, beginning in a rather magnificent style: "*Britannia non minus cœlestibus.*"—Dodd gives the essential passage (*Church History*, iii. 13); but for the facts of the case which it settles he cites the Gallican and Jansenist Du Pin; *Ibid.*, p. 5.—Panzani, in his *Relation*, suppresses the gist of the Brief; Barberini Library, lvi. 136, f. 9ᵛ; and, as to the facts that led thereto, tells a series of stories, without letting it transpire what the bishop's first action really was in the question of regulars and faculties; *Ibid.*, ff. 5ᵛ-7. He speaks with great respect of the Gallicans who entered into the controversy; *Ibid.*, ff. 8, 9.—Brady's short summary of Panzani's account here affords a slight but correct specimen of this envoy's ways; *Episcopal Succession*, iii. pp. 81, 82.—Gillow leaves out the original fact, or *corpus delicti*, which consisted in declaring the confessions heard by regulars to be null and void; he leaves out the essential declaration of the Brief; he seems to think the opinion of the Sorbonne and the Gallican Bishops quite valuable on the subject of the Pope's authority; and, having undertaken in several places to treat Father Edward Knott or Wilson, he leaves him out altogether. Gillow's *Bibliographical Dictionary*, etc., s.v. "Floyd, John;" "Kellison, Matthew;" "Smith, Richard."

[11] General Archives S.J., *Anglia, Historia*, iv. p. 275: in the matter of a *Concordia*.

came, with the notification that they had the Apostolic Brief with them. Dr. Southcot refused to have anything to do with it, or to come down and see them.[12]

Father David, the Benedictine monk.

What followed then, the Benedictine monk of the Cassinese obedience, Father David, will inform us. Writing to the Sacred Congregation of the Propaganda a few months later, he proceeds to speak of the controversy: " Then the resolution," he says, " announced by Brief of His Holiness, with respect to the controversy set on foot by the Right Reverend Bishop of Chalcedon, has come to hand here, both in the original and in authentic copies, having been despatched as well by his Eminence Cardinal Ginetti, Vicar of His Holiness, as by Monsignore the Auditor of the [Apostolic] Chamber; it has, however, been rejected by the secular clergy and not accepted as good, but [held to be] surreptitious; and so too by some of their lay adherents; to the scandal and exciting of public murmurs on the part of many Catholics, at seeing the clergy refuse to recognize any Brief, if they think it is to their prejudice; while, on the contrary, the poor lay gentlemen, to their own great prejudice with the loss of goods and perpetual imprisonment, accepted the Brief of His Holiness which prohibited the oath; although very many of them were of the opinion that the said oath contained nothing against the faith; and they set aside their own private opinion, submitting it to the pontifical decision with all due promptness and obedience. Wherefore, if these factions go on, or if they are permitted to go on, without forcing people to suppress the whole controversy and bury it in its own ashes, there will arise here such a degree of presumption that, whenever in the future Briefs are communicated, every one will be able to presume that they are surreptitious, and will excuse himself from obedience.

" I have seen with my eyes, and your Excellency may believe that I am telling you the truth, because I shall send you a copy by this same post,—I say, I have seen the first personages of England signatories [to a document] against the proceedings of the Right Reverend Chalcedon; such as the Right Honourable the Earl of Worcester, the Earl of Shrewsbury, the viscounts and barons Petre, Abergaueny, Sommersett, Balthimore, and very many others, in numbers much greater than Mgr. of Chalcedon can have on his side; and of knights there are absolutely ten to one, in spite of the

[12] General Archives S.J., *Anglia, Historia*, iv. p. 269: "Declaration of what the four Religious did with Mr. Southcot." This fact is cited in the subsequent petition of the peers; cf. *infra*, § 15, p. 225.

fact that he makes so much account of the protection afforded him by his Eminence, Cardinal Richelieu in France."

After protesting his sincerity, and claiming liberty of speech, the monk goes on to describe the laymen's fixity of resolution, and also a ground of disappointment with them: "Wherefore I say that, as one or more bishops would be a source of comfort to these Catholic gentlemen, if such bishops will consult the quiet and tranquillity of everybody by [simply] giving the consolations of holy Confirmation and holy oils; so, if they will not be satisfied with less than coactive jurisdiction, and that of an Ordinary, your Excellency may be absolutely assured that they [the laity] cannot submit. The particulars, the factions, the fictions, the stratagems, the odium and rancour, the defamation, which have all followed on this pretension of his lordship, baffle description. They are matters to weep over for years and years. And then these lay gentlemen complain that nothing is mentioned in the Brief except what concerns hushing up the controversy, and declaring confessions valid, without touching that point which touches them to the quick, namely, whether he is their Ordinary pastor or no." Here Father David enlarges upon the contrast between what the Brief ordains about taking no further steps except with reference to the Holy See, and what the bishop has now undertaken to do by flying to France, and continuing the campaign by means of the Court there, and of the French ambassador here.[13]

The truth of the monk's account is not invalidated by either the printed or the manuscript literature at hand. Thus Dodd says about the Brief: "This Bull, being only handed privately about among the Bishop of Chalcedon's adversaries, gave strong suspicions to several, that it was either spurious or surreptitious. However, as it was never publish'd in a canonical manner, nor deliver'd to the Bishop of Chalcedon by proper officers, his party took very little notice of it; but still went on in the defence of their cause, supported by the Council of Trent and the general practice of the Church, which requir'd episcopal approbation. Besides, this pretended decree of Urban VIII.," etc., did not agree with the Gallican doctrines, which Dodd goes on to inculcate.[14] This historian, who says that no official communication was made of the Brief, is contradicted by Cardinal Albizi, who reports that Cardinal Bichi, then Nuncio in France, forwarded this Brief to Bishop Smith, who felt

Dodd on the Brief.

[13] Propaganda Archives, *Lettere*, 150, f. 198: London, November 2, 1631.
[14] Dodd, as above, iii. 13, 14, objections 10, 11. The rock, on which Gallican doctrine swung pivoted during many a century, was the question of papal authority, and on it that doctrine finally suffered shipwreck in the Vatican Council.

bitterly disappointed at its contents—went to France—declared that his stay in England, after the receipt of such a Brief, was fruitless; and then resorted to a usual stroke of policy, which may often be successful, but on this occasion signally failed. He offered his resignation to the Pope.[15]

While he is waiting for an answer, which comes in a form either never forecast in his intentions, or at least resented by him afterwards, we may see what the aggrieved lords did; the Brief having come, not a word being found in it regarding themselves, and an account having gone to the Holy Father that they who protested were an insignificant set of nobodies. Some one or more among them proved equal to the occasion. A very able "Information" for the Pope, on the subject of the controversy between Chalcedon and the laity, was drawn up to accompany a "Declaratory Protest," as well for the Holy Father's use as by way of a challenge to all the gainsayers who had endeavoured to mislead His Holiness by a false report.

The aggrieved peers.

§ 15. The Information, accompanying the Protest of the Peers, was entitled "State of the Controversy between the Bishop of Chalcedon and the lay Catholics of England." It mentioned briefly the general subject under debate, and the particular reason for urgency. A recent paper had "audaciously" been given out, and "impudently" submitted to the Holy Father or to the Board appointed by him. Its name was: "A true and sincere Information on the sentiments of Catholics in England towards the Bishop of Chalcedon."[1] Its slanderous and abusive character being described, it is credited here with having caught indeed the gist of the question, when it made the issue depend upon the views of the laity; contending, as it did, that the laymen who stood for Chalcedon were the only ones worthy of notice, and the others were not worth mentioning. It was in view of this contention that His Holiness was requested to suspend judgment till October, when the return of the nobility to town would enable the question to be put to the proof. The gentlemen had proposed to have a double protest drawn up, one of the kind herewith submitted, the other to be put in shape by the opposite party and presented. There have been difficulties attending the

The Information for Rome.
[Oct.], 1631.

[15] Brady, as above, p. 79.

[1] "*Hæc inter scripta cæteris licentius unum prodiit, cui titulus est: 'Vera et sincera Informatio de affectibus Catholicorum in Anglia erga Episcopum Chalcedonensem,' impudenter sane S^{mo} D^{no}, vt fertur, oblatum.*"

project, because of the danger incident to signing such a document; and the loyalty of the opposing party is a very dubious element.[2] Some peers accordingly have not signed, but have signified their adhesion otherwise. The greater number have signed without more ado; and a copy is herewith despatched. This has become the more necessary because of the intrusion of the French ambassador's name and attestation into the question—which, however, he practically withdrew or denied in an interview with Lord Baltimore and Viscount Somerset;—and again because a fraudulent use has been made of six noble names on the wrong side of the question, in the slanderous paper before cited. Of these six, that of George, Baron of Baltimore, is mentioned in the last place. All of these lords affix their signatures to the present document. There are only twenty-six titled Catholic nobles; and twelve sign here. Five will not sign, but have given their verbal adhesion to this document, with permission to use their names. Two more, Paullet, Marquis of Winchester, and Arundel, Baron of Wardour, who are regularly cited as favouring the bishop's pretensions, declare distinctly that they do not see it is the time or place for the authority of an Ordinary, or at least for the exercise of external jurisdiction. Then three hundred of the gentry[3] have affixed their signatures, and time does not allow of procuring more. These have been selected as being most representative in their respective counties.

Baltimore and Somerset.

Here follows a discussion, why they cannot forward a paper attested by a Notary, but must keep the original for private inspection only. A Notary-Apostolic attached to the bishop would not even come downstairs to see the religious who brought him a copy of the Apostolic Brief for authentication. Notaries-Apostolic on the side of the regulars might be thought to be partial. And public Notaries will not suit at all; for communication with Rome in a way to acknowledge the Pontiff's authority exposes the person guilty of it to the penalties of *præmunire;* and therefore they cannot betray themselves to such a public official. Hence, in these straits, they can only keep the original document with the autograph signatures, which will be acknowledged by the signers; while those others, who gave in their adhesion *vivâ voce,* will *vivâ voce* reiterate the same.

The document closes with two significant points; one implying a grievance that the case of the laity should have been slighted as it

---

[2] "*Et ne ab adversariis in discrimen vocarentur, quorum sæpius non tutam fidem experti sunt.*"
[3] "*Nobiles non titulati.*"

VOL. I. Q

was, while that of the regulars was attended to; the other according merited praise to the lay Catholics of England, for having exhibited such a spectacle of faith to the Christian world, although the Sacrament of Confirmation has so long been wanting to them. They say—

"The above being duly considered, the aforesaid Catholic laymen are quite confident that, as His Holiness was pleased to exempt the regulars from the pretended authority of his lordship, although these religious are bound to the Holy See canonically and specially by vows and privileges in a way beyond the duty of the faithful, and they have no fortunes at stake since they possess nothing here, so he will be pleased to comprise in his pontifical solicitude the case of the English laymen, whose interests are imperilled; and he will not require them to acknowledge the power of an Ordinary at this time, when the very persons who aspire to such a jurisdiction (whatever they may have said or written at other times) are forced to admit that, as things stand at present, it cannot be exercised; and this may be proved on the spot by their talk, their answers, their letters.

"In this hope they rest the more confidently as they are sure that His Holiness knows well how far from necessary is the power of an Ordinary, seeing that, during so many years they have approved themselves to the whole Christian world in maintaining the faith— not without glory—which, however, is the gift of God." And, with a confirmatory appeal to the action of Paul V., who in a similar case, and with respect to not dissimilar claimants, left them in peace, the laity close this Information addressed to the Sovereign Pontiff.[4]

The Protest attached to the Information is shorter and perfectly clear. For the reasons alleged, they declare against acknowledging the Bishop of Chalcedon for an Ordinary; they put their signatures hereto or signify their adherence, as elsewhere explained; and they call upon those who dissent from them to draw up a counter-protest and have the signatures affixed— leaving aside all general questions about the necessity of episcopal authority or about the Sacrament of Confirmation being necessary in

The Protest of the peers. [Oct.], 1631.

---

[4] General Archives S.J., *Anglia, Historia*, iii. ff. 372-375: a contemporary copy of *Status Controversiæ inter Episcopum Chalcedonensem et laicos Angliæ Catholicos*. Being intended for Rome, this and the following Protest must have been drawn up in Latin, as here. With respect to the praise of the English laity's confirmed virtue without the Sacrament of Confirmation, compare a passage under date of 1612: "S'aggiunge, che Dio per sua singolar prouidenza può con modo speciale fuori del Sacramento conferir la virtù della Confirmatione, e si uede apertamente ciò esser seguito nei Cattolici d'Inghilterra, poichè niun Regno o Prouincia ha hauuto in questo secolo martiri più costanti, e più illustri." *Ibid.*, ii. f. 400, G. Arcivescovo de Rhodi, Bruxelles, 6 ottob. and 20 ottob. 1612; viz. on the question of appointing a bishop for England, ff. 397-402.

the Church of God at large—points which no Catholic denies—as also setting aside the question concerning the regulars and the bishop.

The names given in the list of autograph signatures are: John Talbot, Earl of Shrewsbury; Henry Somersett, Earl of Worcester; Thomas Darcy, Earl Rivers; James Touchet, Earl of Castlehaven and Baron Audley; William Howard, Lord Naworth; Thomas Somersett, Viscount Cashell; Edward Somersett, Baron Herbert; Henry Nevill, Baron Abergavenny; Thomas Windsor, Baron Bradenham; William Petre, Baron Writle; Thomas Brudenell, Baron Stourton [or Stanton?]; George Calvert, Baron Baltimore. *Names of the Catholic nobles.*

The names of five who acceded without signing are Richard de Burgh, Earl of St. Alban's and Clanricard; Thomas Savage, Viscount Rock-savage; Ulysses de Burgh, Baron Tunbridge; Henry Parker, Baron Morley and Mounteagle; Edward Vaux, Baron Harowdon.

Two are favourable to the bishop, but not to the mixed power which he claims: John Paullet, Marquis of Winchester; Thomas Arundel, Baron Wardor.

One, William Eure, Baron Whitton, is absent. Francis Manners, Earl of Rutland, and Francis Brown, Viscount Montague, do not commit themselves to any opinion, one way or other. Two others are boys, Henry Stafford, Baron Stafford, and Christopher Roper, Baron Tenham. Edward Stourton, Baron Stourton, an octogenarian, does not make profession of his Catholicity; but his eldest son and heir has signed; as also the eldest son and heir—a Catholic—of Viscount Fairfax, who is himself not a Catholic. Henry Constable, Viscount Dunbar, is the only one, who declares absolutely for the bishop. After a general statement regarding the Catholic knights, esquires, and other gentry, who have subscribed to the number of three hundred, with others who have approved without signing, the document closes: "The autographs of all the above are kept for exhibition when called for." [5]

---

[5] General Archives S.J., *Anglia, Historia,* iii. ff. 360, 361, contemporary copy. We are inclined to believe the hand is that of Father Alacambe, *alias* Atslow, etc., *socius* or secretary to the Provincial at this time. The same copyist writes out the Protest and the Information or *Status Controversiæ.* The part which Panzani takes up to discuss in his *Relation,* ff. 35ᵛ–38, from an authenticated copy as he says (f. 12), signed in August, 1631, tallies perfectly with the copy which we cite, and there is no room for doubting that our copy is correct, or that the business was carried through to the very end. This latter point, however, is made certain by other correspondence of the time.—Compare W. M. Brady's sketch of Panzani's performance, comprising that gentleman's characteristic touch about Baltimore and the judgment of God. *Episcopal Succession,* iii. pp. 97–99.—Cf. *infra,* p. 232.

Thus neither laymen nor clergymen nor ambassadors had mistaken the precise point of the question. It was that of numbers and weight. Two years earlier, the General of the Society had expressed his satisfaction to the Provincial, Father Blount, that at length they had entered on the right course in England, and that the chief Catholic laymen were come forward to confirm what only the regulars had affirmed heretofore. And though, when Baltimore and others waited on the Spanish ambassador Coloma and received his attestation, the General expressed his doubts whether the Protest of the peers at that date might not add fuel to the controversy, still he said nothing against its efficacy in conveying the right information to the right quarter.[6] The Protest at that moment, supported by the attestation of the Spanish ambassador in the spring of 1631, had elicited the Brief in favour of the regulars, as the French ambassador in London said in a despairing letter to the French ambassador in Rome, while asking for his immediate and strenuous support.[7] Here it was that the *Désaveu*, or disavowal in the name of the laity, had been attempted, had been endorsed by the French ambassador to retrieve the cause, and was immediately followed by the diplomatic but indignant interview of Baltimore and Somerset with his Excellency. Then, as he only "flipped the paper with his finger," arched his brows in solemn disapproval of such an attempt, said he would see and set things to rights, but never did so, they drew up the present Protestation; and its effect shows us, how quick and far in the settlement of business goes the clear and decisive action of men who know their own minds. The case before us is quite a prototype of several episodes to follow in American history.

An issue of numbers and weight.

Cardinal Albizi reports that, when the Bishop of Chalcedon offered to resign his dignity, the intelligence was very agreeable to the Nuncio and the Pope. Urban VIII. desired the Nuncio to take a formal resignation from the hands of Dr. Smith, and not to allow him back into England. The Bishop changed his mind when he heard that his resignation was so cheerfully accepted, and begged leave to go back to his post. He was refused.[8] And during the next fifty-five years the Vicariate Apostolic of England remained vacant.

Vacating the Vicariate Apostolic.

---

[6] *Anglia, Epist. Gen.*, 1629, August 25; 1631, April 26: General to Blount, Provincial.
[7] Given in Dodd without date, iii. part vi. bk. iii. art. 3 (y), p. 143: "*se fondant sur plusieurs raisons, et particulièrement, que cette authorité étoit préjudiciable aux laïques d'Angleterre, comme il luy* [*viz. au Saint Père*] *apparut par la déclaration, qu'ils en ont faite.*"
[8] Brady, as above, p. 79.

Unhappily for the peace of the Jesuits, their place was not vacated. A policy had been recommended to the Propaganda, as we have seen, by the Bishop of Chalcedon, that, since the regulars had monasteries outside of England, they might betake themselves thither. As to the moral franchise of a good name, that was already in jeopardy, so much so that one acquaintance wrote to another about the Jesuits: "What will or can any man expect of us," said he, "but to write in our defence, and lay open to that end whatsoever we know to their discredit?" which latter words his correspondent duly underlines. After the last protest of Baltimore and the other lords, one very indignant writer proposes to apply the *lex talionis* to the Jesuits as a retribution for the withdrawal of the bishop, and "one petition," he says, "delivered by them, the lay Catholics, to the King for the banishment of the Jesuits, as incendiaries and disturbers of the public peace, would send them all packing hence." This suggestion his correspondent duly emphasizes with a marginal observation, writing the word "Note." Another suggests what he says "will counterpoise the 18 supposed writers against my lords authority," by getting "a dozen or 15 noblemens hands" to what he calls a "Disclaimer." And it is proposed to frighten Rome by setting the Gallican Sorbonne once more upon the track.[9] Meanwhile the Notary-Apostolic who had refused to authenticate the Pope's Brief, put his name, with that of another, to a Declaration against the Protest of the lords; and stated that the English Catholics had been deceived in the matter of the said Protest, and that the great majority desired the very opposite.[10] In Rome a stupendous document of forty-three folios was put together from the correspondence on hand, and distributed in divers copies, the largest application being made in it of the principle already enunciated, that of heaping together "whatsoever we know to their [the Jesuits'] discredit."[11]

The anti-Jesuit campaign.

---

[9] Stonyhurst College MSS., *Anglia A*, viii. f. 99: Fitton to Rant, with compliments to "Sg⁰. Ingola," 1625, January 1.—*Ibid.* f. 224ᵛ: West alias Norton to Fitton, 1631, October 3.—*Ibid.*, f. 74ᵛ: Clerk to [Fitton], 1632, July 13.—*Ibid.*, f. 78ᵛ: [Clerk] to [Fitton] 1634, January 10.—The recipients, Rant and Fitton, were at different dates in Rome, acting as agents for the others. Cf. *infra*, § 61, p. 498.

[10] Dodd, *ubi supra*, art. 4, p. 150; signed John Southcote and G. Farrar, Notaries-Apostolic.

[11] Propaganda Archives, *I Anglia*, 347, ff. 301-343; *Ibid.*, *II Anglia et Scotia*, 297, ff. 1-43.—It was made the subject of a *Compendio breve*, by the Secretary Ingoli, who describes the paper exactly in his title: "*Compendio breve della Relatione dello stato della Chiesa Anglicana data dall' Agente del clero d'Inghilterra in vn Quinternetto di fogli* 43;" *Ibid.*, *I Anglia*, 347, ff. 364, 365.—Several other discourses or opinions of the secretary appear on the same question; *Ibid.*, ff. 359, 360, 362, 363, 381-386, 393-396.—What Ingoli calls a *Relatione* is entitled by the memorialists

It is entitled: "A Brief Account of some abuses introduced into the English Church, of the causes thereof, and of the way to extirpate them, whence is inferred the wretched condition of things, as long as there is no Bishop."[12] An ever-recurring refrain in the nominative case is "a Jesuit," or "the Jesuits;" what they did and did not, what they are doing and do not. Seldom is a statement circumstantial. When a name is vouchsafed, as in about one-fifth of the cases, the other limiting conditions of date, place, and identifying circumstance, are still left out; and the stories, thus floating in the air, if they afford nothing to convince the reader, neither offer a hold to convict the writer.

A Relation of Jesuit doings. 1632.

There are two specimens of stories which relate to our subject— the first about Lord Baltimore, and the other about Father Altham, one of the missionaries who were sent to Maryland in the very next year. The former, recording a public scandal, in the shape of a wrongful separation from his wife whom he repudiates, presents Lord Baltimore as figuring in a circumstance of which we have no trace whatever in history; and, as it is all laid to the account of Father Knott, confessor to both of them, it should have occurred since Baltimore's reception into the Church.[13] As to Father Altham,

themselves *Breve Ragguaglio d'alcuni abusi*, etc. We cite the copy of *II Anglia et Scotia*, ff. 1–43.

[12] The date of the compilation is 1632. Thus, f. 6ᵛ: "*Desumptum ex Supplicatione quadam multorum Sacerdotum missa ad Suam Sᵗᵉᵐ hoc ipso anno* 1632." This extract begins: "*Jesuitæ*" ... *venditant* ... *suo Ordini concessas immensas facultates, indulgentias, privilegia Sodalitatum, participationem immensi spiritualis thesauri* ... *non aliter communicanda* ... *nisi quis habeat a confessionibus Jesuitam* ...; ending: "*Quid tandem de nobis fiet?*" We find on hand in places the originals from which the redaction of this farrago or its materials seem to have been derived.

[13] *Ibid.*, f. 23ᵛ, 24: "*Il Padre Knotto Vice-Provinciale de' Gesuiti consigliò una certa zitella in Inghilterra, che contrahesse matrimonio con il Barone de Baltamour suo padrone, e benchè ella si sforzasse d'evitar queste nozze per l'impedimento dell' affinità spirituale, come dubitava, perchè la prima moglie [Anne Mynne?] di detto suo padrone l'haveva levata dal sacro fonte del Battesimo, nondimeno a persuasione del P. Knotto, qual' era confessore dell' uno e l'altro, contrasse e consumò seco il matrimonio; ma doppo havendo il Barone cominciato ad haverla in fastidio, egli stesso sotto pretesto della detta affinità spirituale voleva disciolger' il matrimonio; et il medesimo P. Knotto, il quale prima haveva dichiarato questo matrimonio valido, per persuadere in tal modo a questa donna d'acconsentire al desiderio del predetto Barone,* ... *doppo, a favore del medesimo, pronuntiò questo matrimonio esser nullo, e giudicò doversi il marito separar dal thoro, reclamante la moglie; e così con publico scandalo dichiarò lo stesso matrimonio hora valido, hora nullo, seconda la libidine di questo Barone suo Padrone*."— According to this, Baltimore should have married his ward after his conversion (1625). Then, after living with her, he should have been divorced, in spite of recriminations; and then, as we know from other documents, he would have married some third lady, whom he took from Newfoundland to Virginia, and whom he lost on the high seas in 1630, "with her children that were left with her." The story put in writing by the Roman agent for the instruction of the Propaganda agrees no better with the known facts and dates of Baltimore's life, than with his character as a Christian gentleman.—For these dates, see above, this Chap. III. pp. 176, 200. In Cecil's statement about his father, as quoted on p. 200, the lady lost with her children in 1630 was "his then second wife."

Whether it will add to the confusion or not, we must needs append the account

§ 15]   MEMORIAL ON BALTIMORE   231

the case reported has no probability on the face of it. If he in confession had refused absolution to a dying gentleman in order to control the penitent's testament and levy on his goods, some authority should have been adduced to show how the secrets of a dying person's confession came to the knowledge of the reporter in the street. But liability to verification or detection does not seem to have formed part of the programme with some of these persons; as one of them wrote to another: " One thing cometh to my mynde about the Supplication, viz. [that] it be carefully kept from any who may impart it. If it came to the Jesuits hands, they will make all use of [it]; yea, other regulars would not take it well." [14]

Then came Panzani, despatched from Rome at the end of 1634, for the purpose of inquiring about the episcopal question. At once he began to despatch summarily all kinds of matters. After giving the proper suggestions to Secretary Windebank, he was able to announce in triumph to the Cardinal Secretary of State, that the King desired Rome to withdraw all Jesuits from England. As soon as he had occasion to hear from the Cardinal upon such topics, he was informed that he had better not offer his services for any communications with Rome, but attend to the affair for which he was sent. Whereupon he offered up his tears

The Roman envoy, Panzani. 1634-1636.

given by Panzani of the same incident, as derived, of course, from the same sources. He names the young person in question Madam Mary Win, and he takes the case from Muskett as if it were a live issue of the time (about February, 1635): " Muskett came to me," he says, " and told me the case; " whereas, if the Baron Baltimore was George Calvert, first Lord, who alone seems to be a possible subject of the story, all the parties were dead for years, and the case itself would be some ten years old. Panzani writes in his Diary: " *Il Sigr Moschetto fu da me coadiutore* [?] *del Vicario, e mi narrò il caso. Baro Baltomor clandestine contraxit per verba de præsenti cum D. Maria Win, famula filiæ Baronis, cujus pater est curtisanus* [*capitaneus?*], *quam prima uxor illius levaverat e sacro fonte. Hunc contractum primo approbavit confessarius illius P. Odoardus Knot Jesuita, Vice-provincialis Jesuitarum; et, cum peteret illa utrum posset reddere Baroni, respondit P. Knot: Baro nihil petet a te quod non sit licitum et ad gloriam Dei; postea tamen pronunciavit matrimonium esse omnino invalidum propter impedimentum cognationis spiritualis, quam ipse falso putabat oriri ex eo quod levaverat e sacro fonte.*"—Vatican Archives, *Nunziatura d'Inghilterra*, tom. 3 A: Diary of Gregory Panzani, February 4, 1634–March 30, 1637, f. 79 (under or after February, 18/28, [1635]).

Father Altham's case is given f. 20ᵛ, and it comes amid an assortment of similar gruesome instances—unnamed Jesuits in some No-man's Land terrorizing the unnamed dying or running away with the trunks of the unnamed dead: " *Il P. Althamo Gesuita negò l'assoluzione ad un nobile moribondo, perchè non volse disporre de suoi beni ad arbitrio suo.*" II *Anglia et Scotia*, as above.

The substance of a domestic difficulty, laid to the account, not of Lord Baltimore, but of Lord Morley, and taken from the *Relation* of Panzani, f. 12, may be seen in Brady, iii. 83.

An account of a common letter sent from England, and apparently one of the most recent quoted by the Roman agent in his extraordinary production (f. 6ᵛ), may be seen in Stonyhurst MSS., *Anglia A*, viii. No. 65; July 13, 1632: Clark, England, to [Fitton, Rome]. Cf. *supra*, Introduction, Chap. II. § 2, p. 53: General to Silesdon.

[14] Stonyhurst MSS., *Anglia A*, viii. f. 126ᵛ: "Jo. Haᵈ.", [England, to . . .] November 9, [1636].

in sincere repentance at the feet of his Eminence, proposed amendment, invoked the proper blessings on the Jesuits, and then relapsed as before. Upon his recall to Rome, after two years of performances, he wrote a *Relation* to justify his errors, those of a man whom his successor, George Con, ranked with *pazzi maligni*, people as foolish as they were mischievous.[15] What Panzani says of George Calvert, in relation to the signature on the last great Protest, is typical of all the rest—

"George Calvert, Baron of Baltimore, signed at the instance of Toby Mathews and Father Knott, Jesuit, but he died a few days afterwards; and by some this was attributed to the judgment of God."[16]

George Calvert had died some eight months after signing; but that was a small matter for Panzani—eight months or a few days. It was the judgment of God that was of consequence. A few months after his arrival in England, he thought he was entering with great insight into the affairs, oaths, and policy generally, of Cæcilius Calvert, second Lord Baltimore. We shall see to what effect. He did make the acquaintance of John Lewger, and received appeals from Father Price on behalf of this newly converted minister.[17]

Hence we part company with the laymen's controversy at this point, where the persons engaged in it enter also into the affairs of the Maryland colony, already more than a year old. Before we shall have seen a decade of years pass over that colony, we may be inclined to infer that, through Cæcilius, second Lord Baltimore, this controversy had an injurious effect on the religious interests of the plantation.[18]

§ 16. In the chorus of sounds which have commanded our attention, only the voices of the Jesuits themselves remain unheard from this time onwards. Besides some official papers, which have

---

[15] Barberini Library, *Lettere Sciolte*, 36: Con, Hampton, January 1, 1637, to Ferragalli.

[16] Barberini Library, lvi., 136, *Relatione dello stato della religione cattolica in Inghilterra, data alla Santità di N.S. Urbano VIII. da Gregorio Panzani*, ff. 36ᵛ, 37. —Cf. W. M. Brady, *Episcopal Succession*, iii. 98.

[17] Vatican Archives, *Nunziatura d'Inghilterra*, 5, ff. 20, 28: Panzani, London, to Cardinal Barberini, March 9 and March 16, 1635; within this space of a week he has the Pope invited by the King to rid England of the entire Jesuit body, or at least to weaken it. His tears begin to flow April 10-20, 1635, and he will be in agony till, after two months, he shall hear he is forgiven: *Ibid.*, f. 33. His blessings upon the Jesuits, with purposes of amendment, June 13, 1635; cf. P. R. O., *Transcripts from Rome*, xvii. Letter begins: "*Conforme al commandamento*..." Con's letters upon him are December 15-25, 1636, to the Cardinal and Ferragalli; and December 23, 1636-January 1, 1637, to Ferragalli: Barberini Library, *Lettere Sciolte*, 36.

[18] Cf. *infra*, § 63, (1), pp. 509-513, third and fourth of Cecil Lord Baltimore's Points.

been referred to in part, we find nothing from their pens. Early in 1631, the order was issued that silence should be kept in this fratricidal war; and the Fathers had to keep it. They pleaded with the General for leave to speak out in self-defence; but he was inexorable. Rome desired it so; their profession bound them to acquiesce; and he bade them see to it, that the example of the unruly did not count for more with them than the rule of duty.[1]

In face of that inevitable expulsion or recall, which, as the new order of the day implied, was but a milder alternative for suppression the Jesuits of England were not unwilling to see the new world open a refuge before them. The occasion of some acute agitation had but to coincide with the occasion of some fit political juncture, and the cause of the Jesuits might be isolated from that of other Catholics and priests; their outlawry become a mere incident without prejudice to others; and their deportation effected in an exceptional and preferential way. In fact, such junctures have occurred; and the latest has been at a date comparatively recent. The earliest was the one which is now before us. In the first and the last case, America was distinctly the land of refuge kept in contemplation. On one or two other occasions it was not excluded. If placed at so safe a distance, the Fathers expected that they might be left in peace.

America a refuge for English Jesuits.

As to this American colony, its projector and designer, George Calvert, while engaged in controversy on the one hand, was deeply immersed in the essential interests of his plantation on the other. He was evolving his charter.[2] He had sued His Majesty for that part of Virginia, "which lyeth between the River of Passamagnus and the present Plantation of Virginia on James River, towards the South." On reference from the King, the Lords Dorsett and Carlisle, Wentworth and Cottington, reported favourably; and, under date of February 23, 1631, his Majesty gave leave for the passing of such a grant. This received the King's signature; but then, upon a counter-petition being reported from the Virginia planters and after a new reference to a special committee, the grant was by common consent resigned. A tract of land, distant to the northward from the Virginia settlement, was now proposed as a substitute. A bill or

---

[1] Cf. *supra*, Introduction, Chap. II. § 9, p. 72.
[2] We assume it as a matter of course, in the evolution of a royal grant of grace, that the King's beneficiary either was the author of the patent or else inspired its provisions. Moreover, intrinsic reasons are quite sufficient to support that postulate in the present case.—Cf. J. V. L. McMahon, *Historical View of the Government of Maryland*, p. 10; also F. L. Hawks, Appendix A to Sabin's reprint of *Relation of Maryland*, 1635, p. 67.

charter was prepared. "His lordship," we are informed, "had caused a blanck to be left in the bill for the name, which he designed should be Crescentia or the Land of Crescence; but, leaving it to his Majestie to insert, the King afore he signed the bill put the question to his lordship what he should call it; who replied that he desiered to have had it called something in honour of his Majesties name; but that he was deprived of that happiness, there being already a province in those parts called Carolana, as is said before: Lett us therefore (says the King) give it a name in honour of the queen; what think you of Mariana? which his lordship excepted against as being the name of a Jesuite that wrote against monarchy; wherevpon the King proposed *Terra Mariæ*, in English Mary-Land; which was concluded on and inserted in the bill.

The draft of a charter for Maryland. [March–April] 1632.

"It passed the privie seale some few days after; but his lordship by Mr. Noys, then Attorney General, advice delayed the passing of it vnder the great seale for some time: and in the interim dyed (viz.) on the 15th of Aprill, 1632, at his lodgings in Lincolns Innfeilds in London."[3]

Death of the first Lord Baltimore. April 15, 1632.

George Calvert was only some fifty-three years of age when he died. His figure had been conspicuous in the history of varied and intricate affairs during a good span of years. That in the conduct of important business public and private, in the handling of practical politics, commercial adventures, and religious controversy, no great error was laid to his account, is no small tribute to his judgment and his prudence. And that, in the busiest period of a life so active, and while enjoying the heyday of professional success, he should have advanced the interests of religion and conscience into the very first place, is a striking testimony to the sincerity and thoroughness of his character. In default of any tortuous policy or dubious ethics, his dexterity and address must have been considerable to direct his course so steadily in such unsteady times. What his son reports of him, as a filial tribute to his

Character of George Calvert.

---

[3] British Museum MSS., *Sloane*, 3662, f. 25, as quoted before.—Also *Calvert Papers*, i. pp. 222, 223: Cecilius, Lord Baltimore, Declaration to the Lords [1634].—As to Baltimore's remark about Mariana's book, *De Rege et Regis Institutione*, published first in 1599, and always acceptable to the Spanish King for whom it was intended, we take Calvert's expression of dissent from Mariana's opinions to be an indication of the political philosophy which he had followed as a Protestant and Secretary of State. It was that of the French Parliament and Sorbonne, which cried down Mariana, his policy, and the doctrine of tyrannicide imputed to him and to the Society. On this occasion it suggested to Baltimore the fitting compliment of a monarchist to a monarch.—Compare Sommervogel, *s.v.* "Mariana," for bibliographical information on the subject.

memory, may probably be taken as literally true of George Calvert's address in dealing with men. Writing to Viscount Wentworth a couple of years after his father's death, Cæcilius makes this remark: "My Lord, I have many occasions from your lordship to remember my dear Father, and now I do not want one: for I must confess, I never knew any man have that way of doing favours unto others, with that advantage to themselves, as your lordship hath and he had."[4]

As a fitting epitaph to his memory, we need but quote some words of his own, those of a Christian gentleman, the height of whose aspirations and the depth of whose feelings need no commentary beyond his own utterance. Writing a letter of condolence to Wentworth, who lost his wife about a year or so after Baltimore had lost his own wife and children on the high seas, the latter says: "There are few, perhaps, can judge of it better than I, who have been a long time myself a man of sorrows. But all things, my Lord, in this world pass away, *statutum est*, wife, children, honour, wealth, friends, and what else is dear to flesh and blood; they are but lent us till God please to call for them back again, that we may not esteem any thing our own, or set our hearts upon any thing but Him alone, who only remains for ever. I beseech His Almighty Goodness to grant that your lordship may, for His sake, bear this great Cross with meekness and patience, whose only Son, our dear Lord and Saviour, bore a greater for you." And, with a devout suggestion that his friend will take "these humiliations" as "sovereign medicines" from the hand of God, the Catholic baron begs the Puritan viscount to "bear with these expressions of affection."[5]

Besides such fugitive expressions, which revealed his heart, he left a monument, which is his memorial in history and a landmark for all time. This was his charter, unique in its kind, and more so in its purpose. It was the work of the first Lord Baltimore, not of the second, who merely inherited it from his father as an heirloom. The statement of Cæcilius himself as to his succession is: "After whose death [that of his father], the now Lord Baltemore became an humble sutor to His Majesty for the continuance of his said royall favor, and His Majesty gaue warrant, dated 21. of Aprill next following, to Mr. Attorney Generall, that then was, to draw a new bill for the granting of the said lands to him and his heires; which passed

[4] *Strafford Letters*, i. 257: Cæcilius Baltimore, London, May 16, 1634, to the Lord Deputy (Wentworth).
[5] *Ibid.*, i. 59, 60: George Baltimore, London, October 11, 1631, to Viscount Wentworth, Lord President of the North.

likewise the Priuy Seale." But on the 7th of June following, a change was made in favor of Virginia, with regard to the southern point of the eastern peninsula, or as it is called the "Eastern Shore" of Maryland.[6] And finally the charter was published under the great seal of England, on June 20, 1632.

As a monument on a dividing line between past and future, the charter of Maryland may well claim a moment's attention even from one who limits his view to the interests of religion alone, as touched on in a document of universal administration. Under this strictly defined aspect we may look at what it states, and at what it means. What it states is prospective, fixing the Maryland of the future. What it means is retrospective, as fixed by the English history of the past.

His Maryland charter a landmark in history.

§ 17. The charter which George Calvert obtained for Maryland was substantially the same as the one which he had devised for Newfoundland. But there were several modifications. He had been a Protestant when drawing up the former. He was a Catholic when drafting the latter. Having passed over from the religion and party which were dominant to the religion and side which were on the defence, he may rightly be considered to have introduced these modifications, no less with a view to meet the new exigencies of his religion, than to embody the dictates of practical wisdom and of personal experience in the colonies. That personal experience itself had not been exempt from some trials incident to his being a Catholic. It had taken in not only the prosaic record of commercial prospects and disappointments, but such a pastoral strain as that of two religious communities worshipping at different hours under his own roof, not to mention the elegiac vein of his being denounced to the home Government for idolatrous connections with Popery. Our attention, then, is rightly aroused to note how this practical man faced such new and unsteady elements, and struck out his course in the altered conditions of the weather.

The charters of Avalon and Maryland compared.

The intolerance which had introduced test oaths into civil existence, and which was fostering the growth at that very moment on the soil of the new world, was not to be found in Calvert's earlier charter for Avalon. Nor had any mention been made there of the Anglo-American formulas about " the superstitions of the Church of Rome." Calvert had merely spoken of " Gods holy and truly Christian

[6] *Calvert Papers*, i. pp. 223, 225.

Religion," which, like allegiance to civil authority, was to suffer no "prejudice or diminution."[1] A fuller and completer development of his principles will be found in the later or Maryland charter. We ought to discover in this instrument some provision made for liberty to practise his religion, as well as liberty to find it in material means—means for its worship, its institutions, its charities, and its education. This latter franchise of being allowed the wherewithal to live should be effective enough to fence Catholic property off from that form of confiscation, which operated unto forfeiture under a fictitious title of "superstitious uses." And there was no reason why it should not also free the Catholic Church in its tenure of property from the factitious and vexatious restrictions of mortmain, not merely the newer and Protestant statutes, but also the older and Catholic laws.

And so, in point of fact, we may just briefly note that the three following measures were sanctioned by the King in Baltimore's new charter: first, an express and absolute liberty to erect and found churches, chapels, etc.; secondly, the right to control as patron all churches of whatever kind that might exist; thirdly, his complete exemption, active and passive, from all Laws of Mortmain. The first and third of these provisions are peculiar to the Maryland charter, as compared with that of Avalon.[2]

Two new religious elements in the Maryland charter.

(1) First, the charter said: "Also We do grant . . . license and faculty of erecting and founding churches, chapels, and places of worship, in convenient and suitable places, within the premises, and of causing the same to be dedicated and consecrated according to the ecclesiastical laws of our kingdom of England."[3] The first part of this clause may well take its meaning and interpretation from the fact that the person so licensed to erect churches, etc., was notoriously a Catholic; in the opinion of some, was fanatically so; and, in the phrase of many nowadays, would be styled bigotedly so. The second part of the clause, to the effect that such houses of worship should "be dedicated and consecrated according to the ecclesiastical laws of our kingdom of England," contained no allusion to Protestantism or Anglicanism, either in its form or its substance; though the Anglicanism

Meaning of "the ecclesiastical laws of our kingdom of England."

---

[1] Scharf, *History of Maryland*, i. 40: charter of Avalon, § xix.
[2] *Ibid.*, i. 34–40: charter of Avalon, in sections i.–xx., April 7, 1623.—*Ibid.*, pp. 53–60: charter of Maryland, in sections i.–xxiii., issued to Cæcilius, June 20, 1632.—For the original Latin text of the Maryland charter, cf. *Archives of Maryland, Proceedings of the Council*, 1636–1667, pp. 3–12.
[3] *Ibid.*, § iv.; wanting in corresponding § iv. of the Avalon charter.

of the day might have adopted such a formula. Elizabeth, for instance, had used this phrase; but she took care to make it quite clear in the context that it was not the ecclesiastical laws of England or the English Church as such that she was speaking of, but the ecclesiastical laws of the rites and doctrine "nowe used to bee receyved in the Churche of Englande," "nowe comonlye used in the said Churche of Englande," "nowe receyved and alowed in the sayd Churche of Englande."[4] Elizabeth and everybody knew perfectly well the difference between the "ecclesiastical laws of our kingdom" and the ecclesiastical laws of a qualified and novel Anglicanism. Legislators and lawyers alike eschewed the good old English terms, which had been in use from Catholic times. They meant something else that was not Catholic, and so had recourse to qualifications, checks, and labels. The "Church of England," as a simple and magnificent title, had passed out of use, *pari passu*, with the importation of the new religion. The new establishment could only presume to use that name now as weighted with several appendages of a species, a difference, and a subdistinction. Thus in the very year when Baltimore was making his first visit to Newfoundland, an Act was passed against Jesuit colleges and Popish seminaries; and Popery was therein distinguished, not from the Church of England simple and grand—indeed, it could not be, for that was what Popery was—but, with laborious legal prolixity, from "the true Religion established within this Realme," from "the present Religion established in this Church of England," from "this Religion established in this Church of England."[5] Naturally, in the course of time, the labels fell off; and the subdistinguished species became brevetted, in common parlance, into the genus from which it sprang. Thus William of Orange, landing from the Netherlands half a century or more later, employed the dignified phrase of simply "the Church of England."[6] Hence, neither in form nor in substance was Baltimore to be understood as implying or connoting Protestantism, when he undertook to have churches "dedicated and consecrated according to the ecclesiastical laws of our kingdom of England."[7] This was that absolute sense in

A Church of England qualified.

---

[4] 5 Eliz., c. 23, A.D. 1562-3: "*An Acte for the due Execution of the Writ* De excommunicato capiendo."

[5] 3 Car. I., c. 3, A.D. 1627: "*An Act to restraine the Passing or Sending of any to be popishly bred beyond the Seas.*"

[6] 1 Gul. and Mar., c. 8: "*An Act for the Abrogating of the Oathes of Supremacy and Allegiance and Appointing other Oathes,*" § xi.

[7] In any case, the liturgy, like the canons, when political interests were not trenched upon, underwent but slight modification at the English Reformation. An age that had known nothing of cathedrals, churches, chapels, and chantries, except to plunder and strip them, and build up houses and found families on the ruins of

§ 17]   PATRONAGE OF CHURCHES   239

which the Tudor Queen Mary had spoken, when, in one of the very first Acts of her reign, that repealing novelties, she spoke of "this Churche of Englande to us lefte by thaucthoritee of the Catholyke Churche," for which "newe thinges" had been imagined and devised by "a fewe of singularitie."[8]

(2) Secondly, Baltimore preserved a clause from his Avalon charter to this effect: "We do grant ... the patronages and advowsons of all churches which (with the increasing worship and religion of Christ) within the said region, islands, islets, and limits aforesaid, hereafter shall happen to be built."[9] Advowson means the right of presentation to a living, or prebend, or benefice. In this manner the Catholic lord was accorded a right, even with respect to Protestant livings, which would enable him to shut out from his estate in the future mischief-makers like the minister Stourton.

Patronages and advowsons

The only difficulty which occurs here is that which a Catholic

religion, was not likely to take umbrage at forms of dedication; for the spirit of destruction is generally out of touch with that of construction. And so too as to the canons. An interesting scene was enacted when the Archbishop of Canterbury insisted on making a visitation of Westminster, which assumption the dean thereof, the then Bishop of Lincoln, stoutly resisted, and produced *papal* Bulls of exemption. But he of Canterbury rebutted him, by producing other *papal* Bulls, revoking the said privilege of exemption. The University of Cambridge likewise defended itself with *pontifical* Bulls. But alas for liberty when the Pope is gone! He of Canterbury replied that the King had now the authority of the Pope; and there was an end of their liberties! We borrow the particulars of these incidents from Panzani, with whom be the responsibility. *Nunziatura d'Inghilterra*, 5, ff. 336, 337: Panzani to Barberini, June 27, 1636, at the end.—Cf. *Documents*, I. No. 10, V.—But the meaning of it is accentuated by many facts, of which the following from Lecky affords a summary statement. He says: "In the old Catholic times, an Archbishop of Canterbury had combined with the barons at Runnymede, and, in opposition to the Pope and to his legate, had wrested the great charter of English liberty from the sovereign; but the Church which succeeded to the sceptre of Catholicism was essentially Erastian, and the instincts of its clergy were almost uniformly despotic." Lecky, *History of England*, i. 8.

[8] 1 Mariæ, stat. 2, c. 2, A.D. 1553: "*An Acte for the Repeale of certayne Statutes made in the time of the Raigne of Kinge Edwarde the Syxthe.*"—Hence statutes and history alike show that the language used by Baltimore in the charter, having an historical and legal significance sufficiently precise and therefore not "vague," renders unnecessary the hypothesis of a "secret understanding between Baltimore and the King," as if the two combined to keep up the appearance of Anglicanism in the charter, while they sacrificed the reality.—Cf. S. R. Gardiner, *History of England*, etc., viii. 179.—However, as regards a variation of this language, when the term "Holy Church" appears in Maryland history (February–March, 1639), the testimony of Dr. Gardiner is valuable, and corroborates what we have said here in the text. Criticizing Neill for supposing that "Holy Church" meant the Protestant "Church of England" as by law established, he writes: "I am sure that Mr. Neill is wrong in saying that the 'Holy Church,' which according to the statute of 1639 was to 'have all her rights and liberties,' was 'that of the charter, the Church of England.' Such a phrase was never, to my knowledge, applied to the [Protestant] Church of England after the Reformation." Gardiner, *Ibid.*, 180, note.—And yet one hundred years after the Reformation it was applied by the freemen of Maryland to the (Catholic) Church of England.—Cf. *infra*, § 53 (2), pp. 440–443; § 54, pp. 450–453; Appendix C, § 74, p. 586.

[9] § iv. Maryland charter; § iv. Avalon.

might raise—whether Baltimore was not rather stretching his conscience to take in such a point. For there is a principle inculcated under the first commandment, that no communication in sacred things must be held with those who are not within the one sacred fold of the Church. And so jealous is this sanctity of reserve, that there can be no such communication with even a member of the Church while temporarily excommunicated by name. How, then, could Baltimore undertake to share in the ecclesiastical business of Protestants, and meddle with the benefices and temporalities of a denomination disallowed by the Catholic Church? One sufficient answer may be given in a few words. The whole question was, in conscience, open to debate; though in practice England had already closed it by law, to the prejudice of Catholic patrons and their vested rights.[10] In the new country, Baltimore might take the benefit of a doubt, in which solid grounds of principle and precedent favoured such a pretension. One reason for doubting was the circumstance that a temporality, of which the incumbent could never be recognized as a member of the Church, had nothing sacred about it; it was only a temporality. As to precedents, facts were not wanting on the continent of Europe to sanction the exercise of such a right vested in a Catholic with regard to Protestant livings.[11]

(3) Thirdly, Lord Baltimore expunged by his charter the Laws of Mortmain. He thereby provided himself and his successors with

The Statutes of Mortmain. unhampered authority to find institutions and charities in temporal means, and to guarantee them in the rights of property and self-control, as against that state of violence and outlawry under which all Catholic life and action were placed by the penal laws of England. He himself being expressly substituted for the King, as the source of all property titles in Maryland,[12] Lord Baltimore and his successors enjoyed "full and absolute license,

---

[10] 3 Jac. I., c. 5, § 13: "*An Acte to prevent and avoid dangers which may grow by Popish Recusants.*"

[11] General Archives S.J., *Anglia, Historia,* vii. ff. 363–370: "*An liceat cuidam Catholico in Anglia habenti ius præsentandi ad beneficium præsentare aliquem hæreticum ad majora mala impedienda?*" This is a very full document, without date; and, in an affirmative sense, it cites the precedent of the Jesuits at Ingolstadt: "*Imo hoc ipsum non semel, sed pluries factum esse a Patribus Societatis Jesu Ingoldstadii degentibus, qui præsentarunt hæreticos ut ab hæreticis conferrentur illis beneficia, ne tale ius amitterent, quod habebant in locis eorumdem Principum hæreticorum.*" Here, besides the proviso mentioned in the state of the question, that of hindering greater evils, there is the distinct fact added that the property to which the advowson attaches is in the territory of Protestant princes; so that nothing can be done in the premises but to treat it and use it as it stands, or else stand the consequences.—Anstey takes it for granted that the Roman Catholic conscience would not permit one to use such a right. *A Guide to the Laws of England, etc.,* p. 13.

[12] Charter, § xviii.

power, and authority" to "assign, alien, grant, demise, or enfeoff," landed property in the new colony " to any person or persons willing to purchase the same;" which said persons were at the same time qualified by the charter, themselves, their heirs and assigns, to hold the property " in fee simple, or fee tail, or for term of life, lives, or years;" all arrangements of whatever kind, conditions or no conditions, being subject to the good will of the Proprietary who gave or sold, and to the acceptance of the person or persons, thus "willing to take or purchase." This enabling qualification, two-sided and unlimited, was itself a tacit exclusion of those Laws of Mortmain which excepted corporations, religious or otherwise, from the franchise of freely acquiring landed property. *Implicit expunging of the Statutes.*

But, to leave no shadow of doubt upon this favourable grant in the charter, a lengthy period was added with an abrogating clause; to the effect that, under whatsoever form of concession the Proprietary of Maryland might convey such property to persons of any description, these latter might " take the premises, or any parcel thereof." And then followed the abrogating clause in these terms: " The statute made in the parliament of lord Edward, son of king Henry, late king of England, our progenitor, commonly called the ' Statute *Quia emptores terrarum*,' heretofore published in our kingdom of England, or any other statute, act, ordinance, usage, law, or custom, or any other thing, cause, or matter, to the contrary thereof, heretofore had, done, published, ordained, or provided to the contrary thereof notwithstanding."[13] *Explicit rejection.*

This clause, as we learn from Lord Coke, allows the absolute alienation of feudal rights over property; and therefore it permits a complete dispensation from the Statutes of Mortmain, which reserved those feudal rights, first as against religious bodies, and then as against all corporations. It would indeed, he says, be " a safe and good policie in the King's licence to have a *non obstante* [clause] also of the Statutes of Mortmaine, and not only a *non obstante* [clause] of the Statute of *Quia emptores terrarum*." But, after all, he adds, there needeth not any such specification by the King of the Statutes of Mortmain, whenever he intends to give what is clearly against such statutes; for it shall never be presumed that the King does not know a law, when he goes against it; therefore, when he goes against it, he dispenses from it.[14] And so, on every account, as well by express statement of his powers in the King's charter, as

---

[13] Charter, § xviii.
[14] Cf. *infra*, Appendix C, § 76 (5), p. 602.

by the King's express derogation from statute, no less than by the intrinsic nature of his position as lord palatine with the privileges of sovereignty, Baltimore was, like the King, " out of the case of the statute " that prohibited the conveyance of landed property in free alms or mortmain to any religious purpose, charity, or institution whatsoever.[15]

It was not out of his own head that Lord Baltimore devised this eighteenth section of his Maryland charter. He was but following history and the statutes. He had a very fair model for his action in the eighth Statute of the first session of the English Parliament under Philip and Mary. In that great Act, which was the repudiation by the whole realm of its previous schism from the See Apostolic of Rome, the fifty-first section speaks of encouraging charitable gifts, after so much havoc and ruin effected under Henry VIII. and Edward VI. " It is to be trusted," says the Act, " that by the abundance of Gods mercy and grace, devotion shall encrease and grow in the hearts of many the subjects of this realm, with desire to give and bestow their worldly possessions, for the resuscitating of alms, prayer, and example of good life in this realm." And therefore it is enacted that lands, etc., may be given or bequeathed " to any spiritual body politick or corporate in this realm or dominions of the same, [whether] now erected or founded, or hereafter to be erected or founded, without any licence of mortmain therein to be obtained, or any writ," etc. ; all Acts or Statutes, heretofore had or made in any wise, notwithstanding. By the new Statute this liberty of amortizing property without further licence was to continue for twenty years. Donors might impose conditions or not, as they chose, and might reserve rights if they desired; " as was used before the estatute of Westminster Third, commonly called *Quia emptores terrarum;* the said estatute, or any other law or custom, now being to the contrary in any wise, notwithstanding." [16]

Precedent under Mary Tudor.

Finally, as all persons were now free to come and acquire all just liberties in the New American colony, so penal laws and restrictions were free to stay away. Both the Avalon and the Maryland charters made profession in the King's name of granting to all liege-men, who should go over there, " all privileges, franchises, and liberties of this our kingdom of England, freely, quietly, and peaceably to have and possess," without let or hindrance from the

Exclusion of penal laws.

---

[15] Co. Litt., 98 : on *Frankalmoigne.*—Cf. Palgrave, *Rise and Progress of the English Commonwealth, etc.*, i. 166 ; on the Palatinate of Durham.
[16] 1 & 2 Phil. and Mar., c. 8.

King that was, or any other that should come to be; any Statute or Act to the contrary notwithstanding.[17] They should carry with them so much of the English law as was suitable to their new conditions; and should add other laws, not repugnant to the former nor at variance with right reason.[18] All other artificial elements or odious incidents of an ancient people that had known strife and sorrow, "the laws of police and revenue (such especially as are enforced by penalties), the mode of maintenance for the established clergy, the jurisdiction of spiritual courts, and a multitude of other provisions, were neither necessary nor convenient for them, and therefore were not in force." [19] And so, with respect to the whole network of penal laws, the Catholic Proprietary left in their native habitat those sanguinary and predatory intrigues, which still found England a happy hunting-ground, and were to keep Ireland a rich preserve for two centuries to come. And, keeping a free hand for equipping conscience and religion with their rights, he assured civil freedom of a respectable and genial home.[20]

[17] § x. in both charters.
[18] §§ vii. and viii. in both charters.
[19] 1 Stephen's *Commentaries*, 102; from Blackstone.
[20] The Rev. James Anderson, Queen's chaplain, has querulously taken exception to the whole style of Lord Baltimore's phraseology and language in the charter. He says: "There is a disingenuousness pervading the whole instrument, which reflects as much reproach upon the King and his counsellors who granted, as upon the nobleman who received, its ample prerogatives." And, after quoting the passages which we have commented upon in the text, he complains: "Is it not clear that every one of these privileges was based upon the assumption that he, upon whom they were conferred, was a faithful member of the Church of England?" Yet he "had forsaken her, and entered into communion with that of Rome." "It is remarkable that every writer of American history, save one, as far as I can ascertain, should have passed over in silence this disgraceful characteristic of the Maryland charter." "The exception to which I refer is that of Mr. Murray, an able writer in the Edinburgh Cabinet Library, who expressly declares it as his belief, that it [the charter] was framed for the purpose of blinding the public mind." The passage commended thus by the Rev. Mr. Anderson is one trifling sentence in a trifling popular book. For our part, we should hope that the observations made in our text will show how far Lord Baltimore was legally accurate and historically true when he spoke as he did, and yet was thinking as a Catholic while he spoke. And we would even allow that the King was an accomplice in the ambiguousness or "disingenuousness;" and all the royal counsellors too—such were the notions prevalent in 1632 about Popery, Rome, and a national reunion therewith. At that time, were it not for fear of the Puritans, the Church of England would again have been Papist. If, however, Baltimore was not still more express in his manner of reducing the charter to form, that was probably because no chance reader had a right to be more distinctly told what no one had a right to know. Should a person of sensitive conscience call this "equivocation," we would invite him to apply such high-strung and poetic morality to his own manner of treating his private affairs in public or in a railway-carriage; and he may find to his dismay that he has been talking the prose of equivocation, and even of mental reservation, half the days of his life; and that the man in the street has been the victim of a "disingenuousness" pervading the entire use of that noble instrument, our sensitive friend's gift of speech.—J. S. M. Anderson, *History of the Church of England in the Colonies*, ii. 113-117.—Murray, *United States*, i. 145; Edinburgh Cabinet Library, xxxv.

CHAPTER IV

FOUNDATION OF THE MARYLAND MISSION, 1633-1640

§ 18. Negotiations for Jesuit missionaries. § 19. Father White as secretary to Lord Baltimore. § 20. The general Conditions of Plantation: 1633. § 21. Conditions propounded to the missionaries: 1633. § 22. Baltimore's views on religious toleration: 1633. § 23. Baltimore's politico-religious instructions: November, 1633. § 24. The proportion of contributions. § 25. Faculties for Maryland: 1633. § 26. Men for Maryland: 1633-1635. § 27. The voyage to America: 1633, 1634. § 28. The West Indies: 1634. § 29. The western populations. § 30. Puritans, Huguenots, and Anglicans. § 31. Propaganda reports on the Islands: (1) Jesuits; (2) Dominicans; (3) Augustinians and Carmelites; (4) Capuchins; (5) Catholic Merchant Companies; (6) The English Islands; (7) The Jesuit Provinces, West and South. § 32. Propaganda documents about the mainland: British colonies and French. § 33. The shores of the Potomac. § 34. The Indian tribes. § 35. The soil and climate: fish, flesh, and fowl. § 36. The first missionary establishment: 1633-1638. § 37. Indented servants. § 38. The second and third missionary establishments: 1638-1640. § 39. The college in prospect: 1640.

Manuscript Sources: Annapolis Records, lib. 1.—General Archives S.J.: *Anglia, Epistolæ Generalium; Anglia, Historia,* iv., v.; *Anglia, Catalogi.*—Georgetown College MSS., *Mosley Papers; Mobberley Diaries.*—(London) British Museum MSS., *Sloane,* 3662; *Additional,* 30,372, 33,029; *Newcastle Papers,* 344.—Public Record Office: *Colonial Papers, America and West Indies; Colonial Entry-Books; Board of Trade.*—(Paris) Archives de l'École de Ste. Geneviève, *Antilles-Guiane,* 1, seq.—(Rome) Corsini Library, codd. 283, 284; Propaganda Archives: *America,* 257, 258; *I America,* 259; *II America,* 260; *America Centrale,* i.; *Antille,* i.; *Lettere,* 132, 133, 139, 141, 142, 145; *Scritture riferite nei Congressi, Irlanda,* ii.—Vatican Archives: *Nunziatura d'Inghilterra,* 4.—Vatican Library, *Ottoboni,* 2536.—Stonyhurst College MSS., *Anglia, A,* iv., v., viii.

Published Sources: J. Boucher, *Discourses.—Bullarium Patronatus Portugalliæ Regum.*—G. W. Burnap, *Leonard Calvert.—Calendar of State Papers, Colonial, America and West Indies,* i., ii., iv., v.—*Calvert Papers,* i., iii.—A. Carayon, *Documents Inédits, Pierre Chaumonot.* — (Propaganda) *Collectanea S. Congregationis de Propaganda Fide.—Compendium*

CHAP. IV] *FOUNDATION OF THE MARYLAND MISSION* 245

Privilegiorum, etc., S.J.—K. C. Dorsey, *Life of Father Thomas Copley.*—W. Douglass, *Summary, Historical and Political.*—J. A. Doyle, *English in America.*—H. Foley, *Records of the English Province S.J.*, i., iii., vii. *Collectanea.*—J. Hammond, *Leah and Rachel.*—A. Hamy, S.J., *Domiciles de la Compagnie de Jésus.*—J. Kilty, *Landholder's Assistant.*—J. Lingard, *History of England*, viii.—(Maryland) *Archives of Maryland, Proceedings of the Council,* 1636-1667; *Judicial and Testamentary Business,* 1637-1650.—*Maryland Historical Society, Fund Publications,* 7; 7 *Supplement.*—P. Mury, S.J., *Les Jésuites à Cayenne.*—E. D. Neill, *Founders of Maryland.*—*Relations, The Jesuit,* lxxi.—*Relation of Maryland,* 1635.—C. de Rochemonteix, S.J., *Les Jésuites et la Nouvelle France au XVIIe Siècle*, i.—J. T. Scharf, *History of Maryland,* i.—J. G. Shea, *History of the Catholic Church in U.S.*, i.—C. E. Smith, *Religion under the Barons of Baltimore.*—*Strafford's Letters,* i.—S. F. Streeter, *Papers relating to the Early History of Maryland.*—J. B. du Tertre, O.P., *Histoire Générale des Ant-Isles.*—J. W. Thomas, *Chronicles of Colonial Maryland.*—*Thurloe Papers,* iv.—*Virginia's Cure.*—J. Winsor, *History of America,* iii., viii.

IN this chapter we consider the foundation of Maryland both as a plantation and as a Mission, since, at the commencement, the two enterprises, the missionary and the colonial, were conjoined in fact. The second Lord Baltimore, by name Cæcilius Calvert, had negotiated for missionaries of the Society of Jesus. In the course of these negotiations and in their first results, there might have been noticed already, though the missionaries do not seem to have been alive to it, the first presage of that misunderstanding which, within a short half-dozen years, widened into opposition and hostility.

As to the general interests of religion, the state of the question became pretty well defined—where it was that Lord Baltimore considered toleration to lie, and with regard to whom he conceived it to operate. Under the head of financial outlay we may discern, not merely what portion others had in Baltimore's adventure, but what fraction his lordship had in his own.

More to our purpose, however, is the view which we are enabled to exhibit of the western world at the time of the Maryland foundation. One part, that which regards the West Indies, is an entirely new chapter of history; while other parts, such as the moral and religious aspects of the populations on the Atlantic sea-board, are probably about as new to many persons, although they are derived from documentary sources already known. All this extensive reach of territory, from New England to the Lesser Antilles, became at one time or other the field of our North American English-Jesuit history.

Thus in this chapter we treat of the islands and the mainland from the funds of the Propaganda archives; of non-Catholic episodes, Puritan, Huguenot, and Anglican history, from British State Papers; and of some natural features in Maryland from remote Jesuit documents. Moreover, within this short period of seven years, we arrive at the development of some three or four missionary establishments in the new plantation, all intended, as far as we can see, to form one collegiate foundation on the plan of the Jesuit institute. In this early period, then, we may discern, with a certain degree of distinctness, some lines of the Jesuit policy in general.

§ 18. The document quoted above, recording the death of George Calvert, stated that the Attorney-General Noys had recommended Lord Baltimore to keep his charter in suspense awhile, before passing it under the great seal; and that in the interim Calvert died on April 15, 1632.[1] Then the document continues: "Whereupon His Majestie was pleased to grant itt to his sonn and heire, the now Lord Baltemore, who was cristened by the name of Cecill, but was afterwards confirmed by the name of Cæcilius."[2] The instrument was thus passed under the great seal on June 20, 1632.

On the fourth day of June a year later (1633), Father Mutius Vitelleschi, General of the Society of Jesus, wrote to Father Richard Blount, Provincial in England: "I understand that your Reverence has had a strong desire for a good while past to obtain from me the requisite authorization for sending some of ours on a mission, in company with English gentlemen or merchants, who are thinking of looking for new abodes in the Indies of the West, beyond the limits of those countries occupied by the Catholic King [of Spain]. Do not be surprised that you have received no answer from me thus far; for you should know that I never heard a word from you about the plan till a year or two ago.[3] Then I replied that a business of this kind needed rather serious deliberation, for fear of offending those who will perhaps claim that such a proceeding runs counter to a right conferred upon them by the Apostolic See. Hence I called for fuller information on the whole project. If you sent such information later, and are now surprised that I returned no answer, the reason of my silence is that I never received the explanation asked for, nor any other letter referring to

The General demurs to a Maryland expedition. June 4, 1633.

---

[1] *Supra*, § 16, p. 234.
[2] British Museum MSS., *Sloane*, 3662, f. 25.
[3] "*Non nisi ante unum alterumve annum.*"

the said subject of deliberation. I might now a second time put off any further consideration of that business till you informed us more fully about it. However, as I understand that your Reverence is very anxious to receive some definite and speedy answer from here, I leave the matter to your own judgment, if the business is so pressing that it will not wait, till you inform us better about the whole plan of that voyage and receive word again from us. So that if, on hearing the opinions of some of the principal Fathers, you judge that such an occasion of advancing the divine glory should on no account be allowed to pass, and that no just cause of offence is to be apprehended on the part of any Catholic prince—a matter about which I have great misgivings—then you may allow some of ours to set out with the said gentry,[4] on a voyage to the country which it is proposed to colonize. But I would much rather, if it can be managed at all, that the enterprise were put off, until you consulted me again and received an answer from here. And with this I commend myself to the holy Sacrifices of your Reverence.—Rome, 1633, 4th of June."[5]

Five days before the General indited this answer, Father Blount had despatched another letter of urgency, which seems then to have taken three months for its journey to Rome. The General replied on August 30, in these terms: "In your letter of May 31, you implied that you were surprised at having received no answer as yet from here, on the subject of sending ours to Virginia. I gave a reason for this in mine of the 4th of June, at the same time informing you of what we thought about that expedition. I trust then that your expectations have already been satisfied, and that I too shall soon receive fuller particulars about the project of those persons who are preparing for the voyage to Virginia. If you consider Father Andrew White to be well fitted[6] for that mission, and if he himself desires it so ardently, I see no reason why I should object to his being sent thither. But one point I cannot do otherwise than commend with all earnestness to your Reverence; it is that, in the choice of those whom you think of sending forth on that new expedition, you not only make much account of their inclination and desire—since, if people are unwilling or are not so well disposed for a long voyage like that, no great good can be expected from them—but also that you scrutinize most diligently their virtue, prudence, and zeal, especially in the case of

The selection of Father White as founder.

[4] "*Cum dictis nobilibus.*"
[5] General Archives S.J., *Anglia, Epist. Gen.*, 1633, June 4: General to Blount, Provincial. This letter was first dated May 28.—*Documents*, I. No. 5, C.
[6] "*Bene idoneum.*"

those who are to lay the foundations of the mission; that they be such as the others who come afterwards may look up to, walking in their footsteps and following their example as a rule and model of action."[7]

The measure of prudence here indicated by the General, that inclinations should be consulted when individuals were to be selected for distant, exposed, and lonely missions, though it might seem not to be on a level with the high devotion professed by every Jesuit, was practically a wise measure, and productive of definite results. Others, not of the Society, observed this. The ecclesiastical official at Lisbon, who was called Collector of the Indies, remarked in a letter to Cardinal Ludovisi about this time, that the Society of Jesus in the East did not require any remedy or reform, "because the Company of Jesus alone," he said, "sends volunteers."[8] This, however, was but a secondary consideration in the despatching of missionaries. Of a primary kind was the character itself of individuals, as the General noted when he called for virtue, prudence, and zeal. There still remained on the part of the Order, which marshalled its men over so wide a field in the world, that close bond which united at the greatest distance superiors and inferiors in vigilance and obedience reciprocally. Thus, of a mission so near at hand as England, the Nuncio in Paris, Du Perron, wrote at this time, that only such missionaries were desired there as remained in contact with superiors of their own; and he mentioned the Society among several Orders that could fulfil this condition.[9]

Consulting inclinations.

Within a few years after the date of the letters just quoted, from the General to Father Blount, several statements were made by the Jesuits relative to the original invitation on which the first missionaries had set out for Maryland. Father Edward Knott, English Provincial in 1641–1642, wrote a Memorial for presentation to the Cardinal Secretary of State or to the Cardinal Secretary of the Holy Office, wherein he introduced an account of the issue between himself and Lord Baltimore, by narrating that, prior to the establishment of the colony, "the said Baron treated with Father

Baltimore's invitation to the Jesuits.

---

[7] General Archives S.J., *Epist. Gen.*, 1633, August 20.—*Documents*, I. No. 5, D.

[8] Propaganda Archives, *Lettere*, No. 98, A.D. 1630, pp. 54–56: Bishop of Gerace, Lisbon, June 8, 1630, to Cardinal Ludovisi: "*Dalla Compagnia di Gesù . . . tutte le altre hanno bisogno di rimedio, perchè la Compagnia manda sola huomini voluntarii, . . . ma in tutte le altre ha spesso gran parte l'amore o l'odio.*"

[9] *Ibid.*, *Lettere*, No. 133, A.D. 1633, f. 24, January 10: an extract: "*Vorrebbe che non si mandassero costì [in Inghilterra] missionarii, che non havessero superiori dell' ordine loro, come Jesuiti, Benedettini e Dominicani, la vita e virtù de' quali fosse ben conosciuta.*"

Richard Blount, who was then Provincial, and he added letters [10] directed to the Father General, earnestly begging that he might have some select Fathers, for the purpose as well of strengthening the Catholics, as of converting to the faith the heretics who were to be assigned [11] for the colonization of that country; as also to the end that the faith might be propagated among infidels and barbarians." [12]

Of the papers meant by Cecil, second Lord Baltimore, for the eye of the General, we have only one. The private letter or letters, referred to by Father Knott, are no longer extant. The one paper which survives is the *Declaratio* or *Account of the Colony*, intended as well for the Catholic public as for the ecclesiastical superiors whom the baron wished to influence. That he desired or urgently asked for priests of the Society at the commencement of the enterprise is affirmed in a Relation which was forwarded to Rome in 1641 by Monsignore Rosetti, Papal Nuncio in Belgium, viz. that at the earnest request of the baron two priests of the Society, with one lay brother, were sent out to Maryland.[13] An historical review of the English Province, drawn up in 1646, makes the same statement in this form, that "a certain English Catholic noble leading out a colony desired to have ours as his colleagues and helpers; and our Very Rev. Father General willingly granted the request." [14]

[Baltimore's own papers.]

§ 19. Coming now to the document called *Declaratio Coloniæ*, "An Account of the Colony of the Lord Baron of Baltimore, in Maryland near Virginia," a document which also propounded for the public the first Conditions of Plantation, we find that Father Andrew White composed this paper. Some six years later, when writing from Maryland to his lordship, Father White mentioned "the Declaration and Conditions of Plantation," and alluded to the circumstance of his having drawn up the written copy, which Baltimore then corrected.[1]

---

[10] "*Addiditque litteras ad P. Generalem enixe rogans.*"
[11] "*Qui ad eam regionem incolendam destinandi erant:*" alluding, no doubt, to the indented servants, who subsequently acquired the full rights of colonists.
[12] Stonyhurst MSS., *Anglia A*, iv. 108K, f. 222.—*Documents*, I. No. 18.
[13] The Vatican copy, or the original Relation, has: "*Illmo Barone obnixe rogante;*" the copy submitted to the Propaganda states the same more baldly: "*Barone rogante.*" Vatican Archives, *Nunziatura d'Inghilterra*, 4, f. 62.—Propaganda Archives, *Lettere*, No. 141, A.D. 1642, ff. 217, 218.—Cf. *infra*, § 61, pp. 496, 497.
[14] "*Nostros desideravit cooperatores adjutoresque, quod Adm. R. Pater Noster libenti animo concessit.*" General Archives S.J., *Anglia, Historia*, v. p. 161.—Also in Stonyhurst MSS., *Anglia A*, v., ff. 65–67.—*Documents*, I. No. 8, D.
[1] *Calvert Papers*, i. 209: White, February 20, 1638/9, to Baltimore: "Seeing in the Declaration and Conditions of Plantation both share in trade and the land runnes in one and the selfe same tenor, and would bee esteemed so if itt weare brought to any

The *Declaratio,* or *Account of the Colony,* begins by mentioning the occasion now offered for establishing a plantation near Virginia, in a province called Maryland, which the King has given by charter to the Barons of Baltimore. It states the primary and secondary objects in view: "First and chiefly, to convey into the said land and neighbouring parts the light of the Gospel and of the truth, where it is certain no knowledge of the true God has ever shed its beams; secondly, for this purpose too, that all who take part in the voyages and the labours may have their share in the profit and honours, and that the sovereignty of the King may be more widely extended." Here, having shown by some testimonies the reasonableness of such an enterprise, the writer lays down in formal terms the Conditions of Plantation for all who will join with the baron in the venture; and then he begins to enlarge upon the primary and secondary objects of the expedition, by showing the advantages, the probabilities of success, etc.

The Account of the Colony. February 10, 1633.

The development of the first point, upon the spiritual object in view, runs as follows: "The first and chief purpose of the Right Honourable Baron is that which should be first also in the minds of others, who shall be in the same ship with him; and it is that, in so fruitful a land, the seeds be sown not so much of fruits and trees as of religion and piety." Then, using a pretty incident in Church lore for turning a phrase about *Angeli* and *Angli,* angels and Angles, the writer proceeds: "Such a purpose is in truth worthy of Christians, worthy of angels, worthy of Englishmen; and never has England, though ennobled by so many triumphs of old, taken up a project more noble or more glorious than this. See, the country lies white for the harvest; it is ready to receive the seed of the Gospel in its fruitful bosom. For this reason they themselves are sending out messengers in all directions to find suitable persons, who will instruct them in the doctrine of salvation, and regenerate them at the sacred font of baptism. At this very date there are persons in the city [of London] who testify that they saw envoys despatched by their kings for this purpose to Jamestown,[2] in Virginia, and infants taken to New England, that they might be purified in the waters of salvation. Who, then, can doubt that many thousands of souls will be brought to Christ by one such glorious undertaking like this? A glorious undertaking I call it, help given

First object in view: spiritual.

---

hearing. I remember when your Lordship corrected the written copie which I made, I gave your Lordship an occasion uppon the graunt of trade to reflecte whether it weare not fitt to limitt the graunt for tearme of life." Cf. *infra,* § 48 (2), p. 398.

[2] "*In urbem Jareli;*" apparently for "*Jacobi.*"

to souls unto their salvation; for this was the mission of Christ the King of glory. However, since all men do not possess such ardour of soul and loftiness of mind as to regard nothing save what is Divine, and contemplate nothing but heavenly things; and since most men are rather captivated secretly or openly by pleasures, honours, wealth, as by a magnetic attraction, so it has come to pass in the singular providence of God that this one undertaking should comprise all the advantages that attract men and all the profits that reward them." [3]

At this point begins the second part of the *Account*, intended to win over not ecclesiastics or religious men, but adventurers or persons having money to invest. The language so far quoted, wherein religious zeal is appealed to, needs but the quotation of chapter and verse from the *Spiritual Exercises* of St. Ignatius on the Kingdom of Christ, or from his *Constitutions* for the Society, to show the contemplation and the paragraphs which were running in the writer's mind and dropping on the paper from his pen. *The second object in view: temporal profit.*

More in the style of a secular noble, but substantially agreeing with the professions made in the *Account* just given, is the manner of expression which Lord Baltimore uses in certain *Instructions* to his Lieutenant-Governor and Commissioners, Leonard Calvert, Jerom Hawley and Thomas Cornwaleys. In the sixth article he prescribes the formalities to be observed on arriving in Maryland and inaugurating the plantation. After a public reading of the Maryland charter, one of the Commissioners or the Governor himself is to "make some short declaration to the people of his Lordshipps intentions which he means to pursue in this his intended plantation; which are, first, the honour of God by endeavouring the conversion of the savages to Christianity; secondly, the augmentation of His Majesties empire and dominions in those parts of the world by reducing them under the subjection of his Crowne; and, thirdly, by [*sic*] the good of such of his countreymen as are willing to adventure their fortunes and themselves in it, by endeavouring all he cann to assist them, that they may reap the *Language of Baltimore's Instructions. November 13, 1633.*

---

[3] General Archives S.J., *Anglia, Historia,* iv. 877–880: a large, closely written foolscap double folio; the hand resembling that of Father N. Southwell (or Bacon), who was then in Rome. This copy is in Latin.—*Documents,* I. No. 9.—Another in the Propaganda is in Italian: "*Il Compendio della Dichiaratione dell' Illmo Signore Milord Baltemor, stampata in Londra, li x. feb^o,* 1633*; intorno la . . . Marilandia. . . .*" Propaganda Archives, *Lettere,* I *Anglia,* 347, ff. 287, 288.—It is no doubt to an English original that the following passage refers: ". . . I send you here a Relation of my Lord Baltemor's new plantation in Mary land, which perhaps you will willingly see." Stonyhurst College MSS., *Anglia A,* viii. f. 71^v: Clerk [England], August 16 1633, to [Fitton, Rome]. Cf. *infra,* § 26, p. 273.—Cf. also § 36, p. 333, note 2.

fruites of their charges and labours according to the hopefulnes of the thing, with as much freedome, comfort, and incouragement as they cann desire. . . ."⁴ In placing thus the spiritual object first, Lord Baltimore probably implied that the spiritual men whom he invited to go out as helpers and partakers should take rank in a relative degree of importance; or at all events that their own estimate of the work before them, and of the facilities due to it, would be admitted as a consideration in his lordship's counsels.

§ 20. It was not only the holy missionaries who were to be helpers and colleagues. The others too, adventurers and investors, are spoken of under the selfsame designation. They are called "companions of his voyages and labours," who are solicited by the attraction of profit and honour; they are "companions and helpers" to whom "he makes the most ample and liberal promises." In this connection the *Account of the Colony* states the first Conditions of Plantation :—

The first Conditions of Plantation, 1633.

"The most noble Baron intends with the help of God to sail for those parts about the middle of next September [1633]; and to those, whom he shall have engaged as companions and helpers in so glorious an undertaking, he makes the most ample and liberal promises.

"Whereof the first and chief is this (to say nothing of the dignities of rank and station which, as the appanage of honour, virtue, valour, and achievements, are to be distributed on a large and noble scale) :—Whoever shall pay one hundred pounds sterling for the transportation of five men (which will be enough to cover the expences of arms, tools, clothing, and other necessaries), whether such person shall think fit to come himself or shall entrust the men and money to those who are to have charge of such matters, or shall commit them to any other person, who shall take care of them and receive the allotment of lands, such person [so investing] shall have assigned to him for all his people and for his heirs in perpetuity the possession of good land to the extent of 2000 acres."¹ This was at the rate of 400 acres per man imported. After the right to a landed estate to be held in fee simple for ever, there follows a most important grant of free trade,—a great privilege in

Land: 2000 acres per every five men.

---

⁴ *Calvert Papers*, i. 136: *Instructions to the Governor and Commissioners*, November 15, 1633, No. 6.
¹ ". . . *possessio agri boni* 2000 *jugerum assignabitur*."

§ 20] INDUCEMENTS TO COLONISTS 253

those days of monopolies and exclusive rights to wares, marts, ports, and even seas and oceans—

"Moreover, if they shall come themselves as companions and lend their assistance in the first expedition, they shall also have their own share, by no means an insignificant one, in a profitable trade — about which more hereafter—and likewise in other privileges. As to these points, they shall receive more particular information, when they call on the said Baron. Note that what has been said above about one hundred pounds sterling shall be understood also to apply to any smaller or larger sum of money in due proportion, whether it be one person alone or several together that contribute and invest it."[2] Thus the enjoyment of the original privileges in their fullest form did not depend upon a certain quantity in the investment. *Trade: a franchise.* *400 acres per head.*

The passage about free trade, just quoted, with its liberal terms, would seem to be the same which Father White six years later was referring to when he reminded Lord Baltimore that he himself, as his Lordship's secretary, had suggested a limitation to this ample franchise; but he subjoined that Baltimore had declined to allow of the limitation: "And notwithstanding this suggestion, your Lordship would have itt goe absolute as the graunt of land."[3] At this latter date the parties had changed sides. It was White in Maryland who was beseeching Baltimore in England to introduce no new policy in the way of limiting free trade, and least of all for those earliest adventurers who had come to settle in Maryland on that express condition. He argued that there was neither right nor expediency in such a new policy.

In the warrant which the Proprietary gave to the Governor a few years later (August 8, 1636) for the discharge of his obligations to the adventurers of 1633, there appears the burden of a "yearly rent of 400 lbs. of good wheat" for every 2000 acres as granted upon the above Conditions of Plantation. For such persons as had transported less than a party of five, the terms of fulfilment were much inferior to the Conditions originally proposed; and again there was a rental of 10 lbs. of wheat yearly for every 50 acres.[4] *Conditions of Plantation, (1633), in the warrant of 1636.*

[2] *Account of the Colony, etc., loc. cit.*—Cf. Maryland Historical Society, *Fund Publication*, No. 7, pp. 46, 47, where, however, the Latin text is imperfect, and the English translation incorrect.
[3] *Calvert Papers*, i. 209.—Cf. *supra*, § 19, note 1.
[4] J. Kilty, *Landholder's Assistant*, p. 30.

In the same warrant, Lord Baltimore authorizes his Lieutenant-General to erect every holding of 1000 acres or more into a manor; and to grant "a court-baron and court-leet, to be from time to time held within every such mannor respectively."⁵

Courts baron and leet.

The registrar of the Maryland Land Office, John Kilty (1808), analyzing this warrant, as containing the only indication he knew of regarding the original Conditions of Plantation, infers as an evident truth from this and other instruments that the title acquired by a settler in Maryland was an absolute one of fee simple; and he comments upon the latter points about the manorial dignity and rights, as being intended to strengthen and elevate the character of the new establishment. He says: "The grants to the adventurers were, as appears by subsequent declarations, to be of *an indefeasible estate of inheritance in fee simple to them and their heirs for ever*; for which the act of immigration, for the purpose of settling in the province, was the sole condition of purchase; but with a perpetual reserved rent in every case; this being the basis of the revenue which the Proprietary meant to draw from his acquisition, independent of the product or profits of those lands which he from time to time directed to be reserved and retained for his permanent estate. Finally, in order to give greater dignity and strength to this new establishment, and pursuing the spirit of the charter in regard to the article of tenure which at that time formed a part of all grants from persons capable of prescribing it, the Proprietary directed that every distinct body of one, two, or three thousand acres, so to be passed and granted to any adventurer, should be erected into a manor by such name as the owner should desire, with the privileges of court-baron and court-leet; for which purpose as well as for common or freehold grants the necessary forms were transmitted."⁶

An indefeasible estate of inheritance in fee simple.

This is all correct, as inferred from the warrant alone or from other similar papers. But it does not quite explain the difference between the offers first made in the *Account of the Colony* and the Conditions thus fulfilled. Still less does it touch upon certain grave difficulties as to the title of fee simple, acquired by any *bonâ fide* settler, and yet soon after disputed by the Proprietary; nor as to certain manorial obligations, which were soon used or invented to crush the lords of manors; nor as to the right of a manorial court, which seems to have been largely or

Subjects of disagreement later.

---

⁵ J. Kilty, *Landholder's Assistant*, p. 31. ⁶ *Ibid.*, p. 32.

completely ignored by the colonial authority. There was another right, that of free trade, originally promised to the colonists, and actually enjoyed by them. In half a dozen years after the first settlement, that too came under the operation of the proprietary pruning-knife.

§ 21. As the colonists helped themselves, and helped Baltimore by doing so, the latter gentleman paid them for their co-operation with land. It was quite otherwise with the missionaries. They expected that, as they were invited to go over, not for the purpose of helping themselves, but of serving the Indians, the colonists, and thereby Lord Baltimore, the latter gentleman would provide for them accordingly; and, while they attended to absorbing duties of the ministry and of charity, they would be treated on the same terms as the clergy in all Catholic and Protestant countries of Europe.

In the midst of his pious declarations and intentions, it soon transpired that he would do nothing of the kind. It is true that he was the prospective Proprietary of ten millions of acres, which were clamouring to be given away. But the co-operation demanded of the missionary clergy, and interpreted by Father White, in his *Account*, to mean aid in extending the Kingdom of Christ, proved to have been groundlessly so interpreted. The co-operation of the priests simply operated in the first place as a good advertisement, inducing pious Catholics to go abroad and extend the palatinate of Lord Baltimore. It proved also to have meant a good substantial contribution of funds and men from the Fathers involved, as if they too were people going out to help themselves and make a fortune. Then a little too late they appreciated what the General had significantly called for—time and deliberation before embarking on the Maryland enterprise. We may now listen to the next Provincial, Father Edward Knott, letting the Papal Nuncio in Belgium know how the scales had fallen from their eyes in the Maryland business, only at the moment when the Jesuits were already compromised.

<small>No provision made for the missionaries.</small>

Knott says, in his *Notanda* or Observations to Rosetti, the Belgian Nuncio (November 17, 1641): "Observation 1. When a colony had first to be led out for the settlement of Maryland, the Fathers of the Society were repeatedly and pressingly asked by the Right Honourable Baron of Baltimore, to be pleased to set out with the colonists; as well for the comfort of those Catholics who were thinking of removing thither, as for the conversion of the infidels among whom a great harvest was expected.

<small>Knott's account to Rosetti.</small>

The Fathers were of their own accord predisposed to undertake that mission, which they knew well would be full of labours and trials; still, without the consent of the Very Rev. Father General, they would not decide. That permission with certain faculties being at last obtained, they yielded to the importunity of the Baron, and determined to go with him. There arose difficulties of one kind or another, which were settled; and then only one remained, and that was: From what source were the necessary means of subsistence to be supplied for the missionaries? For, as to living on alms, there was no hope whatever of that. Yet the Fathers desired not to be preoccupied with the care of providing for their temporal wants; they wished to be free for spiritual things and for the duties proper to their state. The matter was discussed in every sense; but, as to any contribution either from his own funds or from any common source, the Baron could not be persuaded to provide. At length, after a long deliberation, a conclusion was arrived at; the best thing to do seemed to be this, that the Fathers should accept the same conditions, agreements, and contracts [1] as the rest of the colonists, and act accordingly; and that, like them, they should have the benefits of barter on equal terms; and, in the allotment of lands, they should accept of a portion tallying with the conditions and agreements. In this manner they would have wherewithal to support life at present, and then to increase the number of missionaries, for the propagation of the faith and the gospel among infidels. This seemed a hard condition to the Fathers, and not in conformity with their institute, involving a number of difficulties for which they could not discern any easy remedy in the future. Still, such as it was, it seemed a necessary condition to accept, for fear they should look like deserting the cause of God and souls." [2]

The missionaries to be rated as mere adventurers.

In engaging them, however, it may very well have been that Baltimore had taken the measure of the Jesuits quite exactly; not only for the influence which they might exercise, and for the possible amount of contribution which they might throw into the settlement, but especially for the circumstance that Jesuits undertook to go whithersoever the Pope sent them, without asking for viaticum or travelling expenses.[3] This was convenient—although it was not the Pope who was settling Maryland. And so on the first occasion

---

[1] "*Iisdem conditionibus, pactis et conventis.*"
[2] Vatican Archives, *Nunziatura d'Inghilterra*, 4, f. 80.—*Documents*, I. No. 16.
[3] *Constitutiones S.J.*, parte v. c. 3, § 3.—*Examen Generale*, c. 1, § 5.

within about a hundred years, when priests were to be out of the reach of persecution and yet be on soil belonging to England—when Catholics would be able to deal freely, and a Catholic Government to treat openly, with them—the priests so honoured were among the first instances in Christendom, whether Catholic or Protestant, if not the very first, who were left to shift for themselves by the Government that asked for them, and who were put on the footing of mere lay citizens in a community of farmers and traders. *A unique situation.*

§ 22. Lord Baltimore had many grave matters on his hands during the year 1633, not only in the way of organizing a colony, but also of defending his right to organize and his rights to the property itself conferred on him by the charter. We find a pamphlet which was published in this sense. He attended also to litigation before the Lords.[1] He repelled an aggression on his ships.[2] He himself remaining in England to guard his interests, it was only when his ships had cleared the Isle of Wight, that his enterprise enjoyed at last such freedom as the wide ocean afforded, until it should encounter new rocks and shoals in the vicinity of Virginia and in the determined hostility of Captain Clayborne. This latter gentleman, however, had much to say for himself, and seems to have been an injured man.

Amid these fluctuations of Baltimore's fortunes in 1633, only one matter need detain us, and that is a point in his pamphlet, where he expounds some views as to the rights of conscience in the sense of tolerating Roman Catholics, and also as to some fundamental rights of Indians in their own land. These views set forth in the polemical pamphlet may be more precisely defined with the help of further statements which he makes in his *Instructions* (November 13, 1633) to the Governor and Commissioners of Maryland; where likewise are divulged some other principles of conduct governing the baron's policy. *Baltimore's pamphlet in defence of Maryland [1633].*

In the pamphlet entitled, *Objections answered touching Maryland*, we do not discover any intrinsic evidence of its being Father White's production. It is an able and rather political paper, which does credit to the author, whoever he was. There are five objections

---

[1] Cf. *Calvert Papers*, i. 221-229: Cecil's *Declaration to the Lords*, belonging to 1634.

[2] Cæcilius Baltimore, Odiham, January 10, 1633/4, to Strafford.—The *Strafford Letters*, i. 178, 179.

VOL. I. S

proposed in order, and the respective answer is subjoined immediately to each. The first two formulate certain Protestant scruples: first, that the permission granted to Catholics thus to depart from England would dash to the ground the pious hopes entertained of ever seeing them good conformable Protestants; secondly, that the licence thus extended to them would be tantamount to granting idolaters a liberty of worship, which, being reported back from the new country to the old, "would scandalize their bretheren and the common people here." The other three objections are drawn from the damage done to the King's revenue, if it lose so many prime Catholic subjects on whom to prey; from the damage done to the kingdom by the diminution of population and the withdrawal of wealth; finally, from the danger incurred by the good Protestants in Virginia and New England, if these Roman Catholics come down upon them with the help of Spaniards and others. The text may be seen in its proper place.[3] It is in answer to the second objection that a declaration is made, which is perfectly frank in its understanding that there shall be freedom for the Catholic religion in Maryland; and a comparison is instituted between such liberty and that of the Indians, native owners of the soil, who are not to be interfered with by any Englishmen.

Freedom for the Catholic religion in Maryland.

"*Objection* 2. Such a licence will seeme to be a kinde of tolleration of (at least a connivence at) Popery, which some may find a scruple of conscience to allow of in any part of the King's dominions, because they esteem it a kind of idolatry, and may therefore conceive that it would scandalize their bretheren and the common people here.

"*Answer.* Such scrupulous persons may as well have a scruple to let the Roman Catholiques live here, though it bee under persecution, as to give way to such a licence. Because banishment from a pleasant, plentifull and ones owne native country into a wildernesse, among salvages and wild beasts, although it proceed (in a manner) from ones own election, yet, in this case where it is provoked by other wayes of persecution, is but an exchange rather than a freedome of punishment; and perhaps, in some mens opinions, from one persecution to a worse. For divers malefactors in this kingdome have chosen rather to be hanged then to goe into Virginia, when upon that condition they have bin offered their lives, even at the place of execution. And they may with more ground have a scruple of conscience to let any of the said Roman Catholiques

Colonizing as a penalty.

---

[3] Stonyhurst MSS., *Anglia A*, iv. 108E, 8 pp. 16mo.—*Documents*, I. No. 4.

to goe from hence into France (which few or none certainly can have in contemplation of religion only, and this Parliament hath given passes to divers of them for that purpose), that being more properly the Kings dominions then is all that great part of North America (wherein Maryland is included), unto which the Crown of England layes claime upon the title of discovery only, except such part thereof as is actually seated and possessed by some of his subjects. And therefore, in the preamble of the Lord Baltemores patent of Mariland, the enlargement of the Kings dominions is recited as a motive of such a grant; which inferres that it could not so properly bee esteemed his dominions before as when, by vertue of such a grant, it should be planted by some of his subjects. And, if it be all the Kings dominions notwithstanding, then why have not such scrupulous persons a scruple to suffer the Indians (who are undoubted idolators) as they doe, to live there; which if they cannot conveniently prevent (as without question they cannot except by granting such a licence) they may as well suffer those whom they esteem idolators, as those whom they and all other Christians whatsoever repute and know to be so, to inhabite and possesse that country. Moreover, they may also (aswel as in this) have a scruple to treat, or make or continue a league, or to trade with any forraigners of that religion, because in their oppinions they are idolators; or to permit the publique ministers of any such forraigne prince or state to have the free exercise of their religion, while they are in England; and may feare giving scandall to all others by such tollerations or connivences. All which nevertheless we see done even in these times and allowed of, aswel by the Parliament as the King, upon reason of state for the good and safety of this realme. So may this licence bee also thought by such persons a good expedient for the same purpose. And if any (of the weaker sort) should be scandalized at it, the scandal would be *acceptum* not *datum*, and therefore not to be regarded by a wise and judicious prince or state."

In this defence of Maryland as a place of religious refuge and toleration, the conception clearly confines itself to the toleration of Catholics at the hands of Protestants, that is, exemption from such persecution as was rife in England.

§ 23. When the two ships, called the *Ark* and the *Dove*, put in at the Isle of Wight, their last stopping-place before striking out into the Atlantic, the Governor and the two Commissioners received

Baltimore's final *Instructions,* dated November 13, 1633; and on the 22nd of November they weighed anchor and left. If there were any further duties to be discharged or pledges to be given, there was full time for such mutual assurances to be given and taken before starting. But, though the paper of *Instructions* contained a very important item of that kind in its sixth article, still, strangely enough, it adjourned all such matters, though of present urgency, to the time of arriving in Maryland.

The first article required the Governor and Commissioners to suppress in future, both on sea and land, all public profession of the Roman Catholic worship, and all manifestation in social intercourse of Roman Catholic sentiment; but the Protestants in the company were to be as free in all these respects as the mildness and favour of the Governor and Commissioners could encourage them to be. When Lord Baltimore gave this injunction, the character of the incipient colony was already clearly ascertained; the gentry and investors, with their patronage and money, were chiefly, if not exclusively, Roman Catholic; the dependants and indented servants brought over at the expense of the gentry were largely Protestant—

Baltimore's order against the profession of Roman Catholicism.

"Instructions 13 November, 1633, directed by the Right Hon. Cecilius Lord Baltimore & Lord of the Provinces of Mary Land and Avalon unto his well-beloved brother Leonard Calvert Esq., his Lordships Deputy Governor of his Province of Mary Land and unto Jerom Hawley and Thomas Cornwaleys Esq[rs], his Lordshipps Commissioners for the government of the said Province.

"1. Imprimis. His Lordshipp requires his said Governor & Commissioners that in their voyage to Mary Land they be very carefull to preserve unity & peace amongst all the passengers on shippboard, and that they suffer no scandall nor offence to be given to any of the Protestants, whereby any just complaint may heereafter be made by them in Virginea or in England; and that for that end they cause all acts of Romane Catholique Religion to be done as privately as may be, and that they instruct all the Romane Catholiques to be silent upon all occasions of discourse concerning matters of religion; and that the said Governor & Commissioners treate the Protestants with as much mildness and favor as justice will permitt. And this to be observed at land as well as at sea."[1]

Two other articles touch nearly the interests of priests and missionaries. One is the ninth, in which he gives particular directions

[1] *Calvert Papers,* i. 131, 132.

for the building of "a church or a chappel adjacent" to the "convenient house" intended "for the seate of his Lordshipp or his Governor or other Commissioners." There is no mention made of a priest to serve the chapel, or of a chaplain, or of a glebe, or any thing whatever relative to the clergy.[2]

<small>No mention of a clergy.</small>

In like manner, the thirteenth article, while prescribing "that they cause all sorts of men in the plantation to be mustered and trained in military discispline, and that there be days appoynted for that purpose either weekely or monthly," makes no distinction whatever between the clergy and laymen, between the missionaries and the planters, in that phrase, "all sorts of men" who are to be mustered and trained in military discipline.[3] Nowhere in the fifteen articles is there the slightest recognition of priests or missionaries as being in the colony, or of a definite spiritual worship or service to be exercised there.

In the sixth article, his lordship gives an elaborate instruction on the exacting of a certain pledge from the colonists, without which assurance, he says, none were to enjoy the benefit of a share in the colony. This was a public oath of allegiance to His Majesty. Such an important condition for making sure of their investment was to be made known to them only on the other side of the ocean, when they had already paid their price for a plantation, but now might go home bankrupt if they did not choose to fulfil the condition so sprung upon them. For at that time there were oaths of allegiance, which a Catholic could not take in conscience. However, from Baltimore's point of view, it was evident that, whatever became of the Catholic patrons who should reject the imposition of the test, their indented servants would then be already in America, and so have been secured for the colony—

<small>A new condition of colonization.</small>

"6. That, when they [the Governor and Commissioners] have made choice of the place where they intend to settle themselves and that they have brought their men ashoare with all their provisions, they do assemble all the people together in a fitt and decent manner and then cause His Majesties letters pattents to be publikely read. . . .[4] And that at this time they take occasion to minister an oath of allegeance to His Majestie unto all and every one upon the place, after having first publikely in the presence of the people taken it themselves; letting them know that his Lordshipp gave particuler

[2] *Calvert Papers*, i. 138.
[3] *Ibid.*, pp. 139, 140.
[4] Here follows the statement of the triple end in view, as given above, § 19, pp. 251, 252.

directions to have it one of the first things that were done, to testify to the world that none should enjoy the benefitt of His Majesties gratious grant unto his Lordshipp of that place, but such as should give a publique assurance of their fidelity & allegeance to His Majestie." [5]

We notice only one or two more points in this significant series of private directions. In the fifth, he acknowledges that Captain Clayborne has already a landed interest of some kind, "hath settled a plantation," within the limits now covered by the Maryland charter. Amid all the references to his charter, Baltimore makes no allusion to the fundamental condition on which it was given, that the land it covered was said to be "hitherto uncultivated," as expressed in the first period of the instrument. Therefore it could not take in a plantation, allowed by Baltimore himself to be already "settled." [6]

Clayborne and the Isle of Kent.

Finally, in the second article of the *Instructions*, his lordship directs the Governor and Commissioners to set up, while aboard ship, an investigation amongst "the seamen & passengers, to discover what any of them do know concerning the private plotts of his Lordshipps adversaries in England, who endeavored to overthrow his voyage; to learn, if they cann, the names of all such, their speeches, where & when they spoke them, and to whom;" and here follow the items of a minute interrogatory. Then, when Maryland is reached, all whom it might possibly be useful to interrogate further may be taken by them and put upon oath and forced to answer "to such questions as they shall thinke fitt to propose unto them." [7]

An investigation aboard ship.

Neither his brother Leonard Calvert, nor the Commissioners Hawley and Cornwaleys, regarded matters and interests in the same light as Cecil Calvert. They followed their own judgment in the execution of his orders, where sense and circumstance required it. In article the third he told them peremptorily not to approach James Towne in Virginia and not to come within command of the fort at Poynt-Comfort. They did just what he had forbidden them to do. And so we hear nothing more about an oath of allegiance being profferred to the colonists on the American shore, nor about ferreting out secrets aboard ship, or cross-examining informers in a Star-Chamber on land.

[5] *Calvert Papers*, i. 136, 137.
[6] *Ibid.*, 134-136.—Cf. Charter, in Scharf, i. 53.—Cf. Latin original in *Archives of Maryland, Proceedings of the Council, 1636-1667*, p. 3.
[7] *Calvert Papers*, pp. 132, 133.

§ 24. To ascertain what the missionaries were doing at this moment, by way of fulfilling their engagement and taking a place among the contributors, " for fear they should look like deserting the cause of God and of souls," [1] we must note here the proportion of contributions all round. George Calvert, the first Lord Baltimore, had " disbursed neare 20,000 lbs., beside the hazard of his own person in a plantation in Newfoundland," as the Lords were informed in 1634 by the second Lord Baltimore.[2] The latter, not alone, but with his friends, had thrown into the new Maryland enterprise of 1633 only some £10,000; or, in his own words, had "disbursed by himself and his freinds above tenn thousand pounds for the setling of a colony of His Majesties subjects in the said countrey, having sent two of his brothers thither [Leonard and George] (one of whom he hath since lost upon the place), and having seated already above two hundred people there." He therefore humbly besought their lordships to protect him against the pretences of the Virginians and the consequences of further proceedings. "For that would much endanger the overthrow of his plantation, which is now in a good forwardnes to perfection, and consequently his and many of his freinds utter ruine, in respect that the greatest part of their fortunes are thereupon engaged."[3] *£10,000 invested in the expedition.*

The names of many of these friends are attached to the *Relation* of 1635, which was published by his lordship's authority. The list is entitled, "Names of the gentlemen adventurers that are gone in person to this plantation." Besides the two Calverts, Leonard and George, and the two Commissioners, Hawley and Cornewallis, there are thirteen others recorded: a son of Sir Thomas Gerard, a son of Sir Thomas Wiseman, two sons of the Lady Ann Wintour, Messrs. Saunders, Cranfield, Greene, Ferfax, Baxter, Dorrel, Medcalfe, Saire, and Captain John Hill.[4] To these friends should be added the others, who did not go in person, but embarked only their funds in the enterprise; and in this connection we meet with the names of Sir Richard Lechford, Mrs. Constant Wells, Mrs. Eure.[5] The missionaries threw in a substantial contribution, as we shall soon see. And, over and above all this, Cecil Lord Baltimore himself says with candour to Wentworth Lord *Names of the gentlemen adventurers.* *Other contributing friends.*

[1] Knott's *Notanda, supra,* § 21, p. 256.
[2] *Calvert Papers,* i. 222.
[3] *Ibid.,* 228, 229.
[4] *Relation of Maryland,* 1635, p. 56.—Capricious changes of spelling must be allowed for in the documents.
[5] Cf. *Calvert Papers,* i., iii. *passim.*

Strafford, that he cannot lose much, if things go amiss, because others are bearing the burden. He considers that there is "a fair and probable expectation of good success; however," he says, "without danger of any great prejudice unto myself, in respect that many others are joined with me in the adventure. There are two of my brothers gone, with very near twenty other gentlemen of very good fashion, and three hundred labouring men well provided in all things."[6] If to the seventeen names published, including those of Leonard and George Calvert, be added the two names suppressed of Fathers White and Gravener or Altham, the sum-total is just what Baltimore here states—"very near twenty other gentlemen of very good fashion."

An entry made in the plantation records, about the first coming of the missionaries and their subsidy to the colony, is of the following tenor: "Entered by Mr. Copley [as having been] brought into the Province in the year 1633, Mr. Andrew White, Mr. John Altham, etc. Thomas H., etc., to the number of 30."[7] The barest item of expense, at £20 sterling for each of these thirty persons, would be £600. In the year of their arrival, 1634, it is calculated that fourteen assignments were made to the missionaries by other gentlemen, who thus put to the account of the Jesuit missionaries forty-four men of the original *personnel* of Maryland.[8] To this credit of £880 there must be added the church furniture, and the expensive outfit necessary for public worship in the colony, as well as for the prosecution of missionary work among the Indians. What was necessary or might be decent in the matter of religious worship or of the propagation of the faith did not enter into the accounts or liabilities, which the Proprietary considered to be his. Nor did education.[9] Whereas, in the course of a few years, the contributions of men brought in under the patronage of the Fathers, reached such a figure that the claims of land due to them under divers Conditions of Plantation amounted to 28,500 acres; which constituted a fair prospect that, even after the settling of the imported men themselves, religion and education would not fare ill in Maryland.[10] Hence a little more than four years after the first expedition had set out from England, Copley could write to Lord

Contributions of the Jesuit Fathers, 1633.

---

[6] *Strafford Letters*, i. 178, 179.—Cf. copy in Scharf, i. 68.
[7] Kilty, *Landholder's Assistant*, p. 68.—*Documents*, I. No. 30.
[8] K. C. Dorsey, *Woodstock Letters*, xiv. 60: *Life of Father Thomas Copley*.
[9] Here will occur the striking contrast between the liberality of Sir Humphrey Gylberte in his charter, as cited above, § 2, pp. 148, 149, and these features of the Maryland plantation.—Cf. E. D. Neill, *Terra Mariæ*, p. 132.
[10] *Documents*, I. No. 24. As to settling the men, cf. *infra*, § 29, p. 285, 4°.

Baltimore from Maryland: "I will be bold to tell your lordshipe that, though my principal intention be to serve your lordshipe to the prime end, which is the healpe of souls, yet in peopling and planting this place, I am sure that none have donne neere soe much as we; nor endeed are lykly to do soe much."[11]

Among all the entertaining stories of what were called "proprietary" governments in the American Colonies, there is no one, excepting perhaps Pennsylvania, fit to compare with Maryland for the terms on which one man obtained possession of the whole, and for the success with which he then promoted it, as exclusively his own business speculation. Cecil Baltimore's terms were his father's merits, and the felicitous exercise of his father's talents and experience in devising a splendid feudal charter, without feudal encumbrances for the Proprietary. This original advantage he did not dilute, as probably his father would have done, with too much charity and religion. Then came the exploitation of Cecil's own latent resources for company-promoting. He himself made some moderate investment of money, apparently the amount sunk in the equipment of two vessels —one a four-hundred ton ship, the other a forty-ton pinnace. Then he made a large investment of management. He secured a company for all the good there was in it, but no company with any rights that could curtail his, or with any title to a corporate existence; and, within eight years, he used his high powers of absolute lordship and domain to circumscribe and proscribe the rights of corporate existence where his charter had provided for them. And withal he enjoyed at the commencement the advantage of reckoning with a small party of amiable Catholic knights, ladies, and gentry, who formed a striking contrast to the sturdy pilgrims of a more northern colony.

Maryland's place in the roll of ventures.

His success was eventually such that, while Virginia had gone into a state of insolvency, and had seen its old company dissolved, with a slice of its territory given to Baltimore under the name of Maryland; while the proprietors of South Carolina declared at a later date that they could support their establishment no longer, and they sold out to the King; and Connecticut, far from being in the pocket of an individual, was, as an official dryly states, " a sort of republick; they acknowledge the King of Great Britain for sovereign, but are not accountable to the Crown for any acts of government, legislative or administrative;" and Rhode Island, says the same report, "is a sort of republick as well as Connecticut, and governed much in the same

[11] *Calvert Papers*, i. 168.

manner;" different from all these and from other "proprieties," the colonial speculation of Cecil Baltimore not only began in the brilliant manner just indicated, but, when it had become an inheritance of a hundred years' standing in his family (now no longer Catholic), it was described as containing: "Number of white people, 75,000; blacks, 21,000," with the further remark: "The Crown has no revenue in this government."[12]

§ 25. In 1631 there had been due in Rome a meeting of Jesuit procurators or deputies from the provinces of the Society, for the despatch of the business which belongs to that triennial meeting of delegates. Like its numbers, one from each province, so its prime business is very limited, consisting merely in a decision to be given by them, whether a General Congregation or Assembly is to be held in full form by the Society. To this essential commission is annexed a further duty, that of conveying officially to the General such petitions as may be consigned to the respective delegates by the provincial meeting which elected them, by the Provincial superior, or by any member. Wars and pestilence caused a postponement of the meeting in Rome from 1631 till 1632; then again from 1632 till 1633. On April 2 of this latter year, the General sent his notification to the Provincial, Father Blount, that there would be no further postponement. He directed Blount to send his delegate at once to the Continent, that so much of the journey might be accomplished. On a former occasion, neither the deputy nor his substitute had been able to make his way out of the island towards Rome. The delegate, already elected two years before, was Father John Worthington; and, before the end of this year 1633, he safely delivered to the General in Rome a petition about Maryland. It was in the name of the Provincial; it was accompanied by the *Declaratio Coloniæ*, or *Account of the Colony*; and it treated no longer of the men to be sent, but of the powers or faculties requisite. The document and its answer, translated from the Latin, we give here; the text may be seen in its proper place—

The meeting of Jesuit procurators. 1633.

"Answer to the petition of the Father Provincial of England, Richard Blount, entrusted to Father John Worthington, Procurator of England.

Petition about Maryland.

"[The Petition:] Show our Very Rev. Father General the *Declaration* about the Colony, which the Right Hon. Baron of

---

[12] British Museum MSS., *Additional* 30,372: "*Abstract of the Commissions and Instructions formerly and at this time* [1740] *given to the governors of His Majesty's plantations in America*," etc.; large folio vol., ff. 23ᵛ, 28, 28ᵛ, 25ᵛ.

Baltimore is leading into Maryland, situate between Virginia and Florida, discovered first by the orders of Henry VII., and then of others who sailed thither from England. If his Paternity approves, it will be necessary to obtain special faculties; unless perhaps he thinks that those which we have granted us for England will be good also for that part of the world, not only on behalf of the English colonists, about whom there is less room for doubt, but also on behalf of the heathen natives of that country when they shall be converted.

"[Answer:] Father John Worthington has shown us the *Declaration* regarding the above-mentioned expedition. As we hope for a great increase of the Divine glory thereby, and the salvation of very many souls, we cannot but extend to it our full sanction; praying that the Divine providence will favour the pious efforts of the Fathers, who are so prompt in offering themselves to bring the light of faith to nations sitting in darkness and in the shadow of death. And, that they may be equipped with the necessary faculties for so excellent a work, they may use such as have long been granted to the Society by the Apostolic See for the Indies, and are extended to those regions also. Rome. – – – Decemb., 1633."[1] The General's answer. 1633.

In the margin of the Register it is noted: "Faculties for the Indies;" intimating that the decision conveyed in this answer was meant to be on record for future cases. The date appended, "December, 1633," belongs to the formal document intended for communication. There was nothing to prevent the General from giving the same answer earlier by word of mouth to the procurator. Whether it was early enough to reach the missionaries before they left England at the end of November, we have not ascertained. In any case, the next year's convoy would bring the decision to them.

Thirteen months later the General wrote to the Provincial, referring to the same subject: "I am now having copied out for you the faculties as usually granted for the missionaries in the Indies;" and the document was to be sent the following week.[2] A paper of this kind did not mean a mere list, or what is technically called a *tabella* of faculties. It signified little less than a work or digest of privileges and favours: *Breve Compendium Privilegiorum et Gratiarum*, etc.[3] This is the name of the first hand-book published for the use of Jesuit missionaries by order of Father The faculties for the Indies.

---

[1] General Archives S.J., *Anglia, Epist., Gen.*, 1633, December.—*Documents*, I. No. 5, E. On this jurisdiction of the General, cf. *infra*, § 31 (4), p. 309, note 42.
[2] *Ibid.*, 1635, January 20: General to Blount, Provincial.
[3] Cf. *supra*, Introduction, Chap. I. § 8, p. 36, *s.v. Compendium*.

Aquaviva in 1586. The range of application of these faculties, which the actual General, Mutius Vitelleschi, declared were extended to Maryland, might be illustrated from the same Aquaviva's collection of Apostolic letters, published in 1585 for the use of Jesuit superiors. A short notice there prefixed says—

". . . It is important to remember that Pope Gregory XIII., on the 11th of October, 1579, declared by word of mouth (*vivæ vocis oraculo*) that, in the Apostolic privileges heretofore granted to our Society or hereafter to be granted, what is meant by the East Indies is the range of countries and islands from Mauritania towards the South and the East pertaining to Portugal, whether by right of domain or so-called conquest, or of commerce and navigation; and by the West Indies, all that lies to the West, beyond the Canary Islands and those which they call the Azores, pertaining under the same relations either to the dominion of Portugal or to that of the other provinces of Spain." [4]

<small>Maryland technically in the West Indies.</small>

At that time, in 1579, Spain and Portugal were the only two Christian nations whose name and empire could help to define the geography of distant countries East and West. England and France began to operate westward at a later date. And the Spanish monopoly there was supposed to be so complete that, as we have seen above, Father Parsons in 1605, and the General in 1629, objected distinctly to a Catholic scheme of colonization, for fear of giving offence to the Spanish monarchy. But the missionary character of the countries previously identified by reference to the name of Spain or Portugal underwent no change merely because it was England or France that set her foot on the Spanish main. And thus the General Mutius Vitelleschi, in 1635, simply handed the missionaries a copy of the *Privilegia Indica*, the "Faculties" or "Privileges for the Indies."

As to the two divisions of the Indies compared one with another, it made no difference whether it was for India East or India West that powers were originally communicated; because by a Bull of February 10, 1579, Gregory XIII. had declared that all faculties or powers granted by name to the religious of the Society in either direction

---

[4] *Litteræ Apostolicæ*, etc., Romæ, 1585: "*Erit etiam operæ pretium illud in memoriam redigere quod Pontifex Gregorius XIII., die 11 Octobris anno 1579, vivæ vocis oraculo declaravit, in gratiis Apostolicis Societati Jesu concessis, et in posterum concedendis, nomine Indiarum Orientalium intelligi omnes regiones et insulas, quæ ultra Mauretaniam versus Austrum et Orientem ad Portugalliam spectant, sive jure dominii sive conquistæ, ut vocant, sive commercii et navigationis. Nomine autem Indiæ Occidentalis, quicquid eodem jure Occidentem versus, ultra Insulas Fortunatas et eas quas Tertiarias appellant, sive ad Portugalliæ sive ad reliquarum Hispaniæ Provinciarum dominium pertinet.*"—This *vivæ vocis oraculum* may be seen in the *Bullarium Patronatus*, i. 248, where "1577" is printed for "1579."

were thereby bestowed in fact on all Indian missionaries of the Order in both directions.[5]

§ 26. The Fathers and Brothers selected for the Maryland settlement seem to have been within the first two years no fewer than seven, under three different commissions. There was the first band consisting of Father Andrew White, Father John Gravener or Altham, and Brother Thomas Gervase. *Seven Jesuits in Maryland. 1633-1635.* There went out also Father Alexander Baker and Father John Drury, who accompanied a certain gentleman (*cuidam viro nobili*), and then returned after voyaging for eight months. Then there were Father Francis Rogers and Brother John Wood, who came back to England within about two years after the establishment of the colony. There is an eighth named, Father Timothy Hays,[1] whose place seems to have been taken immediately by Father Gravener. The names and dates here given are drawn from the official Catalogues sent by the Provincial to the General. And, as to the going and coming of Baker and Drury, the report appears as well in the Annual Catalogue of 1634 as in the Triennial Review of 1635; besides an account of their voyage, though without any mention of their names, in the Annual Letter of 1634.[2] We pause to look at the characters, antecedents, and acquirements of these men.

Of Father John Altham, or Gravener, or Grosvenor, we know scarcely more than what Maryland history conveys. He was of Warwickshire and was forty-three years of age when he set out with Father White for America. Only ten years in the Order, he had spent all the time of his ministry *Altham, or Gravener, and John Drury.* in the Devonshire and London districts. The review of his studies, if he made any in the Society, must have been as slight as the studies themselves, which had consisted of only two years' philosophy, or, as it was called logic and physics, and of two years' theology, or what was technically called "Cases." Although he was registered as being weak in health, still the one point for which he received special commendation was that he had a bent for the hard missionary life, in which, six years later, the Provincial of the time observed that "he works well."[3]

As to Father John Drury, a native of London, at that time

[5] Gregorius XIII., *Rationi convenit*, February 10, 1579.—Cf. the *Compendium*, or *Litteræ Apostolicæ*, etc., of 1585, pp. 58, 59.
[1] *Alias* John Hanmer or Hamner.—H. Foley, *Records*, vii. 911.
[2] *Documents*, I. No. 8, B.
[3] *Anglia*, Catal. 2, 1639.

twenty-eight years of age, he was too young to have much of a history as yet. He had completed a course of three years in philosophy and of Cases in theology; had just been in charge of the domestic concerns as minister, and of the economical affairs as procurator, in the house at Ghent; was going through his last year of probation, which, as being supplementary to the two years of original novitiate, is called the third year of probation; and just at this point was summoned to join Father Baker.[4]

His chief was a distinguished man and well known under every respect. Alexander Baker, a native of Norfolk, had spent twenty years in the Society, and was now forty-eight years of age. He had completed all the higher studies of the Order; during ten years he had been discharging the duties of a missionary life in England; and he was professed of the four vows, May 23, 1627. He reconciled to the Church, in 1615, the Rev. William Coke, son of the famous lawyer Sir Edward Coke, whose name recalls such evil memories in the history of English Catholics. This alone might have merited for Baker the title which the Commons gave him of being "a known and notorious Jesuit." But he was guilty of other enormities, as a manuscript of his among the State Papers clearly evinces; for he treated therein of Baptismal regeneration as understood by Catholics, in contrast with the conflicting opinions rife among Protestants. Whereupon the Lords and Commons held a conference; and the Lord Archbishop of Canterbury did report to the Lords spiritual and temporal the result of the said conference, which was to the effect that the pious Commons had really thought His Majesty was going to keep his word and advance God's holy religion and suppress the contrary. "Yet at this meeting they find that, on the 12th of July last [1624], his Majesty hath granted a pardon unto Alexander Baker, a Jesuit, and ten other Papists, which, as they are informed, was upon the importunity of some foreign ambassador; and that it passed by immediate warrant, and was recommended from the principal Secretary of State [Conway, Calvert's successor], without paying the ordinary fees." A lady of Dorsetshire, Mary Esmond, in whose house copes, altars, and chalices were found, had also been pardoned, though she had refused to take the oath of allegiance. In view of these irregularities, the Commons formulated a petition, in which the Father's name comes in thus: "one Alexander Baker, a known and notorious Jesuit (who had been formerly released for the like offences)."

[4] *Anglia, Catal.* 3, 1632, 1633, 1634.

The petition, in presenting which the Commons desired the concurrence of the Lords, was read in the course of the Archbishop's report, who then went on to add how much the said Commons were grieved on an inspection of the date of the pardon, and at its dispensing with so many statutes, etc., and at its having been solicited by the principal Secretary of State himself, Lord Conway. "And," continued the Archbishop, "they added these circumstances: That this Jesuit was formerly imprisoned, and, being now at liberty, his conversation will be very dangerous to the perverting of many of His Majesty's subjects; that heretofore, in the time of Queen Elizabeth, if any such were convicted and pardoned (for she pardoned none before conviction, as their fault might be first known), they were banished also, not to return under pain of death, which is prevented by this pardon."

When the Lord Archbishop of Canterbury had ended his lengthy relation of that morning's conference, the Lord Conway began to make excuses on every head. But it is quite clear to any one who reads those minutes, though he have but a fraction of the piety which animated the good Commons, that the Lord Conway's excuses were very lame indeed. And one thing he omitted altogether, nor did the Lords spiritual and temporal, whose names were then subscribed, deliver themselves of any opinion on that most important point, to wit, the elevated policy of Queen Elizabeth, which the Commons now desiderated, but which King Charles and his advisers seemed to be wickedly discarding; inasmuch as she, like a good pious Queen, "pardoned none before conviction;" so that, if the convicted were rarely pardoned and made happy, the innocent were never made so.[5]

This reverend gentleman, Father Baker, went to America, as the Catalogues quoted above inform us. Then the Annual Letter of 1634 states the course of events, but without mentioning his name: "Last year, with the good will of the King and by his authority, a considerable colony of English people, in great part Catholic, was conducted to the hither shores of America under the auspicious patronage of a certain Catholic baron. There went with them two priests of ours, and one coadjutor-brother." These three mentioned in the Annual Letter were White, Altham, and Gervase. The report continues: "Then followed another priest and another lay-brother." These two were clearly Francis Rogers and John Wood. After describing the object of the Maryland expedition, and some domestic

[5] Rymer's *Fœdera*, xviii. 392.—Cf. also H. Foley, *Records*, i. 153, 154.

circumstances attending its departure, the writer proceeds as though to another subject, saying: "Besides, there were granted two priests of ours as companions to a certain nobleman, who had gone (*iverat*) to explore unknown lands. They had an experience of about eight months' voyaging, sufficiently trying. Both were much shaken in health, with spells of sickness. Still, they did their work generously, and gave us good reason to hope for an abundant harvest yet to be reaped in those wide and splendid regions."[6] Now, as the Catalogue of the same year drawn up by the same Provincial's authority puts down the names of Baker and Drury for Maryland, and the next Triennial Review, while reporting two as "sent to Maryland," Father Rogers and Brother Wood, adds that "two priests likewise have returned thence, Father Alexander Baker and Father John Drury," it is perfectly clear that the two companions allotted to the gentleman who went out exploring unknown lands were none other than Baker and Drury.

The special mission of Baker and Drury.

What were these unknown lands in the direction of Maryland, yet apparently different from Baltimore's colony? Writers at a loss to understand what became of George Calvert, who is recorded as an adventurer in the first expedition, assume that he went not to Maryland, but to Virginia; that he operated there, but in whose interest does not appear; and it seems certain that he died within a year.[7] If George Calvert, then, the younger brother of Cecil Lord Baltimore, was the gentleman (*quidam vir nobilis*) whom Baker and Drury accompanied, this subsidiary expedition would point to a plan, political and religious, of working in Virginia, while the main object was being attained in Maryland. At this time Virginia was diplomatically on good terms with the new colony; and to obtain a foothold there, whether as a State Treasurer or otherwise, was a capital point of Lord Baltimore's policy during several years to come. The death of George Calvert, some time after a meeting with the Patuxent chiefs, held on June 20, 1634, would have put an end to this side expedition, and to the immediate purpose which it had in view. The two Fathers were free to return; and a direct voyage to England would have brought them back in time to agree with the vague account: "about eight months of navigation" (*octo circiter mensium navigatione*).

Expedition of George Calvert, jun.

We gather from a letter sent to Rome by the English priest Clerk

---

[6] *Anglia, Historia*, iv. 470, 471: Annual Letter, 1634.—*Documents*, I. No. 8, B.
[7] S. F. Streeter, *Papers*, Fund Publication, No. 9, pp. 62, 69.—G. W. Burnap, *L. Calvert*, p. 39.—J. T. Scharf, *History of Maryland*, i. 66.

on August 16, 1633, that there was apparently an immediate reason of urgency why Father Baker should have withdrawn himself from London at the date of the Maryland expedition. He had just been imprisoned and then released in the same irregular manner which had scandalized the pious Commons on a former occasion. With this information Clerk submits a copy of the Maryland *Relation*, or *Account of the Colony*, issued by Lord Baltimore. He says, after speaking of religious affairs, Anglican and Puritan: "It is generally thought that the times will every day grow better and better for Catholicity, and that the State by degrees will bring all to the same passe as in 3° Elizabethæ, before the chief penall lawes were enacted. The compositions go on slowly [*i.e.* the payment of the blackmail, called 'King's Debts,' on the part of the Catholics, in order to be left alone by the State and its informers]. Pursevants [*i.e.* the officers] do live either in London or in the country. [Items about the royal family.] I heare nothing to any purpose donn by the Judges in their circuitts this summer against recusants or priests; and a little before they began their circuitt one Alexander Baker a Jesuitt, being taken openly in the street and committed to Newgate, was within few daies delivered by my Lord Chief Justice Richardson him self, at the Queens entreaty, to whom meanes was made for it. [Here the writer defends the Queen against the Jesuits' 'followers.'] I send you a *Relation* of my Lord Baltemor's new plantation in Mary land, which perhaps you will willingly see. [Father Francis's book, and the reported conversion of ministers by the Capuchins]."[8]

A reason for Baker's absenting himself from London. 1633

A few years afterwards, on August 24, 1638, Father Alexander Baker died in London. When the Summary of Deceased Members, as quoted before, eulogizes this intrepid missionary for having twice undertaken journeys to the remotest territories of the Indies in the cause of Christ, it must clearly be understood as referring to the Virginia trip, for one of the two journeys; and for the other, just as probably, though not with the same documentary evidence, to the Newfoundland trip of 1629.[9]

As to Father Francis Rogers, who stayed so short a time in Maryland, the explanation of his coming in 1635 with Brother John Wood, and of his going in 1636 accompanied by the same, may possibly be found in the matter of health, Maryland fevers being destined to

---

[8] Stonyhurst MSS., *Anglia A*, viii. f. 71: Clerk, August 16, 1633, to [Fitton, Rome]. Cf. *supra*, § 19, p. 251, note 3.
[9] *Supra*, § 10, pp. 198, 199.

play havoc among all kinds of adventurers on the Chesapeake and Potomac. There is nothing special to remark about either, except that Father Rogers had completed all his studies, was thirty-six years of age, and that he had applied of his own accord for the foreign mission in America. After his return he lived an active life of some twenty-five years on the mission in England. The Brother John Wood who went with him gives a biographer some ground to suppose that he had formerly, under the name of Captain Hill, been an adept of the buccaneering trade, so common to English seamen of that age.[10] He had the health, strength, and experience qualifying him for the manifold occupations of a temporal kind which devolved upon a coadjutor in Maryland.

Rogers, Wood, and Gervase.

Equally efficient with Brother John Wood was Brother Thomas Gervase. He was in the prime of life, being forty-three years of age. But he was doomed to be the first victim of yellow fever among the Jesuits of English America, dying there in the month of August, 1637. It is surmised that he was the Thomas Latham, porter of the Jesuit house in Clerkenwell, London, when the discovery of that residence was made in 1628 by the pursuivants of the Privy Council, and the porter, with all the Fathers caught therein, were duly committed to prison.[11]

§ 27. On the 22nd of November, 1633, the two Fathers White and Altham, being safely aboard the good ship the *Ark*, set sail from Cowes in the Isle of Wight. It is presumed that the Fathers had slipped aboard there at the last moment, when the inquisitorial visits and tests ordered by the Privy Council were finished and duly reported.[1] They had over twenty other persons belonging to their own party; and the history or manner of engaging one indented servant may throw light upon the standing of some among the others, though certainly not of all.

Putting out to sea. November 22, 1633.

The Annual Letter for the year, after mentioning the two detachments of missionaries who went out in "the year just elapsed," 1633,

---

[10] H. Foley, *Records*, vii., *Collectanea*, s.v. "Rogers, Francis;" "Wood, John."—*Ibid.*, the sea-serpent appears in connection with "Captain Hill (once a pirate at sea, afterwards a Lay-Brother with the Jesuits)." We trust that Brother H. Foley has lost his reckoning in reporting this tradition; or we must also call attention to the fact that one of the gentlemen adventurers to Maryland was a "Captain John Hill." See above, § 24, p. 263.—Foley does not seem to have known that Brother Wood was ever in Maryland.

[11] *Ibid.*, s.v. "Gervase, Thomas."

[1] Cf. J. T. Scharf, *History of Maryland*, i. 66-68.

goes on to state that, for the promotion of so religious a purpose as was set forth, "many Catholics showed great liberality, and contributed money as well as servants, these latter being of the first necessity there. Now, as to a certain domestic, it seems to have been a stroke of Divine providence that they who set out last should have lighted upon him. He was one whom our laybrother had known in Belgium, and found to be an industrious and trusty man. Wherefore, while preparing to embark, he took the greatest pains to find the man again; but after a fruitless search he had given up all hope, when, on going aboard of a ship which had a cargo of supplies for various colonies, he all at once lighted on the man. The domestic had fallen into the greatest misery owing to the free confession of his faith, especially because he would on no account take the oath which they call that of allegiance. So he was now in the hands of a certain heretical merchant, who was to take him out of the country, and sell him at will after the usual fashion in some heretical colony. The brother recognizes him, redeems him, and takes him as a companion with him on his own voyage, the poor man being as it were snatched from the very jaws of hell and full of the greatest joy at his deliverance." [2] Then the passage in the Annual Letter goes on to tell of the third detachment, that of Baker and Drury.

A Catholic white slave.

For the voyage over the Atlantic the narrative of Father White is a classical authority, as well because of its being the contemporaneous account drawn up by an eye-witness, as because of the literary style which distinguishes the original Latin. An English version, itself contemporaneous, well composed, and not a mere translation, has lately been discovered. It is seen to be wanting in certain characteristics of the Latin, such as expressions of private devotion and a dominant interest in matters of Divine worship. Both seem to have come from the same pen; and it is plausibly suggested that both were taken from one and the same diary of the voyage. The Latin, which is fuller as a religious man's account, is evidently directed to the General of the Society, who is addressed in one place by his proper designation: "Your Paternity." The English is fuller in matters which could be utilized by the Calverts for advertising among investors in England. To this latter account the Governor, Leonard Calvert, appears to refer when writing from Point Comfort on the 1st of May to his own business partner or fellow-adventurer, Sir Richard Lechford. He says: "And likewise

Two Relations extant of the voyage.

[2] General Archives S.J., *Anglia, Historia,* iv. 470, 471.—*Documents,* I. No. 8, B.

[I have herewith sent you] a more exact journall of all our voyage then I could finde time to deliver unto you in this letter, in respect of my much other business about the – – – the ship homeward and other affaires of the colonie. This I have sent you was writ by a most honest and discreet gentleman, wherefore you may be confident of the truth of it." The account, thus sent and authenticated by the leader of the expedition, being justly considered identical with the English redaction lately discovered, and the English paper being substantially the same as the Latin copy known for nearly a century, we have the trustworthiness of Father White's narrative as an historical document sufficiently vouched for,[3] and the levity of a criticism on the same document as being "picturesque though not always trustworthy" sufficiently stigmatized.[4]

At the moment of starting on the voyage the travellers were not without apprehension that a conspiracy was being hatched, apparently among the crew, to frustrate the expedition; with the natural result that the missionaries would find themselves soon in a London dungeon, instead of being aboard ship ploughing the Western main. But a broken hawser, a lost anchor, a flurry and a flutter in the night, with the pinnace scurrying off to save herself from being run down in the dark, made it necessary for the good *Ark* to follow the flying *Dove*; and the conspirators were foiled by being carried out of the London zone of mischief on to the high sea. Here we may quote a specimen of Father White's religious tone of thought: "This," he says, "happened on the 23rd of November, the day of St. Clement, who, tied to an anchor and sunk in the sea, obtained the crown of martyrdom; and made a pathway for the people of the earth to declare the wonderful things of God." Meanwhile he tells us that, on embarking, "we placed the principal parts of the ship under the protection of God, of His most holy Mother, of St. Ignatius and of all the Angels of Maryland." This act of consecration may have been public.

Piety and religion.

Then followed an exciting race with another merchantman; and the missionary, who was fifty-four years of age, becomes young again as he tells of it. They did not beat the other; but they could have,

---

[3] *Calvert Papers*, iii. 26–45: *A Briefe Relation of the Voyage unto Maryland.*—Ibid., 23, 24: L. Calvert, Point Comfort, May 30, 1634, to Sir Richard Lechford, "Kinde Partner."—*Ibid.*, Introduction by C. C. Hall, 6–12.—Fund Publication, No. 7, *Relatio itineris in Marylandiam.*—For authentic text of this last, see *Documents*, I. No. 8, A.—See reproduction opposite of the *Relatio Itineris*, first page; an office copy. General Archives S.J., *Anglia, Historia*, iv. pp. 413–440.

[4] J. A. Doyle, *English in America;* see *supra*, Introduction, Chap. II. § 11, pp. 80, 81.

RELATIO ITINERIS IN MARILANDIAM.
General Archives S.J., *Anglia, Historia*, iv. p. 413. In a Roman office hand, with additions, lines, and numbers of Father SOUTHWELL's redaction. (⅔ *scale of the original.*)

if they wanted. A terrific storm arose; it was now a contest for life and death; the tiny pinnace showed two lights of distress in the darkness of the night and the fury of the gale; and then she disappeared, to be mourned over and prayed for by the survivors in the bigger ship. In the midst of the three days' storm which continued waxing in fury, all control of the rudder being lost, and the ship drifting helplessly at the mercy of the elements, the Fathers conducted a fruitful mission among the Catholics aboard; and Father White made the first dedication of the new country beyond the seas to the glory of the Redeemer and to the Immaculate Virgin His Mother, as a substitute for the "Dowry of Mary" which England had been and which America was to be.

Fears of Turkish pirates on passing the Straits of Gibraltar, a course past the Canaries, an attempt to take in Boavista of the Cape Verde Islands, with views of the sea, its curiosities and its riches, form the thread of the missionary's narrative, till they are on the point of striking across the ocean and putting in at Barbados. The notion of taking three hundred and twenty passengers out of their way to Boavista was merely in the interest of Lord Baltimore's pocket, that a cargo for the return voyage might be secured there if nowhere else. But more sensible counsels prevailed, and they made for the West Indies. Here again it was largely the provision for the future that led them on this circuitous route; but we have every reason to be grateful for the view afforded of the West Indies, at the moment when these rich islands were taking so prominent a place in the great movement of English and French colonization.

§ 28. Arriving at Barbados, which for voyagers from the African coast is practically the nearest point to reach, and at the same time is one of the most southern among the Antilles, they stayed from January 3 till the 24th of the same month; and here they recovered the *Dove*, their lost pinnace, which, as though come to life again, came sailing in from the high seas just like themselves. In Barbados "some few Catholiques there be, both English and Irish." The Governor was [Henry] Hawley, brother of the Maryland Commissioner; but Mr. Acers, brother-in-law to the said Governor, was just then in charge. Their experiences of this valuable kinship showed them that it was somewhat less than kind. Being sadly in need of necessaries or of those ordinary provisions which to the voyagers were luxuries, they were faced at once with an engrossing

Barbados. 1634.

combination of the most approved modern style on the part of the astute islanders; so that, as the narrator tells us graphically: "Nothing could be had but it cost us our eies; a pig six weekes old was 5 £ sterling, a turke 50 s. and a chicken at 6 s." The only matter whereof the islanders were liberal was the potato root of the best quality, which was so abundant that they would "give cart loades to almost any for the fetching."

Their arrival at Barbados and departure thence was so timed, that they fortunately escaped the danger of an insurrection on the part of servants in the port—that is to say, of Englishmen and Irishmen indented to slavery—and also the risks of a fight on the high sea off St. Christopher between English and Dutch ships on the one side, and Spanish ships of war on the other. In this connection the *Ark* herself is described as a ship "well gunn'd and man'd." The last long paragraph in the Latin account of Barbados is on the glories of the pine-apple, and ends with the remark, in which the General of the Society himself is designated and addressed: "I did wish I could send with this letter just one pine-apple to your Paternity; for nothing but the fruit itself is adequate to the task of showing worthily what it is."

The white slaves, etc.

On January 24, 1634, they weighed anchor in the night and made the next Carib island, Santa Lucia, by noon on the following day. This they left at a safe distance, for the island was "divided in it selfe, the servants (being negroes) against the salvage maisters." His language here in the English account is worthy of notice. Using the generic term "servants," he specifies particularly their kind, "being negroes." At four in the evening they reached the next Carib island, Matalina, Matilena, or Martinique.[1] They dropped anchor, and the missionary had an occasion to view and describe the first Indians of his acquaintance, who came offering their produce for sale. He concludes his account of them in the Latin narrative with the pious wish: "Some one, I hope, will yet have compassion on this forsaken people."

Santa Lucia. Black slaves.

Passing on through the West Indian chain of the Windward Islands, Father White continues: "Next morning by dawneing of the day we made Guadelupe, an Ile so called for the similitude it hath with Guadelupe of Spaine, mountainous almost as the other;" and he adds in the Latin: "I trust also that it is under the guardianship of the same most holy Virgin Mother." "By noone

Guadeloupe.

---

[1] For the rich vocabulary of variations in West Indian names at this date, see above, § 2, p. 151, note 14.

we came before **Monserat**, where is a noble plantation of Irish Catholique[s], whome the Virginians would not suffer to live with them because of their religion;" or, as he expresses it in the Latin phrase: "The inhabitants of Montserrat are Irishmen, who were expelled by the English of Virginia for the profession of the Catholic faith." In this connection we may recall the passage quoted before from an old American record, about the first Maryland missionary "coming hither to the Irish exiles with Lord Baltimore" in 1629;[2] and, if his lordship George Calvert was turned away by the Virginians, it is not unlikely that the "Irish exiles" had themselves to go. *Montserrat, and Irish Catholics from Virginia.*

After leaving Montserrat, "next morneing wee came to **Mævis** [Nevis], an iland infamous for agues by reason of the bad aire. Here haveing staied a day, next morninge we came to **St. Christophers** hard by, where we staied 10 dayes, nobly enterteined by **Sir Thomas Waroner** [Warner] governour, Captaine Jefferson lieuetennant coronell, by two Catholique[s], Captain Caverley and Captain Pellam, and myselfe in particular by the governour of the French colonie." *Nevis, St. Kitts, English and French.*

From St. Christopher, or St. Kitts, as it came to be familiarly known in English history, the voyagers struck out into the high sea, leaving the Virgin Islands, Santa Cruz, St. Thomas, and the others on their left hand, the same which were known afterwards as the Danish Islands. Among those already touched at, the great division between French and English was just then showing itself, to be definitively accomplished, however, only after a long term of years and many vicissitudes of war. The convoy of the *Ark* and *Dove* touched land no more till they arrived at Point Comfort, in Virginia, on the 27th of February, 1634. *The Virgin Islands. The Danish Islands.*

We pause now at the suggestion of Father White's light sketch, to do more justice, for the reader's satisfaction, to the geography and social antecedents of this important element in American Catholic history, that is to say, the West Indian Islands, Windward and Leeward; or, as they are otherwise called, the Lesser Antilles or Caribbees. And as Virginia loosely floated before the mind's eye of the Briton in much the same longitude, latitude, and social bearings as the islands, and, like Maryland, was itself considered to be an island somewhere in the offing to the far far West, we shall include it in this brief review of origin and progress.

[2] *Supra*, § 10, pp. 199, 200.

§ 29. The main body of the Western populations, at the epoch of our Maryland expedition, has been described variously. Unlike the compact uniformity of the Pilgrims in New England, or the modified predominance of one class like that of the Catholic gentry now on their way to Maryland, the composition of the settlements which were being made on the islands or on the mainland was variegated to a degree. Not only were there confessors of the faith, or exiles for conscience' sake, but, as the complaints and protests of the time show, there was a wholesale manufacturing of population by transporting convicts, felons, runaways, rioters, and the like. The Government at home would on occasions offer shiploads of malefactors as its contribution and sign of cordial good will to the well-being of the new colonies.

As to the native Indians, it is remarkable how they melted away everywhere, except where the French and the Spaniards had charge of them. The French intermarried with natives; so did the Spanish colonists in New Spain; and this in honourable and true marriage. A popular Protestant writer of New England in the next century recommended the Protestant missionaries to do the same; though he did not mention the laity in such a connection. He said, "our young missionaries" might "intermarry with the daughters of the sachems and other considerable Indians," and thus "procure a perpetual alliance and commercial advantages with the Indians;" and, he says, "their progeny would be ever a certain cement between us and the Indians;" which political advantage the Roman Catholic clergy could not, he says, secure for a thrifty republic, "because they are forbid to marry."[1]

The native Indians.

With regard to the poor negroes, Father White has mentioned the circumstance of an intestine war in progress between the blacks of Santa Lucia and "the salvage maisters." The cancerous plague of negro slavery, with all its attendant woes, spread in due time through the southern colonies of the adjoining continent, took in Maryland, and to a limited degree invaded the northern colonies also. Both the plague of slavery and the woes of immorality became inveterate under a necessity which imposed black labour on the whites and bound the white masters in economical conditions of life to the blacks. The Stuart kings, or at least the two last of them, were ardent adventurers in the Royal African Company, which secured, conveyed, and delivered cargoes of the unfortunates from the factories in Africa to the cabins in America;

The negroes.

[1] W. Douglass, *Summary*, iii. 138, note.

and nobody inquired scrupulously about the means employed for whipping in the herds of captives from their hearths and homes, and stowing them away in ship-holds. And when, on the other side of the ocean, a thin residue of fever-stricken skeletons were dragged up and out through the hatches to be unloaded in a British-American colony, there was no Peter Claver there in readiness to bandage their wounds and to assuage their sorrows.

If we find among the names of immigrants brought in by Father White, that of "Mathias Sousa, Molato," for the year 1633, and " Francisco, a Molato," for 1635,[2] it is not to be supposed, as a late interpretation has expressed it, that "Francisco brought in by Father White" [in 1635] "was the first slave in the colony of which there is any notice. The Jesuits therefore have the honour of having introduced slavery into Maryland. It has been attempted to pass this distinction on to the Puritans, but justice requires us to refuse to deprive the Jesuits of whatever praise they may be entitled to for their services in this matter."[3] Everything in these half-dozen lines is equally gratuitous with the rest: that the mulatto Francisco put to Father White's credit in 1635 was a slave; that he was the first slave, whereas he came two years after the other mulatto, Matthias Sousa, also put to the credit of Father White, but for 1633; that Father White imported either one or the other, and did not receive them as transferred to his credit in assignments; that, the mulatto Francisco being the "first" of his kind "noticed" in the colony, through him was "slavery" first "introduced into Maryland;" or that any historian living or dead did ever honour the Puritans with the charge of having "introduced slavery into Maryland"—where they themselves did not land. In such documentary matters it would be safer to follow the records in the *Archives of Maryland*, the editor of which observes that, on March 5, 1642, we find "the first reference to the importation of negro slaves," and on July 24, 1644, "perhaps the first recorded purchase of negroes." With these transactions, eight or ten years later, the Jesuits had nothing to do.[4]

Mulattoes imported into Maryland. 1633-1635.

Worse than the cruelties inflicted on the negroes to the prejudice of life and limb was the guilt of systematically denying them Christian instruction and Baptism, in most of the English settlements. Barbados became notorious for its legislation against ever imparting

[2] *Documents*, I. No. 30.
[3] C. E. Smith, *Religion under the Barons of Baltimore*, p. 214.
[4] W. H. Browne, *Archives of Maryland, Judicial and Testamentary Business of the Provincial Court*, 1637-1650, preface, referring to pp. 189, 304.

the benefits of religion to the blacks. At head-quarters in London it was of little avail to make inquiries of colonial governors; to put into the commissions or instructions special clauses about christening the negroes; to hold up for imitation the example of the French and other nations, in the Christian care and charity bestowed on that unhappy class. The Anglican Bishop of London, in due course of time, had a rich assortment of edifying decrees sent over by the Lords of Trade and Plantations. Indeed, that illustrious see is more honoured by the collection of homilies which we find distributed through the archives, than by the selection of ministers which it succeeded in distributing through the plantations; whereof a later governor, writing from St. Christopher, reported that in the entire government of the Leeward Islands, the parishes, he says, " may be at least fourty; and I found, when I came, one drunken orthodox priest, one drunken sectary priest, and one drunken parson who had noe orders, to supply the fourty parishes." [5] And as to ministers not being in orders at all, and yet being allowed to continue in the ministry, another governor jauntily remarked, by way of disputing any one's right to reprove him: The parish loved such a one well, he writes; "but whether he were ordained or not, I cannot say. If he were not, I am sure I could not ordain him." [6]

The negro slaves debarred from Christian instruction.

An important contingent of the population, as well in the West Indies as in the new English colonies on the northern continent, was that which came from Ireland. It was not enough for them to have been banished, kidnapped, spirited away, transported from Europe to America. We have noticed Father White's further observation that, even when in America, " the noble plantation " of Irish Catholics had been banished from Virginia, because the English there would not tolerate their religion. However, it was under the Commonwealth, not long after Father White's voyage, that the great movement of Irish expatriation was designed to flood the islands and the mainland alike with boys and girls, with men and women, in much the same way as the Royal African Company treated their living booty from the Guinea Coast. A few specimens of Orders in Council will show the policy in progress.

The Irish exiles.

"Friday, the 1st of April, 1653. [First business]: That license

---

[5] P. R. O., *Colonial Papers*, xxvii. No. 52, § 16: C. Wheler, governor, St. Christopher, 1671, December 9, to Councell of Forreigne Plantations.

[6] *Ibid.*, xlvii. No. 99: J. Atkins, governor, [Barbados] 1681, December 6, to Lords of Trade.

be granted to Sir John Clotworthie Knight to transport into America five hundred natural Irish men."

September 6, 1653. David Selleck of Boston, New England, who describes his two good ships, one the *Good Fellow* of Boston, George Dalle, master, with twenty-six seamen, the other the *Providence* of London, Thomas Swanley, master, with twenty-four seamen, having petitioned " craveing lycence from the councell . . . in order to their proceeding in a voyage to New England and Virginia, intending to carry 400 Irish children to the said places: it is ordered that a warrant of protection be granted," provided that security be given to the Commissioner of Customs, that they do go to Ireland, and within two months do take in the children, and transport them to those plantations.

Forced deportation. 1653-1655.

September 24, 1653. "That liberty be granted to Richard Netherway of Bristol to transport from Ireland to Virginya 100 of the Irish Toryes."

On the 10th of May, 1655, Jamaica was taken by the English, and five months afterwards the Council ordered : " That one thousand Irish girles and the like number of youthes be sent into Jamaica; and it is reported back to the Committee of Jamaica to consider of the allowances to each of them, not exceeding twenty shillings a head, and the age of such boyes and girles to be fowerteene yeares or under." This business of " transporting youths " runs through divers Council meetings for a year to come, with the names of the noble lords and gallant gentlemen, who were present at the sessions, appearing duly in the minutes. And so the history runs on in its gloomy and tragic course.

For long negotiations, replete with cynical cruelty, one has but to look over the Thurloe Papers, and scan the correspondence between Henry Cromwell in Ireland and Secretary Thurloe in London. In answer to the demand for a thousand Irish girls or young women, the reply comes from Ireland : " Although we must use force in taking them up, yet, it being so much for their own good and likely to be of so great advantage to the public, it is not in the least doubted that you may have such number of them as you shall think fit." In the next letter Henry Cromwell says: " I think it might be of like advantage to your affairs there and ours here [in Ireland], if you should think fit to send one thousand five hundred or two thousand young boys of twelve or fourteen years of age to the place aforementioned. *We* could well spare them, and they would be of use to you; and who knows, but it may be a means to make them Englishmen, I mean rather Christians." Hence different computations heretofore have been made of six thousand boys and women being thus sent over; of their being sold for slaves; of sixty thousand being crowded into ships and sent to Barbados and the islands of America; of over a hundred thousand of both sexes and all ages being relegated to different tobacco islands of the West Indies. Maryland, reputed to be Catholic, seems to have become a colony suspected, as not quite a safe place for Catholic Irish; since "Proposalls for transporting Irish to Maryland" are briefly laid upon the table with the formula: "Respited."[7]

Of a different mould were the contributions in human flesh from England itself, as the following elaborate programme will show. It belongs to a series of representations made by worthy London merchants, as soon as rogues shrewder than themselves began to turn the arts of kidnapping against the kidnappers, and to divert the profits into their own pockets. Then the lamentations arose and became eloquent, and the Aldermen and the Lord Mayor helped to swell the chorus—

White slaves from England.

"Certaine Propositions for the better accommodating the forreigne plantations with servants; reported from the Committee to the Councell of Forreigne Plantations.

"1. It being universally agreed that people are the foundation and improvement of all plantacions, and that people are encreased principally by sending of servants thither, it is necessary that a settled course be taken for the furnishing them with servants.

"2. Servants are either blacks or whites.

"3. Blacks are such as are brought by waye of trade, and are sould at about 20£ a head one with an other, and are the principall

[7] P. R. O., *Dom. Interregnum,* i. 41, p. 45; i. 70, p. 338; i. 76, pp. 318, 319; i. 122, p. 1; i. 93, p. 6, the proposals regarding Maryland, apparently August 12, [1657].—*Thurloe Papers,* iv. 23, *seqq.*; H. Cromwell and Thurloe correspondence, September 11 to November 13, 1655.—Compare Lingard, *England,* viii. 175, 176, 6th edit., from Thurloe, iv. 40, with the computations from Petty, Lynch, Bruodin.— Compare also H. Foley, *Records,* iii. 335 *note,* from Acts of Father John Bathe, S.J., killed by the Cromwellians at Drogheda.—As to dislodging the native population from Ireland, compare Henry Cromwell, Waterford, October 1, 1655, to Thurloe, commending "Mr. Lancelott Stepney and others," for having "transported the number of ten thousand Irish soldiers from hence to Spain, and so having served this country by freeing it of such burthensome people." *Thurloe Papers,* iv. 64.— A modern Liberal, referring to the English dominant caste in Ireland at that time, and speaking of no brutal specimen in the person of Sir William Temple, says of him as an Irish colonist: "He troubled himself as little about the welfare of the remains of the old Celtic population, as an English farmer on the Swan River troubles himself about the New Hollanders, or a Dutch boer at the Cape about the Caffres." Macaulay, *Essay on Sir William Temple.*

and most usefull appartenances of a plantation, and are such as are perpetuall servants.

"4. Whites are such as are diverse waies gathered up here in England; verie few from Ireland or Scotland; and, being transported at the charge of about 6£ a head, are there entertained by such as they are consignd to from hence, or are exchanged for comodities with such as have occasion for them at different rathes [rates] according to theire condicion or trade, by which they are rendred more usefull & beneficiall to theire masters. These after certaine yeares are free to plant for themselves, or to take wages for theire service as they shall aggree, & have to the vallue of tenn pounds sterling to begin planting for themselves.

"5. The waies of obtayning these servants have been usually by employing a sorte of men and women who make it theire proffession to tempt or gaine poore or zole [sole] persons to goe to the plantations, and haveing persuaded or deceived them on shipp board they receive a reward from the person who employed them.

"6. When the shipps is to bee clared at Graves End, ofttymes the servants soe obtayned doe make complaint that they were forced or seduced, and some cunning vogues [rogues], after they have been fedd aboard perhaps a month or longer, doe by this means avoyd the voyage."

In the following paragraphs, 7–12, the document continues to the effect that an Act of Parliament should make proper provision. There are felons. There are those who have escaped condign punishment by privilege of clergie, and have been burnt in the hand; do not brand them so, but send them to the plantations; for, staying at home, they are our chief thieves and robbers. There are the sturdy beggars and gipsies. However, all this is an "ill seed for a young plantation." A system of exchange might be instituted. Relieve towns and villages of those unprovided for. Paragraphs 13–20 are on the Commissioners and their powers.[8]

§ 30. When Governor Wheler, just quoted above, spoke of an orthodox priest and a sectary priest and a parson as dividing the forty parishes of the Leeward Islands among them,[1] we presume that he meant a Presbyterian, a Dissenter, and an Anglican. In any

---

[8] P. R. O., *Colonial Entry Book*, 92, pp. 275–283, [1664?]—Compare *Calendar, America and West Indies*, ii. § 791.—Cf. *Ibid.*, § 769, *seqq.*, on the "spirritts" and their wicked practices in spiriting away young people, 1664, July 12, etc.

[1] *Supra*, § 29, p. 282.

case, the classification agrees closely enough with three main religious castes, which we shall now sketch briefly from Acts and documents of the Western continent and islands, to relieve somewhat with lines of definition the otherwise blank character of a region and a time so obscure to the historical imagination. The three castes or classes are the Puritans, the Huguenots, and the said Anglicans or members of the Established Church.

(1) The Puritans, both as a civil and religious body, were the great power of the North; and from the day they landed they had left **Puritans in North America.** "little or nothing in England to be responsible for them." With their "interest and residence whollye in America,"[2] they grew ever more and more exclusive of England, till a great and successful revolution gave them what they merited and what England deserved. At the time when Lord Baltimore was endeavouring to eject the Jesuits from Maryland, he invited the Puritans of Boston to come and settle in his plantation. He "sent a commission" to Captain Gibbons of Boston, "wherein he made a tender of land in Maryland to any of ours that would transport themselves thither, with free liberty of religion and all the privileges which the place afforded, paying such annual rent as should be agreed upon; but our Captain," continues Winthrop, in his Journal, "had no mind to further his design herein, nor had any of our people temptation that way." This was under the date of October, 1643.[3] Lord Baltimore did admit a persecuted colony of Virginia Puritans about 1649-1650; and within six years afterwards the battle of Providence was fought on the Severn, in which Lord Baltimore's Governor was utterly defeated by the same Puritan colony.[4]

A few months again after this fight in Maryland, whereby Puritans became as well rooted and established there as in New England, and very much better than in Virginia, a paper was

[2] Compare P. R. O., *Colonial Papers*, xi. No. 65, § 4; given in full, *Archives of Maryland, Council Proceedings*, 1636-1667, p. 280: "Reasons of State concerning Maryland in America," [August, 1652]: "4. Fourthly, the Lord Baltemor haveing an estate and his residence in England, this Commonwealth will have a better assurance of the due obedience of that plantation . . . then if the government of that place, att so remote a distance, should be disposed of into other hands, whoe had little or nothing here to be responsible for itt, and whose interest and residence were whollye there." The paper is endorsed in pencil: "See Commons Journal, 31 August, 1652."
[3] E. D. Neill, *Founders of Maryland*, p. 109.—Here may be noticed that use by seventeenth-century Puritans of the term "ours," which some persons have supposed to be a domestic denomination among the Jesuits alone. Cf. also *Documents*, I. No. 20 (the secular priest George Gage, 1642, July 21, to the Bishop of Chalcedon), where the same term "ours" is used by him of secular clergymen.
[4] J. T. Scharf, *History of Maryland*, i. 200-221.

addressed to them in their northern home from the Council of State in London. Cromwell's government extended to them the freedom of the lately acquired Jamaica. The motives and policy of the offer are worthy of attention.

Daniel Gookin,[5] being commissioned by the Council of State to go as envoy to New England, and having £300 advanced him to defray his charges in that service, is provided on September 26, 1655, with instructions to direct him in his "offer to the people of New England." After mentioning the antecedents, how Jamaica was taken by the English on May 10 last, with the other relevant and alluring circumstances of the four months just elapsed, Daniel Gookin is instructed to proceed as follows:— *Cromwell's invitation to Puritans. Jamaica, 1655.*

"6. This being the true state of that affaire and the reality of our intentions therein, we have thought it expedient to send you into the aforesaid colonies and people to explaine & declare these things unto them, and to make them an offer of removeing themselves, or such numbers of them as shalbe thought convenient, out of those partes where they now are unto Jamaica, which wee have done cheifly upon these ensuing reasons amongst many others—

"(a) Our desire is that this place (if the Lord so please) may be inhabited by people who know the Lord & walke in his feare, that by their light they may enlighten the parts about them, which was a cheife end of our undertaking this designe; and might alsoe from amongst them have persons fitt for rulers & magistrates, who may be an encouragement to the good & a terror to the evill doers.

"(b) Out of love & affection to themselves and the fellow feeling wee have alwaies had of the difficulties & necessities they have been put to constest [contest] with, ever since they were driven from the land of their nativity into that desert and barren wildernes for their conscience's sake; which wee could not but make manifest at this tyme when, as wee think, an opportunity is offered for their enlargement and removeing of them out of a hard countrye into a land of plenty.

"(c) Considering that God by providence, through the many difficulties & necessities they are exercised with, had put it into some of their hearts to seeke a new plantation, & particularly them of New Haven, who (as wee are informed) are upon thoughts of removeing into the Bay of De la Ware."

[5] Cf. E. D. Neill, *Terra Mariæ*, pp. 76-78, note.

After these pious motives come eleven heads presenting the Conditions of Plantation, which seem to be liberal enough in giving away the land of an old settled and rich island like Jamaica.[6]

The Puritans stayed where they were and kept concentrated in New England. They were already in Maryland. They never underwent the demoralizing effects of a West Indian island. We pass on to the Huguenots. And, to illustrate their position in the British colonies, we shall take Carolina along with Jamaica and other West Indian islands.

(2) Just about the time when the first Lord Baltimore thought of inspecting the Chesapeake, Antoine de Ridouet, Baron de Sancé, expressed to the King of England his desire to settle French Protestants in Virginia; and he received letters of denization accordingly (June 27, 1629). His proposal assumed the form almost immediately of settling 2000 men within two years in Florida, and thus destroying the power of Spain. The baron had a pension of £100 per annum from King Charles I.; and arrangements regarding Carolina form a conspicuous element in the colonial papers of 1629, 1630. Among the eighty-one persons whom De Sancé expected to take out at once, the first on the list is a minister. The charges for fifty men he estimated at £1000, which comes to £20 a head, as in the first Conditions of the Maryland plantation.[7]

Huguenots for Virginia and Florida. 1629, 1630.

Under the Commonwealth (July, 1657), an interesting proposal concerning foreigners of the Protestant Reformed religion was made by René Augier. They were to be employed in Jamaica or elsewhere in the West Indies; and in the attitude which they were to take up in the face of the Jesuits, we have an outside view of what was being done there by the Order at this time. He says, in his observations on his own proposals—

The Protestant Reformed religion. Jamaica, 1657.

"Primo . . . [That if, according to his proposal in the 8th article, any foreign corporations or colonies shall come to be incorporated into the proposed Society or Companie, for which the patent is to be granted, it shall be especially laid down] that all Jesuists, Missionaries & Muncks shall be excluded from the same . . . [whereupon the said Augier proceeds to shew] the utilitie his said

---

[6] P. R. O., *Domestic Interregnum Entry Book*, i. 76, pp. 304–306; a book with Sir Joseph Williamson's later endorsement: "Usurpers Councell Booke from 3 Apr., 1655, till 21 Mar., 1655/6."

[7] P. R. O., *Colonial Papers*, v. *passim.*—Cf. *Calendar of State Papers, A. & W.I.*, i. 98, *seqq.*

Ser^me Highnesse maye draw by the successe of the said proposall, directly opposed unto the Jesuiticall Society & Companie.

"It is most certaine that the Jesuits fondamentall designe is to settle their empire by their commerce in the one & in the others Indies.

The Jesuitical Companie and Designe.

"[Here follows an exposure of the Jesuits' Constitution on this basis of René's. They are the chief adventurers in divers states, especially in the West Indies; they are the chief merchants, etc.] sucking continually as they doe in all the riches of the East & West, and in soe many purses of Europe by their Congregations de Propaganda Fide, seconded by their chamber men the missionaries & by the muncks their foot-men, their Society which doth alwayes receive without ever expending (living on their thriftynesse & the catchings they make on their schollars & borders) is without comparison become this daye, not only the most riche in monney, but also the overrulers of all the Roman clergy, of the kings, yea & of the Pope him selfe, whome they doe att preasent hold engaged unto the blindfold mentaining of all their passions, namely of their naughty right against the Jansenists.

"[The next two out of Augier's four and a half closely written folio pages are expended on the injured Jansenists; on the great French Jesuitical colonies in the West Indies, especially by the river Orenoque; on the Jesuit empire, the River of Plata, and the great civilization there by mechanicks, dances, games, war, etc. To all this Augier's proposed colony will be a check, for, as he says, he and all other Frenchmen who join will] render themselves not only tributary unto his said Ser^me Highnesse, according unto the conditions which may be regulated thereof, but will also insensibly accommodate them selves for the religion, on such terms as shall be secretly managed with them—regarding amongst others the exclusion of the said Jesuists, missionaries, & muncks, their sworne ennemies; whome they could not avoide to receive at first in the said colonie though in little number; observing them & holding their bridle so short that it will be easie to expelle them when soever they shall have agreed thereof with his said Ser^me Highnesse.

"[Then on Jansenists, Calvinists, and Puritans.]"[8]

The enterprise of Huguenots became an important feature in the settlement of several colonies; and Thomas Dongan, the Catholic Governor of New York, accorded them a kindly reception.[9] They

[8] P. R. O., *Colonial Papers*, xiii. No. 28.
[9] *Ibid.*, lx.: Dongan to Lords of Trade, received May 9, 1687, No. 16.—Cf. Brodhead, *Documents*, iii. 399, 419.

came from St. Christopher and England. But it will furnish a term of comparison between the encouragement afforded such foreign settlers of the Protestant religion and the Conditions of Plantation forced by Lord Baltimore on his invited missionaries, if we take the case of Carolina in 1679.

The Lords Proprietors of Carolina receive kindly a petition of "Protestant and proselyte foreigners," who seek a retreat in the American colonies and particularly in Carolina; and they grant to René Petit and Jacob Guérard each a manor of 4000 acres; and the Lords of Trade and Plantation, besides granting a free passage in two of His Majesty's small ships, advance £2000 to be recovered eventually from the customs on the commodities of Carolina. Four score Protestant families are promised, who can produce silk, oils and wines, and will consume English goods; and they will thus be on the ground as an inducement to receive "yearly a great number of other foreign Protestants, their brethren, who are daily seen to return into Babylon [France], not being able to find in England such employments as might be agreeable with their skill and industry." The Commissioners of the Customs being referred to on the subject of this generosity, had nothing further to say in criticism but that, if the Protestant families in question be already settled in England, they should be encouraged to stay where they are; for too many families already betake themselves to the plantations in America and to the plantation in Ireland, unto the unpeopling and ruin of England; but, if the said families be not yet settled in England, then let all inducements be held out for the success of the colony.[10] (January-December, 1679). And this will suffice for the Huguenots and their prospects. We pass on to the Anglicans.

Huguenots in Carolina. 1679.

(3) The Anglican contribution to America in point of men was largely a subsidiary question, depending upon the tithes and glebes which were to attend the ministry. The ministers of the Established Church professed themselves to be helpless without the money establishment. For this several reasons were adduced in the triple order of a respectable morality, of a political propriety, and of an economic necessity.

Anglicans in North America. A Church establishment.

The moral reason was that, if a clergyman were poor, he would be

---

[10] P. R. O., *Colonial Entry Book*, xx. pp. 143, 144; cv. 308; cvi. 82.—Cf. *Calendar of State Papers, A. & W.I.*, v. §§ 875–1233, *passim*.—For the allusion to Ireland as a colonizing ground offered to needy Englishmen, Scotchmen, New Englanders, Waldenses of Piedmont, cf. Lingard, *History of England*, viii. 176, A.D. 1652.

contemned, and if he were contemned so would his function be; and that Julian the Apostate had stripped the clergy of their goods for this very purpose; since none would apply themselves or their sons to the study of divinity, if they should get nothing thereby to live on.[11] This was a view at Rome, too, among some people.[12] But Rome had always the Orders to fall back upon for priests, if not for poor bishops also; with whom, as the Jesuit Argento said well, the principle was somewhat different: "*Quorum vita despicitur, eorum prædicatio contemnitur*"—"They whose lives [not purses] draw down contempt do expose their ministry to contempt." The political reason which was urged for an establishment ran to the effect that the Anglican ministry had a right to tithes and glebes in England, as by law determined; and therefore it had a right to them everywhere. And the ground of economic necessity was simply this: No tithes, no ministers.

Captain Harvey, Governor of Virginia, set the good example in 1629 of asking that "six grave and conformable ministers be sent thither."[13] Eight years later, no cheery account was given by the Rev. Mr. Lane, who wrote from Barbados to his Grace of Canterbury: "We live," he said, "in the declining age of the world, wherein there is not to be found that youthfull zeale of Gods house, which was wont to eat up men; but on the contrary the world is full of sacrilegious cormorants, that eat up the house of God, which say to themselves: Let us take the houses of God in possession." He went on to describe the impoverished condition in which a minister had to live among the cormorants: ". . . The parishes allow, some 5000 lb., some 4000 lb. of tobacco or cotton wooll by the yeare, which though it may make some sound in England, yet considering our taxes & the excessive rates of commodities here, without other indirect courses, will so keep us here, as we may never hope to see our England againe. . . . For the taxes, they are such as I believe by Christians were never imposed upon the

Virginia, 1629. Barbados, 1637.

---

[11] J. Boucher, *Discourses*, pp. 233, 234, with quotation from Coke's Reports to the same effect.

[12] Cf. Urbano Cerri, *Relazione dello Stato della Congregazione e Missioni di Propaganda Fide*: "*Quando poi [i Vescovi della Congregazione della Propaganda] sono venuti [a Roma, ad limina], bisognerebbe subito spedirli e licentiarli sollecitamente senza che aspettino le risolutioni quali gli si possono mandare; mentre dimorando in Roma, non solo alla Congregatione sono di dispendio, et anco al Palazzo Apostolico, ma portano gran derisione e scredito, vedendosi andar per Roma a piedi accompagnati da un solo prete o servidore, con poco decoro della dignità episcopale, e dell' istessa Congregatione. Onde stimarei, ch' in tal caso fosse bene proibirgli il portar per Roma l'habito prelatitio, che privi di questa apparenza tornarebbero più presto alle loro diocesi.*" Corsini Library, cod. 284, f. 141v.

[13] P. R. O., *Colonial Papers*, v. No. 22.

clergie, being compelled to pay for the very heads upon our shoulders, for the heads of our wives & children above the age of 7 yeares & not borne in the island; no priviledge to ministers more than people: *Tros Tyrius*, &c. . . . Thus at present stands the state of the church here—these the greivances of the clergie: *Laicis semper invisus clerus.* . . . The next is that it [the clergy] is so much greived with exactions, which ought rather to be free, & more added than any thing substracted . . . ."[14] On the whole, however, the laity in Barbados would seem to have done fairly well. Within five or six years past, they had built six churches, besides some chapels. But then they put these in trust with their own vestry-men.

John Hammond, who had been in Virginia nineteen years, described its religious condition at the date of the Maryland expedition. He said, the people began "to grow not onely civil but great observers of the Sabbath; to stand upon their reputations; & to be ashamed of that notorious manner of life they had formerly lived & wallowed in. They then began to provide & send home for Gospel ministers, & largely contributed for their maintenance. But, Virginia savouring not handsomely in England, very few of good conversation would adventure thither, (as thinking it a place wherein surely the fear of God was not). Yet many came, such as wore black coats, & could babble in a pulpit, roare in a tavern, exact from their parishioners, & rather by their dissoluteness destroy than feed their flocks. Loath was the country to be wholy without teachers, and therefore rather retain these than to be destitute. Yet still endeavours for better in their places, which were obtained; and these wolves in sheeps cloathing by their assemblies questioned, silenced, and some forced to depart the country. Then began the Gospel to flourish."[15]

Virginia, 1635-1661.

Speaking more professionally, a writer addressed Guilbert, Lord Bishop of London, his Right Rev. Father in God, on the subject of *Virginia's Cure*, under date of September 2, 1661. Able ministers were wanted there; and an Act of Parliament should be procured "whereby a certain number of fellowships, as they happen next to be proportionably vacant in both the universities, may bear the name of Virginia Fellowships, as long as the needs of that church shall require it; and none be admitted to them, but such as shall engage by promise to hold them seven years & no longer; and, at the end of

[14] P. R. O., *Colonial Papers*, ix. No. 70: Thomas Lane, Barbados, "*pri. non. 8bris,*" October 6, 1637, to Archbishop Laud.
[15] J. Hammond, *Leah and Rachel*, p. 5, A.D. 1656 [corrected, "1655," with further addition in same old hand: "Jan. 29, 1655"].

those seven years, transport themselves to Virginia, & serve that church in the office of the ministry seven years more (the church there providing for them); which being expired, they shall be left to their own liberty to return or not; and, if they perform not the conditions of their admittance, then to be uncapable of any preferment. . . ." Great benefits indeed will accrue to the people from leading lives of virtue; as also great fruit among the heathen; and the writer quotes a well-known Jesuit: " This consideration enforced the accute Acosta, after he had spent seventeen years in conversing with the heathen in that new world (though he was of a church that pleads much for miracles), ingenuously to confesse, that the greatest, & even the only miracle necessary to the conversion of those heathen, is the gracious lives of Christians, agreeable to that Christian faith; & in this he subscribes but to St. Chrysostome. . . ." The writer pleads urgency. He says: "While the grasse growes the steed starves." Hence there should be an immediate enforcement of contributions from "every tythable person" in really good tobacco, for the support and encouragement of ministers.[16]

Such a representation was of the kind used by the Bishop of London at the Board of Trade and Plantations. Hence, while his censor gave an *imprimatur* to the narrative for public reading and edification,[17] the Board of Trade issued instructions to Sir William Berkeley, Governor of Virginia, about promoting the devout and dutiful service of Almighty God throughout the extent of his government. The churches already built were to be kept in order; more were to be added; and houses also for the ministers, of whom each should have one hundred acres of land assigned to him for a glebe. This was a fair allowance in an old colony like Virginia, at the date of September 12, 1662.[18]

Plans for building up the ministry. 1662-1671.

From other quarters other plans were proposed for the building up of the ministry. Sir Charles Wheler, Governor of the Leeward Islands, contended that, the means to support ministers being on hand, the only thing lacking was the power of the bishops to send men out. " I would it were seriously considered," he says, " why it should be a breach upon the liberty & freehold of an Englishman to be sent abroad by the King to preach, any more than to press a souldier & seaman, both being warfares, & the latter [the minister's] of fifty

[16] *Virginia's Cure*, pp. 10, 11, 20-22.
[17] On fly-leaf: " *Imprimatur*, Geo. Stradling, S.T.P., ex æd. Sabaud., Sept. 15, 1662: *Rever. in Christo Pat. Gilb. Episc. Lond. a sac. domest.*"
[18] P. R. O., *Colonial Entry Book*, lxxix. p. 265, *seqq*.

times the consequence to the Crown; for noe good Christian was ever a bad subject; (I meane at long runn, though not upon an immergent occasion when souldiers are prest). But the reason is highly more strong for the commands [command?] of preists; because they are brought up at the King's charge in his colledges, and in the colledges of other good benefactors, which revenue is continued by the grace & piety of the King. And, because I doe serve for an university in Parliament, I am the more bold to affirme (though it may be contrary to their sense) that it would be for the generall good of the universities, if young men, when they come first to practise preaching, were, instead of retireing into remote parts for tenn pounds a yeare, and into schooles to be ushers, and some to teach A B C to children, might be chosen by the universitys to goe into the plantations for five yeares, to have the charges of their voyage backwards & forwards defrayed, and an hundred pounds sterling per annum allowed them while they are there; and His Majesty's countenance at their returne; as usually the chaplaines who goe out with the fleet have been most graciously, some in one kind, some in another, rewarded. But, because I thinke that will not be, I have obtained from the councells and assemblys that I may dispose of the revenues of the church according to my designe, provided I take care to supply them with preaching ministers. And, if I do not take very wrong measures, I shall once in the space of a yeare erect a colledge or two, out of which the government shall be supplyed with able & pious men." [19]

Another plan, like that of Sir Thomas Lynch, ex-Governor of Jamaica, recommended that a couple of considerable prebendaries, such as those of Eton, Westminster, Lincoln, etc., should be attached to the island, for the maintenance of two good, grave, learned men, who, like commissaries, should keep the rest in order; the ministers meanwhile being each provided with £100 sterling a year, or even more.[20]

Jamaica, 1675. St. Christopher, 1680.

Finally, we may touch upon one reason for urgency not yet mentioned. It is stated by the Council of St. Christopher, at the time when the gentlemen thank the energetic Compton, Bishop of London, for his charity and piety in their behalf. They beseech him to send out on the next occasion men of riper years, better read in divinity, than those last young graduates that came hither; for fear,

---

[19] P. R. O., *Colonial Papers*, xxvii. No. 52, § 24: Answer to twenty-four queries of Council for Foreign Plantations; from St. Christopher, December 9, 1671.
[20] Cf. *Calendar of State Papers, Colonial, A. & W.I.*, iv. § 571, [May], 1675.

when a dispute arises between them and the clergymen of the Church of Rome, who are in the French part of the island, the young ministers be foiled in argument; for, without question, the Roman priests there are men of great learning and parts.²¹ So, what with the French missionaries disposing as they choose of the young men's arguments, and a French Knight of Malta, Governor in the French part of the island, always able to turn the English out whenever he chose, as Sir Charles Wheler informed their lordships in 1671,²² the English tenure of land and logic in St. Kitts was somewhat precarious. Priests, knights, and the English in St. Kitts.

What we have said will suffice to determine the bearings of denominational life and activity during a generation or two, before and after the time when Father White made his first voyage. We must now add some lines to the picture from the side of the Propaganda.

§ 31. On a canvas practically blank in ecclesiastical history, we propose briefly to draw a sketch, showing the missionary activity of the Catholic Church in the West Indian islands at the time of their first settlement and development. These islands, in the early part of the seventeenth century, exhibited the general lines of missionary policy which might be seen at this time, and for a century afterwards, governing all the outlying countries of the world. Maryland reproduced at once some characteristic features. Though very much of the literature which supplies the data is of a contentious kind, and therefore not to be taken as history on the subjects of contention, still the principal threads of the narrative appear distinctly enough in the cross-texture.

A paper which purports to be a Relation supplied for the information of the Propaganda (November 23, 1665) describes the beginnings of the Little Antilles in this wise: "The Spaniards who first proceeded to the conquest of Mexico, passing by the islands which lie on the coast of America, called them the Islas Antilas; and the French up to this day still give them the name of Antilles or Caribs, from a barbarous nation of that name who dwelt there. Though the Spaniards landed here, they did not think the islands worthy of occupation.¹ They only took in water

The Little Antilles, 1625.

---

²¹ Cf. *Ibid.*, v. § 1441, p. 572; from St. Christopher, July 12, 1680.
²² *Ibid.*, iii. § 680, p. 291, December 9, 1671.
¹ Compare the statements in the diplomatic controversy between England and Spain under James I. *Calendar of State Papers, Colonial, A. & W.I.*, i. 16,

and supplies, and then went on their way, pursuing greater objects, especially that of reducing the vast continent beyond. It is now thirty or forty years since a French gentleman of Normandy [Nambuc], seeking his fortune by sea, was accidentally driven ashore on one of these islands, at present called St. Christopher, where he began to settle. About the same time an Englishman named Warner came also to the same island and in similar circumstances. The two being equal in strength, they divided the island between them after this fashion; the English occupied the middle of the island and the French the two capes; and so they continue up to the present in peace with one another, without mutual molestation." [2]

This paper, which is attributed to a "Scotch gentleman" unnamed, without any intimation whether or no he drew his information from personal acquaintance with the islands or America, conveys, besides some pregnant passages that seem to have been interpolated, only common items of history, which had just then become public. The Dominican Father J. B. du Tertre, whom we shall have occasion to mention again, had returned from the islands, and published a work on the West Indies in 1654; and in 1658 a César de Rochefort or Francisco Raymundo had produced a similar book at Rotterdam.[3]

On looking at the map, it may be seen that the extensive line of the Little Antilles forms an arc or bow, from near the mouth of the Orinoco in South America to the first of the Great Antilles, Porto Rico; and English politics and geography divide the arc into two sections, the Windward Islands to the south-east and the Leeward to the north-west. St. Christopher, "the mother island," as Colonel Philip Warner, Governor of Antigua, called it,[4] is in the middle of the Leeward or north-west bow of the islands. Guadeloupe and Martinique, which were next in rank as missionary centres, are connecting links of the Leeward and the Windward groups, with Dominica between them. Southward the arc takes in Barbados, Grenada, Tobago, and terminates in Trinidad.

Northwards and west, the line terminates in the Virgin group,

The Antilles, Little and Great.

A.D. 1613, November, seq.—See Map of the Lesser Antilles opposite, adapted from L. Carrez, S.J., *Atlas Geographicus Societatis Jesu*, Chart No. 22, "Les Petites Antilles."
   [2] Propaganda Archives, *America*, 257, f. 78.—Endorsed, f. 81v: "23 Novembris, 1665. America. Relatione delle isole Americane scritta da un gentilhuomo Scozzese, 72. 1. 33."
   [3] Justin Winsor, *America*, viii. 270.—The latter work published at Rotterdam is very little to our purpose.
   [4] P. R. O., *Calendar of State Papers, Colonial, A. & W.I.*, iv. § 861, A.D. 1676, April 3.

including Santa Cruz (Crux, Cruise, Croce, Croix), and then merges into the Great Antilles, that is, Porto Rico, Hispaniola or San Domingo, Jamaica, Cuba. Southwards and east, far distant on the coast of South America, and out of the range of the West Indies is the island called Cayenne, which appears in the French Nuncio's papers of the time as "Carena." Urbano Cerri, in his pamphlet dedicated to Innocent XI. (1677), while improving the account of the "Scotch gentleman" unnamed and uncited, knows so little of what he silently interpolates, that he puts down Cayenne as a West Indian island, apparently between St. Christopher and Martinique.[5]

Cayenne, South America.

According to the Scotchman's date, given as "thirty or forty years" previously, it would be in 1625 that the Frenchman landed in St. Christopher, or as the English called it St. Kitts. This is precisely the date which the histories give.[6] And it is the same which, from his own archives, the Procurator-General of the Society reported in 1659 as the time when Jesuit missions had commenced in St. Christopher. Answering documents referred to him by the Propaganda, that official stated: "The General of the said Society, in virtue of the authority which he has from this Holy Apostolic See, did send, in the year 1625, three Fathers of the same Society to the island of St. Christopher, with the nobleman M. de Nambuc, Governor of the said island, to exercise there spiritual functions and ministries for the good of infidels, heretics, and Catholics, as in fact they have done up to this time."[7] This gentleman, M. de Nambuc (D'Esnambuc), is spoken of as the first French Governor in those parts. His deputies or successors in St. Christopher or Guadeloupe were De Lolieu, Du Plessy, Houël, Aubert; while the Knights of Malta came as viceroys, the Chevaliers De Poinsy, De Toisy, De St. Lawrence. Meanwhile the English waxed strong in the island of St. Kitts; and it was merely owing to the superior prowess of the Knights of Malta, for whom they entertained the profoundest respect, that they did not acquire the predominance for generations. On the contrary, they lost St. Christopher, to the great prejudice of the Irish settlers, who, ranking with the English, lost all with them, while by the English they were ranked as domestic foes, because they were known to sympathize with the French.

Jesuit missionaries in St. Kitts, 1625.

Knights of Malta.

---

[5] Corsini Library, cod. 283, f. 207: "*Isole Antilles: ... In quelle, che si possiedono dal Re di Francia, ch' oltre San Christoforo sono le Caienne, Martinica e Guadalupe, ed altre più piccole.*"

[6] Justin Winsor, *America*, viii. 306.

[7] Propaganda Archives, *America*, 257, f. 56.

(1) In 1639, as Justin Winsor observes,[8] the Jesuit missionary, Father Pierre Pelleprat, was in the West Indies, whence he with Father Méland penetrated by 1652 into the valley of the Orinoco, South America.[9] This is the country which was called Guiana. Father Grillet followed, both in his advent to the West Indies and in his subsequent explorations with Father Béchamel among the natives of the continent.

(1) Jesuits. Guiana, Guadeloupe, St. Christopher, Martinique.

As time advanced (May 29, 1645), the French governor Houël, returning from France, brought over four Jesuits and two Capuchins. The latter remaining in Guadeloupe, the Jesuits moved on to St. Christopher,[10] where, as the French Nuncio reported for 1651 (Paris, January 27), there were three or four Jesuits, six or seven Carmelites, and some secular priests; while in Guadeloupe there were Dominicans; and in Martinique Jesuits.[11]

At this time a memorandum appears in which their Eminences are informed that "the missionaries of the Company of Jesus, who are in the islands and southern parts of America, that is, in St. Christopher, Martinique, and other islands subject to the Crown of France, humbly request that their Superior John Hallé, or whoever else shall be, for the time being, superior of the whole mission, may have those graces accorded him which the Sacred Congregation is wont to grant to the missions of the Indies, in such manner as to be communicable to others of the same mission." Another hand affixes to this memorandum the note: "The same grace, as to the superior for the time being, is asked for Canada."[12] The petitions were submitted for further consideration on the part of the Congregation (May 15, 1651).[13]

Faculties from the S. Congregation, 1651. Also for Canada.

The form of the petition, or of the memorandum, is singular, inasmuch as Jesuit missionaries ask for the "graces" referred to, and not the Procurator-General or Superior-General in their name. The subject, however, of the petition might indeed seem to be the powers or authority of an Ordinary or Prefect-Apostolic. For the Dominican nuns of the Third Order, who come three years later to establish an educational institution in Martinique, state to the Pope that the Jesuit Fathers in the island,

Dominican nuns in Martinique, 1656.

---

[8] *History of America*, viii. 363.
[9] P. Mury, *Les Jésuites à Cayenne*, p. xiv.—Compare Archives de l'École de Ste. Geneviève; 2 *Antilles-Guiane*; 1 *Guiane*.
[10] Propaganda Archives, *II America*, 260, ff. 222-233 : Raymond Breton's Relation, 1656, December 28.
[11] *Ibid.*, ff. 178, 186.
[12] *Ibid.*, "Mem. 1651, 2°."
[13] *Ibid.*, f. 285, "S. Card. d'Este."

"who exercise the authority of an Ordinary here,"[14] have declined to discharge the ministries which the nuns desire at their hands, and have referred them to the Sacred Congregation and His Holiness (March 27, 1656).[15]

Meanwhile the Nuncio informed Cardinal Pamphilj (March 8, 1652) that, "at St. Christopher there are about 8000 French, about 12,000 English and Irish, the latter being chiefly Catholic." In Martinique, he says, "there are 6000 French, and some ancient inhabitants of the islands who are called savages. In Guadeloupe there are 4000 French, and no savages of the former inhabitants. In the other islands adjoining, which are numerous, there are still many of the aborigines." After speaking about Cayenne and the bishopric proposed there by the Duke de Ventadour, "Canon of Notre Dame in Paris," he numbers the missionaries thus: "In the islands near to St. Christopher, Martinique, and Guadeloupe, there are seventeen Jesuit missionary Fathers; and others are sent as needed. There are about five or six Dominicans, and as many Carmelites."[16] The population and distribution of missionaries in the same islands as reported by the same Paris Nuncio three years later (December 31, 1655), differ somewhat from the foregoing: in St. Christopher, he says, 15,000, with "some Jesuits and Carmelites;" in Guadeloupe, 10,000 souls, with "a few Dominicans, and one or other Carmelite and Jesuit;" in Martinique, 15,000 to 20,000 souls, with "Jesuit Fathers;" and Grenada, with "a few Dominicans." He desires more; and he sends a handsome map engraved by the geographer-royal, P. du Val d'Abbeville, with the inscription in French: "Isles of America, called Carib or Cannibal and Windward."[17] An official summary on the state of St. Christopher, Guadeloupe, and Martinique, says of the missionaries, that "the greater number are Jesuits; they live in all three islands; they have there the finest residences, and render the greatest service to the Church of God."[18] Then, after speaking of the other regulars, the document proceeds to treat the question of appointing a Bishop or Vicar-Apostolic in those parts.

Here the account credited to the anonymous Scotch gentleman

---

[14] "*Qui in ea insula Ordinarii locum tenent.*"
[15] Propaganda Archives, *II America*, ff. 362-365, "Sig. Card. Bichi."
[16] *Ibid.*, f. 101.
[17] "*Isles d'Amerique dites Caribes ou Cannibales et de Barlovento.*"—*Ibid.*, ff. 65-68.
[18] Propaganda Archives, *America*, 257, f. 88, s. d.: "*De Gesuiti v'è maggior numero; habitano in tutte tre l'Isole, e vi hanno bellissime case, e rendono maggior servizio alla Chiesa di Dio.*"

ten years later is much more significant and pointed than the Nuncio's;

The Scotch gentleman's account, 1665.
while Urbano Cerri, in his pamphlet, improving on the Scotchman, assumes the air of a connoisseur in West Indian matters. Neither Relation has the credit of contributing new material, save here, where both seem to be original for a purpose. The gentleman is made to say: "In these islands there are missions composed of Jesuits and Dominicans. At St. Christopher there are Carmelites; but they do not exercise any cure of souls in the island, where the Jesuits act as curates; and so do the Dominicans in Guadeloupe. In Martinique are the Jesuits, and in all these parts they are considerably more powerful and numerous than the Dominicans. There are also some secular priests, but without any ecclesiastical government or hierarchy, which the Jesuits will oppose with all their power; and that is no trifle."[19] Following the Scotchman

Urbano Cerri's improvement. 1677.
to the letter, but usually condensing him, Urbano Cerri at this point improves and enlarges on him, and changes the prophecy of future opposition into an actual fact; but the best part of the improvement is the touch where Cerri throws in a remark about the voluptuousness of the islands, implying that the Jesuits want to lead the life of libertines there. He says: "In St. Christopher there are discalced Carmelites, but they do not exercise any cure of souls; there are also some secular priests without any authority or hierarchy, which the Jesuits oppose with all their power, because they should wish, after their usual fashion, to be alone in that island, which is rich to a degree and delicious."[20] That is the style of Urbano Cerri's pamphlet, except that this particular passage does not exhibit all the sentiment which exudes elsewhere.

Passing by the island of Dominica, where, as Raymond Breton says in his report,[21] two Jesuit missionaries had been killed by the savages

---

[19] *Ibid., America*, 257, f. 79ᵛ: "... *alcuni preti secolari, ma senza governo sacro e gierarchia, alla quale s'opporranno i Giesuiti con tutt' il loro potere, quale non è poco* ..." The object of the Relation may be seen a little farther on, f. 8ᵛ, in another insinuation of the same tenor, viz. that the evils prevalent in those parts can be remedied by establishing a "Church formed," that is by instituting an Ordinary; but the Jesuits, who mean to become absolute masters of those islands, temporally as well as spiritually, will oppose the project with all their might, and will not be wanting in artifice to accomplish their purpose: "*ma i Giesuiti, i quali (sia detto tra noi) hanno disegno di impadronirsi tanto del temporale quanto dello spirituale di quelle isole, s'opporranno con tutte le loro forze; ne gli mancaranno artificii di venire a capo di questo loro disegno.*"

[20] Corsini Library, 283, *Isole Antilles*, f. 207ᵛ: "*In San Christoforo vi sono li Carmelitani Scalzi, ma non vi esercitano cura d'anime; vi è anche qualche numero di Preti Secolari senza alcuna autorità e Gerarchia, alle quali s'oppongono i Giesuiti con tutto il loro potere: che vorrebbero secondo il loro costume esser soli in quell' isola assai abbondante e delitiosa.*"—For another specimen of Cerri's manner and style, cf. *supra*, § 10, p. 202, note 20.

[21] Propaganda Archives, *II America*, 260, f. 228.

(1650–1652), we meet with Father John Grillet, who from this time forward is a commanding figure. He appears in a State Paper of William Lord Willoughby, as having received special favour and courtesy from this gentleman, then Governor of Barbados. For the French General, M. de la Barre, saluting Willoughby, who had just sailed into the Nevis Road, thanks him particularly for the attentions paid to Grillet (January 2, 1668).[22] The other replies (January 3): "As to Father Grilliett, he merrited much more of civillity than I was capable to show him; and doubtless it is his goodness if hee doth not complaine; but I am now between the Tropics."[23]

Dominica. Two Jesuits killed. 1650-1652.

Lord Willoughby and the Jesuit Grillet. 1668.

In a letter to the Cardinals indited after he has been liberated from a prison in Holland, Father Grillet, on May 18, 1677, reviews to some extent the history of the past, and presents his petition regarding the conduct of ecclesiastical matters for the future in the three islands of Martinique, Guadeloupe, St. Christopher, and also in Cayenne, situated off the South American shore. He tells of his having been carried off by the Dutch from the missions of America [Cayenne, Surinam, Guiana], and of his being on the point of returning now with three other priests of the Society. He says that "we have been in the islands of the Antilles since the year 1640;" that "at present we number fifteen priests of the Society, besides some lay brothers. We are in the islands of Martinique, Guadeloupe, and St. Christopher, which lie over against the Gulf of Mexico, besides Cayenne detached a little from the continent." He describes how the low state of morals almost extinct among European Catholics has been elevated, and a large number of heretics brought into the fold. As to barbarians, there are the negroes imported as slaves from Africa, and more than 20,000 of them have been instructed in the Catholic faith, with excellent results. Many other heathens have been won to Christ, besides infants baptized before death. Now the way is open into the continent through Cayenne; and the labourers must be ready to face enormous difficulties. There is the hostility of savages and heretics, whereby several of the missionaries have already lost their lives; there is the unhealthiness of the climate, which has forced many others, in spite of themselves, to go back to Europe, whence, however, they have

Grillet's review of the missions, 1640-1677.

---

[22] "*Je suis tout à fait redevable a vostre courtoisie pour les graces et civilités qu'il vous a pleu faire a R. P. Grillet. Je voudrois par quelque service important en mon particulier vous en tesmoigner ma recognoissance. Je le ferois de tout mon cœur.*"

[23] P. R. O., *Colonial Papers*, xxii., Nos. 2, i. ii.

come twice, thrice, to resume their former labours, with whatever little strength they have been able to recover. He himself has been twenty-three years there.

The important part of the letter is that which follows about the faculties. The General's name does not occur. Grillet says: "Since the enemy's fleets hold the sea, the letters of our Superior [Lemercier] have not yet reached us. And therefore in the name of all I humbly and earnestly ask you to confirm or renew the faculties which heretofore the Holy Apostolic See [from the Congregation of the Holy Office] often granted us through your Sacred Congregation; so that with inviolate fidelity as heretofore we may be enabled to assist those who are in need or in danger. But, since that same Superior whom I named, Father Francis Lemercier, is broken down with age, which keeps us in a state of anxiety, it would be a special favour, if not a necessary precaution, in case he vacated his office for one reason or other before the expiration of the faculties, that he had the power of subdelegating his successor in office for the time being (just as in the case of death),[24] until the Holy See, being forthwith informed by the said successor, should provide otherwise."[25]

The petition for faculties. 1677-1680.

---

[24] "*Singularis beneficii necnon necessarii forte quandoque præsidii loco foret ut, si ob hanc aliamve causam ante præfixum facultatibus terminum ab officio discederet, qui succederet ab eo subdelegari ac supplere posset interim (sicut in casu mortis) donec Sancta Sedes Apostolica ab eodem successore certior quam primum facta alio modo provideret.*"—Cf. *supra*, § 30, p. 289; the "Jesuitical Colony" on the Orenoque.

[25] Propaganda Archives, *America, Antille I.*, ff. 256, 257. From the Sacred Congregation of the Inquisition or Holy Office, not from the Propaganda, faculties under twenty-eight heads were granted for fifteen years to Jerome Lallemant, Superior of the Jesuit Mission in Canada; they contained all that is asked for by Grillet; their date was February 20, 1648. In 1651, as mentioned above, Jean Hallé, Superior of the Society in the West Indies, made the general request which has been cited before (*supra*, p. 298); and it was added that the same favour was asked for Canada. In 1657, on May 24, the Holy Office granted faculties under twenty-six heads for seven years to Father Alexander Rhodes, the Jesuit Superior in Persia; but the point of subdelegating does not appear. On the same day it granted the same faculties to Father Nicolaus Poresson [Bresson], Jesuit Superior in Soria [Syria ?], and to Francis Martin, Jesuit Superior at Constantinople. On August 30 of the same year it accorded the same to Henry de Vivier, Jesuit Superior of the Missions and Residences of South America (*Americæ Meridionalis*). Then the whole of this document, with all these concessions, is dated February 4, 1664, as if renewed at that date, the close of the septennium. But the petitioners at this time are John Grillet, S.J., for the West Indies; Jerome Lallemant, S.J., for North America; Joseph Besson, S.J., for Persia; and Nicholaus de Ste. Geneviève, S.J., for Greece; and they ask for fifteen years in their respective petitions, as the summary presented states. Thirteen years afterwards we have the petition of Grillet, as presented here in the text; and a corresponding summary appears, recommending precisely what has been asked for on account of Father Francis Le Mercier, and in his name.—The foregoing documents lie as follows: Propaganda Archives, *II. America*, 260, ff. 76, 82; *Ibid.*, "Mem. 1651 v[?]2°;" *America*, 257, ff. 67, 68; *Ibid.*, ff. 62, 64; *America, Antille I.*, ff. 256, 257; *America Centrale I.*, f. 23.—The whole question of missionary faculties, and of the Jesuit missionaries' dependance on their own regular superiors or other ecclesiastical authorities, may be reserved for a future place in this History.

Three years and a half after Grillet's petition (October 11, 1680), there appears a letter of Father John Paul Oliva, General of the Society, to Monsignor Cybo, secretary of the Propaganda, in which he acknowledges the expression of satisfaction on the part of their Eminences at the work of the Jesuit missionaries in "the islands Caienne." He also thanks the secretary in particular for having sent him, unsealed, the letter directed to Father Le Mercier by the same Congregation, that the General himself might inspect it, and then forward it.[26]

While the rival generals, Willoughby and De la Barre, appreciated Father Grillet, the Count d'Estrées, Admiral of the French Fleet which annihilated the Dutch forces at Tobago, wrote (April 16, 1677) to the Father General Oliva about Père Frémont, who had distinguished himself in an extraordinary manner for his courage during the sea-fight. The admiral tells of the success with which Frémont, while aboard the flagship, converted heretics and brought back Catholics to a good life. And now he cannot but second the good Father's ardent desires of devoting himself to the conversion of the savages of America, and that with the help of some other Fathers, if the General would kindly take the matter into consideration. For reasons of personal friendship he intercedes thus, when perhaps the offices of the Cardinal d'Estrées might have been engaged with more propriety.[27] *Admiral d'Estrées and Père Frémont.*

However, the Superiors of the Society were always of the opinion that even the offices of good admirals might be omitted without any impropriety, in the matter of marshalling Jesuit forces.

(2) As appears by the foregoing account, the Jesuits were not the only missionaries in the field. There were members of the older Orders, the Dominicans, the Carmelites, Augustinians, and Capuchins. There was also mention made of Lazarists, *(2) Dominicans.* or members of the Congregation of the Mission, and of the other Paris Congregation called the Society of Foreign Missions. And there were not wanting secular clergymen, at least from Ireland. To understand in any part of the missionary world the action and interaction of these various forces during the seventeenth and eighteenth centuries, it would be necessary to draw a sharp distinction between certain organic principles of the older Orders and some

---

[26] "*La singolare gentilezza che meco adopera, nell' inviarmi a sigillo volante il foglio diretto al P. Le Mercier dalla Sacra Congregazione, che ancor chiuso sarebbe stato da me trasmesso, con la fedeltà dovuta.*" Propaganda Archives, *America, Antille I.,* f. 262.

[27] *Ibid.,* ff. 259, 260.

new facts which stood out in relation to the Propaganda; as well as, for the purpose of this entire History, to notice certain constitutional differences between other regulars and the Jesuits; and, in all cases, to avoid confounding the Orders themselves with the individuals who might start up in a sporadic way here or there, bearing an Order's name. But, however well-timed such considerations would be when made, this is not the place to make them, while we are hurrying on to our own field of action. Suffice it to have observed that there are such qualifications of principles as distinct from facts, of institutions as apart from persons, and of organizations as strikingly different one from another. And, merely to supplement an observation made before about a supposed antagonism between the secular and regular clergy, we note that, in this rich variety of men and means organized by the Church into the units of regular institutes, there may start a movement of rivalry, which individuals within can set up, and critics without run down, as if it were an essential antagonism between one regular Order and another.

A long account of the Dominican Father Raymond Breton covers the period from 1635 to 1656, some twenty-one years. A company of French merchants, patronized by Cardinal Richelieu, and organized in 1635 by De Lolieu and Du Plessy, was bound by its charter to take over at its own expense four priests for the West Indian service. Reluctantly, says Breton, the Dominican Commissary and Prior of the Novitiate in Paris, Father Carré, granted for the purpose Peter Pellican, a Paris doctor, who was to be Vicar; Peter Griffon, Nicholas Bruchet, and Raymond Breton. They arrived at Guadeloupe on June 29, 1635. In six months Fathers Pellican and Griffon, being sick, returned to France. During the twenty-one years which follow there seem to have gone over about twenty-one Dominican Fathers and five lay-brothers. When Breton himself returned to Europe in 1653, he left two Fathers behind him. All the others had come and gone or died. Guadeloupe was their head-quarters; but Breton had a station also in Dominica.

Relation of P. Breton. 1635-1656. Guadeloupe, Dominica.

One who had come and gone, and had done so twice, was Father J. B. du Tertre, who left in 1642 and again in 1647. Abandoning the missionary life, he devoted himself to writing history,[28] which function, if less heroic than that of the missionary, is still capable of being appreciated by posterity. A

Du Tertre and others. 1642-1648.

[28] Cf. Justin Winsor, *America*, viii. 270; Du Tertre's *Histoire générale des isles de Saint Christophe, de la Guadeloupe, de la Martinique*, 1654; and *Histoire générale des Ant-Isles habitées par les Français*, Paris, 1667–1671.

little after Du Tertre's departure, the superior, Father Armand, O.P., died, and appointed Raymond Breton his successor as Prefect of the mission (1648).

Here begin the troubles which give occasion to the series of relations, petitions, memorials, extant in the archives. Neither the Governor Houël, nor the Jesuit Fathers Hallé and Jacquinot, nor the Augustinian Giles Gendron, nor the Carmelite Claude of St. Joseph, nor all of them together sitting in congress (1652) would hear of Breton's claim to authority. However, Raymond goes on to narrate how almost each and every one of these perverse men either died soon or was expelled by Houël himself, albeit the said Governor never became a friend to Raymond. The visitation on the Jesuits who were involved was that the Rector of the station in Guadeloupe abandoned his place, was kicked by his horse, and died in Martinique; the second died a placid death in Guadeloupe; a third was still surviving, taking care of the Irish, since he was himself an Irishman. While pleading his case in Europe, Breton, with the assistance of his General, obtained a decree from the Propaganda, forbidding priests to administer the Sacraments in those islands, unless they had a legitimate approbation or apostolic faculties; and they were required to show their faculties for the satisfaction of the Prefect of the mission (1655). But this left the question of Breton's claim to the prefecture just where it was; and so he resigned. His paper was dated from the Novitiate in Paris, December 28, 1656.[29]

Breton's authority ignored. 1652, 1655, 1656.

After his return to Europe, four Dominican nuns of the Third Order had sailed for Martinique (1654). A Father accompanied them. Raymond had previously arranged "peaceably" with the Jesuit Fathers and Du Parquet, the Governor, that the nuns should have a station in Martinique. We find several papers or petitions of the good Sisters to the Pope and the Propaganda, begging for the spiritual assistance which the Jesuits, according to their rule, declined to give (March 27, 1656).[30] The attempt which the Dominican nuns made on this occasion at establishing a system of female education in Martinique was about fifteen years after the establishment of the Ursuline nuns in Quebec for the same purpose.[31] Though the petitions of these religious women were under consideration in Rome on March 27, 1656, Breton

Four Dominican nuns. Martinique. 1654-1656.

---

[29] Propaganda Archives, *II. America*, 260, ff. 222–233.—Cf. *infra*, § 58, p. 470.
[30] *Ibid.*, ff. 262–264.
[31] Cf. C. de Rochemonteix, *Les Jésuites et la Nouvelle France*, i. 306.

says, in his paper of December the same year, that they are all dead.[32]

The population. The population of the islands he describes as made up of blacks from Guinea and Angola, Frenchmen, Spaniards, Belgians, Dutch, Portuguese, Danes, Swedes, Greeks, Turks, freedmen not a few, and heretics. "We have fed all these," he says, "with the food of the word."

The end of his paper is an indictment of his own superiors in the Order, unheard-of difficulties being put in his way. This unhappy trait in his communication is only one instance of an everlasting law in operation, to the effect that, in the depositories of administrative bureaus, the tide of representation, remonstrance, or obloquy rises ever in an inverse ratio with the level of success, efficiency, and the spirit of obedience.

(3) Of the Augustinians and Carmelites there occurs but little beyond the incidental notices already mentioned. The Augustinian Giles Gendron, named by Raymond Breton as one of his opponents (1652), had just arrived with René le Bourdagos from Rochelle, whence they had written to the secretary of the Propaganda (August 13, 1651), returning infinite thanks for their appointment to a mission in the islands of America. They were now being conveyed in "an heretical ship;" preachers of the Roman faith, they remarked, being conducted by "heretics of Rochelle, who have already expelled that faith from their hearts and their hearths; and so salvation shall come from our enemies."[33]

(3) Augustinians. 1651.

In like manner, the General of the Carmelites, Fra Girolamo Ari, writing from Paris in 1663 (March 2), takes pains to commend a request, preferred by some of his religious in the West Indies, "to be declared Missionaries-Apostolic with the usual faculties," that is, to be deputed by the Propaganda in its own name.[34] He commends the whole province of Turenne for their missionary work in the islands; where they began with a couple in 1646, under the orders of the General, Buonfiglioli, and had succeeded so well that the Viceroy De Poinsy demanded more of their members; and thither "many of the more fervent being selected were sent by the Provincial and Definitors of the said Province." So they had

Carmelites. 1646-1663.

---

[32] Propaganda Archives, *II. America*, 260, f. 230.
[33] *Ibid.*, f. 42.
[34] Cf. *Collectanea, S.C. de Propaganda Fide*, p. 98, § 278; decree of August 19, 1743, on the name "Missionaries-Apostolic:" "*Denominationem Missionarii Apostolici non competere nisi alumnis Collegiorum Pontificiorum aliisque sacerdotibus ad missiones exercendas deputatis per speciale decretum Sacræ Congregationis.*"

§ 31]   CAPUCHINS AND ST. CHRISTOPHER   307

spread from St. Christopher to Guadeloupe, Capsterre,[35] Cabraira, and the Testuggini [Tortuga], in which places they had been the first evangelical labourers. In 1659 they had obtained from His Holiness the privilege of erecting a confraternity.

In consequence of this commendation, the Sacred Congregation, on the 5th of June in the same year, granted "the erection of a mission of the Carmelite friars in St. Christopher and other islands above mentioned." But, respecting some other matters touched upon in the Congregation, such as "erecting a bishopric for the eradication of abuses as narrated, fuller information is to be obtained, as also what regards the demand for faculties on the part of the Society instituted in France for Foreign Missions."[36] It was on the strength of this decree that the Relation attributed to the "Scotch gentleman" was drawn up; that reports were called for from the Paris Nuncio; and that "Lesley," who may have been the Jesuit Rector of the Scotch College in Rome, was cited in the official summary (November 23, 1665) on behalf of the French Society of Foreign Missions.[37]

The French Society for Foreign Missions. 1663–1665.

(4) The Capuchins have ever been famous missionaries; and in the new era they appear very largely as Missionaries-Apostolic under the Propaganda. For the sake of a case which occurs in Maryland within ten years after the settlement of that plantation, we must take special note of the fullest set of documents which appear at this juncture in connection with the Capuchins, and which have relation at the same time to the Society of Jesus.

(4) Capuchins.

Ten years after the Jesuits had entered St. Christopher with De Nambuc, the Sacred Congregation, on the report of Cardinal Spada, deputed (March 23, 1635) five Capuchins with one lay-brother for a mission to St. Christopher and adjacent islands in America, and four others to Cape Verde in Africa; all being placed under the authority of Father Paulinus, Provincial of the Capuchins in Normandy, who had power to delegate two of the said missionaries as prefects vested with the reformed faculties for Africa and America, and authorized to communicate the same, in whole or in part, to other priests already approved by the Definitors of the said province, etc.[38] The Capuchins entered on the ground, as Raymond

---

[35] *Cabesterre françoise* was only the other end of St. Kitts, away from *Basse terre françoise*, the English having the high ground and shores in the middle. Cf. map, Justin Winsor, *History of America*, viii. 234.
[36] Propaganda Archives, *America*, 257, f. 77 *bis*, 86, 82, 84.
[37] *Ibid.*, ff. 76, 78–80.
[38] *Ibid.*, f. 57.

Breton has informed us; and then, eight years after the former decree, there issued a new one from the same Congregation (June 30, 1643), stating that, on the report of the Cardinal di Sant' Onufrio [Antonio Barberini], the Cardinals issued "a second order to be communicated through the General of the Society of Jesus to his religious, bidding them abandon St. Christopher on the spot, since the Capuchins of Normandy are in that island, which was assigned to them by the Congregation; and this for the sake of avoiding contentions between his religious and the said Capuchins." [39]

St. Christopher. 1635-1659.

No action evidently having been taken on some such "repeated" orders, there appears, about seven years afterwards, a "Relation of all that has been done during six years in the mission of the Capuchin Fathers among the Indians in America, whereof I have been witness, Fra Hyacinth de Longueville, Capuchin of the Province of Normandy. . . ." He supplicates the Cardinals to demand of the Jesuits and Carmelites the restitution of the islands of Martinique and St. Christopher to the Capuchins: "Given in the Capuchin convent of Havre de Grace, March 1, 1650." [40] At this point the circumstances in Rome had changed. Francis Ingoli, secretary of the Propaganda since its foundation in 1622, died in 1649; and the year before (1648) the Prefect of the Propaganda, Cardinal Antonio Barberini, a Capuchin, had also died.

Death of Cardinal Barberini and of Ingoli, 1648, 1649.

Nine years now elapsed when Fra Emmanuel a Ponte Archo, Provincial of the Capuchin Province of Normandy, brought up the old decrees with a formal petition for urging their execution. He said in his denunciation that the Sacred Congregation had assigned the island of St. Christopher in America to the Capuchins; that, whereas the Fathers of the Society of Jesus had intruded upon that field without any authority from the Sacred Congregation, orders had twice been given in peremptory terms to the General of the Fathers of the said Society, to order his men out of the island as soon as possible, for the reasons contained in the decree; whereof a copy was herewith submitted.[41] But since they

[39] Propaganda Archives, *America*, 257, f. 57: "*Copia. . . . Decretum S. Congregationis de Propaganda Fide habitæ die* 30 *Junii*, 1643. ¶ *Referente Eminentissimo Domino Cardinale S. Honuphrii, Eminentissimi Patres jusserunt iterum per Generalem Societatis Jesu præcipi ejus religiosis, ut ab insula S. Christophori, in qua sunt Capucini Normandiæ missionarii, quam primum discedant, cum insula illa per S. Congregationem prædictis Capucinis Norman*[d]*iæ excolenda fuerit assignata; idque ad evitandam discordiam inter eosdem suos religiosos et prædictos Capucinos. Subsignatum, F. Antonius Cardinalis S. Honuphrii. Locus* + *sigilli . . .* 4 *Februarii*, 1659." The former date, 1643, is that of the decree; the latter, 1659, that of the subsequent reference to it.

[40] Propaganda Archives, *II. America*, 260, f. 16: 7 pp. 4°.

[41] "*Et, cum Patres Societatis Jesu absque ulla S. Congregationis auctoritate sese in*

did not obey, and stayed there still, therefore did the said Provincial ask for a confirmation of both decrees, and for the due execution of the latter (February 4, 1659).[42]

Now matters proceeded less summarily. Instead of the third decree asked for, ordering the Jesuits out once more, the proper note was appended: "Refer to the Procurator-General of the Society for

illam insulam introduxissent, per eosdem Eminentissimos Patres fuit absolute bis imperatum Generali Patrum dictæ Societatis, ut ab ea insula suos quamprimum discedere præciperet, ob rationes in decreto cujus copia etiam exhibetur contentas; sed, cum non obedierint. . . ."

[42] Propaganda Archives, *America*, 257, f. 56. Other documents upon this case will serve to show the movement of missionary enterprise towards North America, under the direction of the Propaganda: The Sacred Congregation sanctioned a "mission proposed" for the islands of Guadalupe, Matalino, and Dominica (June 19, 1634). *Acta*, 10, f. 64^v.—The proposal of the Capuchin Norman Provincial, regarding a mission of his men to the "Island of St. Christopher near Affrica, to Cape Verde, and to Cape North in Affrica itself," was referred for inquiry, as to the political dependence of said places, whether they were French or Spanish (January 19, 1635, *coram Sanctissimo*). *Ibid.*, f. 167^v.—Four Spanish Capuchin priests with two lay-brothers were authorized to settle in Guadalupe, Mitallino, and Dominica (November 12, 1635). *Ibid.*, f. 340.—After explorations made in Cape Verde and "the Island of St. Christopher near Affrica," by the Norman Provincial of the Capuchins, the latter was authorized to equip a mission of his French friars, against the Dutchmen found to be in places vacated by the Portuguese [*i.e.* Surinam, Guiana, in South America?] (February 11, 1636, *coram SS^o*). *Acta*, 12, f. 18.—The Cardinal di Sant' Onufrio [the Capuchin Barberini] gave letters to the French ambassador, authorizing the despatch of Norman Capuchins to St. Christopher and Cape Verde (November 5, 1636). *Ibid.*, f. 183.—Five Capuchin priests and one lay-brother were despatched to the "Island of St. Christopher and others adjacent in America, and to Cape Verde in Affrica" (March 23, 1637, *coram SS^o*). *Ibid.*, ff. 265^v, 266.—Considerations on the Spanish Capuchin mission to Guadalupe, Mettalino, and Dominica (June 25, 1640, *coram SS^o*). *Acta*, 14, f. 122^v, 123.—Report of Father Josaphat, Provincial of the Norman Capuchins, on Cape Verde and on Cape North in America [Cape Breton?], and petition of the same that missions of other religious might be prohibited from going to those places where the Capuchins were, to avoid contentions. Answers of the S. Congregation; and to the last point the following reply was given: That the General of the Society of Jesus was the only one against whom the S. Congregation could not provide by direct order; and that therefore steps should be taken to acquire the same control over the Society as over other Orders: "*De prohibitione vero missionum aliorum religiosorum, quia Sacra Congregatio potest providere quoad omnes religiosos cujuscumque Ordinis, excepta Societate Jesu, cujus Generalis facit missiones ad sui beneplacitum sine recursu ad Sacram Congregationem, Eminentissimi Patres jusserunt hæc iterum referri coram Sanctissimo, quia indigent aliqua provisione; quæ illis videbatur fieri posse ut sequitur: Primo, restringenda videtur facultas prædicti Generalis Societatis Jesu, si quam habet ex Bullis pontificiis, eique prohibendum ne missiones faciat ad loca ubi sunt alii religiosi, nisi ibi sint etiam suorum religiosorum missiones; nec ad loca ubi non habet missiones, sine hac Sacra Congregatione ejusque decreto*" (August 20, 1640). *Ibid.*, ff. 137–139.—An order was issued that the Society should restore to the Capuchins the place in Martinique occupied by the Jesuit Fathers after the death of one and the departure of another Capuchin: "*Referente Eminentissimo D. Card. S^{ti}. Honuphrii, Sacra Congregatio censuit, si Sanctissimo placuerit: Primo, missionariis Capucinis in Guinea Affricæ concedendum esse usum jumenti; . . . 2°, eisdem concedendum[am] esse facultatem commutandi ferrum cum pane, vino et farina, dummodo contra Bullam Cœnæ Domini ferrum in dictas partes non deferant; 3°, jussit eisdem missionariis restitui locum missionis, quem habeba[n]t in Insula Martinia prope Americam, et quem, occasione mortis unius ex prædictis missionariis et discessus socii ejus, Patres Societatis Jesu ceperunt* (January 20, 1642, *coram SS^o*)." *Acta*, 15, f. 12^v.—Regarding the licence to barter in the second of these three points on behalf of the Capuchins, compare a decision in the same sense from the General of the Society on behalf of the Maryland missionaries. *Infra*, § 36, p. 339.

information." This official replied that "the General of the said Society, in virtue of the authority which he has from this Apostolic See, did, in the year 1625, send three Fathers of the Society to the island of St. Christopher with the nobleman, M. de Nambuc, Governor of the said island." While they laboured and were already established there for ten years, the Capuchin Fathers, in the year 1635, asked for the same mission, and obtained from this Sacred Congregation decrees, which, like the memorial itself, omitted all mention of the fact that the Fathers of the Society had been at work there, labouring with fruit for the good of souls during ten years; and, what was more, no hearing was given to the Fathers of the Society on the subject; although in particular the sowing of discord was cast up to them, when there was nothing in fact to correspond to such a charge, nor was any proof offered. Wherefore, the supposition being false, the facts of the case being suppressed, and prejudice being done to a third party, no effect could be given to the petition. Moreover, it was not a new thing in the Church of God that divers Orders should work upon the same ground.[43]

Here another official note was appended in due form: "Show this answer to the Procurator-General of the Capuchins." The said official replied that he waived the point of the Jesuits having authority direct from the Holy See, "as they say;" he would only observe that the Propaganda decree in favour of the Capuchins ordered the Jesuits out; how then did the other gentleman say, it was not known they were in, or that they were not heard? It was perfectly well known; and they must have been heard. Then, as to the question of discord, it was a general experience of the Capuchins that dissensions were sure to arise, especially if the district of the mission was small.[44]

This answer was followed by another note, requiring the Procurator-General, who had given it, to explain it by word of mouth, and in particular to state whether it was true or not, that the Fathers of the Society had been in that mission before the first entrance therein

---

[43] Propaganda Archives, *America*, 257, f. 56.
[44] *Ibid.*, f. 59.—"*Lasciando quello che asseriscono della facoltà hauta dalla S. Sede, si mette in consideratione che, mentre il decreto fatto a favore de Capuccini fà espressa mentione dell' iterato commandamento fatto al Rev.mo P. Generale della Compagnia, non si sà vedere come si dica nella risposta, che non si sia fatta mentione da Capuccini nel loro memoriale, che i Padri della Compagnia havessero già missione nella detta isola, e che non siano sopra di ciò stati sentiti; perchè se ciò fusse non si sarebbe fatto commandamento a i PP. che partissero. Dunque si vede chiaro che la Sacra Congregatione era benissimo informato; e che essendogli commandato una volta il partirsene, e non esseguendo il commandamento, gli fù replicato il secondo. Quanto poi alle discordie, l'assertione de Capuccini stà fundata nell' esperienza, quale molto più ha luogo, dove la Missione è ristretta. Tanto dice il Procurator Generale per informatione del tutto à V. S. Ill.ma. Quam Deus, etc. [A tergo] 18 Augusti, 1659.*"

of the Capuchin Fathers and assignment made thereof to the latter by the first decree. The gentleman who had given that previous answer now gave another which settled the debate for good: "The Procurator-General says that he has not the courage [or he does not venture to try] to find out when that mission began." To this the note was appended: "Put the whole matter on the shelf." [45]

About 1649 the Capuchin Fra Francis da Pamplona and two others went by commission of the Propaganda to the island of Grenada, and offered their services to the French Catholics who had no one to administer the Sacraments; but they were rejected, and were required to pass on to the continent.[46] Some seven or eight years afterwards, Fra Joseph da Caravantes [Cacavantes] with others followed in the same path, being deputed for "the islands of Granada, with the condition to pass on farther, and especially into America." After ten years' work on the northern shores of South America, the same Caravantes returned and was authorized to take out an extensive mission of thirteen Capuchin priests and three lay-brothers (May 9, 1667). We have nothing further to do with these missionaries and their fruitful labours, except to note the circumstance that the French Catholic inhabitants of Grenada had no employment for priests, at least if the latter were Spaniards. They could afford to do without any.[47]

Grenada, etc. 1649-1667.

Other papers seem to emanate from the restlessness of adventurers. Some of these described the members of their Order as "disinterested and mortified;" they were justified no doubt in doing so; but the implication, that they themselves were so, is not always borne out by the character of their papers. Two of them reported from Paris (February 20, 1650) the progress of their work during five years in certain parts of the West Indies. They had found that all other regulars whom they had seen in "the West Indies and America" worked only among their compatriots—the Spaniards among the Spaniards, the Portuguese among the Portuguese, the French among the French—" and heretofore no religious has ever thought, or wanted, or been able, to go into those islands, Marigalante, Dominica, St. Vincent, and Granada; or on the continent among the savage and barbarous people; but only we, with the Rev. Father Pacifico di Provins, prefect of the said

[45] Propaganda Archives, *America*, 257, f. 58ᵛ.—"*Dice il Procuratore Generale che non gli bastava l'animo di trovare quando fu il principio di quella missione.* ¶ *Reponatur.*"
[46] *Ibid., II. America*, 260, f. 34: *De Cumanagote y Julio a 23 año 1650.—Ibid., America*, 258, f. 38, Commission from the Capuchin Provincial of Andalusia, June 3, 1647. Faculties from the Holy Office, 12 August, 1649, on behalf of Fra Francis da Pamplona di Provincia d'Aragona, Capuccino.
[47] *Ibid., America*, 258, ff. 36-38, 40-43.

mission, have been the first to work for the salvation of the savages these last five or six years."[48] They say there are twenty thousand barbarians in those islands; and the Capuchin Fathers, that is themselves, are very much loved, and are the only ones desired, because they understand and speak the language of the twenty thousand savages, and "because they are seen to be disinterested and mortified." They wish to keep the said mission for their own Province of Paris; and they ask their Eminences "to give an express order to the Reverend Fathers Capuchin, congregated at present in Rome for the General Chapter, to send us back promptly to the said islands, for the prosecution of the mission, by God's grace so happily begun." In a letter apart, they desire the secretary of the Propaganda to see that the General Chapter "do not make election of other Fathers for this mission, save those of the Province of Paris."[49] They are not distinct in stating why they have "interrupted" their labours and come such a long way to establish a mission which they have abandoned.

It looks like a similar enterprise of adventure when two men try to arrange with the secretary of the Propaganda for the purpose of taking over the island of Cayenne and the mainland beyond, and then establishing a prefecture with the help of four or six others. They write from Genoa on July 10, 1677; and their case is very instructive. We may observe that since 1651 the French Nuncio had sent in reports about the feasibility of establishing a bishopric in "Carena;"[50] he had despatched on August 30, 1652, a favourable report from the superiors of the Jesuits and from M. Vincent de Paul, relative to the fitness of the subjects proposed for the episcopal dignity;[51] the Duke "di Vantador" was ready with the temporal supplies, and desired the Congregation of Missionaries under M. Vincent de Paul to receive some approbation from His Holiness (March 8, 1652);[52] the whole career of the Jesuits Pelleprat, Méland, Béchamel, Grillet, had served to open up the country of Guiana and Cayenne from 1652 onwards, and to start the missions there; and now, twenty-five years behind time, these two men, touching land at Genoa, put in a hurried and urgent claim to

Cayenne and Guiana. 1652-1677.

---

[48] Propaganda Archives, *II. America*, 260, f. 63ᵛ: Fra Joachim de Corbeil and Fra Alexis de Auxerre, O. Cap., to the S. Congregation.—The Italian letters here have "Pacifico di Provino." In another Italian letter, "de Provins" is the signature of Fra Pacifico himself: *ubi infra*, note 56.
[49] *Ibid.*, ff. 17, 33, 63.
[50] *Ibid.*, ff. 178, 186, January 1, 1651.
[51] *Ibid.*, f. 98.
[52] *Ibid.*, f. 100: the Paris Nuncio to the Propaganda.

take over the entire country, without the slightest allusion to the circumstance that there may be antecedent rights and interests already in existence. It is at the moment when Father Grillet has been taken prisoner by the Dutch conquerors of Cayenne, and been brought over to Europe; and only now, after a year, have the French forces been able to recover the place.

These two Normans, then, write to the secretary, saying that there is no regular in the mission of Cayenne; that they desire to occupy it, associating with themselves four or six other Capuchins, fervent and full of zeal; that they have all the faculties necessary from the French King, from the Propaganda, from their own superiors; and therefore they petition earnestly for two distinct decrees in their favour. One should give them the island of Cayenne, the other assign to them the continent of Guiana; the former diploma being intended for use with the French authorities, the latter with the Spanish Government; and, whichever territory they are able to appropriate in fact, they shall reserve the other territory to themselves by right. And, as they understand that the Propaganda has decreed not to answer simple missionaries, they throw themselves at the feet of His Holiness, and expect an answer from the secretary, assuring them of success. A proper endorsement on the letter says that the answer shall be *Nihil* —" Nothing." [53]

(5) In all these movements of missionary enterprise as sanctioned by the Propaganda, one strong element of temporal aid will not have escaped the reader's notice; just as the total absence of it and of all other adventitious resources may have been noticed in Lord Baltimore's missionary policy. That was the concurrence of companies of merchants, who undertook at least to transport the missionaries, if not also to provide for the endowment of religion on the other side of the ocean. Cardinal Richelieu was himself the chief patron of one such company, and put a clause in its charter that it should transport at its own cost four priests for West Indian service. And so liberal was this company that the "Scotch gentleman," in his account, speaks of it as "devoting itself to the propagation of the faith," and negotiating with many English and Irish priests who offered themselves for that service, as well as with the Propaganda itself for the sake of the faculties necessary.[54]

(5) Catholic merchant companies.

The Duke de Ventadour was a benefactor in the matter of sending

---

[53] Propaganda Archives, *America, Antille I.*, f. 258: Fra Epiphanius de Moirans and Fra Bonaventura de Courtray to the secretary.

[54] *Ibid., America,* 257, ff. 78, 80ᵛ, in the Scotchman's Relation.—*Ibid., II. America,* 260, f. 223ᵛ, in Raymond Breton's account.

Fra Pacifico O. Cap. and his companions to Canada or North America (1643–1647).[55] Fra Pacifico himself, in a report from Paris (March 9, 1644) on the affairs of "America, Affrica, and New France," is emphatic as to the necessity of being succoured by a company: "And so," he says, "I come back to the point once more, and say that we shall never do anything without a Christian company which shall stand the expences of the said general conversions." He proceeds to defend himself and Fra Archangelo against the criticisms of brethren who are opposed to the missions.[56]

The French Nuncio (March 8, 1652) makes the question of an American bishopric depend upon the co-operation of those who demand it; inasmuch, he says, as their Eminences might very justly consider it expedient that "before His Holiness accorded the favour, he could oblige those who ask for it to invest a fund for the fit maintenance of the said bishop and of twelve priests, who ought to assist him."[57]

After two years of investigation, upon a reference made by decree of the Propaganda (June 5, 1663), Cardinal Sforza, in a summary or report (November 23, 1665), answers the question regarding a fit subject for the bishopric in favour of the Paris Seminary of Foreign Missions; and then, in a few words, reviews the French commercial companies: "As to the company of Frenchmen which engages in the propagation of the faith, and has on former occasions asked for the necessary faculties on behalf of priests who offer to go on the missions of those islands, Lesley says that this is the same company which supports that very seminary; and that there is, besides, another company of French merchants who trade with the Indies; and when it is time to set sail they should wish to have with them a priest, qualified with the faculties of a missionary, who would then remain there to promote the interests of religion."[58]

(6) The English islands.

(6) Not to pass over the English islands without a word, we state briefly that Captain Henry Hawley, Governor of Barbados at the time of Father White's visit, was indicted later on (July, 1639) by an opposite party in the island; and the last head of the indictment ran thus: "13. That he suffered a Romish priest to escape after he was convicted there [in Barbados]

---

[55] Propaganda Archives, *Lettere di Avignone . . . Inghilterra*, 142, [A.D. 1643], ff. 18, 23.—*Ibid., Lettere di Francia . . . Inghilterra*, 145, [1647], ff. 4–62, *passim*.

[56] *Ibid.*, I. *America*, 259, f. 141ᵛ: "*V. S. I. dica donche a nostri Eminentissimi che lascino gridare questi Padri malissimo affetti a missioni; e che non credino mai che io facci una minima actione indecente alla mia professione. Il R. P. Archangelo si parte . . . a Roma.*"

[57] *Ibid.*, II. *America*, 260, f. 100.

[58] *Ibid., America*, 257, f. 76.—For Jesuit Relations on the Antilles and Guiana, cf. the *Archives de l'École de Ste. Geneviève*; *Antilles-Guiane*, t. 1, *seqq*.

for dispersing Popish books, & seduceing the people, & delivering scandalous words of the Bishoppes here [in England]."[59] This charge against Governor Hawley may refer to the presence in the islands of a missionary sent there by Malachy, Archbishop of Tuam. The action of this prelate in despatching a mission to St. Christopher, for the service of the Irish settlers, was discussed in the Congregation of the Propaganda on January 30, 1638; and was then regulated, with respect to both St. Christopher and Virginia, in April of the same year and in December of the next (April 20, 1638; December 19, 1639). But, at this latter moment, Malachy wrote from Galway, that the two priests whom he had sent were already dead (December 8, 1639). Then the Propaganda authorized him to despatch some regulars, with the permission of their superiors (December 19, 1639). Soon afterwards this permission was extended to comprise either seculars or regulars, of whom he should send two; and the Congregation voted to each sixty *scudi*, with fifty *scudi* for the voyage of both; and directed that the faculties to be obtained of the Holy Office should be for use, not in Ireland, but in the islands only, one of the missionaries being appointed prefect.[60]

Tuam and Irish missionaries. 1638, 1639.

Nearly thirty years later (1667-1669) the Irish priest John Grace, who first wrote from St. Christopher (March 11, 1667) and then reported at home in person, gave a lamentable account of the condition in which he had left his fellow-countrymen. The defeat of the English at St. Kitts by the French had undone the Irish, who, previously well-to-do, were now dying of starvation. While passing through Martinique, Guadeloupe, and Antigua, he heard the general confessions of more than three hundred, of whom fifty died. In Barbados there were many thousands of Cromwellian Irish exiles, who had no priest at all, and very many of them were conforming to Protestantism for want of Catholic instruction or assistance.[61] In the little island of St. Bartholomew there were four hundred Irish Catholics who had never seen a priest in that island. At Montserrat, the Governor, Stapleton, was himself an Irishman and a Catholic; and here was a favourable opportunity to establish missionaries.[62]

Report of John Grace. 1667.

[59] P. R. O., *Colonial Papers*, x. No. 28, i., *In re* Huncks v. Hawley.
[60] Propaganda Archives, *Acta*, 13, f. 17ᵛ, 83ᵛ, 441ᵛ; *Ibid.*, 14, f. 84; *Lettere*, 139 (A.D. 1640), f. 191.
[61] "*Plurimos hæreticorum quibus subjiciuntur ritibus se conformare.*"
[62] Propaganda Archives, *America*, 257, ff. 92-94, 116-119; and *Ibid.*, *Scritture riferite nei Congressi, Irlanda II.*, ff. 141, 147ᵛ, viz. John Grace's own papers, and those of William Burgat, deputy for the clergy of Ireland and then Bishop-elect of Cashel; petitions, reports, letters, dated Rome and Paris, August 8, 1667, to July 5, 1669.

Of Montserrat, prior to the appointment of Stapleton, the Scotchman said that there were four hundred Irish there, all Catholics, who would gladly settle in some French island, where they could serve God publicly and with liberty of conscience.[63] Afterwards, Colonel Stapleton, being appointed to the government of that island,[64] and then becoming Governor-General of all the Leeward Islands, reported the state of religion for 1676 in this wise: The religion most prevalent, he said, was the Protestant. In Nevis there were some Quakers; in Antigua about sixty of them; in both islands as many religions as at home; but most people go to church when they happen to like the parson, or when a fit of "devotion comes upon them; some when common prayer is over. I cannot tell the variety of their religions." In Montserrat most part are Roman Catholics, since it was first settled by those of "that perswasion and continued ever since, untill the French destroyd them all; and are still yet. They give noe scandall" to the Protestants. In fine, the Protestant religion is as eight to one; but in Montserrat the Romish is as six to one Protestant, and no Quaker, for they will let none live amongst them. "They lived loveinge & kind whylest I was amongst them, and doe still, givinge noe more offence the one to the other then what *Meum & Tuum* does betwixt brothers."[65]

Montserrat. Gov.-General Stapleton. 1676.

(7) After this long pause to contemplate men, missions, nationalities, and religions in the West Indies, we need do no more now than point, for the purposes of general Jesuit history, to the background beyond. In the Great Antilles, and on the American continent from what is now New Mexico down through the southern hemisphere, there were divers Spanish provinces of the Society, for which a Propaganda document, without date, gives the number of priests; it mentions neither scholastics nor brothers, but enumerates exactly the professed houses, novitiates, colleges, seminaries, residences, and missions, with the numbers of priests attached to each. This list includes the Philippines, which have become in our days a North American possession; and the period to which it belongs (1625–1683) is the same as we have been considering in this present section. To all these must be added the Portuguese Provinces of Brazil and Maranhão.

(7) The Jesuit Provinces, West and South.

[63] *Ibid., America*, 257, f. 80ᵛ; November 23, 1665.—Cf. the Narrative of Colonel Theodore Cary, *Calendar of State Papers, Colonial, A. & W. I.*, ii. § 1088, i., November 17, 1665; Major Nath. Reade being Governor of Montserrat.
[64] Cf. *Calendar, Ibid.*, ii. § 1788, July 9, 1668: Governor-General Lord Willoughby to the Lords of Council.
[65] P. R. O., *Colonial Papers*, xxxviii. No. 65, p. 31; November 22, 1676.—Cf. *Calendar, A. & W. I.*, ii. § 1152, p. 502.

The sums-total stand as follows:—In the Province of Mexico, 224 priests; in that of New Granada, 90; in Peru, 229; in Paraguay, 111; in the Philippines, 92; in the Vice-Province of Chili, 43.[66] In Brazil we find for one Province, but at a much later date, the number of priests, 228, the scholastics and brothers for the same time being 217; and for another Province (Maranhão), 88 priests with 57 non-priests.[67] If to these be added the French Fathers working in the islands, where, at the early date of Grillet's letter given above, they were 15, we have a sum-total—for dates, however, which do not happen to be identical—of over one thousand priests of the Society (1120) working in the West Indian Islands, in Central America, in South America, and in the Philippines. This number should be doubled to include those who were not yet priests, and are called "scholastics," as well as the lay-brothers; making a total considerably above two thousand.

When the first modest little company of two English Fathers and one Brother coasted the West Indies, they were not only anticipated all round in Spanish, Portuguese, and French settlements by an army of their own brethren, but far to the north, whither they were sailing, they were already flanked by a flourishing mission of heroic French Fathers, among the Hurons and Iroquois of New France, or Canada.

We shall now turn our attention to this northern continent, following the Propaganda documents; and then we shall settle down with the Catholic pilgrims in Maryland.

§ 32. More than half a century before the time of our subject proper, a peaceful invasion had been made of "Florida," that is to say, of the Florida so named to-day, conjoined with Georgia, South Carolina, and Virginia. The expedition which had entered the Chesapeake and the Potomac, ended on the soil of Virginia with the martydom of Father Segura of the Society and seven companions (1569–1571). More successful was the attempt made some years later (1577) by the Franciscan Fathers, who, with St. Augustine as their chief base of operations, evangelized the territory of modern Florida, and organized a civil government. At the beginning of the seventeenth century this mission was visited in person by the Ordinary of Santiago de Cuba, the Dominican Cabezas, twelfth bishop ruling or connected

Jesuit martyrs on the Potomac. 1571. The Franciscans.

---

[66] Propaganda Archives, *II. America*, 260, ff. 7, 9. Chili became a Vice-Province in 1625, and a Province in 1683.
[67] A. Hamy, S.J., *Domiciles de la Compagnie de Jésus*, pp. 6, 7, for the year 1749.

with that see.[1] Thus, but for the intrusion of the English into Virginia (1607) on the south side of the Potomac, the Maryland pilgrims, who set up their abode on the north shore of that great river, might be considered as trespassing on territory occupied by Spanish colonies.

Looking round the horizon of the northern continent, we find allusions in the records to the settlement of the country by "heretics."

New England and Canada. Simon Stock, as we saw before, recommended to the Propaganda a counter-movement by means of his Carmelites. In default of them, the Propaganda summoned English and French Capuchins, through the Procurator of the Order and Father Joseph of Paris, who were to provide for New England no less than for Canada.[2] In point of fact, as to the English department, it was the ubiquitous Jesuits who entered both in Newfoundland and in Maryland.

Similarly, viewing things from the south, a procurator who wrote in his cell at Havana, and called himself Missionary-Apostolic "for the whole of North America,"[3] recommended in the year 1629 that Franciscans and others should be despatched to Florida, "for fear the Indians be infected with the pestilence of the heretics, who frequent those shores, and occupy some regions in those parts." The Franciscans were already there in full possession. But as the writer of this document was engaged here and in other memorials with the divers religious Orders, *omnes fratres et Jesuitæ*, marshalling them over the soil of the new world, prescribing statutes to be enacted for all the provinces of the West Indies, calling for the appointment of a Nuncio, and showing considerable ability on paper in distributing the Augustinian, Franciscan, and Dominican forces through Mexico, Yucatan, New Granada, Quito, Maranhão, and so on towards the south pole, it seems natural that he should also have provided for Florida by sending thither the men who were already there.[4]

---

[1] Cf. J. G. Shea, *History of the Catholic Church*, i. 143, *seqq.*

[2] Propaganda Archives, *Acta,* 7, *Cong.* 132, November 22, 1630, *coram SS⁰*, No. 10, f. 164.—*Ibid., Acta,* 8, *Cong.* 158, May 31, 1632, No. 5, f. 66ᵛ.—Cf. *supra,* §§ 8, 9.

[3] Propaganda Archives, *I. America*, 259, ff. 100–102: "*Il maestro Fra Pietro Nieto Procuratore della Provincia del Messico dell' Ordine Eremitano di S. Agostino e Missionario di questa Santa Sede per tutta l'America Settentrionale.*" This document is a petition against a recent papal constitution ordering the election alternately of Spaniards and Creoles to the office of Provincial.

[4] *Ibid.*, ff. 195, 196, 3 pp. 4to; endorsed, f. 196ᵛ: "*Agosto,* 1629. *Scrittura del P. Pietro Nieto Agostiniano de' mezi da tenersi per propagar la fede Cristiana nell' Indie Occidentali. Per il capitolo generale di 5 Agosto che sarà l'anno seguente.*" It is a document evidently meant for the Propaganda, which was now seven years old, and where, as its secretary Ingoli said at this very time to Agucchi, Nuncio of Venice, every one that wanted had a bureau to write to: *Nell' Indie s'è sparsa la fama di essa [Congregazione], e con grand' allegrezza si darà principio a nuove conquiste de' popoli; solo perchè gl'operaj havranno dove far capo ne' bisogni delle Missioni* . . ." Vatican Library, *Ottoboni,* 2536, ff. 71ᵛ, 72; Francesco Ingoli, Rome, November 3, 1629, to the Nuncio in Venice. The Jesuits come in for some notice with the Havana procurator and prior; he delivers an admonition to them upon apostolic zeal, and on

§ 32] NEW FRANCE, OR CANADA 319

Simon Stock the Carmelite reported from London in 1625 that the Virginian English had "founded a college to carry the infection of heresy through America."[5] This was not so; but people in Virginia had talked about erecting a university and college as early as July 30, 1619.[6]

Virginia.
1619–1625.

Further to the north, on behalf of the French settlement in New France, "commonly called Canada," the Provincial of the Recollects, Province of St. Denis in France, addressed a petition to the Pope, in which he referred to the attack made on Canada a few years before by Captain David Kirke of Newfoundland fame (July, 1629), if he did not allude to a much earlier onslaught by Captain Argal from Virginia (September, 1613). He told of the missionary efforts made recently, and of a new expedition now being organized in which both Recollects and Jesuits were to join. He said that the French "King has driven out the English, and that his Eminence Cardinal the Duke of Richelieu has taken the enterprise to heart, having ordered the Recollect Fathers to go back [to Canada] this year with the Jesuit Fathers, who, two years ago, not only with the consent but at the request of the Recollects, were associated in the said mission; and at the first voyage had lodged in half of the convent of St. Charles of Quebec, the Recollects being in the other half. But all had been expelled by the English; and yet, in spite of the war, they had despatched another mission, but without any happy result; for, having been taken by the English ships, the Jesuit Fathers were conducted to England and then to France, whilst the Recollects, pursued by the Turks, escaped on land under the guns of Bayona in Galicia, whence

Canada.
Recollects and Jesuits.
1629–1635.

the matter of military support, which he discountenances. *Ibid.*, f. 196.—This last point seems to be directed against the Jesuit Joseph Acosta, who, distinguishing several kinds of infidels and barbarians, did not approve of sending men to the slaughter among the "boars and crocodiles" of South America, as he called the savages there, no profit being derived from the loss of men, while the dangers could be sufficiently obviated by the presence or vicinity of an organized force. Other papers of Fra Nieto, "Prior of the Convent of Havana in the West Indies," are on the Gentile rites there, "reported by Cardinal Mellini, November 24, 1628," as also on the necessity of establishing a nunciature in those parts; they were "submitted in October, 1628, by the same Father present *in curia*," and "reported on November 24, 1628, in Congregation 100, in presence of His Holiness, and again November 29, 1628, *Cong.* 101." *I. America*, 259, f. 197, a draft of statutes for all Provinces of the West Indies; *Ibid.*, ff. 213-276, 278-283, on Gentile rites; *Ibid.*, ff. 285-299, on the nunciature.—This zealous man desires the Propaganda to impose his statutes on the General Chapter of his Order, which must pass them as laws; and they include deposition or deprivation of Provincials or Definitors who shall fail to observe the said provisions; while at the same time they smooth the way for missionaries to reach posts of dignity or special privilege. In June, 1633, Nieto brings with him a document from the Mexican Provincial of his Order, commending the bearer to the Cardinals for some signal promotion. *I. America*, 259, ff. 67, 64.

[5] *Supra*, § 8, p. 185.
[6] Cf. *Calendar of State Papers, Colonial, A. & W. I.*, i. 22.

they made their way to France." Apparently it was in connection with this representation that an order was issued by the authority of the Pope, in the Congregation of the Propaganda held January 19, 1635, to the effect that the French Nuncio should procure, if possible, a royal mandate, excluding heretics from Canada; that so the new Christians there, under the care of the Recollects of France, might not be infected with heresy.[7]

The expedition of Jesuit Fathers, thus announced by the Recollect Provincial in 1634, may have been the same which formed the subject of a correspondence betwixt the Propaganda and the General of the Society. In any case, this was the date at which commenced the well-known campaign of the great French missionaries among the Iroquois and Hurons, as told in the *Jesuit Relations*. And another early result of all these movements was the foundation of the first College in North America, that of Quebec dating several years further back than the college of Harvard in New England.[8] The Propaganda sent the following note to the General:—

The Propaganda and the Jesuit General.

"The Sacred Congregation of the Propaganda desires to know from the General of the Jesuits how a mission might be established in North America in the provinces of Virginia, Vermudes, New England, and Nova Scotia, by the Fathers of the Indies who are nearest: because the English have set up a pseudo-bishop in those parts with a large income, to the end that he may infect the regions there with heresy."

Virginia, Vermudes, NewEngland, Nova Scotia.

To this the General replied—

"In the month of April of the present year, there were sent by the Province of France to Canada, which borders on New France, five of the Society, that is, three priests and two brothers, in company with certain merchants, who settled with the intention of planting there the Christian faith. Wherefore they wish to found a seminary, for the purpose of instructing the children of the Canadians in Christian doctrine. Eleven years ago some French merchants wanted to do the same, but they were driven out by an armed force of the English of Virginia, and with them three Fathers of the Society. At the end of the present autumn something will be known about the progress of that mission."[9]

[7] Propaganda Archives, *I. America*, 259, ff. 109–113.—Cf. *Ibid., Acta*, 10, *Cong.* 203, April 23, 1635, No. 35, where it is stated that the Paris Nuncio has obtained from the King an order for the exclusion of heretics in future from the territory of New France.

[8] Cf. C. de Rochemonteix, *Les Jésuites et la Nouvelle France*, i. 221, seqq.

[9] Propaganda Archives, *I. America*, 259, f. 138. A Georgetown College copy among

The fruit of Jesuit labours then gathered in the north is referred to in an account of the Mission of Acadia, presented to the secretary of the Propaganda by Fra Ignatius of Paris, Capuchin. He says of the St. Lawrence that on this great river there are many French people, all Catholics, who receive the whole of their spiritual assistance from the Jesuit missionaries. And, further, of the English heretics he reports on hearsay, that, if they come this way, "they will destroy utterly our holy faith on the great river St. Lawrence, where I believe there are two thousand Christians under the direction of the Jesuit missionaries."[10] The Recollects had not returned to Canada. *The St. Lawrence.*

Finally, coming to the very doors of the Maryland settlement, just at the moment when the English convoy was approaching the Chesapeake and Potomac, we are offered a view of the whole country to the rear as far as the northern confines of New Spain. Fra Alonso Bonavides, a Minorite or Franciscan, in a Relation presented to the Sacred Congregation under date of February 12, 1634, conveys an important piece of information, which in the official summary of the Propaganda is thought worthy of being distinctly inserted for its intrinsic value, as a *ricordo importante*—

. . . "*Noteworthy observation of Father Bonavides.*

"For fear that, from the side of Virginia and other places and islands of North America, the English and Dutch shipping introduce heresy into New Mexico, which borders upon the said places [Virginia, etc.], just in the same way in which it has already been brought in there [Virginia, etc.] by the English and Dutch heretics; Father Bonavides calls attention to the necessity of establishing a mission of Irish Fathers, *New Mexico. English colonies. Irish Friars. 1634.*

the Shea Transcripts has a date attached in a parenthesis, "(*Anno* 1635)." But no such date is on the folio in the Propaganda. The two *bigliettoes* are on one page in two different hands, and in Italian.—Cf. B. A. Carayon, *Documents inédits:* Pierre Chaumonot, p. 199; catalogue at the end. He records the arrival in Canada of three Fathers for 1634, in different months, viz. Perrault, Richard, Buteux. He has five entered for 1635, viz. Dumarché, Quentin, Pijart, Turgis, and Le Mercier, this last being the same whom we encountered above for a later date as being in the West Indian Islands, and who died fifty-seven years after this his first arrival in Canada. The more recent authority of the *Jesuit Relations* (1901) affords grounds for connecting the General's statement rather with 1634 than with any other year about that time. *Jesuit Relations*, lxxi., 139, in *Chronological List of Missionaries.*—But if, discarding any immediate connection between the General's words and the actual foundation of Quebec seminary, we regard only the intention of founding such a college, and if we note the identity of phrase between the Propaganda's remarks to the General and a decree of July 21, 1625, issued upon receiving a report from Simon Stock, we have a date nine years earlier, and the mission of Fathers Brebeuf and Charles Lalemant denoted, and the Argal expedition of 1613 indicated as having taken place "eleven years ago."—Cf. *supra*, § 8, p. 185.

[10] Propaganda Archives, *II. America*, 260, f. 33a; 7 pp. 8vo.—Cf. J. G. Shea, *History of the Catholic Church in U. S.*, i. 225, seqq.

who know the English language; to the end that they may convert not only the Gentiles of those countries to the Catholic faith, but also the heretics, who are gone there from England and Holland, and have become very numerous, taking Indian women for wives; and at the same time [these Irish Fathers] may also bring back the Gentiles already perverted, and prevent the heresy from spreading in New Mexico; and finally may also give assistance to the Spaniards who have been made captive (*schiavi*) in the wars with the said English and Dutch; and help likewise the negroes, whom the Portuguese take to New Spain and sell there," etc.[11] Hereupon a decree was passed to the effect that, after verification of the facts through Cardinal Del Monte, the Sacred Congregation would give its approval to the friar's advice, and would request that Irish friars should be sent over for service in Virginia and other places adjoining New Mexico, within the range of English and Dutch navigation.[12]

§ 33. To return now to the Maryland expedition, which we left at its last stopping-place in the West Indies, there lay to the west of St. Christopher the Virgin group, last of the Leeward Islands; and beyond them the Greater Antilles, Porto Rico, San Domingo, Jamaica, Cuba, which alone among the islands the Spaniards had cared to colonize. North-west there were the Bahama Islands, never specially interesting at any point of history, except in so far as Columbus had first touched land there. Striking out in a straight course from St. Christopher, across one of the deepest tracts of the Atlantic, the voyagers reached Virginia on February 27, 1634.

Point Comfort, Va. Feb. 27, 1634.
To come within reach of Virginian guns, as they did, was "much contrary to my Lord's instructions," says Father White, in the *Briefe Relation* despatched by Leonard, his lordship's brother, for my lord's pleasant reading; just as, a page further on, the missionary tells of the great religious function publicly performed, of which probably he knew not that it likewise

---

[11] Propaganda Archives, *I. America*, 259, f. 152ᵛ. The summary is in Italian. The original memorial in Spanish is 28 ff.: "*Memorial á la santidad de Urbano VIII*. . . . *açerca de las conversiones del Nuevo Mexico* . . . *presentado* . . . *por el P. Fr. Alonso de Benavides* . . . *en 12 de febrero del año* 1634" (*Ibid.*, ff. 158–186ᵛ; incomplete at the end).

[12] *Ibid., Acta*, 10, *Cong.* 192, June 5, 1634, *coram SSᵒ*, No. 28, f. 56.

After this slight review of North and South America, by way of setting the scenes for our much more limited subject in British America, we might satisfy the reader's scientific curiosity by giving a statistical sketch of the whole Western world from Acadia to Chili, in connection with exclusively Jesuit history. But the most limited tableau of the Jesuit colleges, residences, etc., is too ample for a note here. The places occupied and the establishments founded are presented to the eye in various maps of the *Atlas Geographicus Societatis Jesu*, by L. Carrez, S.J. (1900).

was "much contrary to my Lord's instructions;" but which Leonard Calvert, conscious of his own iniquity, sent on to his brother with great indifference, being also conscious of his own good sense in the premises. This contradictoriness to express instructions has given offence to some delicate conscience or other; particularly as the disobedience was exhibited by "ministers of religion," to whom the instructions had never been directed.[1]

In spite of grave apprehension as to the attitude of the Virginians, and dark clouds which were already seen to be gathering in that direction, the new rival colony of Maryland was treated well by Sir John Harvey the Governor; and, without having sustained harm, the convoy sailed up the Chesapeake Bay from Point Comfort, and stood off over against the mouth of the great river Potomac. They seem to have arrived there on the Feast of St. Gregory (March 12) or thereabouts; and the cape to the south, now Smith's Point, was baptized Cape St. Gregories, while the one to the north, now Point Lookout, was called Cape St. Michael, "in honour of all the angels of Maryland." The Potomac itself they named St. Gregories.[2]

The Chesapeake and Potomac.

[1] C. E. Smith, *Religion under the Barons of Baltimore*, p. 167. Out of this deliberate act of "disloyalty" in discharging the functions of their religion, the Jesuit missionaries are discerned by the author to have brought down manifold eventual chastisements on the "innocent" of Maryland, on even Lord Baltimore himself, no less than on themselves the "guilty" (pp. 155, 156). The character of their disobedience to instructions is brought out clearly; that, whereas "Lord Baltimore, as the very first of his parting injunctions to his *deputies in charge of the expedition*, bade them ' cause all acts of Roman Catholic religion to be done as privately as may be . . . '" (p. 148), still, in spite of the fact that (speaking of the selfsame injunctions or instructions) "not twenty-four hours previously the Lord Proprietary *had given the voyagers* written instructions that all acts of Roman Catholic religion were to be done privately . . ." (p. 155), the missionaries did dedicate different parts of the ship to heavenly patrons (p. 154) (which may have been done privately or not); and at the end of the voyage they performed a great religious function, which even charity cannot cover over and excuse, seeing it was one of " a long series of deliberate acts of disloyalty" (p. 155). We have italicized the logic, to emphasize the character of the scruple.

[2] *Relatio Itineris. Documents*, I. No. 8, A.—*Briefe Relation, Calvert Papers*, iii. 39.—As there is an error somewhere in the arithmetic of Father White's narrative, we presume that in his own MS. a word had dropped out, *nonas*; and that then, the English being taken from the Latin, the identical error and miscalculation appeared in the *Briefe Relation*. They arrived at Point Comfort on the 27th of February. They stayed in those waters eight or nine days, and then departed up the Chesapeake. Taking the bay to begin only at its narrower part, near the mouth of the Rappahannock, the narrator states that they entered the Chesapeake on the 3rd day of March—only four days after they had first arrived at Point Comfort, instead of some ten or twelve days according to the premises. Finally they must have come to the Potomac some eleven or thirteen days after the first arrival off the James River. This would be about the 12th day of March.

Now, if, in the original Latin, the word *nonas* had merely dropped out by chance, the dates would stand *tertio nonas Martii*, "3rd before the nones of March," that is, the 5th of March, which would be, by Roman calculation, seven days after their arrival at Point Comfort; and the remaining seven days till the 12th, St. Gregory's feast, might well be spent in feeling their way and sounding, as they went up the

Describing the bay and its affluent, the writer says: "[We] came into Chesapeake Bay, at the mouth of Patomecke. This baye is the most delightfull water I ever saw, between two sweet lands, with a channel 4, 5, 6, 7, and 8 fathoms deepe, some 10 leagues broad, at time of yeare full of fish. Yet it doth yeeld to Patomecke, which we have made St. Gregories. This is the sweetest and greatest river I have seene, so that the Thames is but a little finger to it. There are noe marshes or swampes about it, but solid firme ground, with great variety of woode not choaked up with undershrubs, but commonly so farre distant from each other as a coach and fower horses may travale without molestation."

At the instigation, it was supposed, of the Virginian whites, the local Indian chiefs and the Emperor himself of Pascattoway were in arms against the invaders, who were represented as Spaniards coming to destroy the natives. But the Governor, Leonard Calvert, went up the river to Patowmecke, where he negotiated with the tutor of the young king there; and then farther up to Pascattoway, where the Emperor received the white visitor kindly, and gave the requisite permission for settling in the country.

Patowmecke, Pascattoway, St. Clement's Island.

Meanwhile, before Leonard ascended the river on his embassy, the convoy itself had come to anchor at Heron Island, which they named St. Clement's; and on Lady Day, Feast of the Annunciation, March 25, 1634, they first celebrated Mass on this island—a divine service "never before performed in this part of the world," says Father White. And then, he continues, "having hewn a great cross out of a tree, we took it on our shoulders, and going in procession to the place selected, the Prefect [Governor], the Commissioners, and the other Catholics[3] all assisting, we erected it as a trophy to Christ our Saviour, after reciting humbly on our knees, with feelings of profound emotion, the Litany of the Holy Cross."

In the absence of the Governor, the pilgrims were duly affable and withal cautious. The islands which they had already christened St. Clement's, St. Catharine's, and St. Cecilia's, offered a site for a fort; which, by commanding the river at this its narrowest part (only some four miles wide here), would shut off the whole trade of the upper country from

St. Catharine's, St. Cecilia's Islands.

great bay. The writer's use of the Roman method of calculation in this place would be exceptional with him.

The value, however, of this or any other hypothesis, as, for instance, that a word lost in the Latin was *decimo*, making the text to read: "On the 13th day of March," will lie in its furnishing a clue to determine which MS. was original, the Latin or the English.

[3] "*Cæterisque Catholicis*"—"the rest of the Catholics."

intrusive adventurers. But, on the return of the Governor, they dropped down the river again under Captain Fleete's guidance; and, near the mouth of the Patomecke, as the narrator describes, they came " to a lesser river on the north side of it, as bigge as [the estuary of the] Thames, which we call St. Georges. This river makes two excellent bayes, wherein might harbour 300 saile of 1000 tunne a peece with very great safetie, the one called St. Georges Bay [later St. Inigoes Creek], the other more inward St. Maries. On the one side of this river [St. Maries] lives the King of Yoacomaco; on the other our plantation is seated, about halfe a mile from the water; and our towne we call St. Maries. To avoid all occasion of dislike and colour of wrong, we bought the space of thirtie miles of ground of them, for axes, hoes, cloth and hatchets; which we call Augusta Carolina. It made them the more willing to enterteine us, for that they had warres with the Sasquasahannockes, who come sometimes upon them and waste and spoile them and their country; for thus they hope by our meanes to be safe."[4]

<small>St. George's, St. Mary's Rivers. St. Mary's town.</small>

Here the writer describes the Indians and the country, and tells of the first month's experiences. Of the Indians so much has been written, that we need say but little here. Of the country we must needs say more, since it is the scene of future labours. And of experiences we shall comprise not one month's, but six years' history in a brief sketch of the first struggles with nature and the domestic conditions among the pilgrims themselves.

§ 34. The Susquehannahs, just mentioned as enemies of the Potomac and Chesapeake aborigines, a wild and warlike tribe that came raiding down their splendid river of the Susquehannah into the head of the Chesapeake, belonged to the stock of the Iroquois, whose central territory was that comprised in the modern State of New York, but was then considered as part of Canada, or New France. The ferocious family of the Iroquois took in not only the Five Nations of

<small>Susquehannahs. The Five and the Six Nations.</small>

---

[4] *Calvert Papers*, iii. 38–41, *Briefe Relation;* where "Augusto Carolino" is printed.—In the passage just quoted from the *Calvert Papers*, iii. 38, we have printed "lands" in the clause, "between two sweet lande;" presuming that, in the said publication, a certain sign of the MS. for "s" or "es," resembling an *e* italic, but with the extremity prolonged downwards, and not unlike a Greek *ρ*, has been taken to be an "e." White, for instance, uses this sign in his letter to Parsons (cf. *supra*, § 4, p. 157), "imploiment*ρ*." On this account, in the use which we are about to make of White's and Copley's correspondence, as published in the *Calvert Papers*, i. (*infra*, Chap. V.), we shall use an "s" where the plural number clearly requires it, instead of the "e" which appears several times in the publication.

Senecas, Cayugas, Onondagas, Oneidas, and Mohawks, but also their victims the weaker Hurons, and moreover the Tuscaroras, who, by joining the other five, made what was known in later history as the corporate body of the Six Nations.

The vast Algonquin stock, which spread away far to the north of New England, reached southwards, including the fishing Indians of Maryland and Virginia, with whom our voyagers had to deal; and westward, taking in the Ottawas, Pottawatomies, Shawnees.

<small>Algonquins, Ottawas, Pottawatomies, Shawnees.</small>

Finally, down in the valley of the Mississippi, and that region which in English State Papers was called "the back" of the English colonies, that is, to the west of the Carolinas and Georgia, there roved the Muscogee stock of Natchez, Creeks, Cherokees, Choctaws, Chickasaws.[1] We mention the names of these tribes because they reappear in future parts of our History.

<small>Muscogee Stock.</small>

Leaving the reader to see for himself, in the pages of Father White's English or Latin *Relation,* the pleasant and cheerful account which he gives of the mild, confiding, and docile Maryland Indians, we pass over at once, for the sake of brevity, to another view of them, one much more relevant for showing the course and cause of events which were to follow, and why the Indian missions in Maryland had scarcely sprouted before they were nipped. A *Relation of Maryland* was published in 1635 as an official declaration given out in Lord Baltimore's name, about the state of the new colony, then a year old. The document speaks thus of the Indians—

"Some accounts say that the people are warlike, and have done much harm to the English. Others say that they are a base and cowardly people, and to be despised. And it is thought by some who would be esteemed statesmen, that the only point of policy that the English can use is to destroy the Indians, or to drive them out of the country, without which it is not to be hoped that they [the English] can be secure."

<small>A cynical view.</small>

The dastardly cynicism of this policy, so coldly rehearsed in my lord's name, was not unfamiliar in practice. To destroy people or drive them out of their own country and make room for English interlopers and make these latter comfortable, was already a spectacle to be seen nearer home by Lord Baltimore, no farther off than the

---

[1] Cf. Scharf, *Maryland*, i. 82-97.—Cf. G. Bancroft, *History of the United States*, iii. chap. xxii.; Map of Aboriginal America, east of the Mississippi.—Cf. *Ibid.*, ii. chap. xv., Map of the French, English, Dutch, Swedish, and Spanish Possessions or Claims in the United States, 1655.

Ireland from which he borrowed his title. In Maryland, as almost a unique exception in Western history, this plan of the statesmen was not adopted. But the grounds on which it rested were already accepted in London. The reasons of prepotency and better weapons, for which statesmen justified it, were recounted with approval in the same *Relation of Maryland*. However, a less savage plan than that of using deadly weapons, a plan of palliated enslavement, or an economical estimate of the natives as being " useful to the English," was immediately propounded in the following terms :—

"The truth is, if they [the Indians] be injured, they may well be feared, they being a people that have able bodies, and generally taller and bigger-limbed than the English; and want not courage. But the odds we have of them in our weapons keeps them in awe; otherwise they would not fly from the English, as they have done in time of wars with those of Virginia; and out of that respect a small number of our men being armed will adventure upon a great troop of theirs; and for no other reason [not because the English are better soldiers, but merely because they have muskets]; for they [the Indians] are resolute and subtile enough. But from hence that there can be no safety to live with them is very great error. Experience hath taught us that, by kind and fair usage, the natives are not only become peaceable but also friendly, and have upon all occasions performed as many friendly offices to the English in Maryland and New England as any neighbour or friend uses to do in the most civil parts of Christendom. Therefore any wise man will hold it a far more just and reasonable way to treat the people of the country well, thereby to induce them to civility, and to teach them the use of husbandry and mechanical trades whereof they are capable, which may in time be very useful to the English; and the planters to keep themselves strong and united in towns, at least for a competent number; and then no man can reasonably doubt either surprise or any other ill-dealing from them."[2]

The frame of mind thus betrayed with regard to the Indians, as if these proprietors of the soil and these prospective Christians were good for nothing else but to serve a turn for an Englishman, is illustrated in a peaceable way and without the obtrusion of a musket by Cæcilius Lord Baltimore himself, in a letter to his brother

[2] *Relation*, 1635.—See H. Foley, *Records*, iii. 359.—The Stonyhurst copy of the *Relation* is singularly confused in the original pagination and subsequent binding. Stonyhurst MSS., *Anglia, A*, iv. No. 107.—The British Museum copy has likewise a confused pagination. British Museum Library, 278, C. 30.

Leonard. He had designed a chapel to be built, and in due time he ordered the erection of one. This nobleman who, as history shows us, never gave anything either to whites or Indians in behalf of education or religion, and who, as to the Indians, confiscated the property which they had set aside for their own religious service,[3] did then, when it came to building his own chapel as part of the appurtenances of a residence, express a formal desire that the poor inhabitants of the forest should contribute to the paying for his lordship's chapel; and this on the ground that it would prove the sincerity of their conversion to Christianity.[4]

Baltimore's idea of a Christian Indian.

We cannot pass on and leave the Indians without adverting, in the name of sane history, to an explanation, which has been put forward, of this contempt for Indians and negroes alike, and for every other kind of human being whom brute force could reduce to the condition of a mere thing. The explanation, as offered by a most Rev. Doctor of Boston, is couched in these words: "So slow," exclaims the Rev. Doctor Edward Everett Hale, "had been the development of the spirit of humanity in the sixteenth and even in the seventeenth century, and so ill-defined were the rights of man!"[5] Now, if there is a fact clear in the pages of history during fifteen centuries, it is that the explanation must be just the opposite, and should run in these terms: So rapid had been the decay of the spirit of humanity in the sixteenth and in the seventeenth centuries, and so ill-defined had become with nominal Christians the perfectly well-known rights of man! The English pirates, whose performances on the Spanish main the reverend author reluctantly narrates, and whose character the Council of Jamaica described to the Board of Trade as that of "ravenous vermin;"[6] their congeners on the Anglo-American mainland, whose features are seen to be branded in history with the extinction of all the Indian tribes;—neither the one set nor the other were in any sense a product of moral evolution out of former ages, but were in every sense a devolution of their own age and a product of its moral decadence.[7]

Rights of man in the 16th and 17th centuries.

[3] *Infra*, § 59.
[4] *Infra*, § 60 (3), p. 487.
[5] J. Winsor, *America*, iii. ch. ii., *Hawkins and Drake*, by the Rev. E. E. Hale, D.D., p. 63, in a note referring to Daniel De Foe, "a devoted Christian man," says Dr. Hale, yet an unscrupulous slave-hunter.
[6] P. R. O., *Colonial Entry Book*, xxix. pp. 405–412, May 20, 1680.
[7] While we write, we see the same theory reported as propounded by the eminent physician, Sir James Crichton Browne, on the occasion of the dedication of a chapel at Murray's Royal Asylum, Perth (October, 1904), to wit, that in the old days insanity

§ 35. Father White ends his narrative, both Latin and English, with a short account of the soil and the natural products. "I will end therefore with the soyle which is excellent, so that we cannot sett downe a foot but tread on strawberries, raspires, fallen mulberrie vines, acchorns, walnutts, saxafras, &c.; and those in the wildest woods. The ground is commonly a blacke mould above, and a foot within ground of a readish colour. All is high woods, except where the Indians have cleared for corne. It abounds with delicate springs which are our best drinke. Birds diversely feathered there are infinite, as eagles, swans, hernes, geese, bitters, duckes, partridge read, blew, partie-coloured, and the like; by which will appeare, the place abounds not alone with profit but also with pleasure. + *Laus Deo.*"[1]

The soil, products and game.

About a century and a half later, when the country had been largely despoiled of its original adornments, Father Joseph Mosley portrayed for his amiable sister, Mrs. Dunn of Newcastle, England, some of the natural features which impressed the imagination in his adopted country. Speaking of the farm at St. Inigoes, he said that the soil consisted of a black mould from three to five inches deep; beneath this there was a stratum of stiff clay for several feet; then in many places a layer of fine white sand; and beneath that the clay again. In this soil, the long-leaf white pine and the long-leaf yellow pine, the spruce pine, the white or sweet gum, the black gum, maple, sassafras, persimmon, the white oak, the red, black, and Spanish oaks, the hickory and chestnut, all found a genial soil. Especially did the pine woods luxuriate there as in their natural habitat. Where corn had grown in cleared fields only forty years before, it was found that forest pines occupied the ground, measuring two and a half feet in diameter, springing up to a great height, standing off from one another some eight or fifteen feet apart, and allowing, as Father White had expressed it, a carriage and four to drive through unimpeded. This may partly be seen in the residue of the same forests to-day. Any field left fallow produced such woods; and the largest old pines measured from three to four feet in diameter, their lower limbs branching out at a height of some thirty-five or forty feet from

---

was regarded as the work of the devil, or a sort of demoniacal possession; and those suffering from it, if not cured by the rites of exorcism, somewhat sternly applied, were treated like wild beasts, starved, beaten, done to death, or caged in noisome cells, etc. But how changed was the scene now! Such a theory, if true of some localities, could not be fathered on "the old days," when the insane were invested by Christian charity with a sacred character, and were treated with that tenderness which is insinuated in the very name given them still by Irish charity, that of "innocents."

[1] *Calvert Papers*, iii. 45.

the ground. All sorts of grain abounded; but the heats were excessive for the making of hay. Fruits of every kind were common; and luscious peaches were thrown to the hogs.

"Every bird we see is a curiosity," wrote this Father to his sister. "So is every fish and every beast of the woods. So likewise to our **The birds.** Americans would be your birds, your fish, and your wild beasts. It's like a new world or a new creation to each other. Your common birds in England are not seen here, as the sparrow, the linnets, the finches, the magpie, the starling, etc. Nor are any of our common birds seen in England, as the blue bird, the red bird, the snow bird, the fishing hawk, the eagle, the turkey buzzard (which last the Romans call vulture, but here a turkey buzzard, as it much resembles a large turkey). The same may be said of the fish and wild beasts, except the rat and mouse, which **Two recent adventurers.** are equally here as in England. And these pernicious animals were not, as they say, the growth of this soil, but came in person as adventurers with the first settlers of America. The Indians think us of no better breed, for we have devoured their substance, as the rats and mice do ours." The one bird which Father Mosley identifies as the same on both sides of the ocean is the crow; and yet he declares that to be diminished in size. But, as to the whole series of interesting creatures which sail on either side of the Atlantic under the same name, he pronounces them all to be equivocal things; to wit, larks, swallows, blackbirds, partridges, snipes, pheasants, hawks, doves. He is eloquent on the subject of the humming-bird, "prodigiously small, about the size of a man's little finger to the second joint;" and also on the Baltimore bird; and all their gay phantasies of dress and colour. Nor does he fail to be imposing when he tells of the eagle which he has now in his garden, "as big if not bigger than myself," and which will kill any dog that attacks it.

There were to be found about the new settlement the rabbit, the hare, the fox, the opossum and the raccoon. The banks of the rivers **Other fauna.** and ponds were frequented by the otter, musk-rat, mink, and weasel. In the woods, squirrels were everywhere; of which Father White remarked that the Indians brought in constantly "turkey, partridge, oysters, squirrels as good as any rabbit." The various kinds of goose, duck, and swan, with the sea-gulls mingling among them over the brackish waters, were in abundance. And, peopling the bays themselves, there were perch, aille-wives, shad, rock, fool-fish, flounder, skate, dollar-fish, and eel, with the crocus, drum, and trout. "It is not uncommon there," said Brother Mobberley, half a century later than Father Mosley, "for a man to go out on the trouting-grounds at sunset, and carry home from sixty to one hundred fine trout at late bed-time." Crabs, oysters, turtles do not exhaust the list of natural wealth in the waters, but they must suffice for the list in our records. So we leave them with the porpoise and the shark, which add grimly to the fascination of the scene.

Mosley admired the capabilities of Maryland for commerce. "The country," he says, "is the best laid out for trade of any in the world. The rivers are spacious and wide. The entrance of Chesapeake Bay, or much rather of Chesapeake River, is twenty miles across; Potomack, ten; Patuxent, five or six. Ships by these rivers can sail above 200 miles up into the country." *Capacities for commerce. Climate.*

But the climate—that was another story. The missionaries had not to wait long before they discovered that for themselves. Father White devised a philosophy of his own to account for the sickness and epidemic, which carried off sixteen of the small colony in 1638-1639. As everything good commended itself to the good missionary, so everything bad was really only the effect of something altogether too good: "Really, my Lord," wrote he to Baltimore, "I take the cause of the sickness to bee the overgoodnesse of land, which maketh the viands to [too] substantiall," etc.[2]

Reviewing this period some sixty years later, the Triennial Catalogue would seem to imply that the climate had become much better: "The first comers," it reports, "long led a painful life, sky and air being at that time extremely insalubrious to Europeans, the soil being covered with dense forests, and fertile in none of the products necessary for the colonists. At length, vast quantities of timber being cleared away, a freer and less noxious air was breathed; and gradually this part of the country became dotted with pasture lands and arable fields."[3] However, the Englishman of half a century later quarrelled with the climate in the same way as ever, and the native of a full century afterwards could only pretend to find explanations for what was too evident. Said Father Mosley: "It is very hot and sultry in summer, to a great excess." As to the slow and intermittent fever: "It's the complaint of all us foreigners against this treacherous climate; it's always the fruit of the fall, which chief of us abundantly reap, with the rest of its bountiful

---

[2] *Calvert Papers*, i. 202, February 20, 1639.
[3] General Archives S.J., *Anglia, Catal.* 3, *Rerum*, 1696.—*Documents*, I. No. 8, O².

gifts." The native, Brother Mobberley, looked about for an excuse in the fresh water marshes whither the salt water with its ebb and flow could not penetrate.

Another climatic feature was extraordinary, the suddenness and vastness of the variations; or, as Mosley said, "The changes of weather are prodigiously sudden. On a clear day, a hurricane or a gust, as they call it here, rises in an instant, and will in a few minutes lay down houses and trees in the vein [in which] it blows. Thunder and lightning is, I believe, as dismal here as it is in any part of the world. You can't go two yards in the woods (which composes the great part of the country), but you see some tree or other struck with lightning at one time or other. I've seen it myself strike the trees within very few yards of me."[4]

During the two centuries to come, Maryland fevers were an acknowledged factor in the general management of the country. Governors would ask permission to take a trip to England and shake off the fever which otherwise would lay them low. Between the excessive heat in summer and extreme cold in winter, Governor Hart remarked of the intermediate seasons, that "the vernal and autumnal quarters are attended with fevers, pleurisies, and many other distempers."[5] The Anglican Bishop of London, in the middle of the eighteenth century, when urging the establishment of a bishopric in America, stated among other reasons that, if young men do come for Orders from America to England, "it is with great hazard to themselves, many of them having died here of the small-pox, a distemper fatal to the young people who come from the plantations to England. And many of the young clergy, sent from England to the plantations, have been lost by the distempers of that country, especially by the yellow fever to which they are very subject."[6]

Small-pox in England. Yellow fever in Maryland.

§ 36. Governor Winthrop of Massachusetts was fully justified when he entered in his journal the report just brought to him, that of the Maryland settlers those who came over were, many of them, Papists, and "did set up Mass openly." On Lady Day, March 25, 1634, Father White had sanctified with the Sacrifice of the Mass St. Clement's Island and the waters of the Potomac, believing that

---

[4] Georgetown College MSS.; Joseph Mosley, from Newtown, September 1, 1759; from Eastern Shore, Md., November 5, 1773; to Mrs. Dunn.—*Ibid.*, Joseph Mobberley, *Diaries* in 4to, 1806–1827, i. 23–30.

[5] P. R. O., *Board of Trade, Maryland*, 6, I. 106; received August 26, 1720.

[6] British Museum MSS., No. 33,029, *Newcastle Papers*, cccxliv. f. 63^v; between A.D. 1744 and 1758.

he was the first to do so, and not knowing that Father Segura and other Jesuit martyrs had sacrificed in those parts before him.

After the settlers had made their choice of the district Augusta Carolina, had paid their way and laid out a rough plan of St. Mary's, he tells how one of the better sort of Indian houses or cabins fell to his share, where he and the other Jesuits lived for the time comfortably enough, expecting more suitable quarters. This he thought he "might call the first chapel in Maryland, though its fittings as yet were barely an improvement upon what the house had been as an Indian dwelling."[1]

Thus far we have been guided in the narrative of the first voyage to Maryland by the two classical Relations, one in Latin, the *Relatio Itineris*, the other in English, *A Briefe Relation*, both being referred to Father White as author. While penning his narrative, which he closed one month after the first settlement, neither he in America, nor any Jesuit in England, seems to have been aware of the fact that another mission was being planned to take in Maryland and leave out the Jesuits. Yet so we have to infer from a decree of the Propaganda, under date of April 4, 1634. This states that, at the instance of "the English clergy," whomsoever that term may designate, the Sacred Congregation judged the proposal of sending a mission to Maryland, in the premises, as a measure highly opportune; and it ordered "the agent of the same clergy" to name a prefect and missionaries, or to have them named by the French Nuncio, who in all cases was to report on the fitness of the men designated.[2] *Another Anglo-American Mission. 1634.*

While this business was being broached in Rome, the missionary band in Maryland made a selection of landed property suited to the purposes of their ministry; and they took up a parcel of ground in the heart of the new town. It consisted of "25 acres or thereabouts," and was described in deeds as "lyeing nearest about the new Chappell at St. Maries;" or again, some hundred years later, as "the Chappel Land, on which the Chappel *The "Chappel Land." Other tracts.*

---

[1] *Relatio Itineris, ad fin.*
[2] Propaganda Archives, *Acta*, 10, *Cong.* 191, Apr. 4, 1634, No. 6, f. 45: "6°. *Referente eodem Eminentissimo D. Card. Pamphilio instantiam cleri Anglicani, ut missio in Marilandiam Americæ septentrionalem provinciam, navigationis Anglorum, decerneretur ad convertendos gentiles ac hæreticos Anglos ibi degentes, cum rex Magnæ Britanniæ baronem catholicum ad prædictæ provinciæ gubernat[ion]em destinaverit, Sacra Congregatio occasionem præfati baronis valde opportunam judicans petitioni oratoris annuit; jussitque ejusdem cleri agenti injungi, ut præfectum et missionarios illuc destinandos nominet, vel a clero Galliarum nuntio nominari curet; ad quem scribendum erit, ut de nominatis eorumque idoneitate ad dictam missionem informationes assumat, easque Romam transmittat.*"—Cf. *supra*, Introduction, Chap. II. § 20, p. 133, note 11.

stands at St. Maries, containing about 40 acres."[3] Another tract chosen consisted of " 400 acres of town land about St. Mary's."[4] This tract comprised two parcels of land hard by; one being 255 acres upon St. Mary's Hill in the rear of the new town, and possibly giving rise in Lord Baltimore's correspondence to a by-name for the Fathers, as "those of the Hill,"[5] the other parcel being St. Inigoes Neck on the promontory between St. Mary's River and St. Inigoes Creek. A third tract was on the other shore of St. Inigoes Creek, away from the town, and consisting of the St. Inigoes plantation, 2000 acres; to which was added St. George's Island, with its 1000 acres washed by the Potomac.[6] As at this date there was no urgency enjoined in the matter of obtaining certificates or taking out patents, the particulars of this property do not appear in the official instruments for some years to come. But in 1638, long before any instruments were drawn up, William Lewis appears as Father Copley's overseer for St. Inigoes; and the Father himself speaks, in a letter to Lord Baltimore, of the property which he possesses about St. Maries.[7]

For a topographical view of old St. Mary's City and the environs, with subsequent developments till the city declined, the reader may consult the chart and explanations given below.[8]

As to a chapel already built, used for divine worship, and that exclusively Catholic, the first document which clearly refers to it is some nine years after the commencement of the colony. At that time Father Copley asks the General about the privileges attaching to a church of the Society, whether they can be enjoyed by a chapel that is public, but not consecrated.[9]

A year passed by after the first settlement, and all that could be reported was that there were many difficulties; little fruit, particularly among the barbarians, whose language was being slowly acquired by the missionaries; and that therefore there was scarcely anything to say. Hence the report contented itself with

1634-1636.

[3] *Documents*, I. No. 31.—In the Map, *infra*: d.
[4] *Documents*, I. No. 24.—In the Map, *infra*: 4 and 11.
[5] However, "Hilton" was a cryptic name for Rome.
[6] *Documents*, I. Ibid.—Cf. the Map, *infra*.
[7] Archives of Maryland, *Judicial and Testamentary Business*, 1637-1650, p. 35.— *Calvert Papers*, i. 158; *Ibid.*, 167.—Cf. *infra*, § 46, p. 382; § 49 (3), pp. 414, 415.—As to the name "Iñigo," it is the Christian name which was Latinized by its bearer of Loyola into "Ignatius." Cf. A. Astrain. *Historia de la Campaña de Jesús en la Asistencia de España*, i. 2, 3.—The name "St. Inigoes" is in the full form of declension for the possessive case. Compare "St. Maries," "clergyes," "his Excellencyes," etc.
[8] *Infra*, pp. [567-569], Appendix A: Map of Old St. Mary's City (with Explanations).
[9] *Infra*, § 67, p. 540.

recording that there were five men there, two of them being lay-brothers.[10] These men were Fathers White and Altham with Brother Gervase; and Father Francis Rogers with Brother Wood; both of these two last returning to England by the year 1636. The next year there was no report whatever from the new world; but the Catalogue announced that two new men had gone from England, Fathers Copley and Knowles, filling the places vacated by the Father and the Brother who had returned.[11]

Here the intention was better than the performance—a circumstance of arrested development not unknown to the Catalogues, which manifest sometimes the good thing intended, but give no pledge that they are not belied in the execution. Grave difficulties in England, apparently the incipient phase of Lord Baltimore's opposition, kept Father Copley from setting out till 1637. As the experiences of this missionary introduce the very important controversy of Lord Baltimore with the Jesuits and clergy of the Catholic Church, so the success of young Father Knowles in attaining the object of his petition and being sent out to the Maryland Mission, introduces a refreshing episode from the side of young English Jesuits, whose zeal has left us written monuments of their heroic self-abnegation. *Copley delayed in England. 1636, 1637.*

Before Copley's departure from England for America, his office in London gave him every opportunity to work for the Maryland colony and Mission. He was in charge of the London residence, under the Rector of the community; and he had charge of the temporalities in general; that is, he was both minister and procurator. That he did very well on behalf of Baltimore's colony, and that on his departure he left "a solitude" which was not filled, leaving the Maryland interests in a dormant condition, is what Father White states to Lord Baltimore in 1639, suggesting at the same time that he himself might go back for a year to England, recruit his broken health, and fill the void left by his "Cosen Coplay:" "To assist a solitude," says he, "which since my Cosen Coplays departure thence I conceave the affaires of our colonye are in; and have not many who take them actingly to harte; and even freynds heare our successes as men doe musick, for their owne curiosity; not for our good. And indeede, my Lord, neyther could my Cosen or any body else, tyed to other employments and fixed in the firmament of one place, sufficiently doe the busines we desyre; for itt requires a whole man *His services to Maryland.*

---

[10] General Archives S.J., *Anglia, Historia,* iv. p. 652; *Annual Letter* for 1635.
[11] *Supplementum Catalogi,* 1 et 2, *Personarum,* 1635.

and more; who will take itt to harte, making journey to and fro throughout England to bring in adventurers and putt a new heate and spiritt of action therein; for I have marked that halfe endeavours and want of energye begette delay; and delay workes often dishonour and despayer. I wish I might have Mr. Altam with mee thither [on this year's trip to England], for one who is a true zelante of the good of this place, very active and stirring, and hath many noble freyndes and allies who have sent him since our coming large signes of their love." [12]

At last Father Copley arrived in 1637 with young Knowles, and took over from Father White the care of the mission,—a charge which now required rather business men than missionaries. The younger Father, having attained the object of his desires, reached the foreign mission only to die in the first epidemic of yellow fever. He had been but two months in Maryland, and had won the affection of all; but, stricken down by the plague along with the other three priests in the ministry, he succumbed, mourned by all. Good Brother Gervase, after five years of labour in the colony, and the exercise of the greatest patience, humility, and charity, had preceded Father Knowles to the grave by just one month. He died of the yellow fever in August, and Knowles on the 24th of September, 1637.[13]

Death of Knowles and Gervase. 1637.

Thus far the missions among the Indians were not organized. Some hostile acts had been committed; and the colonial authorities were loth to see any of their priests exposed to danger. Hence a prolonged residence among the natives was prohibited to them. This is one of the explanations which the Annual Letter for 1638 supplies. But, seeing that Mr. John Lewger had just appeared in the Province as Secretary of Maryland, Register of Grants of Land, Collector of the Customs, Receiver of Rents, and Member of the Council, it is not clear whether perhaps his policy against the Fathers, which gradually developed during the subsequent years, had not already begun to operate. Another reason for their being kept among the whites was the prevalence of the epidemic; and certainly the missionaries had enough to do. They served both Catholics and Protestants; and, as they report, with good fruit. They converted all the Protestant adventurers, who arrived in the year 1638. They redeemed four indented servants out of Virginia, and

Exercise of the ministry. 1637, 1638.

[12] *Calvert Papers,* i. 203.
[13] General Archives S.J., *Anglia, Historia,* iv. p. 773; *Annual Letter,* 1638.—*Supplementum Catalogi,* 1 et 2, 1638.—Md.-N. Y. Province Archives, carton A, 16: Fenwick MS.

engaged by the month five handicraftsmen. All of these they converted. The fact of their procuring indented servants at this date, five years after the expedition had started from England, points to the fact that the large family, then brought over at their own expense, had now reached the term of service obligatory by the conditions of contract. And that meant, as we saw before, not merely freedom, but a kind of settlement or a start in life, at the charge of the patron.

Various incidents are told of the conversions, whether to the Church, or to a good life, or to the repentance of a happy death. Mention is made of a gentleman who had sold himself into service within the province of Maryland; of two Catholics who had sold themselves in Virginia, and whom the Fathers redeemed—an example, says the Annual Letter, which other colonists of Maryland followed: "buying thence Catholic servants, of whom there is a number in that place; for every year many sell themselves into servitude; and, living without any spiritual aid, among men of the worst kind of life, they generally suffer shipwreck in their souls."

The death of Jerome Hawley is described; of him, who was the great Maryland Commissioner with Cornwaleys; who then became by royal commission Treasurer of Virginia, cutting out Cecil Lord Baltimore from a similar post; and finally, on occasion of a visit to St. Mary's, made a retreat of the spiritual exercises, as others also of the principal men did, under the Fathers' direction. **Death of Jerome Hawley, and of a noble matron.** He derived the greatest profit from that time of meditation and grace; and was just shaping his life better for the future when he was overtaken by death. His wife Eleanor, too, if it is of her that the Annual Letter goes on immediately to speak as "the noble matron," receives the highest eulogy from the Fathers; just as the same lady is spoken of in the most exalted terms of Christian commendation by the Commissioner, Thomas Cornwaleys.[14] In a few weighty words of the Annual Letter she is commemorated for the fortitude which she had exhibited since the foundation of the colony; for her gift of prayer, her zeal for the good of others, the exemplary management of her whole family, which was itself a perfect model to others; also for her devotedness to the Society, and her liberality towards it at death. Her memory remained in benediction with all, and not least for her tender charity towards the sick.

[14] *Calvert Papers*, i. 180, 181. Cf. *infra*, § 45, p. 379.—Cf. S. F. Streeter, *Papers*, p. 109.

The first will recorded in the colony is that of William Smith, "a member of the Catholique Romane Church" in Augusta Carolina. It is dated September 22, 1635. The spirit of piety which breathes in it is not at variance with the accounts just given of the general religious condition.[15]

First will. 1635.

With the first will and death of a Catholic testator we may connect the first marriage in which Father Andrew White appears, under his newly assumed name of Thomas White, as Lord Baltimore expressly notes: "Mr. Andrew *alias* Tho. White."[16] The parties were John Hollis and Restituta Tue; the witnesses, "Cuthbert Fennick," the faithful agent and trustee of the Fathers, and Robert Perry. The marriage was performed "this instant day by Mr. Thomas White" (June 2, 1639).[17]

The spiritual condition may be sketched in the paragraph, which summarizes the report of 1638: "As to the Catholics, the frequentation of the Sacraments has been such that more devotion is not to be found among people in Europe (*inter Europæos*), in proportion to the number of Catholics. The simpler sort have been catechized, and the more mature have received regular catechetical instructions (*lectiones catecheticæ*), every Sunday; while, on feast days, sermons have rarely been omitted. We have rendered every assistance to the sick and dying, who certainly have been very numerous this year, and whose habitations were very scattered. Not one of them died without the Sacraments. We have buried many and baptized divers persons. And, although there are not wanting frequent occasions of dissension, still during these last nine months no quarrel of any consequence broke out, but we stilled it at once. And there is another comfort we have by the blessing of God, that no vices

The spiritual functions.

---

[15] *Archives of Maryland, Judicial and Testamentary Business*, 1637-1650, pp. 16, 17.
[16] *Calvert Papers*, i. 201.
[17] *Archives of Maryland, Judicial and Testamentary Business*, 1637-1650, p. 52.— Cf. J. W. Thomas, *Chronicles of Colonial Maryland*, p. 209.—Why this gentleman, in the face of Lord Baltimore's statement, should have perpetuated the old account about a Mr. Thomas White, an Anglican clergyman, coming in from Virginia, may be explained by the circumstance that a rev. gentleman who seemed in his preface to be basing his book on the *Calvert Papers* had rehearsed the same history only the year before (1899). See C. E. Smith, *Religion under the Barons of Baltimore*, p. 202. This latter author quotes the "records" for a story about the "Rev. Thomas White of Virginia," in relation to the marriage of William Edwin and Mary Whitehead, on March 26, 1638, where certainly the *Judicial and Testamentary Business of the Provincial Court* has nothing whatever about Mr. Thomas White, or any other person bearing a name nearer akin to the same than Miss Mary Whitehead (pp. 24, 25). The kinship which Lord Baltimore indicates is much more positive, documentary, and rational: "Mr. Andrew *alias* Tho. White." We agree with the reverend gentleman, author of the book just quoted, when he goes on to say, in the same place: "Perhaps, on the whole, the colony might easily have been in a yet worse position."

whatever are taking root even among the new Catholics, although places of this kind are not usually settled by the best sort of men." [18]

The economical department of the Fathers, already involved enough by the original misadventure of their standing on the common Conditions of Plantation, was now made more complex and difficult by a couple of local circumstances. One was that, as money currency did not abound, payment for articles had to be made in kind. The other was that the very necessaries of life, such as corn, had to be procured outside of the colony, either among the Virginians or among the Indians. Thus their bartering and their going abroad to barter had all the appearance of trading; and was spoken of by the missionaries themselves under that name. It was also called truck, and this was the proper designation for barter. Trading for the sake of lucre is strictly prohibited to ecclesiastics by the canons of the Church, howsoever it be carried on, whether directly or indirectly. But mere truck, barter, or purchasing in kind ranks with any other form of purchase. Nevertheless, the question was proposed to the General, apparently by Father Copley, in 1639— Whether in such a case of necessity barter was not admissible? The following answer was returned from Rome, in a letter to Father Henry More, Provincial in England:—

Truck and trade.

"In Maryland I understand there is no money, but only exchange of goods; and, in consequence, that such exchange may be practised by ours without incurring the reproach of trading.[19] And I know that elsewhere too in more places than one it is in use; nor is it blamable, if exercised in just moderation." [20]

This important distinction between trading for the sake of lucre and bartering to obtain the necessaries of life, has not been noticed, when Father Copley is spoken of in terms like these: "He was also engaged in sending out goods for trade with the Indians through the agency of Robert Clarke and others, either for the profit to be drawn from the trade, the support of the mission, or as a means of bringing

---

[18] *Documents*, I. No. 8, G, *ad fin.*
[19] "*Sine negotiationis invidia.*"
[20] General Archives S.J., *Anglia, Epist. Gen.*, 1639, September 3: to More, Provincial.—Also *Ibid.*, same day, to Philip Fisher himself.—*Documents*, I. No. 5, K; No. 5, M.

Compare a licence granted about this time to the Capuchins in Guinea, that they might barter iron for bread, wine, and grain, though they were not allowed to import iron, as being one of the European products forbidden to infidels by the *Bulla Cœnæ*: "*Referente Em° D. Card. S*ti* Honuphrii, Sacra Congregatio censuit, si Sanctissimo placuerit,* 1°, *missionariis Capucinis* . . . 2°. *eisdem concedendam esse facultatem commutandi ferrum cum pane, vino et farina, dummodo contra Bullam Cœnæ Domini ferrum in dictas partes non deferant.*" Propaganda Archives, *Acta*, 15, *Cong.* 284, January 20, 1642, *Coram SS°.*, No. 1, f. 12ᵛ.—Cf. *supra*, § 31, p. 309, note 42.

the missionaries in contact with the natives, learning their language, and facilitating their conversion." [21]

§ 37. The matter of indented service has recurred so often, with the buying and transporting of the white slaves; and they themselves become such an important element in the very next phase of colonial life, that we pause to explain the institution, as we find it characterized in missionary history. Already in 1638, some five years after the expedition first started from England, we come to a pass in Maryland history, when a whole section of the population, which had enjoyed no political status or consideration before, started up into the full franchise of appearing in the assembly, of voting and being voted for, of enacting laws; and this, as Protestants present on subjects intimately concerning the Catholic priests who were absent.

An uncivil element in the colonies. Some of these people were of such a temper that, while still indented servants, they insulted their master in his own house, by reading from a book aloud, and within his hearing, matter "much reproachfull to his religion, viz. that the Pope was Antichrist, and the Jesuits anti-Christian ministers, &c.;" and when the master ordered them to stop that insolence, and reciprocated their compliments for the benefit of other ministers not Jesuit, these servants drew up a solemn protest and a petition for protection to the Protestants of the colony—probably the first time a wedge was inserted between the different faiths, heretofore harmonious in one community. The place where this scene occurred was none other than St. Inigoes, the Jesuit farm across the Creek; and the master in question was William Lewis, Father Copley's own overseer.[1]

There was a very great difference between servant and servant. Some of those who were credited to Father Copley belonged to good families, gentlemen who were employed by him in very responsible positions. Thus Mr. Robert Clerke, who appears as the agent of the Fathers in the Assembly of freemen, is named a "gentleman" in the proceedings of the meeting,

Different kinds of servants.

---

[21] S. F. Streeter, *Papers*, pp. 98, 99. This author had not the letters in the *Calvert Papers*, i., which explain the matter perfectly. His copyist, C. E. Smith, had; but the latter preferred to copy the statement about trade from Streeter, leaving out the explanations suggested by that writer. C. E. Smith, *Religion under the Barons of Baltimore*, p. 203, note.—Compare E. D. Neill, *Founders of Maryland*, p. 123, about the Rev. Wm. Wilkinson: "Like Father Thomas Copley, he engaged in trade, to assist in his support."

[1] *Archives of Maryland, Court and Testamentary Business*, 1637–1650, pp. 35–39, July 3, 1638: "The Processe against William Lewis, Francis Gray, Robert Sedgrave, &c." These latter individuals, the plaintiffs, class themselves among "poore bondmen which are under his [Lewis's] subjection."—*Calvert Papers*, i. 158.

and yet has just been entered in the land records as a "servant to Mr. Copley," brought over by the latter. Mr. Thomas Matthews, future trustee of St. Thomas's Manor, is one transported by the same Thomas Copley. There were other types of servants, such as those mentioned in the Annual Letters. There was the Catholic recusant sold by the English Government to a heretic, for transportation whither and for what purpose the master chose; there was the reduced profligate, sold by himself for a consideration; there were the Catholics who took service in Virginia, and remained utterly at the mercy of abandoned masters. Then, as we have seen in the State Papers, there were the tens of thousands lawlessly marked by the Cromwells, Thurloes, etc., for violent abduction from Ireland; and there were the young people "spirited away" from London. Besides all these, there were the jail-birds, bad-livers, and other litter swept wholesale into the plantation receptacle, with a complete disregard for consequences.

As a matter of publicity and legal regularity, no less than the binding of an apprentice might be, there was published in the *Relation for Maryland*, under date of September 8, 1633, "The forme for binding a servant." [2] By virtue of this indenture, the servant was to "redeem" himself by his work, and make good his master's outlay upon him; and, in view of this self-redemption after the stipulated number of years, the indented servant was called also a "redemptioner." This class was of consequence at the beginning. As time went on, they came to be of little or no consequence; the negroes were better—at least for masters who wished to be quite irresponsible. Still, it was among the redemptioners, even at a late date, that skilled artisans were to be found, and people who could teach something as schoolmasters. Of these latter the Maryland preacher, Jonathan Boucher, said, after the middle of the next century, that in Maryland and Virginia, "two-thirds of the little instruction we receive are derived from instructors who are either indented servants or transported felons. Not a ship arrives, either with redemptioners or convicts, in which schoolmasters are not as regularly advertised for sale as weavers, tailors, or any other trade." The only difference between the skilled artisans and the pedagogical guides for youth was that a man was esteemed, if an artisan; but, if he was good for nothing else, then he was offered and bought up at a lower price to be a schoolmaster.[3]

Indented servant, or redemptioner.

[2] Page 53. The term was usually five years.
[3] J. Boucher, *View of the Causes, etc., of the American Revolution : Discourses*, pp. 183, 184 : *On American Education.*

At the same time as Boucher, Father Mosley gave a description of the indented servant, by way of discouraging some one in England from committing himself. He wrote to his sister: " I must give you an insight of the nature of an imported servant, indented here to be sold. 1°. An indented servant must be publickly sold for a slave, for the term of years signed in his indentures, which brings him for that term of years on a footing with our negroes slaves. 2°. They have no choise of masters, but the highest bidder at publick sale carrys them off to be used at his mercy, without any redress at law. 3°. These masters (as they are chiefly accustomed to negroes, a stubborn dull set of mortalls, that do nothing but by driving) are in general cruel, barbarous, & unmerciful, some worse than others. 4°. The servant's labour is chiefly in the field with an ox, plough, or hoe, with an overseer by them, armed with a cudgel, to drive them on with their work. 5°. Their diet is mean & poor, chiefly some composition of our Indian corn, which at best is very strong & ill-savoured to an European taste, & I think more fit for horses & hogs than Christians, although in my missions I have made many a hearty meal of it. Lastly, & what is the worst of all for Roman C—th—ks [Catholics], by the law of Maryland every indented servant must take the oath on landing, or the Captains of ships pay £5 for each recusant. A law invented to hinder the importation of C—th—k servants. The Captains of ships before landing use the utmost rigour with them to drive them to it. Many have told me that they have for trifling faults been severely whipt to bring them to that one point. Most are brought to it by threats & promises before they come to anchor. I beg of you to use all your interest to hinder any of your acquaintance, especially of our persuasion, from shipping themselves to America; they will bitterly repent it when it is too late. Masters of ships may sing them fine Canterbery stories of this wild country; but as a friend they may believe me, as being an eye-witness of what I say & advance. It has been a fine poor man's country; but now it is well peopled; the lands are all secured; & the harvest for such is now all over. The lands are mostly worked by the landlords' negroes; and, of consequence, white servants, after their term of bondage is out, are stroling about the country without bread." [4]

Mosley on indented service. 1772.

§ 38. The second missionary establishment was at Mattapany on

---

[4] Georgetown College MSS., *Mosley Papers*, 1772, June 5; from Tuckahoe, Eastern Shore, Maryland.

the Patuxent, used as a basis of operations for the Indian missions in that direction, and as a source of supplies drawn out of the Indian country. A new superior, John Brooke or Ferdinand Poulton, with a lay-brother, Walter Morley, had arrived in 1639, and the report for that year, drawn up, no doubt, by Brooke himself, mentioned the origin of this plantation.

He wrote: "There are in this [Maryland] mission four priests and one lay-brother. All are in places far apart, because they hope in this manner to learn the Indian language more quickly and to spread the sacred faith of the Gospel more widely. *The account for 1639.* Father John Brooke, the Superior, stays with the Brother in the plantation of Metapannay. This was assigned us by Maquacomen, King of Patuxent. It is a sort of store-house for the mission, whence most of the temporal supplies are procured. Father Philip Fisher [*alias* Thomas Copley] lives in the chief town of the colony, that which is called St. Mary's. Father John Gravener [Altham] works in the Isle of Kent, at a distance of sixty miles from there. Father Andrew White is more distant still, being one hundred and twenty miles off, at Kittamaquund, chief place of Pascatoa. He stays with the Emperor himself, who is called the Tayac, and has been there since June, 1639. His journey thither was brought about in this wise.

"He had bestowed much time and labour on the conversion of the Patuxent king, a result eagerly looked forward to by all, as well out of gratitude for his beneficence (since, as already observed, he had given a farm to the Society), as on account of his reputation for prudence and the extensive authority he was said to exercise over the barbarians."[1] Here the Annual Letter proceeds to tell of the chief's decline in fervour, and apparently his estrangement from the entire colony. Whereupon the Governor, fearing for Father White's safety, lest he should be killed or held as a hostage, considered that the missionary ought to be withdrawn.

The Indian mission property, however, so well situated on the Patuxent, remained intact. The river itself, as may be seen by the map, enters the Chesapeake on the same western side of the bay as the Potomac, but somewhat more to the north. *The property at Mattapany. [1638.]* The possession of a base there afforded great facilities for operating all through the centre of the Maryland peninsula, which this great river drains; and the long trip was saved round St. Michael's

[1] *Annual Letter*, 1639.—*Documents*, I. No. 8, H.—The modern Mattapany is pronounced with the chief accent on the last syllable, which has the same sound as "eye" (organ of sight). The spelling in the Annual Letter for 1639 does not disagree: "*In prædio Metapannayensi;*" nor that in the Assembly *Proceedings*: "Mattapanient."

Head or Point Lookout from the other base of operations, St. Mary's, situated on an inlet of the Potomac. A subsequent letter, three years later (1642), describes the manner of missionary excursion, which was conducted chiefly by water.[2] By land, this Indian mission property was distant from St. Mary's only a few hours' ride on horseback through the woods. Thus it had quite a strategic value for spiritual ministries among the Indians, for temporal supplies of corn of which the St. Mary's mission stood in need, and for being easily in touch with the latter. Let it suffice at present to add that this Mattapany was the same property which, at a convenient moment, Lord Baltimore seized.[3]

Meanwhile Father White had passed over to the other side of the peninsula, the place called Pascattoway on the Potomac, not far to the south of the modern Washington. Here lived the chief of all the chiefs, the Tayac, or Emperor. And now began a fruitful ministry. The missionary acquired an absolute ascendancy over the mind of this great man, who had indeed killed his elder brother, Uwannus, the reigning Tayac, and had usurped the high dignity.[4] But he became a docile disciple, learnt Christian doctrine, put away all the women about him except his one wife, observed the precepts of the Church, and, on a visit to St. Mary's, asked for Baptism. The Fathers put him off till the next year; and it is a subsequent letter that tells of the great christening (1640). Whitsuntide was the feast designated; and the civil dignitaries of the English colony were to honour the baptism of the Emperor Chitomachon, or Kittamaquund, with their presence and their participation in the functions. The report describes what then took place—

Pascattoway and the Tayac. 1639.

"On the 5th of July, 1640, having been sufficiently instructed in the mysteries of faith, he received the Sacramental waters with solemnity in a little chapel, which for that ceremony and for divine worship he had erected in Indian fashion out of the bark of trees. At the same time, his wife with her infant and one of the chief of his councillors with a little son were regenerated at the font of baptism. The Emperor, who was called Chitomachon [Kittamaquund] before, was now christened by the name of Charles; his wife by that of Mary. The others too, with the Christian faith, received Christian names.

---

[2] Cf. *infra*, § 68, p. 550.
[3] *Infra*, § 59.
[4] *Calvert Papers*, i. 192: Leonard Calvert, 1638, April 25, to Lord Baltimore.

"The Governor [Leonard Calvert] was present at the function, in company with the secretary [Lewger]; nor was anything wanting that our means could supply to enhance the magnificence of the occasion. In the afternoon, the [same] king and queen were united in matrimony according to the Christian rite. Then was erected a holy cross of no trifling proportions. To carry it to the spot chosen, the King, the Governor, the secretary, and the rest lent their hands and their shoulders; two of us meanwhile chanting the Litany of the Blessed Virgin." But the labours and fervour of the occasion brought on Father White a relapse into fever. Father Altham on his part fell into a sickness and decline, of which he died four months later.[5] *Great Christian ceremonies. 1640. Death of Altham.*

This was the third missionary establishment of the Fathers in Maryland; for, as might be anticipated, so good a chief was anxious to have a permanent station for the missionaries among his people. A transaction between Copley and Lewger for 1641 records the certifying and patenting of 400 acres at Pascattoway Creek;[6] and in 1642 Lord Baltimore, writing to the Governor Leonard Calvert, makes mention of a patent recently granted to the Fathers by the latter for one hundred acres of land at Pascattoway.[7] But eventually sickness, revolution, and war prevented the Fathers from making any progress at this new basis of Indian missions.

§ 39. What we have called three establishments may have been rated as four; unless the "four" specially referred to by the General (September 15, 1640) counted in Father Altham's post on Kent Island. Or again, the St. Mary's City establishment, consisting of a chapel lot and 400 acres in two parcels, was separated indeed only by St. Inigoes Creek from the estate, consisting of 2000 acres, which with St. George's Island formed together St. Inigoes Manor of 3000 acres; yet the separation by a half-mile of water or by many a long mile through the woods, and different dates of settlement whether in the city or in the manor, may have given these holdings a double and separate character. In fact, the dates of settlement and the entire origin of this double property may have been so different that, while the city parcels were taken up by the Fathers in their own name, the manor was taken up *The four foundations. 1640.*

---

[5] *Annual Letter*, 1640.—*Documents*, I. No. 8, J.
[6] Annapolis Records, lib. i. f. 118.—*Documents*, I. No. 34.
[7] *Calvert Papers*, i. 219.

by Richard Gerrard, then sold by him to them "at a deere raite," and finally christened St. Inigoes.[1]

In the following letter from the General, who at this date (September 15, 1640) answers one of Father Brooke's (May 2, 1640), there is mention made of four establishments, and of the college which, upon the foundation of one or all, may now, it is thought, be projected. The General says that he will not be behindhand in sanctioning any collegiate plan when sufficiently mature.

". . . As to what you say about the stations fixed in four places (*sedibus quatuor in locis collocatis*), about the good will of the chief prince in that nation, about his disposition for receiving Baptism, and the hope of rich fruit to be gathered, all this has given me the greatest comfort in the Lord. The hope held out of a college I am happy to entertain; and, when it shall have matured, I will not be backward in extending my approval."[2]

This college would clearly have been at St. Mary's City, which was the recognized centre for Indians and whites. Here the Tayac of Pascattoway paid a visit, and stayed awhile under instruction. Then his future successor, a daughter, was sent hither by him to receive an English education, while she was being prepared for Baptism. The King of the Anacostans, a neighbour, was approaching likewise, asking for instruction and for a missionary Father who should remain resident with him.[3] As to the English colonists themselves, the justification of making St. Mary's the seat of a college at that very early date, no more than seven years after the first settlement, will appear at once in the next paragraphs. We merely observe here that this plan would have given us a St. Mary's College, Maryland, within very few years after Quebec College, New France, and within still fewer years after Harvard College, Massachusetts (1637).[4]

The college.

[1] Cf. *Calvert Papers*, i. 164, 3° : Copley, 1638, April 3, to Baltimore.—Cf. Annapolis Records, lib. i. f. 38, assignment made to the Fathers by Gerrard of his original rights in the name of five men transported, which correspond precisely to 2000 acres. As the affair of William Lewis, Father Copley's "overseer" (*Calvert Papers, Ibid.*, 158), shows that in the year 1638 St. Inigoes Manor was already in the hands of the Fathers, since the manifesto of Gray and Sedgrave describes the master there as "William Lewis of St. Inego's" (*supra*, § 37, p. 340), it is not clear why, in April of that same year, Copley, writing to Baltimore, should allude to the two most important pieces of property, Mattapany and "Mr. Gerards Mannor," and mention Mr. Lewis his "overseier" without saying a word of St. Inigoes, if this latter manor was not identical with the former.—For the assignment, cf. *Documents*, I. No. 30.

[2] *Documents*, I. No. 5, R.—Cf. *infra*, § 55, p. 460

[3] Vatican Archives, *Nunziatura d'Inghilterra*, No. 4, ff. 62, 63, *Relation of Maryland;* and f. 64, Poulton's letter, 1641, May 3—Also *Annual Letter*, 1640—See *Documents*, I. No. 8, K, and No. 8, J.

[4] In England there were many "ideal" Jesuit Colleges, which consisted each of divers missionary stations, and, for the present, nothing more. But (1) the very

" To the hopes held out of an Indian harvest," says the Letter for 1639, "there have been added the fruits gathered in the colony among our own people. They have not been insignificant. On the more solemn days of the year sermons are preached. On Sundays the Catechism is explained. Not only Catholics frequent the divine services, but a great many heretics also, who have been rewarded for their pains; since in this year twelve in all, sick of their former errors, have returned into grace with God and the Church. Ours do not omit to celebrate Mass every day, and, as occasion offers, to dispense the Sacraments to all who approach. And we do our best to be ready with counsel, assistance, or in any way we can, to serve those who are well and those who are ill, the afflicted as well as the dying." [5]

In the following year, 1640, the Annual Letter says of the station at St. Mary's, as contrasted with the Indian missions: " Nothing would have been more agreeable to Father Philip Fisher [Copley], who now resides in the colony of St. Mary's, than to have devoted himself to the Indians, if he had been allowed to do so by those who can on no account dispense with his services. He has received a reward for his good will. For, while among the Indians, those five, of whom an account has been given above, are christened in the waters of Baptism, the very same number and about the very same time are by his industry brought back to the bosom of the Church from the errors of heresy. The Catholics who live in the colony are not inferior in piety to those of other countries. But in urbanity of manners, according to the judgment of persons who have visited other colonies, they take the lead of settlers elsewhere. Everything is bright around us with the hope of a harvest. And, while every one of ours is doing his best to give all the help he can, various events occur worthy of note." Here the annalist records two samples, one of Divine mercy, the other of Divine justice.[6]

St. Mary's City. 1640.

---

notion of an "ideal" college, as it started from a real one, terminated also in that as its ulterior object; (2) in England, the ideal college did not become actually a real one of education, merely because the political circumstances were as yet impracticable; (3) the circumstances in Maryland were not only practicable, as much so as in the wilds of Canada, but had always been regarded as practicable for this purpose, since the whole plan of the colony had given reason to expect it.—Compare Baltimore's *Account of the Colony*, drawn up by Father White; his *Objections touching Maryland;* the invitation which he extended to the Jesuits, etc.

[5] *Annual Letter*, 1639.—*Documents*, I. No. 8, H, *ad fin.*
[6] *Ibid.*, 1640.—*Ibid.*, I. No. 8, J, *ad fin.*

CHAPTER V

LORD BALTIMORE AND THE CLERGY, 1635–1640

§ 40. John Lewger. § 41. Baltimore's feudal oath for Maryland : 1635, 1636. § 42. Lewger's introduction into the Church : 1635, 1636. § 43. The freemen's code suppressed by Baltimore : 1635–1637. § 44. Copley, Knowles, and missionary aspirants. § 45. Baltimore, Virginia, and a cleavage of parties : 1635–1638. § 46. Baltimore's code suppressed by the freemen : 1638. § 47. Lewger's refitted code : 1638. § 48. The remonstrances : 1638, 1639 : (1) The parties ; (2) Trade ; (3) Landed property ; (4) Life and limb. § 49. The attack on the clergy : 1638, 1639 : (1) Cornwaleys's protest; (2) Copley's criticism; (3) Copley's requests. § 50. The policy in London : 1638, 1639. § 51. Pressure on the missionaries : 1638, 1639. § 52. The projected Church establishment : 1638–1639 : (1) General standing ; (2) Details. § 53. Mistaken and forgotten data : (1) The *Bulla Cœnæ* and excommunications ; (2) Coke on Church privileges ; (3) The privileges in common and canon law.

Manuscript Sources: General Archives S.J., *Anglia, Epistolæ Generalium; Anglia, Historia*, v. ; *Anglia, Catalogi*.—(London) British Museum MSS., *Harleian*, 980.—Public Record Office : *Domestic, Car. I.,* 278, 303 ; *Colonial, America and West Indies ; Colonial Papers ; Transcripts from Rome*, xvii.—Rome (Vatican Library), Barberini Library, cvii. 21, 22 (*Lettere Sciolte, Inghilterra*, 24, 25).—Vatican Archives, *Nunziatura d'Inghilterra*, 5, 6 ; *Nunziatura di Francia*, 61.

Published Sources : *American Catholic Historical Researches*, xx.—*Ancient Laws and Institutes of England* (B. Thorpe).—J. Anderson, *History of the Church of England in the Colonies*, ii.—T. C. Anstey, *Guide to the Laws of England affecting Roman Catholics*.—Blackstone's *Commentaries on the Laws of England*, i., iii. ; Stephen's *Commentaries*, i., iii.—Bonacina, *Opera Omnia*, iii. : *De Censuris in Bulla Cœnæ*.—J. H. Brodhead, *Documents relating to the Colonial History of New York*, iii.—*Calendars of State Papers, Colonial Series, America and West Indies*, v.—*Calvert Papers*, i.—Coke's *Littleton*; *2 Institutes*.—C. Dodd, *Church History of England*, iii.—K. C. Dorsey, *Life of Father Thomas Copley*.—H. Foley, *Records of the English Province S.J.*, i., vii., *Collectanea*.—J. Gillow, *Bibliographical Dictionary-History*.—H. Hallam, *View of the State of Europe during*

CHAP. V] LORD BALTIMORE AND THE CLERGY 349

the Middle Ages, ii.—J. Cardinal Hergenroether, *Kirchengeschichte*, ii.—
B. T. Johnson, *Foundation of Maryland.*—J. Kilty, *Landholder's Assistant.*
—J. Lingard, *History of England*, viii.—(Maryland) *Archives of Maryland:
Proceedings of the Assembly*, 1637–1664; *Proceedings of the Council*, 1636–
1667.—F. Pollock and F. W. Maitland, *History of English Law*, i.—
Relation of Maryland, 1635.—J. T. Scharf, *History of Maryland*, i.—
Statutes of the Realm.—S. F. Streeter, *Maryland Two Hundred Years ago;
Papers relating to the Early History of Maryland.*—Suarez, *Defensio Fidei.*
—J. W. Thomas, *Chronicles of Colonial Maryland.*—J. Winsor, *History of
America*, iii.—A. à Wood, *Athenæ Oxonienses*.

SOME personal and political elements found their way into the composition of colonial life, and brought about a change in the whole religious aspect of affairs. A new man came to Maryland in the person of John Lewger, who represented in a manifold capacity Cecil Lord Baltimore. Whether he alone gave the new turn to the social and religious history of the colony, or whether he received the impress of his policy entirely from his chief, or how much it may have been that each contributed to a system perfectly suited to both, —all this must be left to the reader's interpretation of Lewger's antecedents and of Baltimore's subsequent action.

The pronounced departure of the two men in what seemed a new religious direction was strictly related to political principles of government. So we shall take note of divers codes of laws, one drawn up by the colonial freemen and rejected by Baltimore; another drawn up by Baltimore or Lewger and rejected by the freemen; both of them to be followed and supplanted by a third, which was devised by the freemen and assented to by the Lieutenant-General in his lordship's name.

With these untoward vicissitudes of laws submitted only to be brushed aside, there coincided a formal attack on the clergy who were then in Maryland; and there was devised by Lewger a Church establishment such as had not been conceived before. In London a policy was formulated, which was said to be countenanced by the Provincial Father Henry More, as it certainly was more than countenanced by the Proprietary Lord Baltimore. In Maryland, persons both lay and clerical became involved in a general campaign, not merely political, but strikingly religious. One or two negative features in the drama will appear somewhat new. First, there is no canon law in the history to constitute the knot of the difficulty between Lord Baltimore and the Jesuits. Secondly, there does not seem to be any political issue about initiating legislation, as between the Proprietary and the freemen. These two conventional elements being eliminated from the history, the whole drama assumes a new cast, different from what we are usually invited to contemplate in the early history of Maryland.

§ 40. As a fellow-student of Cecil Calvert, second Lord Baltimore, there had lived with him at Oxford a young man somewhat older than himself, by name John Lewger. He had entered the University in 1616, when about fourteen years of age. Cecil Calvert, a Protestant and Anglican like Lewger, matriculated soon after, and the two became intimate. Both of them underwent the influences of a University education, and grew up to be men under the Protestant Establishment in circumstances very different, and in religious conditions much altered since the youthful days of Cecil's father, George Calvert. In the older generation, throughout Elizabeth's reign, Catholic influence had been alive everywhere, except in politics, which were largely spent on the effort to kill it. In the younger generation, under James I., not only was a Catholic impress wanting to politics, but Catholic thought was fast disappearing from literature; and, as to law, quite a new shape was being given to the policy of English jurisprudence and to the meaning of laws in past history. Everything was now trained against Popery.

John Lewger. 1616-1634.

Within ten years, when Cecil Calvert had become a man, his father, Sir George Calvert, Secretary of State, entered the Catholic Church. He took his family with him; and Cecil, the eldest son, seems to have entered also in the current or in the wake of the family movement. The colour of his thought, political, legal, and historical, as exhibited in his words and actions during a long and chequered life, would convey the impression that not only his entrance into the Catholic Church had been merely a domestic matter, but that in after-life his chief anchorage in the same Church was only a domestic matter, one of family tradition and association. Indeed, interest alone might suffice to keep him enrolled there, where he could treat on a footing of familiarity with Catholic lords, gentry, and clergy; while his tastes and other associations kept him perfectly familiar with the Protestant world which never deserted him to his prejudice, and which he took no pains to desert.

John Lewger was now an Anglican Rector filling a place in Somersetshire. He was somewhat over thirty-three years of age when he abandoned his living to enter the Catholic Church. This was about 1634, some ten years after the conversion of the Calverts, and at the very time when Maryland was being first settled. He had a wife and at least one child, John; and, on resigning his rectorship, he was reduced to the dire necessity of begging for the means of subsistence. He went about among the priests of London, interviewed the Italian new-comer, a papal envoy by the name of Panzani, and finally was brought into contact with his old acquaintance, Cecil Calvert, now Lord Baltimore. Differing as the latter did from George Calvert, his father, he had nevertheless stepped into his father's place to administer the affairs of a colony under a charter which was not of his own making. John Lewger was to become an important agent in that colonial administration.

The views which Mr. Lewger brought in with him on becoming a Catholic were largely, we may suppose, the same which he had conceived while still a Protestant, and in obedience to which he had sacrificed living and station to conscience. Lewger's views.
Mr. Chillingworth, his friend, a noted divine, had become a Catholic. Mr. Lewger followed. Mr. Chillingworth left the Church and became a Protestant again. Mr. Lewger did not follow, but declared afterwards that his friend was of no meek and winning spirit, that he was haughty and conceited, and therefore unfit for a religion which required humility and obedience. He himself, setting a very fair example of self-denial and of obedience to the dictates of conscience, added to the eloquence of example, as time went on, an explanation of views with regard to the Establishment which he had left. In after-life he published two books, the lengthy names of which are as good as ample propositions for intimating the purport of the publications. The name of the first runs thus: "*Erastus Junior*, or a fatal blow to the clergies pretensions to divine right; in a solid demonstration by principles, forms of ordination, common laws, acts of parliament, that no bishop, minister, nor presbyter, hath any right or authority to preach, &c., in this nation from Christ, but only from the parliament." [1] The name of the second, containing answers to opponents, is in this wise: "*Erastus Senior*, scholastically demonstrating this conclusion that (admitting their Lambeth Records for true) those called bishops here in England are no bishops, either in order or jurisdiction, or so much as legal. Wherein is answered to all that hath been said, in vindication of them, by Mr. Mason in his *Vindiciæ Ecclesiæ Anglicanæ*, Doctor Heylin in his *Ecclesia Restaurata*, or Doctor Bramhall (then called

---

[1] London, 1659–60; two vols. in 4to.

Bishop of Derry, now Primate of Armagh) in his last book entitled *The Consecration and Succession of Protestant Bishops justified*," etc.[2]

Here, as is evident, Mr. Lewger had failed to discover, in the Establishment which he had abandoned, any Divine origin for Orders and jurisdiction. He had found Erastianism instead, or a Church constitution which was not Divine, but merely political. This ecclesiastical condition called "Erastian," which had suggested the names of his two books, *Erastus Junior* and *Erastus Senior*, had been elevated to the dignity of a positive system by the Protestant Erastus, a Professor of Moral Theology at Basle. The theory made headway in England during the seventeenth century. And, as to the lawyers, it suited them admirably, for it made the Christian Church enter into their scheme of jurisprudence just like any department of State which found a chapter in their pages. It meant that the Church was entirely subject to the State in discipline and worship; it was a wheel in the State machinery; it depended on the landlord as the country did, *Cujus regio ejus religio*; and the prince's conscience was the clock to set all other consciences by. Civil fealty towards the King and religious fidelity towards God were so connected that subjects were bound to follow the dictates of the magistrates; since Church and State were nothing but two denominations for the same society.

Lewger and Erastianism. We must infer from this process of Lewger's mature thought, though the books were published some quarter of a century after his conversion, that the gentleman had found in the Catholic Church what he desiderated outside, a primacy of Divine origin, and a Divine source of Orders and jurisdiction. To escape Erastianism he had become a Catholic.

But the difficulty will now occur—Why did he adopt or resume Erastianism when helping Baltimore to govern Maryland? If it was not that he did so merely as an employee of Baltimore—taking his policy from his chief, as Erastians took their religion from their landlord—it may have been that, with the best of intentions, he had not received the best instruction on entering the Catholic Church. Possibly he was too great or too learned to have been a catechumen at all. And, indeed, instruction or no instruction, there was more than one spot at the time where the Catholic culture in the Church was of very much the same growth as Erastianism outside.

---

[2] (London), 1662.—This latter, which we have seen, is an able scholastic production. British Museum Library, 1354, a, 8, very small 16mo, ff. prelim., preface, pp. 104.

Gallicanism was in full process of development; so was Regalism, the future Josephism and Febronianism, with the domination of Parliaments, courts, and ministries, and court-dames, over the Catholic Church and the Papacy.

As we learn from a passage of Panzani's given below, the guides into whose hands Lewger fell certainly favoured him with some very dubious principles of life and action, if the meddling envoy himself was not entirely responsible for at least one immoral principle, the gravity of which he seems not to have recognized. There was a large party at the time that endorsed compromise with the State, compromise with Protestantism,—a party always building the bridges by which other people were to come in, but by which their own people were always pouring out,—friends to foes and foes to friends, the men whom George Con called the *fautori*, or backers of Protestantism inside the Catholic Church. Such persons would not disturb the antecedent views or ill-defined premises in a good convert's mind with what they called the "Puritanism" or Puritanical notions of an exact and exacting Catholicity. Thus a convert to Catholicism might have been a Protestant first, then not a Protestant afterwards; later on he might even be a priest, as Lewger became; but the one important stage totally wanting in the process would still be that he should have become a Catholic at some time or other. When, after his career as a layman in Maryland, and his assumption of the ecclesiastical character in England, Mr. John Lewger applied for admission into the Society of Jesus, he was politely refused. Nothing could be more foreign to the whole spirit of the Jesuit constitution than to shut one's eyes for a moment to the principle of common sense enunciated by Seneca, that "what has gone up without a foundation stands ever ready to topple over"—"*In ruinam prona sunt, quæ sine fundamentis crevere.*"[3]

[3] Wood, *Athenæ Oxonienses*, s.v. "John Lewgar."—Gillow's *Bibliographical Dictionary.*—Cf. Dodd, *Church History*, vi. 106–109, s.v. "Edward Knott," on Chillingworth.—Cf. Hergenroether, *Kirchengeschichte*, ii. 512, 513, 1041, edit. 1879; *Erastianismus*: "*Von dem 1589 als Professor der Moraltheologie in Basel verstorbenen Erastus, der die völlige Unterwerfung der Kirche unter den Staat in Disciplin und Cultus vertrat und ihr jede Selbständigkeit absprach, hat der in England im 17 Jahrhundert viel verbreitete, aber auch bekämpfte Erastianismus den Namen. 'Erastianer sint nicht Christianer' wurde mehrfach gesagt. In Rom und in anderen katholischen Ländern nannte man die Vertreter solcher Ansichten Regalisten, Aulici, Politici. Dem System der Fürstenherrschaft über Religion und Gewissen drückte endlich 1648 der westphälische Friede das Siegel auf.*"—Cf. Hallam, *Constitutional History of England*, i. 309, last note to ch. iv.; about "the principles of what, in the seventeenth century, was called Hobbism, towards which the Erastian system, which is that of the Church of England, though excellent in some points of view, had a tendency to gravitate; namely, that civil and religious allegiance are so necessarily connected, that it is the subject's duty to follow the dictates of the magistrate in both alike. And this received some countenance from the false and

§ 41. Gregory Panzani, a member of the Roman Oratory, was selected by Cardinal Barberini and sent into England by Urban VIII. on what appears to have been his first mission, and was, in fact, his last. He was not made for such a career; and, at this early date in the history of Roman nunziatures, there was not as yet a school of men available at Rome for picking out the right one to discharge a mission of trust. The negotiations for which he was sent were very limited in scope; they concerned the oath of allegiance or fealty, and the differences between the secular and regular clergy in England.[1] Limited as was his mission, his authority was less; in fact, there was little required for such an excursion. His abilities for business seem to have been on a par with his knowledge of English and French; of the former language he knew not a word,[2] and of the latter it is not clear how much he knew. On one occasion at least, in his letters, he recommends that an envoy to England should know French, and be able to deal with people at court.[3] Such being his penury in the means of communication, he made amends for his poverty by an endless capacity for talking and writing. His correspondence in the Barberini Library and in the Vatican, Rome, and the stout quarto volume of Roman Transcripts deposited among the London State Papers, abundantly exhibit his degree of self-control and of ordinary judgment in touching or managing affairs.[4] In his weekly budget he dispenses at large all that he has gathered in from the men who have used him during the

Gregory Panzani.

mischievous position of Hooker, that the Church and Commonwealth are but different denominations of the same Society. Warburton has sufficiently exposed the sophistry of this theory; though I do not think him equally successful in what he substitutes for it."

[1] Thus the General (1635, January 13) wrote to the Provincial, Father Blount : "*Id vero latere non debet R. V^m, fuisse non ita pridem hinc ex curia Romana in istud regnum missum aliquem, quem aiunt virum bonum ac prudentem, non alio fine quam ut tam religiosorum quam ecclesiasticorum et sæcularium etiam ac nobilium virorum animos exploraret; et, an consultum necessariumque judicent ut Episcopus aliquis in regno constituatur, omnium sententias et rationes audiret.*"

[2] Vatican Archives, *Nunziatura d'Inghilterra*, 5, f. 52, London, 1635, April 13: Panzani to Barberini.—Cf. P. R. O., *Transcripts from Rome*, xvii., under same date, f. 4 of letter. Panzani did not pretend to understand the document which he forwarded to the Cardinal about Civitá Vecchia, because the points "were written in English." They contained proposals for free trade with that papal port. Commending his successor, George Con, Panzani noted that among his own principal defects was ignorance of the language. Vatican Archives, *Ibid.*, f. 305^v, 1636, May 28 : Panzani to Barberini, 4th despatch of that date: ". . . *Per esser io conosciuto sacerdote e per mancamento principalmente di lingua, e dell' altre qualità, che io ho notificate a V. Eminenza desiderarsi in un tal ministro.*"—Cf. P. R. O., *Transcripts from Rome*, xvii. under date.

[3] Vatican Archives, as above, f. 200^v, 1636, February 13: same to same.

[4] Vatican Archives, *Nunziatura d'Inghilterra*, 5, 6.—Barberini Library, cvii. 21, 22 (*Lettere Sciolte*, 24, 25); these have now been transferred to the Vatican Library. —London, Public Record Office, *Transcripts from Rome*, xvii., *Barberini*, ii. (Stevenson).

week; and, as the days go on, he says and unsays the same things, as variable as a daily newspaper, and consistent only in the general trend of his love, his fear, and his hate. In the few and short passages which we have discovered relating to Lord Baltimore, the character of the man may be discerned. But for any substantial contributions to history it devolves upon the reader's good sense to discover for himself, in the moist light, and misty medium of the writer's gossip, such matter of fact as floats about partially revealed. *Panzani's weekly budgets. 1635, 1636.*

He has been seven months at work, when he has occasion to mention the Baron of Baltimore in his letter of August 15, 1635. He says: "The Baron of Baltimore has a population—we call it a feudal tenure—in the West Indies; and because, for the instruction of those peoples in the Catholic religion, he has sent thither some Jesuits, and is taking measures to send there Jesuits only, people wonder whether he of Canterbury [Archbishop Laud] will not take that population away from him; since there is reason to fear that the Jesuits will make such a nest there for themselves as to be able to do harm to the State. He is, however, sufficiently favoured by Cottington, whence the other is much afraid." [5]

A week later (August 22) Panzani reports as follows: "The Baron of Baltimore, being wholly devoted to the Jesuits and in a state of affliction for fear of losing his feudal holding in India, should like to win over the King. So, helped by the Jesuits as is believed, he has drawn up the enclosed formula of the oath of allegiance to the King of England. And first he thought fit to show it to a secular priest, perhaps for the purpose of having the seculars also approve of it. It was brought to me, and I said that just to entertain myself I would read it; but for the rest I could not intrude in this business; and I said that every one will be pleased to see Catholics giving satisfaction to the King in matters which are lawful, saving their religious principles. The priest who brought it to me expresses no high sense of approbation for it; which means that people should see to having the Pope's name entirely left out. God grant a good issue to this negotiation." *A Baltimore oath of allegiance. Aug. 22, 1635.*

The next week (August 29) Panzani resumes, beginning with Sir Toby Matthews, whom he takes to be a Jesuit, and whom, says he, the King takes to be mad: "Nevertheless, I am trying to find an occasion for having an interview with him, and pushing him on adroitly, with the precautions intimated by your Eminence, to propose a new

[5] For series of original texts under dates, see *Documents*, I. No. 10, A–W.

formula for the oath—although I believe that he had a hand in the one which the Baron of Baltimore proposes, as I said in my last. In any case, it is hard now to speak to any one till the month of October, because at present London is deserted, and every one is at his villa." This last phrase, borrowed from the society cant of the seventeenth century, is interesting inasmuch as it agrees with the same dialect of three centuries later. Then the city was said to be "deserted" when a few lords went to their villas; now it is said to be "empty" when only five or six millions of people remain behind!

The gentleman continues: "I have learnt that the said Baron, when he showed the said formula to that secular priest, bade him show it to me; but the latter, knowing what I had said to him and to others, answered that I did not want to meddle in the said business under any shape or form. Still he did let me see it privately. I am confirmed in my opinion that the Jesuits have a hand in it. They pretend to keep clear of swearing against the authority of the Pope, to the effect that he cannot excommunicate and depose kings; but [they] only [mean] that whoever swears shall still engage to be faithful to the King, notwithstanding such excommunications and deprivations. Again, I have adroitly exhorted that priest to manage, by all means possible, that the Pope's name do not appear in the new formula."

The next week's despatch (September 5) announces that "the Baron of Baltimore has not yet presented his formula. I am told that he has shown it to the Provincial of the Jesuits, who wants to take counsel upon it. If this is true, we may infer the falsity of the rumour which said that the formula in question came out of the Jesuit mill.[6] In any case, I will diligently observe what goes on in this affair." Here follows some gossip about Toby Matthews. The Provincial of the Jesuits just mentioned was Father Richard Blount, though Father Henry More had already been named for the office. Under the same date (September 5) he returns again to Sir Toby Matthews in relation to Baltimore's oath.

While so long on a wrong scent in taking Baltimore, the oath-framer, to be a creature of the Jesuits, Panzani has also been at fault *A Baltimore draft of laws.* in supposing that the Baron busied himself with English Catholic affairs at all. And from what occurred soon afterwards in Maryland, where a whole full-blown code of laws was received to be planted there off-hand, we infer that the culture which he was known to be developing was not merely the formula of an oath. That could hardly have consumed seven months. Rather it

[6] "*Sia farina de Giesuiti.*"

was an entire feudal body of jurisprudence, whereof an oath of allegiance, whether to the King of England or the Lord Palatine of Maryland, was just one element. And soon afterwards we find, as was noted before, that the new missionary and superior, Father Copley or Fisher, was detained in England by certain difficulties which seem to have arisen from the side of the Proprietary.[7]

Two weeks after giving the last piece of information, Panzani wrote (September 19): "Toby Matthews has not yet come to me. I understand he is at his villa. When he returns I will see and rouse him up to take in hand the business of the oath, or else to lend assistance to Baltimore, who, as I wrote before, had drawn up a formula. I have understood, however, that his formula will serve only for the men of his feudal holding, which they call here a plantation in India; and I have been told he has shown it to the King. I will try to discover more about the whole affair." Here enters the Provincial of the Jesuits; and, trying to divine the meaning of that Father's guarded words, Panzani finds himself adrift again as to the whole tenor of his information.[8] Thus two weeks have passed in learning and unlearning something about the shadowy oath. Two more weeks pass, and leave him in possession of a substantial piece of information, that the good man does not really know anything special about Baltimore's formula (October 3).

Then, a few weeks later (October 24) Panzani has to report the condemnation of the Baron's oath by the Provincial of the Jesuits.[9] Speaking of the latter, he begins by telling the Cardinal that he had asked the Provincial to appoint a learned Jesuit who should draw up the formula of allegiance. The Provincial said that "he knew of a certain Baron, namely, Baltimore, who had in his hands a formula to propose, which he thought would not be acceptable at Rome. Without betraying the circumstance that I had forwarded it to your Eminence, I replied that, if he thought such a formula was bound not to be pleasing at Rome, it were proper to keep it back for a while and make out a good form, and beg him [Baltimore] to undertake the duty of presenting it. For, if the King shall see that the Catholics will not accept a formula proffered by a Catholic, one which he will take to have been composed with maturity, he will become so much the more exasperated against Catholics, and he could start a persecution. This point went home

The Jesuit Provincial.

[7] Cf. *infra*, § 44, p. 368.
[8] *Documents*, I. No. 10, H.
[9] Father Henry More would seem to have succeeded Father Richard Blount in the administration, as Provincial, some little while after this.

with the Provincial, and he promised to look to it. I protested, however, that I gave no opinion nor wanted to give any opinion on the said formula, declaring that it was not my business to enter into matters theological."

In answer to this passage of Panzani's second despatch for October 24, 1635, Cardinal Barberini's minutes say: "From the fact that the Provincial of the Jesuits would not offer to persuade any Catholic to draw up an oath of allegiance, such as would be acceptable to the State without offending consciences, it appears that those most prudent Fathers find great difficulties in the undertaking; and you did well to give the advice that Baltimore's should be suppressed; for here it is not considered admissible."

The correspondence proceeds on this line as on a multitude of others. But, since we are not concerned with anything except the origin of a strange oath which appeared in Maryland some years later, we pass over a month, and then we find the following shred of information: "The Baron of Baltimore wants soon to offer the King his formula of the oath. And I have again besought Laborn, a secular priest, his confidant, to induce him to leave out the name of the Pope or the Pope's authority" (December 5). The Cardinal approves of suspending the Baltimore proposal, and desires a copy of the formula to be sent him privately (January 17, 1636). He then wishes to see it suppressed on all accounts, "especially as long as he [Baltimore] has not consented to leave out the name of the Pope" (January 30). But it was all in vain to think of interfering with Baltimore, when probably he was only attending to his colonial affairs, and, helped by men like Langford or Langhorne, was reconsidering or reconstructing his charter. Panzani said to the Cardinal: "I have made efforts, using a secular priest as intermediary, to get that formula of an oath rightly adjusted, the one which the Baron of Baltimore wants to propose. But he would not withdraw the name of the Pope nor make any change of consequence. I did not want to try again for fear of betraying myself and showing that I knew about it" (December 19, 1635).

At this time, while sinking rapidly in the estimation of his patron at Rome, because of many characteristic performances which were now showing their results, he exhibits the final stage, as he imagined, of the Baltimore production. "Regarding the oath," he writes on January 16, 1636, "I will try to stop Baltimore. This is an affair very aromatic." That was true. Whatever he touched became aromatic. A month later he cries out, "I will do my very best to get Baltimore to drop his formula, and I will try to get a copy and send it" (February 27). At last, in March, he is able to report success: "I have managed to stop the formula of Baltimore; and Labourn, secular priest, a friend of his, has come to tell me that the said lord is resolved not to go about proposing it" (March 12).

So, according to this envoy, seven months at least have been passed by the Proprietary of Maryland, and that at a most busy time, in forming and reforming a model oath for the Catholics of England; and nothing comes of it in the end. Panzani continues in his despatches with other material containing even less substance than we have found in his Baltimore gossip. He has detailed his plans for expelling the Jesuits from England, or for destroying their sodalities of the Blessed Virgin; he has expounded his theories on occult Jesuits and Jesuitism; and he has denounced Puritans and Puritan Jesuits. *A shadowy oath. 1636.*

Now we must borrow his account of Lewger's introduction into the Catholic Church. It is the only one available.

§ 42. Precisely at the same time that Panzani was reconnoitring Baltimore and his oath, he occupied himself on several occasions with John Lewger. On July 11, 1635, he tells the Cardinal that, after many efforts with "these seculars," he has been able to provide for two of the recent converts, who will now proceed to the college at Lisbon. He will try to find relief for another that has been mentioned; "as I have also recommended to Father Philips [the Queen's confessor] a very learned minister, John Leuger, one recently converted, who has had many disputes with these ministers. On his coming to see me, I received him with all marks of affection possible, promising to do for him whatever I could; and he went away satisfied, as I have understood from other persons. He goes about still dressed like a minister, as well because that garb is not held to be distinctive, for it is common even to the students, as because he goes on temporizing thus in order not to lose his income, till he finds something else to live on. The Bishop of London and the Archbishop of Canterbury know that he is converted; still they pretend to be ignorant of the fact, and they tolerate him. In fact, every one tells me that it were necessary to think of providing some fund for these persons; because I am informed that many would be converted if they had wherewithal to support themselves; for they lose their benefices. Nay, this is one of the ways to arrive at the union [of the Churches]; for people of this description, *Panzani and Lewger. 1635, 1636.*

before declaring themselves openly to be Catholics, could so shape their preaching as to prepare the minds of the people. I lay this matter at the feet of His Holiness and of your Eminence."

Seven months afterwards the envoy returns to the charge in the following terms: "Father Leander had already commended to me John Leuger, a converted minister, who having lost a benefice worth 400 *scudi*, has nothing now wherewith to maintain his wife and children,[1] who are become Catholics with him. At present this recommendation is renewed by Father Price. I have tried in various ways to keep up his spirits, and I have spoken several times to Father Philips on his behalf; but I have not been able to get anything of consequence. And a small pittance is not enough for him, since he would wish to have either a large sum paid right down, or an allowance every month; just as the resident minister of Spain, by order of his king, gives allowances, they say, to various persons. I have told him, and I have had others tell him that I was seriously pained at not being able to help him in this manner. And, as he still urged me to send a memorial to your Eminence, I endeavoured to evade the proposal by making as much as I could of the very great expenses which your Eminence has to meet. But, as he still trusted in your Eminence, and seemed to doubt my willingness to do him the service, he resolved to send the memorial to the procurator of the Benedictines. I do not know whether he will do so. I write this to your Eminence that you be not taken unawares" (February 27, 1636).

Three months later, after speaking of Longueville, the same apparently whose acquaintance we made in connection with Newfoundland, he says: "It will be a work of great moment to help John Leuger a converted minister; for I understand that others too would be converted if they could hope for similar aid" (May 28).

Panzani's charitable proposal regarding a converts' aid fund was not at all new at Rome. The same suggestion came from various parts of Europe in the sixteenth and seventeenth centuries; and the Cardinal-Secretary of State might well object, as he did, to having the families of converted ministers throughout Europe attached to his own list of household expenses.

Rather less edifying and more curious was the other suggestion which Panzani had made, and the immoral standard which he seems to have set up before the convert-minister, that the latter might still, for the sake of the living, hold on to his place in the Protestant

[1] "*E figli.*"

Church, occupy the Protestant pulpit, and partake in services which he had already judged to be schismatical or heretical. In Norway, Sweden, Switzerland, and elsewhere, this duplicity had been witnessed during a good part of a century in precisely the opposite direction, when congregations and territories became "reformed" without their knowing it. It was novel to find a papal envoy recommending the same equivocal morality, and that at the cost of a *communicatio in divinis*, or offering strange fire at the altar. But in the case of this peculiar man it will appear less singular when we find him telling the Cardinal with glee that he has forged a paper and told a lie: "I gave to Windebank," he says, "a forged cipher, in which I made up the story that your Eminence desired his son to come to Rome, that you might reciprocate the courtesies which he shows me. And he was jubilant with delight; and he hopes that next Easter will find him there" (August 8, 1635).[2]

Dubious morality.

Such were the auspices under which Mr. John Lewger entered the Catholic Church. Certainly none of the immediate influences that operated on him were of a very puritanical kind. Panzani's great authority, the Father Philips, Queen's confessor, who signed himself "priest of the Oratory of Jesus," and to the surprise of the Cardinal-Secretary and of Spada, the French Nuncio, signed himself also "priest of the Society of Jesus,"[3] is credited by the envoy with a number of extraordinary opinions; as the proposal that Rome should allow of a married clergy, at least for a time, and also allow of communion under both kinds; and, if any one disagreed with the said Father Philips, he should be remanded to go and read the parable of the Prodigal Son![4] This certainly was a compendious sort of theology.

It was from such an environment of infected divinity that, when Panzani went home to write memoirs about himself and Puritans and Jesuits in England, Lewger crossed the ocean as Baltimore's deputy, to regulate the bearings of Church and State in Maryland. Gregory Panzani had spent but two short years in England (1635, 1636), and had not yet learned the English language. John Lewger had spent about two years in the Catholic Church, when he landed in Maryland (November 28, 1637); and how much he had learnt

[2] See *Documents*, I. No. 10, B.
[3] Vatican Archives, *Nunziatura di Francia*, No. 61, ff. 297, 300, 413; 21 June, 15 July, 30 August, 1624. Philips' signature is "*presbyter Societatis Jesu;*" Ibid., f. 297. Cf. *Ibid.*, No. 395, f. 32, where he signs himself "*prêtre de l'Oratoire de Jésus.*"
[4] P. R. O., *Transcripts from Rome*, xvii., under date, second cipher: Panzani, London, June 13, 1635, to Barberini.

of the Catholic Church, of her language and her ways, the sequel may now show.[5]

§ 43. On the American side of the ocean there were two matters of importance which engaged Lord Baltimore's attention during the same years 1635-1637. One was the action of the Maryland gentlemen in legislating for the good of the colony. They drew up a code of "wholesome lawes and ordinances" in a General Assembly held at St. Mary's on February 26, 1635. The other matter was that of his own ambition with regard to Virginia, where he hoped to obtain for himself a dominant and lucrative post. The result of his manœuvres when he was foiled by one of his own Commissioners, Jerome Hawley, reacted upon the affairs of Maryland, and helped to bring about a sharp division of parties, between the official section of the Calverts with their employees on the one side, and the gentry like Hawley with the clergy on the other.

The real occasion for holding the first Assembly of Maryland seems to have been the hostility shown by Captain William Clayborne of Virginia and of the Isle of Kent. Among the "wholesome lawes and ordinances" then passed, "it was enacted that the offenders in all murthers and felonies should suffer such paines, losses, and forfeitures as they should or ought to have suffered in the like crimes in England."[1] This was a statement and application relative to the common law.

Occasion of the freemen's code. 1635.

By the spring convoy of the same year, 1635, Lord Baltimore could have received in England his copy of these laws, submitted for his approval. He disapproved of the whole code absolutely. It is very noteworthy how, in the entire course of colonial history, the same people who claimed all right for England to tax or to persecute, whether they were a Proprietary Government, a Privy Council, or a Board of Trade, did steadily and always set their faces against making or allowing any general statement, that the legal rights of subjects in the Colonies were in no wise different from the rights of subjects in England. They proceeded on an eclectic plan, not at all for the good of the colonists. In many cases they despised even eclecticism, and made discriminating laws against their own plantations, in the same way as against Ireland. So was it in the

Baltimore's disapproval.

[5] As to what Panzani reported that Lewger's petition for alms specified a large sum paid right down, "*una grossa somma adesso*," or at least a regular income, it will be useful to compare the circumstance, if true, with Lewger's enormous appropriation of lucrative offices, from the moment that he was patronized by Baltimore.

[1] *Archives of Maryland, Proceedings of the Assembly*, 1637/8-1664, p. 23: Act of Attainder of W. Cleyborne, March 24, 1638 (N.S.).

Acts of Navigation.[2] The one governing consideration was the King's revenue, or the absent landlord's income, or the London merchant's profits. Under Baltimore's veto in this case fell the application made by the colonists of the English common law in matters of murder and felony.

Within four months from the time when he could have received the code, it was known in London that Lord Baltimore was fabricating something. Panzani, as we have heard, gave out that it was an oath; and then, some seven months after, claimed the credit of having stopped the manufacture of the same.

But one product of the laboratory was ready immediately; and that was simply to authorize the payment of what was due to the adventurers for their having invested in the plantation. The adventurers, during these first years of the colony, were already in three different categories, as having gone out under three different agreements, each of these latter being less favourable to the colonists and more advantageous to the Proprietary, according as the plantation was seen to be more and more assured of success. The clergy had gone out under each of these conditions of contract. But it will suffice to quote a paragraph or two regarding the first category of original adventurers, for the sake of showing the absolute character of the indebtedness which bound Baltimore to the missionaries no less than to the other planters. *Baltimore's warrant to pay the adventurers. Aug. 8, 1636.*

Addressing the warrant to "our dear Brother, Mr. Leonard Calvert, Esq., and our Lieutenant-General of the Province of Maryland, or to any other our Lieutenant-General there for the time being," he formulates the following confession of a debt in the rigorous sense of the term :—

"Whereas the adventurers to plant that our Province of Maryland have made suit unto us that wee would be pleased to grant unto them, under our Great Seal of the same Province, such proportions and quantities of land there, upon such considerations and agreements as we have heretofore propounded and promised to grant the same unto all such adventurors; Forasmuch as we are bound in honour really to perform the same in all points; These are therefore to will and authorise you that presently, upon receipt hereof, you make or cause to be made under our Great Seal of that our said Province unto every first adventuror [that is, of the first settlement], for every five men aged between sixteen and fifty years, which such adventuror did bring

[2] As a sample, see the Order in Council, June 24, 1663. J. R. Brodhead, *Documents relative to the Colonial History of New York, etc.*, iii. 44–46.

into our said Province to inhabit and plant there in the year of our Lord 1633, and unto his heirs forever, a grant of 2000 acres of land of English measure, for the yearly rent of 400 lb. weight of good wheat; and to every adventuror which in that year did bring a less number than five men into that our said Province of the ages aforesaid to inhabit and plant there, and unto his heirs for ever, a grant of 100 acres of land (of like measure) for himself and 100 acres more for his wife (if he brought any), and for and in respect of every servant; and 50 acres for every child under the age of sixteen years, for the rent of 10 lb. of wheat yearly for every fifty acres.

"[Here follow the less favourable conditions for the adventurers of 1634 and 1635, and since, in two categories; also a warrant to erect every 3000, 2000, and 1000 acres into a Manor, with the privilege of holding a court-baron and a court-leet. And for all the foregoing are herewith sent drafts of the relative grants.]

"So we bid you heartily farewell. Given at Portsmouth, the 8th of August, 1636.

"Signed: C. BALTEMORE." [3]

In this acknowledgment of debt and authorization to pay, there is no limit of time assigned within which the payment must be accepted. That is to say, the planters were free to put off the discharge of their obligations attendant upon taking out a patent. There was no prying into conditions behind the contract, as to whether the men, whom Baltimore knew perfectly well, belonged to clubs, or corporations, or fraternities, or societies. In other words, there was no idea of that anti-mortmain legislation, which was in fact excluded by Baltimore's charter. The use too of the term "grant," with regard to liquidating the rigorous debt, may be particularly noticed; because in later times some persons, reading the word "grant" in connection with these original conveyances, proclaimed that the Jesuit missionaries had received free gifts from Lord Baltimore.

Debts and grants.

The warrant just given was dated the 8th day of August, 1636. Three weeks afterwards the Proprietary issued another, to further the interests of a town as distinguished from the mere country settlements. To the same Leonard Calvert, Lieutenant-General, he wrote under date of August 29, 1636—

---

[3] *Archives of Maryland, Proceedings of the Council of Maryland*, 1636–1667, pp. 47, 48.—Cf. also Scharf, *History of Maryland*, i. 121, 122.—Kilty, *Landholder's Assistant*, pp. 30, 31.

"DEAR BROTHER,

"I would have you to pass in freehold to every of the first adventurors, that shall claim or desire it, and to their heirs, ten acres of land within the platts assigned or to be assigned for the town and fields of St. Mary's, for every person that any of the said adventurors transported or brought into Maryland, according to their Conditions first published; and five acres of land to every other adventuror for every other person, which he hath or shall transport thither since that time of the first plantation, till the thirtieth day of August, which shall be in the year of our Lord 1638. And for soe doeing this shall be your warrant. Given under my hand and seal at Warder-Castle in the Realm of England, the 29th August, 1636.

Signed: "CECILIUS BALTEMORE."[4]

Town lots.

The date of these warrants corresponds with the time when John Lewger was in a condition of the direst necessity. Eight months later, he is already Baltimore's secretary, affixing the great seal of the Province of Maryland to the new commission for the government there. In virtue of this new and ample commission, dated April 15, 1637, the Governor, Leonard Calvert, is authorized to declare Lord Baltimore's veto or disassent to all laws heretofore passed in the colony, and to submit for the legislative approval of an Assembly the Proprietary's own code herewith despatched.[5]

§ 44. Since Father White's departure from England at the end of 1633, "Cosen Copley," as he styled his colleague, had been engaged in "putting heat and a spirit of action" into the affairs of the plantation; and, when this business man received orders to set out himself and take charge of the Mission's concerns across the ocean, he was going to leave "a solitude" in London, as White expressed himself to Lord Baltimore.[1] Copley's departure did actually take place just before that of John Lewger, who carried with him the very important consignment of Lord Baltimore's own code of laws, and the Governor's new commission. We pause to take a look at Copley and the other volunteers of this time.

Father Philip Fisher, as he is named in the domestic records of the Society, or Thomas Copley, as he appears in Maryland history,

[4] *Proceedings of the Council, Ibid.*, pp. 48, 49.—Cf. Kilty, *Landholder's Assistant*, pp. 32, 33.
[5] *Proceedings of the Council, Ibid.*, pp. 50, 51, 55.
[1] *Calvert Papers*, i. 203.—Cf. *supra*, § 36, p. 335.

was of a distinguished family. Born in Madrid (1595–96), he had entered the Order at the age of twenty-one. When the Jesuit residence at Clerkenwell was raided by Government agents in 1628, the name of Philip Fisher appeared more than once in the reports.[2] As being procurator of the London mission, besides being in charge of the domestic affairs, he was in the very best position for co-operating with the new American establishment. He had, moreover, some temporal affairs of his father to supervise, and "his own estate" to protect. Fearing that he could not do so in the midst of a horde of pursuivants and spies, who battened on the property of Catholics, he availed himself of a melancholy privilege. He was "an alien born;" and, on English soil, he claimed protection from the King of England. That is to say, he claimed the privilege of not being an Englishman; as so many subjects or citizens under other Governments would be happy to do with their own nationality, when citizenship means only taxation, conscription, and expropriation, and when respect is considered due only to the alien, though he be of the meanest country in the world. Copley's paper ran thus—

Antecedents of Copley, or Fisher.

"To the King's Most Excellent Majesty.

"The humble petition of Thomas Copley sheweth, That the petitioner is an alien born, and therefore doth humbly conceive that for his religion (wherein he was bred) he is not liable to trouble by the laws of this realm. Yet the petitioner, fearing he may be molested by some messengers or other officers in following such occasions which concern his Father (who is very aged and much decayed in health), and his own estate—The petitioner doth humbly beseech your Majesty to refer this petition to one of your principal Secretaries, who finding the truth thereof may signify your Majesty's pleasure to all messengers and other officers, to forbear to trouble and molest the petitioner, that he may follow his urgent occasions and affairs, as aforesaid. And he will ever pray for your Most Sacred Majesty."

A warrant against the priest-hunters.

This petition is endorsed under date of December 1, 1634: "Thomas Copley, an alien born, being troubled by messengers for recusancy.—To be referred to Mr. Secretary Windebank." And again: "At the Court of Whitehall, 1° December, 1634. His Majesty's pleasure is to refer this petition to Sir Francis Windebank, Knight, Principal Secretary of State, to inform himself of the truth

[2] Foley, *Records*, i. 132, 133.

thereof, and to take such course for the petitioner as shall be fit."[3] A warrant was then issued on the tenth of the same month from the Palace of Westminster, securing to "Thomas Copley, gentleman, an alien," the appropriate immunities from persecution.[4]

Within eight months after his arrival in Maryland, Father Copley used language of the following tenor, when writing to Lord Baltimore: "This much I will be bold to tell your lordshipe that, though my principall intention be to serve your lordshipe to the prime end, which is the healpe of souls, yet in peopling and planting this place I am sure that none have done neare soe much as we, nor endeed are lykly to doe soe much."[5] From these words, as well as from Father White's testimony about Copley's activity while in London, we infer that Baltimore and his plantation had profited well by the service of the Fathers and of Copley in particular.

At this time John Knowles was pursuing and finishing the higher studies in the Order. He was twenty-six years of age; he had been nine in the Society, and had taught in the course of humane letters. In 1634, while advancing in his theological studies at Liège, he made known to the Provincial, Father Richard Blount, his desire for the far-off missions of the East. The Provincial presented his name to the General. The latter, replying (June 17, 1634), alluded to Maryland in a manner somewhat singular. Though Father White's expedition had set out for America seven months before, no information would seem to have been communicated to head-quarters. The General speaks thus—

John Knowles.

"To Father Richard Blount, Provincial. That zeal and ardent desire of John Knowles, which moves him to ask for a field of labour in Japan, that he may water it with his blood, refreshes me much. While thinking over so laudable a purpose, this occurred to me among other measures, whether he could not be sent to the Island of Virginia, if indeed any thought is still entertained or any steps are still taken with regard to that expedition. At all events, as mathematical science is very useful and almost necessary for those who go to the East Indies, and urgent demands are made on me for persons so qualified, I should wish to know whether he

---

[3] P. R. O., *Domestic, Car. I.*, cclxxviii., 1634-35, No. 1; endorsed also, "Rd. Freman," etc.

[4] *Archives of Maryland, Judicial and Testamentary Business*, 1637-1650, p. 479.—The appearance of this warrant among the plantation papers so late as 1648, which was the time of Copley's return to Maryland, seems to intimate that he had need then of such a safe-conduct in the colony. It is attested by Wm. Bretton: "*Concordat cum Originali. Ita testor Wm. Bretton.*"

[5] *Calvert Papers*, i. 168, April 3, 1638.

has, and how far he may have, knowledge and experience in the department of mathematics. If I know this, I shall state more clearly my opinion on the subject of his heroic resolution. In the mean time, would your Reverence please make known to him that what I have understood of his pious desires has given me heartfelt satisfaction; and I trust that this fire, which has been kindled in him by the Holy Ghost, will be nourished with the unction of divine grace and burn brighter and brighter. Wishing your Reverence the same gifts, I commend myself to your holy Sacrifices.—Rome, 17 June, 1634." [6]

Two years later, in the summer of 1636, just at the time when Panzani was finishing his reconnaissance of Baltimore's operations, and was making his last appeals at Rome for John Lewger, Copley received orders from the Provincial to embark for America; and the reports issued that year put Knowles down as his companion : " Two have been sent to Maryland, Father Philip Fisher, Father John Knowles. Two also have returned thence, Father Francis Rogers, John Wood." [7] Copley announced his departure to the General, who replied in a most cordial and encouraging letter (September 6, 1636).[8]

Six months after this God-speed from his Paternity, we find that Father Copley is not yet gone, and he receives a note comforting him in his troubles. The General alludes to difficulties which evidently have arisen outside of the Society, and not less evidently from the side of Catholics. The date is March 7, 1637, about the same time when the new commission is being drawn up by Baltimore for his brother Leonard, and a code of the Proprietary's own laws is announced for Maryland. The commission is finished by him and signed by John Lewger, secretary, in the very next month (April 15, 1637). We shall quote a few sentences of the commission relative to the new draft of laws, by way of comparing what Baltimore says with the animadversions implied in the General's letter, on the basis of Copley's representations. And we may find grounds for surmising that the struggle which ensued in Maryland between Baltimore and the clergy was already begun in London between Baltimore and Copley. Whether the new Provincial, Father Henry More, really lent his countenance to the Proprietary in the limited degree for which he was cited by Baltimore,[9] we cannot determine, either from the tenor

Copley detained in London. 1636, 1637.

---

[6] General Archives, S.J., *Anglia, Epist. Gen.—Documents*, I. No. 5, F.
[7] *Catalogus 3. Personarum*, 1636.—*Supplementum Catal.* 1 et 2, 1636.
[8] *Documents*, I. No. 5, G.
[9] *Calvert Papers*, i. 194: Lewger, January 5, 1639, to Baltimore. *Infra*, § 51.

of the General's note or from other premises. But from Father Henry More's subsequent line of action in signing the "Three Propositions," as they were called, of ten years later (1647), we consider the matter dubious and leave it so. More's predecessor, Father Richard Blount, was represented by Panzani as disapproving of Baltimore's oath, whatever that meant. More's successor, Father Edward Knott, has left papers enough to show that at no time did he entertain the newly broached propositions of the Baltimore party. Copley was certainly against Baltimore. Hence, with the exception of an uncertainty on the side of Father More, circumstances point to the conclusion that up to the present time Jesuits were not responsible for the new policy. After the present date, Baltimore had scarcely anything more to do with the Jesuits. He was in other hands for his theological and legal suggestions and consultations.

The commission to his brother Leonard reads thus—

"And we doe further give and grant to him our said Lieutenant, Chancellor, Chief Justice and Chief Magistrate, full and absolute power and authority to assemble the freemen of our said Province or their deputies, at St. Maries within our said Province upon the five and twentieth day of January next ensueing the date hereof, and then and there to signifie to them that we doe dissassent unto all the laws by them heretofore or at any time made within our said Province, as we doe hereby declare them to be voyd; and further to shew unto them the draught or coppy of all such laws and ordinances for the good government of our said Province, as we shall before that time transmitt to him our said Lieutenant under our hand and seal, with our [preliminary] assent for enacting of the same; and likewise, if the said freemen or their deputies soe assembled shall approve of and consent unto all the said draughts or coppies of the said laws and ordinances, in manner as we send the same over, to publish the same as laws under the Great Seal of our Province, that the people and inhabitants of our said Province may take the better notice thereof." [10]

Baltimore's new commission to Leonard Calvert. April 15, 1637.

The General's letter to Copley is as follows:—

"To London. To Father Philip Fisher.

"What it was advisable to do in such a case I see is what your Reverence did, and I am glad of it; so that, although grave difficulties stand in the way of your departure through the agency of the evil spirit, still you must not lose heart, but despise all dangers, relying on Him who strengtheneth you. In that affair I will not abandon

[10] *Proceedings of the Council*, as above, pp. 50, 51; commission, April 15, 1637.

370   COPLEY AND MISSIONARY ASPIRANTS   [CHAP. V

your Reverence; and I shall be happy to give you all the assistance which you ask for from me. And, since no more effectual succour can be had against enemies of whatsoever kind than the most holy Sacrifice, I will contribute liberally from the treasure which the Society places at my disposal, that this mission may be crowned with success and your Reverence be favoured with a happy voyage. And while I do so I beg of God blessings and graces for you in plenty; and I commend myself earnestly to your holy Sacrifices and prayers. Rome, March 7, 1637."[11]

The General to Copley. March 7, 1637.

In the public records of the plantation the entry is then made for five months later: "Came into the Province the 8th of August, 1637, Mr. Thomas Copley and Mr. John Knolls, who transported," etc.[12] Two months afterwards, Father Knowles died of the yellow fever, as mentioned above; and Father Copley wrote to the General (November 3, 1637). The latter replied—

Nov., 1637- May, 1638.

"To Maryland. To Father Philip Fisher, Superior.

"It gave me great pleasure in the Lord to receive your letter of the 3rd of November, telling me about those countries which are white for the harvest, and about the milk and honey of divine grace which are soon to flow there, it is hoped, through the preaching of the faith of Christ. May the Divine goodness give increase to what you and your companions there have planted by your industry and watered with your sweat. It will always afford me particular consolation to be informed of the progress of all and to lend assistance in any way I can. The loss of good Father John Knowles was premature for all of us, and was certainly a great disappointment for you in particular; but let us acquiesce in the dispositions of God's providence, who puts to death and brings to life, and to whom that field of work is an object of more care and love than it can be to us. I am heartily glad to understand that Father Andrew White has recovered his health; and I pray most earnestly that the rest of our members there may be blessed with fruitful labours and a rich harvest of souls. May good Jesus fill you with His Divine Spirit; and, placed as you are in the midst of such plentiful occasions of suffering for His Name, may He keep you mindful of me too in your holy Sacrifices. Rome, May 15 [1638]."[13]

[11] *Documents*, I. No. 5, H.—Cf. also *supra*, § 36, p. 333, note 2; on some rivals.
[12] J. Kilty, *Landholder's Assistant*, p. 66.—For the list of names and claims, including Copley's own, assigned by him to Father Ferdinand Pulton, see *Documents*, I. No. 30.
[13] *Documents*, I. No. 5, J.—In the margin of the Register are the words, "*Resp. de bono statu*," signifying that the letter is an expression of satisfaction at the good account sent.

The young man who had died so prematurely was not alone in his aspirations for a foreign mission. It was a usual ambition in the Society, and one which was amply gratified in the exposed countries East and West. To mention only competitors, so to speak, of the young Father Knowles, there was Nathaniel Bacon, or Southwell, who was called to serve in the English College at Rome. Father White had been thought of for the same place; but he was chosen for the foreign mission. Southwell indited a memorial or petition to the General; and in setting down the date, July 31, 1634, he noted particularly that it is "the feast of our holy father St. Ignatius, before whose altar I have confirmed all this to-day." He asks for the Indian missions East or West, "wherever," he says, "there may happen to be a greater need of labourers in the vineyard and a greater harvest of labours and sufferings for Christ." Then he supports his application with the reasons as follows:— *Nathaniel Bacon, or Southwell.*

"Now the reasons which impel me to this are chiefly the following: First, because this always comes up before my mind, and during prayer too, as the most perfect oblation of all and the greatest sacrifice of myself which I can offer in this life to the Lord, my Creator and Redeemer; and likewise a most complete act of self-abnegation, since it is a separation in fact from all things that are dear to me in this life, without any hope of ever again seeing them; and so it is morally a kind of death suffered for Christ. Secondly, because, though the mission of England is certainly one of great merit, on account of the perils of imprisonment and death which confront one there, nevertheless that vineyard is not so destitute of workmen as some parts of India are; and this appears by the mission which, in point of fact, our Fathers are now fitting out from England for the northern parts of America. Besides, since I feel a very strong inclination of nature towards England as towards my native country, friends, etc., I have always held this propensity in suspicion, doubting whether it came from God, and not rather from nature. So I have never yet ventured to ask for the mission to England; though, on the other hand, I am not so averse to it but that, if holy obedience bade me, I should be ready to go thither; and that on foot too, without any provision for the journey,[14] if it were left to my own devotion to decide. May it please your Paternity to consider the whole matter, and to determine as shall seem best in the Lord. I shall hope that good Jesus will incline you to my desires for His greater glory and the closer imitation of Him in what is hard *Reasons for the foreign missions.*

[14] "*Et pedes et sine viatico.*"

to nature, and for the greater security of my salvation in eternity. Rome," etc.[15]

Father Southwell's career was to take another direction, as he became secretary to the successor of the actual General Father Vitelleschi, and became also a bibliographer of the Society. It is to be observed, by the way, that in this letter of July 31, 1634, eight months after Father White's departure, Southwell in the English College at Rome knew no more of the expedition having actually set out than the General himself knew on June 17 of the same year.

A young man, Father Williamson, made a more successful application, yet not effectual in the end. Writing to the new Provincial, Henry More, on November 15, 1636, at the very time when Father Knowles was supposed to be already on his way to America, the General said: "A desire so pious as that of Father Richard Williamson, and such zeal as he shows in striving to render himself fit for the Indian mission, give me great pleasure. I have already put him down as of the company and number of those who are of the same mind and purpose; and I will not forget him when on some future occasion another colony of missionaries is to go out to those parts. In the mean time, I pray the Lord in His kindness, who inspired him with this desire, to strengthen him with His grace."[16] But, a year and a half later, the claims of Maryland suggest themselves in the first place, especially in view of the loss sustained there by the death of Father Knowles; and another applicant, Father Robert Philips, is spoken of with favour. The General writes to the same Provincial, under date of April 17, 1638—

Richard Williamson.

"I approve of Father Richard Williamson's fervour and his desire of undergoing the hardships of Japan for the sake of Christ. But he and the rest of your English mission have Japan and the Indies in the neighbourhood, an untilled vineyard of the Lord at home, to water freely with their sweat in the name of God, and also, if He grants it, with their blood. Wherefore, just as you choose, you can either apply him to mathematics [for the service of the East], or you can send him to take the place vacated by the good Father Knowles, and so let him seek the crosses of Japan in Maryland.

"Let the same be said of Father Robert Philips, who is asking for Maryland. And, if the needs of that mission are urgent and require his assistance so very soon, I will dispense in his regard with

---

[15] General Archives S.J., *Anglia, Historia*, v. 699; translated here from the Latin.
[16] *Ibid., Anglia, Epist. Gen.*

the third year of probation. But, if he can be kept for a while, it will be better to do so, that with a fuller equipment of the arms of justice he may announce Christ, whom in the retirement of the third year of probation he will imprint still more deeply in his heart."[17] The dispensation regarding a third year refers to a last stage of formation or novitiate in the Society, prior to the final grade which was taken with the last vows. This matter of a dispensation recurs often in relation to Maryland; and, like other licences which might be sought for, afforded in principle and practice abundant matter for the Generals to criticize, even while they were granting what was asked for by the Provincials.

Robert Philips.

A month later (May 15, 1638), in answer to More's letter of the beginning of April, his Paternity signifies his approval of Williamson's absolute appointment to Maryland.[18] Thomas Worthington also, a scholastic of twenty-two years of age, receives encouragement very soon afterwards (July 10, 1638). Writing to the same Provincial, the General says—

Thomas Worthington.

"Not so long ago Thomas Worthington wrote to me from Liège, making known in a petition, happily and piously conceived, his burning desires for the Indies. Although, as I remember having answered already in similar cases, there are the Indies hard by you in Britain, still your Reverence may encourage him in my name; you may foster his pious zeal; and let him know that I will take account of him among others, when occasion offers, according as the Lord shall inspire."[19]

If no one of these applicants landed in Maryland with Father Pulton in 1638, nor at a later period, the reason probably is not far to seek in the troubles which arose between the missionaries and Lord Baltimore.[20]

§ 45. The relations between Maryland and the actual Governor of Virginia had from the first been courteous, if not cordial. There was indeed a party in the Virginian Government, or under it, that was hostile to Maryland as a rival and to Maryland as a nest of Papists. But the Governor himself, Sir John Harvey, was mentioned in Father White's Latin

Friends and foes in Virginia.

---

[17] General Archives S.J., *Anglia, Epist. Gen.*
[18] *Ibid.*
[19] *Ibid.*
[20] For the antecedents and subsequent careers of the men named, cf. Foley, *Records*, vii., *Collectanea*. Father Robert Philips is taken to be identical with Dr. Robert Pugh.

Relation, as anxious to have a bill paid him out of the royal treasury —somewhat of a bad debt on the face of it—and therefore he sought to win favour by honouring the Maryland pilgrims, who were protected by royal letters. Cæcilius, Proprietary of Maryland, had an eye on Virginia, where he thought to make a flanking movement and improve his colonial situation generally. Jerome Hawley, Maryland Commissioner, had his eye too upon the same place. No one of these gentlemen thought it worth his while to consult Virginia itself, which by a process of decline and bankruptcy had come back from the hands of the Virginia Company into those of the King. They were all looking to King Charles, each on his own account; and, having something to gain in the general intrigue, they were willing to trade in mutual favours when needful. However, unlike much of what is meant by Court life, the intrigues here meant nothing dishonourable. They were part of a common struggle for existence in very arduous times.

Thus Lord Baltimore, to show his gratitude for the kindly manner in which the Governor of Virginia, Sir John Harvey, had received the first expedition at Point Comfort, procured the despatch of letters in the name of Secretary Windebank and of the King himself, conveying thanks to the Governor for his humanity, and menaces to other officers who were less kindly disposed (September 15-29, 1634). On the receipt of these letters, Sir John was very happy indeed, as he acknowledged to Secretary Windebank. But, to secure the permanency of Virginian good behaviour towards Maryland, he was quite unable to rule the "exorbitant courses" of his Councillors, such as Captain Sam Mathews, Captain Clayborne, Captain West, and other men, who said "they would rather knock their cattell on the heads then sell them to Maryland." He himself was doing his utmost to comfort the Marylanders; and, says he, "for their present accommodation I sent unto them some cowes of myne owne, and will do my best to procure them more, or anything else they stand in need of" (December 16, 1634). But half a year had not passed when Sir John was marched out of his government by his Councillors, and sent home to England. There were many interesting charges on both sides, such as mutiny charged against his aggressors, and treason against Sir John, "for going about (as they sayde) to betray theyr forte into the hands of theyr enemies of Marylande." But what concerns us more particularly is that he was accused of favouring the Popish religion, and, as the Privy Council minutes express it, of "countenancing the religion in Maryland. Mr. Halley [Jerome Hawley], in the midst of the Mass [!], said that he was come to plant in Maryland the Romish religion. Denied absolutely by Mr. Halley. It is said by Sir John Harvey and Mr. Halley, that there is public Mass in Maryland." The charges on the score of Popery were denied by Sir John. But Lord Cottington, at the Board of the Privy Council where this inquiry was conducted, said that he must make some order upon it (December 11, 1635). Here Lord Baltimore interposed with a suitable memorial on behalf of Sir John, and he called for condign punishment on "the prime actors in the late mutenye in Virginia" (December 22, 1635).[1] Some of them did receive harsh treatment soon enough, at the hands of the London authorities. And so did Lord Baltimore at their hands, when, a few years later, the wheel of fortune had revolved, and the Cromwellians came into power. *The Privy Council. Mass in Maryland.*

In the mean time, it is to be noticed with regard to the scene at the Privy Council Board, that Cottington and Windebank, Secretaries of State, if not already Catholics, were on the threshold of the Church, which they both entered. And so, after this little piece of acting to distract the dogs of religious war who were barking on both sides of the ocean, all parties turned with renewed zest to their own private games.

And now, with the restoration of Sir John Harvey to his government in Virginia, we come to a document perfectly characteristic of Lord Baltimore, and conceived in the same style as the Baltimore Papers which lie in the Stonyhurst archives. The characteristic consists in drawing up papers or petitions, and stamping on them such a character that, if the petition or instrument prove effectual, the benefit and profit shall be altogether Baltimore's, but, if ineffectual, no prejudice whatever can befall him. Thus the papers which will appear later as drawn from the Stonyhurst archives are fathered on the Jesuit Provincial; the benefits contemplated in them redound to the unmixed and unqualified profit of Baltimore; and yet, when they have fallen to the ground utterly ineffectual, and have been picked up later by history, there is not a trace that he ever had a hand in them. *A characteristic of Baltimore's methods.*

On the present occasion, in manœuvring to be appointed Governor

[1] P. R. O., *Colonial Papers*, viii. Nos. 25, 26, 27, 69, 73, 84. *Domestic, Car. I.*, cccii. No. 105. Notes of Nicholas, Clerk of Privy Council, December 11, 1635. —Cf. *Archives of Maryland, Proceedings of the Council*, 1632–1667, pp. 25–40.—Cf. Calendar of State Papers, *A. & W.I.*, i. 216, 1635, December 11.

of Virginia, with £2000 sterling for his annual salary, his own description and exemplification of the policy could scarcely be more picturesque. And if a palpable difficulty checks his manœuvre, that really he cannot become Governor of Virginia, except at the cost of ousting from the same post his dear and devoted friend, Sir John Harvey, who is actually allowed only £1000 per annum,[2] he shows in the same Papers a perfect art in surmounting such an obstruction. He buries his friend in profound silence. The name of Sir John does not drop from his pen.

Writing to Secretary Windebank a little more than a year after the investigation in the Privy Council, he submits a final resolution on the Virginia business, sending his brother-in-law Peaseley with a memorandum for the purpose. And he explains: "I do presume by him also to propose unto you a way of moving the King in this business; such a one as I conceive may be most likely to take effect; or, in case his Majestie for private reasons approve not of the proposition, the refusall of itt in that way will, I conceive, be less prejudiciall to me; but this I humbly submitt to your better judgement" (February 25, 1637). Then the memorandum shows the Secretary what would " bee a fitt way to propound the matter to the King." The way consists in three steps: First, the Secretary will mention to His Majesty that he, the Secretary, has often observed Lord Baltimore to be preoccupied with an ardent desire of showing his gratitude to the King for past favours. Secondly, this preoccupation has led him to take notice of Virginia, and to inform himself of " the great prejudice the King suffers there, by not receiving so much profitt from thence as he ought to have and is due;" whereupon Lord Baltimore has assured Mr. Secretary that he could "undertake to improve his Majesties revenue from thence £8000 yearely, more than now he received for or by reason of that plantation;" and this without any extra taxation. Thirdly (as a mere accidental adjunct of the foregoing), "this advancement of the King's revenue in Virginia" could not be effected unless Lord Baltimore went to reside there for a long time, "which he cannot with his safety well do, except hee bee authorised and enabled by having the government of that country; whereunto though Mr. Secretary perceives the Lord Baltimore hath no ambition or affection, yet for the advancement and perfourmance of this service hee doth verily thinke that, upon his Majesties command, the Lord

His application for the Governorship of Virginia.

[2] J. R. Brodhead (New York), *Documents*, iii. 20: Jerom Hawley, May 8, 1638, to Windebanke, from James Towne, Virginia.

Baltimore would accept of the government, and £2000 yearely for the support thereof, payable out of that improvement of rent," etc.[3]

Now the untoward thing happened. As he was cutting out Sir John Harvey, who in the equity of friendship had all the rights of possession, Mr. Jerome Hawley at that very date had already cut Baltimore out, where the latter had no rights of possession, but still where he had great expectations. Mr. Jerome Hawley, Baltimore's own Commissioner for Maryland, became by the King's gift Treasurer of Virginia; and that on the very same plea which Lord Baltimore bootlessly advanced as a claim for the governorship, to wit, the improvement of the King's revenue in those parts. *Hawley obtains the Treasurership.*

Here begins the melodramatic, if not the tragic phase of early Maryland history. It is to be borne in mind that this very spring of 1637 is the same time when Father Copley, owing to some difficulties in London, is hindered from starting off to Maryland. On all accounts, the spring of 1637 is the turning-point in the early evolution of the Maryland drama. Within a year we find a sharp line of cleavage in the colony. There are the Calverts, Lewger, the Virginian Kemp; later on there comes Langford; and they are all of one colour and one policy, some more and some less. The Commissioners, Hawley and Cornwaleys, with the missionaries, Copley and White, are most distinctly of another colour and policy. Before long, there arises a third party, quite independent of either State or Church, of Catholic priests or baronial Proprietary; and they of the third party carry all before them.

Between January 5 and April 1, 1637, while Baltimore is manœuvring with his "proposition" for the £2000 sterling per annum out of the Virginia treasury, Jerome Hawley, one of the "gentlemen sewers" to Queen Henrietta Maria, is nominated by the King, in a letter to the Governor and Council of that plantation, as Treasurer of Virginia, with powers, privileges, fees, and allowances pertaining to that office; he is to enjoy the precedence belonging to his dignity; formulas are inserted both by His Majesty and Secretary Windebank, about tendering to the new Virginian magnate the oaths of office both as Treasurer and as Councillor, along with the oath of allegiance; and Windebank doubts not that Governor Harvey will admit Hawley to both places, and assist him in advancing the King's revenue. As to the oaths, the Secretary's language runs thus:

[3] P. R. O., *Colonial Papers* ix., Nos. 42, 45.—Cf. *Archives of Maryland, Council*, as above, pp. 41-43.

"His Majesties pleasure likewise is that the said Mr. Hawley be forthwith admitted to the place of a Counsellor of Virginia, & that you give him the oath in such cases accustomed, and likewise the oath of allegiance which he hath already taken heere and promised His Majesty to take there, upon condition whereof he is to be admitted a Counsellor & not otherwise." The letter in the King's name says : " And wee requier you to give him the oathes of Treasurer of Virginea, and allso of one of our Councell there." [4]

In the next correspondence bearing on the subject we find the Calverts beside themselves with vexation. Writing from Virginia itself in the following spring, the Governor of Maryland, Leonard Calvert, impeaches and assails the motives, intentions, and conduct of Hawley, as Treasurer of Virginia and also as Councillor of Maryland ; he speaks to his brother Cecil as to one who " had procured the preferment " for Hawley ; and, as an aggravation of the latter's ingratitude, Leonard adds the pithy circumstance that Hawley ignores any such obligation! He "disclaims," says Leonard, " that he ever sought your help, or had any from you towards his preferment; for he thincketh you did not so much as know he pretended to the place he hath; nor that you knew he had it, untill a long tyme after it was passed to him; thus Captain Cornwaleys telleth me he hath heard him say." Moreover, Mr. Hawley intends to remove his interests " from Maryland and place them in Virginia, and intendeth shortly to remove his wife and family thither: I am sorry it was your ill fortune to be a meanes of so much good to him who is to[o] ingratefull for it." Furthermore, he is " of such greevance unto the Governor and Secretarie of Virginia," Sir John Harvey and Mr. Kemp, " by his draweing all the perquisites of theire two places from them." This last compassionate grievance of Leonard must have touched the heart of Cecil, seeing that at the same date in the previous year he had himself been so deeply engaged in this very enterprise of dislodging Sir John Harvey not only from his perquisites, but also from his place. A further charge is that Mr. Hawley does not believe in Lord Baltimore's right to dislodge Captain Clayborne from the Isle of Kent, seated as it was by that gentleman years before Maryland was founded.[5]

Irritation of the Calvert party.

On the same day (April 25, 1638), the Secretary of Virginia, Mr. Kemp, wrote from " James Cittie," evidently no less under the inspiration of Leonard who was present there, than from a sense

[4] P. R. O., *Colonial Papers*, ix. Nos. 34, 33; 1637, January 10, January 5.
[5] *Calvert Papers*, i. 188, 189: Leonard Calvert, Virginia, April 25, 1638.

of his own wrongs. He declaims at length against Mr. Hawley, and communicates his impressions to Lord Baltimore, because, he says, "I receive from undoubted information that the effect of Mr. Hawlye his busines [viz. the effectuating of Mr. Hawley's business] proceeded from your Lordshipps favour in his behalf."[6]

To judge by some phrases of Captain Cornwaleys in a letter of the same time addressed to Lord Baltimore (St. Maries, April 16, 1638), the latter also was betrayed into "vyolent dis- "Vyolent discourtesyes upon uncertaine suppositions." In this art courtesyes." of discourtesy and violence, whether or no he had already been an adept in it, no one in the near future offered more striking exhibitions than did the Right Honourable Baron of Baltimore, Cæcilius Calvert; until the "whips and scorns of time" taught him to use moderation when speaking to the freemen at least, however much he might indulge his propensity when addressing the clergy. Cornwaleys reads him some very plain common sense while defending Mr. Hawley. He pays a tribute, kindly and merited, to the abilities of Mr. Lewger, the new secretary, who has just appeared in Maryland; and, says the captain, "if hee proves not tooe stiff a maintayner of his owne opinions, and somewhat tooe forward in sugiesting new businesses for his owne imployment, hee may perhaps doe God and your Lordship good service heere." But, he continues: "I should bee sorry toe change Mr. Hawley for him, whoe I perceave stands not soe perfect in your Lordships favoure as I could wish him; which perhaps some takeing advantage at, and willing for toe fish in trobled waters, may by discourteous proceedeings towards him make him weary of unproffitable Maryland, and fors him toe a change more for his peace and proffit." The captain regrets to see that his Lordship is in all probability one of Hawley's declared or "worst enemies." He believes that Baltimore himself will suffer as much as the other if any open hostility be declared. And thus far Hawley has had as much a right to speak plainly in his own defence, against the misapprehensions of mischief-makers, as any body else, and as Captain Cornwaleys confesses that he himself has done and will do: "I must confes I cannot pleade not guilty." He fears that if the new Treasurer removes to Virginia, the loss of Mrs. Hawley, whom Cornwaleys eulogizes in the highest terms for all gifts of virtue, prudence, and industry, "would not a little eclips the glory of Maryland."[7] There is not a little of sound paternal advice in the

[6] *Calvert Papers*, i. 153-155; endorsed by Baltimore: "From Virginea, against Mr. Hawley." [7] *Ibid.*, 179-181. Cf. *supra*, § 36, p. 337.

masculine letter of the captain; and some hints that are very suggestive. "Seldom or never," he says, "have I heard or seene covetousnes decrease with age." [8] But what we have quoted will suffice to show the rift started in Maryland society by the Virginia ambitions of Lord Baltimore and others. More serious causes of disunion are laid bare in the same correspondence.

Mr. John Lewger has arrived with commissions and laws, and a great capacity for creating a stir, or, as the captain expressed it, "sugiesting new businesses for his owne imployment."

§ 46. Father Copley having come into the province on August 8, 1637, John Lewger followed soon after with his wife, and a son John aged nine years, three women-servants, and four men.[1] The date of their coming was November 28, 1637. Lewger's commission made him secretary of the province, and councillor, and recorder of land-grants, and collector and receiver of rents and customs, with a blank margin for other emoluments. Another appointment from the Governor, dated in the following January, made him justice of the peace and commissioner of causes testamentary (January 24, 1638).[2] He became also surveyor-general.[3]

According to the exact terms of the same commission, Governor Leonard Calvert assembled the freemen of the province on January 25, 1638. With many interruptions, this deliberative body sat till the 24th day of March next following. During that time some ninety freemen were present, or were to be represented by proxy—a number which seems to show, not merely the increase of men in the province, but the rapid enfranchisement of servants originally transported. Among the freemen were the three gentlemen, "Mr. Thomas Copley, Esq., of St. Maries hundred, Mr. Andrew White, Mr. John Altham, gentlemen of the same hundred. Robert Clerke, gentleman, appeared for them, and excused their absence by reason of sickness." On the second day, January 26, there were summoned the absentees, "Mr. Thomas Copley, Mr. Andrew White, Mr. John Altham; and Robert Clerke made answer for them, that they desired to be excused from giving voices in this Assembly; and was admitted."[4] It is to be noticed

The Assembly. Jan. 25-Mar. 24, 1638.

---

[8] *Calvert Papers*, i. 175, *med.*
[1] Cf. J. Kilty, *Landholder's Assistant*, p. 68.—Cf. S. F. Streeter, *Papers*, pp. 63, 223, 224, note.
[2] *Archives of Maryland, Proceedings of the Council*, 1636-1667, pp. 53, 54.—*Ibid.*, 60, 61.—Cf. *supra*, § 43, p. 362, note 5.
[3] Cf. S. F. Streeter, *Papers*, p. 256.
[4] *Proceedings of the Assembly*, as above, 1637/8-1664, pp. 2, 5.

how Mr. Robert Clerke is termed a "gentleman" here, an appellation not loosely or carelessly applied in those times; yet his name stood in the provincial records as "servant to Mr. Copley," who had transported others in Copley's name, and had come in the same ship as Lewger.[5]

All the freemen were required to attend at this Assembly meeting. There was no alternative, except to be amerced for non-attendance, or to vest their rights in proxies, who should vote for them. A large part of the business at this Assembly ran in the grooves of proxy voting, a single individual casting as many ballots as were the persons whom he was admitted to represent.

The missionaries did not appear in person. They were excused in a manner entirely different from every one else. They asked to be admitted by proxy, but under conditions such as nobody else proposed. This was refused. And still their presence was not enforced under the penalty of a fine. Hence they occupied the exceptional position of being excused and yet remaining without representation. *Privilege of the cloth for the priests.*

Their overseer, William Lewis of St. Inigoes, sat in the meeting from the first under the title of "planter," that is, generically a freeman. He had proxies in his pocket for five persons, disposing thus of six votes, as many as the Governor himself had been entrusted with, and more than any one else; Secretary Lewger at that time disposing of only two besides his own, and Captain Cornwaleys of only one.[6] Among the proxies of William Lewis we notice one, William Edwine, whose name had appeared as that of a servant assigned to the missionaries by Richard Gerrard.[7] As being overseer of the missionary station at St. Inigoes, and also as being a Catholic whose zeal was pronounced enough to cause trouble a few months later,[8] Mr. Lewis was not likely to vote in such a manner as to prejudice the interests of religion or of the Fathers. The fact that he did so, and lent the weight of his own and his proxy ballots to Lewger's objectionable legislation, shows how obscure to the minds of plain people and ordinary planters was the drift, meaning, and management of the code which subsequently passed. *Planters as legislators.*

These main circumstances of the Assembly are touched upon by

---

[5] J. Kilty, as above, p. 67.—S. F. Streeter, *Papers*, pp. 92, 93.—*Calvert Papers*, i. 184: Leonard Calvert, April 25, 1638, to Lord Baltimore.
[6] S. F. Streeter, *Ibid.*, p. 14.
[7] Annapolis Records, *Lib.* i. f. 38.—*Documents*, I. No. 30.
[8] *Supra*, § 37, p. 340.

Father Copley, in his letter to Lord Baltimore, only ten days after the final adjournment of the house (April 3, 1638). He says: "I will give your lordshipe some accoumpte touchinge the laite Assembly and the proceedings thereof. First then, as I acquainted your lordshipe in my former letter, it was not fitt that we should be there in person; and our proxis would not be admitted in that manner as we could send them; and therfor, as we weare excluded thence, soe we did not intermeddle with them there. Yet Mr. Lugar, conceaving that some that had relation to us weare not soe favourable to his waye as he desired, seemed in some sorte to attribute the same to us. But I will assure your lordshipe that he was much mistaken, for truly we weare noe cause thereof; as he might easily have gathered, in that William Lewis, who is our overseier and had more proxis then all the rest, was ever concurring with him; which could not have binne if we had binne averse. But, howsoever, I canne not heare that ever any of the rest weare averse to any thinge that concerned your lordshipe. And therfor, if he should write any thinge to that effecte, your lordshipe may be confidente that they are meere frivolous suspitions of his owne, without any true grounde." [9]

Though we have not the former letter to which Copley alludes, still the reasons which he had mentioned in it for not assisting at the Assembly in person and for offering proxies only under certain conditions,—under which alone, he says, he "could" offer them—are not difficult to divine, as far as these reasons proceeded from law or custom. The Assembly in which the clergymen were summoned to sit was competent to try causes of blood; and, in point of fact, before it dissolved, it judged and hanged a man, by name Thomas Smith, on a charge of piracy. Every Catholic clergyman is and always has been disqualified both by canon law, and by the civil law in conjunction with the canons, from taking an active part in any such causes. Thus in the very grave case of bringing Titus Oates to justice, half a century later than this, the General of the time prohibited the appearance of any Jesuit on the witness-stand against the sanguinary perjurer.[10] The limitation here on the action of the Maryland missionaries would affect also their proxy or representative in the Assembly.

Reasons for the clergy's abstention.

[9] *Calvert Papers*, i. 158.
[10] General Archives S.J., *Anglia, Epist. Gen.*, iii. f. 366: "*13 Januarii*, 1665. *Perillustri D. Joanni Keinesio, Londinum.* ¶ *Accepi nuper, isthic e Sociis quæri testes, qui perjurii reum apud Judices peragant Oatium—nomen mendaciis ac structis in insontes calumniis ubique clarum. Id fieri nullo modo permittat D.V., cum id a nobis quamaxime sit alienum. Neque enim agitur nunc de protegenda innocentium vita ac fama a falsis calumniatoris criminationibus, sed de pœna perjuro infligenda.*"

§ 46] IMMUNITY OF THE CLERGY 383

A second obvious reason lay in the political character and work of the freemen. From taking part in such deliberations the Jesuit Fathers were inhibited by their own rules and constitutions. There would remain only the land affairs and incidental business for which they could depute a representative.

Besides these general reasons, there were local circumstances which imposed upon the Fathers the duty of abstention; as many, indeed, as there were Indian stations to attend, sick persons to visit, ignorant people that needed instruction, and others in distress who called for assistance. Alluding, however, to the main impediments in the case, Father Copley said very precisely in the passage just quoted, that it was a question of their proxies being admitted or no, "in that manner as we *could* send them."

The Fathers as clergymen received by the vote of the Assembly of Maryland the formal tribute of an immunity or privilege, the first such formal recognition of the ecclesiastical state as such, and one which indicated well enough the general temper and customs of the colony. The missionaries were exempted as no layman was. That was a clerical privilege or immunity. *Clerical immunity or privilege in Maryland.*

The Assembly having been duly organized, the first grave business taken up was his lordship's imported code. It claimed citizenship, like any other transported voyager. But, unlike all others, except perhaps the new secretary, it was fresh from his lordship's bureau, and claimed to govern the lives, liberty, and fortunes of every one in the colony. It formed the business of the morning, on Friday, the second day.

"Then was read out of the draught of lawes, transmitted by the Lord Proprietor, the twelve first acts of the said draught; and were severally debated by the house." In the afternoon of the same day, "then were the acts read througe & severally debated in the reading. And the Lieutenant-General adjourned the house untill Monday morning at 8 of the clock." On the said Monday, third day, 29th of January, 1638: "Then was proposed whether the lawes formerly read should be read againe in the house; or putt to the vote without further reading. Captain Cornwaleys gave his opinion that they should expect a more frequent house. Captain Fleete gave his opinion that they should be read againe. With them concurred Mr. Clerke, Sergeant Vaughan, Edward Fleete, Edmond Parrie, being in all 18 voices with their proxies. On the contrary, that they should be putt to the vote *The imported code. Jan. 26-29, 1638.*

immediately, agreed by the President, Captain Evelin, Mr. Lewger, Mr. Greene, Mr. Snow, Francis Rabnett, James Baldridge, being in all 33 voices. Then were the lawes put to the question, whether they should be received as lawes or no. Affirmed by the President [that is, Leonard Calvert, and] Mr. Lewger, being 14 voices. Denied by all the rest of the assembly, being 37 voices.

"Then, question being moved what lawes the Province should be governed by, it was said by some that they might doe well to agree upon some lawes till we could heare from England againe. The President denying any such power to be in the house, Captain Cornwalers propounded the lawes of England. The President acknowledged that the commission gave him power in civill causes to proceed by the lawes of England; and in crim[in]all causes likewise not extending to life or member. But, in those [in which] he was limited to the lawes of the Province, there could be no punishment inflicted on any enormous offendors, by the refusall of these lawes. Whereupon the commission was produced and examined; &, upon the reading of it, it appeared that there was no power in the Province to punish any offence deserving losse of life or member, for want of lawes. To this they answered, that such enormous offences could hardly be committed without mutinie; & then it might be punished by martiall law."

In the afternoon of the same day, the question was opened again, what laws were to be sent over for the approval of the Lord Proprietor. It was agreed that five committeemen should be appointed to prepare a draft of laws; and, in the election, the Captains Cornwaleys, Wintour, and Evelin headed the list; Governor Calvert came in fourth; Justinian Snow, fifth. Mr. Lewger was left out; but, being secretary, he always had his hand in. The house adjourned for ten days, till the committee should be ready.

A committee of five. Jan. 29–Feb. 8.

Accordingly, at the next meeting on the 8th of February, 1638, the Committee reported that they thought the draft of Baltimore's laws, already rejected, should be read again, "in regard there was found a great deale of misunderstanding of them among the freemen, which made them refuse them." Very good-naturedly the house adopted that view, by 48 voices against 21. And they made an order "that all bills propounded to the house for lawes should be read three times on three severall daies afore they should be putt to the vote." Here the old rejected draft was read through, and this was counted as a second time. "And twenty bills propounded by the Committee were read the first time;" wherein it does not appear how many of these new bills had been slipped through the Committee, out of the residue, as yet unseen, of Lord Baltimore's code, if only twelve of his draft so far had been expressly subjected to the ordeal of examination and rejection.

Now came the final despatching of all. As a code they could not stand the light, neither the twelve already massacred once, nor the other twenty, whencesoever these came. "Captain Cornwaleys desired it might be putt to the vote of the house, whether these lawes at the third reading should be voted severally, or the whole body of them together. And that they should be voted altogether was affirmed by 32 voices; denied by 37." Here every bill was declared amenable to a separate judgment on its own merits. And with that ended Lord Baltimore's code.[11] And with this disaster, on the American side of the ocean, began a state of unfriendliness between Cæcilius Lord Baltimore and the Jesuit missionaries.

In all these legislative dealings there was much common sense on the part of the freemen, and no preconceived notions or passionateness or obstinacy. There was no constitutional question raised about the right or the use of the initiative in drafting and proposing laws. It is true that the manner in which the code dropped down on them from London, with an intimation to pass it bodily, offered a model and precedent in Maryland legislation no wise superior to Poyning's Law in Ireland; according to which, ever since the time of Henry VII., only such Acts could even be proposed in an Irish Parliament as had first been agreed upon between the Lord-Lieutenant in Dublin and the King in London. Of this Irish system a benevolent English author says gently, that it was all conceived out of love for the Irish people, to protect them against their "chief governor."[12] But of the same Irish system no American colony would ever hear a word. And when the long struggle between the home Government and Jamaica was in progress (1679, 1680), whether Poyning's Law, which was good enough for Ireland, was also good enough for Jamaica, His Majesty and the Lords of Trade were told in plain terms that the Irish system was desired by the English to support them against the Irish, but in Jamaica they were all English, and they would have none of it.[13]

No constitutional question raised.

---

[11] *Archives of Maryland, Proceedings of the Assembly*, 1637/8–1664, pp. 6–11.
[12] Lingard, *History of England*, iv. 150.—He says he is following Leland's opinion, II. App. 512–516.
[13] Cf. *Calendar of State Papers, A. & W.I.*, v. 457, No. 6; 1679, December 18:

The fault of the Baltimore code corresponded to the defect of Baltimore's views. He was an intense feudalist for his own benefit; and his code came out made to order, that of a feudal doctrinaire. Whether in that first code he had rounded his notions so completely as to make religion and the Church and the clergy fit into the Baltimore scheme, does not appear, since the text is not forthcoming. But, in Lewger's prompt readjustment of the Baltimore misfit, religion, the Church, and the clergy come trimmed and rounded and finished off in the best style of Erastianism. And where the freemen had said so well that, in the absence of a direct law about "enormous offences," they could still meet an emergency, because "such enormous offences could hardly be committed without mutinie," and then martial law would suffice, Lewger, in the Baltimore code as refitted, brought in the "enormous crimes" expressly, but in such a form and definition as to comprise the discharge of clerical functions by a priest or bishop, unless priest and bishop claimed their spiritual authority from Lord Baltimore, or under him.[14] This was Erastian State tyranny unqualified.

Defect of the Baltimore code.

§ 47. The Calvert party, which in the Assembly had tried to avert the wreck of Baltimore's model ship of state, consisted of two persons, the Governor Leonard Calvert and the secretary John Lewger. One half of this party, and the more intelligent half,—he who knew something of colonial life, as the other the man of yesterday did not,—wrote to the author, Cecil Calvert, Lord Baltimore, and gave his opinion of the code entrusted to their tutelage. Said Leonard Calvert to his brother: "The body of lawes you sent over by Mr. Lewger I endeavoured to have had passed by the Assembly at Maryland, but could not effect it. There was so many things unsuteable to the peoples good and no way conduceing to your proffitt that, being they [the unsuitable laws] could not be exempted from others which they willingly would have passed, they were desireous to suspend them all. The particular exceptions

Leonard Calvert on the codes. April 25, 1638.

Sir Thomas Lynch to Lords of Trade.—J. V. L. McMahon, *Historical View of the Government of Maryland*, pp. 144, 145, propounds this theory that Baltimore's code was rejected because of a constitutional question about the initiative.—So too S. F. Streeter, *Papers*, p. 148.—W. T. Brantley enlarges on it in Justin Winsor, *History of America*, iii. 529.—Any such presumptive issues, if not true, disguise the real issue, whatever that may have been.

[14] *Calvert Papers*, i. 165, 11°.—In a law considered one year later, 1638/9, a clause was introduced which corrected this Erastian assumption of spiritual power. It classed among "enormious offences" the unlawful exercise of jurisdiction and authority "which *ought* to be derived from the Lord Proprietary." *Proceedings of the Assembly*, p. 73.—But even this bill vanished out of sight in the one general Ordinance, which passed. *Ibid.*, pp. 82-84.—Cf. *infra*, § 49 (2), p. 413; § 52 (1), p. 429.

which were made against them Mr. Lewger hath given you an account of in his dispatches to you. Others [*i.e.* other laws] have been passed in the same Assembly and now sent unto you, which I am perswaded will appear unto you to provide both for your honour and proffitt as much as those you sent us did." [1] Here the Governor states that the substance of the Baltimore code, with regard to his lordship's honour and profit, is as well provided for by the refitted model or draft as by the original misfit.

Father Copley wrote by the same mail, and said: "Touching the lawes which your lordshipe sent, I am told that they would not be accepted; and even the Governor and Mr. Lugar said once to me, that they weare not fitt for this colonye. **Copley.** For myne owne parte, seeing noe service that I could doe your lordshipe therin and many inconvenices that I might runne into by intermedlinge, I never soe much as rede them, nether doe I yet know what they contained. For the temporall providence I left my selfe to your lordshipe; and for matter of conscience I supposed that your lordshipe had taken good advise. What occasion then could I have to intermeddle aboute them?

"The lawes which now are sent to your lordshipe [*i.e.* the refitted code] I never knew nor saw till even now, that they weare ready to be sent to your lordshipe. And, there being hast to send them, I only gott a hasty vew of them. Yet diverse things even in that hasty reading occured to me, which I conceaved requisite to acquainte you withall, leaving them to your lordships more serious consideration." [2]

Captain Cornwaleys, too, wrote by the same packet. That his drastic criticism covered the first draft of laws as well as the second, in other words, not only Baltimore's but also Lewger's, appears by such a phrase as the following: **Cornwaleys.** "Nor were it difficult out of the lawes sent over by your lordship, or these that are from hence proposed toe you, toe finde just grounds for toe feare the introdusement of lawes prejuditiall toe oure honors and freedome. Witnes that on[e] act whereby wee are exposde to a remediles suffering of all disgraces and insolensyes, that eyther the pastion or mallis [passion or malice] of suckseedeing governors shall please to put upon us, with out beeing permitted soe much as a lawfull defence for the secureing of life or reputation—though never soe unjustly attempted toe bee taken from us—with out forfeyteing

---

[1] *Calvert Papers*, i. 189, 190; April 25, 1638, from Virginia.
[2] *Ibid.*, 158, 159; April, 3, 1638.

the same and all wee have too boote."³ The policy, which Cornwaleys here alludes to of precluding all remedy at law, as against Baltimore and his agents, was destined to become a favourite method of administration, by means of concordats, new Conditions of Plantation, and even edicts conveyed in private letters.⁴

To relate now the origin and progress of the second code as refitted by Lewger, we observe that, after the demise of Lord Baltimore's first code, a prime interest with all was how to fill the vacant place; and, with the Calvert party, how to secure the succession for a genuine scion of their own policy. The Governor, in the afternoon of that eventful day, quietly gave out that he would adjourn the house and let everybody go home, till "some" should provide a new draft of laws. "Till the lawes," he said, "which they would propound to the Lord Proprietor were made ready; which some would take a care of, & in the meane time the company might attend their other businesses, &c." Thus the whole Assembly of freemen was to be shelved in favour of "some" unnamed persons.

A committee of three elected, Feb. 8, 1638. Lewger alone active.
Captain Cornwaleys put a stop to that manœuvre by forcing a committee upon the president and his secretary. And, as a matter of course, the secretary, Mr. Lewger, did not come into the committee, the votes of the freemen returning Cornwaleys first, the Governor second, and Captain Evelin third. But, as a matter of course again, Mr. Lewger did find his way in as secretary. This was on the 8th of February, 1638. The house was then adjourned for eighteen days, till the Governor and his captains should make an expedition against the Isle of Kent. Adjournments followed till March came, and the Governor with his captains reappeared. During all this time the secretary had the field apparently to himself. And when, on the 12th day of March, the great men gathered again in congress, Mr. John Lewger was ready with a long list of bills, including the twenty lately read a first time.

According to the vote which had rejected Baltimore's code, it was permissible to take the individual bills thereof and present them on their own merits in the new draft. In ten half-days, between the 12th of March and the 24th, the Assembly passed some forty-three bills of general import, besides a couple of indictments that regarded

---

³ *Calvert Papers*, i. 173; April 6, 1638.

⁴ Cf. S. F. Streeter, *Papers*, p. 184: Baltimore, July 14, 1643, to his officers, in the matter of the chapel.—Cf. *Calvert Papers*, i. 219: Baltimore to the Governor, November 23, 1642, in the matter of repudiating his own part of a contract, made under Conditions of Plantation.—Cf. the Baltimore drafts for the Provincial to sign. —*Infra*, § 60 (3), note 15; § 62; § 63 (1); § 66 (1), pp. 529, 530; § 67, pp. 542, 543.

individuals. The law for capital felonies met with opposition from Cornwaleys, Clerke, and Fenwick, who, as we know, were special friends of the Fathers. Another law, for the support of the Lord Proprietor, encountered the same names in opposition.[5] With regard to this last bill for "supportation" of his lordship, the Governor privately told the lordship interested that he had taken steps to buy off Cornwaleys from his opposition.[6]

Of this huge body of jurisprudence, fourteen bills were read the first time on one morning, when miscellaneous business had been finished. They were read a second time, with six others for the first time, on the next morning, in similar conditions. Another morning when they had some moments for legislation, seventeen bills were read for the third time, and passed "by general consent, not one vote dissenting." In the afternoon of the same day, fifteen more were read for the third time and passed. On the next morning, they had legislative leisure to read for the last time six other bills and pass them. And, as if that were not enough, they met again two mornings later, read for the third time six other bills, debated just three of them, and passed them all. Five days afterwards, on the 24th of March, they held a final session, listened to a reading of "the residue of the lawes as they were fair engrossed;" and signed them all, the Governor leading and the others following.[7]

Legislation en masse. March 12-24.

On the 3rd of April, only ten days after the Assembly was dissolved, Father Copley writes a very grave letter to Lord Baltimore.[8] On the 6th of April, Captain Cornwaleys writes a masculine and martial letter, to which reference has already been made.[9] And, on the 25th of the same month, Leonard Calvert writes to his brother from Virginia.[10]

Ominous correspondence. Apr. 1638–Feb. 1639.

Lord Baltimore's consent being withheld from Lewger's code, which came over fulfilling indeed all his desires, but which also came over attended by this correspondence foreboding evil consequences, new measures were tried both in London and in Maryland, as well with respect to the Fathers as with regard to the colonists in general. Not least among these supplementary manœuvres was a concordat, which apparently should, in part at least, supply the place of the suspended legislation, without the odium now attaching to Lewger's

[5] *Archives of Maryland, Proceedings of the Assembly*, pp. 12-22.
[6] *Calvert Papers*, i. 190.
[7] *Proceedings of the Assembly*, pp. 14-24.
[8] *Calvert Papers*, i. 157-169.
[9] *Ibid.*, 169-181.—The endorsement by Baltimore says the "16 Aprill."
[10] *Ibid.*, 182-193.

overreaching code. For this period two more letters are extant—one of Lewger to his lordship, dated January 5, 1639, and one of Father White to the same, of February 20.[11]

All these five letters belong to the year that elapsed between the Assembly just considered and the next session, which reconsidered in large part the handiwork of the former. They enable us to retrace the main lines of the policy, and of the art by which the policy was engineered into the condition of statutory law—under over forty distinct titles, in three distinct readings for each, within the space of some available time on ten half-days—thus allowing the remarkable average of between five and ten minutes per law for planters, who were not constitutional lawyers, to hear, to understand, to digest, to debate at their leisure, and to pass the matter on through each successive stage of parliamentary procedure!

§ 48. The code was denounced in general and in particular. It was criticized under a double aspect as touching lay interests and as concerning spiritual affairs. Under both these respects it was censured by both laity and clergy, as we see textually under the hands of those who wrote, and as we understand by their reports about those who did not write. The clergy on the ground at the time happened to be Jesuits. But it was not the interests of the Jesuits as such that came into question at the outset. It was the interests of the clergy as such. Later on, it became an issue regarding the Order in particular.

The text not having been preserved, the names of the bills as rehearsed in the Assembly minutes[1] help us to identify the separate topics; while the fifty-four pages in octavo print, containing the five letters referred to,[2] supply indications to fill up the bare skeleton of titles, and afford material for understanding the corresponding laws. We can do no more here than point to the results of such a synthesis; and that we shall do for the purpose of following the subsequent trend of events.

Of the two score laws and more, eight are about manors. They regulate the assigning of manors, the peopling and supporting of them; and, strange to say, they contain a prohibition to alienate or part with a manor. There is a law that a glebe shall be settled, or, as we learn from Father Copley, that every manor shall

A sketch of the code.

---

[11] *Calvert Papers*, i. 194-201, 201-211. The passages here and there edited in italics we take to have been underlined only by Lord Baltimore, the recipient.
[1] *Archives of Maryland, Proceedings of the Assembly*, loc. cit.
[2] *Calvert Papers*, i. 157-211.

provide one hundred acres for the support of a pastor; the pastors in question not being Father Copley and the missionaries, nor the manors in question being Lord Baltimore's with his ten million acres, but other people's manors, which they have already bought for themselves. There are laws about building a town, erecting a fort, planting corn, and about securing the titles to lands. There are military duties and services laid to the charge of manors and of freeholds: as well as an oath of allegiance to the Sovereign. At this stage the Baron of Baltimore had not yet put himself forward in the sovereign capacity of demanding an oath of allegiance to himself. The oath here prescribed of fealty to the legitimate Sovereign, King of England, may have had some connection with that which Panzani had lighted upon and written about during seven months, a couple of years before. There are laws about the descent of land, the succession to the goods of intestates, and the probate of wills. Besides, there are criminal laws regarding capital offences; the privilege of clergy for some capital crimes; the arbitrary punishment of enormous offences; and a bill for the support of the Lord Proprietary. This last bill, which was one of the few opposed by Cornwaleys, put back in Lord Baltimore's hands, for his lordship's sole use and behoof, a right of barter and trade, solemnly pledged to the colonists by the Proprietary as a part of the fundamental contract. Leonard Calvert's justification of it is that he had "promised" to buy off the captain's opposition.

Several parts of this code, as is evident, were retrospective, either directly or consequentially, undoing settled conditions on which the plantation of Maryland had proved successful, and recovering for the Proprietary emoluments and vested rights, which he should now wish never to have given away. No doubt as a party, to be charged in some degree with the responsibility of passing this code, the body of planters who voted for it cannot be ignored. But many of them were quite helpless and shiftless in their capacity of legislators, and offered a most ductile material for the managers to do with as they chose. We may listen to the letter-writers describing some things, while others must be sketched in the briefest analysis possible.

(1) Father Copley says to Lord Baltimore: "This I am sure that some here, reflecting on what they have donne, say plainly that, if they canne not live here, they canne live else where, and therfor that they care not much. Others complaine very much that, by the many proxies which the Governor, Mr. Lugar, and there instruments had gotten, they did what they would, without any restraints at all. Others already question the validity of they lawes

(1) The parties.

because they say that they canne proove, that they weare never red thrice in the same tenor. Others say other things. And, if the only apprehension of future consequence already beginne to affright them, what will the consequence[s] themselve[s] doe! Truly I doubte that even in the most flourishing countrys lords of mannors would conceave such lyke laws somewhat burdensom. What then will those apprehend, who shall be soe weake that they shall scarcely be able to stande of themselves? Certainly I conceave that your lordshipe will rather thinke it fit to nourish and support younge sprigs then to depresse them. And to goe aboute to gather frute befor it be planted and ripe is never to have frute."[3]

Captain Cornwaleys tells of the means employed, the same which in modern politics and parlance are attributed to the so-called "wire-puller" or "boss." He desires to see his lordship "at peace with the first adventurers, whoe are, I perceave, no whit satisfyed with theyre last conditions for the trade, theyre harts haveing, it seems, *The expedients employed.* not seconded theyre hands in the agreement; but some for love, some for feare, some by importunety, and the rest for company, consented toe what they now repine toe stand toe. Nor can I blame them, for tis impossible they can be savers by it. Which made mee refuse to beare them company; and therefore am I now the only supposed enemy toe your lordships proffitt; which I disclayme from, unless there bee an antipothy betwixt that and my subcistance on this place."[4]

Father White sketches a well-known class: "relinquishers," he says, "who care little how itt wayeth,"[5] men of recent advent or *Relinquishers. The concordat.* recent enfranchisement, who were willing to sign away anything by a concordat and relinquish everything, because they had nothing of their own to relinquish, and were only helping to sign away other people's rights and goods and trade. These are probably in part the same to whom Copley refers, saying that the profit to his lordship himself would be very uncertain, because other people would come in as middlemen betwixt his lordship and the goods; and, says he, "some that are immediate actors perhaps may gitt some things; but your lordshipe shall be sure, if you your selfe have the profite, to make large disbursments and to receave large accoumpts."[6] In any case, there is a class of people who think that "amonge ruens they shall alwaye find some thinge."[7]

[3] *Calvert Papers*, i. 160, 161.   [4] *Ibid.*, 173, 174.
[5] *Ibid.*, 209, ad calc.   [6] *Ibid.*, 161, post med.   [7] *Ibid.*, med.

As to the concordat, which seems to have been a subsidiary manœuvre for handing over all rights of trade to his lordship, Father White expresses a principle of plain common sense, the necessity for repeating which shows the excesses already committed. He says that, where there is no partnership or common liability, no man nor any ninety-nine in a hundred can sign away another man's property, though he be only the hundredth against ninety-nine. He is his own master and master of his own: "And," says he, "as for the concordate signed by so many who understand little of truck and trade (excepting relinquishers, who care little how itt wayeth), that seemeth to suppose a common stock; which hath not ben since the bad successe of the two former, in which every body was losers; which makes every body protest against itt as an engine and mystery to undoe your lordship and them. From whence itt followeth that, howbeitt all adventurers in England subscribe, yett, heere beeing no guilde nor body of traders, as they say, to carry their right by most voices, though all butt one should forgoe theeir right, yett may that one retayne his. Truely, my Lord, this doth much trouble the thoughts of our colony, who takes this to bee a stepp to take also their land from them in tyme, unles they defend this."[8] It is to be noticed that the "adventurers in England" who were willing to sign papers were gentlemen and ladies, who might well suppose that Lord Baltimore knew best what they should sign. Mrs. Eure was one; but she was of his own family. Mrs. Philpot was probably another; and she was of his family. There were the gentlemen who had come over at first, and had now returned, without of necessity having sold out their rights.[9]

It was not difficult to procure signatures in such a family or society circle; while, on the American side of the ocean, the two managers, Calvert and Lewger, understood one another as perfectly as they understood Baltimore. Governor Calvert wrote with great satisfaction to his brother: "I meane this summer to pass all manner of accounts that are between you and me unto Mr. Lewger; for I have disposed of all my other businesses so, as I may have sufficient leisure to do it in. Mr. Lewger is a very serviceable and diligent man in his secretaries place in Maryland, and a very faithfull and able

---

[8] *Calvert Papers*, i. 209, 210.
[9] Cf. *Ibid.*, p. 196, Mrs. Eure; *Ibid.*, 195, Mr. Wiseman; *Ibid.*, 186, Mr. Philpot. —P. R. O., *Domestic, Car. I.*, ccccxiii., ff. 33, 34; Tho. Arundell, February 17, 1638, to Windebank, on Baltimore, Eure, Philpotts, etc.—*Relation of Maryland*, 1635, list of gentlemen at the end, Henry Wiseman, son to Sir Thomas Wiseman, etc.—J. Kilty, *Landholder's Assistant*, p. 67, the Viscountesse Falkland, etc.

assistant to me."[10] This eulogy was passed just one month after the enacting of the code, and was forwarded with the precious statutes themselves to the person most interested.

The foregoing observations show what kind of parties in Maryland were responsible for the things happening there. The observations which follow will show what kind of things had happened.

(2) They had given away to Lord Baltimore all their rights to trade or barter in beaver and corn, and they were to stay at home and plant tobacco; if corn were wanting, as was usually the case, they could buy of Baltimore or his middlemen, and meanwhile plant tobacco. No one could buy bread of the Indians but through his lordship, who was now made patron-in-chief of what Copley called "these pettye trades and raking out of mens necessitys,"[11] with greedy engrossers under him.[12] The result of this was, says Captain Cornwaleys, that if a man must sit down at home and become a planter of tobacco, an American product which the captain characterizes in the most uncomplimentary and impolite fashion,[13] then, says he, "I must desert the place and busynes, which I confes I shall be loth toe doe, soe cordiall a lover am I of them both; yet if I am forst toe it by discourteous injuries I shall not weepe at parting, nor despayre toe finde heaven as neere toe other parts as Maryland. But I will first doe my endeavor toe compose things soe, as non shall say heereafter that I lost a right I bought soe deere through negligens or ignorans. Other mens imaginations are noe infallible presidents toe mee; nor will the multitude of names nor seales move mee toe bee a foole for company. For what in them was only inadvertens non would tearm less than foolery in mee, whoe might or ought toe know by experiens, that it is impossible toe comply with the conditions mentioned in the lease and bee a saver by them."[14] Nothing would remain for him now but smuggling, and eluding the spies who would be set to watch him, and, he says, "beeing behoulding toe my servants secresy, or goeing with as much cawtion as if I stoale what I gott."[15] He challenges Lord Baltimore's honesty repeatedly: "There is now in you an undoubted powre for toe ratefy your first Conditions with the first adventurers, which I doubt not your lordship will performe toe theyre content."[16] This he will do by correcting the law or bill,

(2) The rights of trade.

The captain's appeal to Baltimore's honesty.

---

[10] Cf. *Calvert Papers*, i. 191, *post med.*   [11] *Ibid.*, 161, *post med.*
[12] *Ibid.*, 167, *ad calc.*   [13] "This stincking weede of America."
[14] *Ibid.*, 176, *med.*   [15] *Ibid.*, 178.   [16] *Ibid.*, 173, *med.*

"that confirmes the trade with the Indians for all comodetyes, toe bee exported, unto your Lordship;" which said bill is only one among "many other absurdetyes I doubt not but your Lordship will finde and correct upon the peruseall of oure learned lawes."[17]

Thus the most influential officer in the colony, by this one letter, on this subject alone, rendered the unqualified signature of the code by Baltimore quite impossible. But there are more implied threats in the long letter, and many more heads of grievance. The "lease" and its conditions, which are so offensive both to the captain and to common honesty, are no doubt the same or akin to those which Father White explains in more distinct terms, when speaking of "the trade of beaver," as secured to his lordship by "the last concordate of five years." He says: "If I understand not amisse, the sharers are to pay the tenth of their cloath and the tenth of theyre beaver for five years, and then to have no more right in trade." Here was a double tithe imposed on the whole colony for the benefit of his lordship's pocket, to be followed after five years by a total withdrawal of their franchise. In arguing against this double imposition, the missionary uses the following language: "I heare men say, that, if the right of truck bee taken from them, first by this covert and after ward by open meanes, they can have no assurance for the lands you give them; seeing, in the Declaration and Conditions of Plantation, both share in trade and the land runnes in one and the selfe same tenor, and would bee esteemed so, if itt weare brought to any hearing [in a court of justice]. I remember when your Lordship corrected the written copie which I made, I gave your Lordship an occasion, uppon the graunt of trade, to reflecte whether itt weare not fitt to limitt the graunt for tearme of life [of each adventurer]; and, notwithstanding this suggestion, your Lordship would have itt goe absolute as the graunt of land. And now, my Lord, this beeing only the specially reward of the first adventurers, who exposed their lives and fortunes and banished themselves from their freynds, allies and country to serve your Lordship in this plantation, doe not blame them, my Lord, if they feele itt and stand for their supposed right, on which their maintenance doth much depend; untill they shall understand how they can loose that, and may not heereafter have their land taken from them too—the form of graunt for each beeing all one."[18]

The concordat. Father White's appeal.

White and the Conditions of Plantation.

How true to the letter this proved to be with respect to the

[17] Cf. *Calvert Papers*, i. *loc. cit.*   [18] *Ibid.*, 209.

missionaries themselves, the subsequent history shows. For the present it may be observed that Father Copley, as procurator, was much more anxious about the corn monopoly, which had been vested in the Proprietary.[19]

On the supposition that the provisions of the code, notwithstanding the more than dubious practice which they sanction, will still become law by means of Lord Baltimore's signature, Captain Cornwaleys asks for the privilege on his own behalf of trading to the amount of £60 worth per annum.[20] Leonard the Governor tells his brother the Proprietary that he has promised to second the captain's petition, as he does for two reasons—because it is thus that he has bought off the captain's opposition to the whole bill, and because he wishes to show some recognition for past services: "which I did as well to decline his hindrance of passing the whole to you, as also to give him incouragement for the many services he hath done you in the colony."[21]—Such was the state of humiliation to which Baltimore's best friends were reduced, that, within six years, they were begging as a pittance for some portion of that which morally and juridically was theirs by an absolute right. It would be an interesting speculation, taking as premises what we know of the Severn in Maryland and of Massachusetts Bay, to infer the probable fate of the baron in his palatinate, if, instead of treating with the Catholic gentry so complaisantly engaged in his enterprise, he had been dealing with Puritans, who so quickly "scrupled" at everything concerning him, his rights, his government, and his titles in Maryland.[22]

Surrender of the captain.

Then, on the strength of the arrangement projected just as if it were already a statutory enactment, Leonard asks his brother to let himself and the captain have the entire monopoly of the trade, granted "to us two," he says, "for two or three years, rent free;" and he promises that the two of them will bring the trade to perfection.[23] Accordingly, eight months later, the secretary, Mr. Lewger, who, as register of grants of land, collector of customs, receiver of rents, commissioner of causes testamentary, justice of the peace, etc., seems to be too much gorged with offices and good things to care for truck in beaver or any other honest calling of a plebeian type, tells his lordship that "the trade of beaver is wholly now in the Governors and the Captaines hands, without any rivall; and

---

[19] *Calvert Papers,* i. 161, *med.*
[20] *Ibid.,* 178, *med.*
[21] *Ibid.,* 190, *med.*
[22] Cf. J. T. Scharf, *Maryland,* i. 201.
[23] *Calvert Papers, ubi supra,* 191.

they are joined partners in the driving of it." [24] This means that the trade had been engrossed without any semblance of a right or title.

Just as the captain begged by way of a pittance for what was his by right, Father Copley begs as a favour for leave to get corn : " I desyre lykwyse from your lordshipe a free grante to buy corn of the Indians without asking leave here; for endeed it will be a greate pressure to eate our bread at there curtesye, who as yet I have found but very little curtuous. Certainly, while the cheife of this colony thus wholy neglect planting [corn], and thinke on nothing but on a pedling trade [in beaver]—certainly in the colony they will still make a scarcity of bread; and in that scarcity, if we shall not be able to healpe ourselves nor the colonye without there leave that make the want, many greate difficultyes may follow." This passage represents the engrossers of the corn supplies as indirectly the creators of the corn famine, calling into existence the demand which they shall supply. He continues : " Certainly I have this yeere planted [corn] much more than the greatest parte of the colonye besyde, and soe intende to continue what I am able; because endeed in planting I place my greatest hope. Yet for some yeers I know that I must buy; and in buying there canne be noe inconvenience to your lordshipe to grante me a generall licence." [25] *Copley's surrender.*

Against the greed of monopoly, and the opinion of those who think that, if his lordship can glut himself with all the good things at once, he will become rich all at once, and the others too, for " the fewer there are the better cheire will be for them," [26] Copley gives the soundest advice about cultivating a steady growth of population, and encouraging the same by all means; and he adds in racy style : " But endeed the old sa[y]ings are true that Roome was not bulte [built] in a day; and that such as will lipe [leap] over style[s] before they cumme at them shall breake there shin, and perhaps not gitt over the still [stile] soe quickly as those who cumme to them [first] before they goe over." [27]

Less safe than Copley in the advice offered is Father White, whose prolix letter manifests the greatest personal devotion, if not a positive affection, for Baltimore. He describes himself as under a " liege duety " of some kind, being " a great partiall and humble servant of your Lordships, who dayly prayeth for your Lordships happines and the good of your province." [28] Now *White's insinuating plea.*

---

[24] *Calvert Papers*, i. 197, 198. [25] *Ibid.*, 168.
[26] *Ibid.*, 161, *med.* [27] *Ibid.*, 162, *med.*
[28] *Ibid.*, 201, 211.

this "great partiall servant," who has spent "some solitarie howers in studie of your Lordships happines," recounts no less than six very great and partial funds of beatitude for his lordship to appropriate; and the second is nothing less than a wholesale series of monopolies on the score of Baltimore's being a kind of sovereign, " as in France, Spaine and Italie the soveraignes doe appropriate the sayle [sale] of certayne things for themselves." And White enumerates the trades of the brick-kilns, of the "carpenters, hatters, sawers, coopers, smiths, etc."[29] The good Father talks in Baltimore's own style of his "lordships infinite charge about this province both abroad and att hoame;" and he adds something about "the mayntenance of your Lordships person after that decent manner as princes are by right of nations mainteyned in splendor according to their place."[30] Whatever all this may mean, one thing is clear, and Father White comes to it at the end of the letter. In the most cautious, gentle, and courteous way, speaking as an old secretary who had drawn up with Baltimore the original Declaration and Conditions of Plantation, he beseeches the Proprietary to be honest and not to swindle.[31] The passage has been given above.[32]

(3) From trade if we pass on to property, we notice several grievances. One regards only Conditions of Plantation for the future, which discourage men in England from ever presuming to obtain a manor in Maryland.[33] A second is retrospective, raising, as it would appear, the rental of the gentlemen who had already acquired their manors on fixed conditions. Father Copley says: "Mr. Greene, one of the gentlemen that camme in the *Arke*, reflecting that, besydes the losse of his halfe share of trucke, he was now to pay tenne barrells of corne for his 10,000 acres, and that only he had three men to raise that and maintaine himselfe and his wyfe, confidently told me that he must necessarily deserte the colonye."[34] A third grievance again is retrospective, inasmuch as men who had acquired their manors under the title agreed on of fee simple, in accordance with the charter of Maryland, were now informed that it was all a feudal holding, which must go back, as improved property, to the lord paramount, Baltimore; and that they could not give, grant, sell, bequeathe their land to any body else; and the only means of conveyance would be under a formal grant anew, and under the seal of the province, from the

(3) Property conditions of tenure.

---

[29] *Calvert Papers*, i. 207.
[31] *Ibid.*, 209, *med.*
[33] *Calvert Papers, ubi supra,* p. 159, *med.*
[30] *Ibid.*, 204, *post med.*
[32] Page 249, note 1; p. 395.
[34] *Ibid.*, 159, 160.

feudal sovereign, and absolute lord, Cæcilius, Lord Baltimore. Of course, there were fees and emoluments connected with such grants, whether original or renewed. So that, whether the absolute lord reclaimed for his own private benefit the improved property of other people, or granted it out again, his finances and privileges, as well as the emoluments of Lewger and other officers, promised to receive a splendid development, and all at the expense of other people.

This rank feudalism of past centuries, now raked up for application in the new world, is fully exhibited in the Stonyhurst documents, by which Baltimore, having failed to impose his tenure *in capite* on the colony at large, endeavoured for years to force it on the Jesuits and their property. *A feudal tenure.* But at the present stage, in the general attempt against the colonists by a law, we have only one sentence of Copley's to show the purport and tenor of the bill, the text whereof is lost. The Father says to Baltimore: "But further, suppose that one should raise men sufficient to git a mannor, yet, when he shall reflecte that, whatsoever happeneth, he canne not sell his mannor, but, by keeping it, he must be necessitated to live where perhaps he hath noe will, I doubte that many will be terrified by that hazard." [35] The reason of his being "necessitated to live where perhaps he hath noe will," must be that of his otherwise losing it by escheat or forfeiture to the lord paramount, Baltimore, if he pretends to get rid of it by any form of conveyance, other than that of passing it back to the said superior lord. The attempt thus made to plant in Maryland the odious servitude, which belonged to an effete system of medieval infeudation, was within twenty-two years of the date when feudal England itself, all bound down as it was by such tenures and servitudes, was about to sweep the whole system away by one comprehensive Act, in the twelfth year of Charles II., 1660.[36] That Act of Charles II. was to settle a revenue on the king in lieu of the perquisites and aids which the old system had afforded him as lord paramount. Baltimore had already the rents; in the Lewger code he was purveying for himself an additional revenue by tithes and trade and monopolies; and withal he was introducing that essential element of feudal servitude, for which in the English system the revenue was to be a substitute and compensation.

[35] *Calvert Papers*, i. 160.
[36] Cap. 24, "*An Act for takeing away the Court of Wards and Liveries and Tenures in Capite, and by Knights Service and Purveyance, and for setling a Revenue upon his Majesty in lieu thereof.*"

The legislative documents on this matter fall probably to the account of the Lewger bill entitled, "Against the aliening of mannors;" if, indeed, two other bills about the "assigning of mannors" were not exemplifications of the same astuteness and artifice." [37]

Now there was another difficulty of the gravest kind, wherein the technical advantage was all Baltimore's, if he was not deterred from abusing it to the damage of the colonists. They had no titles yet, but only a right to titles. It was a strict right by onerous contract, but the patents had not been drawn up and delivered. The colonists had not asked for them, and did not want them yet; no doubt because of fees attendant on the delivery of such deeds, or because of obligations which would naturally arise from a fixed and final settlement, or simply because they wished to sell their claim as negotiable rights. If now the patents, on being applied for, were Retroactive machinery. drawn up in conformity with the retroactive clauses of the new code operating on them, the colonists would find themselves betrayed and undone. They had never come to America on such conditions. On the other hand, as far as the said code may have legislated in favour of the immediate patenting of settlements or of doing so within a certain time, it cannot be said that there was any injustice committed; unless an assurance against such a limitation of time had been part of an original privilege granted to them. Both of these two points, regarding the indefeasible right to take up land, and the time of using that right, are touched upon in the following passage of Father Copley's letter:—

"And touching our temporaltyes. First, I beseech your lordshipe that we may take up and keepe soe much lande, as in my former letters I acquainted your lordshipe to be requisite for our present occasions, according to the first Conditions which we maid with your lordshipe; and that, albeit we now take not up neere our due, yet that herafter we may take it up, when we find it fitt according to our adventures." [38]

It is not easy to understand how men pretending to sit in a deliberative Assembly, or rather to preside over it, men representing a stable authority and not a socialistic anarchy, should Casting lots for other people's property. have conducted business in such a high-handed manner, as to subject their neighbour's property to the ordeal of tossing up or casting lots; should throw this bait out to a hungry proletariate of recently enfranchised freemen; and should

[37] *Archives of Maryland, Proceedings of the Assembly,* p. 20.
[38] *Calvert Papers,* i. 167, med.—The limitation of time came into operation March 25, 1642. *Ibid., Council,* pp. 99, 100.

offer it as a bill and pass it as a law, that people might get by lot the improved property and manors of the first and original adventurers. This incredible bill may have come under the head of what appears in the minutes either as providing "for bounding of mannors," or as determining "the peopling of mannors." In some way or other, the legislators seem to have enacted that no person should have more than one manor. Whence it followed that those having more than one should resign the others. And, to give the proletariate a fair chance and carry their votes solidly with him, Lewger would seem to have proposed tossing up or casting lots for the spoils. Nor was any discrimination made, as indeed it need not have been, between estates derived by grant under Conditions of Plantation from the Proprietary, and those bought outright from some other person already invested with the legal rights to property. It is thus Father Copley comments on this socialistic policy—

"Secondly, by the new lawe we should relinquish what we have, and then cast lotts in what place we shall chooce; and, if our lott proove ill, what we have already may be chosen from us, and soe we may beginne the world anew. And then ether we must loose our buldinge, all our cleering, all our enclosures, and all our tennants; or else, [in case we choose still to remain there, we must lose the privileges of a manor, and] be forced to sitt freeholders, and to pay for every hundred acres one barrell of corne; wheras we are not yet in a little care to gitt bread.

"3dly. Though we should have the best lott, yet, if we should choose [our Indian manor of] Metapanian first, then we are sure to loose Mr. Gerards Mannor, notwithstanding that we have bought it at a deere raite." [39]

Of the same socialistic character were other measures against the gentlemen who had acquired landed property already, under the form and with the privileges of manors. There was a new income tax, violating the Conditions of Plantation. It was an imposition of 20 shillings on every thousand acres. There was mustering in military service, no man being exempted, not even the Catholic priest. There was the drain of seventy-five per cent. of the men on a manor in time of war, leaving only twenty-five per cent. to work, to furnish munitions as called for, and meanwhile to get all supplies out of the ground by planting,

Other socialistic measures.

---

[39] *Calvert Papers*, i. 163, 164.—We have seen reason above for identifying "Mr. Gerards Mannor" so bought with St. Inigoes Manor; *supra*, § 39, p. 346, note 1.

without any permission to provide themselves with necessaries by the avenue of trade. There was the muster master invested with complete authority to inspect the munitions of a manor, to requisition the men and supplies of the manor, and to inflict fines and punishments on the master of the manor. At the same time, he and any other "base baleife" wore a sacrosanct character; so that, if any one being abused by these minions should strike such a sacred personage, the person so abused by the minion should "loose lyfe, lands and goods." [40]

(4) This introduces the new order of grievances on the score of prejudice to life and limb. Captain Cornwaleys denounces the introduction of "lawes prejuditiall toe oure honors and freedome," laws allowing of no remedy against the insolence of passionate or malicious Governors, laws imposing the penalty of forfeiture and death for legitimate self-defence against such tyrants, and laws to boot which left the interpretation of their own rights to the insolent and malicious officials themselves.[41] This is always a dear policy with the despotic, to leave laws indefinite, and to leave them open to the arbitrary interpretation of the parties interested in applying them. Thus one of the bills passed in the Assembly is expressly named: "For arbitrary punishment of some enormious offences." [42] And how comprehensive the term "enormious" was, which placed a man who chose to be "enormious" completely at the mercy of the officials in the province, appears from a definite list, which in the attempt next year to pass a similar law was kindly inserted, in order "that these offences following in this Act and no other shall be judged enormious offences within this province." Nearly a whole quarto page follows full of the enormities; and, in spite of the definiteness pretended, such indefinite crimes as these are included: "scandalous or contemptuous words or writings to the dishonour of the Lord Proprietarie or his Leiutenant-Generall for the time being or of any of the Councill; excerseing within the province any jurisdiction or authority, which ought to be derived from the Lord Proprietary, without lawfull power or commission from or under him; contempts & misdomenors against lawfull ordinances or proclamations; abuses of publique judges or officers." [43] One of these precious officers, the actual sheriff, says Copley, had "formerly bin a pursevante" [44]— which phrase, in the context, seems to imply

(4) Life and limb in jeopardy.

[40] *Calvert Papers*, i. 160.   [41] *Ibid.*, 173, *ante med.*
[42] *Archives of Maryland, Proceedings of the Assembly*, p. 22.   [43] *Ibid.*, p. 73.
[44] *Calvert Papers*, i. 163, *med.* "The shrive (who hath formerly bin a purseuante, and is now a cheife protestante)."

that he had also been a priest-hunter; for such, in Catholic experience and literature, was the meaning connoted in that term of ill omen, " a pursuivant." [45]

Cornwaleys observes that he is in the power of his own servant, as to both person and property, if the servant choose to turn spy and informer while the master is only using his right to trade.[46]

Finally, putting his finger on the revolutionary principle, which had enabled Lewger, backed by the proletariate, to carry this socialistic code through, Copley says: " If we permite this precident, that Assemblys may alter mens rights, noe man shall never be sure of what he hath; but he that canne git most proxis in every assembly shall dispose of any mans estate that he pleaseth; which is most unlawfull in the churches state for any secular man to doe, and for ecclesiasticall persons to permite." [47] And, at the end of his letter, Copley writes a postscript to this effect : " Since the writing of the former letter I am told that Mr. Lugar defends publiquely in the colony, that an Assembly may dispose here of any mans lands or goods as it please. If this weare once bruted and believed, I conceave that none would ether cumme or abide here ; easpecially where, if any factious working man canne but procure an overswa[y]ing number of voices by prox[i]es, he shall undoe whome he please. And none shall be sure of any thinge that he hath; seeing experience hath shewed that one, that would labour for it, may quickly git such a faction and such an overswaing voice of proxis, that he may carry what he will. Really I much feare, that this overbusye stirringe to many new querks and devises will never doe your lord-shipe nor the colony good. I pray God it doe not much harme, according to the old proverbe, that a busy man never wants woe." [48]

Blank socialism.

And here we end the general grievances of the colony, lay and clerical alike. There was another adage indeed which Copley might have quoted, and which Shakespeare uses, about a certain class of people who, being picked up and " mounted, run their horse to death." Here was a legislator who had recently been begging his bread about London. Now no one's property was safe from him.

---

[45] This is the idea conveyed, for instance, by the Catholic peers in the document presented to the ambassador extraordinary of France, Chasteauneuf, as quoted above (§ 11, p. 209, note 14; *Rationes Redditæ*, p. 14). They say : " *Nam hoc ipso quod apud nos reperiatur episcopus qui se appellet Ordinarium, hujus regni satellites hæretici, quos* Poursuivantes *appellamus, majori muniuntur potestate; et per causam vestigandi episcopum penetrant in plurimas domos, atque in plurimos sacerdotes incurrunt, qui alioqui tutiores forent.*"
[46] *Calvert Papers*, i. 177, 178.—*Supra*, p. 394.
[47] *Ibid.*, i. 164, *ante med.*
[48] *Ibid.*, 169.

He was riding his horse to death with Leonard Calvert on the croup. And even Cornwaleys had signified he would be willing to run behind.

§ 49. After giving Lord Baltimore to understand that, as "Roome was not bulte in a day," so a raid on Maryland for spoils will never bring him a fortune out of it, but will leave only ruins in it, Father Copley proceeds: "Many other things to this effect will occure to your lordshipe upon better consideration then I could take; yet these occuring I could not omitte to suggest them. I beseech Almighty God that your lordshipe may make the best use of them, to Gods greatest glorie, and your own temple [temporal]. But now I will say some thinge of the inconvenience fal[l]inge by these lawes of the church of God; which should have binne regarded in the first place, but was not thought of, as it seemeth by the lawe."[1]

With this introduction he opens a remonstrance entirely distinct from that which he has formulated on the account of other landlords, and in his own name as a mere landlord. He and his colleagues were clergymen; and they were the only representatives of the Church in the colony. Yet there was no notice whatever taken of them in the draft of laws, though these had been formulated and carried through by men who claimed to be Catholics, and who were perfectly unhampered by any of the penal restrictions at that time legal in England. The tenor of his remonstrance, as well as of Captain Cornwaleys's upon this subject, shows that the condition now resulting for the Fathers was new in some respects. A certain set of rights or immunities had been silently granted to the missionaries. A proof positive of this is seen in the fact that they had been exempted from attendance at the Assembly, as no layman was; and that without any penalty or protest. Naturally the same set of rights was expected for the future, either silently as before, or at least without any open and contemptuous repudiation. The magistrates, nominally Catholic, were free to follow their conscience in a free country, where Baltimore had guaranteed in express terms "as much freedome, comfort, and encouragement as they [the colonists] cann desire."[2] And, as with Catholics internally there was a rigid principle of duty involved regarding the Church and the clergy, they were bound in conscience, as far as circumstances allowed it, not to violate the principle externally.

Slighting the Church.

---

[1] *Calvert Papers*, i. 162, *med.*
[2] *Ibid.*, 136, No. 6: Instructions, November 13, 1633.—Cf. *supra*, § 19, p. 252.

The estimate to be formed of what circumstances might allow would differ with different men. But, in the remonstrance which follows, Copley is quite clear in contending that no estimate formed by a Catholic, in the actual circumstances of Maryland, could approve of the Erastian contempt for spiritual persons and spiritual interests, which appeared in the new code and was being applied in the new administration. His own estimate of what the circumstances allow is somewhat elastic. He claims nothing absolutely except the principle which cannot be denied by a Catholic, that the Church is not under the State.[3]

However, in laying down the criteria for reducing the principle to practice in Maryland, Copley is more indefinite. He asks that the missionaries "be suffered to enjoy such other priveledges as we may without note;"[4] and this, "while the government is Catholique."[5] He interprets the situation, having an eye to the "satisfaction of the State at home,"[6] that is, the political persecuting State in England. And, though canonical principles and practice are imperative in the Catholic Church, yet he believes that, where an "ecclesiasticall juri[s]diction is not yet setled,"[7] it will be enough for lay magistrates, when deviating from Catholic practice, to respect the principle and "know in private," that what they do with regard to the Church and the clergy is done by them only "as arbitrators and defendors of the Church."[8] Nor does Father Copley seem to look upon the present advantageous situation as anything more than temporary. He implies no term, when probably ecclesiastical jurisdiction will be settled in Maryland; nor any permanency in the government remaining Catholic.

(1) We begin here with the protest of Cornwaleys. The captain's introduction of the ecclesiastical question is much more ample than Copley's. But he omits the particular issues, referring Lord Baltimore for them to the clergy who write by the same mail.[9] He says that a number of Acts are now going over for his lordship's confirmation; but he hopes that the Proprietary will be "more wary in confirmeing then wee have beene wise in proposeing," if he values the happiness of the commonwealth. Captain Cornwaleys proceeds: "Therefore I beseeche your Lordship for His sake, whose honor you and wee doe heere pretend, and whoe at last must judg with what sincerity wee

(1) Plea of Cornwaleys for the Church.

[3] Cf. J. Hergenroether, *loc. cit., supra,* § 40, p. 353, note 3.
[4] *Calvert Papers, ubi supra,* 167, *ante med.*   [5] *Ibid.,* 166, *med.*
[6] *Ibid.,* 167, *ante med.*   [7] *Ibid.,* 166, *ad calc.*
[8] *Ibid.,* 166, *ad calc.*—Cf. *infra,* § 53, p. 442, note 25.   [9] *Ibid.,* 171, *ad calc.*

have discharged it, that you, from whose consent they must receave the bindeing fors of lawes, will not permit the least clawes [clause] toe pas that shall not first bee throughly scand and resolved by wise, learned, and religious divines, toe bee noe waise prejuditiall toe the immunettyes and priveledges of that Church, which is the only true guide toe all eternall happines; of which wee shall shew oureselves the most ungratefull members that ever shee nourished, if, in requiteall of those many favors and blessings that she and her devoute servants have obtayned for us, wee attempt toe deprive her or them of more than wee can give them or take from them, with out paying such a price as hee that buyes it will repent his bargayne.

"What are her greevances, and how toe bee remedyed, you will, I doubt not, understand at large from those, whoe are more knowing in her rights, and consequently more sensyble of her injuryes, then such an ignorant creature as I am. Wherefore now all that belongs toe mee is only toe importune your Lordship, in whose powre t'is yet toe mend what wee have done amis, toe bee most carefull in preserveing His honor whoe must preserve both you and Maryland. Perhaps this fault hath beene permitted in us as a favoure toe your Lordship, whereby you may declare the sincerety of your first pyous pretence for the planting of this desert province; which will bee toe much doubted of, if you should take advantage of oure ignorant and uncontionable proceedeings to assume more then wee can justly give you; and, for a little imaginary honor, throw your self, us and your country out of that protection, which hath hithertoe preserved and prospered that and us beyound humaine expectation. Which noe doubt will bee continued, if wee continue as wee ought toe bee. I never yet heard of any that lost by beeing bountyfull toe God or His Church. Then let not your Lordship feare toe bee the first. Give untoe God what doth belong toe Him; and doubt not but Cesar shall receave his due.

"If your Lordship thinks mee tooe teadious in a discourse not proper toe the part that I doe act, my interest in the whole action must excuse mee. Sylence would perhaps make mee supposed accessary toe these dangerouse positions; which is soe far from my intention, that, as I now declare toe youre Lordship, and shall not feare toe doe the like toe all the world if it bee necessary, I will rather sacrifice myself and all I have in the defence of God's honor and his Churches right, then willingly consent toe anything that may not stand with the good contiens of a real Catholick. Which resolution if your

"The good conscience of a real Catholic."

Lordship doe not allsoe make good by a religious care of what you send over authorised by your consent, I shall with as much convenient speede as I can with draw myself, and what is left of that which I brought with mee, out of the danger of beeing involvd in the ruein which I shall infallibly expect.

"Your Lordship knowes my securety of contiens was the first condition that I expected from this government; which [government] then you thought soe inocent, as you conceaved the propositon alltogether impertinent. But now, I hope, you will perceave the contrary."[10] The captain proceeds to animadvert on the menaces to honour, freedom, and life, without any remedy at law, and "many other absurdetyes" which these "learned lawes" contain. He publicly professes devotion to Maryland, and adds: "Nor will I yet desist from doeing soe, if I may bee soe happy as toe see this differens betwixt the Church and Government well reconsiled agayne."[11]

Referring to Mr. Jerome Hawley, Treasurer of Virginia, who had attended some of the late Assembly meetings, the captain returns again to the Church, as one of the two bonds which have kept Hawley still attached to Maryland: "Well may the dischargeing of the office hee hath undertaken invite him sometimes toe looke towards Virginia; but certaynely not with prejudice to Maryland, from whens hee receaves the greatest comforts that the world affords him both for sowle and body—the on[e] from the Church, the other from his wife."[12] Here follows that high encomium on Mrs. Hawley, already cited by us in conjunction with a passage of the Annual Letter for 1638, and with the account given there of Mr. Hawley's death, who expired in the arms of the Fathers (August, 1638).[13]

Hawley and the Church.

In this warlike declaration from the military chief of the colony, it is not difficult to see the origin of a certain "Act for Church Liberties," which was passed by the freemen in their very first meeting after the date of this correspondence; was passed by them in the very first place among the bills read and engrossed; and, when these taken severally were set aside, was still passed as the very first provision in the comprehensive Ordinance enacted by the freemen, and confirmed by the Governor in the name of the Proprietary (March 19, 1639).[14] In the lengthy passage

Origin of Act on Holy Church.

[10] *Calvert Papers,* i. 171-173.
[11] *Ibid.,* 173, *ad calc.*
[12] *Ibid.,* 180, *post med.*
[13] *Supra,* § 36, p. 337.—Cf. S. F. Streeter, *Papers,* p. 121.
[14] *Archives of Maryland, Proceedings of the Assembly,* pp. 40, 83.

just quoted, the captain formulates a clear statement that, in matters religious and ecclesiastical, there are things which we can neither give nor take away. He was clearly no Erastian; and his words place God and Cæsar just where they ought to be. He claims "immunities and privileges" for the Church, and liberality towards "her devout servants," the clergy; and he dissuades Baltimore from presuming "to deprive her or them" of what these iniquitous laws are attempting to take away. This implies that the state of immunity or privilege claimed was already practically recognized. His remarkable abstention from laying the blame on John Lewger, and his direct summons to Baltimore all through, show that he holds the latter fully responsible for not letting well enough alone. He summons Baltimore to be liberal, and to make good the "pious pretence" of a few years before, when his lordship had posed as a good pious Catholic. The only objective reason for the present change of front is considered by the captain to warrant just the opposite; that is to say, he regards the preservation and prosperity of the colony "beyond human expectation," as calling rather for liberality to God and His Church, than for deprivation and "dangerous positions." And his coupling "the laws sent over by your lordship" with "these that are from hence proposed to you,"[15] both drafts according to him being equally bad, confirms the inference drawn above, that there was a substantial identity between the two—between the triumphant Lewgerism of the freemen's code and the rejected Cæsarism of the Baltimore code. In short, the sharp contrast exhibited in these pages between the "pious pretence" of the astute politician, who had posed as a Catholic for a purpose, and the plain speaking of the military man, who calls himself "a real Catholic" with "a good conscience," is only equalled by another contrast cruelly set forth at the close of the long passage; to wit, between the pious scandal which Baltimore had once taken at the captain's even alluding to illiberality or intolerance in connection with Maryland, and the brutal facts to "the contrary" which the same nobleman, now unmasked, was using his best endeavours to make legal.

(2) We shall sum up briefly the many "inconveniences" which Father Copley notes at length—the same which Cornwaleys styled more forcibly the Church's "greevances," and her "injuryes."

First, no care whatever has been taken in the new legislation to promote the conversion of the Indians; no provision made with

[15] *Calvert Papers*, i. 173.

regard to ecclesiastical persons, nor any favour shown them; no immunity or privilege "preserved" for the Church, such as she enjoys everywhere else. Mr. Lewger even seems to deny the principle that the Church is a Divine institution, with a juridical constitution corresponding; or, in other words, that she has any laws and privileges by Divine right, which a Catholic as such is bound in conscience to observe. The gentleman says that papal bulls and ecclesiastical canons, that theologians and casuists, are all alike to be brushed aside, because they are all *ex parte,* speaking on one side; as if he himself and other gentlemen, who are pulling down the Church, were not *ex parte,* working for their own side. Mr. Lewger holds that privileges, or special laws for herself alone, are given to her only by the State, and there are none that she possesses before the State gives them. Accordingly he, and others who follow him, proceed to treat ecclesiastical persons as laymen. They have granted warrants already against persons in the household of the priests. And, though the sheriff, a man who was once a pursuivant in England, had the decency to request the Father to send the person called for, still he added, even in presence of the Governor, as well as Copley remembers, that otherwise he, the said sheriff, would fetch the man down. Besides, before any one of their new bills has become a law, Mr. Lewger is acting upon them illegally, as if they were laws; and has demanded of Copley a tax for the current year amounting to fifteen hundredweight of tobacco, for the building of a fort. "Wheras I dare boldly say that the whole colony together never bestowed on me the worth of five hundred weight, one would thinke that oven out of gratitude they might free us from such kinde of taxation; especially seing we put noe taxe upon them, but healpe them gratis, and healpe them also in such a manner, that I am sure they canne not complaine." [16]—In point of fact, as to what regards a remedy for the grievance about the warrants and the sheriff and the priests' servants, this was already provided in part by the right accorded (August 8, 1636) in favour of all manors; that the Governor might grant to each one of them in perpetuity a court-baron and a court-leet.[17] But such feudal notions of Lord Baltimore never served any good purpose in the interests of the colonists.—Copley continues with the grievances—

(2) Copley's criticism: Spiritual interests ignored.

Secondly, by the new law the owners of property are to pool

[16] *Calvert Papers,* i. 162, 163.
[17] *Supra,* § 43, p. 364.

what they have with other people; give them a chance by casting lots; in all cases forfeit every manor except one; and, in place of enjoying the purchases made under contract, as well as the improvements made on their property acquired in fee simple, they "may beginne the world anew."

<small>Casting lots for the priests' manor.</small>

Thirdly, if the Fathers choose to reserve as their manor the mission land of the Indians, assigned by the chief of Patuxent for the service of his nation, then, in retaining this property of Mattapany, they must exhibit the absurd spectacle of handing over Mr. Gerard's Manor [St. Inigoes?], which they bought "at a deer raite," to some other party who apparently need not indemnify them. Father Copley considers this socialistic spoliation of other men's estates by any designing politician, "that canne git most proxis" in an assembly, to be intolerable for civil society; but "is most unlawfull in the Churches state for any secular man to doe, and for ecclesiasticall persons to permite."

Fourthly, Catholic priests must go to be trained as soldiers, must provide munitions of war, send to the campaign fifteen out of the twenty men that make the *personnel* of a manor, maintain them in the field by the work of the residue while keeping up the estate, "and others things we should be subjecte to by these lawes, which would be very unfitt for us."

<small>Priests as soldiers; as field-hands.</small>

Fifthly, to satisfy the demands made by these new laws for home-grown corn, the priests themselves must go into the fields and work, and even then they could not meet the demand that "every head plante two acres of corne."

Sixthly, they are arbitrarily deprived of their rights in the barter of beaver and corn; and, when they must needs buy corn for bread, they will be thrown back on the monopolists; and then "upon what extremityes would the[y] quickly cast us; really, I should be very loth to live at the curtesy of other men."

<small>Missionaries forced to beg for corn, but to refuse land.</small>

Seventhly, a converted Indian king may give to the priest who converteth him "soe much land as might suffice to buld a church or a house on." By what right can any one come in between and say nay? "I would desyre your Lordshipe to enquire, whether any one that should goe aboute to restraine ecclesiasticall libertys in this points encurre not the excommunications of *Bulla Cœnæ*."

Eighthly, in every manor one hundred acres must be laid out for glebe land, to maintain pastors. What pastors must the priests maintain? Themselves, and be rooted there, as attached to the glebe, and be forced to leave the Indians and other fields of work alone? Or must they perhaps maintain other priests on their own priests' farms? What would be the meaning of this?— *Priests taxed for a glebe.* Here Father Copley does not seem to have noticed that, as Lord Baltimore had ordered a chapel to be built by way of appendage to his colonial residence, whereunto the Indians should contribute peake and beaver and other things along with their personal labour,[18] so he should need a chaplain or chaplains for his baronial service, as part of his suite. And to the maintenance of the baronial chaplaincy the manors of his neighbours should supply the requisite contributions; just as the poverty of the Indians should have done towards the building of his baronial chapel.[19]

Ninthly, Lewger, in one of his laws, invaded the retired sanctuary of the most private personal liberty; precisely there where the Catholic Church stood prominent and singular on behalf of evangelical chastity. His bill enacted that every woman who did not marry should be disfranchised. As a penalty *Penalty on evangelical chastity.* for not marrying, she should, within seven years after land had fallen to her, dispossess herself of her land, or else forfeit it to the next of kin. If she were possessed of a manor, that went by devolution or escheat to the great feudal lord, Baltimore. Her only salvation lay in getting a husband. "If she have but one mannor," says Copley, "wheras she canne not alienaite it, it is gonne unlesse she git a husband. To what purpose this [wh]ole law is maid, your lordshipe perhaps will see better than I. For my part I see greate difficultyes in it; but, to what purpose, I well see not." However, he says expressly that it is aimed against evangelical chastity: "That it may be prevented that noe woman here vow chastety in the world."

This project of a tyrannous law is only one indication among others, showing what kind of Church, or trend of theological opinion, Mr. Lewger had favoured in his clerical antecedents. Higher Anglican clergymen did not lean that way. In the policy, doctrine, and lives of many at the time, there was much to correspond with the tenor of the following passage, which we find copied out at length by Thomas Gibbons, Esq., in his *Historical Collections*. Entitling the long extract: "Hall on Virginitye," he begins: "Virginity, as the most excellent estate of life which is incident to fraile mortallity, ought to be honoured of all men. Gerson hath taught us not to call it a vertue, but cozen german to a vertue. Neyther doe we think

---

[18] *Calvert Papers*, i. 213, *post med.*
[19] Cf. *infra*, § 60 (3), p. 487.

that the earth affords anything more glorious than eunuchisme for the kingdome of heaven; which is therefore commended by our Saviour not as a thing meerly arbitrary by way of advice, but of charg to the able: *Qui capere potest capiat*," etc.[20]

The mere proposal of such a piece of legislation in the fifth year of the colony's existence cannot be dissociated in the mind from the existence of some provocation, which had excited Lewger's sensibilities. Indeed, it would agree perfectly with the accounts given in the Jesuit Annual Letters, if there were already facts and specimens of high spiritual devotion visible in the plantation. And one of the abuses which appealed at once for reform to the Low-Church or evangelical mind would be this spectacle of the evangelical counsels, sprouting up with the spirit of the Catholic Church, in the new world just as in the old. Hence the proposal of a grievous mulct in the direction of keeping ladies perfectly worldly, or reclaiming them if they were no longer so; of secularizing them, lest piety and the clerical peril should take too deep a root in the Catholic colony; of obviating the danger that, besides four Jesuits already there, even religious women or nuns might loom up on the horizon; and then, as to the predominant interest of money and estate, nothing could be expected but that land and money would go to endow religion, instead of going by escheat to Lord Baltimore, with a discount in favour of his officers. The advent of the rich, influential, and pious Miss Margaret Brent, on November 22 of this same year (1638),[21] would only add to the plausibility of Lewger's repressive policy against such a spread of piety and religion. Still, in justice to Mr. Lewger, notice must be taken of the circumstance that Father Copley's manner of address to Baltimore makes no pretence of courteously excluding his lordship from responsibility in the matter. If, in fact, the bill originated in London before Lewger came over, and had its counterpart in Baltimore's own code, then we must extend the foregoing observations and apply them to Lewger's chief.

Grounds of Lewger's fears.

Tenthly, Copley continues with an objection, which he proposes against another attempt at religious or ecclesiastical innovation. He says that, in the order now prescribed for the payment of debts, there seems to be something amiss. He desires his lordship to have it examined; "for I doubte it runneth not right with that which is ordinarily prescribed

An objection to Lewger's views on restitution.

---

[20] British Museum MSS., *Harl.*, 980, f. 39ᵛ.
[21] J. Kilty, *Landholder's Assistant*, p. 67.—Cf. *infra*, § 68, p. 552.

by casuists as just." Whatever order of payment Lewger's bill prescribed, the theory on which he proceeded, while declining to acknowledge canonical jurisprudence, was no doubt that which he himself stated at this time in the tenth of his Cases, sent over by him to Europe. He affirms, in that tenth Case, that the order of restitution "delivered by casuists (as Bonacina and others)" is "viz. to discharge first the debts due to spiritual persons, and after[wards] lay debts in order as before." And he asks in that case: "Whether a Catholique may refuse such an illegall attempt, and compell the executor and administrator to satisfye creditors, according to the law of England?"[22] This statement is a fair exponent of the solidity of Lewger's learning, if not also of the temper of his judgment at this time of his life. It is a pure fabrication, picked up in no canonist, certainly not in "casuists, as Bonacina and others," but in some of the libellous sources which abounded then; just as in the cyclopædias and Blackstones of succeeding generations similar doctrine has abounded since; an American instance of which, on this very subject, we gave above in the Introduction.[23]

In the eleventh place, Copley calls attention to "the enormous crime" of saying Mass, preaching, hearing confessions, baptizing, if a priest or a bishop has not derived his authority for these spiritual functions from the layman, Cæcilius, Lord Baltimore: "In the 34 law, amonge the enormous crime[s] one is exercisinge juridiction and authoritye, without lawfull power and commission dirived from the lord proprietarie. Herby even by Catholiques a law is provided to hange any Catholique bishop that should cumme hither, and also every preist, if the exercise of his functions be interpreted juridiction or authority." This new offence would be the counterpart of the crime defined by Elizabethan law to consist in deriving spiritual authority from the Pope of Rome and not from her.[24] Supposing that the recent convert to Rome, John Lewger, did not really mean this, we have here a specimen of incompetency in manufacturing laws and saying what he did not mean. And with this ends Father Copley's series of specimen criticisms on the bills.[25]

The crime of exercising spiritual jurisdiction.

He adds: "Diverse other things I doubte not but that your lordshipe will observe, when with better consideration then I have donne

[22] *Documents*, I. No. 11.
[23] *Supra*, Introduction, Chap. II. § 19, pp. 127, 128.—Cf. *infra*, § 60, p. 492, note 24.
[24] But cf. *supra*, § 46, p. 386, note 14; on the limitation introduced into the bill of March, the next year, 1638/9.
[25] *Calvert Papers*, i. 162-165.

you shall read over these lawes. Yet this may suffice to give your lordshipe a caution not to be involved in these grose oversyghts. I hope that Gods grace and good instruction may by degrees make men here more sensable of God and of His Church and of the conversion of infidels, heretofor soe much pretended. But for the present Gods cause is committed to your lordships hands."

Copley here recommends Lord Baltimore to read over the *Bulla Cœnæ*, and know how he stands in conscience as a Catholic; secondly, to take advice of those who are competent to advise in ecclesiastical matters; thirdly, to respect the Church and to provide against the consequences which may issue from bad measures proposed.[26]

(3) He then asks for "a private order," settling the condition of the Fathers as regards colonial officials, so long as the Government remains Catholic. First, that the Church and the priests' houses may be safe from the invasion of sheriff or bailiffs.

(3) Copley's requests: Spiritual.

Secondly, that the Fathers, with their house-servants and half of the field-hands, may be free from public taxes and services; and, while the rest of the field-hands and all the tenants are only in the common condition of colonists, still, in all matters touching the property or family of the ecclesiastics, "privatly the custome of other Catholique countrys may be observed as much as may be; that Catholiques out of bad practice cumme not to forgit those due respects which they owe to God and His Church." Thirdly, that in like manner the magistrates understand in private the principle of respect and immunity due to the ecclesiastical state. Fourthly, that the missionaries may be able to do the work for which they came, of going freely among the savages, abiding and living among them,—without any particular licence from the Governor or other official, as if the priests were smugglers stealing past a custom-house. Lastly, that, when there is question of foregoing rights and privileges proper to their state, and acting prudently in the face of the English Government, still they themselves should be consulted in the matter, and may be left to judge what is prudent in the premises; and meanwhile that they enjoy such other privileges of their condition as they may "without note."

So much for the spiritual condition of the clergy. With regard to the temporalities, wherein they are on the same footing as other colonists, Copley asks: First, that the Conditions of the original contract be observed, in the matter of land. If any part of what he has already taken up be desired for the town of

Temporal.

[26] *Calvert Papers,* i. 165, 166.

St. Mary's, he will show himself accommodating; however, "soe that things be carried in a faire and æquall manner. But I verily believe that, if the lande be left in our hand, the place shall much sooner be bult on and planted, then if it be taken out." Secondly, that, since the Fathers must keep a boat for their missionary expeditions, they should be allowed to employ it in procuring necessaries from outside the colony, without being hampered by the self-made company of engrossers or monopolists. He expresses wonder how any thought could be entertained of interfering with the missionaries in such a matter. Finally, he desires the privilege of being allowed to buy corn for bread from the Indians, without being under the curb of the same pernicious monopolists.

He signs his letter: "S. Maries, this 3 of Aprill, 1638;" and then adds the postscript already quoted about a new proof just come to hand of Lewger's radicalism or socialistic anarchism; to wit that, according to the said gentleman, an Assembly in Maryland may dispose of any man's lands or goods as it pleases.[27]

Upon Copley's letter there are one or two remarks inscribed by Lord Baltimore, to whom it was addressed. These exhibit a disturbed state of mind. Over against Copley's petition, that only half of his planting servants, with all the tenants on the priests' farms, may be held taxable for public assessments and military or other services, while all servants and the priests themselves in exterior matters remain like others subject to the temporal government, Baltimore writes the extraordinary note: "All their tennants as well as servants, he [Copley] intimates heere, ought to be exempted from the temporall government."[28] This is a contradiction to the text which he is annotating. Another observation in the same spirit, exhibiting the same disturbed state of mind, is in the endorsement: "3 Aprill, 1638. Mr. Tho. Copley to me, from St. Maries. Heerein are demands of very extravagant priviledges."[29]

Baltimore's disturbance of mind.

With respect to the "extravagance" of these privileges, especially the one annotated, about all Copley's house servants and half of the planting hands being exempt from taxation and being left to mind the work of the missionaries, there is a very significant fact in the Assembly proceedings of four years later—a fact which gives Captain Cornwaleys an occasion for showing how averse he is to the system

---

[27] *Calvert Papers*, i. 166–169. Cf. *supra*, § 48, p. 408.—On Copley's concession to Baltimore about not taking up land (*Calvert Papers*, i. 164, 7°), cf. *infra*, § 66 (2), p. 532; on the General's confirmation thereof, § 69, p. 558.
[28] *Ibid.*, 166.   [29] *Ibid.*, 157.

of discrimination and favouritism prevalent in the colony. There was the Governor, Leonard Calvert, who had all the privileges and emoluments belonging to his supreme office as lieutenant-general, admiral, commander-in-chief, chancellor, chief justice, chief magistrate, and who by a decree of the Assembly (September 13, 1642) was authorized to use his power and make an expedition against the Susquehannah Indians. This gentleman, in the discharge of his official duty for which he was paid, presumed to demand exemption for his servants and for himself from all services and burdens to the purposes of this Act. The proposal was negatived by a majority of votes under the control of Mr. Brent and Captain Cornwaleys. But, on the next day, Mr. Brent having withdrawn his opposition, the said very partial measure in favour of the chief officer was passed, in spite of Cornwaleys and a number of his proxies. Hence, in a long Act imposing a levy and assessments, a clause stands right in the forefront conferring the favour of exemption on the one man who, by the obligation of his office, was precisely the person bound over to all such services and burdens: "Except," says the parenthesis, "that the Leiutenant Generall and his apprentices are not to be reckond in any hundred to any purpose of this Act." [30]

A lay Governor's demand for a clerical exemption.

Very different from the Church policy of the Calverts was that pursued in the Protestant colony of Virginia at this same time. A law was passed (January, 1640) exempting every member of the Council, as also the Governor with ten of his servants, from all levies, excepting those for Church dues;[31] so that no one was exempted from duties to the Church, though privileged in every other direction. On the contrary, under the Calverts in Maryland, where missionaries were serving gratuitously both whites and Indians, it was on their goods first that levies were made; and on their goods alone, by virtue of bills which never became laws.[32]

The opposite policy in Virginia.

§ 50. After his brilliant success in passing the whole code through the Assembly of freemen, the secretary, Mr. John Lewger, wrote to Lord Baltimore. From what followed in the course of the year, we see that complaints against the missionaries formed an important part of his communications. To the same time belongs also his politico-theological document, called by him "Cases." This paper, whether

Lewger's despatches and his Cases. 1638, 1639.

---

[30] *Archives of Maryland, Proceedings of the Assembly*, pp. 179, 182, 196.
[31] S. F. Streeter, *Papers*, p. 175.
[32] *Calvert Papers*, i. 163 *med.*, 200 *med.* Cf. *infra*, § 51, pp. 426, 427.

as extended in its original form containing twenty heads,[1] or as reduced to the form of nine Questions,[2] expounds a complete system of Catholic Erastianism; that is to say, of a State, especially under the form of a popular Assembly, controlling everything in the Catholic Church, and taking, giving, disposing of every right, whether personal or real, whether of property, life, or limb, if only it concerned an ecclesiastic.

Nine months after the close of the meeting, Lewger wrote to Lord Baltimore (January 5, 1639), expressing his disappointment at not having received as yet a solution of those Cases: "I should have beene glad to have had resolution touching those Cases I sent over—though without any ones hand to it;—because it [the solution] would much have directed me in divers occurrences & difficulties which we meete with here."[3]

The judgment, which was passed by the Jesuits on the difficulties created by Lewger, found expression some years later in a couple of official documents drawn up by the next English Provincial, Father Edward Knott. One is directed to the Nuncio, Monsignore Rosetti (November 17, 1641), submitting the demands then made by Baltimore, and explaining that they are Lewger's. The other, somewhat later, is drawn up for the Cardinal Protector of England. A couple of passages, referring to the secretary and to the doings of the Assembly, may be reported at once as belonging to this present date.

Knott says to Rosetti: "Observation 7. The Fathers of the Society do purposely withhold from subscribing to what the baron exacts of them, because they consider some of the points quite adverse to ecclesiastical immunity; the more so as they know that it is all a production of Mr. Lewger's. This gentleman was formerly a minister among the Protestants, was converted to the faith, became secretary of his lordship, and was his chief instrument in the general Assembly or Parliament. Being imbued with no principles of sound theology, nor equipped with solid erudition, he still maintains those opinions, and openly professes those dogmas, which may well offend the ears of Catholics, and which are extremely disparaging to the dignity and authority of the supreme Pastor, Christ's Vicar upon earth. For example, he holds that the Pope has no external jurisdiction given him by God, but only such as is in the internal domain of

Knott's opinion of Lewger's learning.

---

[1] Stonyhurst College MSS., *Anglia A*, iv. 108B, ff. 198–200.—*Documents*, I. No. 11.
[2] *Ibid.*, 108c: "*Quæstiones quædam propositæ a Domino Leugar, secretario Illustrissimi D. Baronis, de quo fit mentio in Notandis, No. 7.*"
[3] *Calvert Papers*, i. 194, *ad calc.*

conscience; that neither he nor other ecclesiastical persons have a right to any immunity or exemption in person or property, beyond what lay princes and seculars shall be pleased to give to him or them; and other such-like tenets. Nor is he less adrift in doctrine which is of a purely political import; as when he teaches that it is an enormous crime, and one to be visited with punishment, if anybody exercise any jurisdiction whatever, even that of absolving from sins, without a special licence of the baron, from whom all legitimate jurisdiction should descend to others. If any maiden vows virginity, and does not take a husband, then after the twenty-fifth year of her age, she can no longer keep the lands which have descended to her by inheritance from her parents, but must sell them; and, if she refuses, must be forced to do so. As to the General Assembly, which is commonly called a Parliament, he ascribes to it such an extent of power over the property of individuals that, without any qualification, he affirms it is lawful for such an Assembly to take away from any one it pleases whatsoever he hath in this world, or shall have, even to his shirt, if only it be for the service of the State. Let these examples suffice." [4]

To the Cardinal in Rome the Memorial of the English Provincial rehearses precisely the same matter as in the foregoing paragraph; but it adds several points not mentioned there. The writer says that a great door has been opened wide for the further spread of the gospel, through the conversions already made among the Indians, "unless," he continues, "the Fathers meet with obstructions from members of the Christian household.

"Such hindrances have in fact been put in the way. They are of a grave kind; and they have arisen in a quarter where they were least to be expected. For the aforesaid baron, not being able to go in person and govern Maryland, appointed in his stead a certain Mr. Leugar, his secretary, formerly a preacher and a minister, a man still retaining, after his conversion, much of the leaven of heresy."

Lewger's Cases submitted to the Holy Office. Then Knott gives the paragraph just rehearsed above, and adds: "There is other grist of the same mill put up in twenty questions propounded by the same Mr. Leugar; which have been already exhibited to this Sacred Congregation [of the Holy Office or Inquisition] through the hands of its secretary." Here Knott sketches the meeting of Lewger's

---

[4] Vatican Archives, *Nunziatura d'Inghilterra*, 4, ff. 81ᵛ, 82.—*Documents*, I. No. 16.—It is to this Observation or *Notandum* 7 that Knott appends the nine *Quæstiones* in Latin, giving the gist of Lewger's twenty Cases. See note 2, *supra*, this § 50.

Parliament, "made up, with very few exceptions, of heretics." He gives instances of the laws which the gentleman tried to have enacted, "in opposition to the Catholic faith and ecclesiastical immunity;" viz. a bill against any maiden vowing virginity, under penalty of disfranchisement, if she had not a husband in her twenty-fifth year of age; a law that no ecclesiastic be summoned in any cause, civil or criminal, except before a secular judge; that no ecclesiastic enjoy any privilege except such as can be proved from Scripture; nor does the Church enjoy any at all except by the gift of princes; that no one can receive a lot of ground for a church or graveyard, much less any estate, from an Indian king even when converted; that no one may go out of the province without the permission of the lay magistrate, even for the sake of preaching the gospel to the infidels by commission of the Apostolic See; that no one exercise in the province any jurisdiction, if it be not derived from the Baron of Baltimore; and the like. *Further tenets and assertions of Lewger.*

"The Fathers of the Society resisted boldly this infamous attempt, professing that they were ready to shed their blood for the defence of the faith and of ecclesiastical liberty. Very much irritated at this spirit of determination, the secretary reported to the Baron of Baltimore that his jurisdiction was impeded by the Fathers of the Society; and that the government of the province was not practicable as long as they held such doctrine. Whereupon the said baron took offence and became estranged from the Fathers of the Society." Here Father Knott proceeds to tell of the singular and high-handed measures to which Baltimore resorted, between the date of Lewger's first socialistic Assembly and the time when he himself was writing.[5] They belong to a subsequent paragraph here.

We may believe Mr. Lewger when practically he confesses to Lord Baltimore that, in the issue which he has raised between the government and the priests, he does not know the significance of what he is doing, nor where he stands. And the immoral principle too, in which he had been nursed by his advisers on being introduced or shuffled into the Catholic Church—that he might continue for a while filling a Protestant pulpit and insidiously indoctrinating his people with tenets they did not dream of, until he should acquire a subsistence in the Catholic Church which would dispense him from the further use of false pretences,[6]—this principle was now bearing fruit of its own

[5] Stonyhurst College MSS., *Anglia A*, iv. 108K, f. 222.—*Documents*, I. No. 18.
[6] *Supra*, § 42, pp. 359-361.

kind, but in a contrary direction. He was ostensibly a Catholic; had all the money, perquisites, and offices he wanted; but being still a Protestant, and retaining the same principles which had befitted his former pulpit, he was using all the power in his hands to indoctrinate people with a strange creed, or to dragoon them to it by main force.

Thus he writes to Baltimore (January 5, 1639): "For the present we [the priests and ourselves] have no differences at all; and I hope we shall have no more, where either part can avoid them. And for the errors past (which your Lordshipps [letter?] speakes of) on the Governors part and mine, if we knew what or which they were, we should be ready to amend them, & should be glad of the proffer on their part of forgiving & forgetting of them. But we are yet confident we have committed none that we can condemne for errors, either in point of irreverence or disrespect to their persons, or in violation of their liberties, as the present condition of the state there [in England] is. And for my owne part I professe before Almighty God, that I am not conscious of any thing yet done out of disrespect to their persons, functions, or rightfull liberties; & that hereafter they shall find me as ready to serve and honour them as your Lordship can wish."[7] Then he goes on to ask about the Rev. Mr. Price, who had introduced him, it would seem, into the Catholic Church, and who moreover, with Father Leander and Father Philips, had introduced him to Panzani.[8]

Lewger's profession of good will.

The candor transparent in this profession of his mental state is evident if one observes the very phrase he uses in the passage, setting up as a standard for the government of Maryland "the present condition of the state there" in England. It was to escape the state of England that Maryland had been founded; and this gentleman comes several years later to make "the present condition of the state of England" the very foundation of Maryland! But more evident is the condition of his mental equipment, if one will look at the twenty Cases or the nine Questions. He starts with the assumption that "the Cannon law" was not "accepted" in Maryland, which was true; nor was there question of introducing it, as we have seen in Copley's letter; but he adds that neither was the "Catholick religion publickly allowed" in Maryland, which was false.

The calibre of his erudition.

With this preamble, Mr. Lewger asks such questions as the following: Whether the exemptions of the clergy for their "persons, lands, goods, tenaunts, domestiques," etc., "are due to them of divine

[7] *Calvert Papers*, i. 194, 195.   [8] *Supra*, § 42, p. 360.

right by immediate grant from Christ to His Church"? Whether "external coercitive jurisdiction be a part of the powers of the keys left by Christ to His Church"? Whether a magistrate may break a will "in such a country as this," "because it giveth legacyes for Masses to be said for the soule of the deceased, and conteynes in it the profession of the testator to dye a member of the Romane Catholick Church, out of which there is no salvation, with other passages contrary to the religion of England"? Whether a Catholic deputy, "in such a country as this," may vote for disfranchising a female from holding lands, if she do not "marry within a tyme limited"? Whether lands held by religious persons are by that very fact exempt from civic burdens? Whether an Assembly may expropriate the lands of private owners, and of ecclesiastics among the rest, merely because such Assembly judges that the grants of said lands were "prejudiciall to the publick and fit to be reformed"? The rest of the material in Lewger's interrogatory conforms to the calibre of these specimens;[9] from which it is clear that if, when he was a Protestant in religion and an Erastian in doctrine, he had known what James I. and Barclay wrote against Bellarmine, he certainly had no knowledge of what Bellarmine and Suarez wrote to enlighten the minds of James I. and Barclay.

Now, with regard to what happened in London during the year 1638, an interesting question has been started, owing to the theory of a modern Maryland writer. In the effort to account for the controversy between Lord Baltimore and the Jesuits, the worthy author expounds a theory on canon law which is entirely at variance with the principles of ecclesiastical jurisprudence, with the facts of Church history, and with the early Jesuit annals of Maryland. Still, as one element in his theory, he uses the name of Father Henry More, Provincial of the time, and introduces him as being of one mind with Baltimore on the Maryland question, and as even submitting a kind of constitutional agreement, by which he signed away all ecclesiastical rights to the Proprietary.[10] In point of fact, it was Baltimore who submitted the agreement and other papers to the Jesuit Provincial, asking for his signature; wherein he was never gratified. But, as to More's being of the same mind

The developments in London, 1638.

[9] Cf. *infra*, § 63, (1): Third and Fourth of Baltimore's Points, pp. 509-513.
[10] B. T. Johnson, *The Foundation of Maryland, etc., passim,* as above, Introduction, § 19, p. 127, note 9. This gentleman's canon-law theory seems to be spreading now, as accepted and repeated.—Cf. J. W. Thomas, as quoted in Introduction, *loc. cit.*; also B. C. Steiner, in *Report,* American Historical Association, 1901, i. 215, as referred to in *American Catholic Historical Researches,* xx. 95 (April, 1903).

with Baltimore during the year 1638, until he was relieved of his office by Father Knott in 1639, we do no more than call attention to the assumption, and keep it under observation, while events follow one another. However, we may at once supply a trait or two of character, which distinguished Father Henry More from his predecessor in the office of Provincial and from his successor.

With regard to his predecessor, who was Father Richard Blount, the papal envoy George Con described him (1636) as "a Jesuit the most esteemed there is in England; his aspect venerable and his address grave;"[11] and the position, amplitude, and work of the entire English Province at the time might with some reason be considered a monument of Father Blount's consummate prudence, authority, and executive ability. With respect to More's successor, who was Father Knott, the same envoy described him to the Cardinal as "one of the most learned and prudent men in England, by the confession even of his accusers."[12] The high esteem in which Father Henry More himself was held is vouched for by Father Sheldon, of a later generation, in a passage already quoted.[13] But, as to his executive ability in the administration of the Province, several letters of the General, addressed to him personally, intimate where his efficiency might be improved. He was taciturn; towards his official councillors or advisers he was incommunicative, so that they were not informed of the important matters upon which their counsel should have been sought; and, towards other members who sought his advice, he was so sparing of his words and irresolute in his replies that they went away with the same difficulties which they brought for solution. The General suggested that care and industry would adorn his other high gifts with the needed complement of affability.[14] In the active measures taken by his successor, Father Knott, to repair or withstand the evils brought on the Maryland Mission by Lewger and Baltimore, it is very noteworthy how no allusion is made to any steps taken by More, his predecessor, towards obviating the evils in their origin.

Characters of three Provincials.

In the light of these premises the following facts and circumstances become more luminous. By a convoy which set out from England in August, 1638, Father Ferdinand Poulton or John Brooke

---

[11] Vatican Archives, *Nunziatura d'Inghilterra*, 6, f. 70, 1636, October 30: to Cardinal Barberini.
[12] *Ibid.*, ff. 101ᵛ, 102, 1636, December 11.
[13] *Supra*, Introduction, Chap. II. § 6, p. 62.
[14] General Archives S.J., *Anglia, Epist. Gen.*, 1638, June 12: to More, Provincial; 1638, September 18: to same.

was sent over to supersede Father Copley. As in the very next year, before More resigned his office to Knott, there were drawn up Triennial Reports of the Province for transmission to Rome, we have the benefit of Father More's judgment upon the different missionaries who were at this time in Maryland; and we may discern in the estimates formed by More, why it was that he had commissioned Father Poulton for America. He considers Father Copley, though of good talents and sufficient experience, to be deficient in judgment and in prudence. He says that Father White, though excelling in talent, does not excel in judgment, and is of a medium grade of prudence; whereas, in matters of experience, spiritual affairs are his province, and not temporalities. Then Father Altham has not been gifted by nature in any line; but works well as a missionary. The report submitted about Father John Brooke, *alias* Ferdinand Poulton, furnishes these particulars; that he is nearly forty years of age, of which he has spent some seventeen in the Society; that his progress in studies has been eminently satisfactory, though he has not shown distinguished talents in that line; and that he was professed in 1635. His administrative abilities are marked by a sound and practical judgment in matters of business, with both prudence and experience in the conduct of affairs.[15] Father Poulton was accompanied by Brother Walter Morley.

More's characters of the American missionaries. 1639.

It is to be presumed that Father More, either directly or indirectly, communicated his sense of dissatisfaction at the attitude taken up by the Fathers in the face of good Lord Baltimore's policy. For "Mr. Andrew *alias* Tho. White" begins his prolix letter of February 20, 1639, to his lordship with these words: "Right Honorable Sir. Having ended in a former my tedious apologie for my reputation, I reflected that I had troubled your Lordship and my selfe to[o] much and yett had [not] filled the measure of your Lordships expectation," etc.[16] Clearly the good and innocent Father White had been challenged some way to give an account of himself. Similarly, in the course of the following year, before as yet there was any change of Provincial, Father Copley speaks to the General (May 14, 1639) about complaints which he supposes have been lodged against him; for the General, acknowledging his letter (September 3, 1639), says among other things: "I have heard no complaints about the mission [Mattapany?] founded by your Reverence; nor has any thing been done amiss in that

The three missionaries reproved.

[15] General Archives S.J., *Anglia, Catal.*, 1, 2, 1639.
[16] *Calvert Papers*, i. 201.

business, that you should desire me to require you to make amends."[17] And Father Altham too had come in for his share; since White, in the letter to Baltimore, augurs of the same Father, that he "wilbee able to give his disculpa to your Lordship and cleere his innocency."[18]

§ 51. The chief source of information here is to be found in the private communications between Lewger and Baltimore, during the year 1638. We cannot, indeed, verify them with the help of other documents, to see how far they agreed with the communications, for instance, between Baltimore and More. But they are decisive enough as to the view taken, or at least the use made, of Father More's authority by the other two.

On the whole, Lewger, in the course of this year, had every reason to be in high spirits. He had barely arrived in the Province; yet everything was in his hands—his bills gone over to Baltimore for final approval, which would make them statutes; his twenty doctrinaire Cases expected back from his friends with answers worthy of their friendship; he and the Governor, where they were not partners in a monopoly of trade, still partners in a monopoly of nearly all the great offices; and, as a consequence in the direction of the missionaries, such a mastery of the situation, that he might well say to Baltimore, speaking of the Fathers: "For the present, we have no differences at all." He has levied a tribute on them of a tenth, in virtue of a bill which shall never become a law.[1] As Lord Baltimore urges the same plucking for the next year, Lewger ventures to excuse himself on the ground that really there is nothing to pluck; and, besides, for neither year has he had the assurance to levy on anybody else. Others were lay people; these were the only clergymen.

Lewger master of the situation. 1638, 1639.

But best of all are the particulars which he learns direct from Baltimore—that instructions are coming over from London to settle all difficulties with the Fathers. These reverend gentlemen are to have "some temporall person" appointed, that is an agent, who being a layman will impose no duty of personal reverence, and being only their agent can oppose no more obstacle to the exploitation of their rights and goods, than they have succeeded in doing themselves. There are other particulars in these "instructions and directions,"

[17] General Archives S.J., *Anglia, Epist. Gen.—Documents*, I. No. 5, K.
[18] *Calvert Papers*, i. 203, 204.
[1] *Supra*, § 49 (2), p. 409.

which, says Lewger, referring to Baltimore's own statement, are "to be sent out of England for the future comportment of their [the missionaries'] part to your Lordshipps [Baltimore's] right and the government there [in England]." But a singular circumstance, adds Lewger, is this, that Father Poulton himself, who left London and the Provincial so recently, knows nothing about such directions, and has received no letters from Father More of any such import; nor anything which would lend colour to the affirmation of Baltimore, that Mr. More viewed with approval a "Catholique magistrate" using his "discretion" to proceed in Maryland on the same lines as Protestant "well-affected magistrates in the like cases doe in England."

The "like cases," so referred to, were all the matter of English penal laws. Of these we have seen enough in a former chapter, under the heading of the politics and prejudices which drove the first Lord Baltimore to Newfoundland and Maryland, and which allowed to Jesuits in England only a dungeon or a halter.[2] So, while Maryland in general during the year 1638–39 was under the cloud of Lewger's unapproved bills operating as if they were statutes, the Fathers in particular were provided with an importation of the English penal code, to be exercised by a magistrate like Lewger at "discretion." And, to complete the poetic finish of the complacency with which that gentleman at this date regarded himself and his situation,—a man who had been looking about for something to do and to live on, while the Fathers spent money and labour in helping Baltimore to found Maryland,—he now implicitly compared himself, as the guardian of his lordship's weal, with them, and found, as he expressed it, that "they doe now begin to comply with your Lordships service here." *Importation of the penal laws.*

All these matters are delivered as follows in his letter of January 5, 1639:—

"MY GOOD LORD,

"I received your Lordshipps of the 30th July, and the 2d of August; and another since by Mr. Poulton of the 30th July. To answere to the first, I have acquainted Mr. Poulton with what your Lordshipp writes, touching some instructions & directions to be sent out of England, for the future comportment of their part to your Lordshipps right & the government there [in England]. But he made strange *Text of Lewger's letter to Baltimore. Jan. 5, 1639.*

---

[2] *Supra*, Introduction, Chap. II. §§ 13, 14.

at most of them, as if he had received no instructions touching any of the particulars; & [he] desired a note of what was written concerning them, that they might conforme themselves to it in all points, so far as in conscience they might. Neither would he beleeve that Mr. More or any other should give that resolution, that a Catholique magistrate may in discretion proceed here, as well-affected magistrates in the like cases doe in England.

"I should have beene glad to have had resolution touching those Cases I sent over, thoughe without any ones hand to it; because it would much have directed me in divers occurrences & difficulties which we meete with here. For the present, we have no differences at all; & I hope we shall have no more, where either part can avoid them. And, for the errors past (which your Lordshipps speakes of) on the Governors part and mine, if we knew what or which they were, we should be ready to amend them, & should be glad of the proffer on their part of forgiving & forgetting of them. But we are yet confident we have committed none that we can condemne for errors, either in point of irreverence or disrespect to their persons, or in violation of their liberties, as the present condition of the state there [in England] is. And for my owne part I professe before Almighty God, that I am not conscious of any thing yet done out of disrespect to their persons, functions, or rightfull liberties; & that hereafter they shall find me as ready to serve and honour them as your Lordship can wish.

The Cases.

"I sent enclosed in your Lordshipps packett a letter to Mr. Price, but I heare no answere at all of it, nor any thing whereby to guesse that he hath received it. Let me be so much beholding to your Lordshipp, as to lett him know how much I desire from him an answere of my letter; and that the onely cause of my not writing to him this yeare is want of matter to write of. He is one whom I shall ever acknowledge myselfe infinitely obliged to; and I beseech God reward him for all his charity to me & mine." [3]

Further on the writer continues: "For answere to the second letter . . . For the order which your Lordship saith is taken, that they of the Hill [the missionaries] shall have some temporall person, &c., it were indeed a very good course for the avoiding of present difficulties. But Mr. Poulton (whom I acquainted with it) doth not know of any such order taken as yet. . . . For the tenths, I gave your Lordshipp of a generall accompt of that matter in my last; by which your Lordship will find that

Exacting tithes without warrant.

[3] *Calvert Papers,* i. 194, 195.

I have gathred no tenths of any of the rest; & they will thinke themselves very hardly dealt withall to have it exacted of them onely. And besides I am very confident that their gaines of the trade the last yeare will not allow any payment out of it; neither upon the whole trade which they have entred in my booke will the tenth amount to any considerable matter. So that, with your Lordshipps leave I intend to forbeare the exacting of it, till further order from your Lordship; especially so long as they comply (as they doe begin) with your Lordships service here. . . .

" Little els I can think of at this time. My humble service to my Lady, Mrs. Eure, Mr. Peaselie, and Mrs. Peaselie; my prayers to Almighty God for his blessing on our yong Prince and Mrs. Anne; & He multiplie so much happines on your Lordshipps head as is wished by
" Your Lordships most obliged servant
" JOHN LEWGER.[4]
"St. Maries, this 5th January, 1638 [N. S. 1639]."

§ 52. When Lewger wrote the foregoing letter, a new meeting of the Assembly was impending. It would be due within six weeks, on the 12th day of February, 1639. He stated so in this same letter, in which he conferred with his chief about collecting taxes from the clergy; knowing, as his chief knew, that there was not a single law as yet to justify the extortion. For Baltimore **A third draft or code.** had not signed the code of the preceding year; and Lewger himself speaks now of what is apparently a third draft of laws to be engineered through the Assembly once more. He says—

" For the lawes, I have litle to say to them (more than what I have said in my Diarie) till the Assembly be over; which is appointed to begin on the 12th February next."[1]

The laws in question, whether drafted again by Lewger or imported from London, proved to be the last specimen of a code manufactured for the Proprietary. And he himself, as early as the August previously (August 21, 1638), had issued a warrant to his brother the Governor, authorizing him to sign on the spot whatever laws the freemen chose to enact, reserving for himself and his heirs some right of eventual veto.[2]

The code proposed was as seriously entertained by the freemen as

[4] *Calvert Papers*, i. 200, 201.
[1] *Ibid.*, 197, *post med.*—It met only on February 25.
[2] *Archives of Maryland, Proceedings of the Assembly*, p. 31.

the Lewger draft of the preceding year. How much of what appears in the Proceedings belonged to the manufacture indicated by Lewger in the passage just quoted, and how much originated with the freemen themselves, does not appear in the record. Certain it is that, after a session of three weeks, being nine days of deliberative work, the whole body of thirty-six bills, which we can read to-day in their elaborate form, was wrecked.[3] There was some salvage from the wreck; and it consisted in one Ordinance of a temporary nature, resuming in a certain number of short paragraphs the substance of some bills. The discrimination made between the pieces saved and the rest sent adrift is far from having the appearance of either Lewgerism or Cæsarism.[4] The Ordinance was assented to by the Governor in the name of the Proprietary (March 19, 1639), and recorded with an official brevity which answers well to the melancholy dryness of a memorandum on the wrecked bills: "Memorandum, that these bills were engrossed to be read the third time, but were never read nor passed the house. John Lewger."[5]

Life-history of the third code.

As the whole attitude of Baltimore towards the clergy and the Jesuits underwent its last decisive change after this, the final catastrophe in his present course of legislative essays; and the reason for such a decisive change is not hard to divine, on looking at what provisions passed and what did not pass; we pause for a moment on the threshold of this legislation, to understand from an ecclesiastical point of view what kind of institution had been projected for Maryland. For a Church establishment had been projected, as we see chiefly in the papers of John Lewger, and partly in the drafts submitted by Baltimore to the Jesuit Provincial. Nor was it abandoned for years to come, so long as there was a hope, if not of winning the grace of connivance from the Jesuits, at least of ridding the province of their presence, and securing other ecclesiastics in their stead.

(1) Short of dispensing the Sacraments, there was not a point of ecclesiastical jurisdiction or administration, which was not claimed for the secular arm. The Sacraments themselves did not quite escape. For everything was taken over which pertained to external jurisdiction in the Sacrament of Matrimony, such as the power of determining the forbidden degrees of kinship and the right of publishing banns. In the

(1) General standing of the new Church establishment.

[3] *Archives of Maryland, Proceedings of the Assembly*, p. 39, *ad calc.*; pp. 40-81.
[4] *Ibid.*, pp. 82-84: "*Verum recordum.* John Lewger, Secretary."
[5] *Ibid.*, 39, *ad calc.*

matter of baptizing, no ecclesiastic was to go out among the Indians and baptize them, without a permit or pass at every turn from a civil magistrate. The bill "for arbitrary punishment of some enormious offences," [6] did not, as far as the language went, exclude the spiritual jurisdiction of the tribunal of conscience from the category of that usurped exercise of authority, for which hanging was provided;[7] thus anticipating the enactments of some European codes of the nineteenth century against the clerical crime of "disturbing consciences." [8]

Temporally, the new establishment was to be provided both with a glebe and with tithes. For the glebe had already appeared in the former Lewger code, under the title of a "bill for settling of the glebe." [9] A contribution of a hundred acres was exacted therein of every manor; so that, if the manor were only a thousand acres in extent,[10] the allotment to the Church establishment should be no less than a tenth or a tithe of the land. This being exacted of a manor implied that ordinary tithes or other contributions should, as a matter of course, be demanded of less important holdings. Entering thus into the accounts of the public debit, though by no means at the expense of the public treasury or the Proprietary's reserves of land, the ecclesiastical foundation was to be on the same footing, under the head of property, as any other establishment, which was contemplated in canon law and recognized in civil law. It was guaranteed and protected in civic rights; and the taxables were made to pay.

A Church element was judged to be highly important and even necessary in the colony; so much so that the Jesuits themselves, when marked out for expropriation and banishment, were at the same time caught in the grip of a new ordinance, which kept them from moving out of the province, even if they wanted, until substitutes should have been secured. But the freemen put a stop to that exercise of prepotence.[11]

Jesuits apart, the Maryland Church establishment had features of its own minutely defined, as they are traced in the Lewger and Baltimore documents. It might seem, indeed, that some of these

---

[6] *Archives of Maryland, Proceedings of the Assembly*, p. 22.
[7] *Supra*, § 49 (2), p. 413.
[8] Compare the legislation of the Cavour Ministry, Turin, 1856, by which the denial of Sacramental absolution in the tribunal of penance at Easter, or on a deathbed, was brought within the case of an appeal *ab abusu*, the Gallican *appel comme d'abus*. Cf. P. Balan, *Storia della Chiesa*, II. lib. vi. p. 42 (edition 1879).
[9] *Supra*, § 48, pp. 390, 391; § 49, pp. 410, 411.
[10] *Supra*, § 43, p. 364.
[11] *Proceedings of the Assembly*, p. 180, *ad calc.*; September 13, 1642.—*Infra*, § 66, (2), pp. 532-534.

papers were drawn up for the Jesuits alone. But it is to be observed that the signature of the Provincial, which the Proprietary strained every nerve to obtain, would have had the effect of creating an ecclesiastical law for Maryland,—determining the status of ecclesiastics, interpreting canon law, and even limiting the application of papal Bulls; as if the authority of the English Provincial of the Jesuits were that of the sacred Council of Trent itself. Let us follow the tracing of this Church scheme as so drafted.

(2) First, the Maryland Church establishment was a clerical department of State, or a bureau; which, however, as it borrowed its general idea from the Protestant or Catholic establishments of the time, belonged to the category of canonical institutions, as they did. Secondly, according to the programme, it cost the Proprietary nothing; for it was to be endowed with manorial land cleared by the adventurers, at the cost of their labour and sweat, not to mention the further contributions under the head of tithes. Thirdly, all the emoluments incidental to ecclesiastical jurisdiction in the external forum, such as testamentary administrations, probate of wills, supervision of legacies, all matrimonial causes, suits, and dispensations, were withdrawn from the ecclesiastical forum and committed to lay magistrates. There was not the slightest probability that what Lewger pretended in his Cases to treat as but a temporary withdrawal,[12] would ever be made good again to the Church's forum, by calling for a regular ecclesiastical establishment. Meanwhile, such an extension of power was given to laymen over testamentary dispositions as no bishop ever dreamt of in the Catholic Church; for instance, that of breaking Catholic wills for showing therein that one had been a Catholic and was acting accordingly.[13]

(2) Details of the projected establishment.

Fourthly, the clergymen, being citizens, were, like other classes, subject to all civil contributions, taxes, servitudes, and burdens, whether real or personal; and, as to any land of their own, that might be withdrawn from them by vote of the Assembly.[14] Fifthly, the clergymen, not being on the same footing as mere citizens, but being in a canonical state, were deprived of civic franchises. For they were either under the constitution of a corporation aggregate, like a religious Order, or under a corporation sole, in the person of a bishop. In both cases they were disqualified from receiving land, buying it, holding it, under whatever title of

Mortmain.

---

[12] *Cases*, preamble. *Documents*, I. No. 11.
[13] *Cases*, No. 7. [14] *Ibid.*, No. 16.

religion or charity it might have been offered; and, if actually conveyed, it was to be forfeited to the Proprietary.[15] The declaration of the Jesuit Fathers regarding the immorality of this policy barred the introduction of it when it appeared as part of the new Conditions of Plantation, dated November 10, 1641.[16] It was introduced, however, by Baltimore's own authority, in the Conditions of Plantation published seven years later. This act of the Proprietary was a violation of the intentions manifested by his father, who had provided for just the opposite in the Maryland charter by excluding the Statutes of Mortmain.[17] As at first attempted by Cecil, Lord Baltimore, and declared to be in force (November 10, 1641), the said Statutes were of two kinds. They were, first, such as had been passed in the times of Catholic England to regulate the acquisition of property by the Church; and, secondly, they were all the others which had been passed since Henry VIII.'s time, and which made illegal all use of property for purposes distinctively Catholic. This was the penal legislation which classed a Catholic title and right to property under the designation of " superstitious uses." And in this sense were conceived at least three of Lewger's Cases;[18] one of which, the ninth, was so formulated that " spirituall persons " as such, not necessarily being incorporated, were by their very cloth rendered incapable of receiving land from any one save the Proprietary, and were subject to expropriation for the lands which they had acquired otherwise. Insinuating a feudal dependency, as if lands sold in the American plantation of the seventeenth century were gifts from a feudal lord to vassals under feudal obligations, the same ninth Case erroneously denominated the land, sold in America, by the old feudal term for land given in Europe, viz. " lay fee." As the introduction into Maryland of the Protestant legislation on mortmain (November 10, 1641) was reconsidered by Baltimore, he dropped it with its implication of " superstitious uses," which made the religion of his father a " superstition; " and in his next Conditions of Plantation (1648) he inserted the limitation of mortmain as passed in Catholic times only: " The Statutes of Mortmayne, heretofore made in the kingdom of England at any time before the reign of Henry VIII. who was king of that realm." [19]

[15] Baltimore's three papers submitted to the Provincial for signature: The Points; the Surrender or Assignment; the Concordat.—*Documents*, I. Nos. 15, 21, 22.
[16] *Infra*, § 62.
[17] *Supra*, § 17 (3), pp. 240-242.—*Infra*, Appendix C, § 75, p. 596, note 20; § 76(5), p. 604.
[18] *Cases*, Nos. 7, 8, 9.
[19] *Proceedings of the Council of Maryland*, 1636-1667, p. 227, No. 12.

Sixthly, the persons, capacities, functions of the clergy, deputed by their legitimate superiors for service in Maryland, were entirely subject to the inspection and approval of the temporal authorities. Baltimore himself insisted on making the inspection of the gentlemen to be sent by the Provincial from London (September, 1642), as if they were goods passing a custom-house. And he demanded for himself and his heirs the right of ordering out of Maryland any Jesuit whatever, whether one or more [or all ?], without assigning any reason whatever beyond the fact of notification; and then the Provincial was to recall such person or persons within one year; or else the baron would make provision by deportation of the same to some convenient harbour, whither some ship might happen to be going. And the gentleman in the same place intimated that such deportation might be effectuated by him or his heirs " for some other reason than misconduct." [20]

Lastly, in this scheme of a Church establishment, the Pope's authority, as might be expected, met with no recognition whatever. The Council of Trent was not recognized outside of dogmatic definitions.[21] The canonists of the Church were not allowed any standing whatsoever.

This singular scheme, by which just so much religion was admitted into the colony of Maryland as happened to be profitable to the parties admitting it, will be seen to have the merit of being about as far ahead of its time in the development of a bureaucratic Church, as Baltimore's notions of a feudal state in Maryland were behind their time. Still, both the belated feudalism and the anticipated Cæsarism were exactly calculated to put all the profits and influence of either to the account of one gentleman, the Proprietary. And not an obligation of any kind was assumed by him; except, perhaps, in the one case of the generous offer made to the Provincial, that when he or his heirs should demand the recall of one or more Jesuits out of Maryland, for any other reason save that of misconduct, then, if such person or persons went willingly, without creating any trouble, he or his heirs would stand the expense of presenting each with what apparently was hush-money, to the amount of £20 sterling, in cash or in kind, that is, in tobacco or skins.

Merits of the foregoing Church scheme.

For the rest, the scheme was neither Catholic nor Protestant, neither American nor English. In America there was nothing as yet

[20] Baltimore's draft of a Concordat, 5°.—*Documents*, I. No. 22.
[21] *Cases*, No. 2.

that resembled it; and what George Calvert, first Baron of Baltimore, had contemplated for Maryland was altogether different. In England, though the King had made himself head of the Church, there was no such sinking of the ecclesiastical in the temporal administration. A hundred years later, although secularism had made further strides, still Blackstone wrote that the courts of law and equity in England followed the law of the Church's own forum, in matters which had been originally of ecclesiastical cognizance [with the Catholic Church in England]; and, according to the nature of the subject, they adopted the canon or imperial law.[22] The canon law in question was that of the Catholic Church, so far as it had not been modified during the reign of Henry VIII. Short of those modifications, all canons, constitutions, ordinances, and synodals provincial, already existing and not repugnant to the law of the land or the King's prerogative, remained in force as they had proceeded from the Pope's authority, from that of his legates, or the national Catholic hierarchy; and they were binding on both clergy and laity.[23]

§ 53. Five days before the freemen gathered for the fatal meeting of February 25, 1639, Father Andrew White wrote to Lord Baltimore a letter which has been already cited, referring to his former "tedious apologie" for his reputation, and intimating that Father Altham too had been dragged in somehow for obloquy.[1] *Father White's view of the question.* White professes that he will endeavour in this letter to satisfy somewhat "the measure of your Lordships expectation" and "of my liege duety, in signifieng such occurrences and mysteries of the reale publique, which some solitarie howers, in studie of your Lordships happines, have recounted unto mee." Twice has he been brought to death's door, and now he is losing his hearing. He writes "to our great man," that is, the Provincial in London, for leave to return and spend just one year in England, and so undergo treatment for his deafness. This then is an occasion for his lordship to deal with the same Provincial, and secure a couple of missionaries "to come with the next shipps." There is Father Englebey [Augustin Ingleby] who lives in Suffolk, and Father Bennett [Thomas Blackfan] in Dorsetshire, "who both doe infinitely desyre

---

[22] 3 Blackstone, *Commentaries*, 436.
[23] 1 Blackstone, *Comm.*, 82, 83.—1 Stephen, *Comm.*, 66 (7th edition).—Testamentary and matrimonial matters were withdrawn from the ecclesiastical courts only by the Acts of 20 & 21 Vict., cc. 77 and 85. 3 Stephen, *Comm.*, 304, 305.—The jurisdiction had been exercised by the ecclesiastical courts for "more than seven centuries." Stephen, *loc. cit.*
[1] *Calvert Papers*, i. 201-204.

to serve God and your Lordship uppon this place, and have signified their desyres to mee by letter." [2] Father White then advances to the temporal concerns of Maryland; a new style of manors proposed by Captain Evelin; and the "mayntenance of your Lordships person after that decent manner, as princes are by right of nations mainteyned in splendor according to their place. Truely, my Lord, the proposition was well liked," when it was broached by some body. Even " Captayne Cornewallyes" approved of it in the abstract. In the concrete facts of the situation, the captain would prefer to see some "legality" in the manner of going about it; he should like to see the matter treated in Parliament; he should wish the poverty and fewness of the planters to be considered. Still, Cornwaleys was not unwilling that some action should presently be taken in this matter of Prince Baltimore's revenue, though at the cost of other people's labour and sweat.[3]

The good Father continues, in the same strain of intimate friendship which had marked his relations with Baltimore some six years before. He seems to be ignorant of the circumstance that his lordship has changed since then; or else to ignore the fact that his lordship has unmasked himself since then. He writes: " Your Lordship is much beloved and honoured of all. And, so to remaine, I humbly [beg] your Lordship not easily to lend both eares to any information. For emulation wilbee. And this [I] will oversay. I could wish your Lordship a grave unpartiall freynd to write you the truth. *Vis scire cujus rei inopia laborant magna fastigia: qued [quid] omnia possidentibus desit? Qui verum dicat.* [Do you want to know, what it is that splendid fortunes stand most in need of—what it is that is wanting to those who have everything? Somebody to tell them the truth.] So Seneca and an other found none to tell Alexander truth, but his horse; who once, casting him, made him know hee was not Juppiters sonne, when his flatterers chaunted itt to him. Why I say thus, your Lordship shall understand if wee ever meete. In the interim bee itt a riddle. And I returne to the poynt againe." [4]

Father White does return to the point again, in some four long pages, wearisome to the modern reader, but very valuable. The reverend gentleman, who a while ago, when composing for Cæcilius the *Account of the Colony* and first Conditions of Plantation, had contemplated with his mind's eye visions of Christ's Kingdom to be spread among infidels, and of Christian hearts reaping heavenly rewards for their labours on behalf of the poor heathen— the reverend Father who had laid open to the eye of George Calvert's

White's misconceptions.

[2] *Calvert Papers*, i. 202, 203.   [3] *Ibid.*, 204.   [4] *Ibid.*, 204, 205.

astute son the transparent purity of his own apostolic zeal, and had thought he was using intelligible language when he transcribed a meditation from the *Spiritual Exercises* of St. Ignatius into Baltimore's plantation document, did now really descend to plain talk and intelligible things in the succeeding pages which he wrote to that nobleman. He enlarged on beaver, tobacco, and truck, on pease, beans, and mazump, on poultry and turkeys and young calves weaned, and "a breede of swine under a carefull swineyard," not to mention all the wine which, with the bricks, planks, hats, saws, hoops, hardware, "etc.," he would allow his Lordship to "monopolize" "for a tyme" or "for yeares"—as if a monopoly with Baltimore for a time or some years could possibly mean anything else but for evermore and unlimited years.[5] And withal the good Father omitted something, "which," says he, "I will not committe to writing; but will reserve itt to a meeting." And he leaves out other precious things, "which," he remarks, "I dare not committ to letters, which are no better than blabs."[6]

In the same manner in which it appears from this epistle that, though the whole situation had changed, Father White betrayed no knowledge of the facts or else a mistaken appreciation of them, so the reader may rightly infer from this chapter which we are now closing that, in the case of modern historians, many data for early Maryland history have been either unknown or mistaken or forgotten. Some of the mistaken elements have been imported from England; others have been improved in America; and both kinds have lain scattered about at large, as if they were ascertained truths, placed beyond the shadow of a doubt, whether on the field of fact or on that of theory. *The misconceptions of modern historians.*

(1) The Pope has fared ill, even with writers friendly to the Jesuits; still not worse than with the so-called Catholics, Lewger and Baltimore, especially in the diatribe of the latter addressed to his brother Leonard (November 23, 1642).[7] The Pope's name is brought into the controversy, because of a Bull frequently mentioned in the documents, that one named, from the date of its annual publication on Maundy Thursday, the *Bulla Cœnœ*, or "Bull of the day of the Lord's Supper." The meaning of the Bull has been made unwittingly the subject of misrepresentation; and its relevancy in the controversy has been entirely misapprehended. *(1) The* Bulla *Cœnœ misunderstood.*

[5] *Calvert Papers*, i. 205–208. [6] *Ibid.*, 208 *ad calc.*, 203 *med.*
[7] *Ibid.*, 218, 219.—Cf. *infra*, § 66, (2), p. 536.

With regard to the meaning, the following passage from Streeter seems to have been adopted as classical: "By the *Bulla in Cœna Domini*, the Pope asserts full supremacy over all powers and persons, temporal and ecclesiastical. It forbids all persons whatsoever, directly or indirectly, to violate, depress, or restrain the ecclesiastical liberties or rights of the Apostolic See and Church of Rome, howsoever or whensoever obtained or to be obtained, under pain of excommunication; and all who presume to oppose any of its provisions are left under the displeasure of Almighty God."[8] This given as a true, and apparently as an adequate, account of that pontifical document, is ingenuous, inasmuch as it implies that the Bull has not been seen by the writer, or that its Latin has not been understood. It would be just as adequate to say: "By the *Bulla Cœnæ* the Pope asserts no authority save over the faithful of Christ. That decree forbids all persons whatsoever to commit piracy, to rifle shipwrecks, to extort unjust tolls, to increase unlawfully just ones, to forge Apostolic Letters, to supply the Turks with arms against the Christian nations, to impede the access to Rome of travellers and pilgrims, to interfere with the course of justice there." For all these matters are the direct subject of excommunication in the first fourteen sections of the Bull; and the preamble, which assumes the Pope's constitutional position as head of that polity of Christian nations, once called Christendom, makes no assertion whatever regarding "full supremacy over all powers and persons, temporal and ecclesiastical." In the same sections are also condemned heresy, schism, appeals from the Pontiff's authority to a future Council, or to secular courts, obstruction of ecclesiastical business, assaults upon ecclesiastical dignitaries. Of the six remaining sections, three regard secular interference with spiritual jurisdiction, or with the income and possessions of the Holy See. Finally, there are the fifteenth, eighteenth, and nineteenth, which came home to Mr. Lewger, Governor Leonard Calvert, and Lord Baltimore.

Three relevant sections of the Bull. The fifteenth forbids the citing of ecclesiastical persons before a lay tribunal, "outside of the disposition made in canon law" (*præter juris canonici dispositionem*); and condemns all who pass, publish, or use any statutes or decrees, etc., "whereby ecclesiastical liberty is destroyed, or is in any way injured or impaired," etc. The eighteenth prohibits the imposing of taxes, tithes, tolls, loans, and other burdens, on ecclesiastical property

---

[8] S. F. Streeter, *Maryland Two Hundred Years Ago*, p. 32.—Cf. B. T. Johnson, *Foundation of Maryland*, p. 61, quoting exactly the same passage.

without the Roman Pontiff's express permission; and condemns those "who receive such imposts even from ecclesiastical persons giving or granting them spontaneously." This section, referring to imposts which are illegal, forbids the collecting of them under any form, as, for instance, under the semblance of their being a spontaneous offering from the clergy—that kind of voluntary offering, say the canonists, which a man makes when he throws his goods freely into the sea, but only to lighten the ship and save the rest. The censure has no reference to a present or subsidy that is purely and strictly voluntary.[9] The nineteenth proscribes all magistrates and judges, notaries, scribes, officers of any kind, who take part in capital or criminal causes against ecclesiastics, instituting any process against them, arresting them, passing sentence on them, banishing them, except with the specific licence of the Apostolic See; and all those who unduly stretch such licence to cases not contemplated, or who otherwise abuse it; "even though the perpetrators be councillors, senators, presidents, chancellors, vice-chancellors, or by whatever other name they be styled."

Such is the substance of the Bull *Pastoralis Romani Pontificis* or *Bulla Cœnæ*, as published on the kalends of April, 1627, by Urban VIII.—the same Pope under whose pontificate the Maryland Mission was inaugurated. The substance of this document, which was periodically published for the direction of Christendom, dated back to the year 1370, if not rather to 1275 and earlier still;[10] so that it formed part of the canonical institutions in Catholic England from the time of the early Plantagenets, more than two centuries and a half before the Reformation, and three centuries and a half before the foundation of Maryland.

For the excommunication to take effect in any case, it was necessary that the internal guilt of grievous sinfulness against God should have been attended by a public act against the precept imposed. Then followed effects in conscience, the erring party being cut off from the Church's communion; and other effects before the civil law, if the excommunication reached its ultimate and absolute form of branding an individual. For some excommunications, like all those in the *Bulla Cœnæ*, were lesser, binding the conscience before the Church. There was, besides, a greater excommunication, which named a particular person and entailed effects in the eye of the civil law; and

Excommunication greater and lesser. Civil effects.

---

[9] Bonacina, iii., *De Censuris in Bulla Cœnæ*, Disp. I. qu. xix. punctum 1, n. 10.
[10] *Id., Ibid.*, qu. i. *ad init.*

this was reserved exclusively for such public and contagious scandal as, like a cancer in the living body, had to be cut out of the Christian body, Church and State combining to make the excision.

For the way in which these civil effects worked, reference may be made to the Protestant jurists of England; as, for instance, Blackstone on the greater excommunication, and the writ *De excommunicato capiendo*.[11] This greater excommunication hung over the heads of all the Catholics in England, and was applied at will by Protestant bishops and sheriffs. Lord Chief Justice Coke laid it down as the law that under the statute of James I.,[12] " every recusant convict is to be excommunicated, and therefore," he said, " in my circuit I do not admit them for witnesses between party and party, they being no competent witnesses. . . . We have God, the King, and the law of the land on our side; also we have dealt very favourably with you, and not in any rigorous manner. For we may, by the law of the land, attach every one of you by a writ *De excommunicato capiendo*, being by the statute of 3 Jac. c. 5, excommunicated, being convicted; and, if afterwards you do not conform yourselves according to the laws of the land, then we will deal with you according to the rigour of the law, by writs of *Excommunicato capiendo*."—" The whole court agreed with him herein."[13] So that for the first time in Christian history laymen issued the sentence of excommunication; they issued it without presupposing any defined state of sinful conscience, wilfully incurred; they issued the greater excommunication in all its civil effects; and they issued it against a whole population to be applied by any official at will.

A population excommunicated by laymen.

Such was the wholesale dealing in greater excommunication on the part of England at the time. And such was only part of the wholesale importation which Mr. Lewger, at the instigation of Lord Baltimore, had the assurance to announce in Maryland as the law to be followed there with respect to the missionaries; and which, on the unsupported word of Lord Baltimore, he had the hardihood to affirm besides, was the law approved of by Mr. More, their Provincial, as good enough for them: "That a Catholique magistrate may, in discretion, proceed here, as well-affected magistrates in the like cases doe in England "[14]—the tenderness of the application depending entirely upon the kindly dispositions of the men who gratuitously

[11] 3 Blackstone, *Comm.*, 102, 103.
[12] 3 Jac. I., c. 5, § 9.
[13] T. C. Anstey, *Laws of England against Roman Catholics*, p. 42; from 2 Bulstr., 155: The Attorney-General *v.* Griffith and others.
[14] *Calvert Papers*, i. 194, *post med.*

brought the writs, the rack, and the knife over from England to work them.

Not only has the meaning of the *Bulla Cœnæ* itself been unwittingly misrepresented; but its relevancy in the issue between the Proprietary and the priests has been entirely misapprehended.

The importance assumed by the Bull signified merely that the violation of it involved the Catholic conscience; and that the Catholic conscience was an important factor in the public opinion of the colony; and that to go against public opinion, with conscience behind it, was not practicable;—whoever the man might be that offered such an insult to the general understanding. As for the issue involved, and the difficulty arising, Lewger and Baltimore might be Catholics, Protestants, Jews, or infidels. That made no difference in the face of a political expediency. And the interview which Lewger and the Governor had with the Fathers, as well as Lewger's Cases and Baltimore's drafts that came periodically begging for the Jesuit Provincial's signature, all showed distinctly that the question was one of opinion, of public opinion which was too strong, and which was not to be trifled with, in its present state, by any violence done to the tenets of conscience. Even at the beginning of the following century, when the penal legislation had been introduced after the Orange Revolution, complaints were lodged against the Papists of Maryland that they were so capable and influential as to impede the free action of a Protestant government like that of Seymour or Hart. In Lewger's time, they were practically everything, except the venal proletariate, which had the numbers and votes, but nothing more. The votes went largely as proxies into the hands of the two men, Lewger and Calvert, who divided nearly all the official patronage of the colony between them; while of the numbers the same party-manager Lewger said, in the preamble to his Cases, that this was a country "whereof three partes of the people in foure (at least) are heretickes." Bulk was on their side; all the quality on the other.

Relevancy of the Bull in Maryland.

Hence the whole conception formed by some historians or essayists about an issue between the Fathers and the Proprietary, as to whether canon law was to be introduced into Maryland or not, is not only precluded by the facts of the case, but is distinctly excluded by the words and professions of the men. Copley said so in his letter to Baltimore. And the preamble to Lewger's Cases expressly supposes it to be so. It is to be regretted, however, that, in the effort to fill out the contrary theory, liberties

No question of introducing canon law.

should have been taken with some very plain elements of English law and some very certain facts of history, at least to the extent of ignoring them completely in the controversy of Baron *versus* Priests. The Catholic Church of England; her liberties guaranteed by the Great Charter; the protection accorded her by both canon and common law, and much of all this coming down, as Coke says, from " the ancient common law & custome of England;" the common rights due to ecclesiastics precisely as to other freemen; the right to receive gifts of land without impediment, whether before the Statutes of Mortmain or after;—all this matter has been made the subject of historical sketching and criticism, as if it were a festering mass of abuses and evils; while everything in a contrary sense has been built up into a fancied fortification of safeguards and of guarantees for liberty, "which," says one estimable writer, "the experience of Englishmen had demonstrated to be necessary to preserve their institutions, and which their sagacity had devised, their wisdom adopted, and their courage secured." [15]

(2) In a few paragraphs from authorities unimpeachable, and those English, we may clear the ground of obstructions like the foregoing that encumber it at present.

Lord Chief Justice Coke, speaking not of the Church "now by law established," [16] but of the Catholic Church before the reformed establishment, and precisely as it comes in the first place among the clauses of the Great Charter, writes as follows:—

(2) Coke on Church privileges.

"*Concessimus Deo* [beginning of Magna Charta]. 'We have granted to God.' When any thing is granted *for* God it is deemed in law to be granted *to* God; [17] and whatsoever is granted to His Church for His honour and the maintenance of His religion and service, is granted for & to God: *Quod datum est Ecclesiæ datum est Deo.*

" And this and the like were the forms of ancient acts & grants; and those ancient acts and grants must be construed and taken as the law was holden at that time when they were made." [18]

---

[15] B. T. Johnson, *Foundation of Maryland*, p. 62.—Rehearsed with eulogy by J. W. Thomas, *Chronicles of Colonial Maryland*, pp. 88, 89, note.

[16] Cf. *supra*, § 17, p. 238.

[17] This, like much more in old English law, is the language of the Schools. Cf. St. Thomas Aquinas, *Summa Theologica*, $2^{da}\ 2^{dæ}$ qu. 85, a. 3, ad 2^{dum}: "*Bonum exteriorum rerum, de quo sacrificium offertur Deo . . . mediate autem, quando eas communicamus proximis propter Deum.*" And thus Coke speaks: "Here note that the almes and reliefe of poor people, being a work of charity, is accounted in law Divine service; for what herein is done to the poor for God's sake is done to God himselfe." Coke, *Littleton*, 96 b.—On piety as a legal plea, cf. *infra*, § 60 (4), p. 492, note 24.

[18] 2 *Inst.*, 2; at the beginning of the Commentary, pp. 1-78, on *Magna Charta*.

Here, let us observe, some modern authorities quote the ancient jurist Bracton [19] to the effect that gifts were given to God and to His Saints *primo et principaliter*, and only *secundario* to the canons or monks or parsons; and then they add: "We are not entitled to treat these phrases, which seem to make God a landholder, as of no legal value. Bracton more than once founds arguments upon them; [20] and they suggest that land given in frankalmoin [that is, as a free alms to the Church] is outside the sphere of merely human justice." [21] All this is but an application of a principle formulated in civil and canon law: *Summa est ratio, quæ pro religione facit:* "That policy takes precedence which makes for religion."

Sir Edward Coke proceeds on the subject of Church liberties—

"*Quod Ecclesia Anglicana libera sit.* That is, that all ecclesiastical persons within the realm, their possessions & goods, shall be freed from all unjust exactions and oppressions, but notwithstanding shall yield all lawful duties either to the King or to any of his subjects; so as *libera* here is taken for *liberata*. For, as has been said, this Charter is declaratory of the ancient law & liberty of England, and therefore no new freedom is hereby granted (to be discharged of lawful tenures, services, rents, & aids); but a restitution of such as lawfully they had before; and to free them of that which had been usurped and incroached upon them by any power whatsoever." [22]

<small>Church liberties within the realm.</small>

The modern writers just quoted observe that no donation to the Church altered pre-existing obligations on the land, as affecting third parties. "In the donor's hand it was burdened with such service, and so burdened it passed into the hands of the donee. If the donee wished to get rid of the service altogether, he had to go to the donor's superior lords and ultimately to the King for charters of confirmation and release." Hence, "free, pure, & perpetual alms," as expressed in the full formula, was quite compatible with temporal servitudes. The essence of the privilege attaching to such free donations lay, as these authors consider, not in freedom from secular service, but in freedom from secular jurisdiction. And, in practical life and law, all consecrated soil came to be considered as invested with the privilege.[23]

[19] Bracton, f. 12.
[20] F. 12, 286 b.
[21] F. Pollock and F. W. Maitland, *History of English Law*, i. 243, 244.
[22] 2 *Inst., loc. cit.*—Johnson, *ubi supra*, pp. 51, 52, quotes one detached sentence here.
[23] Pollock and Maitland, as above, 250, 251.—Cf. also Suarez, *Defensio Fidei* against James I., lib. iv. c. xiv. nn. 11 *sqq.*; c. xiii. n. 7, etc.; where, under the head of "exemption from civil jurisdiction," he gives a series of exceptions; elsewhere he notes limitations which are dictated by prudence.

The old classical jurist continues, and what he says will serve to explain, not merely the Great Charter as confirmed by Henry III., but the Act for Church Liberties which appears first in the bills, and then in the Ordinance, of the Maryland Assembly for 1639. Coke says—

"*Et habeat omnia jura sua integra.* That is, that all ecclesiastical persons shall enjoy all their lawful jurisdictions & other their rights wholly without any diminution or substraction whatsoever. And *jura sua* [her rights] prove plainly that no new rights were given unto them; but such as they had before hereby are confirmed. And great were sometimes their rights, for they had the third part of the possessions of the realm, as it is affirmed in a Parliament roll." This last remark of the anti-Catholic Sir Edward Coke is somewhat irrelevant to the subject which Sir Edward Coke the jurist is treating.[24] The extent of a possession under a right does not make the right itself larger or smaller, either more or less intense. He proceeds—

<small>Model of the Maryland Act.</small>

"*Et libertates suas illæsas. Libertates* here are taken in two senses. 1. For the laws of England so called, because *liberos faciunt* [they make free], as hath been said. 2. They are here taken for priviledges held by Parliament, charter or prescription more than ordinary. . . . But it is but *libertates suas* [her liberties], such as of right they had before: *Jura Ecclesiæ publicis æquiparantur.* [The rights of the Church are as good as public rights]."

Quoting from older jurists, Coke lays down the principle that, in the matter of keeping her heritage safe and maintaining her rights, the Church is in the situation of a minor, under the tutelage of the sovereign temporal power; and it is contrary to law that she should suffer damage in her possessions or legal claims.[25] He begins then to give specimens of ecclesiastical liberties, commencing thus—

"They [ecclesiastics] are discharged of [the contributions called] purveyance for their own proper goods. And this was the ancient common law, & so declared by divers Acts of Parliament; and there is a writ in the register for their discharge in that behalf. And this is not restrained by the said act of 27 Henry VIII. [after the separation from Rome]."

<small>Exemptions of ecclesiastics.</small>

From this commencement of Coke's illustrative catalogue of ecclesiastical liberties it already appears that, not only did common

---

[24] Cf. *infra*, § 74, note 41.—Stubbs treats such an assertion of the Parliament as unreliable. *Constitutional History of England*, ii. 449.

[25] "*Nec est juri consonum, quod infra ætatem existentes, per negligentiam custodum suorum, exhæredationem patiantur seu ab actione repellantur.*"

law, or canon law as recognized by the common law, guarantee and maintain the Church's rights and liberties, but that the separation from Rome, centre and official basis of the canon law, did not substantially alter its operation in England; although by the separation the very ground had been cut from under canonical jurisprudence.

And, farther on, the same Lord Chief Justice might appear to be commenting on the Lewger and Baltimore code for Maryland. He says: "If a man holdeth lands or tenements, by reason whereof he ought (upon election, &c.) to serve in a temporal office, if this man be made an ecclesiastical person within holy Orders, he ought not to be elected to any such office; &, if he be, he may have the king's writ for his discharge. And the words of the writ are observable;" to wit, that it is not right, and that it has never been done; and that those who are engaged in the spiritual state, *in salubri statu animarum*, should not be so inconvenienced. "By this writ," continues the author, "it appeareth that this was the ancient common law & custome of England, & had a sure foundation: *Nemo militans Deo implicet se negotiis secularibus, ut ei placeat cui se probavit* [26] [' No man being a soldier to God should entangle himself with secular business; that he may please Him to whom he hath engaged himself']. Ecclesiasticall persons have this privilege, that they ought not in person to serve in warre. Also ecclesiasticall persons ought to be quit and discharged of tolles & customes, avirage, pontage, paviage, & the like, for their ecclesiasticall goods; and, if they be molested therefore, they have a writ for their discharge; by which writ it appeareth that this was the ancient common law of England." Here follows the writ; and a list of other privileges, that is to say, special laws for ecclesiastics, with common law writs to guarantee and vindicate them.[27]

(3) Since there was no claim made in Maryland for the introduction of canonical jurisdiction, but merely for the preservation of such common law rights or privileges as might be observed, "to settle our quiet here," said Father Copley to Baltimore; so far as to "be suffered to enjoy such other priveledges as we may without note;" that "privatly the custome of other Catholique countrys may be observed as much as may be, that Catholiques out of bad practice cumme not to forgit those due respects which they owe to God and His Church;"[28] we might pass on without adverting to the field covered by ecclesiastical jurisdiction, in accordance with the principles of English law. But this subject

(3) Privileges in common and canon law conjoined.

[26] 2 Tim. ii. 4.   [27] 2 *Inst.*, *loc. cit.*   [28] *Calvert Papers*, i. 166, 167.

too has been dragged in as part of the Maryland controversy. Suffice it therefore to mention just the heads, not of what has been called in this literature "usurpation," "abuses," "evils, political and social," [29] but of the same matter under its proper common-law designations, which are not abusive but legal.

The Church claimed cognizance of a cause by reason of the matter or of the person. The matter included the whole ecclesiastical status; also the regulation of ecclesiastical corporations, and the internal administration of their revenues. "In this region," says the modern legist, "the one limit set to her claims [by the common law] is the principle asserted by the State that the right of the patrons (*advocati*) of churches are temporal rights; that the advowson (*advocatio ecclesiæ*) is temporal property." [30] Here, if we glance at the charter of George Calvert, first Lord Baltimore, we may observe that it secures to him the "patronages and advowsons" (*patronatus et advocationes*) of all churches to be erected in Maryland; also the right to erect them, as the ground and reason for such patronage. At the same time, it allows him to ask for the dedication or consecration thereof, "causing the same to be dedicated according to the ecclesiastical laws of our kingdom of England." [31] All these provisions were conceived in the exact form of the common law since the time of Henry II.—nearly four hundred years before the Church of the Reformation, as "now by law established," was itself conceived. And so it is apparent that the Queen's chaplain, quoted on a former occasion, was four hundred years out of his bearings, when he assumed that the said language had reference to the Church of England, "lawfully established within this realm" during the sixteenth century; just as he was nine hundred years out of his reckoning when he assumed that the bishopric of Durham, mentioned in the same charter as the model of George Calvert's palatinate, must have been some institution of the same recently organized Church.[32]

Advowson held to be a temporal right.

---

[29] B. T. Johnson, as above, p. 62.

[30] Pollock and Maitland, as above, i. 125.—Cf. *supra*, § 17 (2), p. 240, note 11.

[31] "*Ea[s]que dedicari et sacrari juxta leges ecclesiasticas regni nostri Angliæ faciendas.*"—Cf. Latin text in *Archives of Maryland, Proceedings of the Council, 1636–1667*, p. 4.

[32] J. Anderson, *History of the Church of England in the Colonies, etc.*, ii. 114, 115. Cf. *supra*, § 17, p. 243, note 20. The reverend gentleman introduces the bishopric of Durham in connection with his complaint on the score of religion, as if Baltimore by his charter were put on the footing of a bishop; and as if the bishop in question were a Protestant. But the charter is referring to the bishopric as a palatinate; and history tells us that, as to religion, the Bishop of Durham was a Catholic ever since the days of St. Aidan, A.D. 634; till he adhered in the sixteenth century to the Church "now by law established." Even if the Catholic George

All lands in frankalmoign, or given in free alms, were under the control of the Church; until through an indirect process of law they came into the secular courts. Similarly, all matters of spiritual dues, tithes, mortuaries, oblations, pensions, were left to the undisputed jurisdiction of the courts Christian. More important still, all questions of marriage, divorce, legitimacy, were undoubted subjects of ecclesiastical jurisdiction, although difficulties arose as to the inheritance of feudal lands. The last will or testament was intimately connected with the last Sacraments, and, like intestacy, passed entirely into the Church's courts. Pledges by oath or faith, and the correction or penances of public sinners, belonged to the same tribunal.

Other matters of Church jurisdiction.

As to persons who were by privilege and right referred to the Church's jurisdiction, they were the clergy, and *miserabiles personæ*, that is, widows and orphans.[33]

The canon law "was a wonderful system," says the modern historian. "The whole of Western Europe was subject to the jurisdiction of one tribunal of last resort."[34] And this resulted from two potent factors. The more immediate was the Pope, as the one head of Christendom. The more remote was a divine faith, which bound all in unity to one another, and in union with the Pope as the Vicar of Christ. Under the prelates of the Church, as being themselves the King's justices, "English law," in the twelfth and even the thirteenth century, "was administered by the ablest, the best-educated men in the realm." And, to quote further in the same sense, "it is by 'Popish clergymen' [as Blackstone and the text-books would say] that our English law is converted from a rude mass of customs into an articulate system; and when the 'Popish clergymen,' yielding at length to the Pope's commands, no longer sit as the principal justices of the King's Court, the creative age of our medieval law is over."[35]

Under this double law, common and canon, each operating in its own sphere and having its own forum,[36] the Great Charter left the liberties and immunities of the Church and her clergy, just where they had been placed by the laws of St. Edward,[37] and where subsequently a score of confirmations, accorded by kings to Magna

Calvert, intending to found a Catholic plantation, did mean to insinuate something when he chose for his model a bishopric palatine like Durham, rather than a duchy palatine like Lancaster, he may have had reason enough for the insinuation, as the state of the chaplain's mind seems to show.
[33] Pollock and Maitland, as above, i. 125-131.
[34] Ibid., i. 114.
[35] Ibid., i. 132, 133.
[36] Coke, *Littleton*, 136.
[37] *Ancient Laws and Institutes of England* (Thorpe, 1840), p. 190, seqq.

Charta, reaffirmed that they should remain. With the enjoyment of her liberties we find coupled the guarantee that the city of London and all other cities and boroughs shall have their franchises and customs, which they have reasonably had and used in times past.[38] So did the legislation, warranting the liberties of Holy Church, flow with a full tide till the Reformation.

But with the loss of the papal supremacy in England, and the substitution of a royal supremacy, there was no reason any more for the liberty of a Church; and it passed out of existence. The first opening for liberty that then became visible dated from a hundred years later; when, in the new world of Maryland, the freemen took occasion to make a formal and complex statement, just like those made by Saxons and Englishmen of Catholic times, during the six hundred years gone before. Appealing expressly to the Great Charter, they coupled the Church's liberties with their own. They said, and they decreed as law, that "Holy Church within this province shall have all her rights and liberties;" and then they proceeded in another short paragraph to their own guarantee of freedom: "The inhabitants of this province shall have all their rights and prerogatives, according to the Great Charter of England."[39]

Maryland a refuge for ancient liberties.

Of the clergy taken apart, or found without the protecting arm of freemen, it may be true what Hallam says, meaning indeed to speak of the Middle Ages, but certainly speaking of robber barons: "In times of barbarous violence," he writes, "nothing can thoroughly compensate for the inferiority of physical strength and prowess;"[40] that is to say, for the inferiority of the meekness imposed by the clerical state in the face of brute force riding rough-shod over rights not equally brutal. But it was not by Middle Age barons, or in the old world alone, that barbarous violence could be displayed, whether with an ensign of spare legality and paper formality, or without such an illusive show. We continue with the sequel of our narrative.

Hallam on baronial violence.

---

[38] 14 Edw. III., stat. 1, c. 1.
[39] *Infra*, § 54.
[40] Hallam, *Middle Ages*, ii. 207.

CHAPTER VI

PROGRESS AND CLOSE OF THE FIRST PERIOD, 1639-1645

§ 54. The legislation of February-March, 1639. § 55. Jesuit correspondence on the subject: 1639, 1640. § 56. Applications for the Maryland Mission: 1640. § 57. General applications for foreign missions: 1640-1659. § 58. New Maryland missionaries. § 59. Seizure of Church property by Baltimore: 1640. § 60. Jesuit comments on the seizure: 1641: (1) The Maryland superior Poulton; (2) Copley's assignment to a layman; (3) Baltimore's counter-observations; (4) Knott the Provincial to Baltimore. § 61. A new clergy for Maryland: 1641. § 62. Baltimore's Conditions of Plantation: 1641: (1) Mortmain and the Oath; (2) Baltimore's draft of a Provincial's Certificate; (3) Lewger's Diary on the *Bulla Cœnæ*. § 63. The Provincial Knott on the situation: 1641, 1642: (1) Baltimore's Points; (2) Knott's Observations; (3) Knott's Memorial for Rome. § 64. Expedition of the new clergy suspended: 1642. § 65. Remonstrance of George Gage: July, 1642. § 66. Invectives and violence, September-December, 1642: (1) The Baltimore draft of a Jesuit Assignment; (2) New provisions for ingress and egress; (3) Baltimore's provisions for the incoming clergy. § 67. The chapels. § 68. The Indian missions: 1642-1644. § 69. The General on Maryland: 1643-1645. § 70. Dispersion: 1645.

Manuscript Sources: General Archives S.J., *Anglia, Epistolæ Generalium; Anglia, Historia,* iv., v.; *Anglia, Catalogi.*—(London) Catholic Chapter MSS., 1598-1653.—English Province S.J. Archives, Portfolio 6.— Public Record Office: *Domestic, Car. I.,* 508; *Transcripts from Rome,* xx., xxi.—Westminster Diocesan Archives, xxx.—Maryland-New York Province S.J. Archives, 2, 3.—Rome, Propaganda Archives, *Lettere,* 141.— Vatican Archives, *Nunziatura di Colonia,* 20, 21, 22; *Nunziatura d'Inghilterra,* 4.—Stonyhurst College MSS., *Anglia, A,* iv., vi.; *A,* ii. 24.

Published Sources: *American Catholic Historical Researches,* viii. —P. Balan, *Storia d'Italia,* vii.—Blackstone's *Commentaries on English Law.*—W. M. Brady, *Episcopal Succession in England, Scotland, and Ireland,* iii.—*Calendar of State Papers, Colonial, America and West Indies,* ii., iii.—*Calvert Papers,* i.—C. Dodd, *Church History of England,* ii., iii.—H. Foley, *Records of the English Province S.J.,* vii., *Collectanea.*— H. Hallam, *Constitutional History of England,* i.—J. Kilty, *Landholder's*

Assistant.—J. Lingard, *History of England*, viii.—(Maryland) *Archives of Maryland: Proceedings of the Council*, 1636–1667 ; *Proceedings of the Assembly*, 1637–1664 ; *Judicial and Testamentary Business*, 1637–1650.— *Maryland Historical Society, Fund Publication*, 7.—E. D. Neill, *Founders of Maryland*.—(Oxford, Bodleian Library), *Calendar of Clarendon Papers*, i.—W. S. Perry, *Historical Collections relating to the American Colonial Church*, iii., *Massachusetts.*—J. T. Scharf, *History of Maryland*, i.—C. E. Smith, *Religion under the Barons of Baltimore.*—H. Stockbridge, *Archives of Maryland.*—S. F. Streeter, *Papers relating to the Early History of Maryland.*—J. W. Thomas, *Chronicles of Colonial Maryland.*—*Woodstock Letters*, ix.

THE course of events becomes much more placid in this chapter, as long as we follow the aspirations of young missionaries who claim a part in foreign campaigns of devotion, or while we pursue the veterans themselves in their evangelical work among the Maryland Indians.

But, when we turn an ear to the political authorities, we find that the key of discord was never more harsh. A violent seizure of Church property was made by the lay authority; and secret negotiations were carried on with other clergymen at a distance, to bring them in and to oust the Jesuits. The ejection or eviction of the Jesuit missionaries aimed not only at their persons, but at the proprietorship also of their goods. A complete scheme was broached with notable success in Rome. Two Sacred Congregations were led into error. And only at the last moment, when matters seemed to be perfectly accomplished in favour of the one part and utterly compromised for the other, was the mistake discovered; whereupon certain proceedings, clerical and lay, followed both in London and Maryland, with invectives and violence to boot. The Jesuits, virtually dropping Baltimore and his interests, began to look farther afield, and contemplate an America not cooped up in Maryland.

But at this stage the civil war burst with its side effects on the colony. The very man, whose property in the Isle of Kent Lord Baltimore had expropriated as a first step in Maryland colonization, broke in to expropriate the whole of Lord Baltimore's province, islands and mainland together. Still, howsoever these persons and interests might clash and conflict, there was one expectation cherished by both, and hence, naturally speaking, was not to be frustrated. Whether under Baltimore, or under Clayborne and Ingle, the persons and the goods of the Catholic missionaries were always legitimate prey. Accordingly, two of the Jesuit Fathers were carried off as prisoners to England. Three others, if not prisoners, were reduced to the condition of refugees in Virginia, where all of them died within about a year, whether by violence or of hardship.

§ 54. We have already mentioned, by way of anticipation, the meeting of 1639, and given the life-history of a third code offered for enactment. It was on the 25th day of February, 1639, that the Assembly met at the Fort of St. Mary's City; and it spent ten days in deliberation between that date and March 19. There were present as officials, or as summoned by special writ, six members; and, instead of the whole body of freemen, there attended nine delegates from the hundreds of St. Mary's, St. George's, St. Michael's; from Mattapany and the Isle of Kent. The character of the Assembly was considerably different from that of the general body of all freemen brought together indiscriminately; and there was no question now of exploiting proxies, whether for a valuable consideration or for none. *Assembly of Feb. 25, 1639. The Catholic gentry.*

First and fifth in the attendance of officials or specially summoned members we find the Governor and the secretary, Calvert and Lewger. Next to the President always appears Captain Thomas Cornwaleys, the most influential man in the colony; then the other two devoted Catholics, Messrs. Fulk Brent and Giles Brent; and Mr. Thomas Greene comes in always last or in the sixth place among the special members. Mr. Fulk Brent, who had arrived with the rest of the family in the November previous, returned to England in the very month of March when this Assembly closed.[1] Mr. Giles Brent became Governor later, as did also Mr. Thomas Greene, who was the last Catholic to occupy that high post before Cæcilius Lord Baltimore placed the government of the province in the hands of Protestants.

Thus the whole momentum of influence among the upper gentry, who sat as specially summoned members, was Catholic with an emphasis. The President, Leonard Calvert, was, as we infer, not an unworthy representative of his creed; still he was ever, in the first place, an official representative of his brother, and as such he sometimes joined in measures, legal or illegal, which were worthy of his brother but not of him. The only extraneous element that sat at the gentry's board was John Lewger, secretary.

The code offered for enactment consisted of some thirty-five or more laws; and it was considered with deliberation. The bills

[1] J. Kilty, *Landholder's Assistant*, p. 67.

reached the grade of being "engrossed to be read the third time; but," notes the secretary, they "were never read nor passed the house."[2] After writing this their epitaph, Mr. Lewger had the text of all the bills inserted in the Assembly Proceedings; and then appended the one comprehensive Act which superseded them all. This was named "An Act ordeining certain Laws for the Goverment of this Province." It was passed by the freemen; it was assented to by the Governor in the name and by the authority of the Lord Proprietary; and so it became law "till the end of the next Generall Assembly, or (if such generall Assembly be not sooner called) for three years only." (March 19, 1639.) It is what we name the Ordinance of 1639.

The code abandoned. An Ordinance substituted.

This survival of all the rest preserved in substance several of those abandoned. It saved the substance of the Act for Church Liberties; also of that for the Liberties of the Colonists. It inserted a parallel clause for the Proprietary's rights. It required an oath of allegiance from every one to his Majesty, the King of England. Besides other matters of business, it gave the secretary the power of proving wills and granting administrations with respect to last testaments. It said nothing about matrimonial causes. Nor, in the matter of allegiance, was there any sign of an oath to be taken by the planters in favour of the new royalty, the "prynce" of Maryland, as Lewger called Baltimore in his Cases.[3] Almost all the rest of nearly two score bills departed happily, in the general slaughter of the innocents.

As the bills appear in the Proceedings, they are made to follow a certain order of dignity, which does not correspond with the order of their appearance in the meetings. In both reports, however, the Act for Church Liberties has a pre-eminence. It is the very first in the text of the bills, and runs thus—

"Be it enacted by the Lord Proprietarie of this Province, by and with the advice and approbation of the freemen of the same, that Holy Church[4] within this Province shall have all her rights, liberties, and immunities, safe, whole, and inviolable in all things. This Act to continue till the end of the next Generall Assembly, and then with the consent of the Lord Proprietarie to be perpetuall."[5]

The Bill for Church Liberties.

---

[2] *Proceedings of the Assembly*, p. 39.—Cf. *supra*, § 52, p. 428.
[3] No. 9.
[4] On the use of this term, "Holy Church," cf. *supra*, § 17 (1), note 8; from S. R. Gardiner, *History of England*, viii. 180, note.—Cf. *infra*, Appendix C, § 74, p. 586.
[5] *Proceedings of the Assembly*, p. 40.

The next Act is for swearing allegiance to the sovereign. The formula adopted is simple. But its value comes from another head. It was imitated with improvements by the Proprietary in his effort, two years later, to extract an oath of allegiance to himself. He tried to impose such an oath as an appendage to his Conditions of Plantation (November 10, 1641).[6] Later on, when he was himself about to forswear allegiance to his own sovereign and become a Parliamentarian, abandoning his own royal charter, as it appears, to take out another from Cromwell,[7] he accompanied all this infidelity with the proposal of an oath of fidelity to be taken by laymen and priests to himself—an oath which imposed such a condition of servility, and enjoined such detective duties of spying and informing, that it was quite fit to be compared with other oaths of that age, so full of bad swearing. The text of the legitimate oath to the sovereign runs thus—

"I, A.B., doe truely acknowledge, professe, testifie, and declare in my conscience before God and the world, that our Soveraigne Lord King Charles is lawfull and rightfull King of England and of all other his Majesties dominions and countries; and I will bear true faith and allegeance to his Majestie, his heirs and lawfull successors, and him and them will defend to the uttermost of my power against all conspiracies and such attempts whatsoever, which shall be made against his or their Crowne or dignity; and shall and will doe my best endeavour to disclose and make known to his Majestie, his heirs and lawfull successors, all treasons and traiterous consperacies, which I shall know or heare to be intended against his Majestie, his heirs and lawfull successors. And I doe make this recognition and acknowledgement heartily, willingly, and truely upon the faith of a Christian. So help me God."

A legitimate oath of allegiance.

The third bill in order is entitled "An Act for the Liberties of the People." It consists of two paragraphs. The first bases the liberties and rights of the freemen on the common and statute law of England. The second, in language borrowed from Magna Charta, debars the operation of all penal legislation save such as shall be passed in the province. These two paragraphs of the bill are condensed in the final Ordinance, which, for "the common law or statute law of England" substitutes "the great Charter of England." Since the two principles conveyed in the two paragraphs of the bill were both violated with regard to the

Bill for Liberties of the People.

---

[6] *Infra*, § 62 (1), p. 501.　　　　[7] June 20, 1656.

missionaries by Cæcilius Lord Baltimore, we quote them textually. They are a commentary on the two lines of the Ordinance which did pass into law—

"Be it enacted by the Lord Proprietarie of this Province, and with the advice and approbation of the freemen of the same, that all the inhabitants of this Province being Christians (slaves excepted) shall have and enjoy all such rights, liberties, immunities, priviledges, and free customs within this Province, as any naturall born subject of England hath or ought to have or enjoy in the realm of England, by force or vertue of the common law or statute law of England (saveing in such cases as the same are or may be altered or changed by the laws and ordinances of this Province);

"And shall not be imprisoned nor disseissed or dispossessed of their freehold, goods, or chattels, or be outlawed, exiled, or otherwise destroyed, forejudged, or punished, then according to the laws of this province; saveing to the Lord Proprietarie and his heirs all his rights and prerogatives, by reason of his domination and seigniory over this province and the people of the same. This Act to continue till the end of the next Generall Assembly."

Rights of the Proprietary.

It would be interesting to know what was meant by the reservation here, in the matter of penal legislation; and who it was that had it inserted: "Saveing," it says, "to the Lord Proprietarie" certain rights and privileges, "by reason of his domination and seigniory over this province and the people of the same." This seems to be an appeal to his rights as "prynce" of Maryland, in Lewger's phrase—rights such as the King might exercise. But the King had little power in tightening penal administration. At that date, however, the Habeas Corpus Act was not yet passed, and Catholics and many others were lying in prison without the benefit of judicial relief. And there was the old royal prerogative of issuing a writ, that such and such a person might not go out of the kingdom, *Ne exeat regno*, for defined and special reasons. And, in older feudal times, whole classes of the population were prohibited from passing out of the realm, except with licence.[8] When the Governor, Leonard Calvert, thought to experiment in this style on the freemen of the province—or possibly he may have meant it only for the missionaries—he was challenged by the freemen, to give his reasons; but he declined (September 5, 1642).[9] As to the other point of restraining personal

---

[8] 1 Blackstone, *Comm.*, 264–266.
[9] *Proceedings of the Assembly*, p. 172.—*Infra*, § 66 (2), pp. 532–534.

freedom, seizing and transporting without process of law or even imputation of guilt, we have Baltimore's express order to the same Governor, that he should seize Father Copley and deport him, unless Father Copley seized some one else, unnamed, unknown, and seemingly non-existent (November 23, 1642).[10]

These three bills, much condensed, are inserted in the paragraphs of the Ordinance, or law, as follows; with an adjunct complimentary to the Proprietary himself, who is recognized, indeed, as having his rights and prerogatives, but in a clause that is no saving proviso nor a rider on the liberties of other people:—

"Holy Churches [Holy Church] within this province shall have all her rights and liberties.

"All inhabitants of this province shall take an oath of allegeance to his Majestie.

The comprehensive Ordinance.

"The Lord Proprietarie shall have all his rights and prerogatives.

"The inhabitants of this province shall have all their rights and liberties according to the great Charter of England."[11]

According to the terms of the bills, only the first of these enactments, that about the Church's liberties, was to be perpetual, as soon as sanctioned by the Proprietary, that is to say, by the Governor in the Proprietary's name. The other three were to continue till the end of the next Assembly. But then, being made part of the comprehensive Ordinance actually passed, they were all to last for three years, or till the next General Assembly if held sooner.

So it was held sooner, even in the very next year (October, 1640). And a discrimination was practised. The Act for Church Liberties was passed again in a tone and formula more decisive and categorical than before—

"Holy Church within this Province shall have and enjoy all her rights, liberties and franchises wholy and without blemish."

There was no limitation of time affixed to this bill, which became law.[12] But the fate of the other great constitutional principles was somewhat different in this Assembly of 1640. Thus the last attempt at bolstering up his lordship's prerogatives appears in the minutes under this form—

Act for Church Liberties re-enacted.

"Then was read the third time the Act for Church Liberties passed by all. Lo[rd's] Prerogatives not passed by all but the President and secretary." The bill for the "People's Liberties" met

---

[10] *Calvert Papers*, i. 218, *ante med.—Infra*, § 66 (2), pp. 534–536.
[11] *Proceedings of the Assembly*, p. 83.
[12] *Ibid.*, pp. 96, 95.

with the approval of many; but then disappeared from the minutes.[13] Swearing allegiance to the King did not even find a place in the business, much less the swearing of allegiance to anybody else. This was the condition of affairs in 1640, when the last attempts against the missionaries under the form of public legislation had ceased as being impracticable, and the way of administration had been adopted instead.

Hence to mention briefly the last essays at anti-clerical legislation, whether direct or indirect, we observe the following points among the bills of 1639:—

Under the name of an "Act for maintei[ni]ng the Lord Proprietaries title to the lands of this Province," an obscure clause which denounces the holding or possessing of land received from the Indians, and contains no qualification as to whether the land was for the spiritual service of the Indians themselves or not, would subject the Fathers' previous acceptance of Indian land at Mattapany to the action of this bill as an *ex post facto* law, confiscating their property retroactively.[14]

Indian lands, and trade interests.

An extremely cumbersome Act, or apology for monopolizing all the trade with the Indians, and taking back under the guise of a gift from the freemen the franchise of free trade originally granted to the adventurers, makes a new attempt (by citing the Privy Council, not the words of the charter,) to legalize the engrossing, forestalling, and regrating enterprises of Leonard Calvert and his company.[15]

A bill defining "the authority of justices of the peace" includes among the offences within their cognizance a line of conduct which was essential with the Indian missionaries, and for which they had been invited to Maryland: "Withdrawing of one's self," it says, "out of an English plantation to inhabit or reside among any Indians not christened without consent of the Lord Proprietary or his Lieutenant-Generall; and the offender shall be imprisoned untill he shall find security to perform the order of the judge therein."[16] The missionaries should have to move henceforth with passports in their hands.

In the bill entitled "For the recovering of debts," the fees and claims of a secretary like Lewger, who took such offence in his Cases[17] at an imaginary preference for debts to spiritual persons, stood out extremely well in the order of preferential payment now prescribed. The Lord Proprietary coming first, then "all fees, payments, and contributions, due to publick uses,

Preferential payment of debts.

[13] *Proceedings of the Assembly*, pp. 93, 94.   [14] *Ibid.*, p. 42.
[15] *Ibid.*, pp. 42-44.—Cf. *Documents*, I. No. 17, note 1.   [16] *Ibid.*, p. 53.   [17] No. 10.

§ 54] ANTI-CLERICAL BILLS 455

judges, and officers by any Act of Assembly, shall be paid afore other debts;" and in the remainder of the list for the recovery of debts those "spirituall persons," whom Lewger imagined to be privileged by Bonacina, came in for so little preference that they were not mentioned at all.[18] As far as this bill related to fees, it was expressly saved in the general Ordinance actually passed; and this precise order of preferential treatment was repeated.[19]

Under the heading of an "Act for treasons," there is the offence, "to levy warre against the Lord Proprietarie or his Leiutenant-Generall for the time being (in absence of the Lord Proprietarie), or to come, adhere, or confederate with the Indians of these parts or any forreing prince or governour to the invadeing of this Province or disheriting the Lord Proprietarie of his seignory and dominion therein;" and the penalty is "drawing, hanging, and quartering of a man."[20] This would-be enactment, along with so many other foolish bills, disappeared from the general Ordinance which was passed. But it is to be noted that this very crime, under the same form, is what Cecil Lord Baltimore, only three years and a half after this attempt at legislation, tried to fasten on the Jesuit missionaries. Whether his state of mental excitement was real or assumed, is not easy to determine from the text of his letter. Writing to his brother the Governor, he seems, indeed, to have thought that he was making a large demand on Leonard Calvert's faith; so he begins by informing the gentleman that the Jesuits in Maryland are backbiting Leonard in England.[21] Then he proceeds to aver that they are bent upon an Indian war against Cecil in Maryland. And then, rising to the full gravity of the situation, he assails the Pope, laughing at his excommunications and Bulls, and gloating over some false newspaper item that Rome is, no doubt, sacked already by the Italian barons; for, says Baltimore,

The treason of levying war against the Proprietary.

---

[18] *Proceedings of the Assembly*, p. 69. Lewger's practice in drafting the bill went beyond his theory as stated in the tenth of his Cases. In the latter there was no mention of mere officers being preferred with "the prynce," nor of public contributions voted by any Assembly taking precedence of rigorous debts due to citizens. The order advocated in the Case reads thus: "To discharge first the debts due to the prynce, then executions, then judgements, then recognizances, then bonds, etc." In the bill, there is a rectification restricting the preferential treatment of the Proprietary to debts properly so called; but then comes an extension in favour of the official's pocket, thus: "All fees, payments, and contributions due to publick uses, judges, and officers by any Act of Assembly, shall be paid afore other debts."

[19] *Ibid.*, p. 84. There is one correction, that at least the votes of any socialistic Assembly, making appropriations "to public uses," or presents to greedy officers, are not put distinctly in evidence as giving the title to preferential treatment before *bonâ fide* creditors.

[20] *Ibid.*, p. 71.

[21] *Calvert Papers*, i. 217, *med.*

"hee [the Pope] is thought too weake for them." This, of course—the fault of being too weak to stand up against another—was the capital error and sin which, as Hallam has informed us above, governed the policy of barons "in times of barbarous violence." Baltimore's long passage, full of a mental excitement which would be imbecile, if it were not rather astute, and containing in the middle of a sentence, a parenthesis thirty-two lines long on a printed octavo page, may be read at length as it stands amid newly discovered papers; and it leaves no room for debate whether Cecil Lord Baltimore was a "Romane Catholique," or what kind of a Catholic he was.[22]

The vexatious project about forcing every one to plant a certain quantity of corn, and making every priest become a planter in the field, was attempted again, with a heavy penalty attached. In the Ordinance passed, the penalty was left out; and a brief word about planting corn remained as a kind of exhortation.[23]

Secretary Lewger was gratified by being granted the probate of wills, and all the accessory powers, as well as perquisites belonging thereto.

Lewger gratified with probate, etc.

But the gratification of his pocket did not silence the clamorous and multifarious demands put forward in so many legislative codes, all of them defeated. Considering their manifest tendencies, so pretentious, pragmatical, and anti-clerical, their total failure referable to some body or some interest, the compact state of preservation in which the Catholic clergy and Catholic welfare had survived the ordeal of codes and bills, it is not surprising that legislative attempts should count for nothing henceforth, and administrative acts count for everything; that Conditions of Plantation should be formulated by way of edict, and be made to act retrospectively, *ex post facto;* and that an entire batch of papers should be drawn up by Baltimore for the Jesuit Provincial to sign.

Meanwhile some valuable correspondence has been in progress, and a new generation of missionaries have now come to offer themselves for a life of self-sacrifice in the Western world.

---

[22] *Calvert Papers,* i. 217, 218.—Cf. *infra,* § 66, (2) pp. 534–536. The portion of the invective bearing on an Indian war runs thus: ". . . I am (upon very good reason) satisfied in my judgment that they doe designe my destruction, and I have too good cause to suspect that, if they cannot make or mainteine a partie by degrees among the English, to bring their ends about they will endeavour to doe it by the Indians within a verie short time by arming them, &c., against all those that shall oppose them, and all under pretence of God's honor and the propagation of the Christian faith, which shalbee the maske and vizard to hide their other designes withall."

[23] *Proceedings of the Assembly,* as above, pp. 79, 84.

§ 55. The General, who on occasion of Panzani's mission to England had commended the envoy to Father Richard Blount, Provincial, as a man "said to be good and prudent" (January 13, 1635), had occasion in the following year to mention his successor, the Scotchman George Con.[1] He wrote to Father Knott, Rector in London, saying: "As to Mgr. Con's prudence and equity, and his marked kindliness towards us, it agrees with what I have always thought of him, that his qualities gave every promise of eminence; and, as these hopes become realized, my gratification is great in proportion." After good wishes for the envoy's continued success, the General adds: "As to what Mgr. Panzani is going to say, good or bad, we shall see on his return to Rome. In the mean time, the testimonial which you obtained from him has a right to be appreciated as agreeable to us"[2] (December 20, 1636).

A special occasion for showing benevolence to the Jesuits is described by George Con himself in a letter to Barberini. He tells the Cardinal of his having informed Knott that a book published by that Father had given offence to certain people of state. "After we had conversed at length," says Con, "he complained to me that the charges against his book originated rather with regular priests than with Protestants." Hence the two agreed to quell the turmoil by means of an explanation, addressed by Knott to Con. The envoy continues: "In a note apart he asked me not to allow his letter of justification to be shown to any but Protestants, having only too much reason to fear the criticisms of those Catholics who are abettors, as he considers his accusers to be. Nor is he mistaken therein; because Father Price the Benedictine and Father Francis of St. Clare are those who have been busiest in pushing this matter forward, along with some of the clergy; and, though among these people there is no friendship, they band together readily for enterprises like these." Con proceeds to characterize Knott in terms of the highest respect and praise. He adds that he has himself asked the Father now to write on the infallibility of the Church (December 11, 1636).[3]

Adventures of Knott, the new Provincial.

There was no end to this persecution of Father Knott. And for two or three years the constantly recurring question was, whether he could stay in England at all, and also whether the General could venture to make him Provincial, as successor to Father More. His

---

[1] General Archives S.J., *Anglia, Epist. Gen.*, under date.
[2] Ibid., loc. cit.
[3] See above, Introduction, Chap. II. § 9, note 6.—Cf. also § 50, p. 422.

Paternity took advice; he consulted Mgr. Con, apparently on this topic (July 3, 1638); he substituted Father Silesdon as Rector in London for Knott, whom he made the Provincial's companion or *socius* (February 8, 1639); and finally ventured to send his nomination as Provincial (June 4, 1639).[4] Then the storm broke out. But, fortunately, the Parliamentarians too broke out. The court was dispersed, with its ministers and ambassadors; and, the clergy which flitted round the court being duly scattered, the new Provincial Knott was able to live in peace.

Such were the circumstances under which Father Knott succeeded Henry More in the Provincialship. And, when he looked at the state of affairs relating to Maryland, he found himself charged with building on another man's foundation. This in normal conditions is a usual function, regular and facile. But in the present unsettled phase of the Maryland disturbance, it proved to be the beginning of a ten-years' contention betwixt the Provincial of the Jesuits and the Proprietary of the plantation, filling the whole period of Knott's term of office as well as that of Silesdon's who followed him.

While this change was taking place, Father Copley wrote straight to the General after the legislative assembly of 1639, and received the following reply (September 3, 1639):—

The General to Copley, Knott, More, and White. Sept.-Oct., 1639.

"Your difficulties, as described in your letter of May 14th, touch me deeply; and I do not see how I can help to solve them. However, I derive great comfort from that state of tranquillity which has ensued on the rejection of the laws by the delegates, as well as from the uprightness of that magistrate who, desiring to be reckoned a Catholic, will, I trust, determine on no measure against ecclesiastics without referring to the chief Pastor [the Pope]; since, without him, it is not lawful for them to attempt anything, nor for us to acquiesce, if they did so. He alone and under him the others [ecclesiastical superiors] decide in matters concerning their men, of whatever nation these may be, or in whatever part of the world." His Paternity then approves of the system of barter in Maryland, when ecclesiastics have no currency wherewith to buy. He adds that he has received no complaints on the subject of the mission [Mattapany?] founded by Copley. He continues: "For the rest I will not fail to recommend to Father Provincial the measure of sending your Reverence, if he can, [on a mission] outside of the colony."[5]

[4] General Archives S.J., *Anglia, Epist. Gen.*—All to Henry More, Provincial.
[5] *Ibid.*—Cf. *supra*, § 50, pp. 423, 424.—*Documents*, I. No. 5, K.

On the same day (September 3, 1639) the General wrote to Father Knott, already appointed Provincial, but not yet reported to have entered upon his office: "I see well enough," he says, "in what a critical condition the Fathers in Maryland are placed by reason of the new laws [bills?]. But, if one or other alternative must be taken, then conscience is to be deferred to rather than the clamors of popular cupidity [6] [or the fears of popular odium]. If his Excellency Signor Con could be persuaded to submit the matter to the Holy See, I think it would be worth the trouble." [7]

Principle, not expediency.

Finally, on the same day he wrote also to Father More, Provincial. He spoke of the barter practised by the Fathers; he presented also Father Copley's desires to be liberated from St. Mary's, if the Provincial could send some one to occupy that home post and let Copley go free to the Indian missions; but he added not a word to Father More about the difficulties in Maryland politics.[8]

To Father Andrew White, a few weeks later (October 1, 1639), he said: "Your zeal in seeking souls, and your steadfastness in rejecting unjust laws, as you described in your letter, have refreshed me extremely, and have cheered me up with the hope of the best success yet to attend you." He then proceeded to speak of Father White's History of the Mission, already begun. And he promised to further the interests of their Mission by commending it in his letters to the Provincial and in his prayers to God.[9] Seven days afterwards (October 8), writing to Father Knott expressly as Provincial, he closed his letter with the commendation promised.[10]

Acting upon these repeated recommendations, as also from his own instincts of zeal, the new Provincial indited a letter, to be read publicly where the young men of the Order and of the Province were studying. The answers thereto poured in immediately. We shall quote some in the next section. Before the General could have been informed either of Knott's letter or of the responses called forth, he wrote again on the subject, saying: "I recommend earnestly to the care of your Reverence the Maryland Mission; and I beg of you to send thither the men needed, and to inform me how many you send, and who they are" (July 28, 1640).[11] And to Father Copley, three weeks afterwards, he said: "The letter which you sent under date of

The Provincial's appeal for volunteers.

---

[6] "*Præ invidia populari.*"
[7] General Archives S.J., *Anglia Epist. Gen.*—Documents, I. No. 5, L.
[8] *Ibid.*—Documents, I. No. 5, M.   [9] *Ibid.*—Documents, I. No. 5, N.
[10] *Ibid.*—Documents, I. No. 5, O.   [11] *Ibid.*—Documents, I. No. 5, P.

April 7th gave me great pleasure; and I am in eager expectancy now to learn distinctly the particulars about the baptism of the prince of that nation, for which you say they are preparing [viz. the baptism of the Tayac at Pascattoway]. I hope the superior [Father Poulton] will not omit to send me such a relation. Meanwhile I have earnestly recommended yourself, and the entire Mission, to the Provincial; and I doubt not but he will send you new labourers as soon as an opportunity offers" (August 18, 1640).[12] He exhorts all of them to continue labouring with their usual spirit and diligence. And, on receiving the superior's letter of May 2, he acknowledges it in an answer already cited, speaking of the four foundations or stations, the work among the Indians, and the hope of a future college.[13] Four stations mentioned by Poulton were at St. Mary's, Mattapany, Kent Island, and Kittamaquund or Pascattoway.

We shall now give some extracts from the answers which the young men returned to the Provincial's invitation. His own letter we can partly reconstruct from the references to it in the replies.

§ 56. Father Knott's appeal stated "the happy success of our Mission in Maryland;" the "desire those first Fathers of ours, which were sent into Maryland, have of supplies;" it conveyed an exhortation to the young men "towards Maryland Mission," "a forcible invitement to undertake the happy labor of a mission to Maryland;" and it held forth "the great hope of converting souls to their Lord and Creator." Twenty-four original letters containing answers to this exhortation are extant. They date from about July 17, 1640, till August 6 following. The great house of studies, where the young men of the Province were pursuing their higher courses, was in the city of Liège. From that place many of the letters are expressly dated, and addressed to the Provincial at St. Omer's.[1]

Lawrence Worsly was a theological student of twenty-seven years of age, and seven years' standing in the Society. He wrote—

---

[12] General Archives S.J., *Anglia Epist. Gen.*—Documents, I. No. 5, Q.
[13] *Ibid.*—Documents, I. No. 5, R.—Cf. *supra*, § 39, p. 346.
[1] Md.-N. Y. Province Archives, 2. A superscription reads: "*P. Odoardo Knotto, Soc. Jesu per Angliam Provinciali, Audomarum.*" Nine of them are printed in full, *Woodstock Letters*, ix. 75–89.—Cf. the following entry in the Catalogue of the MSS., etc., of the Maryland Historical Society, by Lewis Mayer, 1854: "7. Copies of letters preserved in George Town College from members S.J., soliciting employment as missioners in Maryland, 1640; pp. 50. Presented by Mr. B. U. Campbell." They were used by Campbell in his *Historical Sketch of the Early Christian Missions among the Indians of Maryland* (January 8, 1848).

"REVERENDE IN CHRISTO PATER.

"Pax Christi.

"I had no sooner heard the relation of the happy success of our Mission in Maryland, and the great hope of converting soules to theire Lord & Creator, but I was surprized with no small joy & compfort; which neverthelesse was but litle, compared with that which I receved when I redd those sweet & no lesse compfortable lines with which your Reverence invited not any one in particular, but all in generall, to employ theire lives & labors in the undertaking of so glorious an enterprize of converting soules to God by means of that mission. And, to tell you the truth, my joy was so great, that no thought nor word for a long time could come from me which resounded not 'Maryland.' The cause of my joy was the hopes I conceved of beeing so happy as to bee one of those who would consacrate themselves to so noble an employment. *Nec vana spes est* [Nor is the trust vain], as I hope; since I doubt not but it is the will of Allmighty God; for, having comended the matter unto Him for some dayes, I still found the same desire I had in the first hower.

Lawrence Worsly's answer to the appeal.

"If your Reverence desireth to know yet farther the joy which was caused in me by this happy niews, I cannot expresse it better than by saying, that it hath bin like an ocean able to drowne all other sorrows & crosses, which by reason of troublesome times might have had no small part in me. Noe crosse ever strook so deep into me as when I saw many able men restrayned from doing such things as weare very suitable to their vocation; but now, seeing such a plentifull harvest prepared for them, sorrows must of necessity give place to joy. I shall thinke my selfe most happy if I might bee thought fitt to be one of those who are to reap God his elected corn. Your Reverence will find, I have no doubt, many both more able & industrious than I am; yet, unless I am deceaved, you will not finde many of better will or helth, to [two] necessary things for the undertaking of hard enterprizes." Here the young man spends another goodly page on similar arguments, calculated to win over his benevolent auditor; and, not least, he insists upon the deleterious effects of procrastination; lest he himself may relent in fervour and zeal, or lest death forestall the designs of the Provincial and the young man's own hopes. Then he comes to a very practical measure at the end of his epistle: "I would willing demaund your Reverence his councell in one thing; and it is, by what meanes I may gett my portion of those corporall goods

Talents of able men left useless.

which by right are due unto me. I would be willing to give all to the furthering of our Mission. The surest way weare to procure some friends to speak to my father. Peradventure my step-mother, who is my Lord Montigue his aunt, will be able to effect it. I leave all to your Reverence his disposing. The 26th of July, 1640.

His patrimony for the mission.

"LAURENCE WORSLY."

John Parker was a young theologian, twenty-nine years of age, and ten years in the Society. He writes—

"REVERENDE IN CHRISTO PATER.
"Pax Christi.
"By reason of yours written concerning the happie successe of our Mission in Mariland, I wished Rev. Father Rectour to signifie unto your Reverence, that I was most willing and desirous to consecrate my weake endeavours to God's servise in those parts. To which alsoe I do not esteeme my selfe a little obliged by reason of a vowe, whereof sometime in manifestation I have spoken to your Reverence. True it is that some condemne mee hier as unfitte for such an imployment, both for want of health & an imperfection in my speech; but I hope that neyther of theese will bee anye impediment unto me. For, allthough my health bee not at this present very good, yet since the ending of my studies it is better than it was, & I hope by the helpe of Villiers will bee much more abettered. At least wais, even the change of aire may much conduce unto it. And, as for the imperfection in my speech, sure I am that, unless in fervour of disputation, especially in a strange language [Latin], it is hardly perceptible. And verily it seems alsoe the custome of Almighty God to make choise of lesse fitte instruments, that whatsoever is donne may bee ascribed to the true author of it. In fine, I am wholy in your Reverence his hands, & soe remain,

John Parker. A vow.

"Rev^{æ} Ves^{æ} servus in Christo,
"JOANNES PARKERUS.

"Leodio, Aug. 6, 1640."

Francis Parker, a young man of thirty-four years of age, tells of his hopes and fears, with respect both to Maryland and to his family. He should wish to bring over the members of his own household to the faith which he has himself embraced. He says—

Francis Parker.

"Reverende in Christo Pater.
"Pax Christi.

"At the very readinge of your Reverence his letter concerninge Mariland, I confesse I found myself very strongly moved to the undertakinge of soe greate a worke; and, allthough I was then in a very quyett moode, as havinge the self same day ended the spirituall exercise, yett, that I might more assuredly knowe the devyne Will in a matter of such consequence, I resolved to take some days of mature consideration before I would wryte unto you. Havinge therefore all this whyle seriously debated the question with myself in the sight of Allmighty God, directinge all my devotions to knowe Jesus his Will in this poynt, after all I fynd in my self a most earnest desyre to live and dye in an employment soe gratefull to his devyne Majesty, soe directly expressinge the holy apostles lyfe, and soe advantageous for the assistinge of soe many poore needy soules as famish there dayly for want of the breade of lyfe.

"The chiefest objections which occurred unto me were these: That, if I went now, perchance I should fynd some difficulty in matter of controversy with heretiques there, havinge yett read but little in that kynde, and had no practise at all. 2ly, That I should want all those spirituall helpes of the third years [novitiate] under Father Stafford, to whose idea in matter of vertue I have ever had a greate ambition wholy to frame myself; and now the tyme just seemed to be come, in which I might most fitly compasse my desyre.[2] Lastly, that my eldest brother, two sisters with their husbands and children are all heretiques; my mother very ould and soe weake a Catholique, that I have just reason to thinke her allmost in extreame want of present help; which many others of my friends, since Father Scroope [Laurence Anderton] came out of those parts [Lancashire], doe allsoe very much stand in neede of; and I seemed now to be come to the poynt when Allmighty God might dispose of me soe, that perchance I might afford them some small succour. Yett for all this, betwixt sweete Jesus and my self, I have soe clearly solved not only these, but alsoe all other objections—of a hard journey, want of all humane comfort, paynes to be necessarily undergone in the gayninge of soules, continuall hazard of lyfe, etc.— that I verily thinke I could securely defend this question without a President. I will not rehearse my motives, because I have allmost infinite; amongst others this is none of the smallest, that herein I

The objections.

---

[2] The third year of novitiate followed the close of all one's studies in the Society.

shall soe neerely resemble glorious St. Xaverius, to whom above all other Saynts I have ever since my conversion bine most especially devoted. Wherefore I doe most humbly prostrate my self at your Reverences feete, and beg of you for the appretiative & tender love you bear to all the glorious Saynts of our Society, and to the pretious blood sweete Jesus shed for all the soules of Mariland, that you will graunt me this jubily of hart for the only favour I begge of you this Jubily yeare,[3] as to employ me freely, if you judge me worthy of so greate a benefite.

"If it be my good hap to be disposed of that way, I should be glad if in your answere you will give me leave to buy some few books for catechisme & preachinge good morall thinges, which I know may be had here and at Antwerp, and scarce any where else.

"Soe comittinge you most hartily to the protection of sweete Jesus, I rest,

"R⁽ᵉ⁾ V⁽ᵉ⁾ Filius indignus et Servus in Christo,

"FRANCISCUS PARKERUS.

"26 July, 1640."

A letter from Matthew Bazier, or Grimes, is worthy of one who, ten years later, died a confessor of the faith, at the age of forty-two, in the dungeon of Newgate. However, not to multiply extracts from the appeals of men who were never sent to America, but whose various springs of action and diverse modes of expression show a marked identity of spiritual attitude in face of an identical call to self-sacrificing service, we shall merely add to the convert's letter just given some extracts from the epistle of a young professor.

Matthew Bazier and others.

Father Christopher Morris, at this time thirty-seven years of age, evidently appreciated his position both as a Professor of Philosophy at Liège, and as a linguist, possessed of eleven languages besides Greek, not to mention other accomplishments which made him useful and brilliant in this world.[4] He begins a letter to the Provincial by telling of the sudden effect produced in his soul on hearing the appeal made; and now, after several days spent in deliberation, he finds himself earnestly moved to "beg as a favour that which heertofore," he says, "I never was able even to thinke on but with repugnance & horrour.

Christopher Morris. His motives.

"The considerations that move me thereunto are these following.

---

[3] 1640, the centenary of the foundation of the Society.
[4] H. Foley, *Records*, vii., *Collectanea, s.v.*

First & chiefly, the great want of succour which those poore soules, as deare unto Christ our Lord & redeemed with as great a price as the best in Europe, do stand in need of, and yet that they for so many yeares since Christ his suffering seeme to have beene so neglected, and as it were forgotten, by the permission of God's secret and inscrutable providence—as if Christ had not suffered for them, but for the Europeans alone, so far they have hitherto been from reaping the fruite of that *copiosa redemptio*, for lacke of external helpes which the Europeans have more then abundance.

"Secondly, the facility which God of His goodness hath bestowed upon me in learning of what language soever, the want of which seemeth to have been the chiefe impediment to the charitable endeavours of such as are already setled there. To which may be added the knowledge of music, which may perchaunce be of speciall use in the beginning of that young primitive Church;—things which heere by reason of aboundance are of no great use unto me, and may be there of special consequence.

"Thirdly, (but this is a motive of another straine, and a grace which I do acknowledge my selfe most unworthy of), the desire of martyrdome. For can the Catholicke Church be firmly established in any country without persecutions and martyrdomes? Will not the devill be as busy in raising oppositions against the Christian faith as well in Maryland as in China, Japony, & other places? At least, if we misse of martyrdome, there cannot want sufferances of labour and afflictions which, joyned to a true desire of martyrdome on my part, I hope will be accepted of Almighty God as part of satisfaction for my manifould former sinnes."

Then the young professor considers the obstacles to the fulfilment of his desires. The "course of philosophy which he has in hand" may readily be picked up and continued either by Father Courtney,[5] or by Father Worsley,[6] or any one else. The writer talks as if he considered his life's work in this respect to be practically over. He speaks of resigning "an employment of credit at such a time as the chiefe labour was overcome and passed, and what remained was rather a glorious crowne of my former paines then otherwise. And if any shall so interprete my desires as to account me rash, in neglecting what commodious and honourable employment I might expect in our Province heere, and inconsiderately covetous of novelty, rather then moved with a true desire of helping soules, I do contemne his judgement and more highly

Obstacles.

---

[5] F. Edward [?] Leeds.   [6] F. Edward [?] Worsley.

esteeme of the teaching of Christ's crosse in all sences in Maryland then of the most honourable chair either in Liège or all Europe besides."

Other dangers and difficulties he has weighed; and, he says, "whether I die by sea in my journey or by land in Maryland, sure I am I shall have as good, yea more glorious sepulcher then in Liège. The cause will ennoble the death. The inconveniences of diet, apparell and lodging will be made easy and supportable by the frequent memory of my Saviours vinegar and gall, nakednesse & hard bed of his crosse. And I hope to feel this stomache that in honourable employment used sometimes to be squeamish, by the influence of the soules hunger and thirst after souls and a good toilsome daies work and labour of body to that effect, to become so hungry as to leape at a browne loaf. He cared little for the want of corporall goods who saied, *Meus cibus est facere voluntatem Patris* ['My food is to do the will of the Father']. If I can gett no meate, I pray God I may starve in so good an employment, & I shall be happy."

With a prayer that God may keep him in these good dispositions, and may inspire the Provincial to order that which is most for God's glory, he adds that if he be chosen, he should wish "to be admonished soone, and to have leave for some bookes of music which shall not cost much, which may be found in these countreys and not in England; as also to buy one Preacher, which I have a great liking unto. More other things I shall beg of your Reverence or let alone, as you shall thinke most expedient. So expecting, till your next letters, upon my knees your Reverence's desired benediction, I rest

"Rᵃᵉ Vᵃᵉ Servus et Filius indignus,

"CHRISTOPHORUS MAURITIUS.

"From Liège, 27 July, 1640."

§ 57. Among the brave young applicants for the Maryland Mission there were several actually selected; and we shall make their acquaintance hereafter.[1] But first, as on a former occasion we took a view of the missionary aspirants who were competitors

---

[1] Besides the four already quoted, the others not chosen among the applicants whose letters are preserved in Maryland, were Matthew Grimes, John Spencer, John Smithson, Francis Matagon (*alias* Matthews), Thomas Atherton, Thomas Owens, T. Humphries, Thomas Mumford, James Monford, William Sadler, Richard Fulwood, Thomas Carew, Thomas Harrison, Francis Line (apparently a professor at the time); and the lay-brothers Francis Maurice and Robert Gray. The persons selected were Roger Rigbie, John Cooper, and the lay-brother Gregory Turberville.

§ 57]   *ENGLISH, WELSH, SCOTCH*   467

of young Father Knowles,² so we ought to take up the same thread here and notice briefly the general movement of zeal for distant missions. Many of the applicants saw neither the countries of the far East nor the continent of the far West, but were deputed, as the General so often said, to find one or other in their own persecuted island of England. Others were successful, and reappeared afterwards in Maryland and St. Christopher; or went to Chili and voyaged to China by way of the Philippines.

And, first, Thomas Owens at Liège, one of the young men who answered Father Knott's letter with reference to Maryland, does also solicit the General's attention during some ten years with his petitions for service in the Indies. After ten years he is in Portugal, only to find that all access to the far East is interdicted.³ Thomas Thompson also asks for the Chinese Mission at different times, the General answering him twice.⁴ After the Welshman and the Englishman very properly comes the Scotchman. William Monteith applies for China four times in two years, and is answered thrice; the first time with the distressing news that, among so many candidates on the lists for China, more must of necessity be disappointed than can be gratified;⁵ and the third time with the benevolent admonition that the former answer had conveyed no promise, but that, if the young man had espied a promise therein, it was because his wish had bodied forth its object—a mistake readily condoned.⁶ Owens, Thompson, Monteith: Welsh, English, Scotch.

Father William Campion asks for the foreign missions at a moment when Japan, China, and the Indies generally are all in a state of disturbance; still the General puts his name down.⁷ The new General, Father Carrafa, answers Father John Smithson, an applicant for the remotest Indies, by representing that others are in the field, and, besides, W. Campion, Smithson, W. Pelham, Rockwood.

---

² *Supra*, § 44, pp. 371–373.
³ General Archives S.J., *Anglia, Epist. Gen.*, 1640, June 2, *passim* to 1650, May 2. One short letter of Father Vitelleschi's to the young man may find a place here as a specimen of simple classical elegance: "*Thomæ Audoëno Leodium.* ¶*Do veniam perlibenter ardori tuo, sive importunum appelles sive imprudentem; nulli venia promptior quam peccato amoris. Verum ego te tui voti non possum facere compotem, dum nulla missionis Indicæ occasio est. Quando ea affulserit, tum demum exploranda nobis Dei voluntas est, cujus exequendæ votum tibi esse primum non dubito; certe esse debet. Tu causam interim tuam apud ipsum age, et me illi in tuis O*[*rationibus*] *comm*[*enda*]. 14 *Junii* [1642]." (The General's own autograph draft without any correction.)
⁴ *Ibid.*, 1641, August 19; 1642, August 16.
⁵ *Ibid.*, [1641], August 24: "*Sero Sinas appellasti, quamvis accuratis litteris tuis; a tam multis enim præventus es, ut eorum plures tam bonæ expeditionis exortes sint futuri quam compotes.*"
⁶ *Ibid.*, 1641, August 24; 1642, October 4.
⁷ *Ibid.*, 1642, March 8.

that for an Englishman India is much nearer; it is to be found in England, where one may yet have to shed his blood.[8] To William Pelham, studying at Bologna, and desiring the Indian Missions in order to be as far as possible removed from ties of flesh and blood, the same General extends the same assurance; and to Pelham's inquiry, when may he renew the application, the reply is that he may do so, when he hears of procurators arriving in Rome from the far East, and that meanwhile he has virtue and letters to acquire in perfection. In all cases England will remain in reserve for his labours.[9] Some twenty-four years afterwards this Father spent the last year or two of his life in Maryland. In similar manner the General answers and gratifies Robert Rockwood, studying at Bologna; but soon afterwards, on learning that this young candidate has engaged the procurator of Chili to carry him off, his Paternity writes, praising him indeed for his vigilance and importunity, but deferring the execution of that plan.[10]

About the same time, the Provincial, Father Silesdon, tells the General of a large number who are in hopes of a call to the Indian Missions; and he receives an answer to the effect that, when the procurators of the missions desire to have these aspirants, the General will not object; but at present the lists are full.[11] Robert White at Liège receives encouragement from the Vicar-General, but no promise of a call to far-off and barbarous peoples.[12] After the short terms of the Generals, Father Piccolomini and Gottifredi, Father Goswin Nickel received such applications with kindness; but, in answering members of the English Province at the time, there was always the obvious reflection to make, that men who wanted martyrdom need not go far from home to seek it; and there were plenty of volunteers in other countries for the blood-stained fields of the far East and far West. In this sense he wrote to George Keynes at Liège; and yet, in the very same year, sent the young man off to China, but, in fact, only to die in the Philippines at the early age of thirty-one.[13] All praise was bestowed on Francis Hawkins, who applied while at his studies, and again at intervals of two years apart when he was already a

R. White,
G. Keynes,
Hawkins,
Nelson.

---

[8] General Archives S.J., *Anglia, Epist. Gen.*, 1646, June 9.
[9] *Ibid.*, 1646, December 1, December 29.
[10] *Ibid.*, 1646, December 22; 1647, February 16: "*Laudo zelum et piam improbitatem qua pulsas fores Indicæ missionis, quaque jam pertraxisti in vota tua Procuratorem Chilensem.*"
[11] *Ibid.*, 1647, May 11.
[12] *Ibid.*, 1649, July 10.
[13] *Ibid.*, 1654, March 17; to Knott, Provincial, 1654, October 31.

priest; but the General finally decided that England was to remain his field of action, the places for the East being all taken up by recruits from other Provinces.[14] Francis Nelson, a student at Liège, received similar directions.[15] What seems a little surprising is that a priest who is already a missionary of standing in England should be an applicant for the Indies. Thus Father Thomas Carey's petition is accepted, but he is recommended to practise resignation, whatever be the arrangement made by superiors in his regard.[16] He died as Rector of St. Omer's some fourteen years later. And Father Francis Bartlett in London applies in 1657, only to be told that England at this date is as full of troubles and as productive of palms as China can be.[17] *Fathers Carey and Bartlett.*

During all this time Maryland and the West Indies had come in for distinct mention as far-off foreign missions. Father Henry Silesdon, writing from the Continent, proposed Father Matajon for the transatlantic mission of St. Christopher. The General, Father Piccolomini, replied (May 28, 1650) that he did not see what good was to be expected in that distant country from one who was not making a satisfactory exhibition of virtue on the mission in England; since the foreign missions required "men thoroughly apostolic at heart, endued with the spirit of submission and obedience;" the only point which the General herewith would determine was that the said Father should not be promoted to his last vows, until the Provincial [Father Foster] had first recalled him from England. Silesdon wrote again some months later, suggesting that Matajon might be sent to Maryland; whereupon the General, addressing the Provincial, notified him rather drily, that as to the two points in Silesdon's letter, one about removing Matajon from the mission in England, the other about sending him to the mission in Maryland, he approved of the former and disapproved of the latter. If the said subject had not the virtue requisite for England, he certainly had not enough for Maryland.[18] *For St. Kitts: Matajon, Buckley.*

At the same time, a ready approbation was being given to the appointment of another Father for the West Indies. The General Piccolomini wrote: " I ratify the mission of Father Robert Buckley to St. Christopher, supposing that he himself does not object;[19] so

[14] General Archives S.J., *Anglia, Epist. Gen.*, 1654, March 21; 1656, May 27; to Barton, Provincial, 1658, February 9.
[15] *Ibid.*, 1659, December 20.
[16] *Ibid.*, 1658, January 5.
[17] *Ibid.*, 1658, February 9.
[18] *Ibid.*, 1650, May 28; August 20.
[19] " *Si quidem ipse non reluctetur.*"

that the desires of the French Fathers may be satisfied, and assistance be given to the souls of his countrymen who are in danger there."[20]

The Irish Father William Mallony seems to have offered himself for Maryland. To the Provincial Knott the General Nickel wrote:

Irish Fathers: Mallony, Christopher Bathe.

"It gives me extreme pleasure to see the charity which your Reverence exercises towards the Irish Mission in its present most afflicted state. I prefer that Father William Mallony should come over to Belgium rather than go to Maryland." He was to succeed Father Thomas Quin in charge of the seminary at Antwerp, the other going back to Ireland as superior of the whole mission.[21]

One other name we may mention as appearing expressly in the Maryland Catalogue. It was that of the Irish Father Christopher Bathe, who was sent to the island of St. Christopher, in 1652, thus probably taking the place designed for the Welsh Father Buckley.[22]

A point in the foregoing correspondence calls for some particular explanation; and that is, how men facing the trials and exposed to the persecutions of the English Mission should be ambitious of the hardships and heroism of the foreign missions, the former being considered by the Generals as equal to the latter under the aspect of tyranny and barbarity. But, irrespective of the great moral fact that, as none are more charitable than the really poor who are worthy objects of charity themselves, so none are more brave than those who are weathering the storms of life already,—there is another reason for this high ambition, which is restless in its craving for heroic self-abnegation; and it was well touched upon by one of the young men in a passage quoted above. There was a condition of enforced idleness, of ostracism in England, when nothing worse was inflicted—men of the first qualifications in talent, culture, and learning, being forced to live in corners and private houses, curtailed of every opportunity which place, chair, pulpit, and even, in large part,

---

[20] General Archives S.J., *Anglia, Epist. Gen.* 1650, April 30.—Cf. *supra*, "Propaganda Reports on the Islands:" § 31 (1); § 31 (2), p. 305; § 31 (6).

[21] *Ibid.*, 1654, August 29.—Cf. Foley, *Collectanea*, s. v. "Malone or Moloney."

[22] A particular interest is naturally aroused by the ardent applications for foreign missions, as revealing the trend of thought and the attraction of motives which animated those courageous spirits. There is a vast collection of such papers or applications, entitled "*Indipetæ*," or "Applicants for the Indies," belonging to the General Archives S.J.; but, having been sequestrated, now to be found in the public *Archivio di Stato*, Rome. In them, the variety of character, the cast of thought, the wealth of pleading, are what might be expected from a score and more of European Jesuit Provinces, abounding in choice subjects worthy of the Society. Yet the essential spirit and motives of the applications are as uniform and family-like as in the specimens just given from a single Province, and that not a numerous one in the roll of the Jesuit Order.

§ 58]   OPEN FIELDS OF ACTION   471

the press itself could afford; while all these advantages, opportunities, and means were at the service of every enemy of their Order and of the Church, with scarcely an opening left for themselves to come forward, to compete and contest. It was the least of the penalties imposed on ability and independence; but it was also the least satisfactory. There was no heroism in inaction. Lawrence Worsly expressed his grief at seeing "many able men restrained from doing such things as were very suitable to their vocation;" whereas, in view of the campaign of zeal to be conducted in Maryland, his "sorrows," he said, "must of necessity give place to joy," at seeing "such a plentiful harvest prepared" for these men.

There is extant an instruction of Father Knott for "Ours," as it is headed, "who are on the English Mission." Chapter the second has these lines, which reveal a whole situation— *Knott's instruction on zeal at home.*

"Pray, are we idle when we pray, study, offer Sacrifice, etc., for the good of our neighbour? The house is building while the foundation lyes under ground invisible. Our Blessed Saviour after thirty years' retirement appeared in the world; Saint Sylvester was called from solitude to a Constantine. Do thy duty & the will of God for the present. He will reserve some great fish for thy net, or at least reward your good desire most amply. The conservation of religion in England is a great good work. This is performing by thy presence in one house, although with a few. If every missioner conserve one family, we shall find that the conversion of several others will follow. And, upon the whole, it will appear that, although, when we consider ourselves alone, we may seem sometimes to be half idle, yet if we look upon the employment relatively, as we are parts of that whole number which God is pleased to make use of in helping our country, we shall find reason enough to content ourselves, and gratitude to His infinite goodness, who has chosen us for a work, than which perhaps in the whole Church there is none of greater importance." The rest of the instruction is chiefly a set of useful admonitions on obviating the evils of so abnormal a kind of life.[23]

We now return to the applications for Maryland in the year 1640, to show the character of the men who were actually chosen for the transatlantic Mission.

§ 58. In 1640 Roger Rigbie was a young priest who a year

[23] Stonyhurst MSS., *A*, ii. 24, No. 4, twelve 4to leaves; a copy [by D. Johnson, 1762?].

earlier had finished his course of divinity at the age of thirty-one. He had succeeded excellently in his studies; possessed a high order of talent, with sound judgment and discretion. Thus far he had shown a special attraction for spiritual ministries, but he was supposed to give promise of success in other lines of activity also.[1] Apparently on his own initiative, he addressed the Provincial with respect to Maryland, and wrote—

Roger Rigbie.

"REVERENDE IN CHRISTO PATER.
          "Pax Christi.
      "I had thought to have petitioned for a favour at your Reverence's last being here; but your sudden, and indeed to me unknowne, departure prevented me. Howsoever, I hope it was not without God Allmighties particular providence, that I might maturely deliberate of soe waightie a matter before I proposed it. My request is only to intreate the happines to bee made partaker of that happie Mission of Maryland. Tis true I conceive the mission not only happie and glorious, but withall hard and humble, in regard of the raw state things as yet are in; yet the love of Jesus neyther feares labour nor low imployment. Your Reverence's letter inkindled in my mind a great desire of this voyage, renewed former good purposes to that effect, and made me in fine resolve upon it. This resolution hath bin verie much strengthened this tyme of holy exercises both in prayer, holy Mass, & other occasions, which I have taken to deliberate of this point. I confesse the deliberation hath bin long; and the resolution, I feare, will come late both for others speedier petitions, and the tyme of the year. Nevertheless, not always first come, first sped; sometimes *novissimi* become *primi* [the last become first]; and, being neare at hand, I confide I may bee ready in due tyme for that voyage the next opportunitie. Besyd's, thoughe others farr better deserving, & more able to found that new spirituall plantation, will have allreadie presented themselves, yet I should be glad to joyne my meanest endeavours with their best; and the little experience I have had gives mee good hopes that my health and strength will bee able to break through occurrent difficulties, and accompanie others in their greatest labours.

"I fear I have hindred your more serious thoughts too long. Wherefore, in a word, I leave the matter wholly to your prudent charitie, desiring you would freely dispose of me as you judge best. If you be allreadie furnished with workmen, it may bee you will want

[1] General Archives S.J., *Anglia, Catal.* 2, 1639.

the next spring to provide for a new harvest; then you know where to find one.

"Thus, with my dutifull respects & best wishes, I humbly crave part of your holy Sacrifices, & rest this 31 of July, 1640.

"Your Rev.'s humble servant in Christ,
"ROGER RIGBIE.

[Superscription:] "R^{do} Patri in Xr^{to} P. Odoardo Knotto, Provinciæ Anglicanæ Soc^{tis} Jesu Præposito, Audomarum."

It appears from this letter that Rigbie was engaged somewhere in the ministry, not far from the port of departure. A younger man by three years was John Cooper, not strong in health, of but moderate talents, equipped with only a short course of studies both in philosophy and theology. Still, he had made fair progress in those branches; he seemed well qualified for spiritual ministries, and would in time make a competent superior.[2] He wrote as follows:— *John Cooper.*

"REVERENDE IN CHRISTO PATER.
"Pax Christi.
"Your Reverences exhortatory letter towards Marylands Mission caused such comfort and joy in my hart, that I was inforced to use no smale indeavour to keep it from breaking forth to others; for I conceived immediatly uppon the reading there of, that there was now hope of compassing my desires in helping to reduce such barbarous people to the knowledg of one God and the true faith of Christ. I have had these many years no smale inclination towards such a mission; but, not finding how to compass it, this litle sparke of zeale for soules was in a manner cover'd with the ashes of dispaire, which now begins againe to shew it selfe; and, by reason of new fewel of hopes added, I find the fier of charity so to increase that I can no longer hold from asking the favour, that I may be sent fortwith into those parts, there to spend *et superimpendere meipsum* in reducing those soules so deare to Christ our Lord, and for His sake more deare to me than my very life. For alas! how is it possible but that I should burne with this fier, beholding with my interiours eyes my dearest Saviour hinging uppon the crosse, and with as many mouths as he had woundes in his virginall body inviting me to this most Christian and truly apostolicall worke? And indeed the confidence I have in His

[2] General Archives S.J., *loc. cit.*

divine providence mak's all apprehension of difficulties to vanish quite out of thought; and, although I might perchaunce have some fals apparent reasons to disswade me from this most holy enterprise, yett of such force I find this present motion that I can admit of none.

"Wherefore I most earnestly beseech your Reverence, out of that affection you bare my souls good, that you will value my health & life no more then I my selfe do value them, who shall be most happy to spend a thousand lives (if I had them) in so good a cause. I would have your Reverence to know that I care not to live nor feare to dye. Death will free me from infinite miseries this world affords; and life is already so distastfull, by reason of my smale increase of love towards Almighty God, that I esteeme it more than a perpetuall death to live any longer. O, how happy should I be eyther to dye in this journey, or in the midst of so glorious a harvest! Verily, Father, I cannot but speake this with much feeling; and so much the more, speaking it to one who I doubt not but understands me.

"But why do I mention death, who perswade myself that life & health will rather be increased then lesned by reason of this journey? For why may I not hope that, as for leaving a father and brother in the world to follow Christ I have found a hundred as wel-wishers in religion, so for hazarding (if I may so term it) my life & health for His love I shall also find both health increased and life prolonged, according unto those His most true words, *Qui perdiderit animam suam propter me inveniet eam* ['Whosoever shall lose his life for me shall find it']. Moreover, my meane parts and small sufficiency will not, as I immagin, prove so beneficiall to Europeians as to thes barbarians, thos of Europe requiring more learning then I for my part professe to have. Besids, this country of Maryland, taking its name from so great a patronesse as is the ever Immaculate Virgin, gives me no smale assurance of doing some thing to her honour and glory, in whose help and assistance I trust next to God.

"I must therfore once more beseech your Reverence, even for Christ's and His most Blessed Mother's sake, that you would approve of this my most humble request, and make me so happy as to be imployed in this most meritorious mission.

"R^{æ} V^{æ} humilis servus et filius in Christo,

"Jo. COOPERUS.

"17 Julii, 1640."

This young Father, receiving no satisfaction in answer to his generous offer, made another attempt two years later. He said (May 9, 1642)—

"HONORED SIR,

"I writ to you an other way, that so at least one [letter] might not faile you. My busines wer only to lett you understand that never was my desire greater for the place ye know then at this present. The more I propose the occurring difficultyes, the more I find my affections inflamed that way, & I hope the very ocean will not squinch this fier. Deer Sir, let me know what hopes there is of obtaining this great happynesse. If you send none this yeare, I must intreat the favour in the interim, you would lett me be where I may imploy the strength & health God hath lately given me, in helping the poore and travelling a foot in that great work. *Cooper again. Hartwell.*

"I am confident I shall be able to performe it, for in experience I find no difficulty in it. Where I live, I am abriged of liberty in doing the good I could wish; which maks me more ernist to be els where imployed. But I leave myselfe to your prudence to dispose, as you shall thinke fitting. Only this I must tell you, that, considering my health is so much increased, I thought it my obligation to propose these motions to you, and so to rest in your advice and counsell.

"Yours ever to be commanded,

"JO. COOPER."

[Superscription, apparently to the same Father Knott, Provincial:] "To his much honored and respected friend, Mr. John Hall."

On this occasion Cooper's request was granted almost immediately; and some while afterwards, in company with Hartwell, he joined the body of missionaries in America, whither Father Roger Rigbie had already been sent a year or more earlier. Of Father Bernard Hartwell, who was then a missioner in the parts about Devonshire, we have no letter extant like those from the young men on the Continent. He would seem to have been naturally a gifted man, though his progress in studies had been only mediocre. His attraction was towards a missionary life; and he was now thirty-three years of age.[3]

Among the applications of 1640 there is a short letter from the Welsh brother Gregory Turberville, then a novice of one year in the Society and twenty-five years of age. He had pursued some humane studies; had good natural talents; and he *Gregory Turberville.*

[3] General Archives S.J., *loc. cit.*

476 NEW MARYLAND MISSIONARIES [Chap. VI

proved himself in the course of time well qualified for the various duties in temporal matters which devolve upon a lay-brother. He wrote to the Provincial in these terms—

"I have had ever (Reverend Father) a certaine innated desier of suffering for my Saviour Jesus; for which end I have left both father & mother, kindred & country; and by entring into holy relligion doe forsake myself as much as possible; and am greately encouraged by the example of our blessed Father, S. Francesse Xaverius, but specially of the thrie holly Japonyan martirs & the protection of holy obedience; which is offered to those whome God Almighty shall call to this Mission to Maryland. I doe most earnestly crave and desier it of you (Reverendo Father), not trusting to my owne ability or deserts; but in the meere goodness of God Almighty & his blessed Mother.

"Gre[gory] Tur[berville]."

This good brother had to wait twenty years before being sent to Maryland. Then he laboured there twenty-four years strenuously and well, and died in the peace of the Lord at his post in 1684, forty-four years after our present date.

Among the thirty-eight persons who have just been mentioned in connection with Maryland or the foreign missions at large, we observe that of the English Province, comprising England and Wales, some twenty-six among the applicants were of the former country, and six of the latter; and that France, Belgium, and Liège each added one to the number of aspirants, all of these being members of the Province. Besides, two Irishmen, Mallony and Bathe, as well as one Scotchman, Monteith, have come forward. Three among the total number were lay-brothers, one being English, and two Welsh.[4] The natives of Wales were Christopher Morris the professor, T. Humphries, Thomas Owens, Robert Buckley, with the brothers Gregory Turberville and Francis Maurice. The one English lay-brother was Robert Gray. Father Francis Matajon, or Matthews, was a native of Liège; Father Bazier, or Grimes, of Rouen; and Francis Nelson, of Brabant.[5]

Nationalities of the aspirants.

[4] Thomas Atherton and Thomas Carew do not appear in Foley's *Collectanea*, but we reckon them as probably English. And some other names like Jas. Monford and T. Humphries are not registered under those forms by Foley. Walter Morris, a Welsh lay-brother, who is registered (*Ibid.*, *s.v.*) as having died in Maryland, seems to be a combination of Walter Morley and Francis Maurice, both lay-brothers.

[5] If the English orthography and style, exhibited in some of the letters, excite attention and criticism, even though there were comparatively few conventional rules

§ 59. While these measures were being taken in Europe to recruit the ranks of the Maryland missionaries and to advance religion, charity, and education in the colony, the Proprietary, Cecil Lord Baltimore, seized by main force the Indian mission property of the Fathers at Mattapany on the Patuxent; and this was understood to be the first step in a general process of expropriation without recourse to law. His agent and right hand in the sequestration would seem to have been his brother, the officer on the ground, a gentleman sworn to administer justice.

There was no legal basis for the act. An attempt, indeed, had just been made in the Assembly of 1639 to supply such a basis, but the bill had suffered shipwreck and disappeared. That attempt at legality had been conceived in these terms: "Neither shall he [any subject of his Majesties the King of England, etc.] obteine, procure, or accept of any land within this province from any Indian to his own or the use of any other then of the Lord Proprietarie or his heirs"—every colonist being thus disabled like a minor, his lordship being the only enfranchised adult. Then, as if to provide a pretext for operating retrospectively, the same bill proceeded: "Nor shall [he] hold or possess any land within this province by virtue of such grant, upon pain that every person offending to the contrary hereof shall forfeit and lose to the Lord Proprietarie and his heirs all such lands so accepted or held without grant of the Lord Proprietarie or under him."[1]

Mattapany. Attempt at legalizing the seizure.

Neither was there anything in the charter to furnish an original justification of the seizure. This was shown by the circumstance that no appeal was made to it in the said bill, which professedly introduced something new. Obliquely there was an insinuation in the heading of the bill about "maintaining" a title, which showed that, if the charter could have been cited directly, it would have been; for the heading runs: "An Act for meinte[in]ing the Lord Proprietaries title to the lands of this Province." Later on,

The charter.

at the time to fetter the hands of writers, one explanation of the circumstance accentuates a point already touched on in the correspondence—that of the handicapping which resulted from ostracism and exile. Father Andrew Pulton, S.J., began a controversial tract with this explanation or excuse: "A. P., having been eighteen years out of his own country, pretends not as yet to any perfection of the English expression or orthography; wherefore, for the future, he will crave the favour of treating with the Dr. [Thomas Tenison, afterwards Archbishop of Canterbury] in Latine or Greek, since the Dr. finds fault with his English." *A True and Full Account of a Conference held about Religion between Dr. Thomas Tenison and Andrew Pulton, one of the Masters of the Savoy*: London, 1687; title-page, verso.

[1] *Proceedings of the Assembly*, February–March, 1638/9, p. 42.

the charter was expressly appealed to as giving such an exclusive right to Lord Baltimore of being the sole hand in the Province. But this appeal to the original patents was in a document for the Jesuit Provincial to sign, who should, as if from himself, let the world know, and thereby lay it down as a principle of Maryland jurisprudence, that Baltimore's charter gave him such a right, which nobody had seen there before.[2]

The acquisition, possession, and enjoyment of the mission property called "Conception" at Mattapany had been so open, regular, and undisputed, that Father Copley, in a letter to Baltimore over two years earlier, had conferred with him about the holding there, and the danger in which the Fathers then were of losing either that property or "Mr. Gerards Mannor." It was on occasion of a certain bill being proposed, whereby they should be forced to "cast lotts" upon their own property, and see what they might keep for themselves and what they must resign to the appetite of the proletariate[3]—an appetite which was afterwards alluded to in a letter from the General under the term, *invidia popularis*.[4] Similarly, as late as the Assembly of autumn in 1640, soon after which date the high-handed act of seizure must have taken place, the Governor who was responsible for the deed, and the Proprietary in whose name it was done, had both figured in a warrant issued to Father Ferdinand Poulton, as being the proprietor of this Conception property at Mattapany. It was in relation to a general election for the October Assembly (1640); and the writ, "given at St. Marys, the 19th September, 1640," began thus—

Mattapany, an undisputed possession.

"Cæcilius, Lord Proprietary, etc., to our trusty and beloved Ferdinando Putton, Esq., of Conception hundred, greeting. Whereas we have appointed to hold a General Assembly at Saint Marys on Monday the twelfth of October next, these are therefore to authorise you, and withall to will and require you, to summon all the freemen of your hundred to assemble at such time and place within your hundred as you shall think fit, then and there to make election of any one Burgess for the said hundred for the said next Assembly," etc.[5]

The meaning of this address to Poulton is clearly to the purport that the said Father was a landed proprietor in Mattapany, and the most conspicuous one there. But there is no question of his having

---

[2] Stonyhurst MSS., *Anglia A*, iv. No. 108H, the Concordat, 1°.—*Documents*, I. No. 22.
[3] *Calvert Papers*, i. 163, 164, 2°, 3°. See above, § 48 (3), p. 401.
[4] Above, § 55, p. 459.
[5] *Proceedings of the Assembly*, p. 88.

owned anything there except the Patuxent Indian mission property of Conception. Hence it was in this capacity that he was addressed by Leonard Calvert, in the name of Cecil Calvert, as late as September, 1640; and this was some two years or more after the first acquisition of what the Annual Letter for 1639 had called *quædam missionis hujus cella penaria*, "a storehouse of the mission," providing most of the temporal supplies.[6] This writ gave the same public prominence to the mission property at Mattapany in 1640, as a similar writ in 1639 had given to St. Inigoes, of which the Assembly Proceedings recorded: "The like summons to all the freemen of St. Michaels hundred to meet the secretary at St. Inego's house on Monday, the 18th February [1638/9]." [7]

The idea of casting lots for the mission property having come to nought, a fit moment was chosen for making a seizure of it; and that was when a certain degree of coldness, if not of enmity, had begun to separate the colonists from Maquacomen, King of Patuxent, who had given the property for the service of his Indians. Father Andrew White had been transferred from Patuxent to Pascattoway, on the other side of the peninsula.[8] This coldness and danger removed the Fathers for a time, and as the event proved for ever, from the side of him who, as real possessor and as donor, would have had something to say in their name, had Baltimore ventured to invade it while the Fathers were in touch with its natural proprietor, the king.

Moment chosen for the seizure.

The use made of the fine tract, which he thus laid his hands on, was not to keep it for himself, but to hand it over to some one else, setting up thereby the semblance of a vested right in another, and raising up an obstruction to recovery by interposing a third party. Baltimore did not save the property for religion, for charity, for education; although it had been given to the Fathers by the rightful owner for religion, for charity, for instruction. Despoiling the Jesuits of it, he did not keep it for the secular clergy, whom at this very time he was engaging in England to go over and supplant the Jesuits. Nor did he reserve it for the Protestant establishment, which might soon be there.

Use made of the tract by Baltimore.

He did not put forward that claim which appeared in his application of the Statutes of Mortmain, to wit, that it was only the

---

[6] *Documents*, I. No. 8, H.—Cf. *supra*, § 38, p. 343.
[7] *Proceedings of the Assembly*, p. 28.
[8] *Documents*, I. No. 8, H.—Cf. *supra*, § 38, p. 343.

licence of higher feudal lords which could authorize the passing of lands from one inferior feudal tenant to another. If he had put that claim forward, he did not act upon such an assumption, and make good the supposed defect by granting the licence, which would have saved such higher feudal rights, while saving the property for the noble purpose intended. It was only too plain that mortmain and feudalism had nothing to do with Baltimore, and Baltimore had nothing to do with them, in face of the Indians, whose absolute rights to their lands as against himself were supposed and therefore guaranteed in the first paragraph of his own charter. The baron of the mailed hand, and of the *fatti maschi* or bold deeds against the clergy, simply took the Indian mission property by main force and handed it over to a creature,[9] ignoring all principles of equity, especially those which in chancery govern the interpretation of a donor's will on lines as near to his intention as possible.[10]

We find no document extant describing the act of seizure itself and Baltimore's agents at this trade, which they might drive with impunity against Catholic priests and Jesuits. But we meet with quite enough about the performance in later documents.

§ 60. (1) On May 3, 1641, Father Poulton or Brooke, superior of the Maryland Mission, wrote a letter, which in part was communicated to the authorities in Rome. It would seem that he had already sent information about the scene of violence in the matter of the Indian mission property; for the trend of this letter is in the direction of saving the whole Mission of

(1) Poulton's letter, May 3, 1641.

---

[9] Knott describes the allotment as made to others, *aliis*, in the plural.—*Infra*, § 60 (4), p. 489, note 16.

[10] *Cy-près*. Compare an application of this doctrine in Hallam, where Thomas Whittaker is cited as advocating it, and the modern liberal-minded author ridicules it. After telling of the "violent courses of confiscation and attainder" which had brought about the dissolution of the monastic foundations in England, and how all that sacred and educational and charitable property was consumed in merely "swelling the fortunes of rapacious courtiers," and how the peers, who in our day are possessed of that same Church property, spend it much better upon themselves, in "even the generous amusements of life," than it could be spent "in maintaining a host of ignorant and inactive monks," with more bad language of the kind, Mr. Hallam here throws in a note logically incoherent, and beginning thus: "It is a favourite theory with many who regret the absolute secularization of conventual estates, that they might have been rendered useful to learning and religion by being bestowed on chapters and colleges. Thomas Whittaker has sketched a pretty scheme for the abbey of Whalley, wherein, besides certain opulent prebendaries, he would provide for schoolmasters and physicians. I suppose this is considered an adherence to the donor's intention and no sort of violation of property; somewhat on the principle called *cy-près*, adopted by the Court of Chancery in cases of charitable bequests." At all this the liberal-minded author sneers, and concludes with a fling at having too many schoolmasters—the same gentleman who in the text sneers at monks being "ignorant"! And then he pursues his merry way. H. Hallam, *Constitutional History of England*, I. chap. ii. 100, 101, 107, 108.

Maryland from being suppressed by the Jesuit superiors. He has evidently received an intimation to that effect. He deprecates "the very thought," as he expresses it, "of recalling us, or of not sending others to help us." The rest of his communication proceeds, in rather the style of an Annual Letter, to describe how affairs now stand; and what seems to be an allusion to the loss of Mattapany is only vague.

The writer tells of the great ceremony at Pascattoway, when the Tayac or Emperor had been baptized on the 5th of July, 1640, the Governor, secretary, and many others of the English colony being in attendance. He describes the new Christian family, consisting of the Emperor himself, chief of many kings, now called Charles, his wife the queen, now christened Mary, and their infant Anna. There was also the chief councillor, Mosorcoques, now become John, and his infant boy Robert. It was only the sudden prostration of Father White, and of Father Altham, in the case of the latter proving fatal, that had suspended the process of wholesale conversion. In February of the present year, 1641, Poulton himself had repaired to Pascattoway with Father White, who, however, suffered a relapse; and so they were in danger of losing their best Indian missionary, who, being versed in the language of the aborigines, had most influence over their minds. The King of the Anacostans now was most forward among promising subjects for baptism.[1] And the daughter of the Tayac, who was to succeed him, resided at St. Mary's, receiving education and instruction for baptism. He continues—

"I hope that by God's favour, if assistance is not wanting, there will be a very great accession to the Christian faith and within a very short time, amid these nations of barbarians. On account of the dearness of supplies we are sorely pinched, our expenses being increased and the resources failing us, whereon we should live." **Resources failing.** As the Annual Letter for 1640 reported, there had been "a famine among the Indians, owing to the drought of the past summer; and, that we might not neglect the bodies of those for the sake of whose souls we had travelled so far, we considered it necessary to relieve their want by supplying them with bread, although corn was sold at an excessive price." Father Poulton's letter of May, 1641, proceeds: In these circumstances, "and while there are none in the colony who either can or will supply us with alms, and Divine Providence shows us that we cannot hope for support either through our own industry or from those for whose salvation we work, whether

[1] Anacostia River and Anacostia the settlement are at present in touch with Washington City, south-east.

Christians or pagans; still I cannot fear but that He will provide us with necessaries—He who feeds the birds of the air that sow not, neither do they reap—and that He, who sent the Apostles to preach the Gospel without wallet or purse, and stood by them in every need, will supply us also, His unworthy labourers, with the means of subsistence, in such manner as shall seem good to His Divine Providence.

"Certainly the very thought of recalling us, or of not sending others to help us in this glorious work of the salvation of souls, would in a manner assail our faith in the Providence of God and His care for His servants, as if He were wanting now where He had not been wanting before. Wherefore, let no such consideration damp the courage of any one, but rather increase and strengthen it; since God has now taken us under His own protection to provide for us Himself; especially as it has pleased the Divine goodness to draw some fruit from our labours. Howsoever it shall seem good to the Divine Majesty to dispose of us, let His will be done. For my own part, I should prefer to work here among the Indians for their conversion, and, destitute of all human aid and reduced by hunger, to die lying on the bare ground under the open sky, than even once to think of abandoning this holy work of God through any fear of privation. God grant me but the grace to do Him some service, and the rest I leave to His Providence."

Deliberate choice of dying by famine.

The Father goes on to state that the Tayac of Pascattoway died on the 7th of March, in sentiments of great piety. And he hopes to find such another chief in the King of the Anacostans, who is asking Poulton to come and make him a Christian. Others elsewhere are sending in similar petitions. Labourers are wanted, men who know the language and are robust in health. The Annual Letter adds here that they did not feel at liberty to run out and apply themselves to new enterprises of conversion, for fear of abandoning prematurely the tender flock in hand; hence the need of labourers, who must not be deterred by fear of temporal penury, since God clothes the lilies and feeds the birds. Finally, Father Poulton concludes his private letter by saying—

"This year we shall not be able to remit anything by way of paying even in part for the food, clothing, and other necessaries which we are asking for; but we must only do as we were forced to at first and practically all through up to this, beg those necessaries gratis for the love of God, or else as a loan." [2]

[2] General Archives S.J., *Anglia, Historia*, iv. p. 847: Annual Letter, 1640.—Vatican

(2) While the superior of the Mission, in his letter to the Provincial, was thus commenting upon the situation, his procurator, Father Copley, was regarding affairs from another point of view, intensely practical. He had already sent a letter to the General (March 8, 1641), in which, to judge by the General's answer, there could have been no mention of so grave an occurrence as the seizure of their Indian mission property. The General simply says in a few lines: "I received your letter of the 8th of March, with its double account blended together of glad news and sad news. But, as the prospect offered by the former seems to promise a longer duration, it has gladdened me much. Your Mission is so dear to me that none other is more so; and whatever I can do to help it I will make good on knowing it."[3] *(2) Copley's action.*

Whatever may have been the form of warrant, if any was issued to seize the Jesuit property, we may note that, at a meeting of the Assembly held a year later, a law was passed on March 23, 1642, in which the Baltimore agency could have found some semblance of a pretext for such a seizure as that of Mattapany. This law was a partial renewal of the general Ordinance passed exactly three years before, when, the Lewger or Baltimore code having been rejected, and Baltimore's claim to being the sole hand in the Province for receiving lands from the Indians having gone by the board, a general complimentary statement was made that the "Lord Proprietarie shall have all his rights and privileges." The said statement held till the following meeting; and then was left out in the two next Assemblies. It came in now as part of a general renewal, to hold good till the next Assembly. This slight matter of Proprietary rights as recognized, being interpreted in the spirit of the old bill about Indian lands, could have supplied just enough of a web of a pretext to insert in the warrant for a seizure.[4]

However that be—and in point of fact it cost Baltimore eight subsequent years of manœuvring to secure some better kind of title to Mattapany than he had or used now—certain it is that, in July, 1641, Father Copley was engaged in the most active and practical measures for saving some portion at least of missionary rights and property, against the operation either of that fictitious pretext or of any other. He *Copley interposing a lay trustee.*

Archives, *Nunziatura d'Inghilterra*, 4, f. 64; also ff. 66, 67, copies of extracts from Poulton's letter.—*Documents*, I. No. 8, J, K.

[3] General Archives S.J., *Anglia, Epist. Gen.*, 1641, July 13.—*Documents*, I. No 5, S.

[4] *Proceedings of the Assembly*, pp. 41, 42, 83 (February—March, 1638/9); 122 (March 23, 1641/2).—Cf. *supra*, § 54, p. 453.

interposed a layman, as a trustee, between Baltimore and the Church property; in very much the same way as Baltimore interposed a third party between himself and the recovery of Mattapany by the Fathers.

It is to be borne in mind, that not even up to this time had the missionaries taken out any patent for their claims. Like other colonists, they supposed and felt sufficiently assured that they were dealing with honest men; and it was certain that any time would do for taking out the grants. But now there was no mistaking the immediate prospect, that the chief authority which had despoiled the Fathers of their Indian mission property would also proceed to expropriate their other property—St. Mary's Hill and the town lots, St. Inigoes and St. George's Island, with St. Gregories at Pascattoway. Nothing was easier just at this moment, seeing that the Jesuit proprietors had not the patents to show. And it so happens that, in a letter preserved, we find Baltimore himself, on November 23, 1642, a year and a half later, calling the Governor's attention to this strategic advantage. He reminds his brother, Leonard Calvert, that the year before he had sent out an order forbidding the said Governor to grant any patents to the missionaries.[5]

In presence of this imminent danger, Father Copley proceeded to secure something from destruction—if not his title to the 28,500 acres which, as is seen in the colonial records, represented the value of his contributions to the plantation,[6] still at least his title to something, to some salvage from the wreck of the educational and religious enterprise, on which eight years of serious work and continuous outlay had now been spent.

On the 27th of July, 1641, he demanded 400 acres of town land, and 3000 acres of land to constitute a manor. On the same day the said Thomas Copley, Esq., "conveyed & assigned all his right & interest in the demand aforesaid unto Cuthbert Fenwick, Gent, and his heirs." Again, on the same day a warrant was issued for the survey of the manor land in such place, not disposed of, as Fenwick should designate. It would seem that Father Copley's property was already plotted. Hence the certificate of survey as accomplished, and the draft of the patent itself followed under date of the very next day, July 28, 1641. In these acts all the parcels of town land (400 acres)

Assignment to Cuthbert Fenwick. July 27, 1641.

---

[5] *Calvert Papers*, i. 219, med. *Infra*, p. 488, note 15.—Compare this exclusion with the simultaneous injunction to take out grants for property, or lose it. *Supra*, § 48, p. 400, note 38; *infra*, § 62, p. 504, note 7.

[6] *Supra*, § 24, p. 264.

as mentioned before, with St. Inigoes and St. George's Island (3000 acres), were described accurately and were vested in Cuthbert Fenwick.[7]

This was the first instance of a trust on behalf of Catholic uses in North America. In conscience and equity the profit and disposal of the property lay with Father Copley, or with the proprietary interest which he represented. In either forum, whether of the civil or of the ecclesiastical law, the case was clearly a *fidei-commissum*, Copley, and through him the Society, being the full beneficiary of the use and trust involved. And it was a very exact augury of the future situation in which the Catholic Church should find herself, as well in the North American continent as throughout the British Empire, that the first allotment of land for Catholic religious purposes on the free soil of America had to be screened under the veil of a trust; and even a layman had to be put forward as the legal proprietor. The most singular circumstance, however, is that this little drama had to be enacted in self-defence against a so-called Catholic landlord. Now, with the layman put forward, the law too would be there. It might easily have miscarried, if the priest or the Jesuit had been required to maintain his claim.[8]

First Catholic trust and lay trustee in N. America.

---

[7] Annapolis Records, lib. 1, f. 115; which is the old lib. F, f. 134.—*Documents*, I. No. 24.

[8] As to the liberties taken with Catholic church property by people representing more or less the British colonial empire, between the date now considered in our text and the emancipation of the North American Colonies, we find some instructive facts just published, relative to the history of the Established Church in Madras, where (1749–1750) two Catholic churches were simply expropriated by the East India Company, and given over to the Rev. Mr. Kiernander, and to others "of the same [Danish or Dutch] mission" as Kiernander; altogether in accordance with the request of the Rev. Messrs. Fabricius and Breithaupt, who had petitioned "that they might have the Romish churches delivered over to their care;" and in absolute agreement with Admiral Boscawen's approving suggestions and encouragement in the matter. F. Penny, *The Church in Madras, being the History of the Ecclesiastical and Missionary Action of the East India Company in the Presidency of Madras, in the 17th and 18th Centuries*, pp. 325–328 (London, 1904). How a similar policy came to fail in Canada, we may see in due time.

With reference to Baltimore's expropriating measures, which were imitated with considerable success two hundred years later (*Documents*, I. *passim*), we may add that his policy, like the case just cited from Madras, and like the projected sequestration in Canada, went even beyond what Englishmen have considered the extremely predacious operations of the French Revolution in 1789. This latter upheaval, possibly because it occurred among a people who had still that hold on substantial principles of civil law which Englishmen seemed to have lost on the same principles in their own common law, took over indeed Church property, but professed to respect original intentions, original proprietary rights, and the obligation of assuming liabilities when appropriating assets. The French senator, M. de Lamarzelle, speaking in the French Republican Senate (November 14, 1905), urged this point with force against the twentieth-century despoilers of Church property with their Law of Separation. He said: " *La théorie que l'Assemblée [Constituante] adopta fut celle du fameux auteur du* Mémoire à consulter, *de l'ennemi invétéré des Congrégations, que vous nous avez si souvent cité ici, la théorie que développa M. de Mont-*

The Mr. Fenwick thus honoured with the first trusteeship on behalf of religious interests, was the same gentleman who, as Cornwaleys's private attorney, received a summons by a special writ to take the place of that absent councillor at the October meeting of 1640.[9] While this writ for that date comes immediately after the warrant to Father Poulton at Conception hundred, Mattapany, requiring the latter, as was mentioned above, to hold in his district an election for the Assembly, it is noteworthy how, in the very next year, Mattapany having been sequestrated, not only is there no warrant to a missionary as landlord in those parts, but there appears instead a certificate of three freemen, Gardiner, Lustick, and Froman, desiring this very same "Mr. Fennick" to represent them for the same Mattapany at the Assembly of August, 1641.[10] This was just about the same time when the patent was being issued in Fenwick's name to save other property of the missionaries from the fate of Mattapany.

Again, about the same date there was another assignment attempted, of which we can divine no satisfactory explanation, unless it were, perhaps, in payment of a debt. It was made by Copley, on August 2, 1641, passing a claim of 400 acres of land at Pascattoway to John Lewger himself, a gentleman who seemed to be no friend of the Fathers. The survey was reported, and the patent drafted between the 2nd and 26th of August. But the grant was "never signed nor delivered."[11]

An assignment by Copley to Lewger.

(3) When Baltimore heard of these transactions, he delivered his sentiments to his brother Leonard, the Governor, in two relays of communication. In the first he said that he had lately heard from a Jesuit in England of Father White having "had a great deale of land given him at Pascattoway not long since by Kittamaquund [the Tayac] before his [the Tayac's]

(3) A Pascattoway grant to the Mission.

---

lozier dans son discours du 13 Octobre, 1789. Voici cette théorie résumée, écoutez-la bien, car le nœud de la question est là. 'La nation, dit M. de Montlozier, peut-elle disposer des biens du clergé? Oui. La nation est-elle propriétaire des biens du clergé? Non. Le clergé peut-il être dépossédé? Oui. Les titulaires peuvent-ils l'être? Non: à moins qu'ils ne soient indemnisés et dédommagés par la nation.' Voilà la théorie adoptée par l'Assemblée Constituante et vous la comprenez: jamais le clergé n'a été propriétaire. Ce qui est propriétaire, ce sont les institutions qui sont chargées de pourvoir aux dépenses charitables, aux dépenses du culte; et le clergé n'est qu'administrateur: et si l'Etat prend l'administration au clergé, ce qui est son droit (toujours d'après la thèse de l'Assemblée), s'il accepte la charge, il aura parfaitement le droit de prendre les biens et d'en disposer aussitôt qu'il les en aura dégrevés. Ce qui prouve que c'est bien cela qu'a accepté l'Assemblée Constituante, ce sont les termes du décret du 2 novembre, 1789, qui porte," etc. Les Questions Actuelles, lxxxiii. 138.

[9] *Proceedings of the Assembly*, pp. 88, 89.

[10] Ibid., p. 106, presented in the Assembly, August 9, 1641: "A certificate from Mattapanient."

[11] *Documents*, I. No. 34.

death;" a grave fact, because, says Baltimore, Pascattoway is "within my Province. By this you may daily perceive what wayes these men goe, and of what dangerous consequence their proceedings are to me." And then his lordship adds his own views about the value of the Indians "who are christened;" that, if they are really Christians, they should come over with "contributions of beaver, peake, &c., for the building of the New Chappell," and out of their poverty save the baron so much expense in the building of a baronial ornament which he calls the "New Chappell." [12]

His second communication was two days later than the former. He has learnt in the interim that Copley has cut him out of further spoliations by anticipating him, and binding down the actual Jesuit farms under a patent from Leonard Calvert, and, worse still, under an assignment and trust to a third party for the missionaries' use. Here the noble gentleman cannot contain himself. He writes a couple of pages on the clergy and the Pope, in that characteristic style of his which one author mildly calls Baltimore's "bluster" and "emphatic epithets;"[13] but in which, with more than bluster, he orders Leonard under a certain pretext to kidnap Father Copley, and ship him out of the Province.[14] Then he proceeds in the following vein, which must on all accounts enter into the extensive literature on blind obedience.

He says: No obligation of justice, which Leonard Calvert conceives to be binding on him, as a Governor sworn to administer justice, has any force whatever, if Baltimore gives orders to the contrary. The reason of this is because, in the exercise of power as Governor, Leonard is discharging an office exclusively derived from Cecil, apparently without any encumbrance of justice or equity. For, says his lordship, the Governor has no reason to suppose but that "some accident" at some time might liberate Baltimore from the obligation to be just; who, in consequence, is always just even when ordering things unjust, or in withdrawing authority lest justice should be done. For affirming this, says he, there are good grounds; but he keeps them within his breast. Nor can they be asked for by the Governor, whose one business it is to practise blind obedience. And he proves this again. He says: If the Governor's obedience were not absolutely blind even in the face of justice, and reasons had to be given him every time he was ordered to do injustice, any other man might come forward, and

Leonard Calvert rebuked for his integrity.

---

[12] *Calvert Papers*, i. 213, London, November 21, 1642.
[13] H. Stockbridge, *Archives of Maryland*, p. 14.   [14] *Calvert Papers*, i. 218 *med.*

by presenting good reasons to the Governor of Maryland for acting reasonably, might induce him thereby to act reasonably and justly. But this, says Lord Baltimore, will never suit him; "for then my power there [in Maryland] were no more then anie mans else, who may with reasons perswade you to doe or forbeare any thing as well as I" [on the score of its being right or wrong]. Hence there must be no demand for reasons. And he concludes a long octavo page and a half of this literature with a peremptory order to the Governor of Maryland, that he must on no account pay any debts to the Jesuit missionaries, unless Lord Baltimore himself sends over to him an "especiall warrant under my hand and seale, to bee hereafter obteyned." So he "rests" Leonard's "most affectionate loveing brother, London, 23th November, 1642."

As this abstract of ours makes a very large demand on the faith of the reader, that any such line of reasoning could have been indulged in by a rational man, we must reproduce the long text itself in a footnote.[15]

[15] *Calvert Papers*, i. 219–221: ". . . I understand that, notwithstanding my prohibition the last yeare, you did passe grants under my seale here to those of the Hill [the Jesuit missionaries], of St. Inegoes and other lands at St. Maryes, and also of 100 acres of land at Pascattoway; some of which, as I am informed, you conceived in justice due unto them, and therefore thought yourselfe obliged to grant them, although it were contrarie to my directions. Which to mee seemes verie strange; for certeinly I have power to revoke anie authoritie I have given you here, either in whole or in part. And, if I had thought fitt to have totally revoked your power of granting anie lands there at all in my name, certeinly no man that is disinterested could thinke that you were bound nevertheless in conscience to usurpe such an authoritie against my will, because in justice divers planters ought to have grants from mee. For, when I have revoked the power I gave you for that purpose, anie man els may as well as you undertake to passe grants in my name, and have as much obligation also in conscience to doe it; and, how ridiculous that were for anie man to doe, I leave it to you to judge. When I did give directions to you, not to grant anie more lands to those of the Hill there upon anie pretence whatsoever, I did so farr as concerned them revoke that power I formerlie gave you of granting of lands there; and it was a great breach of trust in you to doe the contrarie. For I beleeve you would take it verie ill, and with good reason you might, if anie man, whome you should trust with the keeping of your seale, should affix it to anie thing contrary to your direction; although you were bound perhapps in future to cause it to bee done yourselfe. If those persons [the missionaries] had had anie just cause of complaint by haveing grants refused them, it had been your part onlie to have referred them unto me, who knew best my owne reasons why I gave the aforesaid directions. For you are but meerly instrumentall in those things to doe what I direct, and not to compel mee to doe what you thinke fitting. And, for ought you know, some accident might have hapned here, that it was no injustice in mee to refuse them grants of anie land at all; and that, by reason of some act of this state, it might have endangered my life and fortune to have permitted them to have had anie grants at all; which I doe not, Ile assure you, mention without good ground. I shall earnestlie therefore desire you to bee more observant hereafter of my directions; and not expect that I should satisfie your judgment by acquainting you still with my reasons, why I direct anie thing. For then my power there were no more than anie mans else, who may with reasons perswade you to doe or forbeare any thing as well as I. And I doe once more strictly require you not to suffer anie grants of anie lands for the future to pass my seale here to anie Member of the Hill there, nor to anie other person in trust for them, upon anie pretence or claime whatsoever, without

(4) We now state the facts of the spoliation in the brief terms of Knott, the Jesuit Provincial. To Monsignore Count Rosetti, Nuncio (September 22, 1641), Knott passed the following comment by way of explaining the situation:— *(4) Facts of the spoliation.*

"Observation 6. When King Patuxent, at that time a catechumen, had given some lands, etc., of his to God and the Society, with the express condition of maintaining missionaries, who should be bound to instruct the people subject to him in the true knowledge, faith, and worship of God, His Excellency the Baron did by main force wrest the said lands from the Society, and allot them to others, as if he were the Lord and Proprietary thereof—a fact which is notorious." [16]

In a Memorial somewhat later, for the information of the Church authorities in Rome, the same Provincial repeated this statement, connecting it antecedently with Lewger's complaint to Baltimore, "that his jurisdiction was hampered by the Fathers of the Society, and that the government of the Province could not go on with their doctrine;" and adding to it the sequel of Baltimore's subsequent conduct—that he "found certain persons who favoured him and his opinions; and he began to devise a plan for turning the Fathers out of Maryland, and putting [these] others into their place, men who agreed better with the humour of his secretary." [17] Such was the substance of the fact.

The first step taken by the Provincial, on learning of what had happened, was to address Lord Baltimore himself in a letter full of grave considerations, courteous indeed but cogent (September 22, 1641). He had heard, he said, of certain orders being issued, which were ascribed to his Lordship, but were of a kind to disconcert all calculations. In view of the prejudice done to the ecclesiastical state and the laws of the Church, he begged to protest, that Baltimore might indeed do as he wished; but he and the missionaries, while opposing no other force save that of patience, would certainly stand on the defence of remaining strictly *Knott to Baltimore. Sept. 22, 1641.*

---

especiall warrant under my hand and seale, to bee hereafter obteyned from mee for that purpose. So I rest ¶ Your most affectionate loveing brother, ¶ London, 23th November, 1642."

The reasons for all this fencing about plain matters of common sense appear abundantly, when we narrate in the text what Baltimore was just then doing in London.

[16] *Documents*, I. No. 16: "*Ipso facto Societati eripuisse et aliis elocasse, quasi earum dominus esset ac proprietarius, ut palam constat.*" The phrase here, *ipso facto*, which we translate "by main force," is akin to the Italian phrase, *Venirne alle vie di fatto*, "to resort to violence."

[17] *Documents*, I. No. 18.—Cf. *infra*, § 63 (3), p. 516.

faithful to the doctrine and practice of the Catholic Church. Without descending to other particulars, he would advert to this one self-evident principle: that infidels are owners and masters of their own property, and that they can do with it what they choose, and give to whom they like, as much or as little as seems good.[18] And, if any persons whom they have designed to make beneficiaries are said to be incapable of accepting, it is clear that the owners are still owners even though they be pagans, "nor is it lawful for any one to invade that right of theirs, to dispose of their property, or to keep it, or to apportion it out to others without manifest injustice.[19] And will your lordship have this stain attach to your name and your religion, that you would even stop to discuss whether you preferred that infidels kept their property or that the Christian clergy and religious men should have the enjoyment of such goods or lands?" And who dare buy property so taken, and accept on the terms of an absolute bargain what comes with no original title—" but, to state the case as mildly as possible, with a controverted title, and, as your lordship confesses, only a probable one;[20] especially if one consider the piety of the opposing claim, and the religious sentiment of fervent Catholics, who are not going to entangle their consciences in a mesh of scruples on matters of so delicate a nature. Add to all this that the right of possession on which we entered has its value in either forum [civil and ecclesiastical]; and that in the last instance there is a higher tribunal [Rome] common to both parties; and to this higher court the decision of such matters properly belongs." Father Knott adds other considerations like the foregoing, and drops a remark of more relevance perhaps to Baltimore's frame of mind than all the rest put together, when he says that, if the missionaries did but suggest these grounds of doubt to the minds of colonists, his lordship would not find any one to receive what he unlawfully got. This pregnant remark serves to explain the new campaign of papers, which Baltimore opens with the Provincial.

After adverting to the anomalous character of the whole discussion, which might seem to have taken its rise not in positive information sent from Maryland, but in some chimerical notions dropped from

Marginal note: Infidels sole masters of their own.

---

[18] "*Infideles cum fundorum aliorumque bonorum suorum sint veri domini ac proprietarii, integrum illis est ex parte sua libere de iis disponere, statuereque quam parum aut quam multum donare velint, prout ipsis collibitum fuerit.*"

[19] "*Neque cuiquam fas est jus illud invadere, de bonis ipsorum disponere, vel eadem retinere, aut aliis sine manifesta injuria elocare.*"

[20] "*Titulo, ut levissime dicam, controverso et, ut Ill*ma *Dominatio vestra fatetur, tantum probabili.*"

the clouds,[21] Father Knott towards the close of his letter indulges in some light banter, but of considerable gravity like the rest. He begs to "drop one remark, pleasantly, yet in earnest. It is that, as far as I apprehend the situation, the persons [clergymen in England] who are whispering these notions in your lordship's ear, will make all Catholic ecclesiastics in England pass over at last to the Order of the Mendicants, and become in effect and purpose paupers.[22] For, the only conceivable ground of their opinion being certain alleged and ancient laws of England [Statutes of Mortmain], whereby ecclesiastics were rendered incapable of receiving any possessions without the consent of the King—and the fact being certain now that such consent can never be had—it is plain that ecclesiastical persons can effectually receive no further donations of the kind, even irrespective of the modern unjust laws; and in such a case there is no reason why laymen should think of alienating any more what they know can never be conveyed to the beneficiaries, according to their intention."[23] Father Knott dated this letter from Ghent, September 22, 1641.

Status of the clergy in England.

It is clear that, if the land did not belong to the Jesuits, then by no charter, nor by any law heretofore passed, nor by any principle of equity at that time recognized, did the land belong to any proprietor save the Indians themselves, who could never have forfeited to Lord Baltimore what they had never received from him as vassals. For the very same reason, the Indians being masters and patrons, the usufruct did belong to the Jesuits. It may be observed that, when the latter were ejected by the violent entry of the trespasser upon the Indian lands, there is no mention made in the documents either of compensation to the Indians' clerical tenants for the work and improvements of three years' occupation, or of satisfaction for damages suffered in the act of violent entry.

It will also have appeared how supremely important now had become the only colourable pretence left, that of mortmain, as against all whom it might concern, and if possible as acting against the Jesuits retrospectively. On introducing this title eight years were now spent by Baltimore in a variety of restless movements. The one criticism passed by Knott on mortmain, in the letter just cited, could

---

[21] "*Hæc mihi videri non tam informationes e Marilandia allatas, quam vanos ex Utopia rumores aut de Chymeris fabulas.*"
[22] "*Ut universi ecclesiastici in Anglia catholici transeant ad ordinem mendicantium, fiantque et re et voto pauperes.*"
[23] Vatican Archives, *Nunziatura d'Inghilterra*, 4 ff. 94, 95: "*Copia litterarum R. P. Provincialis Angliæ ad Ill. D. Baronem Baltamor; Gandavi,* 22 Septembris, 1641."

have no other value with Baltimore save to render the introduction of it doubly expedient. This criticism was to the effect that, if the Protestant Statutes of Mortmain were in question, they condemned all Catholic uses of landed property as "superstitious;" and inflicted the penalty of instant confiscation for the benefit of the King and of the informer. If the Catholic Statutes of Mortmain were in question—those passed in England before the Reformation—they were incapable now of application to Catholic interests; for, their purpose being to regulate the acquisition of property on behalf of bodies corporate by means of the King's licence accorded, there was no licence now to be had by Catholic ecclesiastics, since the King and State of England had become Protestant.

But further observations on this subject of mortmain, which becomes so conspicuous in Maryland, must be relegated to an appendix.[24]

§ 61. On June 5, 1641, Father Ferdinand Poulton, or Brooke, the superior of the Mission, was shot while crossing St. Mary's River. It was less than five weeks after inditing that letter in which he had said that he preferred rather "to die, lying on the bare ground under the open sky, than even once, through any fear of privation, think of abandoning this holy

Maryland, England, Rome.

---

[24] *Infra*, Appendix C, §§ 74–76.—Knott did also propose, in the letter to Baltimore, a reflection on what he called "the piety of the opposing claim," *pietas causæ oppositæ*, that is to say, of a religious claim as against any other not religious. This, which might seem to be only a pious reflection, had a legal value, and is a maxim in English law: "*Summa est ratio quæ pro pietate et religione facit*," "What makes for charity and religion takes precedence of everything else." It is a little curious that the first application of this maxim, where it appears in the civil law, fits in very well with the Mattapany and Pascattoway questions of the Jesuit claims, and comes down with a crushing effect upon Baltimore's want of a claim. The case is this: Suppose two persons own a field in common; then one can forbid the other to inter a dead body there; since their rights are equal. But let a motive of public utility supervene, and bid me, one of the partners, inter a body there, then my right to do so outweighs his to inhibit it. For, first, my right originally is equal to his, and secondly public utility supervenes. Nay, if my right be dubious, but the public utility be enhanced by a motive of religion, then his right, although a strict one, should give way; for, "*Summa est ratio quæ pro religione facit. L. Sunt personæ, ff. de relig. et sumpt. funer.* (viz. *Digest*, lib. xi. tit. vii.); *ex Papiniano*, lib. viii. *Quæst.: Nam, præter publicam utilitatem, ne insepulta cadavera jacerent, strictam rationem insuper habemus, quæ nonnumquam in ambiguis religionum quæstionibus omitti solet: nam summam esse rationem quæ pro religione facit.*"—For statements of Coke and other lawyers, on the plea of piety and religion as a substantial principle in English common law, cf. *supra*, 53 (2), pp. 440–443.

It is possible that, when John Lewger formulated the tenth of his *Cases*, about "spirituall persons" claiming a preferential treatment in the payment of debts from the estates of testators or intestates, he was thinking of some such principle, relative to the paramount claim of piety and religion; and, having caught it like other points from Copley's mouth without understanding it, he immediately applied it in a subject-matter where it was altogether inapplicable; that is, to the order of liquidation in the matter of strict debts. Cf. *supra*, Introduction, Chap. II., § 19, pp. 127, 128: *History*, § 49 (2), p. 413.—*Documents*, I. No. 11, Case 10.

work of God." The uniform tradition appearing in the Mission documents ascribes his death to an accident.[1]

At the end of July followed the assignment by Copley of the Mission property to Fenwick. On the English side of the ocean, correspondence was being conducted between very different classes of parties regarding the Maryland issue. Baltimore and the Provincial were conferring together; because we have seen, in the letter of September 22, 1641, that Father Knott uses an argument from his lordship's mouth; inasmuch as the latter "confesses that his title is controverted."

But a much more serious correspondence, one entirely novel and meant to be secret, was that which had been started by some secular clergymen in England to support Baltimore and to supplant the Jesuits in Maryland. It had been opened with authorities in Rome. Its fair promise of success would seem to furnish an explanation of Baltimore's domineering attitude towards the Jesuits, now about to be uprooted.

However, to bar the further emigration of Jesuit missionaries, he had not fully developed as yet that bureau or custom-house system which he effectually applied in the following year as an alternative means of exclusion. In 1641 he allowed, though with great difficulty, Father Roger Rigbie to be sent over for work in the Mission. Two other Fathers, Hartwell and Cooper, were likewise ordered by the Provincial to Maryland; but they were stopped by Baltimore, as we shall see.[2] No lay-brother was sent to the plantation for a long time to come. The occasion for making these arrangements was no doubt the loss by death of Father Altham, on November 5, 1640. Four months afterwards died the robust and efficient lay-brother Walter Morley (March 7, 1641). After him, and only three months later, Father Poulton met his death.

Meanwhile in the Roman campaign for the expulsion of the Jesuits from Maryland, the first document which appears is a petition without date. It belongs, at the very latest, to the month of July, 1641, the same time when Copley was making his assignment. Without vouchsafing the slightest allusion to the presence of the Jesuits already in Maryland, the petition informs the Cardinals of the Propaganda that there is a colony called Maryland, governed by a Catholic, the Baron of

The petition to Rome.

---

[1] Cf. *Documents*, I. No. 24.—In the old provincial record of ancient Catalogues, it is said: "*Forte necatus transiens S^{tæ} Mariæ Comit.*" Maryland-New York Province Archives, as above, § 10, notes 15, 16.—Cf. St. Inigoes old Record-book, p. 7.

[2] *Infra*, § 63, p. 506.

Baltimore; that the number of Catholics is increasing there; and the Sacred Congregation is herewith petitioned to send orders to Mgr. Rosetti, Nuncio in Belgium, to the effect that he obtain information about competent secular priests; that he propose the names of at least twelve with a capable prefect; that patents with faculties for the Indies be communicated; "in order," continues the subreptitious document, "that the Catholics who are in the said locality of Maryland, and those who shall yet go there, may have the necessary spiritual assistance of the Sacraments, sermons, Christian doctrine, and other means for the help of their souls; considering, too, that the voyage is long and transport not always at hand, and the need of such assistance is great." The petition then names Dr. Champney as the person to whom these ample faculties for the Indies should be communicated, that he may pass them on to the priests who shall go to the mission.[3]

The secret measure thus adopted is seen to be of the same nature as that of seven years earlier.[4] The time has changed; the colony has expanded; but the manœuvre is identical. On this occasion, Lord Baltimore himself is betrayed in one document as a prime mover, directing the operations.

The urgency of motives in the last part of the petition is directed towards two distinct objects, one that of snatching a commission for Maryland, the other that of obtaining Indian faculties, which were so much ampler than those usually granted for England. On the other hand, the implication in the document is flagrant, both in suppressing the truth relative to Jesuit Fathers who were rendering service to the Catholics, and in suggesting a palpable untruth by those words, that the "need" of assistance was "great." The needs of the Indian tribes were great; but for them Baltimore cared nothing. The one hundred Catholics among the four hundred whites of the colony were in no great need, since of the missionaries one was always tied down to their service at the central station of St. Mary's. Thus in this first of the Baltimore documents meant for Rome we have a complete specimen of the subreptitious and the obreptitious together, by concealment and by false statement. And the manœuvre is identical with that touching St. Christopher, which we described on a former page as being in progress at this very time.[5]

[3] Propaganda Archives, *Nunziatura d'Inghilterra*, 4, f. 56.—*Documents*, I. No. 19, A.
[4] *Supra*, § 36, p. 333, note 2.
[5] Above, § 31, (4), pp. 307-311.

At a meeting of the Congregation on July 2, 1641, Cardinal Spada reported the petition in the name of "the English Catholics living in the island of Maryland, near North America, who were asking for some mission of English secular priests with faculties for the Indies;" and a decree was accordingly formulated, instructing Rosetti to send "information about the said island, the Catholics there, secular priests in England fitted for the mission, and especially one more prominent and learned, who might be appointed prefect." [6]

<small>Rosetti, Nuncio at Cologne.</small>

Monsignore Count Rosetti was in England as late as July 5, 1641. After that, his first letter to Cardinal Barberini, Secretary of State, was dated from Ghent, July 19.[7] He was sent thither to act as Nuncio Extraordinary for the Peace Congress,[8] from which resulted some years afterwards the Peace of Westphalia. On August 17 he acknowledged the receipt of an order from His Eminence, calling for a report of the "Island of Maryland," etc., exactly in the terms of the decree just quoted. He says that he has written to England "to different persons, who are considered disinterested, and are likely to possess good information about the said points." On August 24, the Nuncio reports progress, inasmuch as he is expecting the Relation called for; and on September 7 he despatches it.[9] The Cardinal Secretary of State, Francis Barberini, says (September 14) that he is waiting for it, to put it in the hands of Cardinal Anthony Barberini, Prefect of the Propaganda; he acknowledges the receipt of it a fortnight later (September 28); [10] and then the Relation is found to be in two distinct forms, first as it reached Rosetti himself, and secondly as it was presented in the Propaganda.[11]

On transmitting the Relation "about the Island of Maryland," Rosetti merely stated what the enclosure was, and then added that he inserted also "a note of the names of those who are regarded as best fitted for conducting that mission." Some two months later (November 12, 1641), a decree

<small>Rosetti's report. Decree. Sept., Nov., 1641.</small>

---

[6] Propaganda Archives, *Acta*, 14, *Cong.* 278, July 2, 1641, No. 27, f. 373.—*Documents*, I. No. 19, B.
[7] P. R. O., *Transcripts from Rome*, xx. ff. 275, 289.
[8] Vatican Archives, *Nunziatura di Colonia*, 20, last document.
[9] P. R. O., as above, ff. 368, 374.—Propaganda Archives, *Lettere, di Francia* . . . *Inghilterra* . . . No. 141, [1642], ff. 215, 216.—*Documents*, I. No. 19, C, E.
[10] P. R. O., as above, xxi. ff. 26, 46.
[11] Vatican Archives, *Nunziatura d'Inghilterra*, 4, ff. 62, 63.—Propaganda Archives, *Lettere*, No. 141, [1642], ff. 217, 218.—*Documents*, I. No. 19, D, the *Relation*; No. 19, E, the names of priests submitted; No. 19, F, official summary of Rosetti's communications.

was passed in a general meeting of the Propaganda; wherein cognizance was taken of Rosetti's letter and of the Relation forwarded by him; as also of "fourteen priests named by the same, for the purpose of establishing a mission in Maryland with the fourteen or some portion of them, on behalf of the Catholics at present there or yet to come, and for the conversion of heretics who live in the colony or are emigrating thither. The Sacred Congregation ordered that the matter should be referred to his Eminence Cardinal [Antonio?] Barberini for the purpose of establishing the said mission." A note of Francis Ingoli's, the secretary, directed the sending of an answer in terms of warmest thanks to Mgr. Rosetti, with the phrase that the Congregation does "desire" to establish the said mission in Maryland.[12]

The meaning of this decree will be clearer on inspecting the two editions of the Relation sent by Rosetti, as well as the character of the list submitted.

The paper begins with an exact description of Maryland and its history thus far; also of the mission as conducted there by the Jesuit Fathers, two of their priests and two brothers having died in the service, and only three priests now surviving; "and besides these, it is known that no other priest, whether secular or regular, has been thus far in that colony." The population consists of less than four hundred persons, of whom about one hundred are Catholics; of the rest, the non-Catholics, more than forty have been converted. Here the Relation proceeds to sketch the Indians and their ways; the conversions made and the prospects; the solemn christening of the Emperor and his family, where an original fact is added, that the infant died soon after Baptism. Then, looking at the course of events from the side of England, the narrative tells of the opposition steadily offered to the plantation by the Virginian merchants, who have brought about one notable result, that of impeding the emigration of Catholics by means of an oath of allegiance which is exacted; and it is not known what these enemies may yet effect in Parliament.

The Relation of Maryland. 1641. Two redactions.

Up to this point the document, as submitted to the Propaganda by Rosetti, was substantially identical with that which had come to Rosetti's hands from England. There were some verbal changes; as, for instance, where the original said that at the baron's "earnest"

---

[12] Vatican Archives, *Nunziatura d'Inghilterra*, 4, f. 57.—Propaganda Archives, *Lettere*, as above, No. 141, [1642], f. 361 (cancelled number).—*Ibid.*, Acta 14, Cong. 282, November 12, 1641, No. 47, f. 480ᵛ.—*Documents*, I. No. 19, G.

request two priests of the Society with one brother had travelled with Leonard Calvert to America, the qualification "earnest" was cancelled. More singular still, all the superlatives, which were conceived in true Italo-Latin style, were mercilessly eliminated, and the whole reduced to the plain manner of speaking which is usual in an English dress. Thus *Illustrissimo Barone obnixe rogante* became *Barone rogante*. Here was violence done to the style; and to what purpose does not appear. But the critical result seems plain, that of betraying an English hand, which, manipulating the style in this one respect, seems to have used the opportunity or taken this pretext for manipulating the matter. For where now there should follow at the end the most important statement in the Relation, the entire passage is left out—being first cancelled, and then excluded by transposing from elsewhere, and interposing a natural conclusion, as if the part cancelled had never been there.

The passage thus erased and put out of sight in the official copy submitted at Rome proceeds as follows:—

"On the other hand, there has unfortunately come from another side a cause for delay; and from a side indeed whence it was least feared. For the Right Honourable Baron wanted to have some points established, and to obtain for them the force of laws, which do not agree with the ways, right, and dignity of the Church, the Spouse of Christ. Since the Fathers of the Society would not consent to such propositions, the Right Honourable Baron, taking their resistance to be prejudicial to his profit and dignity, and to be a bad example for others, obtained from some of the secular clergy their written opinions, whereby being reassured in conscience, he ordered that what he had determined on should be carried into effect. Whence it will come to pass that the Society at length may have to abandon the mission begun among the barbarians, for fear of assenting to measures which, as not saving the rights of the Church, cannot be approved. [Here followed the conclusion, which was then transposed:] And such is the present condition as well of this colony as of the mission." [13]

The very essence of the Relation as to the present condition of colony and mission being thus picked out by some one and thrown away, the expurgated official copy was reported in the Congregation

---

[13] Vatican Archives, *Nunziatura d'Inghilterra*, 4, where the two copies stand, ff. 62, 63, the Relation as received from England, ff. 60, 61, the same expurgated and then found in the Propaganda as quoted above. The said volume, No. 4, is a record of Rosetti's own, comprising times much later, when he was Cardinal and Bishop of Faenza.—*Documents*, I. No. 19, D.

(November 12, 1641). The reporter adverted to the necessity of sending missionaries for the service of the Catholics who were in need of priests, and for the help of the heretics as well, whom it was easy to convert, since the Government itself was Catholic; he noticed the fourteen names of competent priests sent on by Rosetti, the first on the list being a Doctor of Theology who might be made prefect; and now the only difficulty was, how to despatch the requisite powers, whether through the Spanish ambassador in London or the Venetian. There was not a word about the Jesuits.[14]

On this report by the Rev. Don Lanucci, the Propaganda decreed that the said matter in hand should be committed for execution to Cardinal Barberini, presumably Cardinal Antonio the Capuchin, Prefect.

The list of eligible priests ran as follows: The Rev. Messrs. (1) Britton, Doctor of Sacred Theology; (2) Fitton; (3) Nelson; (4) Wentworth; (5) Layborne; (6) Harrison; (7) Thomas White or Blacklow; (8) George Gage (Page?); (9) Redman; (10) Trollope; (11) Strickland; (12) Mark Drury; (13) Andrew Biddulph; (14) Holden.[15]

The list of eligible priests submitted.

Several of these names recur in other connections. Thus Messrs. Fitton and Nelson have already been mentioned.[16] Mr. George Gage seems to be the same who indites a long letter on the Maryland expedition, as will appear hereafter.[17] Dr. Holden, likewise, had something to do with Maryland. After advocating the subjugation of Catholic Ireland by the Cromwellian Puritans, and treating with the Cromwellian Government for the reduction of his co-religionists in England, he seemed to be the chief mover, if not the sole instigator, in a plot to exile all Catholics indiscriminately from England and send them off to Maryland, if they did not accept a Gallican and Cromwellian pact, dictated by him from his studio in Paris (1647).[18] Dr. Thomas White, or Blacklow, was the gentleman, whose teachings were repudiated by the English clergy in several formal documents (1657).[19] Under other names in the list there may be comprised two other reverend gentlemen, who within twelve months actually

[14] Propaganda Archives, *Lettere* as above, f. 361ᵛ (cancelled number).—*Documents*, I. No. 19, F.—The reporter's name appears in the *Acta*, 14, f. 480ᵛ, as "Lanuvio."
[15] Vatican Archives, *Nunziatura d'Inghilterra*, 4, f. 57ᵛ.—Propaganda Archives, as above, ff. 315, 316.—*Documents*, I. No. 19, E.
[16] *Supra*, § 7, p. 179, note 7; § 15, p. 229, note 9.
[17] *Infra*, § 65.
[18] To be noted later.
[19] C. Dodd, *Church History*, iii. 355, 356.—*Ibid.*, 354, 355, may be seen Dodd's sympathetic extract of a pamphlet by Dr. Holden, repudiating, not his friend Blacklow, but the censure of Rome.—J. Gillow, *Bibliographical Dictionary of English Catholics*, s.v. "White, Thomas," gives no intimation of his irregularities in doctrine, and s.v. "Holden, Henry," rather makes martyrs of both of them.

went to Maryland, Messrs. Gilmett and Territt. As to Dr. Champney, who was proposed in the original petition to the Propaganda for the charge of receiving the faculties and communicating them to fit subjects, we have a modern bibliographer's view of him, as a champion against "the Jesuit faction"![20]

§ 62. Just at this moment, when the Baltimore ship of state was sailing with so fair a breeze through the channels of Roman negotiations, his lordship issued with his signature new Conditions of Plantation in six paragraphs (November 10, 1641).

(1) The two last paragraphs were conceived so as to strike, not merely the Jesuits who were now supposed to be practically defunct or moribund, but also and chiefly the new men who were helping to make away with the obnoxious Society. For these reverend substitutes no alternative would be left, but to become, as Father Knott had said so pleasantly, professed members of an Order of Mendicants.

In the fifth paragraph Baltimore incapacitated everybody, who could be ranked in the ample category of "corporation, society, fraternity, municipality, body politic, whether ecclesiastical or temporal," from ever acquiring any land in Maryland, in any manner direct or indirect, except through himself; and, if any such description of person did under any pretext make any acquisition of land, the claim lapsed as void into my lord's hands. And, in the sixth paragraph, he incapacitated everybody else from ever giving land in the colony of Maryland to such a description of ostracized persons, or of holding for the use of the same in trust; and this incapacity reached to the full extent covered by "any Statute of Mortmayn heretofore passed in the kingdom of England," whether in Catholic or in Protestant times, whether in the long age when Catholicity was the religion of England, or in present times when the same Catholic religion and its religious uses had become, in the purview of the law, a "superstition," and "superstitious uses."

(1) A double disability for Maryland. Nov., 1641.

It was free for the gentleman as for any other merchant to sell his goods on his own terms, even if these, by collusion with an individual purchaser, cancelled the purpose and object of the eighteenth section in his fundamental charter,

Illegal and irregular.

---

[20] Gillow, *Ibid.*, s.v. "Champney, Anthony, D.D." To Champney's first work on the list, the compiler appends his own descriptive estimate: "Written from his prison in Wisbeach against one of the publications issued by the Jesuit faction." —For the petition, recommending this reverend gentleman as Commissary for the Maryland expedition, see *supra*, § 61, p. 494.

where his father had so carefully provided for the exclusion of mortmain. But under no terms of contract or sale was he legally qualified to make laws, or introduce them, or import them. He was as incompetent there without the consent of the freemen in Assembly met, as the freemen were incompetent without him and his signature. And it shows the helpless condition to which he was reduced, on trying to engineer mortmain into Maryland, that he did so, not through his charter, nor through legislation, but through the postern gate of novel Conditions of Plantation.

The clerical advisers of Baltimore, and prospective successors of the Jesuits, could not possibly escape the application of the ostracism now devised by their patron. For, if their tenure of property was to be referred to a bishop, he would be considered a corporation sole. If they themselves were to be recognized as incumbents in their own name, each one of them likewise would be a corporation sole according to English law.[1] If they presumed to take out claims in their own right, as individual settlers and occupiers under Conditions of Plantation, their rights as citizens would be no more respected by him than those of the Jesuits, who had never been allowed to advance any claim as a body politic, but had been required from the first to act and enjoy rights as individual settlers under the common Conditions of Plantation.

Charles Carroll's view of Jesuit property.

And thus at a later date (October 12, 1717), when Charles Carroll, Esq., answered a formal interrogatory of John Hart, Esq., Governor, who was inquiring by Royal Commission into certain estates within the province, said to be devoted to superstitious uses, the lawyer replied with great precision: "That he doth not know of any lands or sums of money that are applyed to superstitious uses in this province, but believes that some priests in this province are possessed of some tracts or parcells of land, taken up by themselves in their naturall capacities under the comon conditions of plantations, and pursuant thereto, or by those under whom for valuable considerations they derive."[2]

If, notwithstanding such patent facts of Baltimore's own creation, which had rendered a body corporate or body politic impossible, he was now employing every means to create on paper

[1] 1 Blackstone, *Comm.*, 469.
[2] P. R. O., Forfeited Estates, T. 2, ff. 6, 7.—The question proposed, f. 1, was: "Do you know of any lands or sums of mony that are applyed to superstitious uses in the province [Maryland, viz.] for the maintenance of any Popish bishops, priests, Jesuites, or any other regular Order of the Romish Church, or of any seminaries that are for the education of youth in the Romish persuasion?"

a body politic out of the clerical citizens whom he had never recognized as such, and to foist mortmain upon them that he might strike them as the body politic which he was creating on paper for that purpose, it is clear that the new parties were walking into a pass, or an *impasse*, which they had not duly surveyed, when approving of it as good enough for the Jesuits.

But there was still an upper class of Catholics in the colony, and their public opinion was an important factor in Baltimore's calculations. In presence of this Catholic conscience, which had to be reckoned with, the figure of Church law and of censures from Rome loomed up in imposing dimensions. If the new Conditions ran counter to this religious standard of judgment and sentiment, they would fall flat as of no effect. And the only method available for making them agree with the Catholic conscience of the colony was to obtain the approval of the very men, the Jesuits, whom they were designed to hit. This Baltimore tried to effect with the Provincial in England; and his agents tried the same with the missionaries in Maryland.

Besides the Conditions, there was the novelty of an Oath, not one of allegiance to the natural sovereign, the King of England, but one conceived on the same lines, and sworn to him, whom Lewger, in his papers, called "the prynce" of Maryland. This Oath embodied a law which had been distinctly rejected by the freemen in Assembly, that of making the Lord Proprietary the sole hand of the province for receiving lands from the Indians; it bound everybody who took the Oath to become a spy and informer on everybody else in this respect; it purported to undertake the absolute feudal service of defending Baltimore's rights, titles, and privileges; and again the service of spy and informer if any one else did contrariwise. There is no mention made of the basis on which this feudal service rested, of any *quid pro quo*, like that which had governed the whole medieval system. On the contrary, the Oath is expressly designed to be taken at a moment when a sale is being effected, that is, when money is paid for lands, and no gift whatever is made on which a feudal relation or obligation could repose.

An Oath. Allegiance to the Proprietary.

(2) By the irony of fate, then, neither the novel Conditions of Plantation as touching matters of conscience, nor the Oath of allegiance to Baltimore with its medley of obligations resting on no adequate basis, could be advanced further unless they underwent a moral examination, and received the *Exequatur* of the Jesuits themselves. Accordingly, Cæcilius Lord

(2) Baltimore and the Jesuit Exequatur.

Baltimore addressed himself to these moral powers, to the Provincial directly, and to the missionaries in Maryland through his aides-de-camp.

For the Provincial he drew up a paper, which, like the rest of a long series now issuing into officious existence, has been completely misunderstood by American historians. They, reproducing it and the rest, have taken these productions to be the outcome of the Jesuit Provincial's complaisant humour while addressing himself to Baltimore, instead of their being the expression of his lordship's partiality for the rights, goods, and especially the lands of the Jesuits. The documents do not grow less in quantity or biting quality, as the years go on, but rather increase, in much the same way as Cornwaleys had written with an oblique significance to his lordship, that he "never had heard or seene covetousnes decrease with age."[3]

Baltimore's paper runs thus, as preserved in a Latin guise: "I, ---, Provincial of the Society of Jesus in the English Mission, have read through the Conditions of Plantation and the oath as given above, and I do not find anything in them, or in any part of the same, which could subject the Right Honourable Cæcilius Baron of Baltimore for having formulated such conditions or oaths, or could subject any one of his officials, for publishing, executing, or recording them or any one of them by his orders, or similarly any other person or persons, for accepting and admitting the said Conditions and oath, or any portion of the same, within the province of Maryland, to any censure of excommunication in the *Bulla Cœnæ*; or could render the same persons or any one among them guilty of any wrong-doing.[4] In testimony whereof I have hereto appended my signature."[5]

Text of the Provincial's Certificate.

Across the ocean, to obtain a moral and ecclesiastical absolution of the same kind, an interview was held, and it was very instructive. It showed the intellectual capacities of the other Calvert under a new light—that of an expert casuist. We have a brief entry about what occurred, and Mr. Lewger himself is the authority. From this we learn, first, that Baltimore designed absolutely the imposition of

---

[3] *Calvert Papers*, i. 175, *med.*
[4] "*Cujusvis ob id criminis reum.*"
[5] Md.-N. Y. Province Archives, 3, contemporary copy of the Conditions in full, the Oath, and this Provincial's Certificate, all in Latin.—Stonyhurst College MSS., *Anglia, A*, iv. 108A, ff. 194–197; a contemporary copy with the Roman endorsement, f. 197ᵛ: "*Postulata Baronis de Baltimor circa terras, fundos, jura in Marilandia*" [The demands of the Baron of Baltimore, regarding lands, farms, rights in Maryland]. —*Documents*, I. No. 12, A, B, C.

mortmain legislation on the colony. Secondly, that he intended the said Statutes to operate retroactively, in defiance of English law and of all sane law. Thirdly, that all this imposition was to be effected by his own unaided authority, in violation of his charter. Fourthly, that this process being felt to be insecure, his colonial aids proposed a fine casuistical modification. It was in the sense of making the imposition not direct but indirect, inasmuch as every one should be disfranchised for the future who would not subject to the operation of the Statutes all his acquisitions in the past; and, as every one was free to incur the disfranchisement or not, by submitting or not submitting, it was not Baltimore who imposed the retrospective legislation, but it was the individual's own will that graciously assumed it in every case. This certainly was a very fine difference between an absolute imposition and a voluntary assumption of odious laws. It was like the difference between a drawn weapon and the same sheathed; the one being objectionable, the sheath made it excusable; or, again, as between shedding a man's blood and taking a pound of his flesh; the blood-shedding being justly forbidden, the taking a pound of flesh remained as a casuistical amusement. The secretary, John Lewger, resigns all the credit for this hair-splitting to the Governor, Leonard Calvert—which it would be harder to believe if we did not remember that brother Leonard was, after all, an employee of Cecil.

(3) It is thus that the secretary's Diary reports the occurrence, with its development—

Interview with "the good men."

"The Governor and I went to the good men to consult divers difficulties that wee had.

"1. One about the publishing of the Conditions of Plantation by Governor, with that article wherein all grants already passed were charged with the Statute of Mortmaine. To this the Governor found a solution by interpreting the article, not to comprehend grands [grants] already made or due by former Conditions, but that no man should have benefitt by theis new Conditions, unless hee would putt all his land, both that already granted, and that to bee granted, etc., under that condition of not alyening it, etc. And this, being not found to bee an ordination or edict comanding or obligeing anie one, but a meer proposition left to mens liberty, was resolved by the good men not to bee comprehended in *Bullæ Cœnæ*, nor to incurr anie excomunication in the publishers, etc.

"2. Another: Though not excomunication, yet whether it incurred not mortall sinn to bee the active instrument of publishing, negotiating and effecting of such a proposition or contract, as conteyned obligations against piety and good manners, and was mortall sinn in both parties that proffered, and that accepted the contract. And this they resolved, that it seemed so for the present; but they would take time to consider better of it, ere they resolved it peremptorily.

"3. The Oath upon the instructions to bee tendred to all such as were to take land, etc., was resolved to bee evidently against conscience, and to incurr excomunication *Bullæ Cœnæ* to publish it, or administer it, or record anie such oath, or anie other way to be seconding or assisting to it.

"There is a new question rising about the 5th article of the new Conditions of Plantation: That no Society spirituall, etc., shalbe capeable of the conditions—which soundes like an ordination or provision. And, if it be found so, the Conditions, I beleeve, wilbe stopt from publishing or executing; and no body will dare to concurr to the giving them any life or being, for feare of excomunication *Bullæ Cœnæ.*"[6]

It may have been a consequence of this inauspicious report that the formula of a Certificate was solicited by Baltimore from the Provincial, as a subsequent measure, intended to counteract the judgment of the missionaries just as if the Provincial were arbiter of the intrinsic merit of morality, or could modify at will the validity of ecclesiastical censures. At all events, the new Conditions of Plantation were published without their novelties, without the imposition of mortmain, without the ostracism of missionaries, and without the disfranchisement of honourable and pious laymen.[7] Acting upon that last insinuation of Lewger's, to avoid the air of enacting an "ordinance or provision" when smiting a "Society spirituall" with laws of mortmain, Baltimore entered on a side-path for arriving at the same term; he drew up the deeds of voluntary and spontaneous Secularization, of a spontaneous Surrender and Assignment, a spontaneous Concordat,—all executed ostensibly by the Provincial, but all unconditionally in favour of Baltimore.

The new Conditions pruned.

Like the penal conditions, so the formula of servile oath was remanded to a later time, when he could afford to neglect the

[6] Md.–N. Y. Province Archives, 3, "Extracts out of Mr. Lewger's Diary and Letters to the Lord Baltemore;" a contemporary copy, in which, after the paragraph numbered "3," what follows is in another hand, also contemporary.—*Documents*, I. No. 13.

[7] *Archives of Maryland, Proceedings of the Council*, 1636–1667, pp. 99–101; the Conditions were to go into effect "from the Feast of the Annunciation of the Virgin Mary, 1642." The fourth contained the limitation of time for taking out patents.

Catholic conscience in Maryland. Then, at a subsequent date, he was able to take several important steps without great difficulty, though not without eliciting a protest against the output of swearing from his administrative faculty: " with as little swearing," said the freemen, " as conveniently may be.[8] The paragraphs heretofore suppressed were then published with just a slight modification. The oath of servility was taken, when no obtrusive conscience was in evidence to dictate its observance. And the lands of the Indians were declared to be inviolably Baltimore's by right of reversion, when the battle of Providence was soon to teach him that his own lands were no longer inviolably his by charter, or possession, or prescription. Thus the intuitive good sense of the freemen was confirmed by the event, when they said: " Oaths little prevail upon men of little conscience." [9]

§ 63. After writing to Baltimore the forcible letter of September 22, 1641, the Provincial Father Knott treated with the Nuncio Extraordinary, Mgr. Rosetti, and soon had occasion to transmit a formidable document received from the Baron of Baltimore—that which is named his " Points," four in number. As to the point herein which referred to the Indian lands, the Provincial could not have been aware that the baron or his abettors had submitted the case to the very distinguished Doctor of Theology at Doway, Francis Silvius; for the purpose, no doubt, of counterpoising or offsetting the Jesuit opinion, so well expounded in Knott's own letter to Baltimore. The learned gentleman's opinion was given in reply, and was dated some eleven days after the following communication of Knott to Rosetti, which we take up now. The Provincial wrote from Ghent to Rosetti at Cologne in these terms—

" MOST EXCELLENT AND REVEREND SIR,

" With this letter your Grace will receive certain Points, which the Right Honorable Baron of Baltimore has pressed me hard to sign. They are of such a nature as to be, in my judgment, flatly opposed to ecclesiastical immunity, and derogatory in no slight degree to the dignity and authority of His Holiness, as you will see more clearly by consulting my Observations attached.[1] Wherefore, up to this I have declined to

Knott's letter to Rosetti. Nov. 17, 1641.

---

[8] *Archives of Maryland, Proceedings of the Assembly*, p. 242, *ad calc.*, April 21, 1649.
[9] *Loc. cit.*
[1] *Quædam Notanda*, or Observations of Knott.

sign, or to signify any approval by subscribing. It is my opinion that matters have now come to such a pass as to call for reference to the Apostolic See, and for a final settlement by its authority; because the Right Honourable Baron openly declares that he will not allow those to set out for Maryland who hold opinions adverse to him, to his interests, and to the administration of the province. So, of the three Fathers who were to be assigned this year for Maryland [Rigbie, Hartwell, and Cooper], he has allowed only one [Rigbie] to go, and that with great difficulty. The others have had to stay in England."

This measure of Baltimore's, in keeping priests out of Maryland, was certainly in keeping with the tenor of the petition secretly submitted to Rome, where it was asserted that priests were wanting in Maryland. The Provincial continues—

"Meanwhile it has become publicly known, that faculties have been received for secular priests who are to be despatched thither. The Very Rev. Father Philips [the Oratorian, confessor of the Queen,] and the noble baron have taken cognizance of the faculties; and it is the expectation of certain persons that some priests are going to set out soon; unless perchance your Excellency's letter, which arrived at the proper moment, serves to stop them; since you gave orders therein that nothing should be done in this business without apprising you. Equity, as well as respect for your Grace, requires that they should take notice of what you wrote. More on this subject it is not necessary for me to add.

Faculties received for the new missionaries.

"I have received nothing of consequence from England. The King is still detained in Scotland, and some think he is more or less a prisoner in the castle of Edinburgh." Here follow brief allusions to the Queen, to the Very Rev. George Muskett, President of Doway, who had just visited Ghent, and to Rosetti's safe arrival at Cologne. The letter is dated "Ghent, November 17, 1641." [2]

(1) Of the Points enclosed by Knott we have several contemporary copies in Latin and one in English. The title prefixed to the Latin translation is descriptive: "Points drawn up by the Right Honourable Lord Baron of Baltimore, which he insists shall be signed by the Rev. Father Provincial of the Society of Jesus in England, as well in his own name as in that of the missionaries who are in Maryland." [3]

[2] Vatican Archives, *Nunziatura d'Inghilterra*, 4, f. 102.—*Documents*, I. No. 14.
[3] Stonyhurst MSS., *Anglia, A,* iv. No. 108F, f. 210.—Vatican Archives,

§ 63]   INDIAN TRADE AND LANDS   507

The contemporary English begins absolutely without such a title.[4] It starts thus—

"I, A. B., doe hereby declare

"1. That, notwithstanding any former pretences whatsoever, I will not that any of our bodie or Societie within the Province of Maryland shall by themselves, their agents or servants, directly or indirectly, trade or traffique with any Indian or salvage, without the speciall licence of the Lord Baltemore, Lord of the Province, or his Lieutenant-Generall or other Governor of the same for the time being hereafter, to be signified in writeing under his or theire hand & seale. And I doe hereby surrender & disclaime any right or title, which any of our bodie or Societie might pretend, to trade or traffique with the said salvages without such speciall licence aforesaid." (1) First of Baltimore's Points.

Such is the first of Baltimore's Points for the Provincial to sanction in his own name and spontaneously, no sign appearing that his lordship ever suggested, demanded, or enforced the surrender. The style is a fair specimen of that which characterizes the roll of Baltimore rescripts; and the matter is in its way worthy of the rest. The style is that of muniments and protocols in great negotiations; while the matter is that of the jobber's and broker's business, the benefits of which Cecil Calvert the Baron designed as a monopoly for Leonard Calvert the Governor;[5] the secretary John Lewger being, as we have seen, the self-satisfied reporter, who announced to Baltimore that the game of illegally forestalling and engrossing the market was already in full play.[6] And, to ensure this truck for the merchants thus privileged, a bill to that effect having been rejected by the freemen,[7] the missionaries are to be the first that shall freely resign their rights of providing themselves and their dependants with corn and bread.

The second of Baltimore's Points is not unlike the first, except in its subject-matter. It is an enactment against all ecclesiastics of a

Nunziatura d'Inghilterra, 4, ff. 76, 77.—English Province Archives, Portfolio 6, copy taken from Westminster Diocesan Archives, etc.—*Documents*, I. No. 15.

[4] Md.-N. Y. Province Archives, 3, three pages, fol.—It may be noticed by the way that, though we have to draw our information regarding Lord Baltimore's roll of documents from archives which contain them generally in Latin, still we have no doubt that these Latin papers were translations of originals in English. This, which is evident from the character of the Conditions of Plantation, and the Oath meant for adventurers in general, is also clear from the process of translation or correction visible in some Latin manuscripts; as *signorias seu manerias in Anglia* preferred to *prædia seu manerias*, etc., *Illustrissimum* to *Perillustrem*, etc.

[5] Cf. *Calvert Papers*, i. 190, 191.

[6] *Ibid.*, 197, 198. See above, § 48, pp. 396, 397.

[7] Above, § 54, p. 454. *Proceedings of the Assembly*, p. 43; February-March, 1639.

bill rejected by the freemen regarding the Indian lands. It is also a public enactment or proclamation by the Jesuit Provincial against everybody else besides ecclesiastics. Thus it contains two parts, and each part operates in two directions, retroactively in the past, no less than prospectively in the future.

Second Point.

As to all ecclesiastics, Catholic priests or Protestant ministers, and every "person whatsoever within the said Province whether spirituall or lay," the Jesuit Provincial incapacitates them all at all times from acquiring any Indian land, even for the service of the Indians: "No person whatsoever . . . may or ought to purchase, or accept, or make use of any land within the said Province from any Indian or salvage," unless it has first become Lord Baltimore's, who shall have bound it down under ground rent, passed it under the great seal on receiving his fees, and only then allowed it to be used, though the use were that of an Indian chapel. And, as to the Jesuit missionaries, the Provincial does herewith give up Mattapany and Pascattoway by a voluntary act: "I doe hereby disavow and disannull all purchase or acceptance whatsoever of any such land made or to be made by any of our community or Societie there, otherwise then as aforesaid."

As to the lay community at large, the Provincial disqualifies all of them for all purposes mentioned in this point of his proclamation; for he is made to say expressly: "No person whatsoever . . . whether spirituall or lay may or ought to purchase, or accept, or make use." And here too he is made to strip them retrospectively of any goods which fall under his ban; inasmuch as "all other purchase or acceptance of any such land is voide in it selfe." Wherein one may admire the transcendent position of authority accorded by the Lord Palatine of Maryland to the English Provincial of the Jesuits; who by a proclamation is to supplement the defective charter originally granted by His Majesty the King of England, the latter not having disqualified his subjects where the Provincial does! The proclamation likewise serves to redeem the legislation repudiated by the Maryland freemen. And thus we have an Elizabethan or Stuart supplemental method of legislation [8] imported by Baltimore, in the form of proclamation—the exercise and odium of it being all left to rest with his friends the Jesuits. He proffers no request for this lay service at their hands. He slips it into another matter which he is exacting, exorbitant enough, but still ecclesiastical.

It is to be noticed that in these exactions, Lord Baltimore does

[8] H. Hallam, *Constitutional History of England*, i. 321.

not yet demand expressly the gratuitous surrender of all other lands, even those derived from himself under conditions of strict contract, which, as being matter of commutative justice, founds a right against him, much stricter than any derived by himself from his own charter or "gracious letters pattents."

The third of Baltimore's Points is far-reaching in the direction of putting Catholic priests under penal laws, or of importing the penal legislation of England into Maryland. Nor is this part of the Provincial's proclamation, by which all his men and all other priests shall be felons or traitors at the discretion of the Calvert Proprietary and future heirs, allowed to be softened down by the gentle gloss which John Lewger, two years before, affixed then to Baltimore's attempt in the same sense. That secretary had made the statement or model of the proposed Maryland persecution to be, not the conduct of English magistrates and officers and priest-hunters in general, as Baltimore does here, but only that of "well-affected magistrates in the like cases" in England.[9] Following up, then, an unqualified application of penal laws against the priesthood, the Provincial is made to deliver a general sentence of secularization, whereby all gentlemen of the cloth shall be treated as laymen; and a general permit granted to proceed against their persons, lands, or goods, not only for the doing of right to third parties, but "for the mainteyning and preservation of all the rights, prerogatives, & jurisdictions granted to the said Lord Baltemore & his heires within and over the said province & people, inhabiting and being therein, by his Majesties gracious letters pattents, under the great seale of England." For such a violent preservation of whatever may be meant by Baltimore's "rights, prerogatives, and jurisdictions," he and all his officers are herewith to be publicly assured by the Provincial, who is to speak for the Council of Trent and the Pope of Rome, that the *Bulla Cœnæ* shall be dispensed with in their behalf, and the censures thereof shall not light upon them, "although they bee Roman Catholiques." And, to secure the proper machinery for the American duplicating of the English penal laws, the Provincial is made to declare that all acts "made or to be made" by the General Assembly of Maryland, and assented to by Cecil Lord Baltimore or his offspring, shall be perfectly wise and unimpeachable.

Third Point.

The Bulla Cœnæ and its operation.

Lewger's twenty Cases of two years before, which forecast, contained and illustrated all this style of jurisprudence with not a

[9] *Calvert Papers*, i. 194. Cf. *supra*, § 51, pp. 425, 426.

few concrete instances, supply the commentary for this point with several striking examples: to wit, that a General Assembly may "reform" all grants, whether to laymen or ecclesiastics, "resuming" property and rescinding contracts, "without a voluntary surrender or resignation of them [the graunts] by the religious;" that such an Assembly "may make lawes to dispose of the interest and rights of particular persons, as, namely, of clergymen, not being present, nor having proxies in such Parliament or Assembly (though lawfully summoned there unto), nor otherwise holding synods provinciall, wherein theyr consents to such lawes might be expected;" and again that "for any offences against the peace and dignity of the Lord Proprietour," the nature of that dignity not being defined, a "secular judge, being Catholick," may "proceed to the tryall and punishment" of priests "without the incurring of *Bulla Cœnæ*." [10]

The facts which Baltimore was contemplating at the time in England, as the sampler to be copied in Maryland, were quite patent.

The English sampler of penal administration.
Charles I. had repeatedly given orders to the judges, magistrates, and bishops, to enforce the penal laws against priests and Jesuits. Apprehensions had followed, and convictions. One victim died on the scaffold, others perished in prison, some were exiled, while others again were let

[10] Lewger's *Cases*, Nos. 16, 20, 18.—*Documents*, I. No. 11.—In the policy of the second and third out of the Four Points, Baltimore's statements underwent some modification.

1. In the second he avoided mentioning the Statutes of Mortmain, which had been the salient feature in his new Conditions of Plantation (*supra*, § 62). So, too, he omitted all mention of them in his draft of a Surrender or Assignment to be made over to himself by the Provincial (*infra*, § 66 (1)). But in his draft of a Concordat, which belonged to a later date, he returned to the said Statutes absolutely, without any qualification, merely citing those that were now in force in England, *quæ hoc tempore in Anglia vim obtinent* (*Documents*, I. No. 22, 2°); that is to say, both the pre-Reformation and the post-Reformation Statutes, the latter rendering utterly impossible the acquisition of land for Catholic uses, which were now called in legal parlance "superstitious" uses. Finally, in the Conditions of Plantation promulgated in 1648 and 1649, he introduced by his own authority the Statutes of Mortmain, but limited them to such as were pre-Reformation, "the Statutes of Mortmayne heretofore made in the Kingdom of England at any time before the reign of Henry the Eighth who was King of that Realm" (*Proceedings of the Council*, 1636-1667, p. 227, § 12; p. 236, § 10)—a series of statutes which only regulated the acquisition of land for Catholic ecclesiastical uses (*infra*, Appendix C, §§ 75, 76). This is the mortmain which entered into Maryland jurisprudence; and its mode of entry was neither technically nor substantially legal.

2. As to the third of the Four Points, that on the subject of penal laws being set in operation against priests, Baltimore introduced a modification in his draft of a Concordat, to the effect that he and his officers were not to apply such penal provisions against the persons of priests "at the instance of any Catholic," *ob ullius catholici petitionem*, except under the conditions of legal procedure which alone could obtain in Catholic countries (*Documents*, I. No. 22, 3°).

Here may be noted again what has been sufficiently discerned in other ways, that, whenever Cecil Lord Baltimore and John Lewger presume to speak of Catholic ways and the Catholic Church, there is an air of unreality about what they say or imply, which of itself would indicate that neither was a Catholic, though both called themselves so, and one or other no doubt thought he was so.

out on bail.[11] At this very date, Archbishop Laud and the Bishop of Rochester, in quality of judges of the High Commission Court, published a letter, ordering the apprehension of priests and of those who harboured priests, of those found in possession of papistical books, with a long category of other iniquitous persons that followed their conscience, heard Mass, had their children baptized or brought up in the Catholic faith, etc.[12]

There can be no mistaking the immediate objective point of Baltimore's manœuvres. The only doubt arises as to the ulterior good it would have done him, had he attained his object. It is not to be supposed that persecution on its own merits was attractive to him, seeing that he posed as a Catholic himself. Nor could there be any question of criminality on the part of the missionaries, who were held in the highest esteem, and personally were treated with great respect by the Governor and the secretary. Nevertheless, in all his roll of papers he harped upon the application of corporal punishment and of capital punishment to the priests. It was clearly a question of penal laws under their penal aspect.

Not to theorize vainly, we must needs interpret him by his subsequent acts. His deeds of violence performed or commanded, without the help of legislation which failed him, and without a Provincial's proclamation which was refused him, point to a double ulterior object in view, one political, the other economical. The political scope, in view of dangerous times coming, was that he might have those ready and ear-marked whom he could throw out at a moment's notice to the Parliamentary wolves pursuing him, and so purchase immunity for himself. And thus he wrote in the next year to his brother Leonard: "For ought you know some accident might have hapned here that it was no injustice in mee to refuse them grants of anie land at all." [13] He might have added, more explicitly, that in his opinion it could be no injustice in him to throw other people bodily to the wolves or waves, if that was the way for himself to make good his escape or to weather a storm. The economical scope was that of enjoying perfect impunity when he made free with the clergy's property, in such a manner as this History has partly shown and will yet show still more.

Reasons for engrafting penal laws on Maryland.

[11] Cf. Lingard, *History of England*, viii. chap. iv. 182, A.D. 1631.—*Ibid.*, 186, note, A.D. 1634, from Laud's Diary.
[12] Cf. *Ibid.*, 223, A.D. 1640.—Cf. a Latin translation of the letter, "Lamberch," July 2, 1640, in the Barberini papers. P. R. O., *Transcripts from Rome*, xvi. 3 pp. 4to.
[13] *Calvert Papers*, i. 220, *med.*

Finally, the fourth and last of Baltimore's Points treats of testamentary and matrimonial causes. Instead of following the policy of the third Point, it reverses the system, and propounds a policy diametrically opposite. In the third, which regarded the secularization and persecution of clergymen, the custom of England had been set up as the model and standard. In this fourth Point, the custom of England is distinctly rejected and reversed. There was no pecuniary profit in it, if causes testamentary and causes matrimonial remained, according to English custom and Christian usage generally, in the hands of ecclesiastics. Hence his lordship propounds that "untill some ecclesiasticall court be established within the said province with the Lord Baltimores consent," all the matter concerning matrimony and testaments, not only the mixed matter which involves temporal questions—as the laity, with George Calvert among them, had formerly explained to the Bishop of Chalcedon [14]—but some that is purely Sacramental and Divine, shall pass into lay hands. And, for the indefinite usurpation throughout all the time that shall elapse till Baltimore "consents" to the establishment of a competent ecclesiastical authority, the Jesuit Provincial is herewith made to declare that neither the Proprietary nor his officers incur any censures of the *Bulla Cœnæ* or any responsibility in conscience.

Fourth Point.

The commentary supplied here by Lewger's Cases shows that the exclusion of authority as vested in a bishop or other Ordinary was the object of the policy underlying this Point; for a series of those Cases goes to impugn the whole doctrine of England and Christendom at large, relative to the exclusive competence of ecclesiastical courts for such matters.[15] Another series of those Cases trenches on matter that is unmixed or purely ecclesiastical, and even on what is of right Divine. Thus Lewger's seventh Case makes a will superstitious and void if it contains a profession of the Catholic faith, or gives legacies for Masses to be said in the interest of the testator. His eighth sequestrates for profane uses of the State the residue of property designed by the practice of Christendom to pious uses, that is, purposes charitable or religious. His ninth Case annuls the articles of a will bequeathing landed property to the clergy. His eleventh, on matrimony, takes over the publishing of banns, the defining of degrees of consanguinity, questions of divorce. His twelfth meddles with the natural law, and the right

[14] Cf. *supra*, § 11, pp. 204, 205.
[15] *Cases*, 3, 4, 5, 6.—See *Documents*, I. No. 11.

of apprentices to marry, and proposes penalties for "priest or minister solemnizing such mariage," and makes a profession of ignorance "whether such a law be against the liberty of mariage?" The thirteenth enters into the purely Divine order of vowing chastity to God, and means to stop all that by barring "the female from inheriting or houlding of lands, unlesse they marry within a tyme limited" by Mr. Lewger, Cecil Calvert, and the rest of an impeccable and omnipotent local Parliament.[16]

As far as Lewger's Cases or Baltimore's fourth Point impugned the authority of an Ordinary, they did not concern the missionaries. But, since the Catholic conscience was under their direction, the missionaries were just then the great moral power in the colony. And the crime of "troubling consciences" would call imperatively for that large equipment of penal authority which Baltimore sued for from the Provincial, and hoped to receive in virtue of the third Point duly signed. *The moral power then in the colony.* In fact, this moral influence of theirs was a subject about which he was complaining in England; for we find that the chief manager of his intruding body of clergy reported this very grievance as a justification for intruding into Maryland. Said George Gage to the Bishop of Chalcedon (July 21, 1642), when proposing that Gilmett and the others should go without authorization if they could not procure any: "Indeed, it seemes here, that the soules ther must be limited only to Jes[uits]: for theyr confessors; wheras over all the woorld people have liberty to choose what confessarius they please. Besides the case is ther very speciall, in regard the governors find the Jes[uits]: to oppose them openly even in matters of temporalityes; and soe find it a kind of tyranny to bee obliged to use only them for gouvernement of theyr soules, whoe *in temporalibus* are at variance with them."[17]

(2) Father Knott, the Provincial, sent a copy of the Baltimore Points to the Nuncio Extraordinary at Cologne, Mgr. Rosetti, with the letter already quoted (November 17, 1641), calling his attention at the same time to the annexed *Notanda*, or the Provincial's own Observations.[18] In the course of his Observations, Knott sketched Lewger's *dogmata*, or tenets,[19] and attached a draft of that gentleman's twenty Cases reduced to nine main queries in Latin.[20] *(2) The Provincial's Observations and conclusion.*

[16] *Cases*, 7 seqq.—*Documents*, I. No. 11.
[17] London, Catholic Chapter MSS., 1598-1653, No. 159.—See *Documents*, I. No. 20.—*Infra*, § 65.
[18] Vatican Archives, *Nunziatura d'Inghilterra*, 4, ff. 80-83.—*Documents*, I. No. 16.
[19] *Notandum* 7.
[20] *Ibid.*, ff. 78, 79.—Stonyhurst MSS., *Anglia, A*, iv. 108c, ff. 202, 203: *Quæstiones*

The critique contained in the Provincial's ten Observations on Baltimore's four Points could scarcely be more exhaustive and complete. Then follows the conclusion to this effect: That the Fathers of the Society have declined to sign the document. But, if prudent and disinterested persons, and especially the Sovereign Pontiff, who is supreme judge in such matters, consider that the Fathers may licitly and with a safe conscience affix their signature to what the baron exacts, they will find no difficulty in doing so. If, on the contrary, the demands shall be considered inadmissible, then may it please such authorities to state as much, and to declare that neither is it lawful for others to affix their signature and approve of the baron's exactions. "Meanwhile, the missionaries of the Society have been the only labourers thus far engaged in tilling this vineyard of the Lord. By God's grace, they have produced some fruit, and are looking for more as time goes on, especially among the infidels, with the help of Him whose helpers they are, and who, while others plant and water, does alone give the increase."

The Provincial continues: "Two Fathers have succumbed to their labours; also two brothers. There remain still in Maryland three Fathers, to assist whom three others were appointed this year. But the Right Honourable Baron has permitted one only to set out, and that with great difficulty. May Jesus favour with His grace and suggest those counsels to his lordship, which shall be most useful for the Divine glory and the propagation of the faith. If this be the result, whatever be the way, the Society will see its wishes fulfilled."

Baltimore's embargo on Jesuit missionaries.

That last sentiment, intimating indifference as to whatever might be the way, means among other things that Father Knott was ready, if the General authorized it, to suppress the whole Jesuit Mission in Maryland, leaving the ground free for the new-comers. For, just five days after the foregoing letter and documents were transmitted to the Nuncio, he wrote to the General (November 22, 1641) suggesting as an alternative measure the total suppression of the Mission. The General replied (December 21)—

General on abandoning Maryland. Dec., 1641.

"I have received the catalogues which your Reverence sent on the 15th of November, and what you despatched just afterwards on the 22nd of the same month, about the Maryland Mission. The controverted points I will take time to examine, and then I will answer what the occasion

quædam, propositæ a D. Leugar, Secretario Ill^{mi} D. Baronis de quo fit mentio in Notandis, No. 7.

requires. As to the suggestion of breaking up that Mission which has cost ours so much labour, I should be sorry to admit of it, so long as there is hope of gaining souls even at the cost of patience under difficulties. However, if, to obviate greater inconveniences, it becomes necessary to take that step, seeing that secular priests are sailing to the colony, I leave the matter entirely to your prudent judgment." [21]

(3) The manuscripts which the General undertook to examine were no doubt the very same which lie in the Stonyhurst Archives to-day. There is with them an additional document drawn up for a Cardinal " on behalf of the Provincial of the Society of Jesus in England, in the business of Maryland." [22] It is clearly a Memorial for the Holy Office or Inquisition, and the date would seem to be just after the New Year, 1642. The Cardinal in question was probably Francis Barberini, Secretary of State; and the Memorial was intended to bring the question to a final issue with the Sovereign Pontiff, who acted officially as President of the Holy Office or Congregation of the Inquisition. In this paper some new facts appear.

(3) The Holy Office. Barberini, Protector.

It is said that when two Fathers had first gone over to Maryland, "as it were by way of reconnoitring the ground," and had found the fields white for the harvest, " there was presented a few years ago to Cardinal [Francis] Barberini, Protector [of England], a geographical description of that province, with an humble petition that he would be pleased to take under his protection the Fathers who had travelled thither no less than the others who were in England, to the effect that the whole enterprise might excite as little notice as possible,[23] and give no offence to the State authorities in England." This must have meant that the Cardinal, by his diplomatic influence at the Court of Charles I., was to cause the Jesuit establishment in Maryland to be quietly ignored.

After a rapid view of the events which followed, the memorialist comes to John Lewger and his principles, of which he gives specimens, the last being as follows: "That in the General Assembly or Parliament there is vested such a degree of authority over the property of individuals, as to strip any one of everything, even of his shirt, if that be for the service of the State. Other tenets of the same stamp which were comprised in

The Cases before the Holy Office.

---

[21] General Archives S.J., *Anglia, Epist. Gen.*—Documents, I. No. 5, T.
[22] Stonyhurst MSS., *Anglia A*, iv. 108K, ff. 222, 223.—Documents, I. No. 18.
[23] " Quam secretissime."

twenty questions [or Cases] drawn up by the same Mr. Leugar, were submitted to this Sacred Congregation by the hands of the Secretary." [24]

Coming to the campaign instituted against the Fathers for not submitting to Lewger's doctrine, the memorialist arrives at the violent seizure of Mattapany by Baltimore, a property which the King of Patuxent, at that time a catechumen, " had given to the Fathers with the express condition of its maintaining priests, who should be bound to instruct his people in the true knowledge, faith, and worship of God. Then, having found certain persons to abet him in his opinions, the said baron began to consider how he might turn the Fathers of the Society out of Maryland and put others in their places, men who would suit the humour of his secretary somewhat better.

"Accordingly, last year he managed to have a petition presented to the Sacred Congregation of the Propaganda, in the name of the Catholics of Maryland, requesting that faculties might be granted to a prefect and priests of the secular clergy for that mission, without saying a word of the labours of the Jesuit Fathers in that harvest, nor stating the reasons which led him to get new priests in their place." From this statement of the Memorial, made to one who was in a position to verify its truth, we learn that, besides the other affirmations and assumptions in the petition for a new clergy,[25] there was also this implication of its having come from the Maryland Catholics, on whom, if it were eventually rejected, the discredit would of course fall; or, as Baltimore had said so well to Windebank on another occasion, when sending his brother-in-law Peasely to conduct an intrigue about Virginia, he did "presume" to propose the business in such a way that, said he, "the refusall of it in that way will, I conceive, be less prejudiciall to me."[26] Here the prejudice would light upon the far-off Maryland Catholics. And, if his name had to be mentioned, then another principle of his, so well expressed to Strafford, came into play: "a fair and probable expectation of good success," he said, "however without any danger of any great prejudice unto myself, in respect that others are joined with me in the adventure."[27]

The Memorial continues: "To find a new occasion for having the

[24] Card. G. B. Pamphilj [?], afterwards Innocent X.
[25] Above, § 61, pp. 493, 494.
[26] *Proceedings of the Council of Maryland*, 1636–1667, p. 42.—See above, § 45, p. 376.
[27] Cf. J. T. Scharf, *History of Maryland*, i. 68.—See above, § 24, p. 264.

Fathers of the Society withdrawn from the colony, he had certain Points propounded to the Provincial, which in like manner were submitted to this Sacred Congregation [of the Holy Office] by the hands of the secretary. The Provincial was to sign these Points in his own name and in that of the Maryland Fathers. *The Points before the Holy Office.*

"Meanwhile, the Sacred Congregation of the Propaganda, being entirely ignorant of these matters, assented to the petition, and, in the course of August in the year 1641, faculties were despatched by the Sacred Congregation of the Holy Office, and were forwarded to Mgr. Rosetti, now Archbishop of Tarsus.

"However, it is possible that the prefect has not been appointed yet, or that the faculties have not been delivered, but are still, it is hoped, in the hands of Father Philips, the English Queen's confessor. In that case, the aforesaid Provincial most humbly supplicates your Eminence to give orders that the said faculties be suspended and sent back, if they have not gone into effect, or, if they have been delivered, that the departure of the new priests be put off awhile, till the Apostolic See determine what is to be done for the good of souls." *Recalling the new faculties, etc.*

Here the Memorial closes with a profession of perfect submission, as in the Observations made to Rosetti, calling attention to the unreasonableness of turning out men "who were the first to enter that vineyard at their own expense; who have borne poverty and trials for seven years; who have lost four of their men, while labouring with fidelity at their posts even unto death; who have maintained sound doctrine and the immunity of the Church, putting up with the odium and damages thence resulting; who know the country and language of the savages; whereof the priests to be substituted by the Baron of Baltimore are utterly ignorant, with the further circumstance that these latter are going over to countenance and maintain a system of doctrine from which contentions and scandals are sure to arise, and that spark of faith will certainly be quenched which has just been kindled in the hearts of the infidels. Still the Fathers declare that they are ready with all submissiveness either to return from Maryland to England, or to stay there and labour unto death for the faith and for the dignity of the Apostolic See, according as it shall seem good to the prudence, condescension, and charity of your Eminence." In this closing sentence the memorialist intimates that the Fathers are not unwilling, if they be so ordered, to work in the same field with others; as in the case of the St. Christopher Mission, at this same time, we have heard the Procurator-General of the Society observe that it is not unheard of in the Church of God for two sets of priests to work in the same field.[28] But a certain repugnance is shown to seeing the Fathers expelled with injury and ignominy from Maryland, as the efforts of some people were ever bent on effecting in England also. This was a menial service, in which the good Queen Henrietta herself was engaged by those who had her ear.[29]

§ 64. While the Provincial, with his mind perfectly clear on the merits of the question, was carrying the issue to Rome, Dr. De Bois, known most favourably in Catholic and scholastic theology as Francis Silvius (Sylvius), indited an answer or opinion on the subject from the seminary at Doway, under date of November 28, 1641. He treats all the doubts and queries on the ground of pure ethics and natural right; and he reviews a set of answers already suggested or offered, but now presented to him for revision. Analyzing the charter of Maryland, the reasoning based thereon, and the solution already given entirely in favour of Baltimore's claim, Francis Silvius decides on every point against the Proprietary's assumption to be the sole hand or sole consignee of land, as between the Indian aborigines and the whites of his province.

Silvius on the Indian land question.

But in the presentation of the case, with its reasons for uncertainty or doubting, and its queries based thereupon, there is no statement of that circumstance which separated the interests of the missionaries from those of all other whites, and which precluded their action or case from being used as a precedent by any one else. This circumstance was the distinct condition that the mission lands in question were given to them by Indian proprietors for the service of the Indians themselves. And, had this not been distinct

---

[28] *Supra,* § 31, p. 310.
[29] Cf. Oxford, Bodleian Library; *Calendar of Clarendon Papers,* i. 73, 74. Secret instructions for Captain Arthur Brett, sent to Rome by our dearest Consort the Queen. Hampton Court, Oct. 28, 1635: ". . . To get the Jesuits recalled from England, or the King must put the penalties of the law in force against them . . ." Here, too, according to the Panzani gossip, the irrepressible Price appears, still on the track of the Jesuits: "*Ho saputo, che il Vuindibanch ha detto al Bret, che potrà confidarsi con l'agente de' Benedittini in Roma, il che sarà stato per opera del Padre Leandro o del Padre Prisei Benedettino molto favorito d'esso Vuindebanch. Gl'istessi hanno fatto istanza al Bret, che volesse pigliare per segretario un loro confidente, il quale è anche confidentissimo de' Giesuiti; ma egli non l'ha voluto, havendo ricevuto ordine espresso dal Re di non s'intrigare in modo alcuno con li Giesuiti.*" Vatican Archives, *Nunziatura d'Inghilterra,* 5, f. 132; Panzani, London, November 21, 1635 [to Barberini].

§ 64] *MANDATE AGAINST THE NEW CLERGY* 519

as a condition of the gift, still it was understood by the terms of Baltimore's original *Declaratio Coloniæ*, or *Account of the Colony*, as well as by his first Instructions to the Commissioners (November 15, 1633),[1] in both of which the ministry of Christianizing the natives, with its ways and means, was put always in the first place, apart from everything else. In the case submitted to the Doway theologian there is no mention of this circumstance. Hence the opinion of Silvius, peremptory though it be, would be more so if the full state of the question had been presented.

As this hitherto unnoticed paper of Silvius is unique on the North American question, dating from a time prior to the accretions of positive law, and free from the fictions and contradictions with which that law is so grievously affected, we reserve it for a fuller statement in conjunction with Suarez, Chancellor Kent, and others.[2] Meanwhile, judging by the place where we find it, that is, in the Archives of Westminster,[3] we infer that it was duly received by those persons in London who had submitted the case to Doway.

Though for Baltimore this unfavourable opinion only accentuated the necessity of his obtaining from the Jesuits themselves a title to keep the property of which he had relieved them, the mere declaration of a moral point by a theologian had no practical effect whatever on the new expedition and its promoters. They went on their way, either knowing nothing about it or ignoring it. It was not what they wanted. Baltimore's ship of more than royal state, manned with cheerful volunteers, was sailing with a full breeze through the narrows of ecclesiastical jurisprudence. The result was a dramatic crisis: two Sacred Congregations in Rome, within two weeks, issuing two contradictory decrees on the same subject; and, worse than that, the lesser following and contradicting the greater. For, of all the bureaus in Rome, the greatest is that of the Holy Office, presided over by the Pope.

On the first day of February, then, just about the time when the Memorial in Father Knott's name could have been received and appreciated, the great Congregation of the Holy Office or Inquisition despatched an order quickly to Mgr. Rosetti at Cologne. It was conveyed in a letter from Cardinal Francis Barberini, Secretary of State and Protector of England. The Cardinal reviewed the antecedent orders given, by the authority of

Decree of the Holy Office. Feb. 1, 1642.

---

[1] See above, § 19, pp. 250, 251.
[2] Appendix B, §§ 72, 73.—*Documents*, I. No. 17.
[3] Westminster Diocesan Archives, xxx. No. 28.

His Holiness, since the 8th day of August last. Then he proceeded to rescind all in these precise terms—

"Considerations of the gravest import [4] have now come before us, on account of which His Holiness and these my eminent colleagues have thought right to send you word, that, if you have not put in execution what was already enjoined for effectuating that mission, you desist from any further action till you receive new instructions; and, in case you have consigned the same faculties to some other person to execute the commission, that you will be pleased to give precise orders that no steps be taken in any way whatsoever, but that persons wait for new orders from yourself. In short, through your prompt action, we desire to have the mission put off, until such time as this Sacred Congregation shall have examined some points, and determined that which is best to do for the greater service of God ever blessed, and for the propagation of the holy faith." [5]

Soon after, on the fourteenth day of the same February, 1642, Cardinal [Antonio] Barberini, who by the November decree of the Propaganda had been deputed to report on the mission of the fourteen priests to Maryland with a prefect, now presented his statement; and the Sacred Congregation passed a new decree in these terms—

Contradictory Decree of the Propaganda. Feb. 14, 1642.

"On the report of his Eminence Cardinal Barberini regarding the decree of the 12th day of November last about the mission to Maryland, the Sacred Congregation ordered a copy thereof to be forwarded to Mgr. Rosetti, to hear his opinion on the appointment of the prefect for the said mission, on the associates to be given him, and the manner of proceeding with the business, so that the letters patent with the requisite faculties may be issued, and a prefect and missionaries be deputed for the aforesaid Maryland." Signed autograph: "Franciscus Ingolus." [6]

Within about a month from the issuing of these two orders, Mgr. Rosetti had the rare pleasure of receiving both of them. He wrote (March 9, 1642) to the Cardinal Secretary of State, Francis Barberini—

Rosetti's dilemma.

"... Your Eminence was pleased to command me, by a letter from the Sacred Congregation of the Holy Office, to suspend the execution of further measures in the affair of Maryland. Now I am in receipt of a letter from the Sacred

---

[4] "*Gravissimi rispetti.*"
[5] Vatican Archives, *Nunziatura d'Inghilterra*, 4, f. 84.—*Documents*, I. No. 19, H.
[6] Propaganda Archives, *Acta*, 15, *Cong.* 285, No. 35, f. 33.—Vatican Archives, as above, f. 57; a copy among the Rosetti papers.—*Documents*, I. No. 19, J.

Congregation of the Propaganda, by which I am commanded to give information about subjects qualified for that mission, with a view to establishing the same. I humbly beg to inform your Eminence of all this, that I may carry out any orders which you shall be pleased to send."[7]

From March till the latter end of July the convoy of new missionaries waited for the faculties, which they understood Count Rosetti to have. But the faculties never came. Then they lost all patience. And, thanks to this circumstance, we begin to learn something definite about them.

§ 65. George Gage, *alias* Francis Hoard, was a secular clergyman engaged in the English ministry. A few years later than this (1646) he is known to have been secretary to what was called the Chapter of the English Clergy.[1] He is also said by some[2] to have been Vicar-General for a district in England, on behalf of the Right Rev. Richard Smith, Bishop of Chalcedon, who had been formerly Vicar-Apostolic of England till the time of his resignation in 1632.[3] After the acceptance of that resignation by the Sovereign Pontiff,[4] the Right Rev. Richard Smith had no more to do with licences or faculties in England, with Vicars-General or ecclesiastical districts there, than he had with similar attributions in Turkey or China; and any intrusion on his part into ecclesiastical government would differ but little from that of an Anglican at Canterbury or a Jansenist at Utrecht. Nevertheless, in the long letter which we shall briefly summarize here, leaving the text for another place,[5] he is applied to, ten years after he has ceased to have faculties or licences himself, for the favour of a licence at his hands, authorizing an expedition of the clergy to intrude upon Maryland, and that in express defiance of Rome.[6] To him, then in France, where Dr. Smith remained in exile all the rest of his life, the Rev. Mr. Gage wrote in the following sense on July 21, 1642, more than four months after Rosetti had received the final countermand from Cardinal Francis Barberini.

Gage and the Bishop of Chalcedon.

[7] Vatican Archives, *Nunziatura di Colonia*, 21, 1642, March 9.—Cf. P. R. O., *Transcripts from Rome*, xxi. f. 414.—*Documents*, I. No. 19, K.
[1] C. Dodd, *Church History*, ii. 426.—J. Gillow, *Bibliographical Dictionary*, s.v.
[2] The Rev. Secretary, custodian of the Old Brotherhood MSS., 1897.
[3] Cf. W. M. Brady, *Episcopal Succession*, iii. 79.
[4] Cf. *supra*, § 15, p. 228.
[5] *Documents*, I. No. 20.
[6] On this usurpation of ecclesiastical authority, compare J. Gillow, *Bibliographical Dictionary*, etc., where, *ex. gr.*, s.v. "Leyburne, George, D.D." (iv. 222), the compiler betrays no acquaintance with the merits of the question; while s.v. "Smith, Richard, D.D.," the whole matter is passed over in silence (v. 512).

Gage wrote that his lordship knew of the proposed mission to Maryland; how the clergy in England had "been solicited" to undertake it; and how his lordship himself, being solicited in turn, had signified to the said clergy his "good likeing thereof." Faculties had been obtained from Rome; Count Rosetti was to give the approval, when the clergy had made the recommendation of fit persons; the Rev. Mr. Mus[kett, President of Doway College], was to choose a fit prefect and commend him to the said Nuncio; and, when all this had been exactly performed, and Mr. Benson had written several letters to Rosetti, and "our friends in court and myne" were all importuning the Nuncio for an answer, and, says Gage, the "Lord of that Province [Maryland] now calls uppon us for our men," never during two months has a single word come from Mgr. Rosetti in reply. The person named for approval and confirmation is Mr. Gilmett; the time for the sailing of the ships is now six weeks hence; three clergymen are ready for the voyage, "and six or seven familyes resolved to accompany Mr. Gilmett thether in pure zeale to that apostolical man, resolving to sett up theyr rests wher hee imployes his spiritual labours." So they have come to the point now that they must either "damnify notoriously" Lord Baltimore by not giving him the bonus of six or seven families for his colony, or they must "goe thether in virtue only of our owne facultyes, because the Count will not confer the newe [*i.e.* the Indian faculties] uppon any of ours going thether; which wee conceive to proceed out of the Jes[uits'] indeavours, whoe use all meanes possible, not only to oppose the clergy in this businesse, but even to suppresse and keep under the temporal lord of that province, that they may ther have the more absolute rule and power."

The clerical grievances.

So far Gage has expounded the state of the clerical grievance; and we see in what light Lord Baltimore had been exhibiting the Maryland Jesuits, and how he had told his story. We also observe the circumstance that the Jesuits "oppose the clergy" in the Maryland business. It is not the clerical expedition that is opposing the Jesuits and intruding into a place where it has no legitimate footing whatever. The writer continues—

His lordship of Chalcedon is desired to say whether the faculties which these clergymen have for England alone will not suffice for Maryland, since they can procure none others. If the subjects of our own nation over there in America "voluntarily require our assistance in theyr spiritualls," have we not the power and jurisdiction by that very fact? We believe

Faculties without reference to Rome.

that we have, for these reasons: First, there is no bishop over there; therefore we have. Secondly, because our faculties mention only England distinctly; but they "extend to all his majestyes dominions" indistinctly. Thirdly, if the King conquered a country and took us with his army, we should have faculties for the army, and besides for everybody else in the country conquered; and now, in this case, there is no army, there is no conquered people, there is only "a peaceable possession;" wherefore "wee see noe difficulty why the clergy, beeing calld uppon may not (with owt speciall recourse to Rome or licence thence) goe, and exercise theyr functions;" not to mention the temporal advancement or temporal damnification of the lord of that province, by giving him or not giving what he might thus get and what we were arranging *bonâ fide* for so long a time—but all "now hindered by underhand practises of the Jes[uits].

"If therfore your lordship please to approve heer of, it is the clergyes humble sute [suit] at the instance of the Lord of that Province, that you will vouchsafe your licence to such of our bretheren as are ready and willing to go thether; namely to Mr. Gilmett as superiour and two more, such as hee shall best like of seven or eight proposed unto him for his assistants in this service;" and, continues Gage, great urgency is pleaded. The writer proceeds now to set at naught both the Nuncio and Rome—

Licence from Chalcedon instead of Rome. Reasons.

"And many of our bretheren are of opinion that, when the Count sees the clergy is gon thether with theyr owne facultyes independent of him, hee will soone send them order to exercise the newe ones, and approove of such men for the use therof as we shal have sent thether; beecause it will bee more for his honor to have us ther dependent on him then independent. And it seemes (with men carryed agaynst us by the suggestions of our adversaryes), wee must rather use our owne right as farr as wee may, then sett expecting grace and favour from them, which wee stand not in need of; in soe much that many are of opinion, it had been better for us never to have asked any newe facultyes at all, but to have gon thether (beeing called to the harvest of our owne nation) in vertue of our owne facultyes." Then follows the plea quoted before, regarding the oppressed consciences of the colonists and of the "governors" in Maryland, constrained as these are at present to "use only them for gouvernement of theyr soules whoe *in temporalibus* are at variance with them." This last touch of refined consideration, on behalf of delicate consciences, might seem to be from Lord Baltimore himself, whose susceptibility to scruples could have suggested this trait of sympathy, as his fidelity to facts had supplied the elements of Maryland history in this paper.

The last paragraph of Gage's letter exhibits his lordship of Baltimore as playing the same part which we have seen him affect in his letters to Windebank and Strafford; that of using others while hiding his own hand. He now invites the Bishop of Chalcedon to lend him a helping hand; and he makes Gage say:

In Lord Baltimore's name.

"Thus your lordship sees the whole state of the affayre. Please, I beseech you, to oblige the temporal lord of that province (whoe yet dares not write him self in his owne affayre), and your humble servants the clergy heere, by your speedy resolution heerin." [7]

Three weeks later Mgr. Rosetti had heard of the new scheme in England; and he wrote to the Cardinal, saying that Father Philips, the Queen's confessor, had informed him by letter of the pressure which they were bringing to bear in order to secure the faculties for Maryland; "and it seems that, if these do not come to hand quickly, he says they have a mind to use their ordinary faculties, which are *pro dominiis regiis Magnæ Britanniæ* [for the royal dominions of Great Britain]. I have answered him that, as he is on good terms of friendship with the said clergy, he had better persuade them to conform their conduct to what is right; bidding them remember that it is from Rome orders ought to come, and that they look before they leap." [8]

A few days after the receipt of this letter, the Cardinal replied; but, though he noted and answered other points, he took no notice of this.[9]

§ 66. Sir William Berkeley, Governor of Virginia, wrote on one occasion to the Secretary of State, Lord Arlington, saying that in their colony they lived after the simplicity of a past age; and, unless the dangers of the country gave to their fear tongues and a language, they should soon forget all sounds but those that concerned the business and necessities of the farms.[1] Amid these preoccupations of a colonial life, so narrow and monotonous, a letter from the old

[7] London, Catholic Chapter MSS., 1598-1653, No. 159.—*Documents*, I. No. 20.
[8] Vatican Archives, *Nunziatura di Colonia*, 22, 1642, August 10.—*Documents*, I. No. 19, L.
[9] *Ibid.*, 1642, August 20.—Along with these matters there is not a little in the same volume of ciphers relative to the affairs of the Duke of Parma and other Italian princes and barons, touched on in so cavalier-like a fashion by the English baron; Nov. 28, 1642. *Calvert Papers*, i. 218, 219. Cf. *infra*, § 66 (2), note 27.
[1] Cf. P. R. O., *Calendar of State Papers, A. & W.I.*, ii. § 1193; A.D. 1666, May 1.

country, coming by an odd ship now and then, was an attraction, a recreation, a dissipation, beyond anything that files of newspapers can be to us. And so it came to pass that, as there was no public service to protect a mail, the letters entrusted to captains, and entrusted by captains to any one who might make them reach their destination, were snatched up, opened and read as common property. This was an evil common in the colonial period. *Breaking the seals of letters.* And we note the allusion to it and the suggestion made in a letter from Jamaica: "A grand mechiefe to every person or merchant in there letters from there corespondents, which every man takes up & open stiffles as they please; if an office from my lord were establisht for receipt of all letters, both comeing in and out, it would well satisfie the people." [2] Apparently in a sense kindred to this, Father Andrew White wrote to Lord Baltimore in 1639 (February 20), that his provisional return to England for a year would be, said he, "to very good purpose, as well [as] humbly to represent sundry things unto your lordship, which I dare not committ to letters, which are no better than blabs." [3]

At the time of White's so-called "blabs," there were no heavy clouds threatening to break over the Mission. Now there were. And the fact was that, as Father Copley may have divined, the missionaries were practically prisoners in the hands of the Calverts, in a way and for purposes which we shall soon detect;—the one Calvert being an agent of the other, and seemingly an unwilling one; who through the encumbrance of too much personal probity fell short of the other's expectations, as the latter let him know. There could be little doubt but that the letters of the missionaries were liable to inspection, at least from the time when they personally came under surveillance.

To this combination of circumstances we refer Copley's petition in a letter to the General, as far back as March 3, 1642, desiring authorization for a journey to Rome; and from the General's statement in reply, that he did not understand the reasons for such a request, we must infer that Copley had felt it unsafe to speak distinctly even in Latin, and only so far as to develop his petition. The General's answer is dated September 6; and, after expressions of congratulation and condolence on the good and the bad, the fair and the foul weather in the Mission, he approves of the Father's having consulted him about such a step as that of a voyage to Rome, and then courteously waves it aside; for he cannot see what urgency

[2] *Ibid.*, iii. § 231: Richard Browne to Williamson, 1670, August 11.
[3] *Calvert Papers*, i. 203.

there is which may not be met by written correspondence, especially when the absence of one from Maryland would tell so severely on the two missionaries left. He recommends Copley, therefore, to communicate often with the Provincial, who will not be wanting in vigilance. His Paternity is waiting with all eagerness for the Annual Letter. He sends his best wishes to Fathers White and Rigbie.[4]

Meanwhile, on discovering that the whole Roman plot was addled, Baltimore lost all control of himself. The first scene which we are privileged to witness is that of the Peaselys and his lordship; Anne, Mrs. William Peasely, being his own sister. The second is a panorama rather than a single scene, where the cautious gentleman, who could usually hide his hand so well, has betrayed his whole character in a letter to Leonard, covering ten pages octavo in print. The last scene comprises some high-handed acts in a matter of buying and selling, and of obstructing the course of justice, lest redress should be obtained. Since many of these matters appear in American publications, and some of them have been sharply animadverted upon by American writers, we feel dispensed from doing more than stating them, and referring to other published sources. But the conjunction of all these circumstances, as put together and placed aside of the new documents which we have contributed, is of the highest importance for following the course of this history.

A new setting of historical facts.

(1) During a year or two, the Provincial had been providing substitutes for the places left vacant in Maryland. In 1640 his call for volunteers had elicited those twenty-three offers which have been already reported, besides others not comprised in that series. Several men were selected, and deputed to go thither in 1641. Baltimore stopped them in London; and with great difficulty was induced to let one, Father Roger Rigbie, pass his new bureau of inspection, or custom-house.[5] At the same time, he had arranged for the erection of a similar bureau at the Maryland end of navigation, for keeping the men in the province just so long as they might be needed—then to be despatched without ceremony. While thus excluding the other two missionaries deputed with Rigbie for Maryland, his lordship represented at Rome, in the petition of 1641, how destitute the plantation was in point of missionary service, and how it stood in

---

[4] General Archives S.J., *Anglia, Epist. Gen.*, 1642, September 6.—*Documents*, I. 6, A.

[5] Knott's Letter and Observations, *supra*, § 63, pp. 506, 514.

need of men. The Roman plot evolved; and now, when a year later it was time for the winter convoy to depart, as George Gage has mentioned, Lord Baltimore found that his intruding clergy could not be qualified, and he was determined that the Jesuits should not be admitted.

Mr. Peasely, his brother-in-law and London agent, interposed; and wrote on the last day of September (1642) to Mr. Gervis, a Jesuit, stating the result of a conference with Baltimore. This last gentleman would allow of "the present employment of two of yours, as is desired;" but, adds Peasely, there are two conditions. One is that all his exactions shall be forthwith honoured, or, as the phrase stands in Peasely's letter, "that he shall have satisfaction in his just and reasonable demands, and, if it possibly may be, before their departure." The other is that he may inspect the gentlemen designated, speak with them, sound them; as Peasely says, "that he may judge of their disposition and fitness for such a work." Thus was notification conveyed to the Provincial that a bureau for the examination of recruits was established by Baltimore, to pass a final opinion on each candidate's qualifications, theological, canonical, political, and otherwise—"their disposition and fitness for such a work." An answer, said Peasely to Gervis, could easily be obtained from the Provincial Father Knott in time for the adjustment of all these matters before the next ship sailed.

(1) Peasely to Gervis. Sept. 30, Oct. 1, 1642.

The Mr. Gervis thus addressed would seem to have been Father Owen Shelley, procurator in London at that time, occupying much the same position as Copley had held some nine or ten years earlier.[6] The Provincial must have been on the Continent.

The very next day Mr. Peasely wrote again, reporting how Baltimore had suddenly sent word the night before that his mind was changed; how, on a personal interview this very morning, he was not to be moved. He was "stiff in his resolution, saying that he will prepare his demands within these few days;" and an answer from the Provincial might be obtained before a second ship went, a month or so from the present date. Said Peasely: "He is resolute

[6] Cf. Foley, *Records*, vii., *Collectanea*, s.v. "Shelley, Owen."—Cf. Stonyhurst MSS., *Anglia A*, vi. p. 472; where Father Lawrence Standish, writing from Grafton, January 22, 1659, to Mr. John Tirwhit, at "Mr. Brunals in Lincon Inne fields, London," says, in a postscript, "I have spoken to Mr. Jarvis and Mr. Beswick to send their Annualls [Annual Letters]." This was in the Worcestershire district, where Father Owen Shelley served then as a missionary. In the Catalogue for 1638 his office at London is distinctly mentioned : "*P. Odoënus Shellæus Procurator Provinciæ et Consultor Rectoris.*" General Archives, *Anglia, Catal.* 3, 1638, p. 1.

that none shall be sent untill he have satisfaction. This is the substance of all our discourse. I am sorry I have fayled in doing that good and service proposed."

The gentleman encloses Baltimore's note of the night before. It ends with the sentiment: "Howsoever, it was not my fault that the buisness is thus streightned in time; nor that it hath beene so, I wiss, other yeares in the same manner." This remark may allude to his having tried the bureau in the previous year, somewhat too late to be completely effectual in shutting the missionaries out of Maryland.

A lady now entered the lists, his sister Mrs. Peasely, who wrote on October 5, that she had simply wasted her time: "The particulars are not worth relating; for both of us talked too much, since the effect of our discourse proved no more to my content." She closes her note with a pious hope that God "will turn all things to the best;" she is sorry that she cannot wait in person upon her correspondent: "Our time," she says, "is so short and our business so much." This refers, no doubt, to the press of affairs on Mr. Peasely as agent, if not also to his own family interests in the plantation, which required immediate attention on the departure of the ship.[7]

Mrs. Peasely and Baltimore. Oct. 5, 1642.

In the midst of the opposition and disapproval which he encountered all round, from the Peaselys who openly remonstrated with him, from Governor Leonard who silently disregarded him even when ostensibly obeying him, from the Maryland Catholic gentry whose opinion and attitude had more weight with him than the sentiments of his whole family and the rights of all the Jesuits together, it may appear that the one thing which still put nerve into his stubbornness and made him even flighty in running to take up a stand still more obstinate, was some opinion of his or of his advisers, that he had the Jesuits now in his power, and now or never he must bring them to terms. Terms with them meant terms with the whole ecclesiastical body in the future, when not a Jesuit might be left in the province; and, if there were to be anything odious in the ecclesiastical status so arranged, the Jesuits, whether living or defunct, might bear the whole weight of the odium. He would have their signature, resigning ecclesiastical possessions and rights, retrospective and future.

But, more than his reckoning on Rome, his calculations about the

[7] Md.-N. Y. Province Archives, 2; original letters.—Cf. Woodstock Letters, ix. 91-93.

Fathers were completely at fault. Instead of finding in them men who were bent upon staying in Maryland at any price, he had to deal with a Provincial who just then had it in contemplation to withdraw all his men from the place. *Baltimore's, miscalculation.* And a few years later the General came to be of the same mind. Instead of prejudicing the condition of ecclesiastics who might follow them, they were already prepared, as the General had said to Knott in the previous December, to leave everything intact, that others might follow them, and live at peace, if peace and ease were possible for the Church where Cecil Lord Baltimore had anything to say.

The demands of his lordship, which he had told Peasely were so peremptory and indispensable, were indeed imperative and stringent; but they proved to be less indispensable than he thought. We consider them to be the same set of exactions which we find in a certain formula of Surrender or Assignment, drawn up by Baltimore, to be issued as letters patent in the name of the Provincial; the latter being represented therein as informing the world, in a lengthy legal statement, that, for honourable reasons locked up in his own breast, he herewith resigns to Baltimore's sole use and behoof all that the Church has ever acquired for pious uses, and all that the Society has ever acquired by any title in Maryland; and that it contents itself in the matter of right with what Baltimore directly, under his great seal, shall be pleased to accord. The solemn act begins thus—

"To all who shall read, hear, or see these presents, I - - -, Provincial of the Society of Jesus in the English Mission, wish everlasting well-being in the Lord." Then the Provincial is made to recount what he has heard about the acquisition by his men of property at the hands of Indians or other parties, without any interposition of his lordship's grant under the great seal; but he is made to leave out the circumstance that the said acquisition of property from the Indians was in trust for the said Indians' own service. And, in that connection, he is led to imply that Indians cannot dispose of their property, or that they have no property to dispose of, except under some grant or title of Baltimore's passed "legitimately or juridically" to them. The names of the property acquired or of the places in question are given: "Certain lands situated in a place which is called Maltapaniam;" certain "signories or manors, as they say, one of them called the domain or Manor of the Conception, another of St. Gregory, another, etc." Here it would seem that Baltimore's knowledge of localities *Preamble of the Surrender proposed by Baltimore.*

was indistinct; for **Mattapany** and **Conception Manor** were identical; nevertheless, his indistinctness of information did not lead him into any errors which might prejudice his claims to all, for he adds: "another, etc." The St. Gregory's mentioned we understand to designate Pascattoway; and, if there was any positive reason for alluding to "another, etcetera," it could only be the fact that a new missionary residence, rather as a substitute for Pascattoway, was being started at Portobacco. But no land was taken up there by 1642.

After this preamble, the Provincial is made to formulate the body of his act; the reasons for it being stated neither in the preamble nor **Body of the deed.** in the body, but being suffocated in a cloudy phrase about "various honourable causes and reasons."[8] It was by a similar accident of phrase, slipped into something else, that Baltimore had arranged for the disfranchisement of the laity by the Provincial's proclamation, in the great deed of the four Points;[9] ideas sidling into a document when they could not be risked by a direct statement. On the basis of this want of distinct reasons or considerations, the Provincial "grants, assigns, resigns, returns" all that he has acquired in the manner aforesaid; and it is extraordinary with what a luxuriance of phraseology Lord Baltimore, his heirs, any other person or persons—future grantees of his or theirs—are made to enter into the quiet and pacific possession and use of all such property as the "Society or the Church" has or can pretend to have, by whatsoever right, title, or interest.

That is the first step of self-abandonment. The Provincial must proceed now to the very extremity of unconditional surrender, divesting himself of the rights which Baltimore himself acknowledges to be good and legal. He cancels and resigns whatever right or title he may acquire or may have acquired, by treaty with other parties, through act of purchase or confidential trust, in lands legitimately granted heretofore or hereafter to be granted by the said Proprietary to any person whatsoever or to the Society itself. All this he abandons to Baltimore. There is only one thing that he retains, for himself, the Society, and, it is understood, for the Church. That is, purely and exclusively, the right which may have come or shall come direct from Baltimore under the great seal.

And thus by a side wind, without flying its colours, an exaggerated and unhistorical mortmain has sailed back again; the baldest kind

---

[8] "*Ob varias honestas causas et rationes.*"
[9] Above, § 63 (1), p. 508.

of a feudal dependency and servitude being imposed on free citizens, without a single feudal title being advanced by Baltimore, or an obligation assumed, or protection guaranteed; and without even this act of his being acknowledged by himself in the making.[10] *An exaggerated mortmain.*

At a period yet to come some while afterwards, when he was using a more modest tone with freemen, and had learnt by bitter experience the meaning of his own sententious maxim: "Those that wilbee impudent must bee as impudently dealt withall,"[11] he endeavoured to dispel "a strong jellousie raised it seems by some there" against him, as if he were a man who took away with one hand what he had given with the other. He made a solemn asseveration before Almighty God that they were mistaken; as if "by the word Propriety [Proprietary?] all the land formerly granted by us to others in that province should absolutely devolve againe to us in the same manner as if wee had never granted it; which truely wee conceive was a very strange interpretation of that word [" Propriety " or " Proprietary "], and very farr, God knowes, from our intention."[12]

(2) If Lord Baltimore remained stiff in his purpose of not allowing Fathers Hartwell and Cooper to embark until he had received satisfaction, some compromise would seem to have been effected; because, in point of fact, these two Fathers did sail, though not by the first or second convoy which imported the intruding clergy. None of his demands, indeed, *(2) Hartwell and Cooper. Faculties for the Baltimore clergymen.*

---

[10] Stonyhurst MSS., *Anglia A*, iv. 108G, ff. 212, 213.—*Documents*, I. No. 21.—Cf. a translation, B. T. Johnson, *Foundation of Maryland*, pp. 84–86, where, however, one most important clause in the latter part is incorrectly conceived. It is that which imports a surrender not merely of "uses," but of property itself: "*quemcumque titulum, jus, aut nomen, aut repostulationem quamcumque, quam aut Societas nostra vel ulla illius persona directe vel indirecte habet, vel habere prætendere potest, ab ullo Indo vel Indis aut ulla alia persona vel personis, ad ullum usum aut quoscunque usus, ad ullos fundos, tenementa aut hæreditates*" [which should not be rendered as if it were "*usus ullorum fundorum*"]. The bald character of this mortmain, thus foisted upon the Fathers, is made clearer in a later document, which we call a Concordat, where the parenthesis comes in "(*nullo alio admixto titulo*)," "without the admixture of any other title," emphasizing the feudal title, which alone is to be recognized. Stonyhurst MSS., *Anglia A*, iv. 108H, f. 215. See *Documents*, I. No. 22, 1°. In that ample document, besides the disenabling process which the Provincial is made to carry out strenuously against the Jesuits in all lines of franchises and rights, the pains of forfeiture fall heavily on their property, to the full extent as well of mortmain as of the Protestant statutes against the Catholic Church, under the plea of superstitious uses. But this unilateral Concordat belongs, we take it, to a later date. In the Conditions of Plantation published afterwards, when the government had passed into the hands of a Protestant constituency (1648 and 1649), the Mortmain Statutes intended to operate were restricted to those "before the reign of Henry VIII.;" and thereby they excluded the later legislation against the Catholic Church as being a "superstition."

[11] *Calvert Papers*, i. 218.

[12] *Proceedings of the Assembly*, 1637–1664, p. 316, A.D. 1650, August 6.—Cf. oath, *Ibid.*, pp. 305, 306, where the words occur: "Proprietary and Dominion over and in the said Province," etc.

were accorded, beyond what Father Copley had offered to observe some four years previously, when he wrote that he was "resolved to take no land but under your lordship's title." [13]

Still, outside of the written exactions, something was granted him; and it was humiliating enough. His intruding clergy were unqualified and useless. The Jesuits undertook to have them qualified with faculties, if these could be had. And the impelling motive why the Jesuits went out of their way to petition for faculties in Rome on behalf of Baltimore's priests was as little honourable to him as the rest of the proceedings. The General wrote to Father Edward Knott, Provincial, on November 22 (1642): "I myself will see that faculties are asked for from the [Cardinal] Protector, to buy off vexation. If they are obtained, I will let your Reverence know." [14]

The two Jesuits were not despatched even as late as December, for on the 6th of that month we find his Paternity answering the Provincial cautiously: "As to the Fathers to be sent into Maryland, we will give you an answer then when we shall have received the other despatches that you promise." [15] And when these came he replied (December 13): "I am in receipt of what you have sent, the demands of the Right Honourable Cecil Baron of Baltimore; and certainly they cannot be entertained by us. I will see if any better counsel occurs to solve the difficulty. In the mean time suspend all action." [16]

While Lord Baltimore was thus engaged in shutting up the means of ingress from the side of London, his Lieutenant-General, Leonard Calvert, was shutting up the means of egress from Maryland. The Fathers do not appear distinctly as the object of the measure. But it is quite clear that effects not different from those which had oppressed the Catholic clergy under Elizabethan Tudorism were intended to reproduce themselves, one way or other, in the Proprietary's plantation.

The Assembly. July-August, 1642. An Assembly meeting was held in July and August of this year (1642); and on the 23rd of July a bill was introduced about passes as against absconding creditors and runaway servants. It was enacted in due course as a law.[17] But, in the usual furtive manner, it proved to be a tool for striking other people, who were neither absconding creditors nor runaway

---

[13] *Calvert Papers*, i. 164, 7°.—Cf. *infra*, § 69, p. 558; the General's concession.
[14] General Archives, *Anglia, Epist. Gen.*, 1642, November 22.—*Documents*, I. No. 6, B.—This is the entire letter of the General, except four words at the beginning on Father W. Watson. It is incapable of application to England.
[15] *Ibid.*, 1642, December 6.—*Documents*, I. No. 6, C.
[16] *Ibid.*, 1642, December 13.—*Documents*, I. No. 6, D.
[17] *Proceedings of the Assembly*, pp. 133-141.

servants. In fact, it is said that a pass might "not be granted to any one" until he should have given five days' public notice of his intention.[18] So that, to go out of the province at all now, it was necessary to have a pass; and five days of notification and observation sufficed to lay a mine against any man, certainly against the Fathers.

In the month of September the Assembly met again, not by representation through burgesses, but in a mass meeting of all the freemen. In the interval they seem to have discovered where the new law placed them, either with culprits liable to justice, or with serfs, as if they had fallen back into the hands of a Tudor government. Mr. Giles Brent, in the name of the inhabitants of Kent, opened the campaign at the very first session, moving that the house should declare "whether the inhabitants may freely without leave depart out of the province, [not] being engag'd or obnoxious to justice." In a lofty manner, Governor Leonard Calvert declined to propose the motion.[19] The next morning Mr. Brent returned to the charge. Calvert again loftily replied that he would not permit the freemen to determine the matter as judges of the issue; and he refused to put the question. Here John Lewger went against Calvert in a reasoned opinion. The Governor began to give way; but to his condescending answer he attached a rider, where the significant exception was slipped in of a "transcendent cause," evidently belonging to the same genus of political expedients and excuses, as "reasons locked up within one's breast," or *propter rationes nobis notas*, "reasons known to ourselves alone." The gentleman declared "that it is the common right of all inhabitants to depart out of the province at their pleasure, unless indebted or obnoxious to justice, or unless there be some transcendent cause for the safety of the people, for the Lord Proprietary or his substitute to overrule that right in some particular cases for a convenient time."[20] The matter here slumbered for just six days; when Brent came once more to the breach. He was repulsed with the pretext that he must give the names of the parties whom he "pretended to personate." The next morning he was in line with his men; and Calvert was driven out of his last trench. "The Lieutenant-General consented that this should be entered for his answer instead of the former touching that point: That he declareth

---

[18] *Proceedings of the Assembly*, p. 160.
[19] *Ibid.*, pp. 171, 172.
[20] *Ibid.*, pp. 173, 174.

it to be the common right of all inhabitants to depart out of the province at their pleasure, unless indebted or obnoxious to justice." [21] In the maintenance of such a common right it should never have been necessary to assume the offensive with regard to a man who was the chief representative and conservator of peace and justice in the province.

There remained one more movement of Baltimore against the Fathers, and that was expelling them from the province whenever he should think fit. This manœuvre formed the subject of a long paragraph in his monumental Concordat, in which, amid so many other rights to be signed away by the Provincial for the Calverts' unilateral profit, personal immunity from arbitrary coercion was to be resigned. On receiving the slightest intimation from Baltimore or his heirs, and without being accorded the right to ask the reason why, the Provincial was to remove, as the clause had it, the "one or more of our Society" proscribed by the said Baltimore; and, on failure of the Provincial to effect the deportation within one year, the Calverts, that is, Cecil and his heirs, should be at liberty to use the violence, which the gentleman, unabashed, proceeds to describe in the said paragraph.[22] At present, however, not having risen as yet to the necessity of being diplomatic, Cecil Calvert as principal orders Leonard Calvert as his mandatary to commit an act, which, by the common law of England even under the Tudors, was a criminal offence punishable with fine, imprisonment, and pillory.[23] The crime was that of kidnapping.

Summary expulsion without process.

Some one had informed Baltimore that some Jesuit had by some means slipped into Mr. Ingle's ship, and was already on his way to Maryland. Mr. Ingle's ship was the same which carried the first instalment of Lord Baltimore's clergy, in the person of Mr. Gilmett. A second convoy was now to set sail at the end of November (1642), carrying the second instalment, in the person of Mr. Territt, and bearing new despatches. His lordship seems not to have examined whether he was being duped or not. So, bursting into a passion, he was betrayed into writing a manifestation of his character which posterity could ill have spared.[24] By the time that he came to add the postscript he seems to have found out his mistake; for he says quietly that the Jesuits had importuned him for permission to send some of their missionaries

Story of the intruding Jesuit.

[21] *Proceedings of the Assembly*, pp. 179-181.—Cf. S. F. Streeter, *Papers*, pp. 173, 174.
[22] Stonyhurst MSS., *Anglia A*, iv. 108H, ff. 216^v, 217.—*Documents*, I. No. 22, 5°.
[23] 4 Blackstone, *Comm.*, 218.
[24] *Calvert Papers*, i. 216-221.

this season; that he had refused; that in consequence "they have —God forgive them for it—caused a bitter falling out between my sister Peasely and mee, and some discontentment also betweene mee and her husband about it, because I would not by anie meanes give way to the goeing of anie of the aforesaid persons." There is no mention here of the unnamed Jesuit who had slipped aboard with the Gilmett convoy in some unnamed way. We know, too, that, not to mention the unlikelihood of such an absurd story, no Jesuit did actually go till a later period.

Nevertheless, in the emergency, where his honour and his safety are at stake, where he knows the mind of Mr. Territt and knows that of Mr. Gilmett, and has "the opinion and sence which divers pious and learned men here have to this odious and impudent injurie offred unto mee," he issues an edict substantially as follows: The said unnamed Jesuit will either come into my province or not; if he comes, you send him back; if he do not come into my province, you require Copley to bring that man into my province and into your power, that you may send the man back; if Copley do not execute your orders, you kidnap him and send him away instead. The first part of this edict is separated from the second by a stupendous parenthesis of thirty-two lines on an octavo printed sheet.[25]

Baltimore on kidnapping Copley. His excuses.

As an adequate and unimpeachable authority for all this lynch law against priests, the Gilmetts and the Territts, priests themselves, are cited by Baltimore—it is to be hoped with no more absolute certainty than usually attaches to his word. For he goes on to say immediately, as if to lay a requisite salve on his brother's soul: "This I am satisfied here that I may for divers reasons cause to bee done, as the said Mr. Territt and Mr. Gilmett will more fullie satisfie you; and I am resolved to have it done accordinglie." Baltimore had begun the passage with the affirmation that "Mr. Gilmett will I know concurr in opinion with him [Mr. Territt]; for, upon divers consults had here (before hee went), hee was well satisfied what might and ought to bee done upon such an occasion." Whatever persons these were who went under the names of Gilmett and Territt, we should have been glad to believe that they were only Blacklow and Holden; in order not to be forced to infer that there were more Holdens and Blacklows than history has left on record.

Returning to the same subject of either making Copley fetch some one into the province or else of kidnapping Copley and carrying him

---

[25] *Calvert Papers*, i. p. 217, l. 6-9, p. 218, l. 9-14.

piratically out of the province, the worthy lord is very pressing, as if much depended on the crime; and withal is very cautious, implying that, as a consequence, the Jesuits may go about hurting Mr. Territt: "But you must bee verie carefull," says the worthy brother to honest Leonard, "that Mr. Territt receive no prejudice by his communicating my mind to you, or by his zealous affection and fidelity to mee in doeing his best endeavours with you to see my desire herein accomplished. Nor likewise Mr. Gilmett; which I am confident your owne judgment and discretion will incline you to prevent, although I had not mentioned it."[26] And it is in the midst of these recommendations and machinations that the feudal lord plunges into a long tirade against the Pope, apparently on the strength of some gazette item, the exactitude of which is not borne out by history;[27] while the intrinsic merits of the incident, as being a feudal quarrel, should have enlisted the sympathies of the "Absolute Lord and Proprietor of the Province and Country of Maryland" rather on the side of the feudal lord the Pope, than on that of vassals and their accomplices.

Territt's "zealous affection" for Baltimore.

As to this incident of the projected kidnapping, it is worth while observing that, under the aspect of forcible abduction, there is practically no difference between it and a later incident, already noted, when the Orange Lord Bellomont, Governor of New York, privately solicited the Iroquois savages to kidnap their French Jesuit Black-gowns, and pass them over to him, for he was now equipped, said he, with the penal laws of New York.[28]

(3) Baltimore's general recommendation of the clerical gentlemen whom he sends over is quite cordial; and the provision he makes for their comfort, dignity, and independence, befits his wonted foresight. He says of them: "Both whom I recommend in those letters, and do now againe very hartily recommend them to your care; for they are both Ile assure you men of high esteeme heere, and worthy to be cherished and valued by you; in which you shall extreamely much oblige me."[29]

(3) Baltimore's regard for Territt and Gilmett.

It was indeed worth their while to serve with such fidelity the absolute lord who owned all Maryland, by right direct or right contingent, reversionary rights to the Indian lands or rights of escheat to those of many whites, and of all the clergy. The way in which he provided for them was as follows: He desired his brother

---

[26] *Calvert Papers*, i. 219.
[27] Cf. P. Balan, *Storia d'Italia*, vii. c. 47, nn. 1–3, 2nd edition.—Cf. *supra*, § 54, pp. 455, 456.
[28] *Supra*, Introduction, Chap. II. § 15, p. 103.   [29] *Calvert Papers*, i. 212.

the Governor to take care for Mr. Gilmett's "sojourning some where there to his contentment, which I desire," said he, "may be with your selfe for many reasons;" also "his boy that wayted upon him which must also sojourne with him, for he cannot be decently without such an attendance; wherefore I pray take order for him; they have all necessaries of bedding, etc., provided and sent with them." And in like manner "Mr. Will. Territt" is to be accommodated "with a convenient place to sojourne in there. And I shall," adds the magnanimous lord, "as I formerly wrote, pay the charge of it, when I know what it is, if it can not be done otherwise;" that is to say, if some body else, particularly Leonard Calvert, will not himself undertake to do it; "which," continues he, "I hope by your endeavours it may [be done]: and I shall take it very kindly from you," that is, the paying of Baltimore's charges out of another than Baltimore's pocket. But he concludes, facing possibilities at the worst: "Howsoever, you will, I hope, husband my expence herein the best you can, and I shall pay what is necessary for the sojourning of the aforesaid persons by bill of exchange hither."[30] Evidently religion and its ways and means were never meant to be an expensive luxury in the balance of Cecil's accounts.

A year later, this cheap superfluity was still on his hands. And, in a solemn set of "Instructions given by me, Cecilius Lord Baltimore, to my Commissioners for my Treasury in Maryland, dated the 18th day of November, 1643," no fewer than three out of the eight heads deal with the momentous problem, how to lodge the reverend gentlemen and where, without expense to himself and without making them live on air. The absolute lord instructs his Commissioners, who are the "welbeloved Giles Brent, Esq., my Leiutenant-General of the said Province of Maryland, John Lewger, Esq., my secretary, James Neale and Thomas Gerard, Esquires, all of my Counsell there, and William Brainthwait, gentleman,"[31] that "they continue those goods of mine, which were (by my directions) formerly putt into Mr. Gilmett's custody, still in his hands, as long as he staies in Maryland, or I give other directions concerning them. But I would have the Commissioners to demand and keepe a note under Mr. Gilmett's hand of the particulars thereof, acknowledging them to be in his custody." And again he orders that they allow "two steeres to Mr. Gilmet yearly for his expence." And a third time a whole paragraph (No. 7) is devoted to the reverend gentlemen and

[30] *Calvert Papers*, i. 212.
[31] *Archives of Maryland, Proceedings of the Council*, 1636–1667, p. 140.

to Father Copley in the same spirit of absolute economy and lordly parsimony.[32]

But in the mean time, as far as reserves of a secular clergy might be hoped for in Maryland, the whole situation had changed. The new-comers, Gilmett and Territt, had gone over to the side of the Jesuits; which certainly genuine Holdens and Blacklows would never have done. They deserted Baltimore. And perhaps a little knowledge of that gentleman's ways and character, his degree of liberality and the proportion of respect for religion which animated him, had served to disenchant the two imported clergymen. The Annual Letter for 1642 sketches the circumstances. After stating that the Jesuit missionaries in Maryland had declared the anti-clerical bills and penal statutes to be quite at variance with the laws of the Church, the Letter goes on to relate that "two priests were sent over from England to say the contrary. But matters fell out quite otherwise than was expected. For, on hearing our reasons and understanding the question better, they readily fell in with our views, as did most of the laity. By way of epilogue, I add just one circumstance, that two other Fathers [Hartwell and Cooper] have lately come from England to our great comfort. They had a dreary voyage of fourteen weeks, whereas usually it takes no more than six or eight. But about these Fathers, their labours and the fruit, I will write some other time, God willing. We hope indeed that the fruit will be abundant, as we may well presage from their fervour, and from the general union of minds amongst us all; since that is the

The new-comers desert Baltimore.

---

[32] *Archives of Maryland, Proceedings of the Council,* 1636–1667, pp. 141–143. "7. That they use their best endeavours to discharge the bargaine which was made this yeare for Mr. Coplies house at St. Maries, by letting him have his house and land there againe, and a reasonable consideration allowed unto him for Mr. Gilmetts time of being in it; which I would have discharged out of somewhat of mine there. And I desire that, in case Mr. Coply will not be contented to lett the house to Mr. Gilmett till midsommer, which shalbe *anno D*^{ni}. 1645, at some such reasonable rent as my said Commissioners or any two of them (whereof the said Mr. G[iles] B[rent] to be one) shall think fitt; and that Mr. Gilmetts and his families diett cannot be provided & discharged out of my stock and ferme at West St. Maries without any notable prejudice to the said stock, or out of some other profitts belonging to me there (both which I should be very gladd that my said Commissioners could effect for me; and I would willingly allow any reasonable rent to be paid out of my estate there to Mr. Copley for the said house for so long time, but not to be charged to pay anything there for it); then I desire my said Commissioners in that case to take care that some other convenient place there be provided for Mr. Gilmetts and Mr. Teeritts residence & diett there to their contentment, till the time above mentioned, with the best accommodation for them & least charge to me that may be. And I would have them so contrive this business (if possibly they can), that Mr. Gilmett and Mr. Terrett may by all meanes be continued in that province till that time; when I doubt not (by the grace of God) to be able to provide better for them then by reason of the extremity of the present troubles in England I could doe this yeare, which I hope they will consider and have a little patience till then. And this article I doe againe & againe recommend to my said Commissioners care, to give me satisfaction herein."

§ 67]   *THREE CHAPELS:* 1638–1640   539

most infallible sign that He lives in us, He who is perfect unity in Himself and the principle of all union in others." [33]

§ 67. After that provisional arrangement of Father Andrew White's, when he fitted up his first chapel in the Indian wigwam at St. Mary's, or Yaocomico, certain land was taken up by the Fathers in the heart of the new town, and a chapel erected there. In the patent of July 28, 1641, taken out by Copley under the name of Cuthbert Fenwick his trustee, the "New Chappell at St. Maries" was already a landmark. Modern explorers say that it was a brick building, eighteen by thirty feet in extent; that over the altar there was a carved representation of clouds and of the flames of Pentecost.[1] Though there have been difficulties as to what Protestants had to do at "the Chappell" on a Sunday, if the said chapel was distinctively Catholic, or what provision they may have made for themselves at some place which they might have called a chapel also,[2] nevertheless from a Catholic point of view there can be no doubt that the building in question was exclusively

A chapel exclusively Catholic.

---

[33] General Archives S.J., *Anglia, Historia*, iv. 871.—Cf. also C. E. Smith, in a book already alluded to above, *Religion under the Barons of Baltimore, being a sketch of Ecclesiastical Affairs* (1634–1692), pp. 270–272. As a specimen of how history has been and still is written in this age of open archives, a passage of this author, just where he has commended "a love of truth" to his estimable auditory (1899), may here be quoted. After representing the Baltimore drafts as Jesuit deeds, fortified with some promise of executing some other instrument which the gentleman discerns, he conceives that the two secular priests, Gilmett and Territt, who were imported into Maryland, were identical with the two Jesuit priests who were kept out of Maryland at the same time. These four, seculars and regulars together, being reduced by him to the common denomination of Jesuits with the clerical numerator two, he proceeds to write, upon this perfectly plain understanding of the question, in the following sympathetic terms: "On this understanding the [Jesuit] missionaries were allowed to depart. Alas for the trustfulness of Lord Baltimore! As soon as these new [Jesuit] missionaries arrived in Maryland, they repudiated the agreement and became one with their rebellious brethren. In the Jesuit Letter of 1642 the writer thus glosses over this discreditable breach of trust." Here this historian quotes a good page from the Annual Letter about the two secular priests, and he leaves out the passage which follows about the two Jesuit priests. Then, returning from the document, which is correct as far as he quotes it, he resumes his own composition thereupon, which is of a different kind: "So," says he, "the solemn agreement, having served its purpose, was flung aside [by the Jesuits] as the hunter flings aside the burnt cartridge which has brought down his game." Finally, having presented so clearly the *corpus delicti* of untruthfulness and infidelity to deeds and papers, he moralizes in his own person for the benefit of the good people in his flock. The good man exalts for them the love of truth, saying: "As we have seen, these 'good men' did not number a love of truth among the virtues with which they were equipped," etc.; and he winds up the touching passage with a plaintive apostrophe, which he puts in the mouth of the gentle and long-suffering Lord Baltimore: "With the broken pledges of the priests before him, one almost hears Lord Baltimore exclaim: 'Ye disciples of Ignatius Loyola, ye are too hard for me, and I am this day weak, though anointed king' (ii Samuel, 2 [3]. 39)." *Ibid.*—Cf. *Documents*, I. No. 8, L.

[1] J. W. Thomas, *Chronicles of Colonial Maryland*, p. 42.

[2] *Archives of Maryland, Judicial and Testamentary Business of the Provincial Court*, 1637–1650, p. 35: "The Processe against William Lewis," etc.; 1638, July 3.

sacred to Catholic services; and there seems to be no reason to believe but that it was always so. As early as April 3, 1638, we find Father Copley asking the privilege of Lord Baltimore, that "the church and our houses may be sanctuarie."[3] On April 8, 1643, the same Father inquires of the General, "whether our public chapels, not consecrated [as yet, but only dedicated,] have the privileges of those indulgences granted to other churches of the Society;" and his Paternity answers in the affirmative, that the particular solemnity of dedication, which is called consecration, is not necessary for the purpose (August 1, 1643).[4] Neither the request about "sanctuarie" in 1638, nor the question about consecration in 1643, would have been at all pertinent, if the church or the chapel were a mere religious rendezvous, having no exclusive character. The place would have been a hall or meeting-house, not sacred in Catholic eyes.[5] For the situation of St. Mary's "New Chappell," reference may be made to the chart and explanations.[6]

There was besides a chapel with which the name of Mr. Thomas Gerard is connected. It seems to have been a house of his, or a room in his house, by St. Clement's Bay or at least in St. Clement's hundred.[7] And having kindly allowed to the "Protestant Catholicks of Maryland" the use of it for their Divine services, he was otherwise minded some time after, and, "carrying away the books out of the Chappel," he put the key in his pocket, and there was an end of it. By the mouth of David Wickliff, who appears regularly as a delegate or a freeman from St. George's hundred, the parties concerned, believing themselves aggrieved, presented their petition to the House on March 23, 1641. We do not know what lien these people pretended to have on Gerard's property; nor what it was that had aroused the Catholic surgeon's ire against the worshippers. Possibly it was something like the incident of Francis Gray and Robert Sedgrave in the house of the Catholic gentlemen, William Lewis and the Rev. Thomas Copley at St. Inigoes.[8] It was treated by the sapient legislators of St. Mary's in precisely the same manner as they had medicated the Gray and Sedgrave's mischief. They smote the Catholic party. Why they did so, nobody in our age

Gerard's chapel.

The case against Gerard.

[3] *Calvert Papers*, i. 166.
[4] General Archives, *Anglia, Epist. Gen.—Documents*, I. No. 6, F.
[5] Compare the spirit of the Propaganda decree, May 21, 1627, No. 15. *Supra*, § 10, p. 196, note 6.
[6] *Infra*, Appendix A, pp. 567–569.
[7] Cf. *Proceedings of the Assembly*, pp. 127, 128, for April, July, 1642.
[8] *Supra*, § 37, p. 340.

seems wise enough to discover. Possibly because it was the safer party to strike. The House "found that Mr. Gerard was guilty of a misdemeanor, and that he should bring the books and key taken away to the place where he had them, and relinquish all title to them or the house, and should pay for a fine 500 lb. tobacco towards the maintenance of the first minister as should arrive." [9] Whereupon a modern writer observes: "If Mr. Gerard was proprietor of the building in question, the decision of the House, depriving him of his property in punishment for a misdemeanor, seems to have been tyrannical and unjust." [10] In all cases it was tyrannical; for the decision expressly allowed that he was a proprietor; and, even if the complainants had some technical claim or other of tenantship, there was still the alternative of inflicting damages, without thrusting obnoxious people on a man and his property.

A third chapter, a *templum* or *sacellum*, was that erected for the great ceremony of the Tayac's baptism at Pascattoway (July 5, 1640). This Kittamaquund gave land which, as we have seen, was the subject of some tragic declamation in Lord Baltimore's correspondence.[11] The circumstances warrant the belief that expressly or implicitly the assignment was under precisely the same conditions as those of the Patuxents at Mattapany; to wit, that the allotment should be for the service of the Indians themselves, by providing means for the temporal wants of the missionaries. But the incursions of the Susquehannahs made the Fathers transfer their head-quarters from Pascattoway to the safer inlet farther south, called Portobacco Creek.

The chapel at Pascattoway.

Returning now to the first chapel, that at St. Mary's, we note that the Roman scheme for the supplanting of the Jesuits was in full development at the end of 1641. On April 12, 1642, a commission of three appointed by Baltimore bought of Father Copley his presbytery, his house-lot and chapel land. The commission consisted of "the honourable Governor together with John Lewger and John Langford, Esqrs." [12] They gave a bill of exchange for £200 sterling to Thomas Cornwaleys, Esq., whom Copley appointed to represent him in the whole transaction. In principle, there seems to have been no reluctance on the side of the Fathers to part with their chapel rights, in as much as the last

The New-Chapel negotiation. 1642.

---

[9] *Proceedings of the Assembly*, p. 119.
[10] S. F. Streeter, *Papers*, p. 165.
[11] *Supra*, § 60 (3), pp. 486, 487.
[12] *Archives of Maryland, Court and Testamentary Business, 1637-1650*, p. 292.

thing that they relished was being detained in the colony of whites like mere stationary curates. But the negotiation was a sign of something to come, and of some persons to come. A month or so before the contract was effected (March 3, 1642), Copley wrote his letter to the General, asking permission for a journey to Rome. However, it does not appear on the face of it that there was any coercion exercised to force a sale upon the Fathers.

Now followed one of the most damaging little incidents that we may find to anybody's discredit in the conduct of a government. Baltimore protests bills. The man, whose three Commissioners had made the purchase, now had the assurance to refuse payment, to protest the bills original and duplicate, to shut off the course of justice lest reparation, as he himself said, should be ordered " with costs and damages;" and withal he did not hand back the property so obtained. He knew, as he says, that the bills of exchange were not for Captain Thomas Cornwaleys, "whose name it seemes was thought fitt to be used in that business, althoughe the said purchase was not made from him." Nevertheless, sensitive as he himself was to even an imaginary slight on his own honour, he flouted the captain publicly in London by protesting his bills, or, as he says with perfect unconcern: "(As I understand) one or more of them [the bills] are protested according to the usuall manner in such cases." Thus he let them know that it was Copley, not Cornwaleys, whom he meant to damage in his pocket; for which purpose he did not scruple to damage Cornwaleys in his honour. In the same letter in which he made these confessions of his standard of morality, he withdrew from the temporary Governor, Giles Brent, all power of "granting of any more lands within that Province till my arrivall there, when I shall take order to grant to every one their due, who have any just right or claime from me of any lands within that Province." This was half a year or more after the repeated but futile prohibitions, issued to Leonard Calvert, ever to grant patents where the Fathers were concerned, whether in their own names or under that of a trustee.

The cool and placid statement of all this malpractice is made by its author in a ratification of Giles Brent's commission as Governor during the temporary absence in England of Leonard Calvert. The passage in which he restrains the course of justice must now be quoted by way of exemplifying all the rest.

After his reference to the wholesale protesting of bills of exchange, some signed by his own representatives, some "signed," says he, "by the said Captain Thomas Cornwaleys," the right honourable gentleman continues as follows : " Whereupon some directions may perhaps respectively be sent thether to recover a satisfaction of all the said bills to the respective pretenders therunto, together with costs and damages. But because, for divers reasons, true & right justice cannot be done therin without some advises & testimonies from hence, which cannot yet be had: therefore I thought fitt and doe hereby restraine the power of the said Giles Brent, or any other person by authority derived from him, to grant processe or take cognisance of any suit or complaint whatsoever, concerning all or any of the afore said bills of exchange, or to give or pronounce any judgment therin; any thing conteined within the above mentioned or any other commission to the contrary in any wise notwithstanding; but to suspend any proceedings therin till my arrivall there, when I shall not faile to doe unto every person æquall right and justice therin. And doe therefore hereby require the said Giles Brent and all others whom it may concerne to obey my order herein, as they will answere the contrary at their utmost perills. And I doe hereby require the said Giles Brent and my secretary there, or one of them, to cause this my declaration with all convenient speed, after their or either of their receipt hereof, to be recorded & published at the usuall places of publishing orders within the said province for the government there. Given under my hand & seale the fourteenth day of July, 1643. C. Baltemore. To Giles Brent, Esq., my Lieutenant-Generall of my Province of Maryland, & to my secretary & the rest of my Counsell there, and to every of them." [13] Thus all the formalities consecrated to legitimate government and the administration of justice were to seal what a modern author calls " this summary and extrajudicial proceeding;" and were to be applied by a Governor who, in representing Baltimore, " had sworn in the presence of Cornwaleys, immediately after Leonard Calvert's departure (April 15), not only 'to maintain all the interests and royal jurisdictions' of the Proprietary within the province, but 'to do equal justice to the poor and to the rich after his cunning, wit, and power, according to the laws, and to delay nor to deny to any man right or justice.'" [14]

Baltimore's statement of policy. July 14, 1643.

Official malpractice.

But it ought to be observed that the urgency and overbearing

---

[13] *Archives of Maryland, Proceedings of the Council*, pp. 135-137.
[14] S. F. Streeter, *Papers*, pp. 184, 185.—Cf. *Proceedings of the Council*, 1636-1667, p. 210, *med.*

pressure, exercised here by Baltimore to stop the course of right and justice, coincided exactly, both in tendency and time, with the urgency and pressure brought to bear by the same man on the English Provincial, unto the impropriating of the Jesuit lands. It was the time of Baltimore's drafts—of his four Points, and of his great act of Surrender, to be followed in due time by a unilateral Concordat of the most ample proportions, all of them being drafts of his own whereby the Provincial should sign away all his rights to Baltimore; and the last in particular presuming to affirm that Lord Baltimore was incurring great expense "for the propagation of the Christian faith in those parts," and that he had "given no insignificant portion of land in Maryland for the support of ours living there."[15] This was the time also when his men, Gilmett and Territt, living precariously as mere boarders in the colony, at his own expense only in case nobody else would provide for them, were requested by him "to consider and have a little patience" till "midsommer which shalbe *anno Domini* 1645;" while he asked his Commissioners "so to contrive this business (if possibly they can) that Mr. Gilmett and Mr. Terrett may by all meanes be continued in that Province till that time, when I doubt not (by the grace of God) to be able to provide better for them." He gave this document under his hand "at Bristoll, 18 November, 1643."[16]

From a comparison of these dates and facts, it will appear what policy it was that may have underlain his refusal to pay a debt where he hoped soon to receive a gift. His interference with the course of justice, to the prejudice of Jesuit proprietors, would only have been meant to check the prejudice which his pocket would incur if he paid for that which he expected to get for nothing. And "the grace of God," which he invoked as the channel for good things on behalf of Gilmett and Territt, was apparently nothing else than the grace and windfall of the Jesuit property coming to be Baltimore's own. Then the needy gentleman would be rich enough to be generous, and might induce the impatient reverend gentlemen, if possible, to stay for a consideration. But his heyday of great expectations was rudely cut short.

Probable explanation.

In the first place, the new set of Instructions last quoted, and dated on November 18, only four months after the irregular commission and suspension of powers given above, showed by its provisions

---

[15] Stonyhurst MSS., *Anglia A*, iv. 108H, ff. 214, 215.—*Documents*, I. No. 22, 1°, 2°.—Possibly this was the "advises & testimonies from hence;" *supra*, p. 543.

[16] *Proceedings of the Council*, p. 143, No. 7.— Cf. *supra*, § 66 (3), p. 538, note 32.

about paying rent to Copley, that Baltimore felt his method of making free with other people's property to be an ill-advised mode of procedure. In the second place, he was adopting now, not the straightforward measure of paying for what he had bought and of making good incidental damages, but the arbitrary measure of undoing the whole contract with Copley, without speculating further or discounting any other party's losses.

Finally, as he could not keep the courts of justice in quarantine all the time, he was rudely shaken out of his dreams; and, in spite of his temporizing or compromising, he had to face the worst. Captain Cornwaleys brought him and the whole troop of his henchmen into court. *Cornwaleys sues the Government.*

The new instructions which he gave from Bristol (November 18, 1643) to his five new Commissioners (Brent, Lewger, Gerard, Neale, and Brainthwait) for the undoing of the bilateral contract made in his name by the former Commissioners (Leonard Calvert, Lewger, and John Langford), were to the effect that these new men should "use their best endeavours to discharge the bargaine which was made this yeare for Mr. Coplies house at St. Maries, letting him have his house & land there againe, and a reasonable consideration allowed unto him for Mr. Gilmett's time of being in it;" and he, Baltimore, would desire Mr. Copley to rent the same house to Mr. Gilmett till midsummer, 1645, about a year and a half ahead.[17]

Before this attempt to gloss over the late piece of malicious mischief was even penned, Captain Cornwaleys signified that he would have nothing more to do with the man in the old confidential relation of a councillor; he absolutely refused to serve in that capacity or to take the oath (September 16).[18] Then, Leonard Calvert, the Governor, having returned from England in September, 1644, the captain, at the beginning of the new year, pressed forward a suit already instituted against the three responsible parties, Calvert, Lewger, and Langford; he demanded damages to the value of 100,000 lbs. of tobacco and cask; and by his attorney, Cuthbert Fenwick, he prayed the magistrates of the Council to award him the said damages according to justice.

The magistrate, Giles Brent, issued a writ accordingly to the honourable the Governor, desiring him to satisfy the petitioner's demand, or to show cause why not, on some day between this and Monday next. The Governor replied "to the significations both of Mr. Brent and of

[17] *Proceedings of the Council*, p. 143, No. 7.
[18] S. F. Streeter, *Papers*, p. 179.—For the oath, cf. *Proceedings of the Assembly*, pp. 44, 45; *Proceedings of the Council*, pp. 145, 146.

Mr. Lewger per letter, *supra*, that he is not bound to shew cause nor will shew any upon the day, or within the time uppointed, on Monday next." Cuthbert Fenwick then "shewed that his petition to the honourable Governor, for satisfaction of his damages of 100,000 lb. tobacco to his master Captain Cornwaleys, hath beene signified to the said Governor, and that he hath refused to satisfie the damage demanded or to shew cause upon the day appointed him; and therefore prayeth processe of attachment according to the law and common right; and judgment upon his protest according to the law merchant." The magistrate, Giles Brent, awarded attachment on the Governor's goods for the sheriff of St. Maries to execute, and to return the writ by February 1st, sixteen days later. The next day, the same "Cutbert Fennick shewed to the Judge, Giles Brent, Esq., that the knowen Sheriff Edward Packer refused to serve the attachment issued yesterday against the goods of the honourable Governor; and therefore prayed another officer to be appointed. And therupon issued another writt of the same tenor, directed to Thomas Mathewes."[19] Thus, on January 14, 1645, we have Copley's three intimate friends, Cornwaleys, Fenwick, and Matthews, drawn up against the Baltimore party, and apparently in command of the situation; for Fenwick is the attorney whose demands the court is honouring, Matthews is specially appointed as deputy-sheriff for this precise service, and Captain Cornwaleys, commander-in-chief of colonial forces, is the plaintiff here and is conducting the operations. Fenwick was actually trustee of the St. Inigoes Manor; Matthews was to be trustee of St. Thomas's Manor; and it is possible that at this very moment Captain Cornwaleys, by his warrant for 4000 acres "upward of Port Tobacco Creek,"[20] was already holding the future St. Thomas's Manor for the Fathers even then.

It was the misfortune of Governor Leonard Calvert, whatever his own degree of probity and religion may have been, that in presence of his brother Cecil he seems to have conducted himself as a mere employee, one afraid of losing his place; or as a man under a dead weight that dragged him down. Here he was entering on the path of lawlessness because Cecil had gone before; and he refused to appear in a regular process of law.

The writ of attachment issued against the Governor was one of a series extending over nearly a year from the time when Cornwaleys had learnt of his lordship's protesting the bills in London.[21] The

---
[19] *Court and Testamentary Business*, as above, pp. 292–294.
[20] S. F. Streeter, *Papers*, p. 166.
[21] *Court and Testamentary Business*, as above, pp. 263, 266.

three Commissioners lay under writs of execution or of sequestration. To protect themselves, and to pay expenses, they took over the rights to Copley's house and land, acquired by a purchase never made good. And here we may leave them in the hands of Cornwaleys and the law.

§ 68. In the course of 1642—a year noteworthy, as we have seen, for the rise and fall of Baltimore's ambitions regarding a subservient Roman clergy—Father Roger Rigbie, who had been transferred to Maryland at the end of 1641, began his career as an Indian missionary. It soon appeared that for learning the Patuxent language the Mission had acquired in him a man of special talents. But, in the course of his first year, he was stricken down for three months with sickness, no doubt from the country fevers. His station was a "new residence, commonly called Patuxen," says the Annual Letter for 1642. This adjective "new" would seem to distinguish it from the old Mattapany, the Patuxent missionary station expropriated by Lord Baltimore.

Mistaking the character and vocation of a Catholic missionary, the Governor, Leonard Calvert, gave the commission of police officer to Father Rigbie for a defined purpose of arresting some Indians. As this was the first commission of the kind which he put on paper, we presume it was also the last on which he wasted his time and ink. He wrote, under date of July 11, 1642: "These are to desire you to repair to the great men of Patuxent and of the nations adjoyned to them, and of them to demand in my name to deliver without delay unto Simon Demibiel, or Henry Bishop, or any other, the bearer or bearers whereof, the persons of such Indians of any of those nations as shall be named to you by the said Simon or Henry to have done unto them and other English injury in their swine and otherwise; to the end the said Simon or Henry may bring the said Indians before me to answer such complaints as shall be objected against them by the said Simon or Henry or any others. And certifie me what you have done herein as soon as you may. And this shall be your warrant. To Mr. - - - Rigby."[1] *Father Rigbie and the police commission. July 11, 1642.*

Nineteen days afterwards (July 30, 1642) we gather some information of the fate that attended this officious commission. The Henry Bishop thus privileged to be served by a priest who should make a domiciliary visit among native tribes, call out native Indians on the mere naming of them by their enemies, use his sacred authority and

[1] *Proceedings of the Council*, as above, p. 104.

his acquired knowledge of the language for the due reparation to be made on behalf of Simon's and Henry's swine,—this said complainant is found at the Assembly proceedings of a fortnight later; and a petition of his came before the House and was read, "touching a remedy against the Indians of Patuxent for killing his swine;" and he was "answered that he is required to prove his petition, and then he shall have a remedy." [2]

It is noteworthy that, at this same Assembly, an "Act providing for Officers" was going through the stages, and did pass; and by its terms a missionary, as not being exempted, would have been bound to exercise offices imposed by the Lord Proprietary or his Lieutenant-General, and also to execute "any other office or command, so there be reasonable fee allowed for it to be determined by the judge." [3] But, in the very next Assembly of a month later (September 7–11, 1642), Captain Cornwaleys and Mr. Brent fought against the re-enacting of such a bill, which would even have compelled persons to act as common hangmen; and it was thrown out. [4]

The rights and immunities of Indians, original proprietors of the soil, fell into very much the same category as the rights of Catholic missionaries, whether personal or real. And it may be that Lord Baltimore, ordering his brother to kidnap Father Copley, had been informed of a valuable precedent established by the neighbouring plantation of Virginia, where a *lex talionis*, not of an eye for an eye or a tooth for a tooth in a given culprit, but of one man for another, had been genially applied to Indian folk by the court at James City (June 23, 1640); the order being issued that any Indian might be arrested and imprisoned by way of fetching back goods which were stolen not by him, but by some other; just as Lord Baltimore ordered the arrest and transportation of Father Copley, not on his own account, but on that of some other person, whom not even Baltimore knew or could name, and who proved to be non-existent. "Whereas," says the Virginia court record, "Arthur Price hath complained to this Board that he hath lately had stolen from him, by an Indian, one gun, one pair of breeches, and one shirt, the Court hath ordered that said Arthur Price shall have power to detain in his custody the next Indian who shall come to his house, and confess himself acquainted with said Indian who stole said breeches,

[2] *Proceedings of the Assembly*, p. 136.
[3] *Ibid.*, p. 148.
[4] *Ibid.*, pp. 175, 176.

gun, and shirt, until they be brought back by the Indian who stole the same." [5]

This style of administration seemingly appealed to some principle of solidarity supposed to exist among the Indians. Now, on the contrary, if there was a characteristic which lay at the very heart of Indian savagery, it was precisely the absence of solidarity; as the sachems of the Mohawk and fellow-tribes in New York explained more than once, that they had no power to hinder any brave from doing as he chose, individualism being of the very essence of their tribal polity. And, in any case, the exalted grade of Christian solidarity, on which American colonists could plume themselves, might possibly have taken offence at one white man being imprisoned, or evicted, or hanged for another.

But, to sum up the abuses introduced by this high-caste civilization among the poor natives, we need merely observe, with a modern writer, that the proceedings had not always the pretence even of following the laws of war. In 1641 Governor Leonard Calvert issued a proclamation, forbidding the harbouring or entertaining of Indians, and he went on at once to add: "And I doe hereby authorise and declare it lawfull to any inhabitant whatsoever of the isle of Kent to shoot, wound, or kill any Indian whatsoever comeing upon the said island, untill further order be given herein. Given at St. Maries, 10 July 164[1]." [6] *Killing peaceable Indians at sight. 1641.*

Thus much being said about the local government as pitted against the Indians, it will readily be inferred what amount of real sympathy the missionaries might count upon in their efforts to evangelize the natives. In fact, there was no fund either of sympathy or of means under the Calvert dynasty; and the missions had just one assurance of safety, that they lay outside the gloomy and ominous line of direct shadow cast by "the absolute Lord and Proprietor." However, they were still within his district. Before long, one of the missionaries proposed to move outside of the district itself.

Owing to the incursions of the Susquehannahs and the injuries resulting, the Fathers were at that time largely content with excursions; "not a few of which," says the Annual Letter (1642), "we have made this year up the river Patuxent; the fruit whereof was as follows: The conversion of the young queen of the town [Patuxent] having the same name as the river; also of her mother; the conversion, *Missionary labours. 1641–42. Patuxent. Portobacco. Pascattoway.*

[5] S. F. Streeter, *Papers*, p. 156.
[6] *Archives of Maryland, Proceedings of the Council*, p. 99.—Cf. H. Stockbridge, *The Archives of Maryland*, p. 46.

too, of the young Queen of Portobacco; also of the wife and two children of the great Tayac, that is, the Emperor [of Pascattoway] who died last year; and of one hundred and thirty others besides." Here, in connection with the Patuxent and Father Rigbie, an account is given of the method followed in the excursions; and the spirit of self-sacrifice, devotion, and cheerfulness, compare very favourably with the qualities manifested at this same time by their brethren, the French missionaries, beyond the Canadian frontier.[7] The Patuxent language in particular seems to have created special difficulties; and this may have been one reason why Father White had not succeeded so well with the king before he was sent to the Tayac at Pascattoway. In the course of his first year's sojourn among the Patuxents, Father Rigbie composed a short catechism with the aid of the interpreter, and he was in hopes soon of being able to converse in the language. It is noted of him expressly that he had gone to live among these Indians for the purpose of acquiring their tongue more easily.[8]

Rigbie and the Patuxent language.

Father White's experiences were of a different kind in the direction of Potomac town, Pascattoway, and the new station of Portobacco. He took passage up the river in the ship of a New Englander, in whose hands he soon found reason to believe that he himself and the supplies sent with him were in no slight danger. But the ice solved the difficulty, by blocking the ship up and then sinking it at Potomac town; where, in the course of this forced delay, the Father had time to convert the chief of that place, with the principal men, who received faith and Baptism; as also did another chief, with many of his people; a third likewise, with his wife, son, and another person;

---

[7] General Archives S.J., *Anglia, Historia,* iv. pp. 867, 868.—*Documents,* I. No. 8, L.—For a translation, cf. Maryland Historical Society, Fund Publication, No. 7, pp. 83-85.—For a general statement made to Cardinal Barberini of the Fathers being versed in barbarous tongues of Maryland, see *Documents,* I. No. 18, at the end.—Cf. note 8, following here.

[8] The Rev. C. E. Smith discerns in the Jesuit documents some contradictions. In the year 1641, he notes, the Fathers claimed to be "learned in the language of the savages," whereas, in the next year, they confessed their ignorance of the same—a confession which the rev. author bears out with an observation of his own: "A statement," he says, "which is in strict accordance with their practice of always being accompanied by an interpreter."—The gentleman's observations are not in strict accordance with the words of the two passages which he quotes—one place speaking of barbarous language in general, *linguæ barbaræ periti sunt;* the other speaking of the Patuxent language in particular; for the excursions described are those up the Patuxent River, and the missionary immediately referred to is Rigbie in the Patuxent country: "The difficulty of this language is so great that none of us can yet converse with the Indians without an interpreter, although Father Roger Rigbie has made some little progress," etc., *spectata linguæ hujus difficultate.* C. E. Smith, *Religion under the Barons of Baltimore,* pp. 263, 264.—In the same place he makes "Dom Rosetti" a prospective missionary to Maryland.

§ 68]   MISS BRENT AND THE EMPRESS   551

and a fourth, with a personage of some note. These results were well worth his nine weeks of labour; and the Indians in general, moved by the example of so many principal men, were ready to embrace the faith, as soon as the priests should be at leisure to teach them the Catechism.

Meanwhile "the young Empress, as they call her, at Pascattoway," who had been living in St. Mary's, was baptized there. She stayed in the colony still and spoke English well. She was treated as a ward and orphan by the unmarried lady, "Mrs." Margaret Brent; and her own name, properly freighted with a title of dignity, was "Mrs." Mary Kittamaquund. She had reached the age of nine years.[9] No one was more capable than Miss Margaret Brent to protect the young person and vindicate her rights. Thus we find at the end of a suit, instituted on behalf of the Indian ward by her competent guardian, that the demand made upon Leonard Calvert, the Governor, was honoured by Giles Brent, John Lewger, and William Brainthwait, councillors, who paid what was demanded, and gave the necessary guarantee in his lordship's name.[10]

The Indian royalty, Mary Kittamaquund.

This Miss Brent was executrix of Governor Leonard Calvert, and was at one time recognized by the court as well as by the Assembly (1648) in her capacity of attorney to his lordship himself; in which quality she demanded a voice in the House of Assembly, as well as on her own account. When the Governor, Thomas Greene, declined to allow her a vote in the House, she "protested against all proceedings in this present Assembly, unlesse shee may be present and have vote as aforesaid."[11] At the very next Assembly, a year later (April 21, 1649), the freemen had occasion to address his lordship in a letter, wherein they referred to Miss Brent's management of my lord's estate; and they expressed surprise that, in his "tart" letter, he did not express, as they said, rather "thanks from your Honour for her so much concurring to the publick safety, then to be justly liable to all those bitter invectives you have been pleased to express against her." For, said they, "we do verily believe and in conscience report, that it [Baltimore's estate] was better for the collonys safety at that time in her hands then in any mans else in the whole Province after your brothers

The English guardian, Margaret Brent.

---

[9] Annual Letter of 1640, two years earlier: "*septennem filiam.*"
[10] *Archives of Maryland, Court and Testamentary Business,* 1637-1650, pp. 259, 263-265, 270, 271, A.D. 1644.
[11] *Ibid., Proceedings of the Assembly,* January 21, 1647/8, p. 215.

death. For the soldiers would never have treated any other with that civility and respect; and, though they were even ready at several times to run into mutiny, yet she still pacified them; till, at the last, things were brought to that strait that she must be admitted and declared your lordships attorney by an order of court (the copy whereof is herewith enclosed); or else all must go to ruin again; and then the second mischief had been doubtless far greater than the former." [12] On receiving this letter, the "tart" nobleman who received therewith this smart lesson on courtesy, and who in his style of speech seems to have mistaken even a lady for a Jesuit missionary, rose to the level of the soldiers' civility, and spoke of Miss Brent with respect (August 6, 1650). He endorsed everything that she had done in his name up to the date of the freemen's letter.[13]

We have observed already that, though this lady was not actually in the province at the time when John Lewger formulated his doctrinaire Cases,[14] yet she was of the kind whom he was striking at with disfranchisement and confiscation, for the crime of remaining unmarried, or, as Copley expressed it, for reserving the privilege of being able to "vow chastity in the world." In presence of wise and discreet virgins like her, intellectually strong and richly endowed with the goods of this world, there was nothing to expect in the future but the endowment also of charity and religion; just as the Jesuits themselves were incorrigibly bent on doing. Hence the gallant Lewger struck at such ladies with disfranchisement. And, when that failed, the noble and courteous lord struck at them with a Condition of Plantation, inflicting on them an incapacity to give (November 10, 1641). And when, after that, he failed to elicit a disabling sentence to this same purpose from the Provincial, then, the Catholic prodominance in the province having become less, he struck at every one indiscriminately with a sentence of that kind, in his twelfth Condition of Plantation, 1648, which was repeated in his tenth of 1649.[15] It is a loss to the intellectual and moral fund of history, that as much is not known of the Brents as we are forced to know of some other persons.

But, coming back to the Indian ward, we see reason to believe that Miss Kittamaquund found life with the Brents much more

---

[12] *Archives of Maryland, Proceedings of the Assembly*, p. 239.
[13] *Ibid.*, pp. 316, 317.
[14] Cf. J. Kilty, *Landholder's Assistant*, p. 67.
[15] Cf. *Ibid.*, pp. 42, 50.—Cf. *supra*, § 52 (2), pp. 430, 431; § 62 (1); § 63 (1), note 10.

congenial than with her bronzed subjects under the native oaks of Pascattoway; and that a brick house was more commodious than a wigwam of state pitched on " a hill called the Lyon of Jude," with a swamp on the one side and an East Marsh on the other.[16] The Susquehannahs, too, with their unseemly incursions, were adding much to the discomforts of life on the shores of the higher Potomac. So for one reason or other, whether formally or practically, the heiress to that imperial throne abdicated. In fact, we observe that, eighteen years afterwards, the claimant to the imperial succession at the time passed her over rather summarily, as if Kittamaquund the father had no right to appoint "his daughter to be queene, but that the Indians," said the claimant, "withstood itt as being contrary to their custome." Hence, in the person of Weghucasso, they had returned to their old tradition, which was that of continuing the imperial succession, not by sons in a right line, much less by daughters, but by brothers running off laterally, and by the sons of sisters running down obliquely. And so, from the time of the founder of the dynasty, Vttapoingassinem, that came from the Eastern Shore and commanded the Patowmecks and Sasquehannoughs, down through thirteen generations had the government descended without interruption unto Kittamaquund; who did kill the Emperor before him, and then appointed his daughter to succeed him; but the Indians, passing over this heiress, did choose Weghucasso, who had come down from a lateral branch in the far past "(but which of them they knowe not);" and he had then appointed the actual ruler, Vttapoingassinem, who sued for confirmation.[17] And thus does our conjecture seem justified that, for one reason or another, Father White's catechumen and Miss Brent's ward had resigned her rights to the imperial succession.

When these Indian constitutional questions were presented and discussed in 1660–1662, the Governor of the time, Philip Calvert, appointed "Portoback" as the centre for an Indian council. This was precisely the place which, at the present date, in 1642, was described as being newly taken up for a missionary residence. The Susquehannahs were infesting the missionary station at Pascattoway, " slew several men whom we had there, and inflicted great loss on us by carrying off our goods." No protection was to be expected from the plantation of whites.[18] Meanwhile, the town called originally

The Indian imperial title.

---

[16] *Supra*, § 60 (2), p. 486; Copley's assignment to Lewger of 400 acres at Pascattoway.
[17] *Archives of Maryland, Proceedings of the Council*, 1636–1667, pp. 402, 403, 453, 454; A.D. 1660, 1662.
[18] Cf. S. F. Streeter, *Papers*, p. 178.

554   *THE INDIAN MISSIONS:* 1642-1644   [CHAP. VI

Potupaco, but subsequently Portobacco, had in large part received the faith and Baptism. Wherefore as it was situated on the Pamake, almost in the middle of the Indian settlements, and thus was a good starting-point for excursions in all directions, they determined to establish a residence there.

All this belonged to Father White's field of labour (1642); and he adds an interesting account of a marvellous cure wrought in the case of a wounded Indian, and granted to the simple faith and prayers of his neophytes as well as to the application of a relic of the Holy Cross which he himself carried.

His expedition of 1642, which had begun in the New Englander's ship, not without fears of the New Englander's faith, and which had been interrupted at Potomac town by the shipwreck, may reveal in this connection the meaning of a political movement initiated by Baltimore about the same time.

Relations of Maryland with New England. 1642, 1643.

In 1643, the very next year, the Proprietary invited the Puritans of Massachusetts to come down and settle in his plantation.[19] The step seemed singular. However, if there was so much commercial intercourse with men of Massachusetts right on the Potomac itself, the explanation may be easier to give; the more so as Captain or Major-General Edward Gibbons of Boston, to whom Baltimore spontaneously sent a commission for the purpose, is recorded as having possessed a windmill at St. Mary's;[20] and a writer notes of Gibbons that he himself once lost a vessel in the waters of Virginia and Maryland.[21] To these circumstances may be added the kindly treatment of French missionaries in Boston at this early date.

Indeed, to understand the relations between such colonies as Maryland and Massachusetts at the commencement, we must not throw over them the atmosphere and habits of another age. The difference between the earlier and the subsequent periods in Massachusetts is thus touched on by a writer of the next generation, with whom the authority for his statements must lie: "The first settlers," said he, "were a serious good sort of people." He considers them as having belonged to the Church of England; "and at their departure from hence [England] they desired the prayers of the Bishop of London and his clergy for them," and that, too, in a letter sent to the said Bishop "from on board the *Arabella*, and subscribed by Governour, magistrates, and ministers." But, he adds, "they had not

[19] Cf. E. D. Neill, *Founders of Maryland*, p. 109; from *Winthrop's Journal*, October 13, 1643.—Cf. *supra*, § 30 (1), p. 286.
[20] *Archives of Maryland, Proceedings of the Council*, as above, p. 326.
[21] E. D. Neill, *Founders of Maryland*, p. 108.

bin long in the New World before all sorts of people flocked to them, of as different principles as places." And the consequence was that, " even in the space of little more than one generation, near one half of the people are unbaptized." [22]

After Father Rigbie's and Father White's fields of action, the next to be noticed is that of the superior, Father Philip Fisher, or Copley. During the year 1642 he stayed for the most part, says the Annual Letter, in the town of St. Mary's, "to be at the service of the English who are more numerous there, and of the Indians who live in the vicinity, as well as of the others who come thither from other parts." Now, with the arrival of Messrs. Gilmett and Territt, he was set free. He let out his house to them and put the chapel at their service, and went off to the Indians, at least in missionary excursions. He soon enlarged his ambition so as to take in New England. And with this we pass over to the General's letters for the period.

Copley and St. Mary's City. 1642-1644.

§ 69. It is probably to the Annual Letter which we have just been using that the General alluded, when answering Father Knott, Provincial, under date of August 1, 1643. He said that he hoped to find in the accounts now promised of the Maryland Mission some consolation and relief amid the sorrows felt for the Church's losses in Europe.[1] On the same day he answered Father Copley's of April 8, sent from Maryland. He expressed the utmost satisfaction at the wide door now opened for the preaching of the gospel in those parts. He went on to remark : " As to what you say about adversaries, I am not at all surprised at it. The Church has always been hemmed in by them from the very beginning; and they serve virtue as a whetstone, making it sharper and better. I hope that your patience and good deeds will yet overcome the evil ; and the Divine goodness will shed benedictions on your labours." Then, answering the question about chapels not consecrated, as mentioned before, he expressed his good wishes for the widest extension possible of their work and its results.[2]

This Copley packet from Maryland of April 8, 1643, must have announced the arrival of Fathers Hartwell and Cooper in the colony, since we find the fact stated, though without their names, in the

[22] W. S. Perry, *Historical Collections*, iii., Massachusetts, 50, 51; account attributed to E. Randolph, 1689.
[1] General Archives S.J., *Anglia, Epist. Gen.*, 1643, August 1 ; answering Knott's letter of June 16.—*Documents*, I. No. 6, E.
[2] *Ibid.*—*Documents*, I. No. 6, F.

epilogue or postscript to the Annual Letter for 1642.[3] There were now five Jesuit priests in the mission, without any lay-brother. Messrs. Gilmett and Territt were also there; and we find by the Maryland colonial records that Mr. Gilmett's name figured in the Proprietary's accounts as late as May 3, 1644.[4]

Now, a little before the time when Lord Baltimore preached patience to Messrs. Gilmett and Territt, and desired the good service of his Commissioners, that they would "so contrive this business (if possibly they can), that Mr. Gilmett and Mr. Terrett may by all meanes be continued in that province" till the midsummer of 1645, one year and a half later, the Provincial Knott wrote to the General, showing that the baron was campaigning as ever against the Jesuits and on behalf of their property. This was in the autumn of 1643, within a year after the date at which we have placed the act of Assignment or Surrender, administered by the same Baltimore to the same Provincial. To rid the Society of this annoyance, Knott submitted three proposals to the General, the nature of which, in default of the original letter, we may infer from the reply, especially in the light of the same Provincial's Memorial to Cardinal Barberini.[5]

The first proposal would be in the sense of unconditional concession, yielding everything that Baltimore demanded; but throwing the responsibility for doing so on the shoulders of the Roman authorities, while he should be merely acting under orders. The second and third are contained in the General's reply, but are not distinguished there one from the other. The second would seem to be that, without going to the lengths of such uncanonical concessions, the Provincial might undertake an engagement, not to accept of any lands in future, offered to him or to his missionaries, without the concurrent assent of the Proprietary. The third then would be retrospective, containing two elements as to lands already acquired—one being that only the authority of the Pope was competent now to resign such property; the other, that, in view of such a difficulty, the baron might solve it himself, by granting the concurrent consent, or exercising that right to give which he did so much insist upon. For that purpose he had only to regard the property as means of subsistence for the missionaries, and leave it as such; and what else did he want? They did not possess a province or a county. Having a strict right by a bilateral contract to 28,500 acres for work done in settling the province, and value received

Knott's three proposals to the General. Sept. 8, 1643.

[3] *Supra*, § 66, p. 538.
[4] *Archives of Maryland, Court and Testamentary Business*, pp. 275-278.
[5] *Supra*, § 63 (2), pp. 513-515.

already by Baltimore, they had only 4400 acres about St. Mary's town. As to Mattapany, which no one but the Pope could release to its former owner—and that not Baltimore, but the Indian king—if the Proprietary of non-Indian lands did insist upon interposing and concurring to give his sanction also there, let him give his sanction also there. That was not a province, nor a county, but merely a granary or base of operations for the missions among the Indians.

Thus the General writes on October 31, 1643: "I have thought over the difficulties which your Reverence stated in yours of the 8th of September, regarding our Mission of Maryland. I am of the opinion that we should use all means to preserve the good will of the Right Honourable Baron lord of the country, for fear such an excellent harvest should be blighted before it is ripe, and on account of mere temporal things the natives be left destitute of eternal goods. As to an indult from the Apostolic See, such as you desire, there is small hope of getting that. Of the three lines of conduct which you propose, the first does not commend itself to our theologians. The second and third are considered to be licit. Wherefore on the lines so suggested we shall write a letter of the kind that you ask for at our hands, to be shown to his lordship, if you think fit. The difficulty is greater with respect to property already bestowed. That is considered to have passed already under ecclesiastical jurisdiction. And so we are thought to be incapable of ceding it now without the consent of the Pontiff. However, I do not think that it can be of such great consequence; and I suppose his lordship is willing to approve of a fitting subsistence being provided for ours according to our institute; wherefore he will probably consent that the said property serve that purpose. If not, please inform me anew; and I will try whether perchance we may not be able to obtain from the Apostolic See the powers necessary to release our claim." [6]
The General. First letter. Oct. 31, 1643.

Under the same date of October 31, 1643, appears the draft of the other letter, for use with Lord Baltimore. It reads as follows: "From the accounts which your Reverence sent me lately I received much gratification, on learning of the fruit yielded by the evangelical seed which has been sown through the labours of ours in Maryland; besides the well-founded hopes of seeing a plentiful harvest gathered into the granary of the Lord. At the same time, the satisfaction I found in your reports suffered no little diminution by reason of what you went on to relate, with respect to the controversy with the Right Honourable
The General's second letter. Same date.

[6] General Archives S.J., *Anglia, Epist. Gen.—Documents*, I. No. 6, G.

Baron lord of that region, on the subject of not appropriating to the service of the Church any landed property without his consent. I should be sorry if differences about temporal things placed a hindrance in the way of the conversion of souls; or if on account of perishable goods we should be hampered in bringing the natives to goods eternal. Wherefore you may assure the Right Honourable Baron in my name, that we shall not be a source of detriment to his temporal dominion; and that, on the contrary, we shall, as far as the nature of our institute allows us, be always ready to enlarge and promote the interests of his proprietary rights. There is but small hope of obtaining a pontifical brief (such as you ask for), that all donations made heretofore for the benefit of the Church without his consent be nullified. Still, that we may do all in our power to conciliate the right honourable gentleman, let your Reverence adopt this line of conduct: for the sake of peace you will issue an order to all of ours who are working in that vineyard, that they do not accept at all of any landed property offered them, whether by the faithful or by infidels, without the consent of the same Right Honourable Baron. As I have often heard him spoken of with commendation for his eminent piety, zeal, and particular good will towards our lowly Order, I am encouraged to hope that he will be facile and liberal in granting his consent, for such acquisitions as shall appear necessary to support our missionaries according to our institute.

"Please convey my kindliest wishes to him, of whose piety, I am glad to recall, I once had the pleasure of being a witness myself here. And I commend myself to your holy Sacrifices and prayers. 31 October, 1643." [7]

By this letter the principle for which Lord Baltimore had contended was granted to him fully; and that not merely by Father Copley,[8] but by the General himself. All that he had contended for, in trying to force Statutes of Mortmain on the province, was conceded just so far as the Jesuits were concerned. The event proved, however, even for the authorities at so remote a distance as Rome, that it was not merely the principle which the baron was contending for, but it was the property; which, as a modern State might express it, he had an "aspiration" to "incamerate;" in very much the same way as, to his distress, the Virginians and Parliamentarians and the Puritans of the Severn had an aspiration to "incamerate" his province, and did so very soon. We presume that this concession was

---

[7] General Archives S.J., *Anglia, Epist. Gen.—Documents*, I. No. 6, H.
[8] Cf. *Calvert Papers*, i. 164, 7°.—Cf. *supra*, § 66 (2), p. 532.

communicated to him by Father Knott; for we find at once that the baron's appetite increased. As Cornwaleys had said to him: "Seldome or never have I heard or seene covetousnes decrease with age;" and he might have added: "nor decrease with glutting it." [9]

That Annual Letter, which was due in August, was lost on the way. And the General desired Father Knott to send another copy (November 14, 1643). At last, on December 5, he acknowledged with great satisfaction the receipt of the Relation. After congratulations, he added: "Certainly, to the effect that no hindrance may be put in the way by any disagreement about earthly belongings, I have already expressed my mind to your Reverence, that for the sake of peace you should forbid ours to accept any landed property without the consent of the Right Honourable Baron, lord of that region; and I trust that letter will have reached you. I should be sorry indeed to see the first fruits, which are so beautifully developing in the Lord, nipped in their growth by the frost of cupidity." [10] *The General enforces the concessions to Baltimore. Dec., 1643.*

Now they entered on a new year, 1644, with its Relation for the preceding, 1643. Of this we have no copy, nor of any other letter covering the following twelve months. Our information is to be gathered from the General's replies extant. In this interval, the long Generalate of Father Mutius Vitelleschi, which had extended over thirty years, came practically to a close; and a Vicar is seen to be answering letters.

By the reply sent to Father Fisher, or Copley, direct, on July 16, 1644, we learn that he had reported the Baptism of many important people, with hopes of seeing the rest follow. This reference is probably to the Indians. Besides, "Virginia itself had experienced the benefits of the missionaries being so near; and they were thinking of carrying the light of the gospel into the remoter parts of India," *in interiorem Indiam.* The General commends all this, and adds: "As to the excursion which you propose *Virginia. Remoter India. New England.*

---

[9] *Calvert Papers,* i. 175.—Cf.
"*Crescit amor nummi, quantum ipsa pecunia crescit.*"
Juvenal.

[10] General Archives S.J., as above.—*Documents,* I. No. 6, J, K.—Significant of his contempt for the whole issue raised by the colonial Proprietary, the word which the General uses in his draft is *reculæ*: "*de terrenis reculis;*" which we have translated by "belongings." He cancels in his draft an additional barbarous word, "*amobamentiis.*" The former, *recula,* a diminutive from *res,* "a thing," means "a little bit of a thing," a trifle, a *coserella.* The latter seems to be from *amoveo,* "to move away," like *mobilia,* "chattels," from *moveo;* and would class the Proprietary's colonial lands with things that are swept away, as persons come and go—not an inept conception of colonial possessions.

making into New England, I have nothing to say against it. Weigh carefully the difficulties of the undertaking with your councillors; and, if there is a fair hope of success, you have my approval. I will write, however, to Father Provincial, that if anything adverse to the proposal occur to him, he may mention it to you betimes; and do you conform to his advice.

"I regret though that, where the harvest is so great, the harvesters should be so few; and that even for those, few as they are, the necessaries of life are not sufficiently available. He who is the Helper in due season will, I hope, be at hand; and when you seek, and, more than seeking, do also propagate the kingdom of God with such devotedness, He will add the rest. Hence I would approve highly your suggestion about making a foundation, if the consent and good will of the Lord Proprietary of that country can be had for the purpose.

"In any case, however that be, let us not fail in doing good; for in due time we shall reap without fail. Let us imitate our predecessors, those first harvesters of the new soil turned up in Indian climes; and the Apostles themselves, who amid grievous hardships, in cold and nakedness, in hunger and thirst, and amid a thousand perils, scattered the seed of the Word of God. No labours can be so wearing but that eternal rest will be more than enough to requite them with interest. May the grace of our Lord and the charity of God be with you all." [11]

On the same day (July 16, 1644) the General wrote to the Provincial, saying: "The superior of Maryland has inquired of me whether I thought he should make an excursion of some months' duration into New England, whither he says he is invited to go by the hopes of no small fruit. I do not see any obstacle in the way of his going to seek the profit of souls wherever he can find it. But, if your Reverence knows of any, do not omit to give him your opinion on the subject." [12]

To the Provincial, on New England.

The New England in question was at that time all the land north of the Maryland boundary. The Maryland "foundation" under discussion, if it was not the same as had been spoken of before when Father Poulton held out the hopes of a college,[13] must have been some new Indian base of operations, to supply for the loss of Mattapany. And the doubt expressed about the likelihood of eliciting that consent, which Baltimore would make believe he

[11] General Archives S.J., *Anglia, Epist. Gen.—Documents*, I. No. 6, L.
[12] *Ibid.—Documents*, I. No. 6, M. [13] Cf. *supra*, § 39.

Ingle, the captain to whom Baltimore, two years before, had entrusted his first instalment of intruding clergy.[6]

On July 22, 1645, the Vicar-General wrote to Father Knott, who was still Provincial: "I cannot but grieve, as I well may, at the violence which has carried our Fathers off from Maryland, with so much hardship to themselves and such loss to religion in a new-tilled field like that. Perhaps, to reward their labours in that vineyard, the Lord will give them the palm of martyrdom; or, in any case, the glory of confessing the faith more conspicuously in the face of the world, that their virtue may stand out so much the more as an object for imitation."[7]

Thus the two older missionaries, one Father White the founder, the other Father Copley the most prominent man among the fourteen Jesuits who had worked in Maryland, were violently taken away to England. The three new men, who thought they had come to begin a career, were all cut off. They died of hardship or by violence, certainly not in comfort, nor cared for by kind friends. Father Roger Rigbie was carried off to Virginia, and died in the hands of enemies. The Necrology of the Province gives 1646 as the date, and Virginia as the place, of his death.[8] Yet so little did they know in England of his fate, that we find his name in a Catalogue, three years after the date of his death, with the statement that he was professed of four vows on June 17, 1645.[9] Hence his capture and abduction should have been after that date; and he survived but a short time.

Rigbie, Hartwell, Cooper. Death of all. 1646.

Father Bernard Hartwell, who had been sent from England in 1643, became superior of the mission in the following year. His death is reported for the same year as Rigbie's, 1646.[10] Father John Cooper, who accompanied Hartwell to America, is also entered as having met his death in Virginia, day and month unknown, but the year still the same, 1646.[11] The coincidence of three young men dying in the same year, while they lay in the hands of enemies, needs no comment, whether the violence which did away with them was that of hardship or something still more summary. Their very loneliness in the remote distance is made the more conspicuous by the circumstance that, after the date which the Necrology discovered

---

[6] Cf. *Calvert Papers*, i. 211, 212, 216.
[7] General Archives S.J., *Anglia, Epist. Gen.—Documents*, I. No. 6, P.
[8] H. Foley, *Records*, vii., *Collectanea, s.v.*
[9] General Archives S.J., *Catal.* 1, 1649.—*Catalogus* 3, of 1645, from which no doubt the Triennial Report was taken, observes the date to have been *stilo veteri*.
[10] Foley, as above.
[11] *Ibid.*

for their demise, the Annual Catalogue for 1646, if not also for 1647, had continued to report them as in the full administration of the Maryland Mission.[12]

Statistics.

Meanwhile it may be observed that, in the course of twelve years from the day when Father White first set foot on Maryland soil, and founded the English Mission in America, there had died, like soldiers stricken on the field, no fewer than eight men. Two of the survivors were now exiles from Maryland, being presented as traitors to English justice. Four others had come; but of them one couple stayed barely a year or two, and another couple had only attended a gentleman and then returned to England. Thus, among the regular or stationary missioners, the loss of life in twelve years was eighty per cent.

But much more profuse was the expenditure of youthful health and vigour. Father Ferdinand Poulton had just reached forty years of age; Father Hartwell, thirty-nine; Father Rigbie, thirty-eight; Father Cooper, thirty-six; Father Knowles, thirty. Father Altham, one of the original missionaries, was mature in years, being aged fifty-one; Brother Morley, fifty; and Brother Gervase, forty-seven.

[12] General Archives S.J., *Catal.* 3, 1646 *et* 1647.—These words, "*et* 1647," are added on the outside by an ancient hand.

APPENDICES

A. OLD ST. MARY'S CITY
B. INDIAN LAND TITLES
C. STATUTES OF MORTMAIN

APPENDIX A

Text, § 36, p. 334; § 60 (2), pp. 483–485; § 67, p. 540.

MAP OF OLD ST. MARY'S CITY, WITH EXPLANATIONS.[1]

§ 71. Sources of the Map of early properties in Maryland.

§ 71. *Thomas Copley's Properties assigned in trust to Cuthbert Fenwick: Certificate of Survey* [Land Records of Maryland, Annapolis, Md., Lib. 1, fol. 115 (old Lib. F, fol. 134)]: "27th July, 1641 . . . ¶ Laid out for Cutbert Fenwick Gent a parcell of Town land, lyeing nearest about the new Chappell at St. Maries, and bounding on the East with St. Peter's Freehold, on the South with the Town land of Mr. Giles Brent Gent, and a line drawn from the end of the said Town land unto St. Peter's Freehold, on the West with a swamp in St. George's River called the Key Swamp, and on the North with a right line drawn from the top of the hill on the North side of the said swamp, where the rayle heretofore stood, unto that part of the Mill [fol. 116 (134)] Brook, where the Freehold of St. Peter's ends, being about the distance of 45 perches above the place where the mill now standeth, containing 25 acres or thereabouts.

"Further: Laid out for the said Cutbert Fenwick another parcell of Town land, lying together in a Neck making the northern point of St. Inigo's Creek, and bounding on the East with a Creek called St. Peter's Key, on the South with the mouth of St. Inigo's Creek, on the West with St. George's River, and on the North with a line drawn from the head of St. Peter's Key unto a bite distant some 40 perches or thereabouts to the northward from the foreland commonly called Marrill's Point, containing 120 acres or thereabouts.

"[(135)] Further: Laid out for the said Cutbert Fenwick another

---

[1] This is a Map drawn after original surveys, and with acknowledgments due for the chart in *Chronicles of Colonial Maryland*, by J. W. Thomas. The shore-line has been reproduced here as in the map of the U.S. Geological Survey, but, according to actual survey, the northern shore of St. Inigo's Creek should be altered: (1) by prolonging g, the bight or Creek of St. Peter's Key, towards the north-west, as far as the angle formed by the three properties, 10, 11, and the unnumbered tract between, giving a water outlet to all three, with a considerable projecting or pointed front to 10, and making 11, St. Inigo's, a complete neck or peninsula with three sides on the water; (2) by prolonging northwards h, St. Andrew's Creek or bight, as far as the southern junction of 7 and 8, giving a water outlet to 7, a considerable front to 8, and an entire side upon the water to 9. See the inset map in accompanying volume of *Documents*, I. No. 24.

Some modern roads and names have been taken from the same Geological Survey without further comment.

parcell of Town land, lying about St. Maries Hill, and bounding on the East with the Hill Creek, on the South with a branch of St. Inigo's Creek, on the North with a paralell line drawn from the Hill Creek and extending due West up the hill (about the distance of a furlong to the northward from the house now standing) for the length of 160 perches, and on the West with a meridian line drawn from the end of the said 160 perches unto St. Inigo's Creek, containing 255 acres or thereabouts.

"Further: Laid out for a Mannor for the said Cutbert Fenwick one neck of land, lyeing upon the East side of St. George's, and bounding on the North with St. Inigo's Creek, on the South with the mouth of Trinity Creek, and on the East with a branch of Trinity Creek called the Back Creek, and a line drawn from the northermost head of the said branch to the southermost bite of a branch in St. Inigo's Creek called [fol. 117 (135)] St. Luke's Creek, where the Mannor of Cornwaleys Cross ends, containing 2000 acres or thereabouts.

"And further: Laid out one Island, lyeing on the westerne side of the mouth of St. George's River, called St. George's Island, containing 1000 acres or thereabouts."—Here the Patent follows: 28th July, 1641.

(*The localities on the accompanying Map with references to the Land Records at Annapolis, Md.*)—

1. *Governor's Field.* Surveyed as 100 acres for Leonard Calvert, August 13, 1641, Lib. 1, fol. 121 (old Lib. F), also Lib. A, B, and H, fol. 98. Resurveyed for John Mackall, May 1, 1801, Lib. I. C., No. Q, fol. 37, as 70 acres. Lord Baltimore's rent-roll of the date 1707, which is in the library of the Maryland Historical Society, Baltimore, Md., identifies it with East St. Mary's.

2. *The Chapel Lot.* See above, *Thomas Copley's Properties.*

3. *St. Peter's.* Surveyed as 150 acres for Philip Calvert, September 23, 1664, Lib. 6, fol. 277 (old Lib. AA, fol. 491). The survey is notable for giving the length and bearing of the last side, and not saying merely, "thence by a straight line to the point of beginning." At least one of the lines can still be identified. The property must have been granted very early to some one, probably Jerome Hawley or Thomas Cornwallis,[2] as it is mentioned in 1641 in the surveys of the following and the two preceding pieces of land.

4. *St. Mary's Hill.* See above, *Thomas Copley's Properties.*

5. *The Intacke.* Surveyed as 57 acres for Philip Calvert, October 5, 1677, Lib. 19, fol. 510 (old Lib. W. C., fol. 383).

6. *White House.* Surveyed as 63 acres for Giles Brent, October 9, 1639, Lib. 1, fol. 33 (old Lib. F, fol. 58). Resurveyed with adjoining land for Massey Leigh, August 12, 1757, Lib. BC and GS, No. 12, fol. 331.

7. *Sisters' Field.* Surveyed as 70½ acres for Margaret and Mary Brent, October 7, 1639, Lib. 1, fol. 31 (old Lib. F, fol. 56). The southern line can still be identified. At its river end once stood St. Adauctus' Tree.

[2] Cf. *Calvert Papers*, i. 200, *ad calc.*: Lewger, January 5, 1639, to Baltimore.

Greene's Rest. Surveyed as 55 acres, October 15, 1639, Lib. 1, fol. 41, was soon forfeited to the proprietor under an act for deserted plantations.

8. *Clark's Freehold.* Surveyed as 50 acres for Robert Clark, July 21, 1640, Lib. 1, fol. 71 (old Lib. F).

9. *Lewis' Neck.* Surveyed as 30 acres for William Lewis, December 4, 1640, Lib. 1, fol. 46 (old Lib. F, fol. 68).

10. *St. Peter's Key,* or *Van Sweringen's Point.* Surveyed as 50 acres for John Harris, July 15, 1640, Lib. A, B, and H, fol. 82 (Lib. 1, fol. 72). Assigned to Roger Oliver, September 22, 1640 (*ibid.*), and later escheated to the proprietor (rent-roll of 1707, before mentioned). Surveyed again as 50 acres for Garrett Van Sweringen, August 18, 1677, Lib. 13, fol. 103 (old Lib. I.I., fol. 473). The certificate of survey says, "formerly laid out for one Blanchys." This name does not appear elsewhere in the records, and must be a mistake for Harris. There can be no doubt that this is the same land as St. Peter's Key, from the exact correspondence of the descriptions. It was assigned by Van Sweringen in 1675 to Robert Ridgely, Lib. W. R. C., fol. 2. The survey of Chancellor's Point in 1705, mentioned later, speaks of land owned by the widow of Robert Ridgely as being in the position assigned on the map, and the boundary-lines agree with those of the two surveys of the property.

All or most of the land lying to the east of St. Peter's Key, between it and St. Inigo's and St. Andrew's Creeks, was surveyed for Thomas Courtney (1676, Lib. 19, fol. 584) and Daniel Clocker (1681, Lib. 21, fol. 349). But the dividing line or lines are not given on the map, as it is not clear just where they fall.

11. *St. Inigo's Neck.* See above, *Thomas Copley's Properties;* also Lib. A, B, and H, fol. 97. It is very probably the same as *Kit Martin's Point.* The northern line as given seems correct, but it is not quite certain. The boundaries of St. Inigo's Neck make it impossible to place it elsewhere than where our actual survey has placed it; and, as St. Peter's Key Creek is one of its boundaries, the situation of this is made certain also. Corroborative evidence is given under the preceding property.

f. *Chancellor's Point.* Resurveyed for Charles Carroll, November 21, 1705, Lib. DD, No. 5, fol. 719, included St. Inigo's Neck and the land to the west and north of St. Peter's Key.

St. Inigo's Manor and *St. George's Island.* See above, *Thomas Copley's Properties.*

Cross Manor. Surveyed as 2000 acres for Thomas Cornwallis, September 8, 1639, Lib. 1, fol. 110 (old Lib. F). The precise situation of the eastern line is somewhat uncertain.

a. *St. John's Creek.* A survey for John Lewger, September 18, 1639, Lib. 1, fol. 52, places St. John's Creek where the map has it, and distinguishes it from Mill Creek.

m. *Wickliffe's Creek.* Its identification with Carthagena Creek is due to Mr. J. Edwin Coad, whose property lies along it.

APPENDIX B

Text, § 64, p. 519.

INDIAN LAND TITLES

§ 72. Silvius on Maryland. § 73. Kent and others on the general question.

§ 72. WE have stated above the circumstances in which Dr. Silvius of Doway was consulted on the Maryland question of Mattapany. Matters concerning the entire text of his answer, which is in Latin, may be seen in the volume of *Documents*, I. No. 17. We subjoin here, in English, parts of the solution, as translated from the fragmentary Latin manuscript, apparently original and autograph, in the Westminster Diocesan Archives, xxx. No. 28. The passages will serve for a term of comparison with the doctrine of others on the subject, as indicated in the next section (§ 73).

"[Answer to the first *Query*.] . . . Then one asks in general: Whether no person whatever, excepting N., his heirs and assigns, can be the true and absolute lord and proprietary of any part or tract, found there and previously unoccupied, unless N. give his consent? The answer must be the same as before; that no one can be, for the reasons adduced. Besides, it belongs to the lord paramount, such as is the King of England, or else to the lord proprietary, as N. is, to observe and exact the observance of all that conduces to the stable constitution and government of that new plantation, unto the common weal; with the proviso that they do not forbid such persons to travel, trade, dwell there, as shall do so without injury to the English. For, by the natural law of society and human intercourse, others have a right to travel into those provinces, and to trade and stay there, doing, however, no harm to the fatherland or the persons of the English who dwell there; as Victoria shows at large in the lecture cited, 5, section 3. Should any such detriment be reasonably apprehended, the persons who give cause to fear may be prohibited from trading or staying there.

(1) Can any one but Baltimore be proprietary in Maryland?

"Answer to the second *Query*. Of those parts where the barbarians live and have already the right of ownership, anything can be given, granted, or validly sold, to any subject of the King of England by such barbarians, within the limits so allotted to the said N. The reason is, because barbarians have the true ownership of the things they possess; and neither the

(2) Can the Indian proprietors make valid gifts?

King of England nor any one else can take that right of ownership away from them. For, since faith is not the foundation of proprietorship, and furnishes no title of just ownership, it follows that infidels, from the fact of their being infidels, do not thereby cease to be owners of the things which they possess. This is self-evident; and Cajetan proves it well, $2^{da}\ 2^{dae}$ q. 66, ad art. 8,[1] subjoining as a conclusion drawn thence, that no king, nor Emperor, nor the Roman Church, can declare war against them for the sake of occupying their lands, or reducing them to temporal subjection; since there is no motive for a just war. Victoria likewise, in the same lecture, 5, section 1, asserts more than once that there is nothing to prevent barbarians from being true owners; neither their sins in general, nor the sin of infidelity in particular; and that they are owners by public right as well as by private right; nor is there any title here enabling Christians to occupy their goods and lands. Now, the right of ownership means the power of using one's property for any use legally permitted; as may be seen in Dominic Soto, l. 4, q. 1, art. 1, and in Bannez, at the beginning of the treatise on ownership, q. 62, in $2^{da}\ 2^{dae}$.[2] Wherefore barbarians can use their lands and possessions, either by keeping them, or by giving, selling, granting them to whomsoever they will, especially to the English.

"If you say that barbarians cannot make a valid gift, sale, or grant to the subjects of the King of England, not for want of power in the barbarians [to give], but for want of capacity on the part of the subjects [to accept], inasmuch as the King has incapacitated every subject of his to that effect, it appears contrariwise that there is no decree in the royal charter about such a disability; nor can it be satisfactorily inferred from the charter. It is true that he gives, grants, and confirms to the said N., his heirs and assigns, all that part of the peninsula, etc., all the islands, all the soil, all the fields, etc., and that he makes them true and absolute lords and proprietaries of the region aforesaid and of all the premises; and that he grants all this to their sole and proper behoof and use. Whence it truly follows that, by the royal gift and grant, they alone have the dominion and ownership of the region newly discovered, not before settled by them, or granted. But, as to the parts and lands previously occupied and possessed by the barbarians, nothing is decreed, and nothing could be decreed by the King. For those barbarians are not his subjects, nor do their lands and fields pertain to the King's dominion or lie at his disposal; but the barbarians have the dominion and ownership thereof, just as they had before. The King became lord only of the land newly discovered and not occupied by any; not of that land which had its occupiers and owners. It is said, indeed, in the royal charter, that the King enables those who

No disability in any colonist to accept.

---

[1] Viz. of the *Summa Theologica* of St. Thomas Aquinas, as commented on by Cardinal Cajetan.
[2] Viz. of the same *Summa Theologica* of St. Thomas.

shall desire it to receive or buy of the said N. But it does not follow thence that he disenables those who shall accept or buy, not of N. himself, but of the barbarians, such lands, fields, houses, as these had previously possessed and occupied.

"Hence may be gathered the answer to the third *Query*. By the mere fact that the barbarians give, grant, or sell to a subject of the King of England any part of the lands hitherto occupied by themselves, the aforesaid N. does not acquire any true right to that part, so as to be its lord and proprietary; but that person is the proprietary to whom the barbarians granted, gave, or sold it. These, as true owners of that part, have acted according to the power which is in them, when they disposed of the same to that person's use and not to the use of the said N. Nor can any sufficient ground be discerned for saying that the King incapacitated such a person, his subject, from buying or accepting of the barbarians parts of that kind.

<small>(3) Right of the colonist accepting, exclusive of Baltimore.</small>

"The answer to the fourth *Query* follows from what has been said; to wit, that, in case the barbarians give, grant, or sell any such part or region to any subject of the King of England, whether designated (*assignato*) or not by the said N., the latter is bound in conscience to respect and ratify such grant, gift, or sale; nor can he give the property to another, or turn it to other uses. For the grant, gift, sale, has been effected by those who have the legitimate dominion and ownership of these goods; whereas the said N. has not received from any one a power to go about disposing of them otherwise; since the King is not lord of that part or region. For the dominion which accrued to the King by right of discovery extends no farther than the regions and lands newly discovered and uninhabited; it does not affect those which had true lords and owners. The law of nations has it that what are nobody's goods may become the property of the first who occupies them; not that what are somebody's already may be so occupied; for which consult Cajetan and Victoria, as quoted above.

<small>(4) Baltimore bound to respect an Indian gift to a colonist.</small>

"As to the reasons for doubting: To the first one propounded the answer is conformable to what has just been said; that the words of the grant do indeed run, as if N. alone was lord and proprietary of the whole region, of all the tracts, etc. But they have reference to a region uninhabited and to tracts uncultivated; that is, to such as have fallen to the King by right of discovery, not to other lands; because to other lands the King has acquired no right.

<small>The charter, and land unoccupied, etc.</small>

"In the same manner are to be understood the arguments brought forward in the second reason for doubting.

"It is not true what is adduced in the third reason: that the argument which applies to lands not inhabited or occupied by barbarians may also be applied to the parts which the barbarians do possess in that region. For of these lands which they possess they are true lords and

§ 73]   THE RIGHT BASED ON DISCOVERY   573

owners [...] they are not of the others which have been discovered and were no[...] habited by any one.

"As [...] the confirmation: It is of no consequence that the first colonist[...] perchance even the King himself, understood the said N. to be in th[...] manner the sole lord, and to be the only one who had any right to all th[...] region, and to each of its parts; so that no subjects of the King of Engl[...] could accept or buy of the barbarians anything in their possession, ex[...] in dependence on the said N. For, when kings are kindly disposed [...] they are easily imposed upon; and, as to what the first colonists thought [...] that lays down no law.

"So [...] solved at Doway, the 28th day of November, in the year 1641 —defer[...] to a better judgment.

"FRANCIS SILVIUS,
"Doctor of Sacred Theology and
Regius and Ordinary Professor of the same." [3]

The [sc]holastic theologian Victoria, used so largely by Silvius, is also summar[ise]d with sufficient correctness upon this subject by Wheaton, in his [Law] of Nations. This American lawyer says that Victoria [...] asserts the natural right of the Indians to dominio[n] over their own country. He denies the assertion of Bart[olu]s and the other civilians of the school of Bologna, that 'th[e] Emperor is lord of the whole world,' or that the Pope could confer o[n] the King of Spain any dominion over those parts inhabited by infidel [ba]rbarians. He rests their title on what he calls the right of natural [soc]iety and intercourse, as authorizing the Spaniards to sojourn and trade in [th]ose parts of the world without injuring the native inhabitants. The ref[usa]l of hospitality and permission to trade he holds to be a just ground [of] war, which again might lead to the acquisition of sovereignty through [th]e right of conquest confirmed by voluntary cession. He denies the righ[t o]f making war upon the infidel nations for refusing to receive the gos[pe]l; but asserts that they might be constrained to allow its being preache[d t]o those who wished to hear, and [that they might be] prevented from pe[rs]ecuting the new converts." Then Victoria goes on to limit the possibil[iti]es of such latitude being abused by the Christians.[4]

Wheaton's sketch of Victoria's doctrine.

§ 7[3.] Admitting the distinction between a national *dominium* or domain [i]n using a country, and a national *imperium* or empire in governi[ng] the country, we may quote what Vattel says of occupancy: "There [is] another celebrated question to which the discovery of the new world [ha]s principally given rise. It is asked whether a nation may

[3] We[st]minster Diocesan Archives, xxx. No. 28.—*Documents*, I. No. 17.
[4] H. [W]heaton, *History of the Law of Nations*, p. 36.—Cf. Victoria, Franciscus de, [1480-15[...]], "*Relectiones Undecim: De Indis recenter inventis, relectio prior,*" ff. 129ᵛ–[...]2; "*De titulis quibus barbari potuerint venire in ditionem Hispanorum,*" ff. 162ᵛ–[...], edit. Salmanticæ, 1565.

lawfully take possession of some part of a vast country, in which there are none but erratic peoples, whose scanty population is incapable of occupying the whole. We have already observed (§ 81), in establishing the obligation to cultivate the earth, that those nations cannot exclusively appropriate to themselves more land than they have occasion for, or more than they are able to settle and cultivate. Their unsettled habitation in those immense regions cannot be accounted a true and legal possession." This writer then approves of buying the lands from the Indians as the "English Puritans," he says, have done; and so too the Quakers. He quotes the *History of the English Colonies in North America*. Under the name of "English Puritans" here, the credit of Maryland Catholics has been quietly transferred to the wrong party.[5]

Vattel on Indian titles.

The opinions, judgments, and theories reported in different parts of Chancellor Kent's *Commentaries on American Law*, are singularly vacillating and mutually discordant. The judges who have delivered such different opinions at different times would seem to have been influenced in several ways. First, there is conspicuous in latter days a want of familiarity with matters of history and ethical right, as facts evolved and right was understood in the seventeenth century. Secondly, midway in American history, a new set of philosophical notions about man and society originated in the free-thinking and in the revolutions of the eighteenth century. Thirdly, whether as a cause or as an effect of vacillating opinions, the whole policy of the United States Government in dealing with the Indians changed, to the disadvantage of the latter, at a certain period in the nineteenth century. In Kent's *Commentaries* this new departure is dated from 1829. The administration of President Jackson inaugurated the change.[6]

American judges on Indian land titles.

However, some of the opinions delivered by the Supreme Court of the United States will show a substantial agreement in both principle and policy with the statements quoted in our last section from the Doway Doctor of the seventeenth century. The Chancellor reports that the Supreme Court of the United States, in the case of Worcester, reviewed the whole ground of controversy relative to the character and validity of Indian rights within the territorial dominions as they exist now of the United States; and especially with reference to the Cherokee nation, within the territorial limits of Georgia. It declared that the right acquired by Europeans on the ground of discovery was an exclusive right to purchase; which did not deny the right of the Indian possessor to sell.

---

[5] Vattel, *Droit des Gens*, i. § 209, pp. 268, 269; edit. Royer-Collard: "*On ne s'écarte donc point des vues de la nature, en resserrant les sauvages dans des bornes plus étroites. Cependant on ne peut que louer la modération des Puritains anglais, qui les premiers s'établirent dans la Nouvelle Angleterre. Quoique munis d'une charte de leur souverain, ils achetèrent des sauvages le terrein qu'ils voulaient occuper* ('*Histoire des Colonies anglaises de l'Amérique septentrionale*'). *Ce louable exemple fut suivi par Guillaume Penn, et la colonie de Quackers qu'il conduisit dans la Pensylvanie.*"

[6] 3 Kent, *Comm.*, 399, 400, note.

Though [in the course of time] the right to the soil was claimed to be vested in the European Governments, as a necessary consequence of discovery and the assumption of territorial jurisdiction, still such right to the soil was such only with reference to other whites; while, with respect to the Indians, it was always understood to signify only an exclusive preference in being allowed to purchase those lands which the natives were willing to sell. The royal grants and charters asserted a title to the country against other Europeans only, and they were considered as blank paper so far as the rights of the natives were concerned.

In another case, that of Mitchel *versus* the United States, the Supreme Court once more declared the same general doctrine—that lands in the possession of friendly Indians were always, under the colonial governments, considered as being owned by the tribe or nation in common, by a perpetual right of succession. The ultimate fee was either in the Crown or its grantees. The hunting-grounds of the tribes were as much in their actual possession as the cleared fields of the whites. And [in the course of time] individuals had to purchase for themselves by licence or under rules prescribed. This came to be the case in all the colonies.[7] Fiction of law; ultimate fee in the Crown or grantees

Before this came to be the case, by means of law defining the rights of royal grantees to be preferential and exclusive of individual colonists, the latter were as free to acquire as the Indians were to convey their property. Such was the condition of things in Maryland at the time which we have been considering. Indian rights to their own property were recognized, honoured, paid for, and transferred, when Leonard Calvert landed with the first expedition. Then, during fifteen years, there followed a series of Acts, in the name of Cecil Lord Proprietary, to culminate in a law of 1649 about "purchasing lands from the Indians," all of which till that date implied the lack of any exclusive right in the Proprietary; and the last of which at that date conferred on him, for the first time, an exclusive right of being the only person who could receive in the first instance from the Indian possessors of the soil. Much more significant was the course of his private acts with the Jesuit Provincial, soliciting at his hands the transfer of titles acquired by the Jesuits from the aborigines. In the Jesuits, indeed, there was vested at least a double right. They had acquired land from the Indians as any freemen might. And, moreover, they had acquired it in trust for the spiritual service of the Indians themselves.

Besides such facts of the case, which history undertakes to state, there are some fictions which the courts of law assume; to the end that legal decisions in the given subject-matter may have a fixed base of departure and show a continuity of policy. Such a fiction would be that of an ultimate fee in the lands of the Indians being vested in the Crown of England or in the royal grantees; as if *Fictions, more or less plausible.*

[7] 3 Kent, *Comm.*, pp. 383–386.

Indian land were in England. It is probably in the indulgence of some such propensity for presuming legal fictions that we must seek an excuse and indulgence for opinions and statements which are otherwise very inexcusable.[8]

In the inevitable supplanting of native populations by a white race, it may be assumed that the Indians had been occupants only; that they had been displaced, it matters not whether by purchase or by conquest; that they had been incapable of transferring the title of their lands to any other than a white sovereign; that their right and title are absolutely extinguished. These statements may not stand the light of history. Still they place a suitable background behind legal decisions. All parties in actual life agree; and no party who might be injured comes forward to make good his claim. In fact, the jurist speaks expressly of "an assumed but qualified dominion over the Indian tribes, regarding them as enjoying no higher title to the soil than that founded on simple occupancy;" and again of an Indian aboriginal condition, which "would not admit of the application of any more liberal and equal doctrine to the case of Indian lands and contracts. It was founded on the pretension of converting the discovery of the country into a conquest; and it is now too late to draw into discussion the validity of that opinion."[9]

But it was also stated boldly in a decision, that each nation, which discovered the land and discovered the Indians, claimed the right to establish its own relations with these natives; that such relations "necessarily impaired, to a considerable degree, the rights of the original inhabitants; and an ascendancy was asserted in consequence of the superior genius of the Europeans, founded on civilization and Christianity, and of their superiority in the means and arts of war."[10]

Christianity, civilization, etc., conferring no title. Though some reasoning of this kind appeared in the *Relation of Maryland*, as quoted before,[11] still whether propounded in the Maryland *Relation* or in the judicial opinion and precedent, it is of a kind which might be put in the mouth of any bandit; who probably would not malign "civilization and Christianity" by mentioning them in the same breath with a robber's claim. Or still more brutally, quoting the Chancellor's statement, do we find it affirmed that "according to Chalmers,[12] the practice of the European world had constituted a law of nations, which sternly disregarded the possession of the aborigines, because they had not been admitted into the society of nations.[13]

[8] Compare the conflicting opinions in Kent's *Commentaries*, i. 258: Pre-emption of Indian lands; iii. 378: Of the Foundation to Title to Land, (1) By Government Grant; *Ibid.*, 380, 381: (3) Qualified Indian Rights; *Ibid.*, i. 383, 386, as quoted above in the Supreme Court decisions.

[9] *Ibid.*, iii. 381.

[10] *Ibid.*, 379, in Johnson *v.* M'Intosh.

[11] *Supra*, § 34, pp. 326, 327.

[12] Chalmers, *Political Annals*, p. 676.

[13] Kent, *Ibid.*, 388. The text of Kent's *Commentaries* continues here in the line of traditional history; and it quotes in a note (*a*, *389) George Bancroft, i. 400,

And so it was that, in the very year of Leonard Calvert's peaceful descent on Maryland, Roger Williams was denounced at Salem, in January, for a paper which he had written in the neighbouring colony of Plymouth; to prove that a grant of land in New England from an English King could not be perfect, unless the grantees "compounded with the natives." This opinion, says Bancroft, sounded like treason against the charter of the colony. Williams was ready to see the offensive manuscript burned. But he so explained its purport that the court applauded his temper, and declared " that the matters were not so evil as at first they seemed." [14]

R. Williams at Salem. 1634.

as in the next paragraph of our text, without discerning what that historian implies with regard to Roger Williams's theory and the practice of his opponents: "But whatever [*389, *ibid.*] loose opinions might have been entertained, or latitudinary doctrines inculcated, in favour of the abstract right to possess and colonize America, it is certain that, in point of fact, the colonists were not satisfied, or did not deem it expedient, to settle the country without the consent of the aborigines, procured by fair purchase, under the sanction of the civil authorities. The pretensions of the patent of King James were not relied on; and the prior Indian right to the soil of the country was generally, if not uniformly, recognized and respected by the New England Puritans (Bancroft, i. 400). They always negotiated with the Indian nations as distinct and independent powers."

[14] G. Bancroft, *History of the United States*, i. 369, 17th edit.—Here compare the statement just quoted from Vattel, *supra*, note 5.

APPENDIX C

Text, § 17 (3), pp. 240 *sq.*; § 52 (2), pp. 430, 431; § 53 (2), p. 440 *sq.*

HISTORY OF MORTMAIN BEFORE HENRY VIII.

§ 74. General idea of Mortmain. § 75. Statutes of Mortmain in Catholic times.
§ 76. The Catholic statutes and the legal status in Maryland.

Published Sources: Angell and Ames, *Private Corporations Aggregate.*—*Archives of Maryland: Proceedings of the Council,* 1636–1667.—F. Bacon, *Works,* iv.; *Reading on the Statute of Uses.*—J. Bacquet, *Œuvres,* i.—Blackstone's *Commentaries on English Law.*—J. H. Boehmer, *Jus Parochiale.*—G. Bowyer, *Commentaries on Universal Public Law.*—Coke's *Littleton*; 2 *Institutes.*—C. Dodd, *Church History of England,* edited by Tierney, i., ii.—L. Ferraris, *Prompta Bibliotheca Canonica, Juridica,* etc.—W. F. Finlason, *History of the Laws of Mortmain.*—E. Gibson, *Codex Juris Ecclesiastici,* ii.—H. Hallam, *Middle Ages,* ii.—House of Commons, *Report of Mortmain Committee,* 1844.—B. T. Johnson, *Foundation of Maryland.*—J. Kent, *Commentaries on American Law.*—J. Lingard, *History of England,* iv., vii.—F. W. Maitland, *Roman Canon Law in the Church of England.*—T. M. Mamachi, *Del Diritto Libero della Chiesa di acquistare, ecc.,* i., iv.—J. V. L. McMahon, *Historical View of the Government of Maryland.*—F. Palgrave, *Rise and Progress of the English Commonwealth: Anglo-Saxon Period.*—J. Perkins, *Lawes of this Realme.*—Pollock and Maitland, *History of English Law,* i.—F. Sacchini, *Historiæ Societatis Jesu,* pars v.—H. Spelman, *Origin of Terms.*—*Statutes of the Realm,* published by the Record Commission.—*Statutes at Large,* published by Ruffhead.—(*Statutes*) *Ancient Laws and Institutes of England,* published by the Record Commission.—Serjeant Stephen, *New Commentaries on the Laws of England, partly founded on Blackstone.*—W. Stubbs, *Constitutional History of England,* ii.; *Select Charters.*—F. Suarez, *Defensio Fidei,* lib. iv.

IN the Conditions of Plantation issued on November 10, 1641, we have seen that Lord Baltimore inserted a clause which read: "Any statute of Mortmayn heretofore passed in the Kingdom of England."[1] But in a subsequent issue of Conditions (1648) a limitation was introduced: "Statutes of Mortmayne heretofore made in the Kingdom of England at any time before the reign of Henry the Eighth, who was King of that Realm."[2]

---

[1] *Supra,* § 62, p. 499.
[2] *Archives of Maryland: Proceedings of the Council,* 1636–1667, p. 227, § 12.—Cf. *supra,* § 63 (1), p. 510, note 10.

We shall give here a general idea of mortmain; and then we shall sketch the history of the first set of Statutes, or those which were prior to Henry VIII. and to the Protestant Reformation in England. At that epoch, mortmain changed its character, and under the old term conveyed a signification quite new. Hence, if space allowed, it would be proper to review its ambiguous history under the second of its meanings, yes, and under a third and a fourth, down to modern times. Among classical historians and legal writers before our day one may search long, and search in vain, for the essential links in this very tortuous subject.

§ 74. The object and use of Church possessions was stated, in the time of Alexander Severus, seventeen centuries ago, by the first of the Urbans, Pope and Martyr, in the following terms: "The goods of the faithful that are offered to the Lord are not to be diverted to other uses than those of the Church and of Christian or needy brethren; because they are the fulfilment of vows; they are the discharging of penances for sin; and they are the patrimony of the poor."[1] *Object and use of Church possessions.*

Fourteen centuries afterwards (1664), a French lawyer of the regalist or Cæsarist school discerned four reasons why "ancient ordinances and statutes of the [French] kingdom" forbade ecclesiastics and other "people of mortmain"[2] to hold hereditaments or property of an immovable nature in France. The reasons were: first, the example of the Apostles, etc.; secondly, the lapse of such feudal services as could be had only of lay vassals by the higher feudal lords; thirdly, the failure of reserves for national defence, such as laymen could afford; fourthly, the tendency of a great part of the land to come into mortmain.[3]

The classes that make up what this writer calls "people of mortmain" will show what is meant by the term. He enumerates three such classes: first, ecclesiastics, that is to say, archbishops, bishops, abbots, priors, chaplains, ecclesiastical communities; secondly, governors of hospitals, *hôtels-Dieu*, confraternities, etc.; thirdly, secular communities, mercantile, legal, etc.[4]

To describe more distinctly the first class, as pertaining directly to the Church, we may take the commentary of Sir Edward Coke on Littleton's double phrase, "man of religion" or man "of Holy Church."[5] He says: "It is to be observed that of ecclesiasticall persons some bee regular, and some bee secular. They bee called regular because they live under certain rules, and have vowed three things: true obedience, perpetuall chastity, and wilfull *Coke's "men of religion," or "of Holy Church."*

---

[1] Cf. *Breviarium Romanum*, May 25, lect. 9: "*Ipsæ res fidelium, quæ Domino offeruntur, non debent in alios usus quam ecclesiasticos et christianorum fratrum vel indigentium converti; quia vota sunt fidelium, et pretia peccatorum, ac patrimonia pauperum.*"
[2] "*Autres gens de main-morte.*"
[3] J. Bacquet, *Œuvres*, i. 54, 55.
[4] *Ibid.*, p. 57.
[5] "*Un Abbe, Prior, ou auter home de religion ou de Saint Eglise.*"

poverty. And, when a man is professed in any of the Orders of Religion, he is said to be *home de religion*, a man of religion or religious. Of this sort be all abbots, priors, and others of any of the said Order regular. Secular are persons ecclesiasticall; but, because they live not under certain rules of some of the said Orders, nor are votaries,[6] they are, for distinction sake, called secular; as bishops, deanes and chapters, archdeacons, prebends, parsons, vicars, and such like. All which Littleton here includeth under these generall words: *De Saint Eglise*, of Holy Church; and none of these are in law said to be *homes de religion*, or religious."[7]

As to the capacity of these "mortmain people" to acquire or purchase, Coke explains the subject under the head of "Fee Simple," and not as Blackstone does, invidiously and fallaciously, under the head of "Forfeiture;" the latter gentleman implying thereby that the essential idea of mortmain tenure was that of a confiscation or escheat relinquished or condoned by lay proprietors; while the masters of English law show that the title to possess in mortmain was just as good as that of the first lords in the land, and considerably better. This we shall see when inspecting the statutes.

But, as to the capacity of the "people of mortmain," Coke says, explaining Littleton: "Persons capable of purchase are of two sorts, persons naturall created by God, as I.S., I.N., etc.; and persons incorporate or politique, created by the policie of man (therefore they are called bodies politique). And these be of two sorts, viz. either sole [corporation sole] or aggregate [corporation aggregate] of many; againe aggregate of many, either of all persons capable, or of one person capable, and the rest incapable or dead in law [individual regulars or religious], as in the chapter of Discontinuance, sect. 57, shall be shewed. Some men have capacitie to purchase but not abilitie to hold. Some capacitie to purchase and abilitie to hold or not to hold, at the election of them or others. Some capacitie to take and to hold. Some neither capacitie to take nor to hold. And some specially disabled to take some particular thing."[8]

Bodies corporate or politic.

In Coke's time, when all the ancient code of mortmain was complete (not to mention the circumstance that novel statutes of Henry VIII. and Edward VI. had brought new and extraneous elements into this question and under this denomination), the "people of mortmain" fell into the category of those who had "capacitye to take, but not to retayne," unless they fulfilled legal requirements. However, if they did not fulfil the conditions, they did still acquire the right to retain, in case the higher landlords in

Legal requirements under pain of possible forfeiture. Baltimore's requirements.

---

[6] For "votaries," persons under vows, the word "voluntaries" appears in the first edition of Coke's Littleton (A.D. 1628).

[7] Co. Litt., 93 (*b*): On Frankalmoigne.

[8] Co. Litt., *ad init.* 2 (*a*).—To "purchase" here means to acquire.

§ 74]   LEGAL REQUIREMENTS FOR AMORTIZING   581

succession did not use their right to resume possession within certain terms prescribed.[9] It would seem to have been on the basis of this legislation, which was comparatively late as we shall see, and which implied escheat or forfeiture, that Blackstone assigned an original place to mortmain under the head of Forfeiture; though Coke and Littleton treated the same under the head of Fee Simple. And it was this competency "to take, but not to retayne," that Lord Baltimore was trying to impose upon Maryland at the expense of the missionaries. They might receive; but what they received he entered on, three years after date, as "lord of the fee" in the land of the wigwam! Here it is not clear which figure is more curious—that of Blackstone as a lawyer transferring a proprietary title of fee simple over to the head of "Forfeiture;" or that of Lord Baltimore, as a higher "lord of a fee" in an Indian land, observing no vested rights or conditions of time, place, or legality, and so transferring himself bodily into other people's property!

All the kinds of corporations, whether sole or aggregate, ecclesiastical or secular, enjoyed a perpetuity of existence, successors in a line ever keeping up a moral identity in the body politic. Thus it came to pass that by their perpetuity in being, without minority, matrimony, or decease, they furnished no occasion for certain incidental and valuable services, which higher feudal landlords, on occasion of marriages, or successions, or wardships, or escheats, etc., had a right to receive from individual and successive tenants or vassals. Under the aspect of these particular services, property once vested in a perpetual corporation, put on the character of perpetuity in tenure, and became like capital dead—yielding no profit—however useful it might be to the higher landlord in other respects. For, indeed, no property in mortmain did, by the mere fact of its passing into the hands of ecclesiastical or secular corporations, throw off the burdens which were inherent in it, as annexed to the soil. It was only the tenants that showed a different front, under the circumstances of unbroken perpetuity.

It is said that from this fixity or deadness of the permanent corporation the figure of *mortua manus*, or "mortmain" was derived; the phrase signifying a dead hand, which opens no more to release what it holds. But exception has been taken to this figure of speech, as being an antiphrasis, saying the opposite of what is meant; since, in fact, the hand of the corporation is so much alive, that taking it keeps, and keeps the object without changing the subject. Hence, according to this conception, the term should rather have been *manus immortalis*, a hand immortal.[10]

Meaning of the word, "Mortmain," "Amortizing," "Mortification."

---

[9] Co. Litt., *ad init.* 2 (b).
[10] Cf. T. M. Mamachi, *Del Diritto Libero della Chiesa di acquistare, ecc.*, i. 6 seqq.—Cf. Du Cange, *Glossarium ad Scriptores Mediæ et Infimæ Latinitatis*, s.v. "Manus Mortua," where the development of meaning in this term "Mortmain" is given on the line of historical development, which proceeds thus: First, *Manus mortua*, or "the dead hand," signified the release by death of property in the possession of a serf

The act of putting property, donated, purchased, inherited, into the condition of mortmain is "amortizing" the land. However, that term, "amortization," is rather used to designate the fulfilment of legal conditions necessary for such a purpose. Hence it is in the former sense that those are to be understood who speak of Mortmain Statutes as prohibiting the amortization of property, that is, forbidding land to be put into such a condition. And it is in the latter sense that others are to be understood who speak of such Statutes as commanding the amortization of property, that is, commanding the legal steps to be taken for the purpose.[11] The term used in Scots law is "mortification."

Over against the reasons already alleged for not looking favourably on property in mortmain, there are other reasons for approving and commending the same. The French regalist who gave us the former may be quoted for the latter. Bacquet says that property should be in the hands of the Church, to obviate the evil lest ecclesiastics be withdrawn from Divine service to beg their bread; also to put in their hands the means for maintaining the Divine worship, as well as for helping the poor and indigent, since the Apostle St. Paul says that "a bishop should be hospitable;" and again to put them in a condition to help the King in moments of urgency or in war.[12]

Reasons ancient and modern in favour of Mortmain.

To these reasons, which have held throughout the ages, there must be added new grounds in the complex state and needs of modern society, showing that the right to possess in community is an exigency of modern progress. For instance, in the life and work of the Society of Jesus, Father Campano (1584) expounded the matter elegantly and well for King Stephen of Poland, when speaking of colleges. The substance of his argument was that if people called for colleges, they were not asking

attached to the soil, who left no legitimate male children; the hand, which had held the property, relaxing on his decease, and leaving it by escheat to the lord of the manor. This condition of servitude came down from the time of the Roman freedmen. Secondly, "Mortmain" meant the property itself, farms, etc., over which such a right of possession accrued to a lord or to the Church on the death of a serf subject to such conditions. Thirdly, *Homines manus mortuæ*, "men of the dead hand," were the serfs as described. Fourthly, those who were like serfs in this respect, inasmuch as they could not dispose of their property, their benefices, dignities, etc., came to be called by the same name. These were ecclesiastical persons, colleges, communities, etc.; and this is the meaning which prevails in municipal customs and royal edicts: "*Qua notione vocem hanc usurpant fere semper Consuetudines municipales, et Edicta Regia.*" Here Du Cange takes occasion to cite Sir Edward Coke on Littleton, sect. 1, offering the derivation given in our text, which he seems to treat as not proper and historical, but only as literary and explanatory. The first origin of the term in practice and life, as applied to the serf's goods, is left undefined. Du Cange proceeds to discuss with Muratori a meaning of the term in the *Capitulary* of Charlemagne, where he thinks it probable that "*Mortua manus*," "the dead hand," is none other than the king's hand, that of his treasury, the *fiscus*. Now, as the fisc never dies, but always extracts its rights, the term proper to the fisc came by similitude to designate churches, colleges, etc., which are permanent entities.

[11] Cf. Mamachi, *Ibid.*—Cf. J. H. Boehmer, *Jus Parochiale*, c. i. § 23.
[12] J. Bacquet, *Œuvres*, i. 72.

for experiments and tentative essays, but for institutions perfect in their kind; for professors and preachers who were to found great houses; and who, themselves highly qualified and sufficiently numerous, should establish an adequate succession of their own kind. For this it was indispensable that such men should not be taken away from their high duties, to go seeking for the means of subsistence, or soliciting supplies for their establishments. Mendicancy should be no part of a college foundation. Penury would mean only fragmentary and crippled detachments in small and feeble colleges, with obloquy greeting the enterprise of the men, and contempt shadowing themselves. And thus, by the eye of disappointed hope being regarded as intruders where they had come as invited guests, their teaching and doctrine would share the same fate as their damaged reputation.[13]

For such considerations the common law of England regarded the Church possessions in mortmain with great favour, protecting the immunities of ecclesiastical property from every kind of temporal service, when such property had been given to God as free alms, or "in frankalmoigne." Coke states the law thus: "All ecclesiasticall persons may hold in frankalmoigne, be they secular or regular; and no lay person can hold in frankalmoigne." The "freedom" of the alms as thus given distinguishes it from land bestowed upon the Church under conditions, which had the effect of making it "a tenure by Divine service." Its immunities under such a tenure were not so absolute. But the tenants in free alms, says Littleton, "shall doe no fealty to their lord, because that this Divine service is better for them before God then any doing of fealtie; and also because that these words (frankalmoigne) excludeth the lord to have any earthly or temporall service, but to have only Divine and spirituall service to be done for him, etc." Hereupon Coke makes his comments and draws his distinctions, that a tenant in free alms shall not do any fealty "or any other thing, but *devota animarum suffragia* [the devout prayers for the souls departed]," and other prayers, Masses, etc., which are here stated. And, as to Littleton's affirmation that "such Divine service is better for them" than any temporal fealty done to the feudal lord, Coke proceeds: "And it is also said in our bookes, *Que Frankalmoigne est le plus haute service* [That free alms is the highest service]; and this was confessed by the heathen poet—

"Fuit hæc sapientia quondam
Publica privatis secernere, sacra profanis." [14]

---

[13] "*Tum vero quid reliquum fit, nisi ut quorum vita (jure seu injuria perinde hic est) despicitur, eorum et doctrina repudietur?*" F. Sacchini, *Historiæ Soc. Jes.*, pars v. t. i. lib. iv. No. 81.—Cf. J. Argento, S.J., *De rebus Societatis Jesu in regno Poloniæ, ad Serenissimum Sigismundum Tertium*, pp. 129, 130.—Cf. *supra*, § 30, p. 291.

[14] "This was the wisdom of the ancients, to set apart things public from private, things sacred from profane."

And certain it is, that *Nunquam res humanæ prospere succedunt ubi negliguntur divina.*" [15]

These writers go on to show how the spiritual service of prayers and Masses may be enforced, if neglected; that is, in a case of frankalmoigne, by appealing to the Bishop, or, as he is called, the Ordinary, who "ought of right" to see that "such negligence be no more done." The term "Ordinary," says Coke, "we have anciently taken from the canonists." And this leads him to speak of ecclesiastical jurisdiction, which is the very essence of Church immunities. He says: "It appeareth that, for deciding of controversies and for distribution of justice within this realme, there bee two distinct jurisdictions; the one ecclesiasticall, limited to certaine spirituall and particular cases (of the one whereof our author [Littleton] here speaketh), and the court wherein those causes are handled is called *Forum Ecclesiasticum;* the other jurisdiction is secular and generall, for that it is guided by the common and generall law of the realme." And he adds: "Here is implied a maxime of the common law; that, where the right, as our author here speaketh, is spirituall, and the remedy therefore only by the ecclesiasticall law, the conusans [cognizance] thereof doth appertaine to the ecclesiasticall court." [16]

The Bishop's jurisdiction.

Regarding the uses to which the ample possessions in mortmain, monastic and clerical, were put by the Church in the course of generations, the preamble of a single statute passed in the forty-third year of Elizabeth will show a part of the religious and charitable objects to which the funds of the Church were fixedly devoted. This review was drafted at the time when Henry VIII., Edward VI., and Elizabeth herself had spent a good half of a century in squandering upon themselves and courtiers the accumulated funds of the Church and the poor, and when, to fill the enormous void, the new age of Poor Laws and Poor Rates, of vagabondage and philanthropy, was inaugurated. The Act itself, 43 Elizabeth, chapter 4 (A.D. 1601), was the most important of several statutes on Charitable Uses, devised and passed to make some headway against the tide of evil resulting from that accomplished fact, the spoliation of the Church. It was now desired that others should make good again what the Crown and its minions had misappropriated. The title and preamble run as follows:—

History of Mortmain from a Statute: 43 Eliz. c. 4.

"An Acte to redresse the misemployment of landes, goodes, and stockes of money, heretofore given to Charitable Uses.

"Whereas landes, tenements, rentes, annuities, profittes, hereditamentes, goods, chattels, money and stockes of money, have bene heretofore given, limitted, appointed, and assigned, as well by the Queenes moste excellent Majestie and her moste noble progenitors, as by sondrie other

[15] "Human affairs never prosper when Divine rights are set at naught."
[16] Co. Litt., 94–96.

§ 74] *USES OF MORTMAIN: FROM STATUTES* 585

well disposed persons; some for releife of aged, impotent and poore people, some for maintenance of sicke and maymed souldiers and marriners, schooles of learninge, free schooles and schollers in universities, some for repaire of bridges, portes, havens, causwaies, churches, seabankes and highewaies, some for education and prefermente of orphans, some for or towardes reliefe, stocke or maintenance for howses of correction, some for mariages of poore maides, some for supportation, ayde and helpe of younge tradesmen, handiecraftesmen and persons decayed, and others for releife or redemption of prisoners or captives, and for aide or ease of any poore inhabitants concerninge paymente of fifteenes, settinge out of souldiers and other taxes. Whiche landes, tenements, rents, annuities, profitts, hereditaments, goodes, chattells, money and stockes of money nevertheles have not byn imployed according to the charitable intente of the givers and founders thereof, by reason of fraudes, breaches of truste and negligence in those that shoulde pay, delyver and imploy the same. For redresse and remedie whereof, Be it enacted that the Lord Chancellor" shall issue commissions to Bishops, etc., to inquire into the application of charitable funds; commissioners may on such inquiry make order for regulation thereof; etc.

Like all the rest of Tudor legislation on the malversation, misappropriation, and embezzlement of charitable and religious goods, even this charitable Act, in its last section, assures the "Queenes Majestie" that she shall not be touched for anything that she herself, or the others of her Tudor family have seized from the fund of religion or charity, "by Acte of Parliament, surrender, exchange, relinquishmente, escheate, attainder, conveiance or otherwise."[17] Hence there was no restitution to be expected for the poor or other victims from her side.

A similar Act of four years earlier, supplanted by this later one, contained a shorter list of ancient good works, and yet added some other categories, beginning, for instance, thus: "Whereas divers colledges, hospitalls, almes houses and other places within this realme of England, have bene founded and ordeyned," etc.[18]

Not inferior to the testimony of the spoilers themselves, as to what the Church and the religious sentiment of the faithful had done and had intended, is the affirmation of the men, those "noble progenitors" and their Parliaments, who, far from pulling down, had built up in mortmain. In the thirty-fifth year of Edward I. (1307), the statute which legislated against sending out money to alien superiors reviewed in its preamble the causes for the erection of abbeys. It said: "Monasteries, priories, and other religious houses, were founded to the honour and glory of God and the advancement of the Holy Church, by the King and his progenitors, and by the said noblemen [petitioners] and their ancestors; and a very great portion of lands

Objects of Mortmain, 35 Edw. I. st. 1; 2 Hen. V. st. 1, c. 1.

[17] 43 Eliz., c. 4.   [18] 39 Eliz., c. 6.

and tenements have been given by them to the said monasteries, priories, and houses, and the religious men serving God in them, to the intent that clerks and laymen [lay-brothers?] might be admitted in such monasteries, priories, and religious houses, according to their sufficient ability; and that sick and feeble men might be maintained; hospitality, almsgiving, and other charitable deeds might be done; and that in them prayers might be said for the souls of the said founders and their heirs."[19]

Passing over the repetitions of such statements in the English laws, we mention just one more statute, in the second year of Henry V., when the Wars of the Roses had already worked such havoc in the country. The Parliament gathered at Leicester in 1414 treated of hospitals, commanding the Ordinaries to investigate the estates thereof. The preamble rehearses the history that "many hospitals within the realm of England, founded as well by the noble kings of this realm, and lords and ladies both spiritual and temporal, as by divers others estates, to the honour of God and of His glorious Mother, in aid and merit of the souls of the said founders, to the which hospitals the same founders have given a great part of their lands and tenements, therewith to sustain impotent men and women, lazars, men out of their wits, and poor women with child, and to nourish, relieve, and refresh other poor people in the same, be now for the most part decayed," etc.[20]

As to the peremptoriness of the Church's rights in matters belonging to her jurisdiction, to that *forum Ecclesiasticum* of which Coke made mention, let the manner of speech in one statute suffice, precisely in a case where her immunities had been trenched upon in some testamentary matters. A commission of lay judges appointed was abruptly discharged, because, said the statute, process in "causes testamentary and other," which were in question, "notoriously pertaineth to the cognisance of Holy Church;" and the said commission has acted "in blemishing of the franchise of Holy Church."[21]

The forum ecclesiasticum, 18 Edw. III., st. 3, c. 6.

Having thus defined the term, the character, and uses of ecclesiastical property in mortmain, we will add only a slight sketch of its origin and progress, under whatever specific title of free alms or of tenure by Divine service it may have been held.

In obedience to his usual tendency, Blackstone made an assertion that it was always necessary for corporations to have a licence in mortmain from the Crown, and so be qualified for holding lands; and that such licences of mortmain seem to have been necessary among the Saxons, above sixty years before the Norman Conquest. Upon this "fundamental principle" it was easy for him then to imply that ecclesiastics obtained lands illegally;

Mortmain, according to Blackstone, Hallam, Stephen.

---

[19] 35 Edw. I., stat. 1: *Statutum de apportis Religiosorum.*
[20] 2 Hen. V., stat. 1, c. 1.
[21] 18 Edw. III., stat. 3, c. 6.—In connection with these formulas (here *passim*) about "Holy Church," compare Dr. S. R. Gardiner, *supra,* § 17, note 8, p. 239.

§ 74] HISTORICAL DEVELOPMENT 587

because they obtained them without licence. This easy method of writing history saved him from stating how it did come to pass, that, as he admitted, ecclesiastics were honoured with "the largest and most considerable dotations of religious houses within less than two centuries after the Conquest." His imagination ran free with some figures of poetic licence, which have appeared in the encyclopædias and law-books ever since, about the "ingenuity of the clergy" in beguiling the mailed and belted Norman barons somehow; about their "creeping out of statutes;" with other figures about their "inventions" and "devices" and "subtle imagination." [22]

As to a licence being needed before the Statutes of Mortmain imported it, this was a pure imagination. Hallam threw doubt upon the matter for Saxon times.[23] Justice Stephen, an editor and commentator who followed Blackstone implicitly on all such abstruse matters as history and Church affairs, ventured to mention the doubt cast by Hallam.[24] In the mean time, Sir Francis Palgrave had studied that question, and he left no room even for a doubt on the subject of Blackstone's imaginary licence.[25]

In fact, when the Church and the faithful had passed out of the state known to the Roman proconsuls and governors as that of the "Christian superstition," the clergy, or spiritual state, soon came to enjoy a special juridical position, with exemptions which Charlemagne renewed. And the regard in which they were held made St. Boniface, Bishop of Mayence, complain of the comparative "servitude" in which the English monasteries were kept (A.D. 745). Nevertheless, Ethelwulf granted one-tenth part of the land in his kingdom of Wessex for pious uses (A.D. 855), setting it free from the *Trinoda Necessitas*, or triple tax for bridges and highways, for the walls, etc., of strongholds, and for military service in defence of the kingdom. The donations of the Anglo-Saxon kings were derived from two sources—the demesne lands, and the common lands of the townships.[26]

The authentic history according to Palgrave.

"The [monastic] community was created by the association of the brethren; their incorporation and the right of perpetual succession resulted from the nature of the institution; and, until the fifteenth century, it was never thought necessary to confer these privileges by the express clauses of a royal charter. Splendid endowments were bestowed upon all the monasteries and cathedrals; the parochial clergy slowly acquiring an independent establishment. In the sixth century, according to the testimony of Bede, none [no parochial clergy] yet existed; for the missionary itinerancy, which he describes in very forcible

[22] 2 Blackstone, *Comm.*, 269-272.—1 Stephen, *Comm.*, 455 seqq.
[23] H. Hallam, *Middle Ages*, ii. 321.
[24] 1 Stephen, *Comm.*, 455, note; calling Hallam "a writer of great authority."
[25] F. Palgrave, *Rise and Progress of the English Commonwealth: Anglo-Saxon Period*, etc., I. chap. v.
[26] Palgrave, *Ibid.*, I. 157-160.

terms, seems incompatible with the existence of a settled and located priesthood, at least in Northumbria." [27] Palgrave goes on to explain the status of the clergy, the privilege of sanctuary, civil immunities, Church courts, the palatine privileges of Ely and Durham; and he then comes to the heart of the question regarding Church lands—not, indeed, as to how bishops and monks were made the recipients of extensive allotments, but how they could manage to keep them safe from robber barons, and from kings of the same kind, who after all were only first among their peers.

He says: "But the temporal possessions of the clergy were by no means held with security. Abuses prevailed at an early period in the ecclesiastical establishments; and the superiors alienated lands in favour of their friends and relations. This was partially remedied by a canon, which forbade the bishop, the abbot or the abbess from making any grant but for one life; nor was this concession to be made, except with the consent of the communities of which they were the superiors." [28] But the regulation was often evaded or infringed. "Corruption and improvidence were, however, far less destructive than actual force and rapine; and (as in France) the clergy were alternately the objects of liberality and the sufferers from avarice and persecution." Here Palgrave devotes a couple of pages to specimens of this human idiosyncrasy, which had not died out of the race when Maryland was founded. He begins with Ina, "in the most fervid age," he says, "of Anglo-Saxon piety," and goes on to William the Conqueror, who was a model indeed. When the Danes had ravaged the Church lands, it was considered that the lands so ravaged to the damage of their ecclesiastical owners had escheated to the Crown, which thus added damage to damage; and the Crown granted them out again, not to their owners, but to lay landlords. And then, when the Conqueror piously made restitution for spoliations, he set that precedent which was held to be so sacred a duty by the Tudors, Henry VIII. and Elizabeth, five centuries later; he always excepted from the restitution the donations already made by himself to other people. As the author says: "When a tardy restitution of parts and parcels could be obtained [from the Conqueror], the charter carefully confirmed the donations which had been made to his feudal followers. These events, and they were repeated more or less in every country in Europe, show that the influence of the hierarchy has been much overrated. The sword was always suspended over their heads, until they united their interests with the worldly powers." Here the author might have added that, when they did unite their interests absolutely with the worldly powers at the

Abuses from within; and from lawlessness without.

---

[27] Bede, *Hist. Eccl.*, lib. iv. c. 27, etc.—Palgrave, *Rise and Progress of the English Commonwealth: Anglo-Saxon Period*, I. 161, 162.—Bede, however, is speaking here of St. Cuthbert's missionary excursions.

[28] *Synodus Calecuthensis*, A.D. 816.—*Concilia*, i. 170.

§ 74]   PIETY PRIVILEGED AND PROTECTED   589

Reformation in England, then the sword came down with a vengeance, and finished them. After some further observations about the clergy's "cunning," "arts and wiles," and "the crooked policy of the Papal See," as the only defence of the weak "against a turbulent aristocracy or a rapacious sovereign," Palgrave concludes the passage by saying: "For, from the age of Charles Martel down to the reigns of Henry [the Eighth], or Joseph [the Second of Austria], or Napoleon, when could the Pontiff or the priest retain any possessions which the King and the soldier were determined to acquire?"[29]

On the principle, not of spoliation by barons when avaricious and rapacious, but of what their depredations presupposed and proved, the exercise of liberality by barons and others when pious; in short, under the inspiration of Christian faith and devotion, was the Anglo-Saxon and common law formed; and the interpretation of statutes for the future was subjected to those rules of piety, religion, and liberality, which inspired the common law and kept it ever hand in hand with the canon law.[30] These rules are the criterion which, according to Chancellor Kent, governs the construction of statutes in the United States policy; that, whereas it has been always the duty of judges to make such a construction as shall repress the mischief provided against and shall advance the remedy, "this," he continues, "is especially the case as to statutes which relate to matters of public utility, as to establishments of piety, charity, education, and public improvements."[31]

Piety, charity, education, privileged.

The written record of the common law, as descending from the Anglo-Saxon King St. Edward the Confessor, appears expressly in the Capitulary granted by the Norman William the Conqueror, confirming the laws of Edward his cousin, who had received them from his predecessors.[32] The laws thus renewed and continued as the basis of all future jurisprudence "had a double object," says Palgrave—"the security of the right of sanctuary, and the observance of the peace."[33] And it may be noticed that, out of the thirty-nine chapters in all of the Capitulary, the first ten chapters are for the benefit of the Church. They begin with the title: *De Pace et Immunitate*

The common and feudal law combined.

---

[29] Palgrave, *Rise and Progress of the English Commonwealth: Anglo-Saxon Period*, I. 166–169.—For the exemption of the Crown from restitution to charity, education, and religion, see *ex. gr.* 31 Hen. VIII., c. 13, § 17: "*An Acte for Dissolution of Abbeys:*" 43 Eliz., c. 1, § 2: "*An Acte for Confirmation of Graunties made to the Queenes Majestie, and of Letters Patentes made by her Highnes to others;*" 43 Eliz., c. 4, § 8: "*An Acte to redresse the misemployment,*" etc., as above, p. 584.

[30] Cf. Sir H. Spelman, *Origin of Terms*, p. 78. This author (*Ibid.*) likens Canon Law in English jurisprudence to one of its "two Pole-Stars," the other being "the Feudal Law, received generally through all Europe."

[31] 1 Kent, *Comm.*, 464, note.

[32] *Ancient Laws and Institutes of England*, pp. 129, seqq.; *Leges Regis Edwardi Confessoris*, p. 190, seqq.

[33] Palgrave, *Rise and Progress of the English Commonwealth: Anglo-Saxon Period*, II. p. cv.

Sanctæ Ecclesiæ—"On the Peace and Immunity of Holy Church."[34] These provisions, repeated during three centuries by English Parliaments which always guaranteed the rights and immunities of Holy Church, were renewed, as we have seen, by the freemen of Maryland, in the same sense and latitude as during seven centuries before they had been regarded by Catholic ancestors, whether Anglo-Saxon, Norman, or English.

But the Conqueror also introduced a rigid system of feudal law with his barons and vassals. And it was owing exclusively to contact with this feudal law that Statutes of Mortmain were to take their rise. For, while the canon law in English jurisprudence governed "sometimes wholly," says Spelman, "sometimes for the greater part," matters "concerning the Church and Churchmen, legitimation, matrimony, wills, testaments, adultery, diffamation, oaths, perjury, days of law, days of vacation, wager of laws, and many other things;" the feudal law, on the other hand, controlled largely "matters touching inheritance, fees, tenures by knight's service, rents, escheats, dower of the third part, fines, felony, forfeiture, trial by battail," etc.[35] The bestowing of land henceforth on the Church became affected, in its process and method, by this law of feudal tenure, according to which all tenants held of a higher landlord, with duties of military dependency and service; and the higher might hold of higher lords still; till those at the summit, who held in chief, held of the King. The result of the new point of contact between Church rights and the law of the kingdom, as it now stood, is given by Coke in these terms—

"By the ancient common law of England, a man could not alien such lands as he had by discent without the consent of his heire; yet he might give a part to God in free almoigne, or with his daughter in free marriage, or to his servant *in remuneratione servitii*. Our old bookes described frankalmoigne thus: When lands or tenements were bestowed upon God, (that is) given to such people as are consecrated to the service of God. In our ancient bookes these gifts of donation were called Churchesset or Churchseed (*quasi semen Ecclesiæ*); but in a more particular sense it is described thus." Here Coke quotes Fleet in the Latin text, giving the history of the wheat measures bestowed by every one on the Church at St. Martinmas, as well in the time of the Britons as of the Angles. Some great men, however, after the arrival of the Romans, called the offering in Mosaic language by the name of "first-fruits;" as may be seen "in the letter of King Knut to the Sovereign Pontiff; in which they call that contribution *Churchsed*, as it were *the seed of the Church*." Further on, Coke likens a gift in frankalmoigne or free alms to a gift in free marriage; for, says he, it "may be resembled to a Divine marriage."[36]

Coke on this combination. Frankalmoigne.

[34] Cf. 2 Kent, *Comm.*, 501, note (*b*).
[35] Spelman, *Origin of Terms*, p. 78.
[36] Co. Litt., 94 (*b*), 95 (*b*).

§ 74] TESTAMENTS AND BISHOPS 591

It is to be observed that all this bestowal of land and gifts on the Church had to be done during life, because the conditions of feudal tenure did not allow of such gifts by testament or will, unless the heir expressly consented. This shows that the gifts were disinterested; that they were a sacrifice; and that they cost the donor something. They were not given at the expense of heirs unasked, and of others, who might come when the man himself was gone. The prevalence of deathbed beneficence belongs to a much later time.[37]

And it is also to be observed, for the purpose of comprehending the spirit of the times, which was one of faith, devotion, reverence, and charity, that, whether there was a gift at death or not, whether a man died duly shriven or died intestate, not only was the Church regarded as an object of liberality, but the party trusted to do right by every one was the same Church and her ministers; and the widow, children, next of kin, with their claims, as well as the debtors with their rights to payment, were all committed to the Church's solicitude. "And the reason," said Master John Perkins (A.D. 1555), "why spiritual men have the probate of testaments, is because it is to be understood that spiritual men have a better conscience than lay people; and that they have more knowledge what thing is for the profit and benefit of the soul of the testator than lay people have; and that they will attend more than lay people that the debts of the deceased be paid and satisfied with his goods; and they will see that his will be performed as far as his goods will extend." Till all this is done, the officers of the Ordinary are expected to take no fees whatever, either for the probate, or for the record, "or for any other thing concerning the testament."[38] *Testaments under the Bishop's jurisdiction. The reasons. Perkins, A.D. 1555.*

As all these items may appear to be somewhat curiosities of literature, in the light of that vulgarized history of English law and of those laws of English history to which we are accustomed, it may be proper to add plainly what need not be looked for in such history; that is to say, the ultimate basis of the whole system, to which Coke, however, has come pretty near in his way. Suarez, in his book addressed to James I., states it thus: First, that there is in the Church a spiritual power of government distinct from the civil, and of a higher order, conferred upon the Church by the special institution of Christ Himself; secondly, that this spiritual power is not *Ultimate basis of the Christian commonwealth.*

---

[37] Cf. W. F. Finlason, *History of the Laws of Mortmain*, pp. 19, 20.
[38] Master John Perkins, "felovve of the inner Temple, treating of the Lawes of this Realme, etc.," 1555, f. 94, B–G: ". . . Et le reason pur qui les espirituelx homes ount le probate del testamentes est pur ceo que il est destre dentend' que les espirituelx homes sount de meileur conscience que les layes gentes, et que ilz ount pluis conusaunce q[uelle] chose est pur le profite et benefit del alme de le testatour que les laies gentes ount, et ilz voillont pluis attender que les layes gentes que les dettes del mort sount payes et satisfies de ses biens; et ilz voillont veyer son volunte parformed auxi avant sicome ses biens voillont expender," etc. Compare with this the subject of a stricture above, Introduction, Chap. II. § 19, pp. 127, 128.

vested in temporal kings or princes, but in the pastors given by Christ to the Church, and especially in the Sovereign Pontiff who is the Bishop of Rome; thirdly, that this spiritual power is not subordinate to the power of kings, but *vice versâ* kings are comprehended among those over whom Christ gave power to the Church of binding and loosening. Thence it follows that, in spiritual and ecclesiastical causes, the spiritual estate is entirely exempt from the temporal jurisdiction of princes.[39] The Church's immunities and privileges being made concrete in a system of Church and State, the latter or secular power has no competency to disfranchise the Church of her rights acquired.[40] But, as to property, says Suarez, if it were true what the King of England harped upon in his book, that an accumulation of property in mortmain was found prejudicial to the State, then the means to be adopted were obvious; there was the supreme administrator of ecclesiastical goods in the person of the Pope, from whom a remedy in that matter was to be sought, as in any other subject-matter of complaint.[41]

A modern Professor of Jurisprudence at Cambridge adverts to what he calls "the cosmopolitan, the extra-national, or super-national" tone of Englishmen who wrote in pre-Reformation times on canon law.[42] This was a counterpart in their writings of the place which the Church occupied in the world, making Europe what it then was, a Christendom. Hence another modern explains at large and with ability how the Church was collateral with the temporal sovereignty in each and every country; and the law neither of Church nor of State "arose out of or depended on the other, but each had its separate existence and province;" the organism of a State arising out of the natural society of only some families, while the organism of the Church was fitted to the natural society of all families, with which it was and is conterminous.[43]

§ 75. The privileges enjoyed by the clergy could not be claimed by the laity. But the privileges conferred by the clergy, as shared with members of their own household and dependency, were very much coveted by the laity. To hold a fee or be a vassal of an abbot or bishop was to escape from under the direct control of a higher secular lord and live under the spiritual jurisdiction of the Church. In that point, and not in freedom from taxes or other burdens or services, but in freedom from secular jurisdiction, lay the very essence of the Church's privileges of tenure.[1] The Protestant

The laity affecting to be under Church jurisdiction.

---

[39] F. Suarez, *Defensio Fidei*, lib. iv. c. ii. § 2.
[40] *Ibid.*, c. xxx.
[41] *Ibid.*, c. xx. § 32.—When imposing a tax in November, 1380, the Parliament at Northampton threw into the Act a descriptive clause about the clergy, that they occupied the third part of the kingdom. Stubbs considers the statement quite unreliable. W. Stubbs, *Constitutional History of England*, ii. 449.
[42] F. W. Maitland, *Roman Canon Law in the Church of England*, p. 8.—Cf. *supra*, Introduction, Chap. II. § 20, pp. 131, 132.
[43] Sir G. Bowyer, *Universal Public Law*, pp. 134–137.
[1] Pollock and Maitland, *History of English Law*, i. 246, *seq.*

jurist Boehmer quotes the German proverbs: "'Tis good to live under the crozier; the crozier bars nobody out;" and, "To deal with St. Peter pays well."[2] The same author refers the greater part of Church fees or feudal tenures to this precise origin, that estates were offered by laymen to the Church with the intention of taking them back, as holden of the Church in fee.[3] However that be, this practice gave rise to the first English Statute of Mortmain. It appears in the Great Charter of 1217, and is repeated in several subsequent confirmations of Magna Charta (1224–25, 1297).

(1) The first Statute of Mortmain ran thus: "It shall not be lawful from henceforth to any to give his lands to any religious house, to take the same land again to hold of the same house. Nor shall it be lawful to any house of religion so to take the lands of any, to deliver the same back to him of whom they were received to be holden. If any from henceforth so give his lands to any religious house, and thereupon be convict, the gift shall be utterly void, and the land shall accrue to the lord of the fee."[4]

Upon this Hallam remarks that the Church's "tenure was frequently in what was called frankalmoign, without any obligation of service. Hence it became a customary fraud of lay proprietors to grant estates to the Church, which they received again by way of fief or lease, exempted from public burdens."[5] Stubbs explains the statute as "unquestionably called for by the prevalence of an abuse, which had existed from the first day of the Church Establishment in England—the fraudulent bestowal of estates on religious foundations, on the understanding that the donor should hold them as fiefs of the Church, and as so exonerated from public burdens. There is no period of our history at which complaints of this practice may not be found."[6] Another lawyer, while giving a false translation, as is so usual, brings into prominence quite a secondary effect or result of the transaction contemplated by the statute. This result "aimed at," he says, was that "the party giving the land [to the religious house]

(1) The fraud occasioning the first Statute of Mortmain. A.D. 1217.

---

[2] "*Unter dem Krummstab ist gut wohnen; Krummstab schleust niemand aus.*" "*Mit Sanct Peter is gut handeln.*" J. H. Boehmer, *Jus Ecclesiasticum Protestantium*, iii. tit. xx., *De Feudis*, §§ 24, 26.

[3] *Ibid.*, §§ 26–28. Cf. also Ferraris, *Prompta Bibliotheca*, s.v. "*Feuda*," art. 1, No. 41; the *quarta occasio* of Boehmer. This latter gentleman believed in apostolic poverty—for others; and, with the help of Arnold of Brescia and many Latin verses, takes Baronius to task for his sentiment: "*Nulla credebatur auctoritas in egestate*" ["No authority in poverty"]; which, however, is a scriptural position regarding mankind in general (*Ecclus.* xiii. 29); and even of Mendicant Orders may be true on occasion, as we showed above with regard to Jesuit colleges. *Supra*, § 74, pp. 582, 583.

[4] 2 Hen. III., *Magna Charta*, A.D. 1217.—9 Hen. III., A.D. 1224–25.—25 Edw. I., *Magna Charta*, A.D. 1297.

[5] H. Hallam, *Middle Ages*, ii. 204.—This correct statement comes in the midst of an amount of uncritical matter about the frauds of bishops in connection with intestacy, and the frauds of monks in connection with charters, and other raw material of the kind, for the sake of which he seems to have written his books.

[6] W. Stubbs, Regius Professor of Modern History, *Select Charters and Other Illustrations of English Constitutional History*, p. 458.

VOL. I. 2 Q

should not receive any benefit out of it," [but only out of the prayers or Divine service stipulated for by the donor].[7] In this sense the first Statute of Mortmain implicitly sanctioned donations in mortmain. The modern professors, Pollock and Maitland, presenting the statute in its right guise, say: "The mischief prevented seems to be this: Some favoured religious bodies, e.g. the Templars, have royal charters which by general words set free all the lands that they now have, and shall hereafter acquire, from many burdens. A man gives land to such a house, and then becomes that house's tenant; and, as such, he claims immunity under the charter." [8]

These explanations are comparatively recent, and throw sufficient light on the subject. But quite as interesting, and more so because of their historical momentum, are the explanations which have been otherwise than correct, and have enveloped the subject in a becoming cloud of darkness. On all sides the translations to be seen of the text are false; although several confirmations of the Magna Charta have the original text, and old translations perfectly accurate may be seen in the Statutes of the Realm, printed by command of King George III. (1810, etc.).[9] Coke used the correct text, but escaped giving a commentary on it, by skipping to another statute of sixty-two years later;[10] saying that this latter "excellently abridged" and "notably expounded" the former; and, explaining the latter, he said that such was the explanation of the former, because it quoted the same.[11] It did nothing of the kind, as we shall see in a moment. It was quoting something else, of which that classical master of English law knew nothing.[12] And in this error of his the subsequent generations find a technical excuse.

The old translations and commentaries.

To show the tone of all these cyclopædias and law-books, we quote a writer who devotes a short appendix to the Statutes of Mortmain, by way of helping to explain the controversy between Baltimore and the Jesuits in Maryland. His account of the first statute is this: "The second of Henry III.'s great Charters prohibited acquisition of lands by religious houses." [13]

That is all! Precisely the contradictory is true—that the said charter implied a sanction for the acquisition of lands by religious houses. What it forbade was the pretended acquisition by a religious house, but a real retention by the lay personage who pretended to give. And the chastisement inflicted was

The layman punished for the fraud.

---

[7] R. Matthews, barrister, before Mortmain Committee of the House of Commons, 1844, *Reports of Committees*, (6), p. 70 (588).
[8] Pollock and Maitland, *History of English Law*, i. 333.
[9] *Statutes of the Realm*, I. (1810) pp. 19, 25, 118.—The variations of the old correct translations are given there in notes; and we have made our choice above.
[10] 7 Edw. I., *De Viris Religiosis*.
[11] 2 *Inst.*, 74, 75, on *Magna Charta*, c. 36.
[12] Pollock and Maitland, as above, i. 334, note.
[13] B. T. Johnson, *Foundation of Maryland*, p. 181, Appendix F.

to let the feudal laws take their course. As a gift, the conveyance or alienation should "be utterly void" which did no harm to the religious house; but it should operate against the layman as a forfeiture or escheat, which did justice to his superior feudal lord: "The land shall accrue to the lord of the fee."

And thus the Statutes of Mortmain began with what Hallam calls "a customary fraud of lay proprietors."

(2) The second statute on the subject introduced a formality of consequence into donations bestowed on religion. It was some forty years later than the previous law. "In 1258," says Maitland, "at the Oxford Parliament the barons prayed remedy, that men of religion may not enter the fees [estates] of earls and barons and others without their will, whereby they lose for ever their wardships, marriages, reliefs, and escheats.[14] In 1259 the Provisions of Westminster ordained that it shall not be lawful for men of religion to enter the fee of any one without the licence of the lord of whom the land is holden;"[15] or, as the text says, "of whom the fee is immediately holden."[16] *(2) A licence to be had from the landlord interested. A.D. 1259.*

Here is the introduction of a licence which is now required to put land in mortmain. As is clear, it is a question of obviating damage to the antecedent rights of a third party. There is no mention of prejudice against mortmain as such, because of the absorption of property in "dead hands," or because of another supposititious motive invented later about landed property lying *extra commercium*, "outside of circulation;" as if land were meant to circulate, and not the produce of land. Coke himself reports the authentic reasons, derived from the feudal privileges alleged; but he makes no mention of the spurious motives, which were not as yet invented.[17] It was to be Blackstone's happy phrase, reported but not approved by the commentator Stephen, "that the circulation of landed property from man to man began to stagnate;"[18] which cannot be said of the circulation of his phrases; and which, it is to be hoped, shall always be said of landed property in any well-ordered and conservative State.

(3) This rule about obtaining a licence was not observed. Hence, twenty years later, a new and important law was passed. "In 1279," says Maitland, "the Statute of *De Viris Religiosis*,[19] after referring to the Provisions of Westminster, as though they were or had been law, put a check upon alienations in mortmain." Here the writer explains Coke's mistake, in supposing that the reference made by this statute was to the *(3) The licence made subject to all feudal interests involved. A.D. 1279.*

---

[14] *Petition of Barons*, c. 10.
[15] *Provisions*, c. 14. Pollock and Maitland, *Ibid.*, i. 333.
[16] *Statutes of the Realm*, as above, i. pp. 8–11: 43 Hen. III., A.D. 1259, c. 19.
[17] 2 Inst., 75.—Cf. 1 Stephen, *Comm.*, 456, note (f).
[18] 2 Blackstone, *Comm.*, 269, 270.
[19] Stat. 7 Edw. I. For the parallel French ordinance of 1275, see Langlois, *Le Règne de Philippe le Hardi*, 206, *seqq.* Esmein, *Histoire du droit français*, 278.

first Law of Mortmain, sixty-two years earlier; Coke being ignorant of the Provisions of Westminster, which had introduced the element of a licence only some twenty years before. By this new statute, not only the landlord immediately above, but all other parties interested in maintaining the feudal privileges of a fee, up to the lords paramount and the King above all, were authorized to take the requisite steps. If, as religious men had still continued to do, they entered into feudal holdings or into their own personal fees, without observing the recent provision regarding a licence, then the immediate lord next in rank above might enter into the said property within a year, and take it over or back as forfeited; and, in his default after a year, the next highest in turn, and then others upwards even to the King, had a right to enter.[20]

This regarded only feudal lands because of their feudal burdens and privileges. It did not touch property held in gavelkind, or on burgage tenure, or in copyhold. "And, even within its limited scope," observes Finlason, "the statute does not absolutely prohibit the alienation, at least so as to make it void; but only enables the lord to make it void [for the religious house] by entering upon it [himself]. And this he would not do if he received an adequate fine for the alienation, which on ordinary feudal principles he was entitled to on any alienation, and which would satisfy the purview of the statute as declared in the preamble, namely, that religious men should not enter into the fees of any, *without licence and will of the lord.*" [21] In other words, it meant the introduction of an indemnity. Maitland remarks: "The King and the other lords, if any, whose interests were concerned, could bind themselves to take no advantage of the statute; and licences to acquire land in mortmain were somewhat easily obtained.[22]

The indemnity.

The preamble said that religious men had been entering into "their own fees;" which seems to mean that the heirs of feudal houses, having become religious men, had entered in due time upon their inheritance; which thus became the property of the religious community and came

---

[20] 7 Edw. I., stat. 2, *De Viris Religiosis:* "*Nos super hoc pro utilitate regni congruum remedium provideri volentes, de consilio prelatorum, comitum et aliorum fidelium regni nostri de consilio nostro existentium, providimus, statuimus et ordinavimus, quod nullus religiosus aut alius quicumque terras aut tenementa aliqua emere vel vendere, aut sub colore donationis aut termini vel alterius tituli cujuscumque ab aliquo recipere, aut alio quovis modo, arte vel ingenio sibi appropriare præsumat sub forisfactura eorumdum per quod ad manum mortuam terræ et tenementa hujusmodi deveniant quoquo modo. Providimus etiam, quod si quis religiosus aut alius contra præsens statutum, quoquo modo, arte vel ingenio, venire præsumpserit, liceat nobis et aliis capitalibus dominis . . . ingredi . . . tenere. . . .*" As to the feudal basis of such a law regarding an alienation, which is declared to be irregular and is visited with forfeiture, cf. L. Ferraris, *Prompta Bibliotheca Canonica, Juridica, etc.,* s.v. "*Feudum,*" art. iii. Nos. 15, 16. To estimate rightly the importation of feudal ideas into Maryland, or of such feudal language as a "lay fee" (*supra*, § 52 (2), p. 431), it should be borne in mind that feudal tenures, fiefs, or fees, were essentially favours, trusts, granted under conditions; they were lay "benefices," and were spoken of as such in feudal law: "*beneficium amittit,*" "*beneficio carebit.*" Ferraris, *Ibid.*, No. 17.

[21] W. F. Finlason, *Laws of Mortmain,* p. 25.

[22] Pollock and Maitland, *History of English Law,* i. 334.—Cf. F. Hargrave, note, 108, on Co. Litt., 98 (*b*).

into mortmain.[23] By this new law the feudal rights were asserted even against these religious heirs. But no imputation was cast upon them or on the monastery, because men entered on their own heritage. Nor is Hallam's implication borne out that monasteries were very improper and "indecent" and grasping, because sons followed their fathers. He says: "If the wealth of ecclesiastical communities had all been as fairly earned [viz. by cultivating deserted tracts, by husbanding resources, by not wasting revenues in dissipation], we could find nothing in them to reprehend. But other sources of wealth were less pure; and they derived their wealth from many sources. Those who entered into a monastery frequently threw their whole estates into the common stock; and even the children of rich parents were expected to make a donation of land on assuming the cowl. Some gave their property to the Church before entering on military expeditions; gifts were made by some to take effect after their lives, and bequests by many in the terrors of dissolution. Even those legacies to charitable purposes, which the clergy could with more decency and speciousness recommend, and of which the administration was generally confided to them, were frequently applied to their own benefit." And he quotes in a note a passage from Muratori to prove the charge; but the note scarcely proves it.[24] The whole of Hallam's indictment would show that the state of the monasteries and of the clergy must have been excellent indeed, if their iniquities in land-getting presented no worse a case for him to "reprehend." And, if he implies that mere death-bed bequests of feudal land were at that time customary, his accuracy is on a par with the rest of the spirit manifested.

Hallam's criticism on heirs succeeding, if religious men.

The stage herewith arrived at, with respect to the acquisition of feudal lands, is that which Coke described as the "capacitie to take but not to hold," and this became general afterwards for all corporations in the following limits. He says: "If any sole corporation or aggregate of many, either ecclesiasticall or temporall (for the words of the statute [25] be, *Si quis religiosus vel alius*) purchase lands or tenements in fee, they have capacitie to take, but not to retayne (unlesse they have a sufficient

---

[23] "Where of late it was provided, that Religious Men should not enter into the Fees of any without licence and will of the chief lord, of whom such fees be holden immediately; and, notwithstanding, such religious men have entered, as well into their own fees as into the fees of other men, approprying and buying them, and sometime receiving them of the gift of others; whereby the services that are due of such fees, and which at the beginning were provided for the defence of the realm, are wrongfully withdrawn, and the chief lords do lose their eschetes of the same." —(End of the preamble; then follows the enactment as above. Translation taken from Ruffhead's *Statutes at Large*.)

[24] H. Hallam, *Middle Ages*, ii. 202, 203.—As to heirs, and through them monasteries succeeding to a feudal tenure, the laws governing various cases of capacity or incapacity may be seen in L. Ferraris, *Prompta Bibliotheca Canonica, Juridica, etc.*, s.v. "*Feudum*," art. ii. Nos. 33–40.—As to Hallam's implication here regarding devises of land by will or on a death-bed, cf. *infra*, § 76, (9) (a), p. 611, from Palgrave.

[25] Viz. *De Viris Religiosis*. See note 20, here *supra*.

licence in that behalfe); for, within the yeare after the alienation, the next lord of the fee may enter."[26]

(4) Legislation now worked in two directions: on the one hand, to save the lay fees or estates for feudal services; and, on the other, to save the Church fees or property in mortmain for Divine service. The former or lay fees were obstructed by the apparatus of licence and indemnity from coming into mortmain, and that under pain of forfeiture. The latter or Church foundations were not merely obstructed—they were absolutely barred, under the same pain of forfeiture, from ever being disposed of into lay hands, to the prejudice of their spiritual burdens, and of the spiritual rights acquired by the donors who had created them. This did not mean then, and has never meant, that Church property was transcendentally inalienable; but that, on the one side, a Church fee was inalienable to the prejudice of spiritual rights, which by going into lay hands were certain to be lost, and, in point of fact, were lost at the Reformation; while, on the other side, the lay fees were inalienable also, as far as their transfer went to the prejudice of feudal rights, which by conveyance into spiritual hands were sure to suffer diminution.[27]

(4) Saving lay fees. Saving Church fees.

Mr. Burge, giving evidence before the House of Commons Mortmain Committee (1844), observed with regard to a series of statutes which he enumerated,[28] and which we are now considering, that "they originated, not in any design to prevent religion or charitable institutions from receiving gifts, but in the desire to preserve to the Crown and the mesne lord those feudal rights, of which they would be unquestionably deprived, if property was permitted to be given to a body which was incompetent, after having once acquired it, ever again to part with it." This description by the lawyer is not quite accurate in its reference to inalienability. He continues: "The law recognized and enforced the reverential feeling of our nature, that property, which had been once devoted to the service of the Almighty, was sacred and could not be withdrawn from it. The law would not allow the Church to part with any property it had acquired. It became therefore inalienable; and the Crown and the mesne lord lost all those incidents of escheat, relief, and other feudal profits which were of considerable value. Hence the policy was, not to declare the alienation void, but merely to permit the Crown or the lord to enter for the forfeiture. But according to the principle, *Quilibet potest renunciare juri pro se introducto* ["Any one may resign a right introduced in his favour"],

[26] Co. Litt., 2 (b).
[27] Cf. T. Mamachi, *Del Diritto Libero della Chiesa di acquistare*, etc., IV. lib. iii. c. 1, § 14, pp. 134, *seqq.*, Thesis: "*Egli è per altro falsissimo, che i beni ecclesiastici sieno assolutamente inalienabili. Molti di già per le urgenti necessità della Chiesa e degli Stati sono stati di fatto alienati.*"
[28] "I apprehend the origin, the object, and tendency of these statutes have been misrepresented. The Statutes of Mortmain properly so called, that is, the statutes prohibiting the alienation of land in mortmain, and to which I am now referring, are: Magna Charta, 9 Hen. III., c. 36; 7 Edw. I., s. 2, c. 1; 13 Edw. I., s. 1, c. 32; 13 Edw. I., s. 1, c. 33; 34 Edw. I., s. 3; 18 Edw. III., s. 3, c. 3; 15 R. II., c. 5."

the Crown and the lord might remit the forfeiture; and they did so, on receiving an equivalent or compensation."[29]

Having in view these alternate safeguards, as they were devised for the maintenance of respective rights, we may note how the legislation proceeded on such lines. The Statute of Westminster the Second (A.D. 1285) contains several laws exactly to the purpose.[30] One is against putting property in mortmain under judgments obtained by collusion; where the party giving allowed himself to be brought into court as a defendant holding Church property; then made no defence; and judgment was delivered in favour of the Church. This practice of fictitious recovery, or *pia fraus*, "pious fraud," as Blackstone calls it when speaking of the use of it by laymen among themselves,[31] was treated by the new law with great simplicity. A jury should sit upon the case. If the recovery was genuine, and the religious house really owned the property so "recovered," there was an end of it; the house entered into possession. If the recovery was fictitious, then the tenant who was parting with it, to the prejudice of his higher landlord, lost it by forfeiture.[32]

Saving lay fees from collusive alienation. A.D. 1285.

Similarly, tenants put up crosses on their lands, claiming " the privileges of Templars and Hospitallers; it is ordained," says another statute, " that such lands shall be forfeit to the chief lords or to the King, in the same manner as is provided for lands aliened in mortmain."[33]

On the other hand, there was the abuse of sacred property in the sense of alienating it to laymen. That is treated peremptorily, as follows : " Our Lord the King hath ordained that, if abbots, priors, keepers of hospitals and other religious houses, founded by him or by his progenitors, do from henceforth aliene the lands given to their houses by him or by his progenitors, the land shall be taken into the King's hands, and holden at his will; and the purchaser [to whom it was alienated] shall lose his recovery as well of the lands as of the money that he paid. And, if the house were founded by an earl, baron, or other persons, for the land so aliened he, by whom or [by] whose ancestor the land so aliened was given, shall have a writ to recover the same land in desmesne, which is thus: *Præcipe tali abbati*. In like manner, for the lands given for the maintenance of a chantery, or of a light in a church or chapel, or other alms to be maintained, if the land given be aliened. But, if the land so given for a

Saving Church fees from lay hands. A.D. 1285.

---

[29] House of Commons, *Mortmain Committee Report* (6), x. 1844, pp. 164 (682), 165 (683).—Upon the statement about inalienability, Finlason passes the criticism : " *Quære*. Whether ecclesiastical corporations could not at common law alienate; in the reign of Elizabeth, Acts were passed to prevent them. But they could not *die* ; and, of course, no corporations could render personal services, being bodies *politic*." W. F. Finlason, *Laws of Mortmain*, p. 177, note.

[30] 13 Edw. I., Stat. Westm., cc. 32, 33, 41.
[31] 2 Blackstone, *Comm.*, 117.
[32] 13 Edw. I., c. 32.
[33] *Ibid.*, c. 33.

chantery, light, sustenance of poor people, or other alms to be maintained or done, be not aliened, but such alms is withdrawn by the space of two years, an action shall lie for the donor or his heir, to demand the land so given in demain," etc.[34]

From these samples it is evident that, at the end of the thirteenth century (1285), the maintenance of land in mortmain for Divine service was as jealously watched and protected as that of the lands in lay fee for feudal service ; and somewhat more so ; since it was much easier to bring feudal estates into ecclesiastical mortmain, than to bring Church lands out of mortmain. This will be seen still more clearly in what follows, which has especial reference to Maryland.

§ 76. At this point all that was essential in the legislation was complete. There remained only the further organizing of formalities ; as well as the application of these laws touching ecclesiastical communities to a new kind of community which had now arisen, the lay corporation.

In fact, with the next statute, that of *Quia emptores* of only five years later (1290), the age of giving to the Church feudal lands in free alms or frankalmoigne was virtually over. And the whole system of licence and indemnification was implicitly reaffirmed.

The very beginnings of Maryland bring us into contact with the main points here. We encounter the statute *Quia emptores* in the charter itself. As that statute practically swept away all frankalmoigne or free alms to the Church, so the charter of George Calvert, first Lord Baltimore, expressly swept away that law and everything else of its kind. And, as to the lay corporations, since the same lord left them perfectly free by the same paragraph of his charter, the next lord, Cecil Calvert, threw a net about them, to catch them like the Church, and discriminate against them in Conditions of Plantation.

(5) Since a general breaking-up of the old tenures was now inevitable, and, by allowing their inferior landlords to divide and subdivide into smaller feudal holdings, the greater or higher lords were left in the background, and out of touch with the actual tenants of the soil, it came to pass, says the new statute of *Quia emptores* (A.D. 1290), that the same chief lords lost their escheats, marriages, and wardships, belonging to the fees ; which thing seemed very hard and extreme unto those lords, and moreover manifest disinheritance. The remedy was simple, but it brought about a political and economical revolution which was not foreseen.[1]

(5) Setting land free for buying and selling. A.D. 1290.

The remedy was that of allowing every freeman to sell as he chose, without, however, his acquiring thereby any feudal relation to the

---

[34] 13 Edw. I., c. 41.
[1] Cf. W. Stubbs, *Select Charters, etc., of English Constitutional History*, pp. 458, 478.

purchaser: "It is ordained that it shall be lawful to every freeman to sell his lands at his own pleasure; and that the feoffee [the new purchaser] shall hold the same of the chief lord of that fee by such services as his feoffer [the tenant vendor] held them." Thus the chief and remoter landlord retained his feudal rights, into whatever lay hands the estates passed. Church hands had to be excepted, if the incidental damages regarding marriages, escheats, etc., were to be prevented. Hence the statute added: "And it is to be understood that, by the said sales or purchases of lands or tenements, or any parcels of them, such lands or tenements shall in no wise come into mortmain, either in part or in whole, neither by policy nor craft, contrary to the form of the Statute [of Mortmain] made thereupon of late [*dudum editi*]." [2]

(*a*) Now the Statute of Mortmain, which was thus appealed to, meant, as has been seen, the necessity imposed of obtaining a licence in order to amortize property; and that for the purpose of maintaining feudal rights and claiming the reimbursement of positive damages.

(*b*) Moreover, the legal status of any subordinate lay tenant now left him no longer in a condition to bestow on the Church any part of his tenure, under the old feudal aspect of free alms, or frankalmoigne.

These two observations will enable us to understand Coke's commentary on the statute *Quia emptores*. It is to the double effect, first, that the age of "free, pure, and perpetual alms," [3] was virtually over, that form of donation being possible henceforth only with the chief lords or the King, chiefest of all; but, secondly, that under this new statute, no change whatever was made with respect to the facility of obtaining a licence or dispensation. *Coke on this Statute Quia emptores.*

Then, as to practical life, it follows that, if it was still as possible as ever to obtain a licence or dispensation for disposing of property under the new statute, still more easy was it to dispose of property when the whole statute itself was dispensed with and swept away. Then not even a licence was necessary. This Queen Mary did (A.D. 1554) for twenty years; and the first Lord Baltimore did in his Maryland charter (A.D. 1632) for ever.

Sir Edward Coke (A.D. 1552–1634) says—

"If a man grant at this day to an abbot or to a prior lands or tenements in frankalmoigne, these words, 'frankalmoigne,' are void; for it is ordained by the statute which is called *Quia emptores terrarum* (which was made Anno 18 E. 1) that none may alien nor grant lands or tenements in fee simple to hold of himself." Hence, as the purchaser [that is, the person who acquires] must hold "of the same lord of whom his grantor held, and shall not hold of his grantor in frankalmoigne, by reason of the same statute," it is only by prescription now, or by express gift of the King, that frankalmoigne, or free, pure, and perpetual

---

[2] 18 Edw. I., stat. 1, c. 3: *Quia emptores*.
[3] Pollock and Maitland, *History of English Law*, i. 245.

alms in land, can be given any more. The King, adds Coke, "is out of the case of the statute." Then, after quoting Littleton's text, he proceeds—

"Here Littleton speaketh of a licence or dispensation [to put land in mortmain], within the said statute of *Quia emptores terrarum* (and mentioneth no other statute); which may bee done by the King and all the lords immediate and mediate, for it is a rule in law: *Alienatio licet prohibeatur consensu tamen omnium, in quorum favorem prohibita est, potest fieri* ['Though alienation be forbidden, it can be effected with the consent of all those in whose favour it has been forbidden']; and *Quilibet potest renunciare juri pro se introducto* ['Any one can forego a right granted on his behalf']. And the licence of lords immediate and mediate in this case shall inure to two intents: viz. to a dispensation both of the statute *Quia emptores terrarum*, and of the Statutes of Mortmaine, as Littleton here implyeth; because their deeds shall be taken most strongly against themselves. But it is a safe and good policie in the King's licence to have a *non obstante* also of the Statutes of Mortmaine, and not only a *non obstante* of the statute of *Quia emptores terrarum*. But it appeareth by Littleton (which is a secret of law), that there needeth not any *non obstante* by the King of the Statutes of Mortmaine; for the King shall not be intended to be misconusant [ignorant] of the law; and, when he licenseth expressly to an abbot, etc., which is in mortmaine, he needs not make any *non obstante* of the Statutes of Mortmaine; for it is apparent to be granted in mortmaine. And the King is the head of the law; and therefore *Præsumitur Rex habere omnia jura in scrinio pectoris sui* ['It is presumed that the King keeps all laws registered in his bosom'], for the maintenance of his grant to be good according to the law; for which cause of purpose Littleton maketh no mention of any licence in Mortmaine." Then, after some further commentaries, to the effect that, if the abbot and convent alienate the gift, all the emoluments shall revive at once accruing to the lord, Coke proceeds—

"*Nota* (Reader): Since Littleton wrote, a man may either in his life time, or by his last will in writing [4] give lands, tenements, etc., to any spirituall bodie politicke or corporate, to be holden of himselfe in frankalmoigne or by Divine service, as by the statute 1 & 2 Phil. & Mariæ (which endured for twenty years) appeareth; which statute since that time hath been favourably and benignly expounded." Again citing his text, Coke continues—

"It is to be understood that a man seised of lands may at this day give the same to a bishop, parson, etc., and their successors in frankalmoigne, by the consent of the King and the lords mediate and immediate of whom the land is holden; for the rule is, *Quilibet potest renunciare juri pro se introducto*." [5]

[4] 1 & 2 Phil. & Mar., c. 8.
[5] Co. Litt., 98, 99.

If now we consult the statute of Philip & Mary as cited by Coke, we find the very model of George Calvert's Maryland charter, in the matter of letting property go into mortmain. The Queen Mary's statute referred to is that momentous one by which the English nation made its reconciliation with Rome; but at the cost to the Church of recognizing as good the expropriation of sacred property, incalculable in value, which had been seized by lay hands during the two preceding reigns. All these fruits of rapine being released by the Church, the statute, in its last sections, contains the provisions for making compensation and for building up again religion and charity out of the universal ruins. Frankalmoigne and every form of gift are rehabilitated in perfect freedom for an initial period of twenty years. And, to guarantee the legal effects, one statute is dispensed with by name; that is, *Quia emptores*. Here this Act of Queen Mary and the charter for Maryland agree in form and in effect.

Dispensing from Statutes of Mortmain, by suspending Quia emptores, 1 & 2 Phil. & Mary, c. 8.

It is thus that the said sections in Queen Mary's Act run—

"XXIII. And forasmuch as, after this reconciliation and unity of this noble Realm to the body of Christs Church, it is to be trusted that, by the abundance of Gods mercy and grace, devotion shall encrease and grow in the hearts of many the subjects of this Realm, with desire to give and bestow their worldly possessions for the resuscitating of alms, prayer, and example of good life in this Realm ; to the intent such godly motions and purposes should be advanced : Be it therefore enacted by authority of this present Parliament, that it shall be lawful to such as shall be seised of any manors, lands, tenements, parsonages, tithes, pensions, portions, or other hereditaments whatsoever, in fee-simple, in possession, reversion, or remainder, in their own rights, not being copyhold, may thereof make feoffments, grants, or any other assurances, or by his last will and testament in writing may bequeath and give in fee-simple all and every the said manors, lands, tenements, parsonages, tithes, pensions, portions, or other hereditaments, to any spiritual body politick or corporate in this Realm or Dominions of the same, nowe erected or founded, or hereafter to bee erected or founded, without any licence of mortmain therein to be obtained, or any writ of *Ad quod damnum* to be sued out for the same; the Acts *De terris ad manum mortuam non ponendis*, or any other Act or statute heretofore had or made in any wise notwithstanding. Saving to the lords of the fee all rentes, services, due or going out of any of the said lands, tenements, or hereditaments, so to be amortized, as aforesaid." Here there follows a proviso, limiting the operation of the statute to twenty years; and then another section, saving the ancient prerogatives, as well of the Sovereign of England as of the Sovereign Pontiff; and finally comes the passage with the derogating clause about the statute *Quia emptores terrarum*. It reads as follows:—

"XXIV. Provided always, and be it enacted by the authority aforesaid, that in and upon every such giftes and devises to be made to such spiritual corporations or persons, as is aforesaid, the donor, feoffor, or devisor thereof may reserve to him and to his heirs forever a tenure in frankealmoigne, or a tenure by Divine service; and to have all remedies and actions for and upon the said gifts or devises, and tenures; in like manner or form as was used before the estatute of Westminster Third, commonly called *Quia emptores terrarum*: the said estatute or any other law or custom now being to the contrary in any wise notwithstanding." [6]

The invitation here extended to all classes of persons was quite clear; not merely to benefactors that they might give, but to wrongful possessors that they should restore: "Parsonages," says the Act, "tithes, pensions, portions." It was clear and strong enough for a Blackstone, not only to see and note, but to sneer at in characteristic fashion; about the policy of Henry the Eighth's "next popish successor;" and how, "in order to regain as much of them [the abbey lands] as either the zeal or timidity of their owners might induce them to part with, the Statutes of Mortmain were suspended for twenty years, by the statute of 1 & 2 Philip & Mary, c. 8; and during that time any lands or tenements were allowed to be granted to any spiritual corporation without any licence whatsoever." [7] For conferring this extensive franchise, it sufficed, just as Sir Edward Coke had indicated, to derogate from the statute *Quia emptores terrarum*.

And so, as we observed in a former paragraph,[8] Baltimore's charter had at least this model before it, and certainly operated in the same sense. The very amplitude of his language in the part of his charter relating to the subject covered every form of conveyance, grant, and donation. If anything were conceived as still wanting to set up in Maryland a counterpart of the eminent prerogatives inherent in the Crown, and smooth the way for mortmain—a point on which Coke insisted so much in the matter of dispensations—that too was there in the palatine privileges or sovereignty of the Proprietary. So the Statutes of Mortmain were by the fundamental charter excluded from Maryland, not for twenty years but for ever; and the possession of landed property in mortmain was organically legal.

The first Lord Baltimore, and the second.

The reaction of Cecil, second Lord Baltimore, against this part of his father's charter, bore an aspect of inconsistency; but really it was only an expression of his animus against all expenses in favour of the Church, charity, and education. As to his inconsistency, it should be noticed that the same law, 18 Edw. I., stat. 1, c. 3, *Quia emptores terrarum*, which was so carefully set aside by Queen Mary and the first Lord Baltimore, not only had the effect of stopping the general practice of free alms in mortmain,

---

[6] 1 & 2 Phil. & Mar., c. 8.
[7] 2 Blackstone, *Comm.*, 273.
[8] *Supra*, § 17 (3), p. 242. Cf. also § 52 (2), pp. 430, 431.

but also buried the whole practice of creating manors on the part of inferior landlords.[9] George Calvert having exhumed the old system by derogating from the statute, and having expressly restored for Maryland the right of erecting manors and manorial courts,[10] his good son, Cecil Calvert, took the effete manorial system to work it assiduously for a while; and yet at the same time he buried again the whole system of free alms or beneficence, which in its nature is never effete. He insisted, too, on the right of unqualified and unconditional forfeiture or escheat into his own hands of what had never been received from him, and even of what had been bought from him for purposes of religion, charity, and education. For such pretensions he had no model whatever in the statutory history or social life of Catholic times. The sample which he was really following belongs to the later history of mortmain after Henry VIII.

In the mean time we finish the last few stages of Catholic beneficence as it appears in the statutes.

(6) Nine years after the enactment of the foregoing statute *Quia emptores*, another was passed under the same able prince Edward I. (A.D. 1299), showing to clerical and monastic institutions the process by which they were to put land for their own service in mortmain; that is, how they were to " amortize " legally. It states that such [laymen] as would purchase new parks, and men of religion that would amortize lands,[11] shall have writs out of chancery to inquire upon the points accustomed. If the lands in question be found to be worth more than twenty shillings yearly, the inquest " shall be returned into the exchequer, and there they shall make fine for the amortizement or for the having of the park," supposing that the inquest made is favourable ; and from thence a certificate to the effect shall be sent into chancery; and so, too, if the property is found to be worth less than twenty shillings a year. The chancellor or his lieutenant shall take a reasonable fine, according to the quantity of the thing, and then deliver them.[12]

<small>(6) How to amortize legally. A.D. 1299.</small>

The writ issued for the inquiry by the chancellor was called *Ad quod damnum*. And a sample of such a writ will show what was the spirit of the laws in Catholic times, even after the Statutes of ecclesiastical Mortmain had reached almost their complete development. The following is its form :—

<small>The writ inquiring into the prejudice done: *Ad quod damnum*.</small>

"We command that you inquire if it will be *to the damage* of us or others, if we grant to B. that he [the donor] may give a messuage, etc.,

---

[9] W. Stubbs, *Select Charters, etc., of English Constitutional History*, p. 478.
[10] *Archives of Maryland, Proceedings of the Council*, 1636–1667, Charter, p. 11; sentence immediately following the one which derogates from the statute 18 Edw. I., stat. 1, c. 3.
[11] " *Et gentz de Religion qe vodreint terrez ou tenementz amortir.*"
[12] 27 Edw. I., stat. 2, sect. 1.

to a certain chaplain, to celebrate Divine service for the soul of him and the souls of his father, mother, and ancestors, and of all the faithful departed, in the chapel of the Blessed Mary of Westminster, or in the parochial church of the Blessed Mary of Southwark every day, to have and to hold to the said chaplain and his successors, celebrating Divine service in the church aforesaid, or in the chapel aforesaid every day, etc. And, if it be to the damage of us or others, then *to what damage [ad quod damnum]*, etc.; and of whom the said lands, etc., are held; and by what services; and how much they are worth, according to the true value of the same; and if the lands remaining to B. [the grantor], beside the donation aforesaid, be sufficient for the customs and services owing to be done, and all the other charges he sustains, and hath been used to maintain, as in suits, aids, tallages, fines, amerciaments, contributions, and other charges." [13]

The tenor of this writ serves to show the point of Sir Francis Palgrave's criticism on the whole story of mortmain, as propagated by Blackstone, and by those who have copied him. Testifying before the Mortmain Committee of the House of Commons (1844), Palgrave, in the first place, declined to accept the aforesaid story, with regard to the scope and purpose and operation of the earlier Mortmain Laws. Then, arriving at the present stage of legislation, where we now are, with its more stringent conditions than before, that eminent authority continued: "Now, in considering what the evil was which it was necessary to remedy, far too narrow a view is taken, if it be supposed that the legislature sought only to protect the pecuniary or military incidents of tenure. At that time, there were a great many civil obligations connected with land, which could not be discharged unless the freehold was in possession of laymen. If religious persons had an undue proportion of land, there would be a deficiency of persons to attend the view of frank-pledge; a deficiency of persons to be put in assize as jurors. Attendance upon assizes in early days was exceedingly burdensome. It was so burdensome that it was a very common thing for persons to obtain a remission of that duty. These duties were very onerous; and, if there were but few freeholders, it became a great hardship upon them." Here the gentleman adduced a parallel case from Ulster, in the matter of the grants to London Companies; and he continued: "Thus one of the objects, though not expressed in the statute preventing alienation of land to persons in religion or to religious houses, was to prevent a diminution in the number of persons in the county or hundred able to perform those services to the community. We learn this from the writ *Ad quod damnum*." The jurist gave an abstract of the statute which we have just reported with the writ; and he added: "Parks were subjected to the same rule,

The wide range of prejudice done to lay tenants.

[13] W. F. Finlason, *History of the Laws of Mortmain*, p. 28.—Cf. E. Gibson, *Codex Juris Ecclesiastici Anglicani*, ii. 668.

because, by absorbing the smaller tenants, they might lead to the same evil; and accordingly, from that time until the writ of *Ad quod damnum* was rendered unnecessary by the statute of William & Mary, no mortization was to be made except by such previous inquiry. The inquiry was to be made by a jury; and, according to their verdict, a licence was to be granted or refused. There were other statutes relating to purely feudal principles; that is to say, providing that the consent of different intermediate lords should be obtained. They do not, however, very much bear upon our present subject [that is, the new kind of mortmain under George II.], except that the general tenor of them is to show that there was no great vigilance on the part of the lords to exercise their rights.

"It is rather remarkable that the very same classes of society, who legislated against those alienations, are the classes who furnished the means for their evasion [that is, by ever making new endowments in behalf of religion, charity, and education]. However, so it was. It is a contradiction we frequently find. The classes to whom legislation belongs endeavour to evade the laws they themselves have made."[14]

No special care in enforcing Statutes of Mortmain. Reasons.

The contradiction which the jurist here noted and the explanation which he furnished, appear to have been much less real and patent than he thought. As to the contradiction of classes in society legislating and then neglecting their own laws, he should have mentioned that laws do not proceed so often from a class as from a few agitators in a class; a few nobles against the clergy; a few clergymen against some clerks regular; a few disappointed prelates against the Pope. Still more grave was the omission in his explanation to note a fact as broad and wide as medievalism, as deep and significant as the very name of those "Ages of Faith." This fact was the faith of those barons—their Catholicity—their devotion. Even the worst among them had lucid intervals; and their intervals of goodness were made lucid by the light of Divine faith, hope, and charity. It does not serve any purpose to omit mentioning so palpable a fact, merely because the jurist may have disliked the implication of English law and of English writers in the seventeenth and eighteenth centuries, that this Divine faith of Catholicity was a "superstition." Such implication, if worthy of his notice, did not change in the least the relevancy of the fact, which therefore he should not have omitted. Anything may be thought to be anything by some people; so much so that Queen Elizabeth herself, in trying to reconstruct charity, by the statute of Charitable Uses, omitted to bring in religious chaplains or ministers of worship as an object and means of charity, because she was afraid, says Sir F. Moore, author of the Act, that her own Protestant religion might one day become a superstition, and her charities would then go by the board; as the Catholic religion of her ancestors had

[14] House of Commons, *Mortmain Committee Report*, etc., 1844, pp. 8 (526), 9 (527).

been a superstition with her, and she had seen to it that their charities went into her pocket.[15] In point of fact, the Protestantism of the Tudors has already become a "superstition" in the nineteenth and twentieth centuries, a new creed of faith or science claiming and obtaining the right of succession.

Sir Francis Palgrave proceeds to a very important element in the history of mortmain, that of other persons than religious communities being contemplated in the Acts. First in the matter of 13 Edward I., c. 32 (A.D. 1285), "this statute," he says, "speaks of religious men and *other ecclesiastical persons*, who implead or bring actions against parties, who make default by collusion." He observes again: "They begin to feel some inconvenience attending the granting of lands to the *secular clergy*. Thus, in connection with the writ, *Ad quod damnum*, there is a specific case in the 18 Edward I. which will show how the general law was practically worked." The King refused licence to some, granted licence to others; the ground of discrimination being the capability of the tenant with the residue "to bear the common burdens of the country." The jurist then proceeds to "a new era, the reign of Richard II."[16] But two stages intervene—

The secular clergy brought under Mortmain Statutes.

(7) Seven years after showing people of religion and of the Church by what legal process they were to put lands in mortmain, another law (A.D. 1306) prescribed that, in effectuating the process, nothing should be done, where there were any intermediate lords, except with their consent, which should be shown to the King under their patents; and no licence should pass where the donor retained no residue of his feudal holding for himself.[17]

(7) Supplementary formalities for amortizing. A.D. 1306.

(8) A generation later (A.D. 1344), under Edward III., witnessed another Act regarding mortmain. It was in the sense of protecting the clergy, when they had fulfilled the legal requirements; and, even if they had not done so, still protecting them in the sense of allowing them now to fulfil conditions wanting: To wit, that if prelates, etc., are impeached for purchasing lands and putting the same in mortmain, and then they "shew our charter of licence and process thereupon, made by an inquest of *Ad quod damnum*, or of our grace or by fine, they shall be freely let in peace,

(8) Condoning deficiencies in mortmain titles, etc. A.D. 1344.

[15] W. F. Finlason, *History of the Laws of Mortmain*, p. 50: "[Of the Statute of Charitable Uses] its author and expositor, Sir F. Moore, said: 'But a gift of lands to maintain a chaplain or minister, to celebrate Divine worship, is not within the letter or meaning of the statute; for it was of purpose omitted in the penning of the Act, lest the gifts intended to be employed upon purposes of charity might, in change of times (contrary to the minds of the givers), be confiscated into the King's treasury. For, religion being variable according to the pleasure of succeeding princes, that which at one time is held orthodox may, at another, be counted superstitious; and then such land is confiscated, as appears by the statutes of charities [the Statute of Chauntries], 1 Edw. VI., c. 14.'—Duke on Charities."

[16] *Infra*, (9).—House of Commons, *Mortmain Committee* (1844), as above, *loc. cit.*
[17] 34 Edw. I., stat. 3.

without being further impeached for the same purchase. And, in case they cannot sufficiently shew that they have entred by due process after licence to them granted, in general or in special, that they shall be well received to make a convenient fine for the same, and that the inquiry of this Article shall wholly cease,[18] according to the Accord comprised in this Parliament." [19]

From this Act it appears that there was "grace" distributed in the way of allowing amortization without any legal process; that there were "general" licences given, not merely "special;" and that, as late as the middle of the fourteenth century, when Wycliff was just about to preach down the clergy, there was no difficulty whatever in the way of amortizing land for the service of the Church, even if clergymen had imprudently taken the risks of overriding the law, to escape the inquest and expense.

(9) We come now to the last of the Mortmain Statutes in the genuine sense of the term; and one of the most important for several reasons. The legal element of Uses and Trusts on behalf of religion comes under statutory notice. Besides, lay fraternities or corporations are brought into line with religious communities. For the first time also it would seem that there was a political object in a Mortmain Statute—as against the lay corporations, not as against the Church. With regard to the Church, while the statute extends the operation of licences to lands held for a sacred use, even though not held in the clergy's name; and also extends the same operation to estates acquired under the plea of being intended for churchyards; still the very same process of obtaining the licences prevails as before, no change being introduced in that matter. The date (A.D. 1391) was that of the Lollard agitation against the clergy and against all upper classes of society, and that of an extreme weakness in the Papacy, owing to the great Western schism.

(9) Enlarged application of Mortmain Statutes. A.D. 1391.

The statute then of 15 Richard II., c. 5, recited that some spiritual persons had entered into lands adjoining to their churches, and by sufferance of the tenants had made churchyards thereof, and had hallowed the same in virtue of Bulls from "the Bishop of Rome," but had no licence from the King or the lords. It declared that such land was subject to the provisions already made in the Statute *De Religiosis*, 7 Edward I. The Act then proceeds to the matter of uses, enacting with regard to all those who are possessed by feoffment or by other manner of lands, tenements, etc., to the use of religious persons "to amortize them, and whereof the said religious and spiritual persons take the profits, that betwixt this [the morrow after All Souls] and the Feast of St. Michael next coming, they

---

[18] "*Et en cas qils ne pourront sufficialment monstrer qils ne soient entrez par due processe apres la licence a eux grante, en general ou especial, qils soient bonement resceuz a faire covenable fym, et qe lenquerrie de cest article cesse de tout.*"
[19] 18 Edw. III., stat. 3, c. 3.

shall cause them to be amortized by the licence of the King and the lords; or else that they shall sell and aliene them to some other use between this and the said feast; upon pain to be forfeited to the King and to the lords, according to the form of the said Statute of Religious, as lands purchased by religious people;" and that from henceforth no such purchase be made, to the uses of religious or spiritual persons, [otherwise than as subject to the Mortmain Statutes]. The Act then proceeds to comprise lands purchased for guilds, fraternities, offices, commonalties, or for their use; the reason assigned being that mayors and commons of cities or boroughs have perpetual commonalty, and others have offices perpetual; and therefore they are as perpetual as people of religion. All now are under the ordinary Statutes of Mortmain.

It is to be observed that no restriction is imposed upon the spiritual and religious persons, except that of reasserting the necessity of taking out a licence. Moreover, the ground common to all the legislation, as brought to bear on the laity and confirmed with regard to the clergy, is said to be the perpetuity, not of the land under a fixed tenure of possession, but of the moral person, who possessed the land so as not to die, never to marry, never to be a ward, and who thereby withheld so many items of feudal service and subsidy.[20]

The common ground of the legislation.

Now, this statute, both as prohibiting trusts even in favour of religion except with a licence, and as prohibiting the possession of land by any body politic, religious or lay, except with the same licence, supplied the basis for Cecil Calvert's policy in the Conditions of Plantation published in 1648—the same which he had tried ineffectually in 1641.[21] Then prohibiting secret trusts, on behalf of any person whatsoever, he even introduced a political motive, saying that "all secret trusts are usually intended to deceive either the Government or State where they are made, or some other persons."[22]

The model of Cecil Calvert's policy.

With the aid of a few authorities, we shall see the merits of Cecil Calvert's policy, which has most points of contact with this last of the Catholic Mortmain Statutes, though it has also been illustrated by antecedent Acts of the same series. In them there has been no trace of politics, of the State for motives of public policy taking up an attitude with regard to the Church; it has all been a feudal and civic policy, adjusting property rights and difficulties by means of legislation, like any other municipal question. Here, in the statute of Richard II., politics enter for the first time into mortmain legislation, but with respect to laymen. It is only in the next stage of mortmain so called, from Henry

---

[20] Perpetual commonalty: "That is, 'perpetual succession' as corporations. It is not said the land is as perpetual, but the bodies politic holding it." W. A. Finlason, *History of the Laws of Mortmain*, p. 31, note.

[21] See above, § 62, p. 499.—Cf. § 63 (1), note 10, p. 510.

[22] *Archives of Maryland, Proceedings of the Council*, 1636-1667, pp. 227, 228, §§ 12, 14.—Cf. *Ibid.* for 1649, pp. 236, 237, §§ 10, 11.

VIII. to our day, that politics enter into the relations with the Church as a motive permanent and dominant.

(a) As to politics. In the examination of the general question before the House of Commons Mortmain Committee (1844), Sir Francis Palgrave came to this statute, and, after reciting it, continued thus: "I am reading the statute, and, as far as I have read [with respect to uses of land in favour of spiritual persons] there is no departure from the spirit of the earlier statutes, which we will call, if you please, the Feudal Statutes; and so far only the petition of the Commons extended.[23] The ancient statutes are the result of the petitions of the Commons and the answer of the King. Generally speaking, the Crown granted less than the Commons asked. It was not so in this case. When King Richard II. gave his answer to this petition, he gave them a great deal more than they asked. All the remainder which I am about to read is not the prayer of the Commons, but the grant of the King; and the two together have formed the statute. The statute, being the King's expansion of the petition of the Commons, extends to 'all lands, tenements, fees, advowsons, and other possessions purchased or to be purchased to the use of guilds or fraternities; and moreover it is assented,' [that mayors, bailiffs, etc., which have perpetual commonalty or offices perpetual, shall be subject to the same laws, etc., in amortizing as religious]."

(a) Former statutes feudal.

Palgrave continued: "Circumstances had greatly changed since the earlier statutes were made. There had been, with the exception of burghs and some other places where the custom prevailed, no power of devising by will and disinheriting an heir. An individual might part with land in his lifetime, though at that early period he could only do so with the consent of his heir. He had no power of devising by will. Therefore in those times there could be no abuse as to a devise by [of?] land. But by degrees the custom had grown up of conveying land to uses, which became the indirect means of doing that which the law did not permit. And extensive use was made of this evasion in devising land to all kinds of charitable purposes; in particular to guilds and fraternities. Now, at this period, which was quite a revolutionary era, the Crown became jealous of guilds; so much so that they were ordered to return their regulations or by-laws into Chancery." Here the jurist explained the growth of political influence on the part of the guilds, trading companies, etc., of the time, and the reaction of the Crown's influence by putting a restriction on lay communities, never thought of before. He considered these restrictions purely political. He said—

The new conveyance of land to uses. Political objects.

"There were no corporations, in the strict sense of the term, till the time of Henry VI.; and therefore, whatever property the communities we now call corporations took, they must have taken as communities [of laymen]. I do not find any restriction preventing any civil body having

[23] 15 Rich. II., *Rolls of Parliament*, iii. 291.

perpetual succession taking land, till we come to this statute; and therefore I think this additional restriction was purely political, for the purpose of preventing an increase of power in bodies which were using such power in an adverse manner to the King. With respect to the returns of the guilds required by Richard, he gained little information. The returns could not indicate the sentiments of the members of the guilds, which were ostensibly for charitable objects.

"After this period, however, not much attention was directed to the subject, until we come to the reign of Henry VIII. (23 Henry VIII.), when there is a statute to prevent certain gifts in mortmain, principally for companies or brotherhoods. No further mortmain restrictions were enacted in the reign of Henry VIII. It was not likely that gifts would be made at a time when religious and charitable foundations were the bait for cupidity and the objects of general spoliation. In the time of Elizabeth we come to a totally different era." [24]

If we are to accept this jurist's authority on the subject, as supported by an examination of the statutes, we have to conclude, as to the motives of the statutes: That there was no political motive in any part of the mortmain legislation, as regarded the Church; that the first time politics entered was in the last mortmain law (A.D. 1391), and then it was with exclusive reference to lay fraternities; that from Henry III.'s Magna Charta of 1217, to Richard II.'s mortmain law of 1391, and then during the long interval from 1391 till Henry VIII.'s law of 1532, there was never any restriction whatever for a political motive on the acquisition of property by the Church, by her religious communities, or clerical corporations, whether aggregate or sole; that during the same long period of mortmain legislation, consisting of 315 years, the only restrictions were those which came from the formalities imposed by feudal necessities, as the great lords conceived them; and that such formalities or feudal safeguards scarcely hampered in any direction the enormous development of religion, charity, and education, to which the statutes themselves, subsequently enacted for the spoliation of the great system or for a partial reconstruction of it, bear ample witness.

Summary of the political history. 1217-1532.

As to the life-history of the Mortmain legislation, we have also to conclude: That, in the terms of Hallam, it was a "customary fraud of lay proprietors," which originated the first Statute of Mortmain as against laymen, and, according to the explanation of Sir Francis Palgrave, it was the hostile and revolutionary tendencies of lay fraternities which gave the political cast to the last Statute of Mortmain, as directed against the laymen; and that of the old fable about the English State being arrayed against

Summary of errors in the life-history of Mortmain.

---

[24] House of Commons, *Mortmain Committee Report* (1844), pp. 9 (527)-11 (529).—Cf. a digest of this evidence, W. F. Finlason, *History of the Laws of Mortmain*, pp. 170, 171.

§ 76] USES AND TRUSTS 613

the Church, about "the bishops and clergy" on one side being against "the nobility and laity" on the other,[25] nothing further remains than the suggestion to record it as archaic and obsolete, belonging to a darker age. Still it remains in the books. Chancellor Kent did not escape the force of tradition.[26] Angell and Ames, on the Law of Private Corporations Aggregate, rehearse the substance of the fable.[27] A Maryland writer is sententious in the brevity with which he refers to the story as a simple and self-evident episode of history; and with it he can afford to illustrate something else less evident: "We cannot cite a better illustration of this," says J. V. L. McMahon, "than that which is found in the history of the Statutes of Mortmain, the simple object of all of which was to prevent the alienation of lands to the all-absorbing clergy, whose ingenuity, prompted by their avarice and thirst for dominion, for ages kept the statute law lagging behind them."[28]

(b) As to uses. Cecil Calvert introduced into a plantation document about buying and selling a political reason for excluding thenceforth all secret trusts from his plantation. Such an insertion of a doctrinaire reason into a business paper would seem to imply that at least he felt the necessity of alleging some excuse. He said: "Because all secret trusts are usually intended to deceive the Government or State where they are made, or some other persons," etc.[29] His view on the subject was the same as that of Henry VIII.; and the plan of campaign which he followed against ecclesiastical, charitable, and educational property was not very different from that of Henry VIII., although on an infinitesimal scale, where the Tudor monarch had proceeded on a gigantic plan. In the twenty-seventh year of his reign that monarch destroyed the whole existing system of uses, by a statute which transformed the beneficiaries of trusts into the legal owners, cutting out at one stroke all the intermediaries or trustees to uses.[30] At once he and his ministers had the Church, charity, and education at their mercy, without any intermediaries to mask the beneficiaries; and in the same year the destruction of the monasteries commenced. Bacon, in his account and defence of the Statute of Uses, puts this matter very gently and pleasantly. The time of the statute, he says, "was in 27 Henry VIII., when the King was in full peace, and a wealthy and flourishing estate; in which nature of time men are most careful of their possessions, as well because purchasers are most stirring," as because of the needs of providing for children with good assurance, etc. "About that time the realm likewise began to be infranchised from the tributes of Rome,

(b) Cecil Calvert's dislike of uses and trusts. His model: 27 Henry VIII., c. 10.

[25] Cf. *supra*, Introduction, Chap. II. § 19, p. 127.
[26] 2 Kent, *Comm.*, 282, *seq*.
[27] Angell and Ames, p. 113.
[28] J. V. L. McMahon, *Historical View of the Government of Maryland*, p. 110.—Cf. *supra*, Introduction, § 19, p. 128.
[29] *Archives of Maryland, Proceedings of the Council*, as above, *loc. cit.*
[30] 27 Hen. VIII., c. 10.

and the possessions that had been in mortmain began to stir abroad; for this year was the suppression of the smaller houses of religion, all tending to plenty and purchasing."[31] However, as Henry VIII. had also attacked pious trusts, given where there was no mortmain at all,[32] and therefore where there were no feudal rights to be protected, another author is driven to explain the matter by more psychological reasons. He considers it to have been enlightenment and the great spirit of enterprise in the noble prince. "As the age became enlightened," says Reeves, quoted approvingly by Justice Stephen, "gifts of this kind [for a pious purpose] were viewed with a less favourable eye. These sentiments, concurring with the designs of the enterprising prince upon the throne, contributed towards the general attack which was soon afterwards made on one branch of such institutions" (those erected for devotion)—the "religious houses."[33] At a moment when Blackstone, and Justice Stephen after him, happen not to be speaking of the clergy or the Church or religion, they call Henry VIII., in plain terms, "the rapacious prince then reigning."[34] And Palgrave, as we have heard, places the whole history on its right basis, saying of the age that it was "a time when religious and charitable foundations were the bait for cupidity and the objects of general spoliation."

Uses thus expelled by Henry VIII. came back under the form of trusts. And there is no need of our rehearsing the vindication thereof by the jurists.[35] We merely advert to the following matters of fact. It was a trust which put a stop for the moment to Cecil Calvert's attempt at despoiling the missionaries of Maryland. Were it not for secret trusts and uses, not an acre of land probably would have remained in the hands of the rightful Catholic owners in Ireland, except at the price of their religion—owing to the English legislation of Cecil Calvert's own time, and of his own kind.[36] And if, since the time of the Protestant Reformation to our day, any Catholic estate in England has been enabled to serve the purposes of the ancestral religion, it has been only because of the operation of trusts so secret as to be called "spiritual."[37] Hence we may safely dismiss the scruple of the Maryland Proprietary on the score of danger to his paternal government arising from the secrecy of uses and trusts, as any similar scruple of Henry VIII. on matters of morality might with perfect safety be dismissed.

Trusts. Their value in Catholic history.

There is nothing material now to add on the subject of the ancient

---

[31] Sir Francis Bacon, *Works*, iv. 180, 181; *Reading upon the Statute of Uses*.
[32] 23 Hen. VIII., c. 10.
[33] 1 Stephen, *Comm.*, 459, note; from Reeves, *History of English Law*; iv. 237.
[34] 1 Stephen, *Ibid.*, 249, on 26 Hen. VIII., c. 13.
[35] Cf. 4 Kent, *Comm.*, 290, *seqq.*
[36] J. Lingard, *History of England*, vii. 199, note, A.D. 1638.
[37] W. F. Finlason, *History of the Laws of Mortmain*, pp. 92, 93.

Catholic statutes, except that if, in the friction with canonical rights, the legislators strained too far the feudal rights, that was a matter for the canonists, the chancellor, and the King's Bench to settle among themselves, according to the fixed principles which all admitted. The tradition of Christendom in this direction was diverted and broken off in England only at the time of the Reformation. It continued straight on its course in other countries of Europe, both Catholic and Protestant. These did not lose their hold so rapidly upon history.

Understanding between Church and State. Popular sentiment.

In the House of Commons Mortmain Committee of 1844 Viscount Clive asked the well-known lawyer and writer, Mr. Burge: "Have you ever found in old books any popular complaint that the law allows undue disherison of heirs, or anything to indicate that the powers of charitable bequests existing at any period were viewed by the community with distrust?" Mr. Burge: "It has been represented, but I think erroneously, that the Statutes of Mortmain were passed for the purpose of protecting the people of England against the rapacity of the clergy and against their ignorance and superstition." Viscount Clive: "You have not met with any statement in old books which would lead you to suppose that the popular opinion took that line?" Mr. Burge: "No, I have not. I should say most probably the writers and historians were misled; and I am referring particularly to those who have spoken of the gross ignorance of the clergy." And here the distinguished gentleman proceeded to give an instance of gross falsification in the pages of Robertson's *Charles V.*, and of Hallam copying him.[38]

During the Wars of the Roses, many expedients were adopted for recouping the losses to the Treasury; and among them was the "resumption of grants,"[39] a piece of policy advocated by Lewger for Maryland, and practised by Cecil Calvert on the missionaries. There was also wholesale confiscation and forfeiture, inflicted on enemies; and that too was tried in Maryland, though not on enemies. But towards the Church those sanguinary houses of greedy kings, who slaughtered and robbed indiscriminately in the Wars of the Roses, behaved themselves very differently indeed; and in this respect they were not imitated by Cecil and Lewger. When Edward IV. clambered to the throne (A.D. 1461) through a sea of blood, with a wholesale wreckage by confiscations and forfeitures, he revoked in general the grants made by the three "usurping" kings of the House of Lancaster;[40] but, with regard to the Church, the very first statute ordained that any Acts which concerned corporations, religious establishments, etc., should hold; and that all gifts in mortmain bestowed on any

Favour shown to ecclesiastical Mortmain.

---

[38] House of Commons, *Mortmain Committee Report* (1844), p. 172 (690).—Cf. *supra*, Introduction, § 11, p. 81, note 5.
[39] J. Lingard, *History of England*, iv. 68, 70.
[40] *Ibid.*, p. 70.

persons by the aforesaid "pretensed kings" should be perpetually valid.[41]

As the length of this Appendix prohibits our pursuing at present the subject of Mortmain into its two next English and American stages of Superstitious Uses and Charitable Uses, as well as into its fourth and last European stage of the twentieth century, which is that of Mortmain Nondescript, we cut it short and omit the rest of this interesting question, unless it be called for in the sequence of our historical text.[42]

[41] 1 Edw. IV., stat. 1, c. 1, §§ 1-4, 6.
[42] Dodd, edited and annotated by Tierney, devotes two pages in the text to the Statutes of Mortmain, with some notes and an appendix by the editor. These writers discern in the said statutes scarcely anything more than a rightful subjugation of the monasteries, and a vindication of parochial rights and clergy as against monastic progress; but with the unfortunate result that the Mendicant Orders came into the field. Now, it was against the Mendicant Orders that the Statutes of Mortmain were filed! Hence Dodd signifies his cordial approval. Dodd's *Church History of England*, edited by M. A. Tierney, i. 128, 129.—As to Tierney's note, *Ibid.*, introducing into the question of mortmain "parochial tithes" alienated in favour of monasteries, compare Blackstone for a similar reference to "the intrigues of the regular clergy, or monks of the Benedictine and other rules," and a sympathetic allusion to the defrauded "secular or parochial clergy (a much more valuable set of men than themselves [the monks])," etc. Herewith compare Finlason's lively note on the juridical competency of Justice Blackstone when touching such a subject; he shows it to be quite on a par with that of his chiefs and leaders—Lord Hardwicke and Lord Chief Baron Gilbert. W. F. Finlason, *History of the Laws of Mortmain*, pp. 72, 73, note.—Like all such pieces of Blackstone, the Justices Stephen, father and son, reproduce the very words of that gentleman, for the sake of preserving such a "relic" from "perishing" with the rest of "a work now falling into decay." The whole passage properly mounted for preservation may be seen in 2 Stephen, *Comm.*, 724, 725, on Tithes.—Cf. *supra*, Introduction, Chap. II. § 15, p. 100.

INDEX

[*Arabic numbers designate the pages; roman numerals, the notes.*]

A

ABBOT, *Archbishop of Canterbury*, 122; *v.* Copley, John

Abstention of clergy from Assembly, 382; reasons for, 382, 383; from witness-box, 382, x.; *v.* Oates, Titus; as a privilege, 383

Account of the Colony; *v. Conditions of Plantation*, Declaration

Acers, *Mr.*, Barbados, 277

Acts of Assembly, Maryland; *v.* Assembly, Bills

ACTS OF PARLIAMENT: 2 Hen. III., Magna Charta, 128, xii., 593, iv.—9 Hen. III., Magna Charta, 128, xii., 593, iv.—43 Hen. III., c. 19, 595, xvi.—7 Edw. I., stat. 2...594, x., 595, xix., 596, xx., 597, xxv.—13 Edw. I., cc. 32, 33, 41...599, xxx., xxxii.-xxxiv.; c. 32...608—25 Edw. I., Magna Charta,128, xii., 593, iv.—35 Edw. I., stat. 1...585, 586—14 Edw. III., stat. i., c. 1...131, vii., 446, xxxviii.—15 Rich. II., c. 5, 609-612—2 Hen. V., stat. i., c. 1...586—23 Hen. VIII., c. 10...614, xxxii.—27 Hen. VIII., c. 13...589, xxix.—31 Hen. VIII., c. 2...239, viii.—1 & 2 Phil. & Mar., c. 8...602, 603, 604—5 Eliz., c. 23...238, iv.—13 Eliz., c. 3...90, 147, iv.—14 Eliz., c. 6...91, xxi.—23 Eliz., c. 16...145, 146 —27 Eliz., c. 30...90—29 Eliz., c. 6...87, vi.—35 Eliz., c. 1...87, vi.—39 Eliz., c. 8 ...584, 585, xviii.—43 Eliz., c. 1...589, xxix.—43 Eliz., c. 4, 585, xvii., 589, xxix.—3 Jac. I., c. 5...88, xv., 240, x.—7 Jac. I., c. 6...88, xv.—21 Jac. I., c. 4... 90—3 Car. I., c. 3...238, v.—3 Car. I., c. 8...90—12 Car. II., c. 24...399—1 Gul. & Mar., c. 8...113, xiii.; 238, vi.—11 Gul. III., c. 4...88, xvi.—34 & 35 Vict., c. 48...116, xxiii.

Act of Toleration, Quebec, 91

Advowsons, temporal property, under common law, 444; Calvert, possessor of, 444

African Company, Royal, 282

Agucchi, John Baptist, Nuncio at Venice, letters to, from Ingoli, 183, 194, 195, v., 197, ix., 318, iv.; his answer, 198, x.

Alabaster, *Mr.*, 159, xi.

Albizi, *Cardinal*, on Bishop of Chalcedon, 202, 203, 221, 228

Alexis de Auxerre, *Fra, Capuchin*, letter from, to Propaganda, 311, 312

Algonquins, comprise Ottawas, Pottawatomies, Shawnees, 326

Allen, *Dr.* William, President of English College at Rheims, on sending S.J. to England, 144, 145

Altham; *v.* Gravener

Ambassador, French, endorses the Disavowal, 228; Spanish, endorses Protest of peers, 228; *v.* Fontenai, Coloma

America, Central and South, Provinces S.J. in, 316, 317

Amortizement; *v.* Mortmain

Anacostans, *King* of, a catechumen, 481, 482

Anderson, *Rev.* James, *Queen's Chaplain*, his criticism on the disingenuousness of the patent for Maryland, 243, 244, xx.; on the bishopric of Durham, 444

Angell and Ames, on anti-clericalism and Mortmain, 613

Anglican Church and the Puritans of Massachusetts, 554

Anglican clergy in North America: Atkins on Leeward Islands, 282; their presence depending on tithes and a glebe, 290, 291; Board of Trade's instructions, 293; Wheler on pressing the clergy for colonies, 293, 294; Lynch on appointment of prebendaries, 294; Council of St. Christopher asks for a more learned and older clergy, 294, 295

Anglo-American mission of secular priests, exclusive of S.J., 333

Anna; *v.* Pascattoway

Annual Letters, sent to Provincials and Generals S.J., 50; recounting conversions, 51; schedule for, 53, 54; redaction of, for a History, 60, 61

Antigua, divers religions in, 316

Antilles, Spanish and Portuguese provinces S.J., 317
Antilles, Little, 1625, range on the map described, 296; Relation for Propaganda on, 295, 296; their first occupation, by Nambuc and by Warner, 296; *v.* West Indian Islands
Antwerp, seminary, 470
Apostacy, rewards for, 88, 89
Apostolic Letters, define Maryland to be in West Indies, 268
Appeal *ab abusu*, under the Cavour ministry, 429, viii.
Aquinas, *St.* Thomas, on grants made *to* God, 440, xvii.
Archangelo, *Fra, Capuchin,* 314
ARCHIVES, register and notices of fifty, 1-3, 7-29; published, 3-7; and Maryland legislature, 29-31; guide to principles of narrative, 46; value and importance of, 46; broken into, 55; at era of 1700...56; private correspondence, 64-66; Propaganda, few communications from S.J., 75; Vatican, few communications from S.J., 75
Argal, *Captain,* 319
Ari, *Fra* Girolami, *Carmelite General,* on Carmelite missionaries-apostolic, 306
Ark, the ship, Father White, S.J., sails in, 274; arrives at Point Comfort, 279
Armand, *Father, O.P.,* Superior, Guadeloupe, appoints Raymond Breton his successor, 305
Arnold of Brescia, quoted by Boehmer, 593, iii.
Arundel of Wardour, Thomas, *Baron,* 179, 180, viii., 225, 393, ix.
Arundel, Thomas Howard, *Earl* of, 180, viii.
Assembly of Maryland,
 1638: Clerke, agent of S.J., in, 340, 380; clerical privilege for priests, 381, 382, 383; F. Copley's letter to Baltimore on absence of clergy from, 382; business, the imported code of laws, 383-385; adjourned by Governor, 388; committee of three elected by, Lewger secretary, 388; *v.* Committee of Assembly, 1638; composed chiefly of non-Catholics, 419; its enactments Erastian, 418, 419
 1639: members of, 449; attempt to legalize land seizure by Proprietary, 477; Act for Church Liberties, 450, 453; Act for Rights of Proprietary, 453; Act for Liberties of People, 454
 1640: Poulton's summons to, quoted, 478
 1642: law on passports for all, 532, 533; Act providing for officers, 548
 1648: expresses opinion of Mrs. Brent, 551, 552; *v.* Laws of Maryland

Aubert, *Governor* of St. Christopher, 297
Augier, René, on Huguenots in Jamaica, 288, 289
Augusta Carolina, bought from Indians, 325
Augustine, *St.,* hypocrisy in penal laws, 111
Augustinians; *v.* Missions
Avalon, *Province* of, Newfoundland, patent granted to Lord Baltimore, 177; letter from Ingoli on, 183; Stock on, to Propaganda, 185; Lord Baltimore's expedition to, 188; Stock's account of, 191, 192; Jesuit Fathers sent to, 192; Propaganda and Capuchins, 193; Baltimore brings Hacket to, 193; James and Stourton leave, 193; its description, 193; report from Nuncio on sending priests to, 195-197; F. L. Rigby, missionary in, 199
Azores and Canaries, boundary between East and West Indies, 268

B

BABTHORPE, *Sir* Ralph, and sodality of the Immaculate Conception, 215, vi.
Bacon, on penal law, 91, 110, 111; on Statute of Uses, 613, 614
Bacquet, his reasons for Mortmain, 582
Bailiffs, their prepotence in Maryland, 402, Baldridge, James, freeman, 384
Baltimore, George Calvert, first *Lord,* his controversy with Jesuits, 53; silence imposed on Fathers S.J. in his controversy with Bishop of Chalcedon, 70, 71; and Lewger, 77; his conversion, 94; colonization of Maryland, 94; a refugee from persecution, 95; situation under penal laws, 98, 99
 Married to Anne Mynne, 155; his son, Caecilius [Cecil], 155, 156; his antecedents, 176; his marriages, 176, ii.; *v.* Win, Maria; negotiations for the Spanish match of Charles II., 176; his conversion to Catholicity, 178; its date, 179, vii.; Goodman on his devotion, 179; resigns his post as Secretary of State, 179; marriage, 179, 180; letter to Strafford, 180; brings Hacket to Avalon, second expedition, 193; denounced by Stourton, 193, 194; his counter-accusation, 194; leaves Avalon for Virginia, 200, 201; applies for Jesuit missionaries, 201; correspondence with F. White, 198; his signature in letter of Catholic peers to Chalcedon, 206, vii.; goes to Newfoundland, 1628, leaves it, 1629...206; sends three sons to St. Omer's, 206; refuses the Council of Virginia the oath of allegiance, 207; his letter to Wentworth, 207; compromised with Jesuits in the Chalcedon controversy, 207; and the Declaration of Lay Catholics, 208; his

INDEX

letter to Lord Petre, on the Disavowal, 209–211; information for Rome, 225; story concerning, 230; *v.* Muskett, Win; Panzani on death of, 232; his application for a part of Virginia, 233; patent for Maryland granted, 233, 234; his death and character, 234–236; analysis of the Maryland charter, 236–243; rights of patronage in Maryland, 239; this a case of conscience, 240; document S.J. on the case, xi.; *v.* Charter of Maryland

Baltimore, Cecil, second *Lord*, son of George, first Lord, his quarrel with S.J., 126, 127; traditional interpretation of his controversy with S.J., 126–128; McMahon on his introducing Mortmain into Maryland, 128; issue explained by Davis, 131; 155, 156; controversy and the religious interests of his plantation, 232; letter to Wentworth, on his father, 235

Invites missionaries S.J., 248, 249; his papers on Maryland, 249; Account of the Colony, and the situation of the missionaries in contrast with it, 255–257; organizes his expedition, 257; pamphlet, *Objections answered*, 257; his *Instructions*, 257, 260–262; *v.* Clayborne; with friends invests £10,000..263; his business success, 265; invites Puritans to Maryland, 286; consequences in the battle of Providence, 286; his injunction to commissioners on privacy of religious functions disregarded; interpretation by C. E. Smith, 323; official *Relation of Maryland*, 326; policy regarding the Indians, 327; criterion of their conversion, 328; letter from White on Copley, 335, 336; letter on patent to the missionaries for Pascattoway, 345

His Maryland Mission of Jesuits, according to Panzani, 355; draws up an oath of allegiance, 355, 357; or rather a body of laws, 357; vetoes the Maryland Assembly's laws, passed 1635..362; his first warrant to pay adventurers by land grants, 363, 364; the grant, a payment of debt, 364; his second warrant, 365; letter from Copley to, 367; his or Lewger's code, 1638..381; petition to Windebank for a Governorship, 375, 376; withholds assent from the code passed in Assembly, 389; criticism of Cornwaleys, White, and Copley on the code,—all rights of trade given to Baltimore, 394; Cornwaleys's appeal, 394; Concordat and rights of trade, 395; White's appeal, 395; Cornwaleys on the Church, 405–408; letter on the code from F. Copley,—eleven criticisms and eight requests, 408–415; his opinion of the requests, 415; measures against S.J., 419; on an agent for Fathers S.J., 425; his third code of laws 1639..427; issues warrant for L. Calvert to sign it, 427; rejection of the code, 428

His third code reviewed, 449–456; oath of allegiance to, 451; his tirade against the Pope, 455, 456; seizure of Mattapany, 477–480; writ to Poulton, as proprietor, 478; gives the property away, 479, 480, x.; Copley interposes lay trustee, 484–486; letter to L. Calvert against S.J. missionaries, 486–488; comments on the Pope, 487; orders Copley to be deported, 487; himself to be the source of justice for L. Calvert, 487; forbids the granting of patents to S.J., 484; stops Hartwell and Cooper, missionaries, in London, 493, 526, 555; his attitude towards Mortmain, 1641,—introduces statutes through plantation documents, 500; his mission of secular priests and Mortmain, 501; desires approval of Fathers S.J. for measures against them, 501–503; his four Points, 506–513; employs G. Gage, priest, 524; his demands granted by Copley, 532; his draft of Surrender for the Provincial S.J., 529, 530; protests bills of exchange for New Chappell, 544, 545; favour towards Gilmett and Territt, 544; G. Brent issues writ of attachment on behalf of Cornwaleys, 546; his principle of Mortmain conceded by the General S.J., 556–558; concession enforced, 559; his loss of Maryland, 562, xvi.; *v.* JESUITS, Knott; his right, according to Silvius, of being sole proprietary in Maryland, 570–573; against frankalmoigne, 605; his views those of Henry VIII., 613; *v. Instructions*, Laws of Maryland, Maryland

Bancroft, George, quotes Sarpi and Grotius, 93; his prejudices, 123, 124

Bannez, Treatise on Ownership, 571

Barbados, *Governor* Henry Hawley, 277; White's narrative, 277, 278; the clergy in 1637..292; Irish missionaries and exiles, 314, 315

Barberini, Antonio, *Prefect of Propaganda*, 75; letter from Ingoli to, regarding Stock on missions, 190, 191; his report on Capuchin and S.J. mission in St. Christopher, 308, xxxix.; his death, 308; 309, xlii.; report on approving the mission of secular priests to Maryland, 520

Barberini, Francis, *Cardinal Secretary of State* and *Protector of England*, 191, 231; correspondence with Panzani, on the Manifestation against the Jesuits, 208, xiii., 358; Panzani to, on Jesuits and the Protest of Catholic Peers, 211, ii.; reports Bishop of Chalcedon's letter in Propaganda, 220; on expelling S.J. from England, 231; Panzani to, on Anglicans and Papal bulls, 239, vii.; comment on F. Blount's condemnation

620   INDEX

of Baltimore's oath, 358; letter from Con to, on F. Knott and his book, 457; Rosetti's relation to, 495, 496; Knott's memorial to, 515-517; letter from, to Rosetti, on stopping mission of secular priests to Maryland, 520, iv., v.
Barclay against Bellarmine, 421
Baronius, Boehmer *versus*, 593
Barter; *v.* Truck
Bartolus of Bologna, 573
Baxter, adventurer to Maryland, 263
Bede, on monasteries, 587, 588
Bellarmine, 421; *v.* JESUITS
Bellomont, *Governor*, desires Iroquois to deliver up Fathers S.J., 102, 103, 536, xxviii.
Benefices; *v.* Mortmain
Bentivoglio, *Cardinal*, 197, viii.; report of Belgian Nuncio on Avalon, 194, 195-197; Mass said in heretics' place of worship, 196
Berington, *Rev.* Joseph, on multiplicity of oaths, 116; refers to tract by Porteus, 134
Berkeley, *Governor* of Virginia, instructions to, from Board of Trade for building up the Anglican ministry, 293, xviii.; on colonial life, 524, i.
Bichi, *Cardinal, Nuncio* in France, 223
Biddulph, Andrew, proposed for mission of seculars to Maryland, 498
Bills of Assembly, for Liberties of the Church, 450; for Oath of Allegiance, 451; for Liberties of the People, 451; for Proprietary's rights, 451; and title to land, 453; for Indian trade monopoly, 454; touching authority of J.P.'s, 454; and payment of debts, 455; for treasons, 455; for planting, 456; *v.* Assembly
Bills of exchange, for New Chappell, Baltimore protests them, 542; order to G. Brent, Governor, 543
Birds of Maryland, 330
Bishop, Henry, petition against Indians, 547, 548, ii.
Bishop, William, first Bishop of Chalcedon, 202, i.
Bishopric, American, Propaganda recommends Paris Seminary of Foreign Missions for, 314
Blacklow; *v.* White, Thomas
Blackstone, *Justice*, on Catholic affairs, 100, ii.; traditionary opinions of, 125; *v.* Palgrave; on greater excommunication, 438, xi.; on Mortmain, 586, 587, xxii.; on "circulation" of land, 595, xviii.; on "pious fraud," 599, xxxi.; on Henry VIII., 614, xxxiv.; on Mortmain and subjugation of the regulars, quoted by Stephen, 616, xl.
Blanchys, 568
Blethersden, Kent, 122; *v.* Copley, John
Board of Trade, instructions to Governor Berkeley for building up ministry in Virginia, 293, xviii.

Boavista, Cape Verde Islands, 277; *v.* Voyage
Boehmer, on apostolic poverty, *versus* Baronius, 593, iii.
Bologna, 468
Bonacina, interpreted by Lewger, 413
Bonaventura de Courtray, *Fra*, Capuchin; *v.* Missions, Capuchin
Bonavides, *Fra* Alonso, *Minorite*, his Relation to Propaganda on North America, and need of Irish friars, 321, 322, xi.
BOOKS; *v.* SOURCES
Boscawen, *Admiral*, approves seizure of Church property, 485, viii.
Boucher, Jonathan, on indented servants, 341
Bourdagos, René de, *Augustinian*, 306
Bowyer, P., quoted on nature of State Church, 131; *v.* Hooker, Gladstone
Bozman, John Leeds, historian of Maryland, 104; spirit of his *History of Maryland*, 117, 118; Bayle quoted by, against Catholics, ii.
Bracton, on grants to God through the Church, 441; Maitland and Pollock on the term "Deo," *to* God, in grants to the Church, xix., xx., xxi.
Brantley, W. T., on Baltimore's code, 386, xiii.
Brazil, numbers of S.J. in, 317, lxvii.
Breithaupt, *Rev. Mr.*, 485, viii.
Brent, Fulk, in Assembly of 1639...449
Brent, Giles, freeman and *Governor*, opposes Calvert's demand for exemption from conscription, 416, xxv.; in Assembly of 1639...449; against law of passports, 533, xix.; 537, xxxi.; 542; issues writs against Governor, 545, xvii., 546; White House, 568
Brent, *Mrs.* Margaret, 412, xxi.; in charge of Empress of Pascattoway, 551; executrix for Governor, 551; refused a vote, her protest to Greene, 551, xi.; Assembly's opinion of her, 551, 552, xii., xiii.; attempt to disfranchise her, 552, xv.; Sisters' Field, 568
Brent, Mary, 568
Breton, Raymond, O. P., his Relation on West Indies, 298, x., 304-306; two missionaries S.J. killed in Dominica, 300, xxi.; stationed in Dominica, 304; Prefect of Mission, troubles, resignation, 305; arrangements for nuns of Third Order, 305; indictment of his superiors, 306
Brett, *Captain* Arthur, instructions for, against S.J., 518, xxix.
Bretton, William, 367, iv.
Brief, Papal, of 1631, respecting Bishop of Chalcedon's jurisdiction, 220, 221, ix., x.; *v.* Dodd, Gillow; JESUITS, More; Panzani, Regulars
Britton, *Dr. of Theology*, proposed for mission of seculars to Maryland, 498, xv.

INDEX 621

Browne, *Sir* James Crichton, on rights of man, 328, vii.
Browne, John, priest, his forged confession, 98
Bruchet, Nicolas, O. P., goes on West Indian Mission, 304
Bruodin, 284, vii.
Bulla Coenae, land laws and the, 410, 414; misunderstood, 435; Streeter's exposition of, 436; real scope of, 436; articles relevant to Maryland laws, 436, 437, 439; *v.* Lay tribunals; excommunication and the Catholic conscience in Maryland, 439; and *Conditions of Plantation*, 502, 504, vi.; and Mortmain, 503; and Baltimore's Four Points, 509, 510, 512
Bulls, Papal: Coke's fictitious Bull, 96; forgery of 1605...97; produced as canon law after the Reformation, 239, vii.; *v.* Panzani
Buonfiglioli, *General* of Carmelites, 306
Burgat; *v.* Cashel
Burge, William, on fraudulent use of references, 81, v., 82; reinforces Palgrave's evidence on Mortmain, 126, v.; 615; on saving Church fees for the Church, 598, 599, xxix.; on scope of Mortmain Statutes, 615, xxxviii.
Burleigh, *Lord*, William Cecil, advice on penal law against Catholics, 91, 92; justifies persecution, 93
Butler, C., 134, xv.

C

CABRAIRA, 307
Caesar, *Sir* Julius, *Chancellor of Exchequer*, his papers on revenue from persecution, 87
Cajetan, 571, i., 572
Cajetan, *Cardinal*, 221
Calais, German Lutheran troops called out from, 86
Calvert, Cecil [Caecilius], second Lord Baltimore; *v.* Baltimore, Cecil
Calvert, George, first Lord Baltimore; *v.* Baltimore, George
Calvert, George, *jun.*, 263, iv.; his supposed expedition to Virginia, 272
Calvert, Leonard, Lieutenant-Governor of Maryland, *Instructions* to, 251, 260; disregards instructions, 262; reference to White's narrative, 275, 276, 323; visits Indian Emperor, 324; at baptism of Tayac, 345; Baltimore's warrants to pay adventurers in land, addressed to, 363–365; commission of 1637 to, 369
Assails Jerome Hawley in a letter to Lord Baltimore, 378; calls Assembly, 1638...380, iv.; defence of Baltimore's code, and comment on, 386, 387; his committee to draft laws, 1638...388; his letter to Baltimore on the code, 389, x.; commends Lewger, 393, ix.; seconds Cornwaleys's petition for privilege of trading, 396; and Assembly of 1639, 449; assents to Ordinance, 450; challenged in matter of penal legislation, 452; addresses F. Poulton, S.J., as proprietor of Conception, 479; required to hold Baltimore's orders as a rule of justice, 487; *Conditions of Plantation*, interview with Fathers S.J. to obtain consent to, 502, 503; holds Fathers S.J. under surveillance, 525; and law of passports, 533, xix., xx.; receives orders to kidnap F. Copley, 534, 535; and suit of Mrs. Mary Kittamaquund, 551, x.; returns from England, 1644...561; his commission from Charles I., 561, 562, xvi.; his situation on his return, 562; his property, Governor's Field, 568
Calvert, Philip, Governor of Maryland, 176, ii.; names Portobacco for Indian Council, 553; his property, St. Peter's, 568
Calverts, three boys captured at sea with Jesuits, 206, viii.
Canada, missions, Propaganda summons Capuchins for, 318, ii.; Recollects and S.J. in, 319
Canary Islands, with Azores, boundary of West Indies, 268, iv.
Canon law, unrecognized in Lewger's Church establishment, 432; recognized in England according to Blackstone, 433, xxii.; testamentary and matrimonial matters in England withdrawn from, xxiii.; *Bulla Coenae*, part of, until Reformation, 437; no question of introducing it into Maryland, 439; *v. Cases*, Lewger; touched divers matters and persons, 444; limit set to, in patronages and advowsons, 444, xxx.
Canon and common law, on liberty of the Church, 445, xxvi.
Canterbury, George, *Archbishop* of, a patentee under the Virginia Charter of 1612...152; on Father Baker's pardon, 270, 271
Cape Breton; *v.* Cape North
Cape North, Capuchin Mission at, 309, xlii.
Cape Verde, acts of Propaganda touching, 309, xlii.; four Capuchins deputed to, by Propaganda, 307
Capitulary of William I., 589; on Church privileges, 590, xxxi.
Capsterre, St. Christopher, 307, xxxv.
Capuchin, *Fathers*, proposed by Propaganda for Avalon, 193; in Virginia, according to Cerri, 202, xx.; Procurator-General, correspondence with Propaganda on mission S.J., St. Christopher, 310, xliv., xlv.; barter or truck allowed to, 339, xx.; *v.* Alexis de Auxerre; Archangelo; Barberini; Emmanuel; Francis de Pamplona; Hyacinth; Joachim de Corbeil; Josaphat; Joseph da Caravantes; Pacifico di Provins

622   INDEX

Caravantes; *v.* Joseph da
Carena; *v.* Cayenne
Caribbees; *v.* West Indian Islands
Carlisle, *Earl* of, patents of West Indian Islands granted to, 150, xiv., 151; on the Maryland Charter, 233
Carmelites revise Stock's account of Avalon, 184, vii.; General's orders to Stock, 188, ii., 202, xx.; *v.* Missions
Carolina [Carolana], colony of, projected by French Huguenots, 1630...150; Carolana, name proposed for Maryland, 234; Huguenots in, 290
Carré, Father, *O. P.*, Paris, appoints missionaries O. P. for West Indies, 304
Carroll, Charles, his view of Maryland property S.J., in answer to Governor Hart, 500, ii.; Chancellor's Point, 569
Carthagena Creek, 569
Cary, Colonel Theodore, his narrative on West Indies, 316, lxiii.
Cases, Lewger's, 416; Knott's *Quaestiones*, giving gist of, 418, iv.; submitted to Inquisition, 418; questions asked in, 420, 421; preamble, and the assumed issue on canon law, 439; on the "prynce" of Maryland, 450, iii.; a commentary on Baltimore's four Points, 509, 510, x., 512, 513, xx.; a memorial to the Inquisition on, 515, xxii.
Cashel, William Burgat, *Bishop-elect* of, on the West Indies, 1667–1669...315, lxii.
Casuists; *v.* Bonacina, Lewger
Catechism, in Patuxent, Rigbie's, 550, viii.; *v.* Language
Catholics, English, residue of, in 1700, 111, 112
Caverley, *Captain*, a Catholic at St. Christopher, 279
Cavour ministry, and appeal *ab abusu*, 429, viii.
Cayenne, its situation, 297, v.; *v.* Cerri; bishopric proposed for, by the Duke de Ventadour, 299; request from Capuchins for mission in, 312, 313; superiors S.J. and St. Vincent de Paul on appointing a bishop for, 312, li., lii.; *v.* Congregation of Missionaries, West Indian Islands
Cayugas, family of Iroquois, 326
Cecil, *Sir* Robert, political enemy of Catholics, 155
Cerri, Urbano, *Secretary to Propaganda*, his memorial to Innocent XI., reviewing Virginia, New England, Avalon, and Maryland, 202, xx.; on Cayenne in West Indies, 297; on missionaries S.J., 300, xix.; quoted on *Isole Antilles*, xx.
Chalcedon, William Bishop, first Bishop of, 202
Chalcedon, Richard Smith, second *Bishop* of, *Vicar-Apostolic* in England, Stock requests to live under obedience of, 189, iv., vi.; Stock's letters on Chalcedon's differences with regulars, 191, 192; his controversy with the regulars, decree of the Inquisition, 201, 202; makes regulations, 202, ii., 203; remonstrances to, from laymen, 203, iv., 204; admonition to, from Urban VIII., 203; *v.* Albizi, JESUITS, More; a Papal Brief on his affairs with the regulars, 212; Catholic laymen send an Information to the Pope concerning, 212, iii.; his controversy, Stock's suggestions to Propaganda on, 213, i., ii., iii.; charges Jesuits with Gunpowder Plot, heresy, error, sedition, etc., 213, 214, iv.; complains of his cause being transferred from Propaganda to the Inquisition, 215; his complaints of regulars, 215, vi. 216; as being "pedagogues," or hirelings, 216, viii.; Jesuits' sodality, 217; real issue misunderstood by peers, 217, 218; letter on his own jurisdiction, his estimate of Catholic lords, 219, i., ii., iii.; attributes a blasphemous publication to the Jesuits, 220, v., vi.; vacates Vicariate, 228; his policy against S.J., 229; *v.* Brief; G. Gage to, 1642...513, xvii.; *v.* Gage; his powers in 1642... 521, vi.; *v.* Information, Remonstrance
Chalmers, on land titles of barbarians, 576
Champney proposed for communicating faculties to mission of seculars for Maryland, 498, xx.
Chancellor's Point, 569
Chancery and doctrine of *cy-près*, 480, x.
Chapel at Pascattoway, 541, xi.; lot, 567, 568; *v.* Property
Charitable Uses, statute of, 607
Charles I., 94 506, 561; his pension to De Sancé, 288
Charles II., 69
Charles V., 93; *v.* Bancroft
Charles Martel, 589
Charter of Maryland, authorship of, 233, ii.; *v.* Baltimore, George; a landmark in history, 235, 236; comparison of, with Avalon Charter, 236, i., ii., iii.; its exemption from Mortmain Statutes, 237, 238; its exclusion of penal laws, 242, 243, xvii.-xx.; issued to Cecil, second Lord Baltimore, 246, ii.; *v.* Noys; rights of ecclesiastical patronage reserved to Baltimore, 239, ix.; expunges Mortmain Statutes, 240, 241; its precedent in 1 & 2 Phil. and Mar., c. 8...242, 603, 604; secures advowsons and patronage for Calvert, 444, xxxi.; dispenses from Statutes of Mortmain, by suspending *Quia emptores*, 600–604
Charters for colonies, fifty-nine given by the British Crown in eighty years, 150; religious clauses in, 151, xvi., 152; oaths of allegiance and supremacy in, 152; *v.* Gylberte
Chatham, *Lord*, approves of penal laws against Catholics, 91

INDEX 623

Cherokees, their rights to the land, 574
Chesapeake, Mission S.J. enters, 317, 323; 331
Child, G. W., on the Catholic reaction, Tractarian Movement, 118, 119, 120
Chili, priests S.J. in, 317, lxvi.
Chillingworth, Knott's book published for, 71; his conversion and lapse, 351
Chitomachon; *v.* Kittamaquund
Church acts and grants, by English law granted *to* God, 440, xvii., 441; *v.* Aquinas, Bracton, Coke
Church in Maryland passed over in legislation, 405–409; *v.* JESUITS, Copley; Cornwaleys
Church legislation, scope of, 444; its limits, 444, xxx.; lands in frankalmoigne, marriage and testamentary matters, and persons under, 445, xxxiii.; forces that formed the system, 445, xxxiv., xxxv.
Church liberties, Coke, Maitland-Pollock on, 441, xxi.-xxiii.; Church free from secular jurisdiction, not from secular service, 441, xxiii.; mean freedom from diminution or subtraction of her rights, according to Coke, 442, xxiv., xxv.; ecclesiastics exempt from purveyance, 442; permanence of the same legal conception after separation from Rome, 443
Church privileges, Suarez on exceptions and limits of, 441, xxiii.; Anderson and some dates of, 444, xxxii.
Church of England, title of, passes from Catholic Church to Anglican, 238, 239
Churchill; *v.* Marlborough
Churchesset or Churchsed, first-fruits, 590
Ciphers, use of, unsafe in 1705...67
"Circulation of land," Stephen on Blackstone's phrase of, 595, xviii.
Civil law, and Baltimore's Points for the clergy, 509, 510, x.
Civitá Vecchia, free trade with, proposed from England, 354, ii.
Claude of St. Joseph, *Carmelite,* and Breton O. P., 305
Clayborne, *Captain* W., Virginian *Councillor,* his hostility to Baltimore, 257; his plantation, settled before Maryland, 262; attainder of, 362, i., 374; invades Catholic colony, 562
Clergy brought under penal laws by Baltimore's Points, 509; *v. Bulla Coenae*
Clerk, *Rev. Mr.*, priest, letter to Fitton, on Smith and other ex-Jesuits, 181, xii.; 229, ix.; letter to Fitton, Rome, on F. Baker, 272, 273; sends copy of Maryland Relation or Account of the Colony to Rome, 273
Clerke, Robert, servant and gentleman, 340, 341; *v.* Assembly; represents S.J. in Assembly, 380, 381, v., 383; opposes several bills in Assembly, 1638...389, v.; 569

Clitheroe, Margaret, her martyrdom, 88, xiv.
Clive, *Viscount,* in Committee on Mortmain, 615, xxxviii.
Clotworthie, *Sir* John, his licence to carry off Irishmen to America, 282, 283
Coad, J. Edwin, 569
Code; *v.* Acts, Assembly, Bills, Laws
Coke, *Sir* Edward, justifies intolerance in penal laws, 96, 97; on Winslade, 153; and penalty of greater excommunication for all Catholics in England, 438, xii., xiii.; on Church acts and grants, 440, xvi.-xviii.; on Church liberties, 441, xxii., 442; *v.* Johnson, B.T.; on frankalmoigne, 580, 583, xiv., 584, xv., xvi.; on first Statute of Mortmain, 594, x., xi., xii.; *v.* Bulls, Gunpowder Plot; JESUITS, Southwell
Coke, William, son of Sir Edward Coke, reconciled to the Church by F. Baker, 270
Colleges S.J., property necessary for, 582, 583, xiii.
Coloma, Spanish Ambassador, attests the Protest of Peers against Chalcedon, 209, xiv.
Colonies, propagation of religion a motive in founding, 142; Gylberte's charter and liberality towards religion, 148, 149, viii.; their foundation, 149, 150; their expansion, fifty-nine charters in eighty years, 150, xiii.; order of settlement, 150; their range, 150; varying names of West Indian Islands, 150, xiv.
Colonization, persecution an incentive to, 146; Gerrard's, Gylberte's, and Peckham's enterprises, 146–149
Commission to Governor, 1637...365, 369; *v.* Calvert, Leonard
Commissioners for Treasury, Maryland, orders concerning Gilmett, 537, xxx.
Committee of Assembly, Maryland, 1638: Cornwaleys, Calvert, Evelin, Lewger secretary, 388; adjournments, 388; forty-three bills of statutory law, 389
Committee of House of Commons on Mortmain, 1844...598, 599, xxix., 611; *v.* Burge, Clive, Palgrave
Common lands and demesne, source of donations to the Church, 587
Common law, its writs to safeguard Church privileges, 443, xxvii.
Commonalty or perpetual corporate existence, 610, xx.
Commonwealth, the Christian, Suarez on the ultimate basis of, 591, 592, xxxix.-xl.
Companies, Catholic merchant, transport missionaries, 313; Richelieu, patron of, 312; Fra Pacifico de Provins on, 314, lvi.
Compton, *Bishop of London,* requested by Council of St. Christopher to send more learned and older clergy, 295

624   *INDEX*

Con, George, Papal envoy, 71, vi., vii.; succeeding Panzani, 232; letters on Panzani to Ferragalli, 232, xvii.; a commendation of, by Panzani, 354, ii.; commended by General S.J., 457, i.; defends F. Knott's book; his letter to Barberini, 457, 458; and the Maryland anti-clerical laws, 459

Conception, mission property S.J. at Mattapany, 478; Copley's letter to Baltimore on danger of losing, 478, iii.; Baltimore's writ to F. Poulton as proprietor, 478, v.; a storehouse for the mission, 479, vi.; *v.* Mattapany

Concordat [*Concordia*] among regulars: England, 71, vi.; Maryland traders': F. White on trade rights in, 393–395; Baltimore's draft for a Jesuit: modification of his Points, 510, x.

Conditions of Plantation in Maryland, 1633: allotment of land, 252; free trade, 253; 256, 388, iv.; and land tax, 401; 1641: introducing Mortmain, declaration of Fathers S.J., 431, xvi.; *v.* Mortmain; and disabilities for all corporate bodies, 499, 500; draft of Certificate for Provincial's signature, 502, v.; interview of Calvert and Lewger with Fathers S.J. to obtain consent to, 502, 503; all grants charged with Statutes of Mortmain, 502; against piety and conscience, 504; and disfranchisement of unmarried ladies, 552; and Mortmain, 578; Statute of Mortmain, 1391, model of, 610

Confirmation, sacrament of, wanting under persecution in England, 226, iv.

Confession, forged; *v.* Browne, John

Congregation of Missionaries, St. Vincent de Paul's, and bishops in Cayenne and Guiana, 312

Connecticut, colony of, 1636...150; a republic, 265

Conquest, right of, and Indian lands, 576

Conscience, Catholic, Panzani's recommendations for converts, 359, 361; a factor under Baltimore's government, 439; impeded Seymour and Hart in Protestant government, 439; views of Protestant historians, 440; Baltimore's policy in view of, 501; and *Conditions of Plantation*, 504, 505; in Maryland, G. Gage on, 513, xvii.

Conscription, indiscriminate, 401; effect on priests of, 410; clerical exemption for field servants and tenants, 415, 416; L. Calvert demands the privilege for himself, and is opposed by Cornwaleys, 416

Constitutions S.J., language of, in Account of the Colony, 251

Contract under *Conditions of Plantation* repudiated by Baltimore, 388, iv.

Converts, list of, sent to Propaganda, dangers of betrayal and suppression of names, 51; Indian, in Maryland, 549, 550, 559, *passim*

Conway, *Lord*, and F. Baker's pardon, 270, 271; parliamentary conference on the pardon, 271

Copley, John, priest, confused with Thomas Copley, S.J., 122; Rector of Blethersden, 122; *v.* Abbot, Neill, E. D., Smith, C. E.

Copley, Thomas; *v.* JESUITS

Corn, Lord Baltimore's monopoly of, and F. Copley, 396, xix.; 397, xxv.

Cornbury, *Governor* of New York, his character, 102

Cornewallis; *v.* Cornwaleys

Cornwaleys, Thomas, Commissioner of Maryland, *Instructions* to, 251, 260–262; 263, iv.; 378; defends Hawley, his letter to Baltimore, 379, 380; his votes in the Assembly, 1638...381, vi., 383–385; criticism on Baltimore's code, 387, 388; on precluding redress, 388; member of committee on laws, 388; opposes bills, 389; his letter to Baltimore on the code, 389, 391, 392; appeals to Baltimore's honesty, 394, 395; opposes bill to support Proprietary, 391; Calvert seconds his petition for trading privileges, 396; denounces despotic laws, 402; his plea for the Church, 404–407; reference to Hawley and the Church, 407, 408; opposes Calvert's demand for exemption from conscription, 415, 416; opinion on Baltimore's revenue, 434; on Assembly of 1639...449; Fenwick as his proxy in Assembly, 1640...486; agent for F. Copley in sale of New Chappell, 541; Baltimore protests bills made in name of, 542; sues Government, 545; leaves Council, 545; Fenwick, his attorney, 545; sues out attachment against Governor from Brent, magistrate, 546, 568; St. Peter's or Cross Manor, 569

Corporations, Coke on capacity of, 580; perpetuity of, 581; *de facto*, monasteries as, 587; and tenure of property, Coke on, 597, xxv.; Finlason on, 599, xxix.; rise of lay, 600; *Conditions of Plantation* discriminate against, 600; distinct from communities, their rise, 611

Cottington, *Lord, Secretary of State*, 233; and Baltimore, 355; reconciled to the Church, 375

Council, Indian, Portobacco chosen for, 553

Councillors of Maryland: Brent, Lewger, Brainthwait, and suit of Mrs. Mary Kittamaquund *versus* the Governor, 551, x.

Court-baron, privilege of, 364

Court-leet, privilege of, 364

Courtney, Thomas, St. Peter's Key, 569

Cowes, Isle of Wight, F. White sails from, 274, i.

INDEX

Cranfield, adventurer to Maryland, 263
Cranmer attacked by Macaulay, 119
Crescentia, name for Maryland, 234
Cromwell, Henry, his correspondence with Thurloe on transporting Irish children to West Indies, 283, 284, vii.
Cross Manor, 569
Crown, the, and guilds, 611
Customs, Commissioners of, criticism on Huguenot colony for Carolina, 290, x.
Cybo, *Monsignor, Secretary of Propaganda*, letter to, from Father Oliva, General S.J., 303
Cy-près, doctrine of, Hallam and Whittaker on, 480, x.

D

DALLAS, R. C., upholds loyalty of Catholics, 108, iii.
Dalle, George, master of ship *Good Fellow*, 283
David, *Father, O.S.B.*, letter to Propaganda on Brief touching faculties of regulars, 222, 223
Davis, G. L., on supremacy of State over the Church, 131; explains issue between S.J. and Lord Baltimore, 131; cites Magna Charta, 131
De Bois; *v.* Silvius
Debts, bill for preferential payment of, 1639...454, 455, xviii., xix.; Lewger's theory and practice, xviii.; ecclesiastical claims passed over, 455; *v.* Restitution
Declaration; *v.* Protest of the Peers
Declaration of the Colony [*Declaratio Coloniae*], objects propounded, *Conditions of Plantation*, 250; development of first object, spiritual, 250, 251, iii.; development of second object, temporal, 251; later repudiation of, 254, 255; Baltimore's, contrary to his Points, 519
Deeds; *v.* Documents
De la Barre, *General*, thanks Lord Willoughby for attentions to F. Grillet, 301
De la Ware, Bay of, 287
Delegates in Assembly, Catholic members summoned, 449
Del Monte, *Cardinal*, 322
De Lolieu, Governor of St. Christopher, 297; organizer of a French West Indian Company, 304
Delolme, traditionary opinions of, 125; *v.* Palgrave
Demesne lands, 587
Demibiel, Simon, 547
De Poinsy, Knight of Malta, viceroy in St. Christopher, 297, 306
De St. Lawrence, Knight of Malta, viceroy in St. Christopher, 297
De Toisy, Knight of Malta, viceroy in St. Christopher 297

VOL. I.

Discovery, rights belonging to, 572; and right of purchase, 575
Disraeli, on mythical Popish Plot, 102, vii.
Documents: S.J., preservation of deeds, etc., 55; transmission of, 78; material difficulties, ink, paper, etc., 78; present condition of, 78, 79; Hallam on cause of the lack of, 124, 125
Dodd, views on F. Arrowsmith's admission into the Society, 162, 163, vi.; on Alexander VII.'s Brief about secular clergymen and religious orders, 163, vi.; cites Gallican and Jansenist authorities on the faculties of regulars, 221, x.; on Urban VIII.'s Brief concerning faculties of regulars, 223, xiv.; approves Statutes of Mortmain as subjugating regulars, 616, xiii.
Domain, distinct from empire, 573
Dominica, two missionaries S.J. killed in, 300, xxi.; acts of Propaganda touching, 309, xlii.
Dominican nuns of Third Order in Martinique, 1656...298; missionaries S.J. decline ministries to, 299, xv.; four sail for Martinique to found schools, 305; petition for spiritual assistance S.J., 305; their death, 306, xxxii.
Dominicans; *v.* Missions
Dominis, Mark Anthony de, F. Floyd's book against, 58
Dongan, Thomas, Governor of New York, 289
Dorrel, adventurer to Maryland, 263
Dorsett, *Lord*, 233
Douglass, William, *Dr.*, advocates persecution of Catholics, 104, 105; on fate of oaths, 115, xx.
Dove, the pinnace, meets the ship *Ark* at Barbados, 277; arrives at Point Comfort, 279
Doyle, J. A., on F. White's Relation, 80
Drake, buccaneer, 150
Drogheda, F. Bathe killed at, 284, vii.
Drury, Mark, priest, proposed for mission of seculars to Maryland, 498
Du Cange, history of the term "mortmain," 580, x.
Dudley, Paul, *Chief Justice* of Massachusetts, on Church of Rome's infallibility, 106, 107; J. Mayhew's Dudley lecture, 105, 106
Dunn, *Mrs.*, letters to, on Maryland, from F. Mosley, 329-332
Du Parquet, *Governor* of Martinique, 305
Du Perron, *Nuncio* in Paris, 248, ix.
Du Pin, Jansenist, 221, x.
Du Plessy, *Governor* of St. Christopher, 297
Duresme; *v.* Durham
Durham [Duresme], William, *Bishop* of, patentee under Virginian charter, 152
Durham, bishopric of, privileges palatine of, 177; model for Maryland colony, 444, xxxii.; Anderson on, 444, xxxii.

2 s

E

East India Company expropriates Church property, 485, viii.
East St. Mary's; *v.* Governor's Field
Edward III., an era in mortmain, 608; *v.* Acts of Parliament
Edward IV. revokes grants, except to the Church, 615, 616, xl.
Edward VI., 584
Edwin, William, marriage, 338, xvii.
Edwine, William, indented servant S.J. and freeman of Assembly, 381
Elias, *Fra, Carmelite*, 184
Eliseus, *Fra, Carmelite*, 184
Elizabeth, policy of, against Catholics, expounded by Coke, 96; insists on principle of persecution, 93; 584; and restitution to the Church, 588; Sir F. Moore on her charities and religion, 607, 608, xv.; 612
Emancipation, hopes of Catholic, destroyed in 1790...56
Emmanuel, Ponte Archo, *Capuchin Provincial* of Normandy, his letter on St. Christopher and S.J. to Propaganda, 308, 309
Emperor; *v.* Tayac
Empire, distinct from domain, 573
Empress at Pascattoway, *alias* Mrs. Mary Kittamaquund, conversion of, 551; ward of Mrs. Brent, 551; gains suit against Governor, 551, x.; her abdication, 553, xvi., xvii.
End, the, justifies the means: a principle applied by Hallam to the English Reformation, 114, 115, xviii.
England, state of, in 1645...562, i., v.
English Islands; *v.* West Indian Islands
English Mission, enforced inaction in the, 471; Lawrence Worsly on, 461, 470, 471; F. Knott on, 471, xxiii.
Epiphanius de Moirans, *Fra, Capuchin*, 313, liii.; *v.* Missions
Erastianism, 352, 353, iii.; in Lord Baltimore's code of laws, 386; a bill modifying the principle of, 386, xiv.; *v.* Establishment, Lewger, *passim*
Erastus, Professor of Moral Theology at Basle, 352, 353, iii.
Esmond, Mary, petition of the Commons against her pardon, 270
Esnambuc, d'; *v.* Nambuc
Establishment of Church, Lewger's plan and claims, all jurisdiction and administration to be secular, 428; interference in administering sacraments, 428; its provision, glebe and tithes, 429; the Provincial's signature for, 430; details of endowment, 430; takes over all testamentary and matrimonial jurisdiction, 430; clergy to be taxed, but not to be landholders, 430, 431, xiii.; *v.* Mortmain; provision for surveillance over clergy, 432; for right of deporting clergy without reason assigned, 432; no place for canon law, 432
Estrées, *Count d', Admiral*, his letter to Oliva, General S.J., on F. Frémont, S.J., 303
Ethelwulf, 587
Eure, Mrs., contributor to Maryland enterprise, 263, 393, ix., 427
Eury; *v.* Ury
Evelin, *Captain*, freeman of Assembly, 384; on committee of laws, 388; a new style of manors proposed by, 434, iii.
Excommunication, greater and lesser, 437; civil effects, 437, 438; Blackstone on writ, *De Excommunicato capiendo*, 438, xi.; Coke on greater, and its application by laymen to Catholics in England, 438
Exemption, clerical, Calvert's demand for, on his own behalf in Maryland, 416, xxx.; granted to no layman in Virginia, 416, xxxi.
Exile; *v.* Orders in Council, Thurloe
Extermination of Indians, 549, v.

F

Fabricius, *Rev. Mr.*, 485, viii.
Faculties for the Indies, 1633, granted for Maryland by the General, 267; a digest of them for missionaries, 1635, 267; *Privilegia Indica*, 268, iv.; petition for, from missionaries S.J. to Propaganda for West Indies and Canada, nature of, 298, xii., xiii.; granted by Inquisition to S.J. for Canada, for Persia, for Syria, for Constantinople, for West Indies, 302, xxiii.; for Irish missionaries, 315; from Holy Office for Fra Francis da Pamplona, Capuchin, 311; for mission of seculars received by F. Philips, 506; not delivered to mission of seculars, 521, vii.; for mission of seculars, licence from Chalcedon, not Rome, 522, 523; irregular, 524; *v.* Regulars
Faith, the motive of endowments, 607, 608
Famine in Maryland, 481
Farrar, G., *Notary-Apostolic*, 229, x.
Fauna of Maryland, 330, 331
Febronianism, 353
Fees; *v.* Property
Fenwick, Cuthbert, 338; opposes bills, 1638...389; lay trustee for property S.J., 484, 485, vii.; proxy for Cornwaleys in Assembly, 1640...486, ix.; for three other freemen, 1641...486; attorney for Cornwaleys *versus* Government, 545, 546; trustee for F. Copley, 567, 568
Ferdinand, *Emperor*, protests to Elizabeth against persecution, 93

Ferfax, adventurer to Maryland, 263
Ferragalli, letters to, from Con, 232, xvii.
Feudal rights, reserved to chief landlord by *Quia emptores*, 600-605
Feudal Statutes of Mortmain, Palgrave on, 610, 611
Feudalism, second Lord Baltimore's policy of, for Maryland, 386; manner of its introduction in spite of first Lord Baltimore's charter, 600, 604, 605; operation of *Conditions of Plantation* in Maryland, and last of Mortmain Statutes in England, 610
Fictions, legal, on expropriation of Indian lands, 575, 576
Finlason, on Statutes of Mortmain and regulars, 616, xlii.
First-fruits, or Churchsed, 590
Fisher, George, 221
Fitton, priest, agent in Rome for clergy, letter to from Clerk, on Smith and other ex-Jesuits, 181, xii.; 229, x.; 273, viii.; proposed for mission of seculars to Maryland, 498
Fleet, quoted by Coke, 590
Fleete, *Captain*, 325; freeman of Assembly, 383
Florida, comprised Georgia, South Carolina, and Virginia, 317; mission S.J. and its martyrs, 317; Franciscan mission at St. Augustine, 317
Fontenai, *Marquis de, French Ambassador*, action with Catholic Lords, 209, xiv.; gives his attestation to the General Disavowal, 209; interview of, with Lords Baltimore and Somerset, 210, 211
Foreign Missions; *v.* Paris Seminary of
Forgeries; *v.* Bulls, Papal
Forum ecclesiasticum, 586, xxi.
Franchise, civic; *v.* Mortmain
Franciscans; *v.* Bonavides, Missions
Francisco, mulatto immigrant, 281, ii.; *v.* JESUITS, White, A.
Francis da Pamplona, *Fra, Capuchin*, with companions in Granada and South America, 311, xlvii.; his commission and faculties, xlvi.
Francis of St. Clare, *Fra*, 457
Frankalmoigne, lands in, 441, xxi.; directly under Church law, 445; Coke defines people of mortmain under, 580, vii.; Coke explains English law of, 583, xiv., 584, xv., xvi., 590, xxxvi.; new era of, with statute of *Quia emptores*, 600, i.; provided for in Maryland by Baltimore's charter, 600
Freedom of trade in Maryland for adventurers, 253
Freman, Rd., 367, iii.
French Revolution, rights of Church property respected during, 485, viii.
Froman, freeman, 486
Froude, J. A., on liberal opinions as reactionary, 119

G

GAGE, GEORGE, priest, *alias* Hoard, Francis, employing term "ours," 286, iii.; proposed for mission of seculars to Maryland, 498; on the Catholic conscience in Maryland, 513, xvii.; and Bishop of Chalcedon, 521; letter to Chalcedon on mission of seculars and faculties, 522; writes in Baltimore's name, 524, 527
Gallicans, and the Jesuit policy of silence in controversy, 76, 77; *v.* Inquisition S. Cong., Sorbonne, 221, x., 223, xiv.
Gardiner, freeman, 486
Gardiner, S. R., title of "Holy Church" never applied to Anglican Church, 239, viii.
Gates, *Sir* Thomas, patentee under Virginian Charter, 151, xv.
Gendron, Giles, *Augustinian*, and Breton, O. P., 305, 306
Gentile rites, reported on by Cardinal Mellini, 319
Georgia; *v.* Florida
Gerace, *Bishop* of, Collector of the Indies, on volunteers for missions, 248, viii.
Gerard, Richard, sells St. Inigoes, 346, i.
Gerard's [Richard] Manor, Copley to Baltimore, on danger of losing, 478, iii.; *v.* St. Inigoes Manor
Gerard, *Sir* Thomas, incited to colonize by persecution, 1574...146; contract with Gylberte, 147; his son an adventurer to Maryland, 263
Gerard, Thomas, *Commissioner*, 537, xxxi.; withdraws from Protestants the use of his chapel, 540; found guilty of misdemeanor, 541, ix., x., 545, xvii.
Germany, employing brute force against members S.J., 134, xiii.
Ghent, 49, 170, 491
Gibbons, *Major-General* Edward, Mass., the commission offered him by Baltimore, 554; a proprietor in Maryland, 554, xx., xxi.
Gibbons, Thomas, on evangelical chastity, 411, 412
Gilbert, *Lord Chief Baron*, 100, ii., 616, xli.
Gillow, Joseph, his *Bibliographical Dictionary*, etc., of English Catholics, and its materials, 163, vi.; quotes Sorbonne and Gallican authorities on questions touching the Pope and regulars, 221, x.; *v.* JESUITS, Knott; on Chalcedon's authority, 521, vi.
Gilmett, priest, secular missionary for Maryland, 498, 522, 523, 544, xv.; Baltimore's regard for, 534-537; to have F. Copley's house, 538, xxxii.; he deserts Baltimore, 538; *v.* Smith, C. E.; to rent F. Copley's house, 545
Ginetti, *Cardinal*, 222
Gladstone, State Church coextensive with the State, 131; adopts Hooker's opinion, 131

Glebe, priests taxed for a, 411, xviii.
Gondomar, *Count*, 179
Good Fellow, ship, Dalle, master, 283
Goodman, *Bishop of Gloucester*, on Lord Baltimore's faith and devotion, 179; his Catholic leanings, 179, viii.
Gookin, Daniel, envoy from Council of State to Puritans, 287, v.
Governor's Field, 568
Governors, of Barbados, *v.* Willoughby, *Lord*; of Guadeloupe, *v.* Houël; of Jamaica, *v.* Lynch; of Leeward Islands, *v.* Wheler; of Martinique, *v.* Du Parquet; of Maryland, *v.* Brent, Calvert, L., Calvert, P., Greene, Hart; of Massachusetts, *v.* Winthrop; of Montserrat, *v.* Reade, Stapleton; of New York, *v.* Bellomont; of Virginia, *v.* Berkeley, Harvey
Governors of St. Christopher, the French Knights of Malta make English tenure of land precarious, 295; 297
Grace, John, Irish missionary, report on Irish in English West Indian Islands, 315, lxii.
Granada, New, priests S.J. in, 317, lxvi.
Grant of land, by Baltimore, liquidation of a debt, 364
Gray, Francis, process against W. Lewis, 340, i., 343
Great Charter [Magna Charta], 442, 451, 453; and first Statute of Mortmain, 593, iv.; 594, viii.; *v.* Acts of Parliament
Greene, Thomas, adventurer to Maryland, 263; his losses, 398; in Assembly of 1639...449; as Governor of Maryland, refuses Mrs. Brent a vote in Assembly, 551, ii.
Greene's Rest, 568
Gregory Nazianzen, *St.*, 95
Grenada, Capuchins in, 311, xlvi.
Griffon, Peter, *O. P.*, and the West Indian Missions, 303
Guadeloupe, 278; Dominican and Capuchin missions, 298, 299, 304; 1652, population, 299; acts of Propaganda touching, 309, xlii.; *v.* West Indian Islands
Guérard, Jacob, Huguenot, 290
Guiana, Fathers Pelleprat and Méland, S.J., in, 298
Guilds and the Crown, 611
Guinea Coast, 282
Guizot, quoted by Palgrave on historical traditions, 125
Gunpowder Plot, exploited by Coke, 96
Gylberte, *Sir* Humphrey, his colonial enterprise, 1578...146; his patent derogatory from the *Acte against fugytives*, 147, v.; his contract with Peckham and Gerard, 147; denounced to Walsingham, 147; his liberal provisions for religion in his colony, 148, 149, viii.; takes possession of Newfoundland, 149; his adventures, 149, ix., x.; his charter, 264, ix.

H

Hacket, priest, brought to Avalon by Baltimore, 193; denounced by Stourton, 194, 199
Hakluyt, Richard, *Prebendary of Westminster*, patentee under Virginian charter, 150, xv.
Hale, *Dr.* Edward Everett, on rights of man, 328, v.
Hallam, H., on fraudulent use of references, 81; Macaulay on, 84; and logic, 87; his *Constitutional History of England* on persecution, 86; Paget to Somerset, 86; the rack, 86; martyrs and confessors, 86; penal legislation, 86; execution of priests, 88; ostracism of Catholics, 91, xxii.; the Catholic conscience, 92; denial of Habeas Corpus writ to Catholics, 92; persecution, 93; diffidence of Catholics towards Protestant king, 94; Coke's intolerance, 96; Southwell's death, 96; charge of idolatry against Catholics, 107; hypocritical pretext for persecution, 111; intolerance stifling literature, 124, 125; on times of barbarous violence, 446; on *cy-près*, 480, x.; on a licence for Mortmain in Saxon times, 587; fraud occasioning the first Statute of Mortmain, 593, v.; on frankalmoigne, 593, v.; on property coming to the Church through heirs, 597, xxiv.
Halley, 375; *v.* Hawley, Jerome
Hallier, Francis, in the Chalcedon controversy, 216, viii.
Hammond, John, on lack of good Anglican clergy in Virginia, 1655...292, 293; *v. Virginia's Cure*
Handwriting of documents S.J., 78; of F. White, 325, iv.
Hardwicke, *Lord Chancellor*, 100, 616
Harris, John, St. Peter's Key, 569
Harrison, priest, proposed for mission of seculars to Maryland, 498
Hart, John, *Governor* of Maryland, on the climate, 332, 439; interrogatory to Charles Carroll on property S.J., 500, ii.
Harvey, *Captain, Governor* of Virginia, his request for ministers, 291, 323; favours Maryland Mission, 373, 374; his fall, 374; charges against, of Popery, and his restoration, 375, 378
Havre de Grace, Capuchin Convent, 308
Hawkins, buccaneer, 150
Hawks, *Dr.*, on apostacy, 89
Hawley, Eleanor, her life and death, 337; eulogy of, 379
Hawley, *Captain* Henry, *Governor* of Barbados, 277; indicted for suffering a priest to escape, 314, 315; *v.* Irish missionaries
Hawley, Jerom, *Commissioner* of Maryland, *Instructions* to, 251, 260; disregarded, 262; adventurer to Maryland, 263; his death, 337, 362, 376;

INDEX 629

Councillor and Treasurer of Virginia, 377; assailed by the Calverts, 378; upholds Clayborne, 378; defended by Cornwaleys, 374, 379; St. Peter's, 568
Hebb, Vernon, 568
Henrietta Maria, *Queen*, 94, 377, 506, 517, 518, xxix.; gave name to Maryland, 94
Henry II., common law from time of, touching Church privilege, 444
Henry IV. of France, 94
Henry VI. and the rise of corporations, 611
Henry VIII., six dogmas imposed by him on the nation, 143, 584; and restitution, 588, 589; few Mortmain restrictions in reign of, 612; his views adopted by Cecil Calvert, 613; attacks trusts outside of Mortmain, 614; described by Stephen and Blackstone, 614
Herbert, *Lord*, Bishop of Chalcedon on, 219
Heretics in North America, Capuchin mission sent to counteract, 318, iii.; Franciscans suggested for Florida by Fra Nieto, 318, iv.
Herne Island, named St. Clement's, 324
Hill, the [St. Maries Hill], 426
Hill, *Captain* John, adventurer to Maryland, 263; and John Wood, S.J., 274, x.
History, critical sense in reading, 79, 80; conditions of writing, 134, 135; assumption of falsity in Jesuit writers, 135; barrenness of authentic published, 135
  Materials for: materials chiefly used, Jesuit archives, 47; letters to members S.J. on collecting matter, 47, 48, 49; solidity rather than speed in writing, 58; documents to Generals, 65; from Generals, 65, 66; special importance of, 66; loss of, through violence, 66, 67, i.; loss of, from Savoy College under F. Tidder, 67; loss of, by deliberately burning papers, 1718–1733...68, 68, v., 69; loss of, at Suppression of the Society, 69
History, Jesuit and Catholic, threefold attitude towards, 82; prevalent traditional views, 82, 83
History of Maryland, materials for, desired by the Maryland Legislature from Jesuit archives, 1636...29–31; schedule for, 54, 55
History of S.J., translation of it into English forbidden, 73, 74
Hoadly, *Dr.*, publishes memorial of Urbano Cerri, under the name of Steele, 1715... 202, xx.
Hoard, Francis; *v.* Gage, George
Hobbism, Hallam on, 353, ii.
Holden, priest, against Leyborne, 72, viii.; proposed for mission of seculars to Maryland, 498
Holden, *Member of Parliament*, on persecution under Test Act, 1736...108

Hollis, John, marriage, 338
"Holy Church," Gardiner on the term, 450, 586, xxi.
Hooker, his opinion on State Church, 131, 354; adopted by Gladstone, 131
Horsmanden hangs Ury for a fictitious plot, 103; his letter to Colden, 103, xiii.
Houël, *Governor*, St. Christopher, Guadeloupe, 297; brings Jesuits and Capuchins to West Indies, 298; and Breton, O. P., 305
Howard, *Cardinal*, of Norfolk, letters from J. Warner, S.J., to, 76, l.
Huguenots, proposal from De Sancé to Charles I. on colonizing Virginia and Florida, 288, vii.; proposal by Augier to Cromwell about Jamaica and West Indies, 288, vii.; in Carolina, 290; *v.* Carolina
Hurons, Indians, 326; *v.* Iroquois
Hyacinth de Longueville, *Capuchin*, on mission in St. Christopher and on S.J., 308

I

Idolatry, charge of, against Catholics, 107, x.
Ignatius Loyola, *St.*, 143
Imposts for clergy, forbidden by *Bulla Coenae* to lay tribunals, 437
Ina and Church property, 588
Income tax and *Conditions of Plantation*, 401
Indented servants, 337; their condition and temper in Maryland, 340; their petition to fellow-Protestants, 340; types of, 341; *v.* Clerke; form for binding, 341; description of, by Boucher and F. Mosley, 341, 342
Independents; *v.* Puritan
Indians, European marriages with the, contrast between English and Latin America, 280; *lex talionis* applied to, 548, 549; extermination of, 549; Kent and American law on their land titles, 574
Infidels, true proprietors of their land, 571
Information of the Catholic laymen to the Pope on the Bishop of Chalcedon, 212, iii.; on misrepresentation regarding Baltimore and other lords, 212; and Protest of the Peers, 224, i., 225, ii., iii.
Informers, their fees, 87
Ingle, Mr., 534; invades Catholic colony, 562, 563
Ingoli, *Dr.* Francis, *Secretary of Propaganda*, correspondence with Fra Simon Stock, 181, 182; and with Agucchi, on Avalon, 183; his letter to Card. Antonio Barberini, on Stock and missions, 190, 191; letter to Agucchi, on Newfoundland, 197; his minutes of Propaganda

meeting on missions in Spanish and Portuguese Indies, 197, ix.; on Jesuits in universities, and on Jesuitesses, ix.; and Stock, 215; and Chalcedon, 221, viii.; death of, 1649...308; to Agucchi, 318, iv.; 520, vi.

Inquisition, *Sacred Congregation* of, decree on Chalcedon controversy, 201; admonition to Bishop of Chalcedon, 203; and the Chalcedon controversy, 214, 221; grants faculties to Fra Francis da Pamplona, Capuchin, 311; receives Lewger's *Cases*, 418; memorial to, on Lewger and Baltimore, 515-517; and Propaganda, contradictory decrees of, 519-521

Inquisition, Spanish, 93

Instructions, Baltimore's, to Governor and Commissioners of Maryland, 1633...251, 252, 257; *v.* Calvert, Cornwaleys, Hawley; forbid open profession of Roman Catholicism, 260; no mention of a clergy, 261; military discipline for all men, 261; oath of allegiance, 261, 262; cross-examination ordered on board ship, 262; on Jamestown and Poynt-Comfort, 262

Intacke, the, 568

Intolerance and suppression of documents, Hallam on, 124, 125; reappearing in Maryland history, 126, 127, 128; *v.* Persecution

Intruding Jesuit, story of an, 534, 535

Ireland as a colonizing ground, 290, x.; Poyning's law for, 385

Irish Catholics, expelled from Virginia, settled at Montserrat, 279; their transportation, 282, 283

Irish missionaries in English West Indian Islands, 315; Irish friars for Virginia and other places, 322

Iroquois, sachems refuse to betray French Jesuits to Bellomont, 103; family of, comprise first five, then six nations, 326, i.

Irving, Washington, 124

Isle of Kent, Maryland, 343, 448, 460

Islands, Windward and Leeward; *v.* West Indian Islands

J

JACOBITISM, Catholicism a sign of, Paley's argument, 109, 110, iv.; and penal laws, 111

Jamaica, taking of, 283; Order in Council for transportation of Irish to, 283; *v.* Thurloe

James I., 94; answer to Commons concerning Recusants, 94, xi.; against Bellarmine, 421

James II., oath of allegiance to, and disloyalty towards, 113

James, *Rev. Mr.*, Protestant minister in Avalon, 193

James River, Virginia, 201, 233

Jamestown, Virginia, 250, 376, ii., 378; Maryland adventurers forbidden to approach, 262

Jansenism, and the Society of Jesus, 74; letters from the General on, 74; anti-Jesuit literature of, 209, i.

Jansenists, Augier to Cromwell on behalf of, 289

Jefferson, *Captain*, Lieutenant-Colonel of Nevis, 279

Jesuit, in tradition, indictment of, 120, 121; an exception in the indictment, 121, 122

Jesuit writings, assumptions regarding, 135; theology presupposed in, 135, xvi.; *v.* Mejer

Jesuitesses, 197, ix.

JESUITS—

1. Generals—

Partial list of, 32, 33; Aquaviva, Claudius, his handbooks on faculties for missionaries and for superiors, 268, iv.; Carrafa, Vincent, letter to F. Smithson and others on foreign missions, 467, 468; De Noyelle, Charles, on memoirs, 49; on literary excellence, 58; Gonzalez, Thyrsus, on materials for S.J. history, 56, v.; Gottifredi, Alexander, 468; Nickel, Goswin, on Annual Letters, 49, 50; on F. Alford's Annals, 60; on F. More's English Jesuit History, 64; and Propaganda on St. Christopher, 308; letters to applicants for foreign missions, 468-470; Oliva, John Paul, 49, vii.; on Annual Letters for the Propaganda, 51, ix.; on saving archives, 55, iii.; on literary excellence in publications, 57, i., ii.; on the employment of talent, 59, vii.; on legible writing of letters, 78, vi.; on choosing fit subjects for the Society, 168, xiv.; letter to Cybo, Secretary of Propaganda, on West Indian S.J. Mission, 303, xxvi.; letter to, from D'Estrées French Admiral, on F. Frémont, 303; Piccolomini, Francis, 55, i., ii.; on F. Matajon and foreign missions, 469, xviii.; on F. Buckley for St. Christopher, 469, 470, xx.; Retz, Francis, F. E. Plowden, procurator, burns the letters of, 68, v.; *v.* History, materials for; Tamburini, Michael Angelo, F. E. Plowden, procurator, burns the letters of, 68

Vitelleschi, Mutius, on authentic history, 47, 48; on controversial briefs, 53, xv., xvi.; finds fault with hasty publication, 58; uses Latin tongue, 58; urges solidity against speed, 58, 59, iv.; and F. Floyd on the *Astrum inextinctum*, 59, v., vi.; desires Campagnoni to collect historical materials on the Maryland Mission, 64, x.; imposes silence in controversies, 70-74; on handwriting, etc., of More, Knott, and others, 78; and the deciphering of the Peers' Remonstrance

INDEX

JESUITS (*continued*)—
to Chalcedon, 206, vii.; comment on Protest of the Peers, 228; demurs to sending out a Maryland Mission, 246, 247; gives faculties for the Indies, 267, i.; *v.* Faculties; correspondence with Propaganda on mission in North America (1625), 320; decision for Maryland, on barter or truck, 339; to F. Poulton [Brooke], on the Maryland foundation for a college, 346; to F. Copley, disclaims having sent a reproof, 423, 424, xvii.; to F. Knott, on George Con, and on Panzani's testimonial, 457, i.; to FF. Copley, More, and White, on Maryland ecclesiastical politics, on truck, on a mission into New England, on new men for Maryland, 458, 459; letter to Thomas Owens, applicant for foreign missions, 467, iii.; letters to F. Copley, commending Maryland Mission, 483, iii.; letters to FF. Knott and Copley, on Baltimore's policy, on conversions in Maryland, on mission into New England, 555–560; grants Lord Baltimore's demands regarding Mortmain, 558, viii.; enforces the concession, 559, x.

Vicar-General Sangrius, letter granting Baltimore's demands, 561, xv.; on imprisonment of FF. Copley and White, 562, vii.

2. Provincials—

Barton, Richard, 64, 469; Blount, Richard, 228, 246, 247; letter to, from General, on providing historical materials, 47; on avoiding controversy, 71, iv., 73, 162, iii.; letters from General to, proposing F. Andrew White for divers posts, 170; on the application of Baltimore for American missionaries, 201, xix.; condemns Baltimore's oath of allegiance, 357; Card. Barberini's comment, 358; letter from General to, on F. Knowles, 367; character of, 422, xi.; Courtney, Edward, *alias* Leeds, 51, 60, ix.; supplies historical particulars, 62; letter from General to, on choosing fit subjects for the Society, 168, xiv.; 465, v.; Foster, Francis, 49, 55; Gray, George, 50, 53, iii., 74, xix.; Harcourt, Thomas, martyr, 56; Keynes, John, 58, iii.

Knott, Edward, 50; 78, iv.; disapproves of Baltimore's policy, 369; character of, 421, xii.; letter from General to, on Con and Panzani, 457; his book and controversies, 457, 458; contentions with Baltimore, 458; letters to, from General on Maryland, 459, x.; 468, xiii.; his instruction on enforced inaction in the English Mission, 471, xxiii.; 475; his documents on seizure of Mattapany, 489–492; protest to Baltimore, 489–491; his letter to Rosetti and Observations on Baltimore's Points, 505, 506, i., 513, 514; his readi-

JESUITS (*continued*)—
ness to dissolve the Maryland Mission, 514; his proposals to grant Baltimore's demands, 556; letters of the General to, embodying the proposals, 556–558

More, Henry, historian S.J., 61, 78, 94, ix., x., 221, x., 339, xx., 425; death, 61; History of the English Mission and Province of the Society, 62, 63, vii., 64; 71; on the Bishop of Chalcedon's regulations, 203, iii.; his policy regarding Maryland, 349; and the "Three Propositions," 369; character of, 422, xiii., xiv.

Silesdon, Henry (*alias* Bedingfield), letters from General to, on accuracy of historical materials, 48, iii.; on the carping of persons ill disposed towards the Society, 73, xiv.; to General, on applicants for Indian missions, 468, xi.; proposing F. Matajon for St. Christopher, 469, xviii.; Simeon, Joseph, receives instructions from General on gathering records, 48; on caution in transmission of Annual Letters to Propaganda, 52; on not leaving talents unemployed, 59, vii.; Turberville, John, to G. Thorold, on readmisson of Br. Clemson in Maryland, 161, i.; Warner, John, 49, vi.; 53; and historical materials, 56, iv., 62, 67, iii.; 76, i.; Warner, Sir John (*alias* Clare), 78

3. Fathers—

Acosta, Joseph, quoted in *Virginia's Cure*, on Christian good example for infidels, 293; on military support for missions, 319, iv.; *v.* Nieto, *Fra*; Aegidius, 169; Alegambe and historical materials, 62; Alford, Michael, and revision of his writings, 59, 60; Altham, John (*alias* Gravener), story concerning, 230, 231, xiii.; 264, 335, 336; in Isle of Kent, Maryland, 343; freeman of Assembly, 380, iv.; 423, xv.; reproved, 424, xviii.; death of, 481, 493; Anderton, Laurence (*alias* Scroope), 463; Antonie, *v.* Rivers; Argento, J., 291, 583, xiii.; Ashby, Richard, 57; Atherton, Thomas, applicant for the Maryland Mission, 466, i., 476, iv.; Babthorpe, Thomas, his Thomism, 174, 175; Bacon, Nathaniel, *v.* Southwell, Nathaniel; Bacon, Thomas, *v.* Southwell, Thomas; Baker, Alexander, his journeys to the Indies, 198, xiii.; his voyage to America, 269, ii.; Baldwin, 157; Bartlett, Francis, volunteer for foreign missions, 469, xvii.; Bartoli, and historical materials on England, 62; Bastard, Robert, 161; Batford, 169; Bathe, Christopher, sent to St. Christopher, 470; Bathe, John, killed at Drogheda, 284, vii.; Bazier, Matthew (*alias* Grimes), applicant for the

JESUITS (*continued*)—
Maryland Mission, 466, i.; in Newgate, 464; Béchamel, explorations in Cayenne and Guiana, 298, 312; Bedingfield, H., *v*. **Provincials**, Silesdon, 48; Bellarmine, 77, 421; Bernard, Roger, *v*. Smith, Anthony; Besson, Joseph, 302, xxiii.; Beuerige, Thomas, 160, 161; Blewett, Thomas, *v*. Smith, Anthony; Blundell, James, 160, 161; Brebeuf, 321, ix.; Brooke, Robert, and Governor Seymour, 89; Brooke, John, *v*. Poulton, Ferdinand; Brown, Charles, 72, xii.; Buckley, Robert, for mission to St. Christopher, 469, 470, xx., 476; Buteux, 312, ix.; Butler, *v*. Lanman; Campano, on reasons for endowing colleges, 582, 583, xiii.; Campion, Edmund, *B*., 143-145; Campion, William, applicant for foreign missions, 467, vii.; Canisius, Peter, *B*., 168, xiv.; Cappecius, *v*. Copley; Carew, Thomas, 466, i.; 476, iv.; Carey, Thomas, applicant for foreign missions, 469, xvi., 476, iv.; Carwell, Thomas, 74, xviii.; Colford, Thomas, 174

Copley, Father Thomas (*alias* Fisher, Philip), More's account of his trial in London, 64, viii., 562, iv.; travesty of his character by C. E. Smith, 121, 122; accused of trading, 330, xx., 340; proprietor of St. Inigoes, 1638... 334, vii.; his antecedents in Europe, and services to Maryland, 334-336; transaction about land at Pascattoway with Lewger, 345, vii.; reconciles five heretics, 347, vi.; detained in England, 357; business in London, 365; his antecedents,—his petition against priest-hunters, 366; warrant in his favour, 367; letter from him to Baltimore, 367, iii. iv.; detention in London, 1636...368, viii.; General's letters of approval to, 369, 370; arrival in Maryland, 1637... 370, xiii.; freeman of Assembly, 380, iv.; his letter to Baltimore on the absence of clergy from the Assembly, 1638...382, ix.; on the code of laws, 387, ii.; letter to Baltimore on Lewger's code, 389, viii., 390, 392, iii.; fears about corn monopoly, 396, xix.; asks for a licence to buy corn, 397, xxv.; his advice on fostering population, xxvi.; on new conditions imposed regarding manors, 398, xxxiv., 399, xxxv.; his requests to Baltimore, 400, 401; criticizes despotism and socialism in the laws, 402, xliv., 403, xlvii., xlviii.; remonstrance on omission of Church interests from the code, 404, 405; illegal tax collected by Lewger from the missionaries, 409; his remarks on getting property by lot, 410; on marriage law and evangelical chastity, 411; on Lewger's bill for payment of debts, 412, 413, xxii.; on deriving authority for spiritual functions from civil head, 413, xxiv.;

JESUITS (*continued*)—
admonitions and advice, 414, xxvi.; requests spiritual and temporal, 414, 415, 443, xxviii.; More's estimate of his character, 423, xv.; reproved, the General's disclaimer, 423, xvi.; his plan to enter New England, 458, 459; Baltimore's order to seize and deport him, 453; conveys land to lay trustee, Cuthbert Fenwick, 483-485; attempted conveyance to Lewger, 486, xi.; his deportation ordered by Baltimore, 487; accedes to Baltimore's demands, 532, xiii.; rents his house to Gilmett, 538, xxxii., 545; sale of New Chappell to Baltimore's Commission, 541; asks leave of General to go to Rome, 542; labours at St. Mary's City, and with the Indians, 555; reports conversions, 559; the Vicar-General on his sufferings, 563, vii.

Cooper, John, chosen for the Maryland Mission, 466, i.; 473, 474, 475; debarred from Maryland by Baltimore, 493, ii.; sails for Maryland, 531, 532; arrival in Maryland, 538, 555; his death, 563, xi.; Coppleius, 78; *v*. Copley, Thomas; Crathorne, John, 169, 172, xv., 174; Cresswell, Joseph, named in British statutes, 170; advocates promptness in publication, 58; Crombach, H., 60; De Conick, 169; Drury, John, missionary to North America, 269, ii.; studies and career, 270; Dukes, John, ex-Jesuit, 181, xii.; Dumarché, 312, ix.; Fisher, *v*. Copley; Fitzherbert, Thomas, Rector of English College, Rome, 171; Floyd, John, author, his book against De Dominis, 58; chosen by General to answer *Astrum Inextinctum*, 59, v.; 159; and the Gallican question about regulars, 209, i., 216, viii.; Forcer, Francis, 78, v.; Foster, 60, ix.; Galloway, missionary in Martinique, 69; Garnett, Henry, martyr, 153, 158, vii.; Garnett, Thomas, martyr, 160; Gerard, John, letter to, from F. White, 156; Gervis, 527, vi.; *v*. Shelley; Grant, 57, ii.; Gravener, *v*. Altham; Grene, Christopher, his comment on Parsons' criticism of the Norumbega project, 154, iv.; his industry in saving documents, 157, iv.; Greene, Richard, White's letters on his behalf to Gerard and Parsons, 156-158; Griffith, *v*. Alford; Grillet, John, missionary in West Indies, 298; General de la Barre, thanks Lord Willoughby for attentions paid to, 301, xxii., xxiii.; in a Dutch prison, 301; on missions and faculties to Propaganda, 301, 302, xxiv.; taken prisoner by Dutch, 312, 313; Grimes, *v*. Bazier; Hall, confessor in English College at Rome, 171; Hall, John, 475; Hallé, Jean, Superior in West Indies, petitions

INDEX

JESUITS (*continued*)—
Propaganda for faculties, 302, xxiii.; ignores Breton's claims, 305; Harrison, Thomas, applicant for the Maryland Mission, 466, i.; Hartwell, Bernard, 475; debarred from Maryland by Baltimore, 493, ii.; sails to Maryland, 531, 532, 538, 555; Superior of the mission, Maryland, 563; his death, 555, x.; Hawkins, Francis, applicant for foreign missions, 469, xiv.; Hays, Timothy, 269; Hunter, William, and Governor Seymour, 89; Humphries, T., volunteer for Maryland, 466, i.; Jacquinot, missionary in West Indies, 305; Keynes, George, at Liège, volunteer for foreign missions, dies in Philippines, 468, xiii.

Knott, Edward, 60, ix.; his publications, 70; his book against Chillingworth, etc., 71; animosity against, 71, v., vi., vii., 72, viii., ix.; proposed for confessor in English College, Rome, 171; 209, i., 216, viii., 230, xiii.; Panzani on, 232, xvi.; his memorial to Rome on issue with Lord Baltimore, 248, x., xi., xii.; Observations to Rosetti on Baltimore's policy, 255, 256; letter to Rosetti on Lewger and his views, 417; memorial to Card. Francis Barberini, 418, 419

Knowles, John, 335, xi.; death, 336, xiii., 370; applicant for foreign missions, 367; letter of commendation from General to Provincial, 367, 368, vi.; Lalemant, Charles, 321, ix.; Lallemant, Jerome, Superior in Canada, faculties granted to, for Canada, 302, xxv.; Lanman, Henry, 160, 161, *v.* Butler; Lathwait, Thomas (*alias* Scott), 160, 161; Laymann, Paul, 59, v.; Le Mercier, Superior of West Indian Mission S.J., petition to Propaganda for faculties, 302, xxv., 321, ix.; Lessius, Leonard, 169; Line, Francis, volunteer for Maryland, 466, i.; Mallory, William, applicant for the Maryland Mission, 470, xxi., 476; Mariana, 234, iii.; Martin, Henry, Superior in Constantinople, petition to Propaganda for faculties, 302, xxiii.; Matajon (*alias* Matthews), 466, i.; not approved for foreign missions, 469, xviii., 476; Méland, in Guiana, 298, ix., 312; Monford, James, volunteer for Maryland, 466, i., 476, iv.; Monteith, William, applicant for the Chinese Mission, 467, v., vi.; Morgan, William, 49, vii.; the General Oliva on the use of his learning, 59, vii.; Morley, George, 172; Morley, Henry, *v.* Lawrence, Rigby; Morley, Walter, 476, iv.; death of, in Maryland, 493; Morris, Christopher, volunteer for Maryland Mission, 464, 476; his letter of application and arguments, 465, 466; Morris, Walter, 476, iv.; Mosley, Joseph,

JESUITS (*continued*)—
letters to Mrs. Dunn, on Maryland, its capabilities and climate, 329, 330, 331, 332; on indented servants, 342, iv.; Mumford, Gervase, 49, vii.; Mumford, Thomas, applicant for Maryland, 466, i.; Nelson, Francis, applicant for foreign missions, 469, xv.; 476; Orlandini, 73; Owens, Thomas, applicant for Maryland, 466, i.; volunteers for Indies, and goes to Portugal, 467, iii., 476

Parker, Francis, volunteer for Maryland, 462; his letter of application and arguments, 463-465; Parker, John, volunteer for Maryland, his letter of application, his vow, 462; Parsons, 143, 144, 145; opinion on a Catholic colony to Norumbega, 153, 154; 268; Pelham, William, applicant for foreign missions, 468, ix.; Pelleprat, Pierre, in Guiana, 298, ix., 312; Percy, John, 70; Perrault, 321, ix.; Philips, Robert, applicant for Maryland, 372, 373, xviii., xx.; Pijart, 321, ix.; Plowden, Edmund, procurator, burns papers, 68, v., 69; *v.* History; Poresson [Bresson], Nicolaus, Superior S.J. in Syria, faculties for, from Propaganda, 302, xxiii.; Poulton, Ferdinand (*alias* Brooke, John), Superior in Maryland, 343; on Maryland foundation for a college, 346; sent to supersede Copley, 423; report on him, 423, xv.; 425, 426, 460; warrant to, for election of burgess, 478; his letter to the Provincial on the Mission, 480, 481; shot by accident, 492, 493, i.; Price, John, 169, 170; Pulton, Andrew, 476, iv.; Pulton, Ferdinando, ex-Jesuit, 181, xii.; Quentin, 321, ix.; Quin, Thomas, 470, xxi.; Pugh, Robert, *v.* Philips; Rhodes, Alexander, Superior, S.J., in Persia, faculties for, from Propaganda, 302, xxiii.; Richard, 321, ix.; Rigbie, Roger, chosen for Maryland Mission, 466, i.; his career, 472, i.; his application for the Maryland Mission, 472, 473; allowed to go by Baltimore, 493, 526, iv.; at Patuxent, 547, 550; a police commission sent to him by L. Calvert, 547, i.; composes a catechism in Patuxent, 550, viii.; *v.* Smith, C.E.; death of, 563, viii., ix.; Rigby, Lawrence, and Avalon, 199, xiv.; Rivers, Anthony, 158; *v.* Smith, Anthony; Rockwood, Robert, applicant for foreign missions, 468, x.

Rogers, Francis, missionary in Maryland, 269, 273; returns to England, 335, 368, vii.; Rookwood, Robert, ex-Jesuit, 181, xii.; Roper, 94, ix., x.; Sacchini, historian S.J., 62; Sadler, William, volunteer for Maryland, 466, i.; Sanders, Francis, letter to, from General, 67; Sanctarelli, 77; Ste. Geneviève, Nicholaus de, Superior in

JESUITS (*continued*)—
Mission of Greece, faculties for, from Propaganda, 302, xxiii.; Scott, *v.* Lanman; Scroope, *v.* Anderton; Segura, and seven companions, martyrs on the Potomac, 1571...317; Sheldon, Henry, on materials for history, 56, vi.; 421, xiii.; Shelley, Owen, 172; letters to, from Peasely, 527, 528; Smith, Anthony (*alias* Rivers, Bernard, Blewett), ex-Jesuit, 180, x., 181, xii.; missionary in Avalon, 181, xii., 189, 190; Smithson, John, applicant for foreign missions, 466, i., 467, 468, viii.; Southwell, Nathaniel (*alias* Bacon), and historical materials, 62; his redaction of More's History, 63, 78; 171, 173, 251, iii.; petition for foreign missions, 371, 372; Southwell, Robert, arraigned by Coke, 96; Southwell, Thomas (*alias* Bacon), 172, 174; Spencer, John, volunteer for Maryland, 466, i.; Stafford, 171, 463; Strange, Thomas, his wit on the rack, 86, vi.; 159, xi.; Suffren, J., 72, ix.; Suarez, 77, 421, 591, 592, xxxix.; Talbott, Thomas, letter to Silesdon on new novitiate at St. John's, Louvain, 159-161, xv.; Tanner, historian, 62; Thomas (Southwell *or* Babthorpe), applicant for the American Mission, 174, 198, xii.; Thompson, Thomas, applicant for the Chinese Mission, 467, iv.; Thomson, Francis (*alias* Yates), 161; Thorold, George, 161, i.; Turgis, 321, ix.; Tidder, Edward, 67, ii.; Victoria, Vienna, letter from, to B. Peter Canisius on choice of subjects, 168, xiv.; Vivier, Henry de, Superior in South America, faculties for, from Propaganda, 302, xxiii.; Wading, Peter, 169; Walley, *v.* Garnett; ix.; Watson, W., 532, xiv.

White, Andrew, 247, vi., 264, 269, 271, 314, 335, 525, 526, iv.; General to, on History of the Mission, 47; date of his death, 61; his *Relatio Itineris*, 62, iv., 63, 64; More on his arrest and trial, 64, viii.; J. A. Doyle on his Relation, 80; secular priest, 155; exiled from England, 156, 159; enters S.J., 156, 157; his letters, 156, iii.; to Gerard, 156; to Parsons, on behalf of F. Greene, 157, 158; his admission into novitiate, 159-161; sent to England, his final vows, 168; professorial and missionary duties, 1619-1629...168-174; designated twice for the English College, Rome, 171; General's letter to, on the American Mission, 174, xviii., xix.; changes name Andrew to Thomas, 175, xx.; first Lord Baltimore to, 198, xi.; connection with White's Neck in America, 199, xiv., 200, xvi.; composes the Declaration of the Colony, 249; Lord Baltimore's revision, 249, i.; sails from Cowes in

JESUITS (*continued*)—
the *Ark*, 274; his narratives of the voyage to America, Latin and English, 274, 275; *v.* Voyage; accused by C. E. Smith 'of having introduced slavery into Maryland, 281; his *Briefe Relation* sent to England by Leonard Calvert, 322; his handwriting, and *Calvert Papers*, 325, iv.; on Maryland, 329; letter on Copley to Baltimore, 336, xii.; first recorded marriage in the mission performed by, 338; his *alias* Thomas, 338, xvii.; conversion of the Tayac at Kittamaquund, 343-345; after Copley's arrival in Maryland, 370; freeman of Assembly, 380, iv.; letter to Lord Baltimore on laws of Maryland, trade rights, the Concordat, *Conditions of Plantation*, monopolies, 390, x., 392-395, 397, 398; More's estimate of his character, 423, xv.; reproved, 432, xvi.; on revenue, 434, 435; his History of the Mission, 459; transferred from Patuxent to Pascattoway, 479, 481; at Pascattoway, 550; marvellous cure of an Indian, 554; carried prisoner to England, 562, iii.; his trial, 562, iv.; Vicar-General on his trials, 563. vii.; death, 563, viii.

White, Robert, applicant for foreign missions, 468, xii.; Williamson, Richard, applicant for missions, 372, xvi., xx.; Worsley, Edward, 465, vi.; Worsly, Laurence, 460; volunteer for the Maryland Mission, his letter of application and arguments, 461, 462; on inaction in the English Mission, 471; Worthington, John, 266; Worthington, Thomas, applicant for the Indian Mission, 393, xix., xx.; Yates, *v.* Thomson

4. Coadjutors—
Clemson, Ign., 161, i.; Fettiplace, *v.* Laward; Fulwood, Richard, applicant for the Maryland Mission, 466, i.; Gervase, Thomas, in Maryland Mission, 269, 271; death of, by yellow fever, 274, 335, 336, xiii.; Gray, Robert, volunteer for Maryland, 466, i., 476; Griffith, Francis, 160; Latham, Thomas, 274, xi.; Laward, John, 160; Maurice, Francis, volunteer for Maryland, 466, i.; Walter Morris, 476, iv.; Mobberley, Joseph, on Maryland, 331, 332; Morley, Walter, 343; Rigbye, Edward, 160; Roper, Michael, 160; Sheldon, Hughe, 160; Turberville, Gregory, chosen for Maryland Mission, 466, i.; his application for foreign missions, 475, 476; his death in Maryland, 476, i.; Wood, John, in Maryland, 269, 271, 274, x., 335, 368, vii.

Joachim de Corbeil, *Fra, Capuchin*, letter to Propaganda on West Indian Missions, 312

John; *v.* Mosorcoques

Johnson, B. T., his theory on canon law in Maryland, 421, x.; on F. More, S.J., 421, x.; and Coke on Church liberties, 441, xxii.; on first Statute of Mortmain, 594, xiii.
Johnson, *Dr.* Samuel, on the mythical Popish Plot, 102
Josaphat, *Capuchin*, on African Mission, 309, xlii.
Joseph da Caravantes, *Capuchin*, in Granada and South America, 311
Joseph II. of Austria, 589
Josephism, 353
Jubilee year, first centenary S.J., 464
Julian the Apostate, on religion and treason, 95; reason for despoiling the clergy, 291

K

KELLISON, MATTHEW, his theory that regulars are "pedagogues" and hirelings in the Church, 216, viii.
Kemp, *Secretary* and *Councillor* of Virginia, 378; assails Hawley, 379, vi.
Kent, *Chancellor*, and discordant opinions of American law on Indian land titles, 574, 576, viii.; on Mortmain, 613
Kent, Isle of, station S.J., 460
Kidnapping of Copley ordered by Baltimore, 534, 536
Kiernander, *Rev. Mr.*, 485, viii.
King of England, lord of unoccupied land only, 571
Kirke, *Captain* David, attack on Canada, 319
Kit Martin's Point, 569
Kittamaquund, name of Tayac, 343, 344
Kittamaquund, Pascatoa, Maryland, 343
Kittamaquund, *Mrs.* Mary; *v.* Empress
Knights of Malta, viceroys in St. Christopher, 297
Knott, Edward; *v.* JESUITS
Know-nothings, in America, 102
Knut, King, on first-fruits, 590

L

LAMARZELLE, M. de, on rights of Church to property under French law of separation, 485, viii.
Land, allotment of, promised in Maryland, 252, 253; for missionaries only as colonists, 255, 256; tenure of, in Maryland, 364, iii.; conditions for adventurers, 364; grant of, as payment of a debt, 364; unoccupied, and royal charters, 571, 572; *v.* Town lots
Lane, *Rev. Mr.*, his letter to Laud on clergy in Barbados, 291, 292
Langford, John, *Commissioner*, 358, 545; and purchase of New Chappell, 541
Langhorne, 358

Language of the Indians, the Jesuit missionaries and C. E. Smith on, 550, viii.
Latin, commonly used in literature, 58; used for communications of Generals S.J., 58, v.; the usual means of communication among the learned, 85
Laud, *Archbishop*, letter from Lane, 291, 292; judge of High Commission Court, 511, xii.
Law, canon, meaning of its terms in Catholic times, 237, 238; terms qualified for use in Anglicanism, 238, viii.; *v.* Church of England; papal and pontifical Bulls produced by Anglicans after Reformation, 239, vii.; *v.* Panzani; Maitland on, in pre-Reformation times, 592
Law, canon and civil, on exemption of clergy from taking part in causes of blood, 382
Law, common and feudal combined, 589, xxxiii.; Spelman on, 589, xxx.; Coke on frankalmoigne in, 590, xxxvi.
Law, feudal, in union with common law, 589, 590; Mortmain derived from, 590
Law of England, basis of Maryland liberties, 451
Law, Poyning's, for Ireland, 385, xii.
Laws of Maryland. First Code, 1635... 362; their character, 362; submitted to Lord Baltimore, 362; his veto, 363; commission to L. Calvert for new laws to be signed, 369

Second Code: 1638, Baltimore's imported Code of, first read in Assembly, 383; rejected, 384; English laws suggested, 384; second reading, 384, 385; third reading, and rejection, 385; consequence of rejection regarding S.J. and Lord Baltimore, 385; defects of the Code, feudalism and Erastianism, 386; initiative in proposing, McMahon and Streeter on, 386, xiii.; Leonard Calvert's defence of and comment on, 386, 387; comments by Cornwaleys and Copley, 387

Second Code refitted by Lewger: precludes redress at law, 388, iv.; Assembly committee of three, and Lewger secretary, 388; forty-three bills passed, 389; letters to Baltimore from Copley, Cornwaleys, and Calvert, 389; Baltimore withholds assent, 389; law and spiritual interests in, 390; *v.* Trade; sketch of Code, 390, 391; oath of allegiance, 391; *v.* Panzani; bill of support for Proprietary opposed by Cornwaleys, 391; land tenure laws in the Code, 396; criticism on, 400, 401; touching life and limb, 402, xlii.; revolutionary character of, 402, 403, xlv.; disfranchising single women, 411; debts, order of payment, 412; Lord Baltimore invested with spiritual authority, 413; sections of *Bulla Coenae* relevant to, 436, 437, ix.

Third Code: thirty-six bills wrecked, 427, 428; an Ordinance substituted, 428; 449, 450; v. Assembly, Bills; Ordinance of 1639...450; becomes law until next Assembly, 450; v. Ordinance
Ultimate basis of justice to be Baltimore's orders, 487, 488; Baltimore's text hereupon to L. Calvert, 488, xv.; act for officers, 548, iv.; for Indians, 548, 549, v., vi.; v. Lay tribunals, Imposts for clergy, Property

La[y]borne, Leyborne, Leyburne, priest, letter against, by Dr. Holden, 72, viii., 521, vi.; and Baltimore's oath of allegiance, 358, 359; proposed for mission of seculars to Maryland, 498

Lay communities, brought under Statutes of Mortmain, 609-612

Laymen, their Articles or Questions, and letter on Chalcedon's regulations, 203, iv.; Information to the Pope concerning Chalcedon, 212, iii.

Lay tribunals, *Bulla Coenae* limits the citing of clergy before, 436, 437

Lay trustee, 484; first in North America for Catholic property, 485, viii.

Lazarists, or Congregation of the Mission, and the West Indies, 303

Leander, *Father*, 360, 518, xxix.

Lechford, *Sir* Richard, contributor to Maryland venture, 263; business partner of Leonard Calvert, 275

Lecky, W., his account of Paley's conscience, 136, xvii.; Catholic spirit of the great Charter of Liberty, 239, vii.

Leeds, *Sir* Thomas, and sodality of Immaculate Conception, 215, vi.

Leeward Islands, state of Christian ministry in, 282

Legislation; v. Assembly, Bills, Laws, Maryland

Leicester, Parliament at, 586

Leland, quoted by Lingard on Poyning's Law, 385, xii.

Lesley, Rome, 307; on French Catholic merchant companies, 314

Letters, Annual, method and material, 49-55, and *passim*; private, of the Generals S.J. and members, 64-66, and *passim*

Letters to Propaganda from Bishop of Chalcedon, 215, 219, 220; to Bishop of Chalcedon from Propaganda, 220, 221; v. Barberini; Inquisition

Lewger, John, 77, 232; Panzani's account of, 42; v. Baltimore; and Bonacina, on restitution and payment of debts, 128, x.; Secretary of Maryland, etc., his posts and policy, 336, 388; at baptism of Tayac, 345; patent of land to, from F. Copley, 345; at Oxford, 350; Anglican rector, and conversion, 351; his books, 351; his Erastianism, 352, 353; refused entrance into S.J., 353; Panzani on him, 360, 362, v.; Baltimore's secretary, 365, 368; his arrival and offices in Maryland, 380; his commission, 380; and proxies at the Assembly, 381, 382; letter to Baltimore on the Jesuits, *Cases*, etc., 390, xi.; Calvert's commendation of, 393; to Baltimore on monopoly of trade, and Cornwaleys, 396, 397; his socialism, 403, 404; and Church interests, 409; unauthorized tax on missionaries, 409; bill against religious life, marriage law, 411, 412; on casuists and restitution, 413; his despatches and *Cases*, 416, 417; F. Knott's letters on, 417, 418, 419; his tenets, 419, 420; his view of the situation, 1639...424; letter to Baltimore, 425-427; on third code of laws, 427; and the greater excommunication, 438; in Assembly of 1639...449; on payment of debts, 455, xviii.; granted probate of wills, 456; Copley's attempted conveyance to him of Pascattoway land, 486; and the preferential claims of piety, 492, xxiv.; and Fathers S.J., on *Conditions of Plantation*, 502-504; against L. Calvert on law of passports, 533, 537; a commissioner to buy New Chappell, 541, 545; St. John's Creek, 569

Lewger, John, *jun.*, 351

Lewis, William, overseer of St. Inigoes, for F. Copley, 346, i.; process against, by indented servants, 340, i., 539, 540; freeman of Assembly, 381, 382; Lewis's Neck, 568

Liberality of opinion with respect to Catholicism, growth of, 117-123

Liberties of the Church, bill for, 450, 453; v. Assembly, Bills

Liberties of the people, bill for, its basis and policy; the Ordinance, 1639...450-453

Liberty, guarantees of, in canon and common law of England, 445; Maryland a refuge for, 446

Licence for putting lands in mortmain, 595-601; v. Mortmain

Liège, College, S.J., 168, 169, 468, 469

Lisbon, seminary, 168

Littledale, R. F., a writer on S.J., 118, iii.

Littleton; v. Coke

London, Anglican *Bishop* of, on Maryland climate, 332, vi.

London, Guilbert, *Bishop* of, addressed by author of *Virginia's Cure*, 292, 293; his censor's *imprimatur*, 293, xvii.

London: Places: Lincoln's Inn Fields, 234; St. Paul's Churchyard, 162; Tyburn, 162
Prisons: Bridewell, 159; Clink, 86, 159; Fleet, 86; Gate House, 98, 159; King's Bench, 159; Marshalsea, 159; Newgate, 86, 159, 464; Tower, 86, 159, xi.

Longavilla; v. Longville

INDEX

Longfellow and prejudice, 124
Longville, Thos., *alias* Longavilla, sent on first mission to Newfoundland, 180, 181, 360; Stock's account of, 189, 190
Lookout Point, called Cape St. Michael, 323
Lord Mayor and aldermen, on English white slaves, 284, 285, viii.
Lots, bill for distributing private property away by casting, 410
Loyola; *v.* Ignatius
Ludovisi, *Cardinal,* letter from Bishop of Gerace to, on missionary volunteers, 248
Lustick, freeman, 486
Lynch, 284, vii.
Lynch, *Sir* Thomas, 1675, ex-Governor of Jamaica, on prebendaries for colonies, 294, xx.; on Poyning's Law, 386, xiii.
Lyon of Jude Hill, 553

M

MACAULAY, *Lord,* on Macintosh and Hallam, 84; on Cranmer, 119
Macintosh, *Sir* James, on Saurez, 84; Macaulay on, 84
Mackall, John, Governor's Field, 568
McMahon, J. V. S., on the initiative in Maryland legislation, 386, xii.; on history of Mortmain, 128, xi., 613, xxviii.
Maevis; *v.* Nevis
Magna Charta; *v.* Great Charter
Maitland, on pre-Reformation canon law, 592, xliii.; *v.* Pollock
Malachy; *v.* Tuam
Manifestation, the; *v.* Price
Manors, grievances of landlords, 402
Map of Old St. Mary's City, 567; of America, 326, i.
Maquacomen, King of Patuxent, 343, 479
Maranhão, number of S.J. in, 317, lxvii.
Marlborough, *Lord,* his perjuries, 113, xv.
Marriage law, and a penalty on evangelical chastity, 411, 412
Marriage, matters touching, under Church legislation, 445; first recorded, in Maryland, 338, xvii.
Martinique [Matalina, Matilena], Caribbee island, 278; missionaries S.J. in, 298, 299; population of, 299; F. Breton, O. P., missionary in, 304, 309, xlii.; *v.* West Indian Islands
MARYLAND—
English penal laws reproduced in, 88, 89; principle of Orange revolution carried out in, 114, 115; repudiates State Church, 132; founded 1633...150; patent of, a variation from the colonial type, 153; *v.* Assembly, Bills, Laws of Maryland
Draft of Baltimore's patent for, 234; names proposed for, 234; granted under privy seal, 1632...236; *v.* Charter for Maryland; estates of inheritance in, 254; £10,000 invested in, by Cecil, second Lord Baltimore, and his friends, 263; contributions of Fathers S.J. to, 264, ix., 265; and business success compared with Virginia, South Carolina, Connecticut, Rhode Island, 265, 266; no revenue for the Crown, 266; technically in West Indies, as defined in Apostolic Letters, 268, 279; *Proposalls for transporting Irish to,* "respited," 284; climate of, 331, 332; soil and products, birds and fauna of, 329, 330; commercial capabilities, 35, 331
Baltimore invites Puritans from Massachusetts to, 554; Silvius on land tenure in, 570; *v.* Assembly, Bills, *Conditions of Plantation,* Henrietta Maria, Laws of Maryland
JESUIT MISSION: Jesuits applied for by Baltimore, 201, 248, 249; correspondence between the General and the English Provincials, 246-248, and *passim ;* on footing of ordinary colonists, 256, iii., 257; 1633, seven Fathers in, 269; F. Copley to General about privileges, 334; the ministries, 336; conversions, 337; redemption of slaves, 337; functions, 338, 339, xviii.; truck and trade, 339, xx.; Mattapany, 343; foundations in Maryland, 345, 346, i.; collegiate foundation, and the plan of, 346, ii.; nature of, 346, iv.
Secular agent of, to be appointed, 424, 426; volunteers, Provincial's appeal for, 459, xi.; twenty-four answers extant, 460; text of some letters, 461-466, 472-476; nationalities of aspirants to, 476, iv., v.; Mattapany seized by Baltimore, 477-480; suppression of, F. Poulton's letter, 481, 482; famine in, 481, 482; men S.J. wanted for, 482; property S.J., extent of, in 1641...484
Abandonment of, General's letter to Knott on, 514, 515, xxi.; expulsion of Fathers S.J., Knott on, 515-517; Fathers S.J. under surveillance, 525; missionaries stopped by Baltimore in London, 526, 528; Patuxent, 1641-42, 549, 550, vii.; *v.* Baltimore, Cecil; JESUITS, Copley, Knott; Cornwaleys
Mass, sacrifice of the, in Maryland, 324; first offered by F. Segura, S.J., and companions, 333
Massachusetts, Puritan colony of, its character, 554, 555
Massey, Leigh, White House, 568
Mathews, *Captain* Sam, Virginian Councillor, 374
Mathews, *Sir* Toby, 232; and Baltimore's oath of allegiance, 355, 356
Matthews, Thomas, 341
Mattapany, mission S.J. at, 342, 460, xiii.; description of property, 343, 344; pronunciation of, 344; seized by Baltimore, 477-480; seizure of, 483, iv.;

no patents taken out for, 1642...484; Indians rightful proprietors in default of S.J., 491; "piety" of the claim S.J. in English law, 492, xxiv.
Mauritania, most western country of East Indies, 268, iv.
Mayhew, *Dr.* Jonathan, on toleration of Catholics, 105, 106
Mead, 193, i.
Medcalfe, adventurer in Maryland, 263
Mejer, Otto, on Jesuits, 135, xvi., 142, i.
Mexico, number of priests S.J. in, 317
Middleton; v. Clitheroe, Margaret
Mill Creek, 569
Millini, *Cardinal,* reports to Propaganda on Avalon, 186; on Gentile rites, 319, iv.
Missionaries treated as adventurers, 255
Missions, Augustinians from Rochelle, sent by Propaganda to West Indies, 306; Capuchins, missionaries-apostolic, 307; in St. Christopher and Cape Verde, 307; controversy with S.J., 308-311; acts of Propaganda concerning, 309, xlii.; papers to Propaganda on their mission, 311, 312; and Propaganda, Cayenne and Guiana, 312, l.-liii.; Carmelite, in the West Indies, 306, 307; Dominican, provided under charter of a French West Indian Company, 304; their names and numbers and labours, 304, 306; Franciscan, in Florida, 317; Irish friars for New Mexico, 322, xii.; the earliest to Newfoundland begun by Smith and Longville, 180; *v.* Canada, New England, Secular clergy mission to Maryland
Mohawks, 320
Monasteries, as corporations, 587
Monopolies, recommended to Baltimore by F. White, 398
Monopoly of trade, claimed by Baltimore in his Points, 507; in corn, effects of, on mission, 410
Montague, *Lord,* John Copley, priest, domestic chaplain of, 122; connection of L. Worsly, S.J., 462
Montserrat, colony of Irish Catholics from Virginia at, 279; Stapleton's report on religion in, 314, 315, 316
More, priest, 94, ix., x.
More, H., S.J., on arrest of Copley and White, 562, i.; *v.* JESUITS
Morley, *Lord,* 231, xiii.
Mortification, or amortizing, 582, xi.; *v.* Mortmain
Mortmain, introduced by Lord Baltimore, McMahon's explanation of, 128; first origin of statutes, 129; *v.* Stubbs; legislation, not yet in Maryland, 1636... 364; pre-Reformation and post-Reformation, proposed for Maryland, 1641... 430, 431; and seizure of Mattapany, 491, 492; in Baltimore's draft of Surrender, for the Provincial S.J., 531, x.; Lord Baltimore's demands conceded by Copley and General, S.J., 532, 558, 559, x.; in *Conditions of Plantation,* 578, ii.; meaning of, 579-581; people of, 579; ecclesiastics, 579, iv.; different theories of Coke and Blackstone on, 581; Baltimore's practice agreeing with neither, 581; reasons for, 582, 583; *v.* Bacquet, JESUITS, Campano; history of, from statute 43 Eliz., c. 4, and others, 584, 585, 586; according to Blackstone, Hallam, Stephen, 586, 587; authentic history according to Palgrave, 587-589; Suarez on supreme administrator of ecclesiastical property, 592, xli.
Mortmain Statutes: Baltimore's patent exempting from, 241, 242, 431; precedent for exemption, 242; imposition of retroactively, violation of charter by, 502, 503; modifications of Baltimore's policy, 510, x.; derived from feudal law, 590, xxxv.; First Statute, fraud occasioning, 593, iii.; comments on, by divers authors, 593, 594; a licence required before putting lands in Mortmain, 595, 596; *v. Provisions of Westminster;* enumeration of the Statutes, 598, xxviii.; Committee of House of Commons on, 1844...598, 599, 611, xxix., 615; privileges of Templars claimed for lands in, 599, xxxiii.; relaxed in practice, causes, 607, xiv.; and politics, 610, 611; political history of, 612; errors in history of, 612, 613, xxvi.-xxx.; charity, religion, and education under, 612, 615, 616; uses and trusts, 613, 614; Burge on popular favour to, 615, xxxviii.; favour shown to, by English kings, 615, xxxix., xl.
Mosorcoques, chief councillor of Tayac, his baptism, 481
Mulattoes, imported into Maryland, 281; *v.* Francisco, Sousa
Mun, *Conte de,* on French law against religious congregations, 102, vii.
Muscogee Indians: Natchez, Creeks, Cherokees, Choctaws, Chickasaws, 326, i.
Muskett, George, 94, ix.; story about Lord Baltimore, 231, xiii.; 506; to choose prefect for mission of seculars, 522
Muster-master, his powers, 402
Mynne, Anne, married to George Calvert, afterwards Lord Baltimore, 155, 230, xiii.

N

NAMBUC, DE (*also* Esnambuc), divides St. Christopher with Warner, 296; first French Governor, 297, 307, 310
Names, Christian, and patron saints, 175, xxi.
Napoleon, 589
Narratives; *v.* Voyage
Neale, James, *Commissioner,* 537, 545, xvii.

INDEX 639

Negroes, enslaving of, under Stuarts, 280, 281; legislation debarring plantation slaves from Christian instruction, 282; in the West Indian Islands, 1677, 20,000 instructed Catholics, 301

Neill, *Rev.* E. D., on documents S.J., 81; confuses John Copley, priest, with Thomas Copley, S.J., 122

Nelson, priest, 94, x.; proposed for mission of seculars to Maryland, 498

Netherway, Richard, his licence to carry Irish Tories into exile, 283

Nevis [Maevis], 279; Quakers in, 316

Nevis Road, 301

New Chappell, Indians to be taxed for, on behalf of Baltimore, 487; Jesuit, at St. Maries, account of, 539, 540; bought by commission from Copley for Baltimore, 541

New Chappell lot, S.J. property, survey of, 567; *v.* St. George's Island, St. Inigoes, St. Mary's Hill

New England, divers colonies, patents beginning 1620...150; Propaganda orders a mission to, 1625...185: Propaganda summons Capuchins for, 318; its boundaries, 560

Newfoundland, taken possession of by Gylberte, 149, ix.; patent granted, 152, xviii.; oath of supremacy for, 152; first mission by Smith and Longville, 180, xi., xii.; or New England, nomenclature of 1630...194, 195, v.

New Haven, Puritans of, 287

New Mexico and the colonies, English, Dutch, 321, 322

New York, its penal laws, 18th century, 102, viii.

Nieto, *Fra, Augustinian*, Havana, correspondence with Propaganda on American Missions and regular orders, 313, 319

Nieuport, 206

Nonconformity, crime of, not to be condoned, 145, 146

Norton; *v.* West

Norumbega, coast of Maine, 149; a Catholic colony projected for, 153-155

Notaries, apostolic and public, 225

Notary-apostolic; *v.* Farrar, Southcote, *Dr.*

Nova Scotia, Propaganda orders a mission to, 185

Noys, *Attorney-General*, on Baltimore's patent, 246

Nuncio, at Brussels, on Stock's missionary project, letter to Propaganda, 186, xii.; report on Avalon, 194-197; *v.* Bentivoglio; at Paris, 203; reports on West Indies, 299; on mission in Cayenne, 312, i.; *v.* Bichi

O

OATES, TITUS, monograph concerning plot, 49, 56, iv.; no witness S.J. to appear against, 382, x.

Oath of allegiance, and colonial charters, 152; impossible to Catholic conscience, 152; and of supremacy, exacted of Puritan pilgrims, 196, 197; in Baltimore's *Instructions*, 261; Baltimore's, 355, 356, 357; Provincial S.J. condemns it, 357; Cardinal Barberini against it, 358, 359; bill for, 451; model of similar oath to Proprietary, 451, 505; text of legitimate, to King of England, 451; to Baltimore, its feudal characteristics, without feudal basis, 501

Oath of supremacy, and charters of Newfoundland and Virginia, 152, xvii.

Oaths, enforced by Test Act, 112, 113; breaking, abrogating, and appointing, 113

Objections answered, Baltimore's pamphlet on toleration of Catholics, 256, 257

Observations of F. Knott, Provincial S.J., on Baltimore's Points and Lewger's tenets, 505, 513, 514

Occupancy, right of, 576; *v.* Titles

O'Leary, 134, xv.

Oliver, Roger, St. Peter's Key, 569

Oneidas, 316

Onondagas, 326

Orange Revolution, principle of, the end justifies the means, 114, 115, xviii.; imported into the Colonies, 114, 115; endorsed by G. Bancroft, 115, xviii.

Orders, Holy, and secular offices under common law, 443, xxvii.

Orders in Council to transport Irish girls and boys to Jamaica, 283; *v.* Clotworthie, Irish Catholics, Netherway, Sellech, Thurloe

Ordinance, Assembly of Maryland, 1639, and the abandoned bills, 450-453

"Ours," a term used by S.J., Puritans, and secular clergy, 286, iii.; *v.* Gage

Ownership, right of Indian, 571-577; *v.* Bannez, Cajetan, Kent, Silvius, Soto

Oxford, John, *Bishop* of, patentee under Virginian Charter, 152

Oxonford; *v.* Oxford

P

PACIFICO DI PROVINS, *Fra, Capuchin*, Prefect of West Indian Mission, 311, 312, xlviii.; on merchant companies and temporal aid, 314, lvi.; *v.* Ventadour

Paget, to Somerset, 86, ii.; on the English people and reformed doctrines, 111

Paley, *Dr.*, his argument for penal laws against Catholics, 109, 110, iv., 111; his philosophy of life, according to Lecky, 136

Palgrave, *Sir* Francis, on traditionary opinions in history, 18, 118, 125, 126; on religious spoliation, 612, 614; and authentic history of Mortmain, 587-589; on feudal Statutes of Mortmain,

611, xxiii.; on political objects of last statute, 611, 612; *v.* Blackstone, Burge, Delolme, Guizot, Robertson; Smith, Adam

Pamphilj, *Cardinal,* report from Nuncio at Paris on West Indies, 299, xvi., 516, xxiv.

Pamplona da; *v.* Francis

Panzani, Gregory, *Oratorian,* envoy to England under Urban VIII., correspondence with Barberini on the Manifestation against Jesuits and Chalcedon documents, 208, xiii., 211, ii.; suppresses gist of the controversy concerning faculties of regulars, 221, x.; his part in the anti-Jesuit campaign, 231, xiii., 232, xv.; his own Relation, comment on Baltimore, 232, xvi., xvii.; Con's comment on, 232; anecdote on Papal Bulls as post-Reformation canon law, 239, vii.

    His character and qualifications, 354, 355; his letters and gossip, 355–359; his theories on Jesuitism, 359; account of Lewger, proposal of a converts' aid fund, 360; a forgery, 361; General S.J. on, 457, i.; *v.* Con, Ferragalli

Paper, qualities of, in letters, 78

Paraguay, priests S.J. in, 317, lxvi.

Paris, novitiate O. P., 305, xxix.; Seminary of Foreign Missions, recommended for American bishopric by Cardinal Sforza, 314, lviii.; supported by a merchant company, 314

Parkman, Francis, and prejudice, 123, 124

Parrie, Edmond, freeman of Assembly, 383

Pascattoway [Kittamaquund], station S.J., 324, 460, xiii.; F. White transferred to, 479, viii.; Anna princess of, her baptism, 481; Mary, Queen of, her baptism, 481; F. White at, 550, vii.

Passamagnus, River, in Virginia, 201, 233

Passports, a bill for, 454; and five days' notice of departure, bill for Maryland, 532–534

Patent for Maryland; *v.* Charter for Maryland

Patents; *v.* Charters

Patowmecke, 324, 583

Patrons, temporal rights of, in ecclesiastical property, under common law, 444, xxx.; Calvert, possessor of, by charter of Maryland, 444, xxxi.

Patuxent, meeting with chiefs of, 272; 331; mission S.J. in, 343; 478, 479

Paulinus, *Fra, Capuchin,* Provincial in Normandy, his faculties for missions in Africa and America, 307, xxxviii.

Peasely, Anne, *Mrs.* William, sister of Lord Baltimore, 427, 526; her interview with Baltimore on behalf of mission S.J., 528

Peasely, William, Baltimore's London agent, 376, 427, 526; and the bureau of inspection for Fathers S.J., 527, vi.; announces Baltimore's embargo on their departure, 528

Peckham, *Sir* George, incited to colonize by persecution, 1574...146; contract with Gylberte, 147

"Pedagogues," or hirelings, theory about regulars, advanced by Bishop of Chalcedon, the Jansenists, Kellison, Hallier, and others, 216, viii.

Peers, names of Catholic, 227; *v.* Information, Protest

Pellam, *Captain,* a Catholic at Nevis, 279

Pellican, Peter, *O. P.*, West Indian Mission, 304

Pemberton, *Lord Chief Justice,* on Catholic religion, 99; *v.* Plunket

Penal law, and Baltimore's Points against clergy, and Concordat for Provincial S.J., 509, 510, x., 511; enforced in England, 510, 511, xi., xii.; injustice of, *v.* Augustine, St.; Bacon, Jacobitism, Macaulay, Waldeck-Rousseau

Penal laws against Catholics, Habeas Corpus writ withheld, 88–92; barring Catholics from public offices, 91; identified with the interests of religion, 99, xix.; for recusants in New York and Virginia, 18th cent., 102; defended by Paley, 109, 110, 111; *v.* Test Act; antecedent to Jacobitism, 111; history fabricated by Paley to support them, 111; *Acte agaynst fugytives over the sea,* 147; Gylberte's patent derogating from, 147; *v.* Acts of Parliament; renewed severity of, 178; *v.* Tankard

Penal legislation, debarred from Maryland, 451; attempted introduction into Maryland, 452, 453

Perjury, justification of, by Hallam and Hume, 113, 114, xvi.

Perkins, *Master* John, on spiritual men and testamentary administration, 591

Perry, Robert, 338

Perry, W. S., and the character of Puritans in Massachusetts, 554, 555, xxii.

Persecution, reasons for, discussed, 86; Reformed Churches established by means of, 86, 87; revenue from, 86, 87; literature on revenue from, 87; for theoretical possibilities, 88; causes of, not in the alleged customs of the times, 92, 93; contrary to practice of Catholic countries, 94; stipulation by Spain against, 94; stipulation by France against, 94; special, advocated by Wm. Douglass against American Catholics, 104, 105; by Jonathan Mayhew, 105–107; decline of, 117

Persons, clergy and *miserabiles,* privileged under Church legislation, 445

Peru, priests S.J. in, 317, lxvi.

Petit, René, Huguenot, 290

Petition about Maryland, to General S.J., from Provincial F. Blount, 266, 267; granted with Faculties for the Indies, 267, i.

INDEX

Petre, *Lord*, 209, 211
Petty, 284, vii.
Philip and Mary, 1 & 2, c. 8, their statute repudiating the English schism from Rome, and suspending *Quia emptores*, 242, 602, 603, 604, vi.
Philippines, priests S.J. in, 317, lxvi.
Philips, *Father*, his opinions, 360, 361, ii., iv.; receives faculties for mission of secular priests, 506, 517; on faculties of the seculars, 524
Philpot, *Mr.* and *Mrs.*, 393, ix.
"Piety," interests of, legal principle violated by *Conditions of Plantation*, 504
Pirates, English, their character, 328
Planting corn, bill to enforce, 456, xxiii.
Plots, Gunpowder, 151; Bishop of Chalcedon charges Jesuits with, 214, iv.; Oates', condemnation of Archbishop Plunket by Pemberton, 99; fictitious Popish, in America, 101; in England, 102; *v.* Disraeli, Johnson, Dr.; John Ury hanged for, by Horsmanden, 103
Pluckley, 122; *v.* Copley, John
Plumer, *Member of Parliament*, attempts to have Test Act repealed, 1736...107-109
Plunket, *Archbishop*, condemned by Pemberton for complicity in Oates' Plot, 99
Plymouth, New England, 186, 200
Point; *v.* Poynt
Points, Baltimore's four, drafted for Provincial S.J.'s signature, 506, 507; substance of, 507-512; criticism of matter and style, 507, v.-vii., 508, viii.: I. no barter of missionaries S.J. with Indians, 507; II. no acquisition of land from Indians by any colonist, 508; III. clergy placed under penal laws, 509; modified in Concordat, 510, x.; IV. testamentary and matrimonial matters taken over into lay hands, 512; copy sent by Provincial S.J. to Rosetti, 513
Policy of silence, S.J., in controversy, 69-76; imposed by General S.J. in Chalcedon controversy, 70; three effects of, 76; effect on published literature, 76, 77
Pollock and Maitland, criticism on Blackstone, 126, 127; on First Statute of Mortmain, 594, viii.
Poole, William, denounced for baptizing his child a Catholic, 194, ii.
Poor laws and rates, their origin, 584
Pope, the, Lewger and Baltimore on, 435; President of Holy Office or Inquisition, 515; and the right of ownership in infidels, 573; supreme administrator of ecclesiastical goods, 592, xli.
Popes—
Alexander VII., his brief on secular clergy becoming regulars, Dodd's gloss in the title of it, 163, vi.
Clement IX., Coke's fictitious Bull of, 96

Clement XIV., Suppression of S.J., 69
Gregory XIII., 221; territorial range of Faculties for the Indies, 268, 269, v.
Gregory XV., institutes S. Congregation of Propaganda, 188
Innocent X., memorial to, from Cardinal Albizi, 202
Innocent XI., memorial to, from Cerri, reviewing Virginia, Avalon, and Maryland, 202, xx., 297
Paul V., 221, 226
Pius VII., restoration of S.J., 69
Urban I., martyr, on uses of Church property, 579, i.
Urban VIII., 75, 223; issues decree through S. Cong. of Inquisition on the Chalcedon controversy, 201; admonition to Bishop of Chalcedon on the limits of his faculties, 203; suppresses Price's Manifestation, 208; controversial works condemned by him, 214, iv.; resignation of Bishop of Chalcedon, 228
Population, of West Indian Islands, 306; F. Copley to Baltimore on wealth by increase of, 397, xxvii.
Portobacco, station S.J., 553, xviii.; chosen for Indian council, 553; situation, 554
Port Tobacco Creek, 546
Post-office in colonies, want of, 525, ii., iii.
Potomac Mission, S.J., 331; its martyrs, 317, *v.* JESUITS, Segura; description of, 324, 331
Poverty, religious, Anglican view against, 291; view of Urbano Cerri, 291, xii.; *v.* JESUITS, Argento, Campano; general maxim regarding, 593, iii.; *v.* Boehmer
Poyning's Law, for Ireland, 385, xii.; repudiated by Jamaica, 385, xiii.
Poynt Comfort, Maryland colonists forbidden by Baltimore to approach, 262, 275; *Ark* and *Dove* arrive at, 279, 323, ii.
Prerogative; *v.* Rights of Proprietary
Presbyterian; *v.* Puritans
Price, William, *O.S.B.*, his Manifestation, 208; suppressed by Urban VIII., xii.; 232, 360, 457, 518, xxix.
Priest-hunters; *v.* Warrant
Priesthood, Hallam's commentary on its nature, 129, i.; position of, in Church and history, 130, 132
Privilege of clergy, granted to missionaries S.J. by Maryland Assembly, 383, 588; coveted by laity, 592; Boehmer on, 593, ii., iii.
Privileges of the Church, William the Conqueror's Capitulary on, 589, 590, xxxiv.
Propaganda, *Sacred Congregation* of, 50; occasioning the foundation of Protestant societies for propagation of religion, 50; Annual Letters S.J. received by, 51; confused by non-Catholic societies with Religious Orders, 51, vi.; Prefect of, Card. Antonio Barberini, 75; foundation

VOL. I.   2 T

642 INDEX

of, 181; on missionaries for Newfoundland, 182, i., ii.; action regarding Virginia, Vermudes, New England, Nova Scotia, Philippines, China, East Indies, 185, x.; on conduct of missions, 186, xi., xii., xiii.; sends faculties to Fra Simon Stock, Carmelite, 187, xiv., xv., xvi.; on Capuchins for Avalon in the place of Jesuits, 193; forbids missionaries to use heretical places of worship, 196, vi.; acknowledges Nuncio's report on Avalon, 197, viii.; orders a Capuchin mission for Avalon, 197; Cerri's memorial from, to Innocent XI., reviewing Avalon, Virginia, and Maryland affairs, 202, xx.; v. Hoadly, Steele; and Stock on Chalcedon controversy, 213, i., ii., iii.; and the Inquisition on the Chalcedon controversy, 214; letter from, to Bishop of Chalcedon, 220; decree respecting S.J. sodality of Immaculate Conception, 221, vii.; and documents against English Jesuits, 229, xi.; petition to, from missionaries S.J. in West Indies and Canada for faculties, 298, xii., xiii.; faculties from, for S.J. missions, 302, xxv.; on a mission of Carmelites for West Indies, 307; on a bishopric, 307; and Society for Foreign Missions, 307; v. "Scotch gentleman;" decrees on S.J. and St. Christopher in favour of Capuchins, 308, xxxix.; and Capuchin mission for Cayenne and Guiana, 312, 313, liii.; on Irish missionaries for English West Indian Islands, 315, lx.; correspondence with Fra Nieto, Augustinian, 318, iii., iv.; its function as a bureau for missionary correspondence, 318, iv.; on excluding heretics from Canada, 320

Decree on a Maryland mission of secular priests from England, 1634... 333, ii.; misled on the subject of Maryland, 448; on proposal of a new secular priests' mission to Maryland, 1641...493-494, 516; instructs Rosetti to gather information, 495, vi.; Rosetti's Relation, two redactions, 496, 497; deliberations on the mission of seculars to Maryland, 498, xiv.

Propaganda and Inquisition, contradictory decrees of, 519-521

Propagation of Gospel in New England and America, Society of, 50

Propagation of religion a motive in founding colonies, 142

Property, rights under *Conditions of Plantation*, 400, 401; missionaries disqualified to acquire, 410; no disability in colonist to accept, 571, 572; purchase of feudal, set free by statute *Quia emptores*, 600, ii.

Church: Government and Catholic religious proprietors, 56; Urban I. on the uses of, 571, i.; Bacquet on, 579, ii., iii.; vicissitudes of, 588; Stubbs on, 592, xli.; feudal character of, 596, xx.; tenure of, through heirs becoming regulars 596, 597, xxiii.; Hallam on, 597, xxiv.; saved by statute from alienation into lay hands, 599, 600, xxxiv.; East India Co. and expropriation of Catholic churches,—its rights of, respected in French Revolution, 485, viii.; v. Corporations

Lay: saved by statute from collusive alienation into religious hands, 599, xxx.-xxxiii.

Tenure of, in Maryland, grievances, 398, xxxiii., xxxix.; feudalism imported into, 398, 399; Lewger's bills on, 400, xxxvii.; casting lots for manors, 410; assailed by Lewger, 415, xxvii.; General Assembly's socialistic powers, 418; reclaimed for Proprietary, 454, xix.; restricted for clergy by Baltimore's Points, 508; partial concession to Baltimore by F. Copley, 532, xiii.; and by the General, 558, viii.; essence of Church privilege in, 592, i.; capacity of corporations regarding, 597, 598; attempts to legalize seizure of missionary, 477, 478

Proprietary of Maryland, his claim to enforce penal legislation, 452; rights and prerogatives, 453; preferential payment of his debts, 454; Baltimore sole, of land found unoccupied, 570, 571; bound to ratify gifts from Indians, 572; v. Baltimore, Cecil

Proprietors, Indians true, 570, 571

Protest of the Peers, in the Chalcedon controversy, 224, 226-228; names of nobles signing, 227; elicits the Papal Brief, 228, vii.; v. Information; Southcote and Farrar sign a Declaration against, 229

Protestant, origin of name, 93

Providence, ship, 283

Provisions of Westminster, and Mortmain, 595, xvi.

Pugh, R., on irresponsible controversialists, 72, viii.

Puritans, of Massachusetts, and oaths of allegiance and supremacy, 196, 197; in North America, 286; invited by Lord Baltimore to Maryland, 286; invited by Council of State to Jamaica, 287, 288; of Massachusetts and the Anglican Church, 554; and Indian land, 574

Pursuivant, meaning of term, 403, xlv.

Purveyance, exemption of clerics from, in English law, 442

Q

QUAKERS, and Indian land, 574
Quebec, Convent of St. Charles, 319, 320, viii.

Quia emptores, statute of, derogated from in Maryland charter, 241; effect on frankalmoigne, 600–605; *v.* Baltimore, Cecil; Mortmain

R

RACONIGIO, *Fra* Angelo Raffaele da, on English Jesuits, 218, xi.
Rabnett, Francis, freeman of Assembly, 384
Raleigh, *Sir* Walter, 150
Rant, priest, 229, ix.
Raymundo, Francisco; *v.* Rochefort, César de
Reade, *Major* Nath., *Governor* of Montserrat, 316, lxiii.
Recollects, and Canada, 319; *v.* Richelieu
Reculae, meaning of, 559, x.
Recusants, Popish, penal laws for, 88, 89; terms of acquittal for, 89, 90; tests for, 91; House of Commons on, under James I.; *v.* Penal laws
"Redemptioner;" *v.* Indented servants
Redman, priest, proposed for mission of seculars to Maryland, 498
Reeves and Stephen on the spoliation of religious houses, 614, xxxiii.
References, fraudulent use of, 81; *v.* Burge, Hallam, Robertson
Reformed Church, the, imposed on the English by force, 86, 87
Regalism, 353
Regulars, their character, 132; apparent antagonism to secular clergy, 133, xi.; Bishop of Chalcedon on, 218, xi., *v.* Raconigio; number of, in England, 218, x.; not dependant on Chalcedon for faculties, 221, x.; enumeration of missionary Orders in the West Indies, and apparent antagonism amongst, 304; *v.* Pedagogues; Coke on, 579, v., 580, vi., vii.; alleged subjugation of, by Mortmain Statutes, 616, xlii.; *v.* Blackstone, Dodd, Finlason, Tiernay, Stephen
Relations, or Annual Letters, 32; of New France, 52; on Lesser Antilles, by a Scotch gentleman, 295, 296; to Propaganda on Maryland, 495, 496; revised redaction of, 497; of Maryland, 1635, names of original adventurers, 263, iv.; on Indians, 326, 327; form for binding indented servants, 341; *v.* Panzani
Relinquishers, and trade, 392, v.
Remonstrance to Bishop of Chalcedon, 204–206; exceptions to the mixed power, 205, 206; signatures of Baltimore and other lords, 206, vii.; Jesuits accused of forging, 207, 208; *v.* Jansenism, Sorbonne
Rental, of wheat, in Maryland, 253; *v. Conditions of Plantation*
Restitution, Lewger's order of, 413, xxiii.
Revisers of Jesuit history, 64, ix.

Rhode Island, colony of, 1636...150; a republic in part, 265
Richard II., an era in Mortmain, 608, xvi.; *v.* Acts of Parliament
Richardson, *Lord Chief Justice*, delivers F. Baker from prison, 273
Richelieu, *Cardinal*, intimacy with Bishop of Chalcedon, 220, 223; sends Recollects and Jesuits to Canada, 319
Ridgeley, Robert, St. Peter's Key, 569
Rights of man, 328, v., vii.; *v.* Browne, Crichton; Hale
Rights of Proprietary, 452; Act for, 453; and the seizure of Mattapany, 483
Robert, son of chief councillor of Tayac, his baptism, 481
Robertson, *Dr.* W., traditionary opinions of, 125, 126; *v.* Palgrave
Rochester, *Lord*, Judge of High Commission Court, 511, xii.
Rookwood, *Mr.*, 159, xi.
Roper, priest, 94, ix., x.
Roses, the Wars of the, 615, xlvi.
Rosetti, *Papal Nuncio* in Belgium, 249, xiii.; Knott's *Notanda* or *Observations* to, 255; orders received by, from Propaganda on the mission of secular priests for Maryland, 495, vi.; his Relation, 495, viii.–xi.; letter to, from F. Knott on Baltimore, Lewger, and the mission of seculars to Maryland, 505, 506; and the contradictory decrees of Inquisition and Propaganda, 519–521; and faculties for mission of seculars, 522, 524

S

SACRAMENTS, enforced by Test Act, 112, 113
St. Adauctus' Tree, 568
St. Alban's Seminary, Valladolid, 154
St. Augustine, Florida, Franciscan missions in, 317
St. Bartholomew, Island of, Irish exiles without a priest, 315
St. Boniface, Bishop of Mayence, 587
St. Caecilia's Island, 324
St. Catharine's Island, 324
St. Christopher; *v.* St. Kitts
St. Clement's Island, Mass at, 332; *v.* Herne Island
St. Clement's Bay; *v.* Gerard, Thomas
St. Cuthbert, 588, xxvii.
St. Cyran, *Abbé de*, 216, viii.
St. Edward the Confessor, 589
St. George's Bay, later St. Inigoes Creek, 325
St. George's Island, 334, vi., 484; survey of, 568; S.J. property, 569
St. Gregories, Pascattoway, 484
St. Gregories, Cape; *v.* Smith's Point
St. Inigoes Manor, S.J. Property, 334, vii.; indented servants at, 340; sold by Gerard, 346, i., 401, xxxix.; 479, vii.; 484; survey of, 568

644

INDEX

St. Inigoes Creek; *v.* St. George's Bay

St. Inigoes Neck, 569

St. John's College, S.J., Louvain, 158, viii., 159

St. John's Creek, 569

St. Kitts [Christopher], 279; Council of, asks Compton, Bishop of London, for more learned and older clergy, 294, 295; loss of, by English, 296, 297; missionaries S.J. and Carmelite in, 297–299; *v.* West Indian Islands; population of, 299; Capuchins deputed to, by Propaganda, 307; Fra Hyacinth's Relation on, 308, xl.; defeat of English by French at, 315

Santa Lucia, Carib Island, trouble with black slaves, 278; *v.* Voyage

St. Mary's Hill, S.J. property, 484; survey of, 567, 568

St. Mary's City, 325, 460, xiii.; chart of, 334, 567; town lots in, assigned by warrant to adventurers, 365, iv.; *v.* New Chappell

St. Michael's Cape; *v.* Lookout Point

St. Michael's hundred, 479

St. Omer's College, S.J., a depository for documents, 56; printing-office in, 56

Sant' Onofrio, Rome, Agucchi's tomb in, 198, ix.

St. Peter's, Maryland, 568

St. Peter's Key, *alias* Van Sweringen's Neck, 569

St. Thomas's Manor, 546, xx.

Saire, adventurer to Maryland, 263

Salisbury, Robert Cecil, *Earl* of, patentee under Virginian Charter, 151, xvi.; patron of G. Calvert, 176

Sancé, Antoine de Ridouet, *Baron de*, proposal to Charles I. on Huguenot colony for Virginia and Florida, 288, vii.

Santiago de Cuba, Cabezas, *Bishop* of, visits Florida Mission, 317, 318, i.

Sarpi, Fra Paolo, quoted by Bancroft, 93

Saunders, adventurer to Maryland, 263

Savoy, 58, iii., 69

"Scotch gentleman," Relation on West Indies and missionaries S.J., 296, 297, 300, xx., 307; Cerri's improvements of Relation, 297, 300

Secretaries of State; *v.* Baltimore, George; Burleigh, Cottington, Walsingham, Williamson, Windebank

Secular clergy, in apparent antagonism with regulars, 133, xi.; in Northumbria, 587; brought under Statutes of Mortmain, 608

Secular clergy mission to Maryland, 1641, to supplant S.J., 493; petition to Propaganda for, 493, 494; Rosetti's Relation on, 495–497; *v.* Rosetti, Spada; list of priests submitted to Propaganda, 498; Baltimore's intended use of it, 501; faculties received by F. Philips, Oratorian, 506; faculties not conveyed, 521; G. Gage to Bishop of Chalcedon, on disappointment and delay, 522, 524; unqualified for want of faculties, 527; General S.J. on faculties for, 532, xiv.

Sedgrave, Robert, process against, 340, i., 343

Selleck, David, his licence to deport Irish children, 283

Seminaries; *v.* St. Alban's, Seville

Senecas, 326

Servants, indented, 337

Severus, Alexander, 579

Seville, seminary at, 154

Seymour, *Governor* of Maryland, address of, to FF. Brooke and Hunter, S.J., 89; 439

Sforza, *Cardinal*, on Paris Seminary of Foreign Missions for American bishopric, 314

Ships, Lord Baltimore's, the *Ark* and the *Dove*, 259

Signature of Provincial S.J. desired by Baltimore for papers submitted, 430, 431, xv.; the Certificate, 502, 504, vii.

Silence in controversy, policy of; *v.* Policy

Silvius, *Dr.* Francis, Douay, 169; Baltimore's case on Indian land titles submitted to, 505, 518; his solution received in England, 519, iii.; text of the solution, 570–573

Sister's Field, 568

Slave, a Catholic white, redeemed, 275, ii.

Slaves, English, white, Lord Mayor and aldermen on, 284, 285; redeemed by Fathers S.J. and others, 337, xiv.; *v.* Indented servants, Smith, C.E.

Slavery in New Spain, 322; *v.* Negroes

Smith, Adam, 125

Smith, Anthony, priest, in Avalon, denounced by Stourton, 194; 199

Smith, *Rev.* C. E., accuses Father Copley of libertinism, 121; quotes Neill, 121; his comments on "disloyalty" of S.J. missionaries to Lord Baltimore, 323, i.; confounds truck with trade, 340, xxi.; charges Jesuits with introducing slavery into Maryland, 381, iii.; on Jesuit missionaries and Indian languages, 550, viii.; confounds Gilmett and Territt with priests S.J., 539, xxxiii.

Smith, Thomas, condemned for piracy, 382

Smith, William, will of, the first recorded in Maryland, 338, xv.

Smith, New York historian, commends penal laws against priests, 102

Smith's Point, called Cape St. Gregories, 323, 324

Snow, Justinian, freeman of Assembly, 384

SOCIETY OF JESUS—

Its adversaries, 69, 70; Suppression of, loss of books, papers, and archives, 69; English terms and phrases about, 84, 85, iv.; dealt with by brute force in

INDEX

Germany, Switzerland, 133, 134; violence of accusations against, by Jansenists, 209, i.

Literary and scientific excellence an object of institution, 57, i., 58, ii.; priests and regulars, 129, 132; contrasted by non-Catholic writers with the Catholic Church and secular priesthood, 132, 133, x., xi.; *Constitutions*, 135; identified with the Roman Catholic Church by O. Mejer, 135, xvi.; theology, philosophy, policy of, 135–137; novel experiences of, in Maryland, 137; prospective destiny of, 137, 138; formation of the members, choice of subjects, novitiate, rules, vows, etc., 163–168; *Spiritual Exercises*, 251; Provinces in Central and South America, 316, 317, lxvi., lxvii.; applications for foreign missions, 460–476; for mission of Maryland, 461–466, 471–476

English Province: its elements, 161; lay brothers not in England, nor for Maryland, 161, i.; total membership, 1580–1633...161, 162; charged with Gunpowder Plot, heresy, etc., by Bishop of Chalcedon, 212, iv., 220, v.; sodality of the Immaculate Conception in England suspended, 215, vi.; *v.* Babthorpe, Leeds; Card. Cajetan commissioned by Propaganda to treat of, 221; campaign against, in England, 1632...229, 230, xii., xiii.; *v.* Propaganda; America a refuge for, 233

Society, Camden Publication, 122
Society of Foreign Missions, 303, 307, xxxvii.
Society, Maryland Historical, 568
Society; *v.* Propagation of Gospel
Somerset, Paget to, on repugnance of the English people to the Reformed religion, 86, ii., 111
Somerset, *Viscount*, 72, 209, 225; Bishop of Chalcedon on, 219
Sorbonne, 76, 221, x., 229, ix.; *v.* Gallicanism, Inquisition S. Cong.
Soto, Dominic, 571
SOURCES: *v.* ARCHIVES; Literature published, 220 works tabulated, 34–44; other works cited: *v.* names of authors at large, and under JESUITS
Sousa, Mathias, mulatto, 281
South Carolina, 265; *v.* Florida
Southcote, *Dr.* John, on first missionaries to Avalon, 180, x.; 221, 222, xii., 229, x.
Southcote, *Sir* John, 180
Spada, Nuncio at Paris, 202, 361
Spain, Court of, offers Masses for young Prince of Wales, 207, x.
Spires, protestation at, 93; *v.* Protestant
Spoliation, religious, Reeves, Stephen, and Palgrave on, 614
Stapleton, *Governor* of Montserrat, 315, lxii.; *Governor-General*, report on religion of Leeward Islands, 316

State Church, and the priesthood, 130; Bowyer, Davis, Gladstone, Hooker, on, 132; repudiated in Maryland, 1639, 132, viii.
Statute of Uses, Bacon on, 613, 614, xxxi.
Statutes of Mortmain; *v.* Acts of Parliament, Mortmain
Steele, *Sir* Richard; *v.* Hoadley
Steiner, 421, x.
Stephen, *Serjeant*, 614, xxxiii., xxxiv.; and Blackstone's text, 100, 101; on licences for amortizing, 587, xxii., xxiv.; 595, xviii.
Stephen, *sen.* and *jun.*, 616, xlii.
Stephen, *King* of Poland, 582
Stepney, Lancelott, 284, vii.
Stock, Simon, *Fra*, Carmelite, correspondence with Ingoli, and the Propaganda, on Amerian missions, regulars, Jesuits, Bishop of Chalcedon, 181–193, 198, 202, xx., 213, i., ii., 318; his letter, 1631, February 4, to the Cardinals of Propaganda on Chalcedon and the regulars, 214, 215; *v.* Ingoli
Stourton, Erasmus, on Lord Baltimore in Avalon, 193, 194
Strafford, Thomas Wentworth, *Earl* of, 180, ix.
Streeter, S. F., on Baltimore's code and the initiative in legislation, 386, xiii.; on *Bulla Coenae*, 436, viii.
Strickland, priest, proposed for mission of seculars to Maryland, 498
Stubbs, on extent of ecclesiastical property in England, 442, xxiv., 592, xl.; on origin of Mortmain legislation, 129, xiv., 593, vi.
Suarez, 84, iii., 421; on exceptions and limits to Church privileges, 441, xxiii.; on basis of Christian commonwealth, 591, 592, xxxix., xl.; on Mortmain, 592, xli.
Surrender, deed of, drafted by Baltimore for the Provincial, 529–531; exaggerated principles of Mortmain, 530, 531, x.
Surveys of Copley's properties, 567, 568
Susquehannahs, 325, 553, xviii.
Swanley, Thomas, 283
Switzerland and S.J,, 134
Synodus Calecuthensis, 588, xxviii.

T

TANKARD, THOMAS, recusant, 178, v.
Tayac, Indian Emperor, 343; conversion of, by F. White, 344, 345; baptism of, at Pascattoway, 460, xii.; daughter of, a catechumen, 481; his death, 482
Templars and Mortmain, 599, xxxiii.
Temple, *Sir* William, 284, vii.
Tenison, *Archbishop*, challenged by F. A. Pulton, 476, iv.
Tenure of property in Maryland, Dr. Francis Silvius on, 570–573; *v.* Silvius

Terra Mariae; *v.* Maryland
Territt, priest, sent on mission of seculars to Maryland, 498, 534, 535, 536, 537, 544; *v.* Smith, C. E.
Tertre, J. B. du, *O.P.*, 296
Test Act, attempted repeal of, 1736...107, 108; *v.* Holden, Sacraments, Walpole
Test oaths in the colonies, 115–117; *v.* Acts of Parliament, Berington
Testaments, under Church legislation, 445; Church franchise in, 586, xxi.; under ecclesiastical jurisdiction, 591, xxxviii.; growth of power to devise by, 611
Testuggini; *v.* Tortuga
Thomas, J. W., 421, x., 567, i.
"Three Propositions," the, 369
Thurloe, *Secretary*, and H. Cromwell on transporting Irish children to West Indies, 283, 284, vii.
Tierney, M. A., 616, xlii.
Tithes in Maryland, 395, 429, 616, xlii.
Title; *v.* Tenure
Titles to land, Vattel on Indian, 573, 564, v.; not conferred by Christianity, civilization, etc., 571, 573, 576, x.–xiii.; Kent and American law on, 574; ultimate fee in the Crown, 575; assumed foundation of, 576, vi.; true foundation of, 573
Titles to property in Maryland, no limitation of time for taking out patents, 1638...400, xxxviii.
Tobago, French victory over Dutch at, 303
Tortuga, 307
Town-lots in St. Mary's, grant of, 365, iv.
Trade, distinct from truck, 339, 340, xxi.; and "relinquishers" in Maryland, 392, 393; and truck, reserved to Baltimore by the code and Concordat, 395, xviii.; Cornwaleys, his privilege of, 396; with the Indians, bill for monopoly of, 454; forbidden to S.J. in Baltimore's Points, 507; rights of; *v.* Monopolies
Transportation; *v.* Irish Catholics, Orders in Council, Thurloe
Treasons, bill for, 455; its provisions and disappearance, 455; S.J. accused by Baltimore under, 455
Trollope, priest, proposed for mission of seculars to Maryland, 498
Truck, method of colonial exchange, 339, *v.* Capuchins, JESUITS, Vitelleschi; Missions; right of, given by Concordat to Baltimore, 395
Trusts, secret, prohibited by Baltimore, 499, 510, x., 610, xx., 613, 614; *v.* Uses; their value in Catholic history, 614, xxxvi.
Tuam, Malachy, *Archbishop* of, sends Irish missionaries to English West Indian Islands, 315, lx.
Tuckahoe, 342, iv.
Tue, Restituta, 338

Turenne, Carmelite province, 306
Tuscaroras, 326
Twickenham [Twittnam], 210

U

University projected for Virginia, 319, vi.; *v.* Stock
Ury, John, Anglican minister, hanged by Horsmanden for New York Popish Plot, 1741...103
Uses and trusts, 613, 614

V

VALLADOLID, St. Alban's Seminary at, 154
Van Sweringen, Garrett, 569
Van Sweringen's Point; *v.* St. Peter's Key
Vattel on Indian titles, 573, v.
Vaughan, Sergeant, freeman of Assembly, 383
Vaughan, *Sir* William, sells land in Newfoundland to Lord Baltimore, 177
Ventadour, *Duc de*, Canon of Notre Dame, Paris, 299; and temporal aid for missionaries, 313
Vermudes, Propaganda orders a mission to, 185
Vicariate-Apostolic, in England, vacant, 228
Victoria, Francis de, scholastic theologian, on land tenure, 570, 571, 572; Wheaton on, 573, iv.
Vincent de Paul, *St.*; *v.* Congregation of Missionaries
Virginia, 150; religious clauses in charter of 1606...151; charter of 1612...152; oath of allegiance added to oath of supremacy, 152, xix.; Propaganda orders a mission to, 185; *v.* Stock; Baltimore petitions for part of, 200, 201, xvii.; patent for part of, 233, 265; legislates against recusants, 102
Supposed expedition of George Calvert, *jun.*, to, with Fathers Baker and Drury, 272; included among West Indian Islands, 279; Huguenots proposed for, 288; lack of Anglican clergy in, 292, 293; *v.* Hammond, *Virginia's Cure*; university in, 319, vi.; *v.* Florida; Lord Baltimore's petition for the Governorship of, 375, 376; clerical exemptions and laymen, 416; mission S.J. to; *v.* Maryland
Virginia's Cure, J. Hammond to Bishop of London on lack of ministers in Virginia, 292, 293, xvi.; *imprimatur* of censor, 293, xvii.
Virginity, Hall on, 411
Vitus; *v.* JESUITS, White, A.
Votaries (voluntaries), 580, vi.

Voyage to Maryland, Father White's double narrative, 275-279
Vttapoingassinem, 553

W

WALDECK-ROUSSEAU, and penal laws for Religious Orders, 111, x.
Walpole, *Sir* Robert, and the Test Act, 1736...108, 109
Walsh, *Friar*, 134, xiii., xv.
Walsingham, and Gylberte's enterprise, 147, vi.; Gerrard and Peckham's petition to, 148
Warder Castle, 365, iv.
Warner, *Sir* Thomas, and F. White, 279; divides St. Christopher with De Nambuc, a Frenchman, 296, ii., 297; Governor of Antigua, 296, iv.
War, right of waging, against infidels, 573
Waroner; *v.* Warner
Warrant, for F. Copley, against priest-hunters, 366, 367, iii., iv.
Warrants, Lord Baltimore's, for land grants, 363-365
Watson, W., priest, 120
Watten, 48, 58, 59
Weghucasso, 553
Wells, *Mrs.* Constant, contributor to Maryland enterprise, 263
Wentworth, *Earl of Strafford*, 233; letters to, from George, Lord Baltimore, 207, x., 235, v.; from Cecil, Lord Baltimore, 235, iv.
Wentworth, priest, proposed for mission of seculars to Maryland, 498
Wessex, a tithe of its land granted by Ethelwulf to the Church, 587
West, *Captain*, Virginian Councillor, 374
West, *alias* Norton, priest, 229, ix.
West Indian Islands, charters for, to Earl of Carlisle and Lord Willoughby, 150, xiv., 151; names of, 151, xiv.; range of, defined in Apostolic letters, 268; Windward and Leeward, 279, 296; population of, and missionaries, 280, 299; mission S.J., 298-303, 313; Irish missionaries in, 315, lx.-lxii.
Wheaton, his view of the Church, 84; on Francis de Victoria, and infidels' rights of property, 573, iv.
Wheler, *Sir* Charles, *Governor* of St. Christopher, on state of the clergy, 282, v., 285; on the pressing of Anglican clergy for the colonies, 294, xix.; on the precarious tenure of English land in St. Christopher, 295, xx.
White, Andrew; *v.* JESUITS
White House, 568
White, Thomas, Anglican clergyman, Virginia, 338, xvii.

White, Thomas, *alias* Blacklow, *priest*, 221; proposed for mission of seculars to Maryland, 498; censured by Rome, 498, xix.
White's Neck, chapel at, 199, 200
Whitehead, Mary, 338, xvii.
Whittaker, Thomas, and the doctrine of *cy-près*, 480, x.
Wickliffe's Creek, 569
Wilkinson, William, Protestant clergyman, 340, xxi.
William I. and Church property, 588, 589
William III., oath of allegiance to, 113; *v.* Acts of Parliament
Williams, Roger, on land titles from Indians in New England, 577, xiv.; *v.* Kent, Chancellor
Williamson, *Sir* Joseph, 288, vi.
Willoughby, *Lord, Governor* of Barbados, and F. Grillet, S.J., 298; patent for West Indian Islands granted to
Will in Maryland, first recorded, of W. Smith, 338, xv.
Wills, Lewger's *Cases* on breaking Catholic, 430, xiii.
Win, Maria, alleged to be wife of Lord Baltimore, 231, xiii.
Winchester, Paullet, *Marquis* of, 206, vii., 225
Windebank, *Sir* Francis, *Secretary of State*, 231, 366, 374; Panzani's forgery to, 361; reconciled to the Church, 375; petition to, from Baltimore, on Governorship of Virginia, 376; letter of, on Hawley, Treasurer of Virginia, 377, 378, iv.; 518, xxix.
Winslade, his plan for a Catholic American colony in Norumbega, 153, i.; Coke on, 153; Parsons' criticism on the plan, 153-155
Winthrop, *Governor* of Massachusetts, on advent of Catholics to Maryland, 332
Wintour, freeman of Assembly, 384
Wintour, *Lady* Ann, two sons, adventurers to Maryland, 260, iv.
Wiseman, *Sir* Thomas, a son of, adventurer to Maryland, 263, iv.
Wiseman, Henry, 393, ix.
Worcester, Henry, *Bishop* of, patentee under Virginian Charter, 152
Writs: *Habeas Corpus*, 92; *Ad quod damnum*, 605, 606, xiii., 607, 608; *passim*; *v.* Mortmain
Wyslade; *v.* Winslade

Y

YOACOMACO, King of, 325; *v.* St. Maries

END OF TEXT, VOL. I.

DOCUMENTS

VOL. I

WITH MAPS AND FACSIMILES

SECTION I

PRELIMINARY, ADMINISTRATIVE, NARRATIVE, CONTROVERSIAL
1605–1670

§ 1. Preliminary Documents, 1605–1633

No.
1. Parsons on American Catholic Colonization, March 18, 1605.
2. White's letter to Gerard, Oct. 27, 1606.
3. George Lord Baltimore to Lord Petre, Aug. 8, 1631.
4. Objections answered touching Maryland, [1632, 1633].

§ 2. Administrative: Letters of the Generals S.J., 1629–1744

(*Anglia, Epistolae Generalium*: 3 tt.)

5, A–T. Extracts from Vol. I. 1605–1641. Latin.
6, A–K^4.   „   „   Vol. II. 1642–1698. Latin.
7, A–V^3.   „   „   Vol. III. 1698–1744, and Supplement. Latin.

§ 3. Narrative: Annual and other Letters, 1634–1773

8, A–X^2. Transcripts and Extracts. Latin.

§ 4. Controversial: in the Dispute with Lord Baltimore, 1633–1670
On Property and Civil Rights

9. Account of the Colony, with first Conditions of Plantation, 1633. Latin.
10, A–W. Panzani Papers, 1635–1636. Italian.
11. Lewger's Cases, [1638].
12, A–C. Baltimore's new Conditions, Nov. 10, 1641, and documents annexed. Latin.
13. Extract from Lewger's Diary on the same, [1642].
14. Knott to Rosetti, Nov. 17, 1641. Latin.
15. Baltimore's Points submitted to the Jesuit Provincial, [1641]. Latin.
16. Knott's Commentary on the same. Latin.

No.
17. Silvius on the Indian Land Titles, Nov. 28, 1641. Latin.
18. The Provincial's Memorial to the Holy Office, [1642]. Latin.
19, A–L. Rosetti Papers, 1641, 1642. Italian; Latin.
20. George Gage to the Bishop of Chalcedon, July 21, 1642.
21. Baltimore's Draft for a Jesuit Surrender of property, [1642]. Latin.
22. Baltimore's Draft for a Concordat with the Jesuits. Latin.
23, A, B. Agretti and Airoldi on Baltimore, 1670. Italian.

SECTIONS II.—VII

DOCUMENTARY EXCURSUS, NARRATIVE AND CRITICAL, ON JESUIT PROPERTY AND ITS USES IN NORTH AMERICA, COLONIAL AND FEDERAL, 1633–1838

SECTION II

ORIGINAL ORGANIZATION, 1633–1773

§ 5. THE ORIGINAL COLLEGE FOUNDATION IN MARYLAND, 1633–1727

24. St. Inigoes Manor, 1633–1693.
25. St. Thomas's Manor, 1649–1693.
26. Britton's Neck and Outlet, or Newtown, 1668–1693.
27. The same three estates, 1693–1727.
28. St. Xaverius and other tracts: Bohemia, Eastern Shore, 1706–1732.
29. Attwood's Observations on preserving these estates, 1727.

§ 6. PARTICULAR GRANTS, DEEDS, BEQUESTS, IN MARYLAND, 1633–1727

30. Claims of land by Conditions of Plantation, 1633–1638.
31. The Chapel Land, St. Mary's City, 1641–1727.
32. Britton's Neck and Outlet, 1668.
33. Loss of land by erosion, 1640–1894.
34. Pascattoway, 1641.
35. Confidential trusts to save the property, 1641–1693.
36. Bequests during the first half-century, 1635–1685.
37. Londey's devise of land, Eastern Shore, [1686–1693].
38. Beginnings of Bohemia estate, E.S., 1706.
39. Additions to St. Thomas's Manor, 1711–1780.
40. Specimen of measures to save personal property, 1717.
41. Second part of Bohemia, 1721.
42. Father Robert Brooke's patrimony, 1723, 1724.
43. The legal case on behalf of Father Brooke, 1729.
44. Decision in the case, 1729.
45. Quantico on the Patuxent, 1725.
46. Slaves and Catholic owners.
47. Thorold's conveyance to Attwood of the foundations, Western Shore, 1726.
48. The entire quantity of Jesuit landed property, 1727.
49. Devises of land made to the Jesuits, 1633–1727.

§ 7. PARTICULAR BEQUESTS AND BENEFACTIONS, 1727-1780

No.
50. Settlements by individual Jesuits, 1727-1741.
51. Release of debt by the parent Province, England, 1728.
52. Another such release, 1738.
53. An accumulated debt to the same English Province, 1754.
54. Funds sunk in the Mission of Maryland by the same Province, 1758-1763.
55. Policy of independence in the ministry.
56. The Provincial Corbie's Ordinations, 1759.
57. Contributions of the missionaries to the Mission, 1755-1779.
58. Bishop Carroll's statement on the foregoing policy.
59. The same on Jesuit property titles.
60. Archbishop Marechal's statement on the same subject.
61. The ultimate and juridical basis of Jesuit tenure.
62. White Marsh: devise of James Carroll, 1728.
63. ,, ,, legacies to Carroll's nephews, Jesuits, 1628-1774.
64. ,, ,, Thorold's two wills, 1729, 1737.
65. Father Ignatius Brooke's patrimony, 1732.
66. Joseph Gates's gift of landed property, 1740-1779.
67. Father Gilbert Talbot, Earl of Shrewsbury: Longford estate, 1744.
68. Legacies in money, 1745-1756.
69. Father Robert Knatchbull's devise of land, 1748.
70. Sir John James's foundation for Pennsylvania, 1740-1751.
71. A Hunter legacy, 1759.
72. Father Joseph Semmes' patrimony assailed, 1763-1770.
73. The Thomas Shea life-annuity, 1764.

§ 8. THE COLLEGE FOUNDATION IN MARYLAND, 1727-1780

74. The system of wills and bonds prescribed.
75. The line of descent, 1727-1793.
76. Additional lands in Charles County, 1729-1778.
77. The solemn placing of boundaries.
78. Mountain Prospect on Little Pipe Creek, 1742-1800.
79. Small chapel lots acquired.
80. Assignment to save property in 1746.
81. Edenburgh: value of tenure in the name of individual Jesuits, 1771.
82. Bohemia, E.S.: quieting and completing the possession, 1731, 1732.
83. ,, ,, violent attempts at expropriation, 1773.
84. Deer Creek: beginnings of the estate, 1750-1773.
85. ,, ,, development of the plantation, 1779-1793.
86. ,, ,, dedication to the Corporation of the R.C. clergymen, 1793.
87. ,, ,, sale of the plantations, 1801-1815.
88. ,, ,, further sales, 1816-1822.
89. ,, ,, controversy and certificates, 1821.
90. Concordata between the Maryland Mission and the English Province, 1759.
91. Frederick and environs, 1765-1780.
92. Old St. Peter's, Baltimore—acquisition and use, 1764-1806.
93. ,, ,, ,, and the new cathedral, 1808-1816.
94. ,, ,, ,, —a new chapter of history, 1816-1824.
95. St. Joseph's, Tuckahoe, E.S., 1764-1822.
96. Appendix: Mill Creek, Delaware, and New West Chester, 1772-1810.
97. Official report of the Maryland Mission and property, 1765.
98. Old index of some title-deeds in Maryland.
99. Carroll and Marechal on the foregoing endowment of religion.

§ 9. The College Foundation in Pennsylvania, 1740–1822

No.
100. General view of the prospects, 1740, 1741.
101. Cost of living in Pennsylvania, 1740, 1741.
102. The land purchases effected, as appearing in the wills, 1742–1814.
103. Statement of the Vicar-General, Louis de Barth, on the same.
104.   ,,   ,, procurator, A. Marshall, reaching to 1824.
105.   ,, in the C. Neale-B. Fenwick Memorial sent to Rome, 1822.
106. Official report of outlay and income, 1765.
107. Reference for further particulars, 1740–1830.

§ 10. Paring away the Property in Divers States, 1793–1830

108. Waste in Pennsylvania: Goshenhoppen.
109. Liquidation in Philadelphia and New York.
110. Marshall's account of missionaries as farmers, 1824.
111. Philadelphia: St. Mary's.
112. Lancaster, Pa.
113. White Marsh: Bitouzy, and Carroll, 1813–1815.
114. Condition of the plantations, 1824–1830.

SECTION III

CHARGES AND CLAIMS AGAINST THE FOREGOING ORGANIZATION

§ 11. Propaganda and other Documents

115. Baltimore. Marechal's Memorial to the Propaganda, Aug. 19, 1820. Latin.
116, A–E. Rome. Letters of Marechal and the General, Jan. 18–Feb. 12, 1822. Latin.
117, A–F. Notes (1–6) of Marechal on the last letter of the General. Latin.
118. Report submitted by the General to the Propaganda, [March–May], (1822). Italian.
119. Notes of Marechal on the General's report and Rozaven's letter. French.
120. Questions submitted by Marechal to the Propaganda on the Jesuits. Latin.
121. Marechal to the Propaganda: *Breves Responsiones*, April 20, 1822. Latin.
122. The General to the Maryland Superior, C. Neale, July 26, 1822. Latin.
123. Baltimore. Marechal to C. Neale, Nov. 27, 1822. French.
124. C. Neale to Marechal, Dec. 9, 1822, with comments by the latter. Latin.
125. Marechal to C. Neale, Dec. 14, 1822. French.
126. C. Neale to Marechal, Dec. 23, 1822, with comments by the latter. Latin.
127. Marechal to Gradwell in Rome, Jan. 4, 1823. French.
128.   ,, ,, ,, ,, ,, Jan. 17, 1823. French.
129.   ,, ,, ,, ,, ,, Jan. 28, 1823. French.
130.   ,, ,, Card. Della Somaglia, July 21, 1824. Latin.
131.   ,, ,, Card. [Fesch], Nov. 4, 1824. French.
132.   ,, ,, Card. Della Somaglia, Dec. 21, 1824. Latin.
133.   ,, ,, Card. [Fesch], July 14, 1825. French.
134. Card. Fesch to Marechal, Aug. 27, 1825. French.
135. Marechal's Twenty-three Propositions on Maryland Jesuits, Jan. 15, 1826. Latin.
136. Marechal to Card. Della Somaglia, Oct. 17, 1826. Latin.
137.   ,, ,, Card. [Fesch], Oct. 17, 1826. French.
138.   ,, ,, Gradwell, Oct. 18, 1826. French.
139.   ,, ,, Card. Della Somaglia, Nov. 6, 1826. Latin.
140.   ,, ,, Gradwell, Nov. 28, 1826. French.

SECTION IV

REORGANIZATION, 1773-1792

§ 12. PROVISIONAL ORGANIZATION TO PRESERVE THE PROPERTY, 1773-1793

No.
141. The fact and form of Suppression, 1773.
142. Inaction during ten years, 1773-1783.
143. Father John Carroll's plan of organization, [1782].
144. Carroll's personal views, 1783-1788.
145. The Select Body of the Clergy and its Chapter, 1783, 1784.
146. The Form of Government, 1784-1805.
147. Jesuit rights to the property, 1784-1786.
148. Current business at the Chapter of Oct., 1784.
149. Carroll's reports to the Propaganda, 1784-1786.
150. The Chapter of 1786.
151. The Academy, the Bishopric, and Incorporation, 1786.
152. Opposition, 1787.
153. The title of Jesuit ownership discussed, 1787.
154. Unconditional surrender of the opposition, 1787.
155. Revival of the Society projected, 1788, 1789.
156. The Chapter and the incoming clergy, 1789, 1790.
157. The Chapter of 1789 and the Bishopric.
158. The same Chapter and the Academy, 1789.
159. The same Chapter and Incorporation.

§ 13. THE SEE OF BALTIMORE AND THE JESUIT ESTATES, 1790-1822

160. Carroll's Declaration of no right accruing to his See, May 26, 1790.
161. Father Ashton, the reputed occasion of Carroll's Declaration.
162. Ashton and Marechal's claims, 1792-1806.

§ 14. THE LEGISLATURE AND THE CORPORATION, 1792-1808

163. The beneficiaries in equity, 1792.
164. Act of Maryland Assembly creating a Corporation, Dec. 23, 1792.
165. Act of Assembly in confirmation of the same, Jan. 28, 1806.
166. Acts of 1808 and 1894.
167. Declarations of Fathers Walton, Molyneux, and Ashton, Oct. 3, 1793.
168. Constituent meeting of the Select Body under the new Charter, Oct. 4, 1793.
169. Name of new Board: "Corporation of the R.C. Clergymen," Oct. 5, 1793.

SECTION V

THE ENDOWMENT OF RELIGION, 1792-1830

§ 15. THE ENDOWMENT OF RELIGION BY THE FOREGOING SELECT BODY 1792-1830

170. Provision for the Sulpicians, 1792-1799.
171. Tessier on the ex-Jesuits' benefactions, 1792-1799.
172. The Select Body. Membership, 1793-1816.

No.
173. The Executive Board or Corporation. Pensions and aids, 1794–1800.
174. Aid for the seminarians, 1800–1802.
175.   „   „   1802–1805.
176. Pensions and aids, 1801, 1802.
177.   „   „   „ 1803–1805.
178. Carroll's statements on the Jesuit titles, 1800–1815.
179. Pensions and aids, 1805–1815.
180.   „   „   „ 1816–1820.
181. End of the eleemosynary disbursements, 1820–1825.
182. The expropriation announced: Marechal to C. Neale, Dec. 14, 1822.
183. Rebuttal by the Corporation, 1822–1830.
184. Review of the period 1792–1830.

SECTION VI

CONCORDATS, 1793–1826

§ 16. CONCORDATS: MARYLAND AND MISSOURI, 1798–1826

185. A list of Jesuit stations, 1798.
186. An attempted contract: Carroll-Molyneux, Sept. 20, 1805.
187. Dr. J. G. Shea's contributions to the Controversy hereupon of 1818–1822.
188. The L. Neale-Grassi Concordat, April 3, 1816.
189.   „   „   „   text.
190. The ecclesiastical status, 1818–1822.
191. Fate of the Concordat of 1816.
192. Marechal's accounts to the Propaganda, 1820–1826.
193.   „   „   „   „   St. Patrick's Church, Washington.
194. Dubourg and Missouri, 1815–1821.
195. Marechal on Missouri and Dubourg, 1823, 1824.
196. The Upper Louisiana Concordat: Dubourg-C. Neale, March 19, 1823.

SECTION VII

CRITIQUE AND SEQUEL

§ 17. CRITICISM OF THE DOCUMENTS IN THE PROPAGANDA, ETC.

197. The controversial literature from Dr. Marechal to Dr. Eccleston, 1818–1838.
198. The original land titles of the Jesuits.
199. The grounds for the expropriation.
200. Gradwell's and Poynter's contributions to American history, 1818–1822.
201. Gradwell's agency for Marechal, 1822–1824.
202. Card. Fesch in the controversy, 1822.
203. Fesch's Concordat, June 18, 1822.
204. Fesch's Concordat and the Papal Brief of July 23, 1822.
205. Text of the Concordat and of the Brief.
206. Lay contributions to the controversy, 1822–1824.
207. Messrs. Brent, Ironside, etc., 1824–1826.
208. Gradwell, Marechal, and the Jesuit Roman College.
209. Marechal's Twenty-three Propositions on the Maryland Jesuits, January 15, 1826.
210. The Marechal-Propaganda documents, 1820–1826.

No.
211. Last session of the Propaganda on the controversy, June, 1826.
212. Text of the final authentic documents, June 27–Dec. 24, 1826.
213. Documents of the new period, 1827, 1828.
214. Whitfield and Gradwell, 1828.
215. Whitfield and Wiseman, agent in Rome, 1828–1834.
216. Eccleston and Wiseman, 1834, 1835.
217. Eccleston: Fathers McSherry and Mulledy, 1835–1838.
218. Temporalities and reputation.
219. Anti-Corporation documents from other parts.

APPENDIX

ANALOGIES

220. Ireland: preservation of the Jesuit property, 1773–1814.
221. England: vicissitudes, 1773–1829.
222. Canada: Jesuit incorporation, 1887.
223. Other non-Catholic countries and Jesuit property during the Suppression.
224. Juridical decision in Rome (1836), on permanence of Jesuit property rights, notwithstanding the Suppression.

PRINTED BY WILLIAM CLOWES AND SONS, LIMITED, LONDON AND BECCLES.